FIFTH EDITION

THE SOCIOLOGY OF HEALTH, HEALING, AND ILLNESS

Gregory L. Weiss
Roanoke College

Lynne E. Lonnquist
Mary Baldwin College

PEARSON

Prentice
Hall

Upper Saddle River, New Jersey 07458

Library of Congress Cataloging-in-Publication Data

Weiss, Gregory L.
    The sociology of health, healing, and illness / Gregory L. Weiss,
Lynne E. Lonnquist.—5th ed.
      p. cm.
    Includes bibliographical references and indexes.
    ISBN 0-13-192840-6
    1. Social medicine—United States.   2. Medical ethics—United States.
3. Medical care—United States.   I. Lonnquist, Lynne E.   II. Title.
    [DNLM: 1. Sociology, Medical—United States.   2. Ethics, Medical—United States.
3. Delivery of Health Care—United States.
WA 31 W429s 2005]
RA418.3.U6W45 2005
306.4'61—dc22

2005015563

To Janet   To Dan

Editorial Director: Leah Jewell
Executive Editor: Christopher DeJohn
Supplements Editor: LeeAnn Doherty
Editorial Assistant: Kristin Haegele
Senior Marketing Manager: Marissa Feliberty
Marketing Assistant: Anthony DeCosta
Prepress and Manufacturing Buyer: Mary Ann
Gloriande
Cover Art Director: Jayne Conte

Cover Designer: Maureen Eide
Cover Image: Stock Illustration Source, Inc.
Director, Image Resource Center: Melinda Reo
Manager, Rights and Permissions: Zina Arabia
Manager, Visual Research: Beth Brenzel
Image Permissions Coordinator: Joanne Dippel
Photo Researcher: Elaine Soares
Full-Service Project Management: Kelly Crooks,
TechBooks/GTS

This book was set in 10/12 Times Roman by *TechBooks/GTS* York, PA Campus. It was printed and
bound by Courier Companies, Inc. The cover was printed by Courier Companies, Inc.

Photo Credits appear on page 379.

Pearson Education LTD.
Pearson Education Singapore, Pte. Ltd
Pearson Education, Canada, Ltd
Pearson Education—Japan

Pearson Education Australia PTY, Limited
Pearson Education North Asia Ltd
Pearson Educación de Mexico, S.A. de C.V.
Pearson Education Malaysia, Pte. Ltd
Pearson Education, Upper Saddle River, New Jersey

10 9 8 7 6 5 4 3 2 1
ISBN 0-13-192840-6

CONTENTS

CHAPTER FOUR
SOCIETY, DISEASE, AND ILLNESS   59

CHAPTER FIVE
SOCIAL STRESS   87

PART III
Health and Illness Behavior

CHAPTER SIX
HEALTH BEHAVIOR   109

CHAPTER SEVEN
EXPERIENCING ILLNESS AND DISABILITY   129

PART IV
Health Care Practitioners and Their Relationship with Patients

CHAPTER EIGHT
PHYSICIANS AND THE PROFESSION OF MEDICINE   153

CHAPTER NINE
MEDICAL EDUCATION AND THE SOCIALIZATION OF PHYSICIANS   177

CHAPTER TEN
NURSES, MID-LEVEL HEALTH CARE PRACTITIONERS, AND ALLIED HEALTH WORKERS   197

CHAPTER ELEVEN
COMPLEMENTARY AND ALTERNATIVE MEDICINE   219

CHAPTER TWELVE
THE PHYSICIAN-PATIENT RELATIONSHIP: BACKGROUND AND MODELS   244

CHAPTER THIRTEEN
PROFESSIONAL AND ETHICAL OBLIGATIONS OF PHYSICIANS IN THE PHYSICIAN-PATIENT RELATIONSHIP   268

PART V
The Health Care System

CHAPTER FOURTEEN
THE HEALTH CARE SYSTEM OF THE UNITED STATES   286

CHAPTER FIFTEEN
HEALTH CARE DELIVERY   311

PREFACE

The United States—like all countries around the world—is in a seemingly constant state of change with regard to disease and illness, health- and illness-related behaviors, the health care professions, and the health care system. The fifth edition of this text has been written to update our description and analysis of these dynamic processes and the work in medical sociology that helps us to understand them.

In preparing this fifth edition, we have sought to retain and strengthen the emphases and features of the earlier editions; to thoroughly update patterns, trends, and statistics; and to present new material that reflects important changes in health care in society and important advancements in medical sociology.

KEY EMPHASES WITHIN THE TEXT

This edition of the text maintains the same five emphases as the earlier editions. **First, we provide broad coverage of the traditional subject matter of medical sociology and include both new perspectives and new research findings on this material.** The core areas of medical sociology (the influence of the social environment on health and illness, health and illness behavior, health care practitioners and their relationships to patients, and the health care system) all receive significant attention within the text. Naturally, statistics throughout the text have been updated to provide timely analysis of patterns and trends. Recent research findings and thought have been incorporated in every chapter. Attention devoted to relatively new areas in the field has not reduced coverage of traditional areas such as social stress,

illness behavior, and the physician-patient relationship.

Second, we have continued to emphasize emerging areas of analysis in medical sociology and recent work within the field. Recent health care reform efforts in both the public and private domains continue to have dramatic effects on almost every aspect of health care. We describe these effects throughout the text.

We also continue to incorporate key medical ethics issues throughout the text. These issues represent some of the most important health-related debates occurring in the United States today, and many medical sociologists have acknowledged the importance of understanding these policy debates and setting them within a sociological context. We have attempted to provide balanced and comprehensive coverage of several of these issues (especially in Chapters 13 and 16 and in the Discussion Questions and Cases at the end of chapters).

This fifth edition also provides extended analysis of a wide range of topics including:

- *The SARS epidemic.*
- *The sociology of mental health.*
- *The multidimensional consideration of stressors.*
- *The increasing problem of obesity.*
- *The contributions of animals to human health.*
- *Medical malpractice.*
- *The Terri Schiavo case.*
- *Recruitment of nurses to the United States from other countries, including Third World countries.*
- *The effect of race concordance on satisfaction with physician care.*
- *The Medicare prescription drug benefit.*

- *Concerns about pharmaceutical companies.*
- *Recent court decisions regarding managed care companies.*
- *Significant recent developments in the health care systems of China and Great Britain.*

Third, the extensive coverage of gender, race, and class issues as they relate to health, healing, and illness has been maintained. Throughout the textbook, we examine issues in light of race, class, and gender. We want students to constantly be exposed to the important influence of these factors on matters related to health and illness. The chapters on social epidemiology, social stress, health and illness behaviors, the profession of medicine and medical education, and the physician-patient relationship all give special emphasis to these matters.

Fourth, we continue to emphasize key social policy questions. Timely questions and issues addressed in the earlier editions are continued and updated here. Examples include the provision of clean needles to people using injectable drugs (Chapter 4), the reconfiguration of traditional responsibilities of hospital nurses (Chapter 10), the social acceptance and legitimation of complementary and alternative healers (Chapter 11), the legal status of medical marijuana (Chapter 11), the influence of managed care on physicians and patients (several chapters), the effects of trends toward consolidation and merger among American hospitals and the pressures placed on the viability of public hospitals (Chapter 15), and the use and possible abuse of advanced health care technologies (Chapter 16).

Fifth, we have attempted to prepare a text that is informative, readable, and interesting. We want readers to become aware of many of the understandings of health, healing, and illness drawn from the field of medical sociology. We want readers to become intrigued by the provocative issues and debates that exist in medical sociology and in the health care field. We want readers to find this book readable and interesting.

Both of us enjoy structuring our classrooms to enable as much reflection, critical thinking, and student participation as possible. We have found that there is simply not time for some of the classroom activities that we most enjoy (e.g., reading and then discussing a provocative paperback, watching a good documentary and critically analyzing it together, or using student panels to introduce issues) if we feel obligated to lecture on all of the material in each chapter. On the other hand, we do want students to become familiar with the important contributions of the field. When we use this book, we do spend some time lecturing on parts of it, adding to certain discussions and presenting some of the material in an alternative manner. But, our students are able to grasp much of the book on their own, enabling us to supplement and to create additional types of learning experiences.

What are the key pedagogical features of this text?

- *Clear organization within chapters and a clear writing style.*
- *Interesting boxed inserts ("In the Field") that provide illustrations of key points made in the chapters.*
- *Interesting boxed inserts ("In Comparative Focus") that examine a selected health topic or issue in another country or countries.*
- *Meaningful tables and charts with the most recent data available at the time the book is being written.*
- *Illustrative photographs, most of which were taken specifically for use in this book.*
- *Chapter summaries.*
- *End-of-chapter "Health on the Internet" references and questions.*
- *End-of-chapter "Key Concepts and Terms" sections.*
- *End-of-chapter "Discussion Cases."*
- *References conveniently provided at the end of each chapter.*

Three additional facets of the book are important to us and help to describe its place within the field. **First, we consider a strength of the book to be the large number of research studies cited to illustrate key points.** We do this to constantly demonstrate to students the empirical basis of sociology, the origin of sociological knowledge, and the fascinating types of research conducted in medical sociology. We hope it inspires students to consider interesting research projects.

We have worked hard to identify theoretically meaningful and methodologically sound studies that contribute important knowledge to our understanding of health, healing, and illness. While making heavy use of research conducted by medical sociologists, we also include appropriate material from the other social sciences, from the government, and from the medical professional literature. We believe that this is helpful in forming the most comprehensive understanding of the topics covered in the book.

A second facet of our book that is important to us is that we provide balanced coverage on key issues. That does not mean that our book lacks critical perspective or analysis. In fact, readers will find no shortage of critical questions being asked. But, we believe that students learn more when they are exposed to arguments on both sides of issues and are challenged to consider the soundness of reasoning and quality of evidence that are offered.

Finally, we hope that this text reflects a genuine understanding of some very important and complex issues. Both of us have had many opportunities to experience various dimensions of the health care system. Between the two of us, we have been able to apply and extend our medical sociological training through work in a free health clinic, a family planning clinic, in family counseling, in hospital bioethics groups, on the human rights committee of a state psychiatric hospital, on the Navajo reservation, and in voluntary health agencies. While we have not substituted our personal experiences for more general understandings developed through sound theory and research, we believe that our experiences have helped us to develop a better understanding of certain issues and have assisted us in being able to illustrate important concepts and patterns.

Ultimately, our hopes for student-readers remain the same as with the earlier editions—that they gain an appreciation for how the sociological perspective and social theory contribute to an understanding of health, healing, and illness and for the manner in which social research is used to study these processes. In addition, we hope that readers perceive some of the many wonderfully exciting issues that are studied by medical sociologists.

ACKNOWLEDGMENTS

We are deeply grateful to the many people who have made helpful suggestions and comments to us about the first four editions of this book and/or about this fifth edition. Our appreciation is extended to: James R. Marshall, S.U.N.Y.-Buffalo, School of Medicine; Lu Ann Aday, University of Texas, School of Public Health; Paul B. Brezina, County College of Morris; Janet Hankin, Wayne State University; Naoko Oyabu-Mathis, Mount Union College; Judith Levy, University of Illinois at Chicago; Mike Farrall, Creighton University; John Collette, University of Utah; Raymond P. Dorney, Merimack College; C. Allen Haney, University of Houston; Arthur Griel, Alfred College; Larry D. Hall, Spring Hill College; Patricia Rieker, Simmons College; Deborah Potter, Brandeis University; John Schumacher, University of Maryland, Baltimore County; Lisa Jean Moore, College of Staten Island.

We would also like to thank Janet Jonas and Chris Rowley for their terrific photographs and the Health Sciences Library at the University of Virginia.

We are indebted to several people at Prentice Hall for their assistance and support throughout this project. Publisher Nancy Roberts, Executive Editor of Sociology Chris DeJohn, and Senior Marketing Manager Marissa Feliberty have all been very helpful. Our thanks also go to Kelly Crooks, Production Manager at TechBooks/GTS, and Joy E. Dickerson, Copyeditor.

Gregory L. Weiss
Lynne E. Lonnquist

1

A BRIEF INTRODUCTION TO THE SOCIOLOGY OF HEALTH, HEALING, AND ILLNESS

Through much of the first half of the twentieth century, matters pertaining to health, healing, and illness were viewed as being primarily within the domain of physicians, other health care practitioners, and scholars in the chemical and biological sciences. Neither medicine nor sociology paid much attention to each other. This changed dramatically in the second half of the century as the paths of sociology and medicine increasingly converged. This chapter presents a brief introduction to the sociology of health, healing, and illness—a subfield of sociology commonly referred to as medical sociology.

DEFINITION OF MEDICAL SOCIOLOGY

Ruderman (1981:927) defines **medical sociology** as "the study of health care as it is institutionalized in a society, and of health or illness, and its relationship to social factors." The Committee on Certification in Medical Sociology (1986) of the American Sociological Association (ASA) provided the following elaboration:

Medical sociology is the subfield which applies the perspectives, conceptualizations, theories, and methodologies of sociology to phenomena having to do with human health and disease. As a specialization, medical sociology encompasses a body of knowledge which places health and disease in a social, cultural, and behavioral context. Included within its subject matter are descriptions and explanations or theories relating to the distribution of diseases among various population groups; the behaviors or actions taken by individuals to maintain, enhance, or restore health or cope with illness, disease, or disability; people's attitudes, and beliefs about health, disease, disability and medical care providers and organizations; medical occupations or professions and the organization, financing, and delivery of medical care services; medicine as a social institution and its relationship to other social institutions; cultural values and societal responses with respect to health, illness, and disability; and the role of social factors in the etiology of disease, especially functional and emotion-related disorders and what are now being called stress-related diseases.

Clearly, the focus of medical sociology is broader than just "medicine." In fact, the title of this book was intentionally selected to connote that medical sociology includes a focus on

1

IN THE FIELD

THE SCOPE OF MEDICAL SOCIOLOGY

The field of medical sociology is an extraordinarily broad and exciting arena in which one can pursue an unusually wide range of interests, from social psychology and social epidemiology to health policy, social movements, and political sociology. In what subfield is there more theoretical and methodological diversity?

. . . The vitality of medical sociology cannot be explained only by its intellectual content, the energy of members, or even by the availability of funds for research and training. Part of the explanation resides in the fact that today's health sector constitutes an extraordinarily broad and vibrant arena of society. Hardly any sociologist could ignore today's health sector with its relevance and implications for the rest of society, its share of the GNP and workforce, its manifold influences on the occupations and professions, and its essential metaphors and definitions which guide our understanding of everyday life. The health sector is large and powerful and pervades the whole of the society (Levine, 1987).

---

health (in the positive sense of social, psychological, and emotional wellness), healing (the personal and institutional responses to perceived disease and illness), and illness (as an interference with health).

HISTORICAL DEVELOPMENT OF MEDICAL SOCIOLOGY

Setting the Foundation

It is difficult to identify any specific event as the "starting point" of the field of medical sociology. Certainly, some of the basic insights of the field were present among society's earliest philosophers and physicians. Many physicians in ancient times (see Chapter 2) perceived an essential interrelationship among social and economic conditions, lifestyle, and health and illness. This understanding has been an integral part of medical thinking in some (though not all) civilizations since then. Often cited as a key historical figure who paved the way for medical sociology is Rudolf Virchow, the great mid-nineteenth century physician (and founder of modern pathology). Virchow identified social and economic conditions as being primary causes of an epidemic of typhus fever in 1847 and lobbied for improved living conditions for the poor as a primary preventive technique. Arguing against biomedical reductionism—attempting to reduce every disease and illness to a biological cause—Virchow contended that medicine is largely a social science that needs to consider the influence of social structure on creating both health and illness.

The Turn of the Century

The last decades of the nineteenth century and the first decades of the twentieth century were a time of heightened awareness in both the United States and Europe of the need for social programs to respond to health crises. These were years of social upheaval caused in part by the effects of the Industrial Revolution and rapid urban growth (and, in the United States, a tremendous influx of largely poor and unskilled immigrants). In 1915, Alfred Grotjahn published a classic work, *Soziale Pathologie*, documenting the role of social factors in disease and illness and urging the development of a social science framework for working with communities and providers in reducing health problems. The term **social medicine** was coined to refer to efforts to improve public health.

However, an important crosscurrent was occurring simultaneously. The discovery of the germ theory of disease enabled physicians to more successfully treat the acute, infectious diseases which plagued society. This reinforced a belief that medicine could rely solely on biological science. The discipline of sociology was still in its infancy and was not able to provide sufficient documentation of the need for a complementary focus on social conditions.

The Early to Mid-Twentieth Century

Several important precursors to the development of medical sociology occurred in the first half of the 1900s. Social surveys became an important research technique, and many focused on health and living conditions. Sociologists often worked with charity organizations and settlement houses, which also became subjects for study. By the 1930s and 1940s, many sociological studies of the medical field, including Talcott Parsons's 1939 work on the medical professions, appeared. Political scientist Oliver Garceau (1941) contributed to the political sociology of medicine by analyzing the political life of the American Medical Association. George Rosen (1944) studied increasing specialization in medicine. Oswald Hall (1946) studied the informal organization of medical practice in an American city (Rosen, 1976).

The 1950s and 1960s: The Formal Subdiscipline Emerges

The emergence of medical sociology as a field of study occurred in the 1950s and 1960s. The most important developments pertained to changes in health, healing, and illness; to external recognition of the field; and to its institutionalization within sociology.

Changes in Health, Healing, and Illness. Based on analysis by Rodney Coe (1970) and others, the development of medical sociology was facilitated by four changes that had occurred or were occurring in medicine in the 1950s and 1960s. These were:

1. *Changing patterns of morbidity and mortality.* During this time, the primary causes of sickness and death shifted from acute, infectious diseases (e.g., influenza, tuberculosis) to chronic, degenerative diseases (e.g., heart disease, cancer). Because the factors that lead to degenerative diseases are more obviously interwoven with social patterns and lifestyle, the necessity for sociological contributions became more apparent.

2. *The impact of preventive medicine and public health.* In the 1800s and early 1900s, the field of public health focused primarily on bacteriology (linking particular germs to diseases) and immunology (preventing disease occurrence). As the twentieth century progressed, however, it became apparent that protection of public health also required consideration of social factors such as poverty, malnutrition, and congested living areas—all of obvious interest to sociologists.

3. *The impact of modern psychiatry.* The development of the field of psychiatry led to increased interest in the psychophysiological basis for many diseases and illnesses, in the importance of effective interaction between patients and practitioners, and in the use of patients' social environment as part of therapy.

4. *The impact of administrative medicine.* Throughout the twentieth century, the organizational complexity of the medical field—in the settings in which care is delivered, in the ownership of medical facilities, in the bureaucracies that were created to regulate and finance medical care—enormously expanded. The abilities of sociologists to analyze organizations and structures, to identify those who are harmed as well as those who gain by various arrangements, and to examine the consequences of alternative techniques were increasingly useful skills in organizationally complex environments.

External Recognition and Legitimation. Two key events during the 1950s and 1960s contributed to the increased interest in and legitimation of medical sociology. First, medical schools began to hire sociologists for their faculties. Although medical sociology was not always well integrated into the curriculum, the move symbolized an increasing recognition of sociology's potential contribution to understanding disease and illness. Second, government agencies and private foundations initiated significant financial funding for medical sociology. The National Institutes of Health and the National Institute of Mental Health sponsored sociological research in medicine and subsidized training programs for graduate students in sociology. (Both authors of this book received fellowships from the U.S. Public Health Service for their graduate education.) The Russell Sage Foundation provided significant funding of programs to increase the use of social science research within medicine.

Institutionalization of Medical Sociology. Finally, two additional events are especially noteworthy in the institutionalization of medical sociology. In 1959, medical sociology was accepted as a formal section of the American Sociological Association—an important step in bringing recognition to the field and enabling recruitment of new members. Second, in 1965, the ASA assumed control of an existing journal in medical sociology and renamed it the *Journal of Health and Social Behavior*. Now the official ASA journal for medical sociology, it is a key mechanism for medical sociologists to share their research findings.

Since then the field has flourished. The ASA section on medical sociology currently has approximately 1,000 members (there are about 15,000 ASA members) and is the second largest special interest section within the association. Medical sociologists publish in a wide variety of journals in sociology, public health, and medicine and are increasingly employed in health planning, community health education, education of health professionals, and health care administration in addition to colleges and universities. See the box, "Major Topics of Analysis in Medical Sociology," for one way of organizing the major topics within medical sociology.

Emerging Areas of Interest

As occurs in any dynamic field of inquiry, the amount of attention medical sociologists devote to specific topics varies over time. Typically, this happens as new areas of interest emerge and as former areas of study are reopened or are more vigorously pursued. Two such areas in medical sociology are issues related to medical ethics and issues related to managed care and health care reform.

Issues in Medical Ethics. Technological advancements in medicine in the last few decades have raised important and provocative ethical questions. Sociological analysis and insights are extremely important in genuinely understanding these matters. In recent years, medical sociologists have become more active in studying: (a) values, attitudes, and behaviors of people relative to ethical issues in medicine (e.g., attitudes about genetic research and human cloning) and how they are influenced by various social factors; (b) social policy questions (e.g., on new reproductive technologies or on the termination of treatment for the terminally ill); and (c) social movements (e.g., the pro-life and pro-choice movements) that have developed around interest in ethical issues in medicine. DeVries and Subedi (1998:xiii) describe sociology's role as "lifting bioethics out of its clinical setting, examining the way it defines and solves ethical problems, the modes of reasoning it employs, and its influence on medical practice."

Issues in Managed Care and Health Care Reform. Concerns about the high costs of health care and about the lack of access that millions of Americans have to quality health care have led to health care reform efforts in the United States. Though a comprehensive national health program failed in Congress in 1994, the massive shift from traditional health insurance plans to managed care networks, such as health maintenance organizations, has had tremendous repercussions throughout the health care system. Many of these areas (e.g., the declining autonomy of physicians, the increasing use of nonphysician providers such as nurse practitioners, the stability of physician–patient relationships, the structure of hospitals) are examined in chapters throughout this book.

IN THE FIELD

MAJOR TOPICS OF ANALYSIS IN MEDICAL SOCIOLOGY

The four major categories of interest in medical sociology with specific topics of analysis and sample research questions (that will be answered in the appropriate chapters) are as follows:

Category #1: The Relationship Between the Social Environment and Health and Illness

Social Epidemiology—the study of patterns and trends in the causes and distribution of disease and illness within a population. Research question: Why is the infant mortality rate higher for African Americans?

Social Stress—the study of the imbalance or unease created when demands on a person exceed resources to deal with them. Research question: Why do women report higher levels of stress?

Category #2: Health and Illness Behavior

Health Behavior—the study of behaviors intended to promote positive health. Research question: Why does society focus on changing individual behaviors rather than the social circumstances which influence individual behaviors?

Experiencing Illness and Disability—the study of the ways that people perceive, interpret, and act in response to illness. Research question: What factors cause people to interpret medical symptoms in very different ways?

Category #3: Health Care Practitioners and Their Relationships with Patients

Physicians and the Profession of Medicine—the study of medicine as a profession and the role of medicine within society. Research question: What consequences has the surge in medical malpractice cases had for medicine and for society?

Medical Education and the Socialization of Physicians—the study of the education and socialization of physicians in medical schools. Research question: What are the key value orientations that students learn in medical school?

Nurses, Mid-Level Health Care Practitioners, and Allied Health Workers—the study of issues pertaining to nonphysician health care providers. Research question: Why are physicians more supportive of physician assistants than they are of nurse practitioners?

Alternative and Complementary Healing Practices—the study of healers and healing practices outside conventional medicine. Research question: Why do many people simultaneously use both medical doctors and alternative healers?

The Physician-Patient Relationship—the study of patterns in the way that physicians and patients relate to each other and factors that influence these patterns. Research question: Do male and female physicians interact differently with patients?

Category #4: The Health Care System

The Health Care System—the study of the organization, regulation, financing, and important problems in the health care system. Research question: What effect is health care reform having on the health care cost crisis?

Health Care Delivery—the study of the organizations and agencies (including hospitals) that provide health care services. Research question: What are the consequences for society of for-profit versus not-for-profit hospitals?

The Social Effects of Health Care Technology—the study of the social consequences and public policy choices of new health care technologies. Research question: What are the supporting and opposing arguments for legalizing physician-assisted suicide?

Comparative Health Care Systems—the study of health care systems in other countries. Research question: Why are most health care systems around the world currently undergoing significant change?

SOCIOLOGY'S CONTRIBUTION TO UNDERSTANDING HEALTH, HEALING, AND ILLNESS

Sociology may be defined as "the scientific study of human society and social interaction" (Robertson, 1987:5). It is the discipline with primary responsibility for studying social interactions among people, groups and organizations, and social institutions and examining how these interactions influence and are influenced by the larger culture and social structure of society.

Three particular aspects of sociology contribute in important ways to understanding health, healing, and illness: (1) the sociological perspective, (2) the construction of social theories to explain why things happen as they do, and (3) the scientific foundation of the discipline.

The Sociological Perspective

Sociology is just one of many perspectives that are used to acquire knowledge about the world. History, biology, chemistry, anthropology, psychology, economics, political science, philosophy and religion, clinical medicine, and other disciplines all contribute to our understanding of the medical field. Sociology's primary focus is understanding social interaction, groups and organizations, and how social context and the social environment influence attitudes, behaviors, and social organization.

The **sociological perspective** requires an ability to think about things in a manner other than that to which many individuals are accustomed. Often, we think very individualistically about human behavior. If a particular teenager begins smoking cigarettes, or a particular man is reluctant to see a physician when ill, or a particular medical resident feels abused by superiors, we may attempt to understand the behavior by focusing on the particular individual or the particular situation. However, sociology attempts to understand these behaviors by placing them in social context; that is, by looking for social patterns and by examining the influence of social forces or circumstances that have an impact on individual behavior.

C. Wright Mills, an enormously influential sociologist, referred to this ability to see how larger social patterns (public issues) influence individual behavior (personal troubles) as the **sociological imagination** (Mills, 1959). The fact that most smokers began as teenagers, that men generally are more reluctant than women to see a physician, and that many students feel they have been abused during medical school are social patterns that transcend individual attitudes and behaviors. Sociologists attempt to understand these patterns by examining social forces that have an impact upon them; that is, to identify and explain the "public issues" that lead to the "personal troubles."

The Construction of Social Theories

Sociology is an effort to identify and describe social patterns and then to find cause-and-effect relationships that explain the patterns. In *Invitation to Sociology* (1963), Peter Berger describes sociology as searching for the general in the particular—attempting to determine how particular facts or individual behaviors may generate as well as reflect social patterns. Whether the focus is delinquency, family interaction, or medicine, sociologists attempt to identify patterns in attitudes and behaviors.

> All science, natural and social, assumes that there is some underlying order in the universe. Events, whether they involve molecules or human beings, are not haphazard. They follow a pattern that is sufficiently regular for us to be able to make generalizations—statements that apply not just to a specific case but to most cases of the same type. . . . Generalizations are crucial to science because they place isolated, seemingly meaningless events in patterns we can understand. It then becomes possible to analyze relationships of cause and effect and thus to explain why something happens and to predict that it will happen again under the same conditions in the future. (Robertson, 1987:6)

Major Theoretical Orientations in Sociology That Guide the Effort to Find Explanations. Three major theoretical orientations have dominated the field of sociology. These orientations are fundamental images of society that guide sociological thinking and the process of searching for explanations (Ritzer, 1983).

Functionalism (or structural-functionalism) views society as a system (a structure) with interdependent parts (e.g., the family, the economy, medicine) that work together to produce relative stability. Each of these parts is assumed to have positive consequences (or functions) and may have negative consequences (dysfunctions) for the society as a whole. When each part operates properly, a stable and relatively harmonious society exists.

Given this image of society, functionalists are adept at identifying the effective integration of societal parts. For example, functionalists might identify the manner in which the value that America places on science and discovery has led to significant advancements in medical knowledge and to the development of new forms of medical technology.

Conflict theory views society as a system largely dominated by social inequality and social conflict. Societies are viewed as being in a constant state of change, characterized by disagreements over goals and values, competition among groups with unequal amounts of power, and hostility. Conflict theorists perceive whatever societal order exists to be dictated by the most powerful groups, rather than being based on the value consensus envisioned by functionalists.

Given this image of society, conflict theorists are skillful at utilizing a critical perspective about society and at identifying social inequities. In this regard, medical sociologists have an opportunity to comment critically on perceived problems and inequities in the health care system and to offer a critical perspective on the functioning of the system. For example, conflict theorists point out that a primary reason that many low-income women conceive premature, low-birth-weight babies is their inability to access adequate prenatal care.

While functionalism and conflict theory view society from a macro perspective (examining society as a whole), **interactionism** (or symbolic interactionism) focuses on small-scale, day-to-day interactions among people. Society is viewed as the ultimate outcome of an infinite number of episodes of interaction each day in which individuals interpret social messages and base their responses on these interpretations.

In medicine, interactionists have shown how physicians sometimes use particular communication strategies (e.g., using brief, close-ended questions; interrupting patient comments) to reinforce dominance and to bolster role distance.

The Scientific Foundation of the Discipline

Charon (1998) has stated that sociology rests on both an objective and a critical foundation. Sociology is a social science, and through much of its formative years, researchers typically followed the same basic model of science and scientific research as did their colleagues in the natural and physical sciences. These techniques rely on empirical procedures used to obtain quantifiable data designed to test specific hypotheses. Scientists are expected to maintain objectivity in the conduct of their research; that is, to attempt to prevent biases from influencing the conduct of the work or the conclusions drawn.

The Scientific Process. A model of the scientific process is provided in Figure 1–1. According to this model, once a particular

Figure 1–1 The Scientific Process

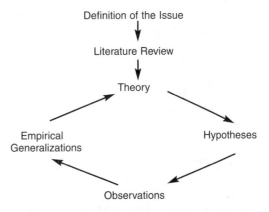

Source: Adapted and reprinted with permission from Walter L. Wallace (ed.), *Sociological Theory: An Introduction.* New York: Aldine de Gruyter. Copyright © 1969 by Walter L. Wallace.

sociological question is identified, the researcher scours the literature (typically books and journals) to learn what research has already been done and to determine what is already known about the subject. This work guides the researcher in formulating a *theory*, or general explanation, about why things happen as they do.

Based on this theory, the researcher deduces one or more specific *hypotheses* (specific statements predicting what will be found in the research). These hypotheses must be capable of being found to be accurate or inaccurate. Research is then designed to test the accuracy of the hypotheses; a sample of people is selected from the population for study and data are collected.

Once the data have been collected and analyzed, the researcher seeks to draw empirical generalizations from the research. Conclusions are drawn about the accuracy of the hypothesis and appropriateness of the theory that guided the research. The research may lend additional credence to the theory, may suggest the theory needs to be modified, or may be so inconsistent with the theory that a major revision is needed. If the results of the research are published or presented, the study will join others on the subject and be available for the next researcher doing a literature review in the area.

Data-Collection Techniques. Some of the most important data-collection techniques used by medical sociologists are briefly described here. Other techniques, such as specific epidemiological techniques, are described where appropriate in the text.

1. *Survey Research.* **Survey research** is the most commonly used data-gathering technique in sociology. It involves the systematic collection of information about attitudes and behaviors through personal or telephone interviews or self-administered questionnaires. Survey research is particularly helpful in studying attitudes or values—subjects that cannot easily be studied in other ways—and in obtaining self-reported data on health and response to illness.

Proper sampling techniques must be followed so that the sample is representative of the population of interest.

2. *Experimental Research.* **Experimental research**—seeking to identify cause-and-effect relationships between specified variables in carefully controlled conditions—is typically conducted in a laboratory but can be done in natural settings. In the ideal case, two groups—the experimental group and the control group—are formed. The groups should be as similar as possible, except that only the experimental group receives the independent variable (the potential "cause"). Whatever change occurs in the dependent variable (the potential "effect") from the beginning to the end of the experiment can then be attributed to the independent variable. Experimental research can be used in health settings for purposes such as testing health education materials, innovations in teaching medical students, and new payment mechanisms.

3. *Observational Research.* **Observational research**—the systematic observation of people in their natural environment—has also been a valuable data-collection technique for medical sociologists. Although it is more difficult to be systematic in using this technique (though an extensive array of techniques to support systematic study is available), it does enable observation of actual behaviors rather than reports of behavior or behaviors performed in artificial settings. Important observational studies have been conducted in such diverse settings as general care hospitals, mortality review conferences, and in patient self-help groups.

4. *Use of Existing Statistics.* Many demographers (those who study population size, composition, and distribution) and other medical sociologists study health problems and society's reaction to them by drawing upon recorded vital and social statistics. Researchers may examine birth and death records, medical charts and insurance forms, and any compiled statistics on mortality, morbidity, medical resources, or any other aspect of health care systems.

Limitations of the Scientific Method.
Although the scientific method continues to dominate in sociology, most sociologists acknowledge that reality is often more subjective than objective. These perspectives direct sociology to help us to understand the "socially constructed" nature of belief systems about health, illness, and healing practices. Cultures vary in their perception of what constitutes good health, in factors that shape health (e.g., the Chinese belief in the presence of a vital spirit in the body), and in views of appropriate healing procedures (e.g., the importance of social support in Navajo healing). These perspectives are examined further in this text in chapters on social stress, illness behavior, and alternative healing practices.

THE ROLE OF THE MEDICAL SOCIOLOGIST IN THE TWENTY-FIRST CENTURY

What will the future role of the medical sociologist be? Perhaps three aspects will be most important.

First, the most important objective of the medical sociologist will continue to be to demonstrate and emphasize the important influence of cultural, social-structural, and institutional forces on health, healing, and illness. Medical sociologists must be ever more vigilant in using their "theoretical and methodological skills to address interesting and important questions" in order to ensure that the sociological perspective continues to influence public discussion (Pescosolido and Kronenfeld, 1995:19).

Second, medical sociologists need to maintain their spirit of free and critical inquiry (Bloom, 1990). Responding to an article that suggested some physicians were concerned about sociologists' more liberal ideology, Mechanic (1990:89) wrote:

> It seems clear that these commentators . . . prefer a sociology that is adjunct to medical activity and accepting of its basic premises. Such a sociology would simply be a servant to medicine not fulfilling its larger responsibility to understand medicine as a social, political, and legal endeavor; to challenge its curative and technological imperatives; to examine equity of care in relation to

class, race, gender, age, character of illness, and geographic area; and to study the appropriate goals and objectives for health care in the context of an aging society with an illness trajectory dominated by chronic disease.

Finally, medical sociologists should continue to seek interdisciplinary collaboration. In the early years of the field, medical sociologists debated whether their primary focus should be on the **sociology of medicine** (i.e., advancing sociological theory and method through research in the medical field) or on the **sociology in medicine** (i.e., making practical contributions to the practice of medicine) (Straus, 1957). Although many medical sociologists clearly have identified more with one of these approaches than with the other, the distinction has blurred over time, and today most researchers understand that good sociological research can simultaneously contribute to the development of medical sociology *and* to improved health care (Bird, Conrad, and Fremont, 2000). Straus (1999) has recently suggested that it is even possible to take a critical perspective while working in a medical setting, so long as it is perceived to be constructive, objective, and not blatantly antagonistic.

Mechanic (1995:1492) recently noted that "the major health problems facing national systems are complex and multifaceted and not easily amenable to analysis from the perspective of any single discipline." Coe (1997:6) has encouraged working with other social scientists (as well as others involved in health research) as a way of creating "opportunities to strengthen a sociological perspective" and deepening "our understanding of the complexities of human behavior in the context of health and illness." Zussman (2000) has written persuasively about how genuine understanding of ethical issues in medicine can be derived by utilizing both normative reflection (the primary approach of medical ethics) and empirical description (the primary contribution of sociology). Although discouraging biological reductionism, Fremont and Bird (1999) have emphasized the importance of understandings that integrate social and biological explanations of matters related to health and illness.

SUMMARY

Medical sociology emerged as a scholarly field of inquiry in the 1950s and 1960s. Four factors were primarily responsible for this emergence: (1) a shift from acute, infectious diseases to chronic, degenerative diseases as major sources of morbidity and mortality; (2) increased focus on behavioral factors related to health and illness; (3) increased recognition of the importance of the patient-physician relationship; and (4) the increasingly complex structure of the health care system. Simultaneously, outside agencies (e.g., medical schools, government agencies) were taking increased interest in the field, and medical sociology was becoming institutionalized as a special interest section in the American Sociological Association.

Sociology's contributions to the study of health, healing, and illness emanate from the sociological perspective (the understanding that human behavior is largely shaped by the groups to which people belong and by the social interaction that takes place within those groups); sociology-based theoretical approaches (functionalism, conflict theory, and interactionism); and from the scientific foundation of the discipline.

Perhaps the most important tasks of medical sociology are to demonstrate and emphasize the influence of cultural, social-structural, and institutional forces on health, healing, and illness and to maintain a spirit of free and critical inquiry while recognizing the interdisciplinary basis of health and illness.

HEALTH ON THE INTERNET

Learn more about the Medical Sociology Section of the American Sociological Association at:

http://dept.kent.edu/sociology/asamedsoc/

KEY CONCEPTS AND TERMS

conflict theory
experimental research
functionalism
interactionism
Journal of Health and Social Behavior
medical sociology
observational research

scientific process
social medicine
sociological imagination
sociological perspective
sociology in medicine
sociology of medicine
survey research

DISCUSSION QUESTION

To understand better the approach and work of medical sociologists, select a recent article from the *Journal of Health and Social Behavior* or *Social Science and Medicine* or any journal assigned by your professor. Identify its main subject, theoretical approach, data-collection technique, and main findings.

How does the approach of a medical sociologist differ from that of a medical journalist or that of a layperson attempting to understand some subject related to health, healing, and illness? Identify a specific question related to medical sociology or an issue that you might be interested in studying.

REFERENCES

ASA Committee on Certification in Sociology. 1986 *Guidelines for the Certification Process in Medical Sociology.* Washington, DC: American Sociological Association.

Berger, Peter L. 1963 *Invitation to Sociology: A Humanistic Perspective.* New York: Doubleday.

Bird, Chloe E., Peter Conrad, and Allen M. Fremont. 2000 "Medical Sociology at the Millennium," pp. 1–10 in *Handbook of Medical Sociology,* 5th ed., Chloe E. Bird, Peter Conrad, and Allen M. Fremont (eds.). Upper Saddle River, NJ: Prentice Hall.

Bloom, Samuel W. 1990 "Episodes in the Institutionalization of Medical Sociology: A Personal View." *Journal of Health and Social Behavior,* 31:1–10.

Charon, Joel. 1998 *The Meaning of Sociology,* 6th ed. Upper Saddle River, NJ: Prentice Hall.

Coe, Rodney M. 1970 *Sociology of Medicine.* New York: McGraw-Hill.

———. 1997 "The Magic of Science and the Science of Magic: An Essay on the Process of Healing." *Journal of Health and Social Behavior,* 38:1–8.

DeVries, Raymond, and Janardan Subedi. 1998 *Bioethics and Society: Constructing the Ethical Enterprise.* Upper Saddle River, NJ: Prentice Hall.

Fremont, Allen M., and Chloe E. Bird. 1999 "Integrating Sociological and Biological Models: An Editorial." *Journal of Health and Social Behavior,* 40:126–129.

Garceau, Oliver. 1941 *The Political Life of the American Medical Association.* Cambridge, MA: Harvard University Press.

Grotjahn, Alfred. 1915 *Soziale Pathologie.* Berlin: August Hirschwald Verlag.

Hall, Oswald. 1946 "The Informal Organization of the Medical Profession." *Canadian Journal of Economic and Political Science,* 12:30–44.

Levine, Sol. 1987 "The Changing Terrains in Medical Sociology: Emergent Concern with Quality of Life." *Journal of Health and Social Behavior,* 28:1–6.

Mechanic, David. 1990 "The Role of Sociology in Health Affairs." *Health Affairs,* 9:85–97.

———. 1995 "Emerging Trends in the Application of the Social Sciences to Health and Medicine." *Social Science and Medicine,* 40:1491–1496.

Mills, C. Wright. 1959 *The Sociological Imagination.* New York: Oxford University Press.

Parsons, Talcott. 1939 "The Professions and Social Structure." *Social Forces,* 17:457–467.

Pescosolido, Bernice A., and Jennie J. Kronenfeld. 1995 "Health, Illness, and Healing in an Uncertain Era: Challenges From and For Medical Sociology." *Journal of Health and Social Behavior,* Extra Issue: 5–33.

Ritzer, George. 1983 *Sociological Theory.* New York: Appleton-Century-Crofts.

Robertson, Ian. 1987 *Sociology,* 3rd ed. New York: Worth Publishers.

Rosen, George. 1944 *The Specialization of Medicine.* New York: Froben Press.

———. 1976 "Social Science and Health in the United States in the Twentieth Century." *Clio Medica,* 11:245–268.

Ruderman, Florence A. 1981 "What Is Medical Sociology?" *Journal of the American Medical Association,* 245:927–929.

Straus, Robert. 1957 "The Nature and Status of Medical Sociology." *American Sociological Review,* 22:200–204.

———. 1999 "Medical Sociology: A Personal Fifty-Year Perspective." *Journal of Health and Social Behavior,* 40:103–110.

Wallace, Walter L. (ed.). 1969 *Sociological Theory: An Introduction.* Chicago: Aldine Publishing Company.

Zussman, Robert. 2000 "The Contributions of Sociology to Medical Ethics." *Hastings Center Report,* 30:7–11.

2

THE DEVELOPMENT OF SCIENTIFIC MEDICINE

Today's healing practices and health care systems are evolutionary products of centuries of efforts to understand disease and illness and to find effective means to protect and restore health. Understanding this historical development is important both as an end in itself and as a means to a better understanding of current patterns.

Compiled histories of medicine are not in short supply. But few of these histories attempt to place the development of medicine within a societal context. In 1970, Thomas McKeown argued for a "sociological approach to the history of medicine." He suggested the following topics for the social historian: (1) people's understanding of causal forces in disease and illness (what may be called the "sociology of medical knowledge"); (2) activities in which physicians engage, including diagnosis, pathology (understanding of disease), disease prevention, disease cure, prognosis, and palliation (relief from suffering); (3) reasons for improvement in human health and the relative contributions of sanitation, nutrition, and medical technology; (4) the evolution of medical practice, including medical specialization; (5) the history of public health and the pub-

lic health service; and (6) the development of hospitals and their changing role within society.

This chapter focuses primarily on the first of these objectives by describing the historical development of scientific medicine and tracing the ascendancy of scientific medical authority in America. However, several additional themes should emerge from a close reading of this chapter:

1. The "constantly shifting character" (Cassady, 1991) of medicine as understanding of disease causation shifts between a supernatural and scientific basis; as the role and popularity of alternative healing philosophies ebbs and flows; and as the emphasis within medicine centers more on preventive care or curative care.
2. The constant struggle of physicians and medical researchers to discover causes of disease and effective cures for them and the typically long time lag before major discoveries are accepted and have any impact on patient care.
3. The important impact on medicine of other major institutions in society including the government, the church, the family, and science.

4. The constantly evolving view within societies of the nature and inevitability of disease and of the patient's responsibility for self-care.

A BRIEF HISTORY OF MEDICINE

The crucial event in the development of scientific medicine—"that all disease is materially generated by specific etiological agents such as bacteria, viruses, parasites, genetic malformations, and internal chemical imbalances" (Berliner, 1984:30)—is Louis Pasteur's formulation of the germ theory of disease in the 1860s and 1870s. Prior to this time, both lay and professional understanding of the causes of disease and illness had evolved through a multitude of approaches and explanations. The first part of this chapter traces this history in a very brief "sociology of scientific medical knowledge."

EARLY HUMANS

Although the first forms of writing did not appear until between 4000 and 3000 B.C., paleontologists have used such human remnants as teeth, bones, and mummies, as well as works of art, to study early disease and its treatment. They have learned that disease and injury are as old as humankind (and the presence of bacteria and viruses far older). There is evidence of tumors, fractures, parasitic diseases, arthritis, osteomyelitis, and dental caries that predate written communication.

How did early humans interpret these medical calamities?

> Primitive man, noting the rising and setting of the sun and moon, the progress of the seasons, the birth, growth, and inevitable death of plants, animals, and humans, did not take long to arrive at the supposition that these phenomena did not occur by chance . . . it seemed logical to suppose that they were ordered by some all-powerful god, or gods, and equally logical was the belief that fortune and misfortune were signs of the gods' pleasure or displeasure. (Camp, 1977:11)

Supernatural Belief Systems

These "magico-religious" or **supernatural explanations of disease** evolved into complex belief systems. Diseases were caused either by direct intervention of a god or spirit or through a sorcerer (a mortal in control of supernatural forces) or through the intrusion of some foreign object into the body. This "object" might have been a spirit or demon or even something more tangible such as a stone or pebble (Ackernecht, 1982).

Early humans used several divination procedures (e.g., crystal gazing or trances) to read the

---

IN THE FIELD

THE CONTRIBUTIONS OF IMHOTEP AND ANCIENT AFRICANS TO WESTERN MEDICINE

A considerable body of knowledge attests to the fact that Africans in antiquity made significant contributions to medicine and may have been the originators of medical practice. Though current medical history texts give little attention to the contributions to medicine of people of color, Greek philosophers, historians, and physicians (who are given much credit) wrote of what they learned from the writings and oral traditions of Africans.

Some now refer to Imhotep—an African engineer, architect, scribe, priest, and physician who lived around 3000 B.C.—as the "Historical Father of Medicine." He is known to have instructed many Greeks in the art of medicine, possibly built the first hospital, and recorded his observations and knowledge about surgery, anatomy, pathology, diagnosis, and experimental scientific observation (Pickett, 1992).

intentions of the supernatural. Once diagnosis was made, appropriate cures were employed. Religious rituals such as prayer, magic spells, and exorcism were used when the origin of the disease was traced to supernatural forces, and more physical means, including a "sucking-out" procedure, artificially induced vomiting, and "bloodletting" (draining blood from the body to extract the foreign presence or redistribute the blood—a practice that survived for centuries), were used in cases of object intrusion (Ackernecht, 1982).

The most amazing procedure used was skull **trephination**—using sharpened stones to drill or carve a hole in the skull. The exact purpose of trephination is unknown, but many believe it was done to release evil spirits. The holes drilled were of various sizes and configurations depending upon the diagnosis. Fossil studies demonstrate that many of the patients survived the surgery, and some of them received additional trephinations years after the original one (Green, 1968).

The First Physicians

Specialists (often religious figures) emerged to serve as intermediaries with the gods. Known as the **shaman** (or the "witch doctor" or "medicine man"), this was typically a highly revered, much feared individual who often provided effective medical care. Many were adept at observing animals and noting the plants and herbs they used for relief, and many practiced trial and error medicine—experimenting with a variety of substances or procedures till the most effective were identified. The kinds of diseases most common in early societies—rheumatic diseases, digestive disorders, skin diseases, and gynecological disorders—are problems more amenable to cures available at the time than would be epidemic diseases, such as typhoid, measles, and smallpox, which many believe were not yet present.

Of course, these techniques were only part of the medical arsenal of the shaman. Prayer and incantation, ritualistic dancing, and sacrifices were also used to capture the attention of the gods. These techniques also increased the patient's confidence in the cures being attempted—an important psychotherapeutic benefit (Camp, 1977; Ackernecht, 1982).

THE EGYPTIAN CIVILIZATION

Of the various ancient civilizations whose medical practices have been studied in some depth, Egypt has received the most attention. This is due to Egypt's reputation as an especially healthy civilization and to an abundance of written material and other forms of evidence (medical writings preserved on the papyrus reed and well-preserved mummies) that exist from the 3000-year old Egyptian civilization.

The most important development in Egyptian medicine is the evolution of physicians into specialists, since most of them focused on a particular disease or on a particular part of the body. Physicians were also religious leaders, and each was devoted to a different god. As a result, they tended to focus on whatever diseases were associated with their deity. Not surprisingly, given the hot and dusty desert conditions, most physicians specialized in eye care (Camp, 1977).

Egyptian medicine also produced two noteworthy documents: the **Code of Hammurabi** (a Babylonian King who lived from 1728 to 1686 B.C.) which is possibly the first codified set of guidelines regarding responsibilities of physicians, and the Ebers Papyrus—a type of medical textbook summarizing extant knowledge about several disease categories that offered tips on diagnosis, prognosis, and therapeutic measures, including over 800 specific prescriptions (Ackernecht, 1982).

GREEK AND ROMAN SOCIETIES

One of the most remarkable civilizations of all was that of Greece during the last 2000 years B.C. The substantial contribution of the Greeks to medicine is consistent with their contributions to philosophy, art, theater, sculpture, government, and other areas.

In the beginning part of this era, religion and medicine were still inextricably linked. Apollo, the sun god, was also god of health and medicine and believed to be the inventor of the healing art. According to Greek legend, Aesculapius was the son of Apollo and such a brilliant healer that by the eighth century B.C. he was considered the Greek god of health. Temples called "asklepieia" were created where priest-physicians practiced the healing ceremony of incubation or "temple sleep."

Patients who came to the temple would purify themselves (bathe), fast, read about the cures of former patients, and make offerings to Aesculapius. They would be given drugs to induce sleep. During the night, harmless "sacred" snakes would crawl around the patients and lick their wounds after which attendants would apply salves. Lore has it that cures were invariably produced (Hastings, 1974).

Hippocrates—The "Father of Medicine"

Simultaneously, a more empirically based medicine was developing and many physicians enjoyed favorable reputations. The most renowned of these physicians is certainly **Hippocrates** of Cos (460–377 B.C.)—the "father of medicine." Hippocrates was born in Cos, was well educated, became a successful and much beloved physician, and was an esteemed teacher. He is best known for three major contributions:

Hippocrates of Cos, the "father of medicine," advocated natural rather than supernatural explanations for disease. (Copyright The British Museum).

1. *The principle of natural, rather than supernatural, explanations for disease.*

   Hippocrates taught that disease is a natural process and that symptoms are reactions of the body to disease. He further emphasized that the chief function of the physician is to aid the natural forces of the body. With this principle, sick people ceased to be considered as sinners and sinners began to be thought of as sick people. Hippocrates emphasized that the body possessed its own means of recovery and that a healthy man was one in a balanced mental and physical state because of complete harmony of all of the humors. (Green, 1968:31)

   Hippocrates subscribed to the **humoral theory of disease**—a dominant approach for centuries. The humoral theory postulates that

there are four natural elements in the world (air, earth, fire, and water) and four natural properties (hot, cold, dry, and wet). In the body the elements are blood (hot), phlegm (cold), yellow bile (dry), and black bile (wet). A person is healthy when these four humors are in balance and when the individual is in balance with the environment. Therefore, one seeks moderation in life so as not to upset the balance. Sickness is created by imbalance. These imbalances are detected by physical symptoms. A warm forehead (fever) indicates excessive heat; a runny nose is a sign of excessive phlegm. Appropriate cures seek to restore balance. For example, cold food was a remedy for heat-related diseases, and a very dry environment was created for the patient with excessive phlegm.

2. *His writings.* One of the most important sets of medical writings ever collated is the *Corpus Hippocraticum*, more than 70 books, monographs, and essays covering a variety of aspects of medicine. Hippocrates wrote of the importance of observing disease progression and described his own copious note taking of medical histories, symptoms, and reactions to therapy when treating his patients. He encouraged physicians to treat the whole patient, not just a particular organ or particular symptom (Ackernecht, 1982).

3. *His teaching of human compassion and ethical standards as illustrated in the Hippocratic Oath.* The first section of the **Hippocratic Oath** expresses reciprocal commitments made by physicians and their apprentices and establishes teaching as a primary obligation of the physician. The second portion of the oath is a brief summary of ethical guidelines. Some of the pledges—for example, against doing abortion, cutting for stone, and facilitating a suicide—raise questions since all were common practice at the time and were activities in which Hippocratic physicians are known to have engaged (Nuland, 1988). Nevertheless, the oath commanded significant attention then as it does now (even though most physicians no longer pledge to it).

Despite the popularity of Hippocrates, Greece could be described as an "open medical market place" that was comprised of several types of religious, magical, and empirical medical practitioners. Because there was no medical licensing, anyone could be a healer, and patients used the services of practitioners representing a multitude of medical philosophies.

IN THE FIELD

THE HIPPOCRATIC OATH

I swear by Apollo the physician, and Aesculapius, Hygeia, and Panacea and all the gods and goddesses, that, according to my ability and judgment, I will keep this oath and this covenant:

To reckon him who taught me this Art equally dear to me as my parents, to share my substance with him, and relieve his necessities if required; to look upon his offspring on the same footing as my own brothers, and to teach them this Art, if they shall wish to learn it, without fee or stipulation; and that by precept, lecture, and every other mode of instruction, I will impart a knowledge of the Art to my own sons, and those of my teachers, and to disciples who have signed the covenant and have taken an oath according to the law of medicine, but no one else.

I will follow that system of regimen which, according to my ability and judgement, I consider for the benefit of my patients, and abstain from whatever is deleterious and mischievous.

I will give no deadly medicine to anyone if asked, nor suggest any such counsel; and in like manner I will not give to a woman an abortive remedy. With purity and with holiness I will pass my life and practice my Art.

I will not cut persons labouring under the stone, but will leave this to be done by such men as are practitioners of this work.

Into whatever houses I enter, I will go into them for the benefit of the sick, and will abstain from every voluntary act of mischief and corruption; and, further, from the seduction of females or males, of freemen and slaves.

Whatever, in connection with my professional practice, or not in connection with it, I see or hear, in the life of men, which ought not to be spoken of abroad, I will not divulge, as reckoning that all such should be kept secret.

While I continue to keep this Oath unviolated, may it be granted to me to enjoy life and practice the Art, respected by all men, in all times. But should I trespass and violate this Oath, may the reverse be my lot.

Roman Medicine

Medicine did not flourish in Rome. Roman households ministered to the sick in their own families, often using treatments similar to those used in early societies (Hastings, 1974). Beginning in the third century B.C. (Rome was founded in 753 B.C.), Greek physicians began filtering into Rome. At first, these physicians were persecuted, partly out of a jealousy that Rome was not producing its own physicians. Cato the Censor (234–149 B.C.), the man given credit for being the first important writer in Latin, prohibited any in his family from using these physicians (he relied instead on raw cabbage taken internally and rubbed on the body as a medicinal cure). Pliny the Elder himself is said to have remarked, "The honour of a Roman does not permit him to make medicine his profession, and the Romans who begin to study it are mercenary deserters to the Greeks" (Camp, 1977).

Perhaps for this reason, physicians openly competed for status and reputation. Aggressive self-promotion and public humiliation of rivals were not uncommon. Physicians sought out medical cases that had been difficult to solve and attempted public, spectacular diagnoses or cures that would be widely publicized and, when successful, would lead to improvement in social standing (Mattern, 1999).

Asclepiades

The arrival of Asclepiades (a Greek physician born in Asia Minor in 124 B.C.) initiated a general increased regard for physicians. Skeptical of the idea of the "self-healing" potential of the body, Asclepiades believed that health and illness were determined by the condition of the pores. If the pores were either too open or too closed, illness resulted. He prescribed massage, diet (wine was a common recommendation), and baths as techniques to alter the structure of the pores (Camp, 1977). Asclepiades became a popular figure, founded a school that survived his death in 60 B.C., and influenced Julius Caesar to decree in 46 B.C. that

Greek slave-doctors were free and had full rights of citizenship.

Roman Contributions to Medicine

Rome's major medical contributions were to the field of public health. Recognizing that unsanitary conditions contributed to the spread of disease, the government constructed a system of aqueducts to obtain pure water, built an elaborate system of public baths, passed ordinances requiring street cleanliness, and established a system of hospitals to tend to the sick.

Galen

The other pivotal figure of this era is **Galen**, a physician whose ideas dominated much of medicine for the next 12 centuries. Born in Asia Minor in A.D. 131, he studied Hippocratic medicine (and its rival theories) and eventually migrated to Rome at the age of 34. There he became famous as a physician, author, and medical researcher.

Galen made extensive contributions to the understanding of anatomy. Since he was prevented by Roman law from using human cadavers for study, Galen relied on the dissection of monkeys and pigs and on the study of the skeletons of criminals. Based on these studies, he refuted several common medical notions (e.g., that the heart was the origin of the nerves, that blood vessels originated in the brain) and added to the existing knowledge about bones, muscle groups, the brain, and various nerves. Yet he could not be dissuaded from his belief in "pneuma"—that certain vital spirits (but not blood) circulated throughout the body (Green, 1968).

Galen, an extremely dogmatic individual who was absolutely convinced that his ideas were accurate, vehemently discouraged others from further investigating his work. Though we now know many of his theories to be false, they were extremely influential during his time and for several subsequent centuries. On the other hand, his title as "the Father of Experimental Physiology" seems well deserved, as he was probably the foremost medical experimentalist until the 1600s.

THE MEDIEVAL ERA

The end of the Western Roman Empire is generally pegged at A.D. 476 when the conquest of Europe by the barbarians was completed. In the East, the Byzantine Empire (based in Constantinople) survived and became a center of civilization. The time period between (roughly) A.D. 500 and A.D. 1500 is referred to as the Medieval Era.

Monastic Medicine

Medical practice in the first half of this era is referred to as **monastic medicine** because medicine was based in the monastery. Medical practice was officially controlled by the Church in Byzantium (the early Christian church), which was extremely hostile to physicians. This hostility was based on two precepts: (1) disease and illness are beneficial in that they test one's faith and commitment to God and the church, and (2) all illnesses occur as punishment by God, possession by the devil, or the result of witchcraft.

These religious causes required religious cures, typically prayer, penitence, or intercession with saints. Particular diseases and body parts were believed to have a patron saint who could inflict pain and enact cure. Thus, if one had a toothache, prayer was made to Saint Apollonia; lepers appealed to Saint Gete; and those with plague prayed to Saint Sebastian (Hastings, 1974; Ackernecht, 1982). According to the church, private physicians represented a form of blasphemy in their efforts to cure disease apart from religious intervention (Camp,

1977). In reality many people from all stations in life considered secular healing to be an appropriate complement for religious healing and often used the services of herbalists, midwives, wise women, and lay specialists. These practitioners are largely responsible for preserving much of the medical knowledge that had been passed on to them and ensuring its transmission to later generations (Bennett, 2000).

Arabic Medicine

The commonwealth of Islam was founded in 622 by Mohammed. During the next 100 years, his followers conquered almost half of the world known at that time. By 1000, the Arab Empire extended from Spain to India. The Arabs were intensely interested in medicine. They built famous teaching hospitals, bestowed high prestige on private physicians, and basically served as the link between Greek medicine and Renaissance medicine (Hastings, 1974).

Scholastic Medicine

The second half of the Medieval Era is referred to as the time of **scholastic medicine**. In 1130 a proclamation from the Council of Clermont forbade monks from practicing medicine because it was too disruptive to the peace and order of monastic sequestration (Ackernecht, 1982). Rather than shifting medicine to the private sector, medical practice became the province of the secular clergy, and universities began to play a prominent role in the education of physicians. Though it is impossible to fix the precise date at which universities in the modern

IN THE FIELD

A MEDIEVAL JOKE

If you want to be cured of	Apply it
I don't know what	I don't know where
Take this herb of	And you will be cured
I don't know what name	I don't know when

sense first developed, twelfth- and thirteenth-century schools became centers where a variety of disciplines were taught (probably the most important legacy provided by the Middle Ages) (Green, 1968).

Two other occurrences during this era are significant: (1) There were numerous devastating epidemics (leprosy reached a peak in the thirteenth century; epidemics of scurvy were common; the Bubonic Plague—**Black Death**—caught hold in Europe in the 1340s and killed an estimated 43 million people in 20 years) that made clear the total helplessness of physicians to restrain disease (Green, 1968); and (2) the earliest hospitals developed in the monastic period (though they were mostly places of refuge for the poor, the clergy did provide caring concern for those who came to them).

MEDICINE IN THE RENAISSANCE

The fifteenth and sixteenth centuries—the Renaissance—represent a rebirth in the arts and philosophy, scientific endeavor, technological advancement, and medicine. The scholarly blinders of the Middle Ages were discarded in favor of *humanism*, which stressed the dignity of the individual, the importance of this life (and not solely the afterlife), and spiritual freedom.

Andreas Vesalius

A key early event of the Renaissance was the refutation (at long last) of many of Galen's ideas. Andreas Vesalius (1514–1564), a product of a Brussels medical family, contradicted Galen's description of anatomy. Using corpses purchased from grave-robbers, he discovered that Galen's descriptions accurately portrayed monkeys but, in many respects, not humans. For centuries, people had believed Galen's conclusions were based on human dissection, yet they were not. Vesalius contended that if Galen was wrong about anatomy, he might be wrong about his other medical conclusions (e.g., pneuma). Yet allegiance to Galen's ideas was so strong that Vesalius was dismissed from his university posi-

tion for this heresy, and his career as an anatomist was finished (though he later became a court physician). It was not until 1628 that Englishman William Harvey demonstrated conclusively that blood circulates throughout the body in an action stimulated by the heart (Hastings, 1974).

Paracelsus

The humoral theory of disease also came under attack. Philippus Aureolus Theophrastus Bombastus von Hohenheim (1493–1541)—Paracelsus, for short—held that God revealed medical truth to humans through revelation. A devotee of astrology and alchemy (the chemistry of the day), he criticized the humoral theory and spent much of his life searching for specific pharmacological remedies and produced some modest successes. Though often disliked for his attacks on Galen, and known as a thoroughly contradictory fellow, Paracelsus is nevertheless an important figure in medical history.

Medical Specialization

During the Renaissance, the medical specialization that had begun to develop in the ninth or tenth century became more pronounced. *Physicians* were those who had graduated from a school of medicine. They provided diagnosis and consultation and were expected to bear themselves as gentlemen so as to match the demeanor of their wealthy patients. *Surgeons* were lower in status because they practiced skills learned in apprenticeship. Their primary responsibilities were to treat external complaints (e.g., wounds, abscesses), to repair broken bones, and to perform minor surgeries. In some areas, *barber surgeons* were available to perform major surgery (often on war wounded), and many also practiced bloodletting. Approximately equal in prestige to surgeons, *apothecaries* dispensed herbs and spices prescribed by physicians and, especially in the countryside, often took on the physician's duties. Nevertheless, self-medication and lay healing were very common in the Renaissance, and families placed priority on staying well.

MEDICINE FROM 1600 TO 1900

The Seventeenth Century

The development of modern science is the key event of the seventeenth century.

> This scientific revolution replaced previous concepts with new ideas of matter and its properties, new applications of mathematics to physics, and new methods of experimentation. By 1700, a "new world" view had taken form. Modern science rested on interchange and mutual verification of scientific ideas and information by investigators in many countries and these needs were satisfied by the development of scientific societies and publications (Green, 1968:83).

In part, this scientific revolution was stimulated by several scientist-philosophers of the century, most notably Francis Bacon (1561–1626) and René Descartes (1596–1650). Bacon argued for "natural" explanations for events that could be understood through systematic observation and experimentation. Descartes invented analytical geometry and, through his work on momentum, vision, reflex actions, and a mind–body duality, laid the basis for a science of physiology.

William Harvey. The most important physiological advancement in the century was Englishman William Harvey's (1578–1657) confirmation of the circulation of blood. Though the idea had been suggested by others earlier in history, Harvey was the first to offer experimental and quantitative proof.

Throughout his life, Harvey was a clinician-researcher. He maintained a clinical practice of medicine (in his later years being physician to kings and other members of the aristocracy) while he devoted himself to medical investigation in anatomy and physiology. Primarily through analysis of dissected and vivisected animals, observation of the weakening heartbeat of animals as they were about to die, and various forms of experimentation on human heartbeat, Harvey proved that the contraction of the heart drove blood into the major arteries toward the body's peripheries (and that cardiac valves prevented blood from reentering the heart through the arteries). When the heart is resting between beats, it is filled with blood that has been carried to it by the veins. Though Harvey's finding removed a key obstacle to medical progress, the discovery was met with skepticism by some and open hostility by others. It had little influence on the treatment of patients during Harvey's time (even in his own practice) as physicians waited for further substantiation of his main ideas (Nuland, 1988).

Clinical Medicine. How did all of this scientific theorizing affect patient treatment? Not much. Even those theories now known to be accurate were met with skepticism, and the process of incorporating new knowledge or techniques into medical practice was quite slow. Medical superstitions were common, routine treatments often dangerous, and quackery quite prevalent. On the other hand, some seventeenth-century physicians focused their attention on the physician–patient relationship and on the body's self-healing capacity, and in this way, maintained the Hippocratic tradition.

The Eighteenth Century

The eighteenth century, the "Age of Enlightenment," is marked by efforts to collate the advancements of the preceding century and to further refine knowledge in all fields including medicine. People perceived that they were living at a special time of rapid growth; more open intellectual inquiry; advancement in the arts, literature, philosophy, and science; and freer political expression.

Development of a Modern Concept of Pathology. Though medical progress had been achieved in many areas, understanding of disease causation in the early eighteenth century was little different than it had been 2,500 years earlier. Many still advocated the humoral theory or some variation of it; others traced disease to climactic conditions or focused on structural explanations such as the condition of the pores.

The understanding that diseases are attached to particular organs is traceable to Giovanni

Battista Morgagni (1682–1771), an Italian physician and Professor of Anatomy at the University of Padua. Based on his systematic and thorough note taking of patients' symptoms, Morgagni developed the **anatomical concept of disease**—that diseases could be traced to particular pathology or disturbance in individual organs. Hence, he directed medicine to seek the originating localized disturbance in a particular organ. It may seem strange to us today that for so long physicians did not connect patients' symptoms with the corresponding pathological condition. And even those who challenged the prevailing notions of the day, like Andreas Vesalius and William Harvey, relied primarily on the old ways in the actual treatment of their own patients.

The Emergence of Public Health and Preventive Medicine.   The eighteenth century also witnessed a return to interest in public health. Attention was focused on the unsanitary conditions that prevailed in industry, the armed forces, prisons, and hospitals. The lack of public sanitation in cities and contaminated water supplies were seen as significant threats to health. Individuals were encouraged to attend more to personal hygiene.

The foremost accomplishment of this movement was the discovery of an effective preventive measure against smallpox, a leading cause of death among children. Edward Jenner (1749–1823), a British country doctor, had heard that milkmaids infected by cowpox developed an immunity to smallpox. Through experimentation (on humans), Jenner demonstrated that persons inoculated with cowpox (vaccinated) would not develop the disease. Though initially regarded with suspicion, it was a signal event in the history of preventive medicine (Ackernecht, 1982).

Alternative Paths of Medicine.   In discussing the advancement of ideas later confirmed by science, competing theories and treatments of the day often are overlooked. The discoveries of Morgagni and Jenner, for example, do not mean that medicine was not simulta-

neously taking alternative routes. For example, William Cullen of Edinburgh (1712–1790) founded a medical system based on "nervous forces"—that all diseases were a result of overstimulation or an inability to respond to stimulation. Appropriate cures were found in stimulants and depressants (Ackernecht, 1982). Edinburgh-trained James Graham established a "Temple of Health and Hymen" in London. The temple was filled with beautiful young virgins attired in skimpy costumes who would sing to the sick—an approach that seemed logical to Graham who believed that illness could only be cured in the presence of beautiful sights and sounds (Camp, 1977).

The Nineteenth Century

Many eighteenth- and nineteenth-century inventions stimulated a rapid growth in the iron and textile industries and led to the Industrial Revolution. Industrialization began in England and spread to the rest of Europe and the United States. The development of large industries with many jobs pulled large numbers of workers into concentrated areas. The world was not prepared to deal with the consequences of this urbanization process. The cities that grew up around the industries were severely overcrowded, typically unsanitary, and often lacking safe procedures for food and water storage. These conditions produced a very unhealthy living environment.

Hospital Medicine.   The first half of the nineteenth century is known mostly for the importance physicians and medical researchers attached to clinical observation. Ackernecht (1982) suggests that in the Middle Ages medicine had centered in libraries; in the following three centuries (as in antiquity) it centered on the individual sickbed; in the nineteenth century, for the first time, it centered on the hospital.

Hospitals had existed for centuries but increased rapidly in number in the 1800s in response to the massive number of people migrating into the newly developing cities. Communicable diseases became commonplace; many of the urban migrants contracted typhoid fever and tuberculosis. Admission to a hospital was the only resort. These patients provided an unprecedented opportunity for clinicians and researchers to observe the sick and to search for common patterns in their symptomology, disease progression, and response to medication. By the 1830s, especially in Paris, physician-researchers were increasingly taking advantage of the opportunity to separate patients by condition and to specialize in particular conditions in order to expand medical knowledge (Weisz, 2003). Simultaneous advances in science and technology (e.g., the invention of the stethoscope by Laennec) were extremely important events of this era, but the immediate course of medicine was more strongly influenced by clinical observation in hospitals.

Laboratory Medicine.   The laboratory became the focus in the second half of the century. The work of Morgagni and others had fixed attention on pathology in particular organs. But no one knew what caused something in the organ to go awry. Many theories existed, and each sought "the" answer to unlock this key mystery. The absence of a correct answer to this question was repeatedly made obvious by the absence of effective cures.

> They bled their patients, and they puked them and purged them and blistered them as their professional forefathers had always done; they confused the metabolisms of the sick with dazzling combinations of botanicals whose real actions were only partially known, and often not known at all. They stimulated in cases whose cause was thought to be too little excitation, and they tried to induce a touch of torpor when the opposite was the case. In short, except when the need for amputation or lancing was obvious, the healers didn't really know what they were doing. (Nuland, 1988:306)

Discovery of the Cell.   The answer to the mystery is, of course, the cell, and credit for its discovery and interpretation goes to the German pathologist Rudolf Virchow (1821–1902). Virchow pinpointed the cell as the basic physiological matter, and understood that disease begins with some alteration in the normally functioning, healthy cell. Effective treatment depends on restoring the cell to normality (or, at least, terminating its abnormal development).

Ironically, while Virchow's discovery of the human cell appropriately led to study of the physiological changes involved in disease progression, Virchow was a leading proponent of the importance of environmental influences on health and illness. He understood that one's social class, occupation, and involvement in social networks had as much to do with creating sickness as cellular changes. He referred to medicine as a "social science" and as the "science of man" and sought to influence societal conditions that negatively impact human health (Ackernecht, 1982). The final 30 years of his life were largely devoted to explorations in the fields of anthropology and archaeology, to the development of public health measures in his hometown of Berlin, and to advocating for democratic reform and political and cultural freedom in Germany. He was a much beloved figure in Germany at the time of his death.

The Germ Theory of Disease.   One more question remained. What causes a cell to begin to change? What substance or what condition initiates the disease process? At various points in history, medical researchers had speculated on the existence of microorganisms, but the speculation never inspired any substantial following. From the 1830s through the 1860s, various researchers observed bacteria under the microscope (minute organisms were first observed under a microscope by its inventor, Leeuwenhoek, in 1675), but the significance of the organisms was not understood at the time.

The key figure in the development of the **germ theory of disease** is Louis Pasteur (1822–1895), a French chemist, now called the "Father of Modern Medicine." In 1857, Pasteur countered prevailing understandings by demonstrating that fermentation (he lived in the wine region) was not solely a chemical event but was the result of various microorganisms. By 1862, he had disproved the notion that bacteria were spontaneously generated.

However, not until 1877, after 20 years of research on microorganisms, did Pasteur turn to human diseases. He identified the specific bacteria involved in anthrax and chicken cholera, and, with several of his pupils, identified other disease-causing bacteria and developed effective vaccinations against them (Ackernecht, 1982). By 1881, the germ theory of disease was generally accepted.

With the impetus provided by Pasteur, one bacteriological discovery after another occurred over the next 10 years. Between 1878 and 1887, the causative agents for gonorrhea, typhoid fever, leprosy, malaria, tuberculosis, cholera, diphtheria, tetanus, pneumonia, and epidemic meningitis were discovered (Ackernecht, 1982).

The success of these efforts inspired an exciting period in medical history. Researchers would focus on a particular disease, identify the organism that caused it, determine how it invaded the body, and identify a vaccine that would prevent it. At first, it was understood only that vaccines worked. It required another 10 years to understand why—that the body produces antibodies in response to the presence of a disease and that these antibodies remain in the body to fight the disease on future exposures (Hastings, 1974).

Progress in Surgery. Considerable progress in surgery also occurred during this time due to three essential advancements: (1) an understanding of the "localized" nature of disease (when surgeons believed that diseases were caused by generalized forces, like humors, it made little sense to remove a particular area or organ); (2) an ability to control the patient's pain in the surgical process (which occurred in incremental stages based on trial and error throughout the nineteenth century); and (3) an ability to prevent wound infection. Throughout history, surgeons recognized that almost all surgery (even "successful" surgery) resulted in a frequently fatal infection in the wound site. ("The operation was a success, but the patient died.") Surgery performed in hospitals was especially likely to result in infection.

The importance of "asepsis" (surgical cleanliness) was discovered by Sir Joseph Lister (1827–1912), an English surgeon. Lister's concern

was prompted by the very large percentage (almost half) of his amputation patients who died as a result of infection. At first convinced that infection was caused by the air that came into contact with the wound, Lister altered his thinking when he read descriptions of Pasteur's work. By the mid-1860s, he realized that sepsis was caused by bacteria in the air rather than the air itself. Lister learned that applying carbolic acid to the wound, his hands, the surgical instruments, and the dressings used to close the wound prevented sepsis from occurring (Hastings, 1974).

THE ASCENDANCY OF MEDICAL AUTHORITY IN AMERICA

Early America

The earliest explorers to America found that native Americans relied mostly on supernatural explanations for disease and illness. Treatment of the sick typically was assigned to a "medicine man" who could intercede with the gods and, it was hoped, drive off evil spirits. Among the most common ailments were those related to the active and difficult lifestyle: fractures, dislocations, and wounds.

The Early Colonists. The earliest colonists endured an excruciatingly difficult voyage across the ocean (typically requiring three or more months) only to be met with tremendous hardship upon arrival. Though warned about the danger of disease by their sponsor, The London Company, the Jamestown settlers in 1607 were more concerned about being attacked by Indians. They selected a site for their new home that had a military advantage (being able to see up and down the river) but that was limited by an inadequate food supply and brackish water. Six months after arrival, 60 of the 100 who landed had died from dietary disorders or other diseases (Camp, 1977).

The Plymouth Colony in Massachusetts had a similar experience. Due to an outbreak of scurvy and other diseases, only 50 of the 102 arrivals survived the first three months. Epidemics and other infectious diseases (e.g., malaria, dysentery, typhoid fever, influenza, smallpox, scarlet fever, yellow fever, consumption [tuberculosis]) were the primary killers during the colonial years (Green, 1968).

The colonists also brought with them from Europe several contagious diseases (e.g., measles, smallpox, mumps) that had been unknown in the Americas. Lacking immunity to these diseases, Native American populations were decimated by them in continuing outbreaks. Some historians estimate that up to 90 percent of Native Americans died in this process (Cassady, 1991).

Though health problems were rampant in the colonies, conditions for enslaved people were especially bad. Subjected to massive overwork; poor food, housing, and sanitation; and inadequate medical care, their health was very poor in both an absolute and relative sense.

Early Medical Practitioners. Medical care was provided by colonists (often clergy) who had some formal education (not necessarily in medicine). The only known medical work published in America in the 1600s was by Reverend Thatcher of the Old South Church in Boston. The Rev. Cotton Mather (1663–1728) (precocious, vain, and fanatical about witches) is often called the first significant figure in American medicine. Though a full-time clergyman, Mather read widely about medicine, wrote numerous treatises and books on anatomy and therapeutic medicine, and is known for an understanding of inoculation far beyond that of his contemporaries.

There were a few trained physicians and surgeons who had migrated to the colonies from Europe, and it was common for young men to attach themselves to these physicians as apprentices (typically, for four to seven years). But, in colonial America, people from all walks of life took up medicine and referred to themselves as physicians. Many added the physician's duties to another job such as food merchant, wig maker, or cloth manufacturer (Starr, 1982). Much medical care was delivered by the apothecary. Although apothecaries primarily made their living by providing drugs and medical preparations, they also

gave medical advice, dressed wounds, and even performed amputations (Ford, 1965).

Obviously, in such conditions, there was little in the way of professionalized medicine. The first comprehensive hospital in the United States (The Pennsylvania Hospital in Philadelphia) was not built until 1751 (and the second not till 20 years later in New York); the first efforts to license medicine came in 1760 (in New York); the first formalized medical school (at the College of Philadelphia) was established in 1765; and the first state medical society (in New Jersey) organized in 1766.

Domestic Medicine. Given these conditions, it is not surprising that families assumed primary responsibility for protecting the health of family members and providing therapeutic agents when sick. Women stored medicinal herbs just as they did preserves, made up syrups and salves and lotions, bandaged injuries, and were expected to tend to sick family members. They called on other family and friends in the community for advice and sometimes sought the assistance of an older woman in the community known for her healing knowledge (Starr, 1982; Cassady, 1991).

Domestic medicine was supported by an ideology that individuals and families were capable of providing for the ill. Texts on domestic medicine (typically written by physicians) were available as was advice through newspapers and almanacs as well as word-of-mouth. Medical jargon was criticized as being unnecessary and discouraging people from family treatment.

The Revolution to the Mid-1800s

Though there were only about 3,500 physicians in the country at the start of the Revolutionary War (and only 400 had a university medical degree), medicine was making progress. Many of the physicians were as competent as the times allowed, and they took their responsibility to apprentices seriously.

Americans who could afford formal medical education often travelled to the University of Edinburgh, then considered the world's finest medical school, or other European centers. By the

IN THE FIELD

THE DEATH OF A PRESIDENT

In December 1799, he went out riding and got caught in a cold, freezing rain. When he returned to the house, he neglected to change immediately out of his wet clothes. He quickly came down with a cold, and within two days was experiencing throat pain and respiratory distress. Unable to swallow, he had trouble talking.

Three physicians were called in, and a short time later, a bloodletter was added to the team. At 7:30 a.m., the bloodletter removed 12 to 14 ounces of blood from the patient. A mixture of molasses, vinegar, and butter was provided, but it brought on nearly fatal choking. At 9:30 a.m., an additional 18 ounces of blood were removed, and at 11:00 a.m., another 18 ounces were removed. The patient tried to gargle with sage tea mixed with vinegar, but he was unable to cough it up and almost suffocated. Despite continued pleadings by his wife for caution,

another 32 ounces of blood were let at 3:00 p.m. At 4:00 p.m., calomel (mercurous chloride) and tartar emetic (antimony potassium tartrate) were administered.

After a brief spell of improvement, his condition began to weaken. Various poultices and compresses were applied. Around 10:00 p.m., he whispered burial instructions to a friend. A few minutes later, the recently retired first President of the United States, George Washington, died.

Did the attempted cure kill the former president? It is clear that the bloodletting did not help and probably hastened Washington's death. It is now generally agreed that Washington had acute bacterial epiglottis. The youngest of the three physicians had argued unsuccessfully to do a very new technique at the time, a tracheotomy, to assist Washington's breathing. That might have worked and prolonged his life (Morens, 1999).

turn of the century, the country had established four medical schools (Pennsylvania, Columbia, Harvard, and Dartmouth), each of which sought to offer excellence in medical training (but with a minimum of faculty members; Dartmouth had a one-man medical faculty for over a decade).

The most famous American physician of this era was Benjamin Rush (1745–1813), who after serving an apprenticeship in the colonies, earned a medical degree from Edinburgh. Rush, a signer of the Declaration of Independence and a strong advocate for temperance and the abolition of slavery, wrote extensively on his medical observations and made substantial contributions to the understanding of yellow fever and psychological problems. He argued against the common stigmatization of the mentally ill and urged that those with mental health problems be treated with kindness and humaneness (Marks and Beatty, 1973).

Nevertheless, he preached and practiced many of the medical errors of the day. He believed all symptoms and sickness were trace-

able to just one disease—a "morbid excitement induced by capillary tension," and he recommended and used bloodletting and purging as common cures (Ackernecht, 1982).

America's experience in the Revolutionary War highlighted the lack of accurate knowledge about disease causation and treatment. The annual death rate in the Continental Army was approximately 20 percent; 90 percent of war deaths were the direct result of disease (Green, 1968).

Frontier Medicine. In the early nineteenth century, many of America's most important contributions to medicine occurred in the expanding midwestern region of the country. This is explained by the extremely difficult life lived by those on the frontier and their susceptibility to disease. Life was difficult; food was often in short supply (Marks and Beatty, 1973).

While families typically practiced homemade remedies (based on both trial and error and superstition), there were some remarkable medical achievements. Ephraim McDowell (1771–1830), an Edinburgh-trained physician practicing in Danville, Kentucky, was the first to successfully practice ovariotomies (in 1809, he removed a 22-1/2 pound ovarian tumor from a woman who originally had thought herself pregnant). William Beaumont's (1785–1853) experience with a young accidental gunshot victim led to experiments on digestion (Green, 1968). Daniel Drake (1785–1870) wrote about the influence on health of physical and social environmental factors (e.g., climate, diet, ethnicity, lifestyle, occupation), encouraged collaboration among physicians, and was a strong proponent of physician licensure.

The Status of Medicine. Despite these advancements, medicine remained a very downgraded occupation. Physicians had little genuine understanding of disease causation and few effective treatments. Sometimes their cures were helpful (e.g., using willow bark, a source of aspirin, or rose hips, the ripened fruit of the rose bush and a good source for vitamin C, for fevers). Other remedies may not have been helpful but neither were they harmful (e.g., using fried daisies for a compress or putting feverish patients in a tent with burning tobacco). Some cures, however, were very harmful (e.g., bleeding, purging, amputation for any broken limb, trephination).

Alternative Philosophies. For a variety of reasons, physicians were poorly paid (and often not paid at all). These reasons include (1) the fact that family medicine was preferred by many; (2) the difficulty in seeing a substantial number of patients in a day (people lived far apart and efficient transportation was lacking); (3) the inability of many patients to pay for care (much care was provided on credit but never reimbursed); and (4) the fact that many people offered themselves as physicians (without licensure requirements, there was virtually unlimited entry into the field). Given these conditions, many could not justify the cost of formal education. Through the first half of the 1800s, then, physicians enjoyed little prestige (Starr, 1982).

Many alternative healing philosophies (medical sects) competed throughout this time period. "Thomsonianism" was created by Samuel Thompson (1969–1843), a New Hampshirite, who had unhappy experiences with "regular" physicians. He believed that disease resulted from insufficient heat and could be countered by measures that would restore natural heat (e.g., steam baths that would promote massive sweating, "hot" botanicals like red pepper) (King, 1984). Over three decades, Thompson's influence grew, and he attracted many followers.

A second important medical sect, **homeopathy**, was founded by a German physician, Samuel Hahnemann (1755–1843), who viewed diseases as being primarily of the spirit. Homeopaths believed that diseases could be cured by drugs that produced the same symptoms when given to a healthy person (the homeopathic law of "similars"—like cures like). The rationale was that a patient's natural disease would be displaced after taking a homeopathic medicine by a weaker, but similar, artificial disease that the body could more easily overcome (Starr, 1982).

1850 Onward

At least three events of major significance during the second half of the nineteenth century and the first half of the twentieth century combined to "professionalize" medicine.

The Civil War (1861–1865). As has frequently occurred, war dramatizes both the technological strengths and weaknesses of a society. Despite the ferocity of battle between the Union and Confederate forces, disease and illness represented the most lethal forces of the Civil War. An estimated 618,000 persons were killed during the Civil War—one-third from battle fatalities and two-thirds from disease and illness. Diarrhea and dysentery were the major killers, while numerous deaths were caused by smallpox, typhoid, yellow fever, pneumonia, and scarlet fever.

The wounded often lay on the battlefield for days until a conflict subsided and they could be moved. Wounds commonly became infected. Surgery was primitive; though anesthesia was often used, it typically took the form of alcohol

Medical tools of the late 1800s, like this amputation knife, reflect the still primitive nature of medicine at this time.

or opium. In some instances, the patient was hit in the jaw to knock him out; at times, the patient would simply bite down on a piece of wood or even a bullet (hence the expression, "bite the bullet") as a distraction.

To remove a bullet, the surgeon would put his unwashed hand in the open wound, squish around until the bullet was found, and pull it out. Scalpels used for amputation (there were approximately 60,000 amputations during the Civil War—three-fourths of all operations) were not washed; the blade was often dull; and what sharpening occurred was done on the surgeon's boot sole. Surgeons bragged about the speed with which they could amputate a limb (the best were called 1-1/2 minute men). Almost everyone got infections; many died from them. For comparison purposes, in Vietnam, 1 in every 75 wounded soldiers died; in World War II, 1 in 33 wounded died; in the Civil War, 1 in 7 wounded died.

Professional nursing began during the Civil War as a means to assist in the treatment of wounded soldiers. The ambulance corps was initiated to move the wounded from the battlefield to field hospitals. These experiences helped medical personnel learn about sanitation and other public health measures.

Medical Advancements. As discussed earlier, the discovery by Pasteur that microorganisms cause disease is considered by many to be the single most important medical discovery ever. Coupled with Lister's recognition of the

importance of sepsis and Wilhelm Roentgen's (1845–1923) discovery of X-rays and their diagnostic utility in the 1890s, much improved disease diagnosis was possible. These advancements meant that knowledge existed which required specialized training.

The germ theory of disease stimulated a massive and effective assault on infectious disease through prevention (immunization) and treatment. The decades of the 1920s through the 1940s represent years of peak pharmacological success—a time when one "magical bullet" after another was discovered. Insulin was discovered in 1921. Vitamin C was isolated in 1928 (enabling better understanding of vitamin deficiency diseases) the same year that a vaccine for yellow fever was produced. The potential for sulpha drugs (in preventing the growth or multiplication of bacteria) was realized in the 1930s, and the ability of penicillin to kill bacteria was fully understood in the 1940s. For a time, great optimism was engendered that all diseases and illnesses could be eradicated.

An unfortunate consequence of this focus on germ-caused disease was the turning away of attention from the "whole person." Some of the most valuable lessons to be learned from the Hippocratic tradition, such as the influence of lifestyle, the importance of inner harmony and moderation in life, the mind-body connection, and the importance of person-oriented medicine, were lost in the rush to identify microorganistic culprits and methods of conquering them. It would be decades before the importance of these themes would be remembered.

The Organization of Professional Medicine. During the first half of the nineteenth century, several localities and states formed professional medical societies. While there was considerable variation in their objectives and activities, each primarily focused on promoting the professionalization of medicine. On May 5, 1847, 250 physicians representing many of these medical societies and some medical schools met in Philadelphia to establish a national medical society, the **American Medical Association** (AMA).

The motivation to establish the AMA was part ideological and part economic. Competition from homeopaths and other alternative healers was limiting financial success for physicians and reducing pride in the field. Physicians openly sought more esteem and condemned those with alternative approaches (King, 1991). In part, the motivation for creating the AMA was similar to Hippocrates' motivation for writing his famous oath: to establish visible standards for the practice of medicine so as to gain a greater confidence from the general public.

The AMA identified its chief goals as the (1) promotion of the science and art of medicine; (2) betterment of public health; (3) standardization of requirements for medical degrees; (4) development of an internal system of licensing and regulation; and (5) development of a code of medical ethics.

However, it would be years before the AMA would develop into an important force in medicine. Several states and some medical schools opposed uniform standards in education and licensing requirements. There was sentiment in the general public against legitimizing a particular medical orientation as it was not clear that the brand of medicine offered by the AMA was superior to the many alternative healing philosophies in existence.

Forces Stimulating Professionalization

Three pivotal events strengthened the position of the AMA in medicine. First, the discovery of the germ theory of disease offered medical schools a sound approach to disease causation and treatment and a clear rationale to the public for preferring formally trained physicians.

Second, the AMA was eventually successful in achieving one of its key goals: **medical licensure** requirements. The AMA and the country's top medical schools argued that licensure would restrict the practice of medicine to those who had been formally trained and were able to demonstrate competency. Opposition stemmed both from those who wanted to maximize the choices people had available for medical practitioners and from the administrations of many of the lower quality medical schools who feared their graduates would not be able to pass a licensure exam. By the early 1900s, the battle had largely been won as most states required a license to practice medicine.

These two events were necessary but not sufficient in the AMA's drive for professional authority. By 1900, there were approximately 110,000 physicians in the United States, but only 8,000 belonged to the AMA. Reorganization of the AMA in 1901 (tightening the relationship among local, state, and the national associations and increasing the power of the AMA's governing board) provided a boost to the association, but one thing more was needed—control of medical education.

In the late 1800s and early 1900s, there was considerable variation in the quality of America's medical schools. More than 400 medical schools had been created in the United States in the 1800s. Some, like Harvard and Johns Hopkins, offered sound training in the basic sciences and substantial clinical experience under close supervision, as well as excellent resources. The majority, however, were not linked to a university and did not have access to the faculty, library resources, and facilities provided in the better schools. In many cases, admission standards were nonexistent, and there was no training provided in the basic sciences and little or no clinical supervision. As late as the 1870s, one physician was quoted as saying, "It is very well understood among college boys that after a man has failed in scholarship, failed in writing, failed in speaking, failed in every purpose for which he entered college; after he has dropped down from class to class; after he has been kicked out of college; there is one unfailing city of refuge—the profession of medicine" (quoted in Numbers, 1985:186).

The Flexner Report. The AMA contracted with the Carnegie Foundation to study the quality of medical education. They hired Abraham Flexner to conduct a comprehensive study of all the medical schools in the United States and Canada. Upon hearing of this study, many schools closed immediately rather than being condemned. Flexner's team visited the 155 remaining schools. His final report, the **Flexner**

Report, issued in 1910, praised the efforts of many schools (Harvard, Western Reserve, McGill, Toronto, and especially Johns Hopkins) but lambasted those offering inferior programs. He recommended that the number of schools be reduced to 31 and that medical education be subjected to formal regulation.

The "Great Trade of 1910"

The only national standards available for accrediting medical schools were those that had been prepared by the Council on Medical Education (CME) of the AMA. In 1910, the states and the federal government made a deal with the AMA. In return for providing the best and most efficient health care system, the states and the federal government gave the CME monopoly over the production and licensing of physicians, including the power to establish standards for medical schools. In this "**Great Trade of 1910**," the AMA was given a near-exclusive right to regulate the medical profession. With the power of knowledge supplied by the germ theory of disease and the organizational legitimacy provided by the states and the federal government, the powerful position of the AMA was secured. In turn, the AMA institutionalized scientific medicine as the foundation of America's health care system.

PERSPECTIVES ON THE ASCENDANCY OF MEDICAL AUTHORITY

Attempts to interpret and explain the ascendancy of medical authority in the United States have followed various lines. Two contrasting approaches, that of Paul Starr and Vicente Navarro, are summarized here.

Paul Starr

Paul Starr's *The Social Transformation of American Medicine* (1982) is a fascinating and well-documented description and analysis of the evolution of the medical profession in America. Starr (who won the Pulitzer Prize for this work) describes the rise of medical authority in America,

as medicine was transformed from a relatively weak and poorly regarded occupation into a powerful and prestigious "sovereign" profession, and how the efforts of medicine to maintain professional autonomy by limiting government control have left it open to being taken over by corporatization. The second of these points will be examined in later chapters; the first point addresses the bases for the ascendancy of medical authority in America and is discussed here.

Starr acknowledges the synergistic relationship between the advance of science and the professionalization of medicine but contends that something more than the former is needed to explain medicine's acquisition of economic power and political influence in America and its ability to shape the health care system. Paul Wolpe summarizes this point.

> A profession's power rests on its consensually granted authority over a specific, cultural tradition. Knowledge and maintenance of that tradition is the profession's social capital, and it must guard that capital from challenges while projecting an aura of confidence, competence, trust, and self-criticism. Professions institutionalize control over social capital by establishing licensing procedures, internally-run educational institutions, and self-regulation. But institutional legitimacy, while somewhat self-sustaining, also depends on ongoing public acceptance of a profession's claim of exclusive expertise over a realm of specialized knowledge. Lacking broad coercive powers, professions have developed strategies to protect their socially granted right to interpret their particular cultural tradition. (Wolpe, 1985:409)

Starr suggests that professions develop authority in order to maintain their position. This includes social authority (Max Weber's notion of controlling actions through commands; authority typically is built into laws or rules or bureaucratic protocol) and **cultural authority** (which Starr defines as, "the probability that particular definitions of reality and judgments of meaning and value will prevail as valid and true") (Starr, 1982:13). Cultural authority is manifested in the "awe and respect from the general public and legislators" that allows medicine to set its own conditions of practice (e.g., site of care and payment mechanism) (Anderson, 1983:1243).

While social authority can be legislated, professions must "persuade" publics that they are deserving of cultural authority.

> The triumph of the regular profession depended on belief rather than force, on its growing cultural authority rather than sheer power, on the success of its claims to competence and understanding rather than the strong arm of the police. To see the rise of the profession as coercive is to underestimate how deeply its authority penetrated the beliefs of ordinary people and how firmly it had seized the imagination even of its rivals. (Starr, 1982:229)

What structural changes in medicine resulted from this "social transformation"? Starr (1982) delineates five key changes: (1) The growth of hospitals created a desire for hospital privileges and referrals which caused physicians to become more colleague-dependent and less patient-dependent; (2) Gaining control of medical education and the licensure process enabled the profession to restrict entry into the field and shape the evolution of the profession; (3) Having medicine viewed as a special type of field legitimated the expenditure of enormous sums of public money for hospital construction, medical education, medical research, and public health; (4) Physicians gained nearly complete control over conditions of medical practice (e.g., the setting of fees) and established significant political influence; and (5) Medicine established very clear professional boundaries that were to be respected by others.

By the 1920s, the ascendancy of medical authority was clear. Though the sovereignty of medicine would not peak for several decades (probably around 1970), its prominent position and ability to control the health care system were firmly established.

Vicente Navarro

An alternative view of the ascendancy of medical authority in America is presented by sociologists and medical historians who follow a social conflict approach. Vicente Navarro, a Marxist scholar who has written extensively about medicine, disagrees with three assumptions he finds in Starr.

Starr's interpretation of America sees the past and present structure of power in the United States as reflecting the wishes of the majority of Americans. To see the structure of power in America as the outcome of what Americans want, however, is to beg the question of which Americans. If by Americans it is meant the majority of Americans, then two assumptions are being made. One is that the majority of Americans share a set of beliefs, values, and wants that provide an ideological cohesiveness to the totality of the unit called America. The other assumption is that the majority of Americans have had and continue to have the power to determine what happens both in the private sector of America (through the market forces) and in the public sector (through the representative public institutions). To these two assumptions Starr adds a third one: the dominant ideologies and positions become dominant through their powers of persuasion rather than through coercion and repression of alternative ideologies and positions. (Navarro. 1984:515)

Navarro emphasizes that Americans have been and continue to be "divided into classes, races, genders, and other power groupings, each with its own interests, set of beliefs, and wants that are in continuous conflict and struggle" (Navarro, 1984:515). These groups have different levels of power and interact within a dominant-dominated framework. In society in general and within medicine, powerful groups (typically) are decisive due to the resources they have acquired. They get their way not because they successfully persuade, but because they coerce and repress the less powerful.

According to Navarro, the ascendancy of medical authority occurred (and the corporatization of medicine is now occurring) not because people willed it and not because they were persuaded it was in their interests, but because it served the interests of powerful societal groups (the government, those sufficiently wealthy to afford medical education and private health care, the corporate sector). These groups determine what options are provided for society and ignore values and preferences (such as for universal coverage for health care) that they judge not to be in their interest.

SUMMARY

The study of the history of medicine is important both to understand earlier peoples and events and to decipher ways in which modern ideas and practices have evolved. Understanding of disease shifted from supernatural explanations in early humans, to a slightly more empirical basis in Egyptian society, to natural causes in the Greco-Roman era. Hippocrates, the "Father of Medicine," encouraged careful observation of sickness in patients, a close relationship between physician and patient, and ethical guidelines for physician behavior.

The centrality of religion's role in medicine re-emerged during the Medieval Era, but ultimately became overshadowed by the scientific perspective during the Renaissance. Particularly important was Pasteur's discovery of the germ theory of disease.

Diseases were common in colonial America, trained physicians were few, accurate medical knowledge was limited, and most families cared for their own sick members. Physicians had lit-tle training, low prestige, and earned little money. The gradual implementation of the germ theory of disease led to other medical discoveries, much-improved medical care, and widespread public health and disease prevention programs.

The American Medical Association was established in 1847, though it did not become a powerful voice for medicine for several decades. The two key events in the institutionalization of the AMA were (1) the establishment of licensure requirements in states, thus controlling entry into the field; and (2) the federal government's granting of authority to the AMA to control standards in medical education.

Paul Starr emphasizes that medical authority ascended in the United States because the medical profession persuaded people that such power was in their best interest. Vicente Navarro contends that the profession of medicine and the health care system have evolved in ways desired by powerful groups.

HEALTH ON THE INTERNET

There are several informative Web sites about Hippocrates, his writings, and recent updates of his work. Read the "Introductory Note," the "Oath of Hippocrates," and the "Law of Hippocrates" at:

www.bartleby.com/38/1/

Consider the following questions:

1. The final paragraph of the Introductory Note contains an aphorism about the art of the physician. What is the meaning of this statement? What does it say about the physician-patient relationship? Have you observed any occasions in which a physician seemed to be practicing this art?

2. Point five in the Law of Hippocrates includes with the statement, "Those things that are sacred, are to be imparted only to sacred persons; and it is not lawful to impart them to the profane until they have been initiated into the mysteries of science." What is meant by this statement?

3. In what ways is the "Law of Hippocrates" consistent with the "Oath of Hippocrates," and in what ways does it differ?

KEY CONCEPTS AND TERMS

American Medical Association
anatomical concept of disease
Black Death
clinical medicine

Code of Hammurabi
cultural authority
domestic medicine
Flexner Report

Galen
germ theory of disease
Great Trade of 1910
Hippocrates
Hippocratic Oath
homeopathy
humoral theory of disease

laboratory medicine
medical licensure
monastic medicine
scholastic medicine
shaman
supernatural explanations of disease
trephination

DISCUSSION QUESTION

In his seminal work, *The Structure of Scientific Revolutions* (published in 1962), Thomas Kuhn describes the history of science as a series of eras, each guided by a dominant paradigm (i.e., a theoretical perspective or general understanding of things). This is "normal science," and it is sustained through education and research apprenticeships, whereby young scientists are socialized into the prevailing paradigm.

Occasionally, new theoretical insights or empirical findings appear that question the dominant paradigm. If these "anomalies" are infrequent or isolated occurrences, consensus around the dominant paradigm will be undisturbed. However, if these contradictory perspectives persist and are replicated, a "scientific revolution" may occur wherein the old paradigm is replaced by a new one. Kuhn sees scientific progress as occurring through revolutions rather than evolutions.

Based on your reading of this chapter and other familiarity you have with the history of medicine, would you say Kuhn's view is or is not applicable to the advancement of medical knowledge? Has the progression of medical knowledge occurred incrementally in an evolutionary process? Or, has there been one or more revolutions in understanding disease and illness from which new paradigms have become accepted?

REFERENCES

Ackernecht, Erwin H. 1982 *A Short History of Medicine.* Baltimore: Johns Hopkins University Press.

Anderson, Odin. 1983 "Book Review of *The Social Transformation of American Medicine." Medical Care,* 21:1243–1245.

Bennett, David. 2000 "Medical Practice and Manuscripts in Byzantium." *Social History of Medicine,* 13:279–291.

Berliner, Howard S. 1984 "Scientific Medicine Since Flexner," pp. 30–56 in *Alternative Medicines: Popular and Policy Perspectives,* J. Warren Salmon (ed.) New York: Tavistock.

Camp, John. 1974 *Magic, Myth, and Medicine.* New York: Taplinger Publishing Company.

———. 1977 *The Healer's Art: The Doctor Through History.* New York: Taplinger Publishing Company.

Cassady, James H. 1991 *Medicine in America: A Short History.* Baltimore: Johns Hopkins University Press.

Ford, Thomas K. 1965 *The Apothecary in Eighteenth Century Williamsburg.* Williamsburg, Virginia: Colonial Williamsburg Foundation.

Green, John R. 1968 *Medical History for Students.* Springfield, IL: Charles C Thomas.

Hastings, Paul. 1974 *Medicine: An International History.* New York: Praeger.

King, Lester S. 1984 *American Medicine Comes of Age, 1840–1920.* Chicago: American Medical Association.

———. 1991 *Transformations in American Medicine.* Baltimore: Johns Hopkins University Press.

Kuhn, Thomas S. 1962 *The Structure of Scientific Revolutions.* Chicago: University of Chicago Press.

Marks, Geoffrey and William K. Beatty. 1973 *The Story of Medicine in America.* New York: Charles Scribner's Sons.

Mattern, Susan P. 1999 "Physicians and the Roman Imperial Aristocracy: The Patronage of

Therapeutics." *Bulletin of the History of Medicine,* 73:1–18.

McKeown, Thomas. 1970 "A Sociological Approach to the History of Medicine." *Medical History,* 4:342–351.

Morens, David M. 1999 "Death of a President." *New England Journal of Medicine,* 341:1845–1849.

Navarro, Vicente. 1984 "Medical History as Justification Rather Than Explanation: A Critique of Starr's *The Social Transformation of American Medicine.*" *International Journal of Health Services,* 14:511–527.

Nuland, Sherwin B. 1988 *Doctors: The Biography of Medicine.* New York: Knopf.

Numbers, Ronald L. 1985 "The Rise and Fall of the American Medical Profession," pp.185–196 in *Sickness and Health in America: Readings in the History of Medicine and Public Health* (2nd ed.), Judith W. Leavitt and Ronald L. Numbers (eds.). Madison: University of Wisconsin Press.

Pickett, Anthony C. 1992 "The Oath of Imhotep: In Recognition of African Contributions to Western Medicine." *Journal of the National Medical Association,* 84:636–637.

Starr, Paul. 1982 *The Social Transformation of American Medicine.* New York: Basic Books.

Weisz, George. 2003 "Medical Specialization in the Nineteenth Century." *Bulletin of the History of Medicine,* 77:536–575.

Wolpe, Paul R. 1985 "The Maintenance of Professional Authority: Acupuncture and the American Physician." *Social Problems,* 32:409–424.

3

SOCIAL EPIDEMIOLOGY

The field of social epidemiology focuses on understanding the causes and distribution of diseases and impairments within a population. Early in the history of the field, epidemiologists concentrated primarily on identifying microorganisms responsible for epidemics of acute, infectious diseases. Utilizing the germ theory of disease (see Chapter 2), epidemiologists achieved much success in identifying the agents responsible for these diseases.

However, the narrow focus on disease agents made it difficult to establish broader understandings of disease. For example, sole reliance on disease agents could not explain why outbreaks of many diseases ebbed and flowed nor why only some people who were exposed to various bacteria manifested the disease while others did not. And, as infectious diseases declined, the traditional focus on agents proved less successful in explaining chronic, degenerative diseases such as coronary heart disease and cancer.

Gradually, the focus of **epidemiology** broadened to include characteristics of the person (including gender, race, social class, and lifestyle) in whom the disease agent settled and

characteristics of the physical and social environment (including employment status, stress, and exposure to toxic substances) in which the person (and agent) existed. This expanded focus on social and cultural factors related to the risk of death and disease is often referred to as **social epidemiology** and now represents a major thrust of many (though not all) epidemiologists, whatever their disciplinary background.

THE WORK OF THE EPIDEMIOLOGIST

The work of the epidemiologist has been compared to that of a detective or investigator. Epidemiologists scrutinize data on death and disease within societies, often searching for patterns or linkages within population subgroups (e.g., among men or women or among people living in cities or in rural areas) or other meaningful changes over time. If a pattern or trend is discerned, the task of the epidemiologist is to explain it—that is, to identify a cause-and-effect relationship. This may require understanding how the disease is contracted, how it has been or could be spread, and why it is more common among some groups of people than others.

The focus of epidemiological investigation typically targets disease agents, the environment, and the human host.

> *Disease agents* include (1) biologic agents, such as insects, fungi, bacteria, and viruses; (2) nutrient agents, such as fats and carbohydrates; (3) chemical agents, such as gases, dust, and solid particles in the air; and (4) physical agents, such as radiation, temperature, and humidity. The *environment* includes (1) the physical environment, such as weather factors, climate, and geography; (2) the biological environment, involving the presence or absence of known disease agents cited above; and (3) the social and economic environment of socioeconomic status, type of occupation, location of home, etc. Finally, the *human host* is a consideration of demographic factors such as age, sex, and race as well as physical condition or constitution, habits and customs, and styles of life. (Coe, 1970:41–42)

Many contemporary epidemiologists subscribe to a "web of causation" approach based on their belief that most disease patterns can be explained by a complex of factors involving all three traditional research targets. However, many believe that current changes in global health patterns, such as the AIDS pandemic, and developing technologies, such as in genetics research and information systems, will cause the field of epidemiology to continue to evolve. In the future, epidemiology's focus may be both more sociological (e.g., examining the ways in which social policies impact on risky behaviors) and more biological (e.g., eliminating or reducing the number of genetic diseases) (Susser and Susser, 1996). Accordingly, McKinlay (1996) has suggested adding a fourth target: social systems. Thinking of influences such as government reimbursement policies, priorities of hospitals and other organizations, and the behavior of health providers, he argues that individual health behaviors cannot sensibly be separated from system influences.

In conducting their work, epidemiologists use a variety of data-gathering techniques including (1) examination of medical records and data bases from physicians, hospitals, schools, employers, insurance companies, public health departments, and birth and death records; (2) systematic clinical evaluations; (3) health-focused surveys; and (4) experimentation (typically with animal subjects) under tightly controlled conditions.

In the 1990s, CDC added a new weapon to its arsenal: PulseNet—a national computerized system that allows data about disease agents to be instantly shared around the country. For example, in 1998, officials at the Massachusetts Department of Health used PulseNet to transmit the DNA pattern of E. coli bacteria from scattered cases of individuals in Boston experiencing an intestinal disorder. When the same pattern was discovered in cases in New Hampshire, Maine, and Connecticut, investigators were able to trace the bacteria back to a particular batch of hamburger which was then quickly removed from stores in the Northeast. The system is similar to that used in computer transmission of fingerprints or human DNA, but in this case the culprits are nonhuman.

None of these techniques is without concern. For example, much terminology that is used in medical recordkeeping lacks precision, and operational definitions of some key concepts vary from state to state. Analyses have demonstrated that the accuracy with which data bases are maintained varies considerably. Health interview data have been extremely beneficial in understanding the general health of the population, but they sometimes have low correspondence with data collected through clinical examination. Drawing conclusions must be done with extreme care.

Until 1950, the United States lacked a nationwide system of disease surveillance. In that year, techniques were developed at the Disease Center in Atlanta (later to be called the Centers for Disease Control and Prevention) to provide ongoing evaluations of disease conditions and systematic responses to these conditions. Through this national surveillance system, data are now analyzed to define outbreaks of disease, to characterize the extent of the outbreak, and to determine likely effects of the disease on the population. The Centers for Disease Control and Prevention report these data weekly to health departments, government agencies, academic facilities, and the public through the *Morbidity and Mortality Weekly Report (MMWR)*.

THE EPIDEMIOLOGICAL TRANSITION

Prior to large-scale migrations and urbanization, the threat of infectious disease and epidemics was minimal. However, once people began to move from one region of the world to another, and once crowded and unsanitary cities emerged within nations, diseases spread more quickly and lingered longer.

As societies develop and modernize, the patterns of morbidity and mortality change systematically. Early stages of development are characterized by high risks of death at relatively young ages from **acute, infectious diseases** (e.g., pneumonia, smallpox). As societies advance, there is a greater likelihood of dying at older ages from **chronic, degenerative diseases** (e.g., heart disease, cancer). To capture this **epidemiological transition**, Omran (1971) divided the mortality experience of humankind into three stages: the Age of Pestilence and Famine, the Age of Receding Pandemics, and the Age of Degenerative and Human-made Diseases.

The Age of Pestilence and Famine existed throughout the world for thousands of years and still exists today in many of the world's developing countries. Factors including lack of proper nutrition, poor sanitation, and unclean drinking water lead to almost unceasing epidemics of infectious and parasitic diseases such as influenza, pneumonia, diarrhea, smallpox, and tuberculosis.

Infants, children, and women of reproductive age are at particularly high risk during this era and are even now often the victims of nutrition-related diseases or other diseases to which they are more susceptible because of continuing inadequate nourishment. Infant mortality rates remain very high today in many developing countries, in which more than one baby in every 10 dies in the first year of life. Moreover, adult health in developing countries is a serious and continuing problem. Data reveal that in industri-

alized market-based economies, the risk of death between the ages of 15 and 60 is 12 percent for males and 5 percent for females. The corresponding figures in sub-Saharan Africa, a developing area, are 38 percent for males and 32 percent for females. Historically, life expectancy during the Age of Pestilence and Famine was between 20 and 40 years, though life expectancy in most of the world's developing countries today exceeds that. In several African countries, however, life expectancy remains less than 50 years.

As today's modern countries progressed through the Age of Receding Pandemics, improvements were made in sanitation and standard of living, and advances in medical knowledge and public health led to a decline in the number of people dying from infectious and parasitic diseases. The development process for every country has some features particular to that country, but many epidemiologists believe that there is a standard progression of changes in disease patterns as modernization occurs. In response to their own efforts and, in some cases, from technical assistance (e.g., in agricultural or industrial techniques) provided by the United States and other countries, many developing countries today are lowering mortality rates. As the frequency of acute, infectious diseases declines, people begin to survive into older age when they are more likely to experience and to die from chronic, degenerative diseases like heart disease and cancer. Historically, during this stage, life expectancy was about 50 years.

As mortality from acute, infectious diseases stabilizes at a relatively low level, and the most common causes of death become chronic, degenerative diseases, the Age of Degenerative and Human-made Diseases arrives. Mortality rates drop considerably from earlier times, and life expectancy reaches approximately 70 years or more.

At one time, it was generally believed that the decline in mortality experienced during the third period put life expectancy at about its biological limit. However, in the mid-1960s, an unexpected and rapid decline in deaths from major degenerative diseases such as heart disease occurred. These declines first affected middle-aged people, but today the lives of older people are being extended as well.

Olshansky and Ault (1986) suggest that modern societies have entered a fourth period of epidemiological history, which they label the Age of Delayed Degenerative Diseases. During this era, the risk of dying from chronic, degenerative diseases is pushed back to older ages. Both reduction in behavioral risk factors (e.g., a decline in cigarette smoking) and recent advances in medical technology are responsible for this shift.

The Age of Delayed Degenerative Diseases raises new questions about the health of the population. Will prolonging life result in additional years of health or additional years of disability? Will healthier lifestyles and the postponement of chronic disease retard the aging process? Will death increase from other diseases (Olshansky and Ault, 1986)? Will there be continued outbreaks of epidemic disease (e.g., AIDS and the recent increases in rates of tuberculosis) that represent an inconsistency in this fourth period? The box, "Disease Epidemics of the Future?," describes a recent case of a disease epidemic.

One thing is certain: during the period of Delayed Degenerative Diseases, all segments of

---

IN THE FIELD

DISEASE EPIDEMICS OF THE FUTURE?

In May, 1995, a 36-year-old man was admitted to the hospital in Kikwit, Zaire, with a fever and diarrhea. Soon, however, blood began seeping out of every orifice of his body, and his internal organs became liquefied. He died on the fourth day, the same day that a nun and a nurse who had cared for him became ill. Others on the hospital staff became sick. Epidemiological experts in lethal viruses (who were referred to by one author as "disease cowboys") stationed at the World Health Organization collected their equipment and materials and immediately flew to Kikwit. They gathered samples and dispatched them to the Centers for Disease Control and Prevention. Their verdict, as feared: Ebola virus.

Ebola first surfaced in 1976 in Zaire and the Sudan. It is not known where it resides in nature, how epidemics get started, or why they do not occur more frequently. It is known that the virus is spread through bodily secretions and that the fatality rate is between 50 percent and 90 percent. There is no vaccine and no treatment. Ebola was contained in this episode within a couple weeks but only after it had killed 228 of 289 victims.

Is Ebola outbreak a rare and unduplicated experience? No. In the last couple decades, more than 20 fearsome viruses have surfaced around the world, including HIV (which had caused more than 20 million deaths in the world by 2000) and Lassa (which affects between 200,000 and 400,000 annually in West Africa). Many observers believe that these outbreaks are due to the unceasing devastation of the ecosystem—including destruction of the ozone layer and the rain forest and the continual accumulation of chemicals in the environment—which has opened these viruses to the human host (Lappe, 1994). In 1989 a strain of Ebola virus was transmitted to a laboratory in Reston, Virginia (the subject of Richard Preston's *The Hot Zone* and Laurie Garrett's *The Coming Plague*). Some researchers there developed antibodies to the virus though none developed symptoms. What may be new strains of Ebola are currently thought to be simmering in dense, African rain forests (Thacker, 2003).

On the other hand, perhaps the alarm that these killer viruses have created in many people in modern nations should also be of sociological interest. During the same time period that Ebola was claiming its 200-plus victims in Kikwit, hundreds of thousands of children in developing countries were dying from drinking impure water—a far less exotic but far more serious threat to the health and lives of people in Zaire and other developing countries.

the elderly population are expected to increase dramatically in absolute numbers. The Centers for Disease Control and Prevention has projected that the U.S. population age 65 and over will increase to 71.0 million in 2030 (having been only 16.7 million in 1960 and 35.0 million in 2000).

Recent Alarming Increases in Infectious Diseases

In the last few years epidemiologists have discovered a pattern that could be tremendously disruptive to the epidemiological transition: several infectious diseases, including tuberculosis, syphilis, gonorrhea, and bacterial pneumonia, are becoming increasingly resistant to the antibiotics that have been successful in defeating them. Malaria (spread by a parasite) was all but eradicated in the world in 1965; today, it infects an estimated 270 million people annually and kills up to 2 million. Diphtheria is very rare in the United States, but in the mid-1990s, it affected more than 50,000 Russians each year. Tuberculosis (TB), the most common fatal infectious disease in the world (a death toll of 2.5 million per year), has reemerged in the United States after a 30-year decline. In the early 1990s, more than 25,000 cases of TB were being reported annually in this country (the number was still about 12,000 per year in 2002).

Several patterns related to infectious disease are evident. First, they represent a global problem.

IN THE FIELD

HAS SARS BEEN VANQUISHED?

The first new infectious disease of the 21st century was SARS—Sudden Acute Respiratory Syndrome. SARS apparently originated in rural China in late 2002 and was first reported in February, 2003. The disease was soon spread by international travelers to Europe, North America, and throughout Asia. As the world recognized that SARS was often fatal, considerable panic occurred, especially in areas like Singapore, Hong Kong, and Toronto, where the biggest outbreaks occurred. In these cities, some schools closed, entire families were quarantined, people wore surgical masks to reduce the likelihood of contracting the disease, some hospitals closed, and some students studying abroad were brought home. Some experts postulated that SARS could become an uncontrollable pandemic. However, by July, the first emergence of SARS was all but vanquished. More than 8,000 contracted the disease: 10 percent of them died from it.

How was control of SARS achieved? Success stemmed from a worldwide collaborative effort of epidemiologists and public health experts who were led by the World Health Organization and the Centers for Disease Control and Prevention. They quickly identified the source of the disease as being a particular virus. They determined that people who died were either attacked by a more virulent strain or already had weak immune systems. They discovered that the virus originally latched onto animals and that genes in the virus mutated, enabling it to then latch onto human tissue. Measures were enacted to control the virus within hospitals, to learn how to best treat patients, to do laboratory studies, to discourage travel to cities with the most occurrences, and to quarantine patients. Most agree that without these measures, SARS could have become a tragic worldwide cause of death.

What was learned from SARS? That the world is one place and that all areas are affected by what is happening elsewhere. That more effective public health measures are needed around the world. That traditional infectious disease control programs can have success (Henley, 2003). That infectious diseases are powerful and are very difficult to eliminate altogether, as was proven when some cases of SARS re-emerged in China in 2004.

SEVERE ACUTE RESPIRATORY SYNDROME (SARS)
Self declaration of symptoms

SEVERE ACUTE RESPIRATORY SYNDROME (SARS)
Pengisytiharan sendiri tanda-tanda sakit

严重急性呼吸系统综合症
自我申报病症

சார்ஸ் நோய் (கடுமையான மூச்சு குழாய் நோய்)
வியாதியின் அறிகுறிகளை உடன் கூறவும்

College of Family Physicians
Singapore

Please declare to the clinic receptionist on registration if you have

- Fever
- Travelled within 10 days of onset of symptoms to high risk areas/countries
- Close contact with anybody admitted to hospitals for SARS or suspected SARS
- Cough, shortness of breath or difficulty in breathing

Thank you for your co-operation

Tolong beritahu kepada kerani diwaktu pendaftaran jika anda ada

- Demam
- Mengembara dalam jangkamasa sepuluh hari dengan tanda-tanda sakit SARS ke negara-negara yang ada risiko tinggi SARS
- Berdekatan dengan sesiapa yang dimasukkan ke hospital untuk penyakit SARS atau disyaki mempunyai penyakit SARS
- Batuk, sesak nafas atau susah bernafas

Terimakasih atas kerjasama anda

38°C

请在注册待诊时，
向诊所接待员我报以
下病症：

- 发烧
- 发病症十天内去过高危区
  与任何证实或怀疑有该病症而入过医院的人士
  ，有过近距离接触者
- 有咳，气促或呼吸困难者

多谢合作

சாரஸ் நோய் பரவுவதை தடுப்பதற்கு உங்கள்
ஒத்துழைப்பை பணிவுடன் நாடுகிறோம்.
கீழ்க்காணும் எவையும் உங்களுக்கு
பொருத்தமாக இருந்தால், கிளினிக் தாதியிடம்
தயவுசெய்து முன் கூட்டியே கூறவும்:

- உங்களுக்கு காய்ச்சல் (ஜுரம்) பிடித்திருந்தால்
- நீங்கள் சென்ற பத்து நாட்களுக்குள் நோய் பரவிய வெளி நாடுகளில் இருந்து வந்திருந்தால்
- நீங்கள் சார்ஸ் நோயால் பாதிக்க பட்டவருடன் நெருங்கிய பழக்கம்/ தொடர்பு கொண்டிருந்தால்
- உங்களுக்கு இருமல் அல்லது சுவாசிக்க சிரமமாக இருந்தால்

உங்கள் ஒத்துழைப்புக்கு நன்றி.

This poster is released by the College of Family Physicians Singapore on 29th March 2003.
The document is downloadable from *www.cfps.org.sg*.
以上壁报乃新加坡家庭医生学院在三月二十九日发报.
可以在 *www.cfps.org.sg* 下载

Severe Acute Respiratory Syndrome (SARS) emerged in 2002. Prompt and effective work by epidemiologists and public health experts prevented a worldwide pandemic.

During the decade of the 1990s, about one-third of all of the deaths in the world were attributable to infectious disease—the single biggest killer. Second, these diseases (which include respiratory tract infections, blood diseases, kidney and urinary tract infections, and others) are becoming an increasing threat in the United States. Combined, they now represent the third leading cause of death in the United States, and the mortality rate from infectious disease has jumped in the last 15 years. Third, many of the antibiotics that have been effective against these diseases no longer are effective. Some infectious diseases have become resistant to traditional drugs, and more will become so. And, finally, the response to infectious disease must be at the worldwide level. Yet, both the CDC and the World Health Organization are on record that the state of preparedness for outbreaks of disease epidemics is inadequate.

This chapter offers an introduction to several key concepts and measurement techniques in epidemiology—life expectancy, mortality, infant mortality, maternal mortality, morbidity, and disability—and examines current rates and trends within the United States.

LIFE EXPECTANCY AND MORTALITY

Life Expectancy

Based on current mortality data and projections, **life expectancy** rates reflect the average number of years that a person born in a given year can expect to live. Due to variations in rates among segments of the population, life expectancy typically is calculated separately for males and females and according to race or ethnic background.

Trends.   Since 1900, life expectancy in the United States has increased approximately 30 years from 47 to 77.2 (in 2001). However, this increase does not mean that a significant increase has occurred in the life span (the maximum biological age). In the early part of the century, death for males and females often occurred in the first year of life and often during

TABLE 3–1   Life Expectancy in the Year 2000 in Countries with 5+ Million Persons

Country	Life Expectancy in 2000
Japan	80.7
Australia	79.8
Switzerland	79.6
Canada	79.4
Sweden	79.2
Italy	79.0
France	78.8
Spain	78.8
Israel	78.6
Greece	78.4
Netherlands	78.3
Belgium	77.8
United Kingdom	77.7
Austria	77.7
Germany	77.4
Finland	77.4
Jordan	77.4
United States	77.1 (18th)
Lowest 10:	
Zambia	37.2
Mozambique	37.5
Malawi	37.6
Zimbabwe	37.8
Angola	38.3
Rwanda	39.3
Niger	41.3
Uganda	42.9
Cote d'Ivoirie	45.2
Ethiopia	45.2

Source: United States Bureau of the Census, Population Division, International Programs Center, *International Data Base, www.census.gov/ipc/www/idbnew.html,* 2003.

childbirth in females. These deaths significantly reduced average life expectancy. Males and females who survived these stages could expect to live on average almost as long as males and females do today. Table 3–1 identifies life expectancy in the year 2000 for some of the world's countries with 5+ million persons.

Greater life expectancy together with a lower fertility rate (i.e., the rate of reproduction of women in their most fertile years—ages 15 to 44) has resulted in a larger proportion of the United States population being over 65 years of age. Just 4 percent of the population was 65 or older in 1900; the corresponding

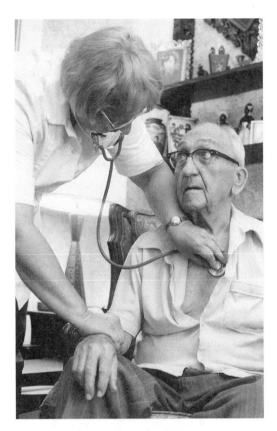

Life expectancy in the United States now exceeds 77 years, and an increasing percentage of the population is 65 years of age or older.

figure today is 13 percent, and persons 65 and older are the fastest increasing segment of the population.

This "aging" of the American population has many implications. The greater number of elderly persons will require significant increases in the supply of ambulatory health care, short-term hospitalization, and extended care. Their number will also provide a formidable voting bloc and lobbying force to ensure that their needs will not be overlooked. Because extended care can be expensive, increasing numbers of the elderly may need to reside with their adult children, thus requiring a family member to take on a full-time caregiving role, or necessitating the use of home health care services (an important development in the United States that is dis-

cussed in Chapter 15). Many elderly persons and their families will be faced with having to determine the relative value of quality versus quantity of life and the extent to which high technology medicine will be employed.

Mortality

Mortality refers to the number of deaths in a population. While death itself is easy to document, determining the actual cause can be problematic because death may result from a combination of many factors. In the United States, an attempt is made to classify each death according to the *International Statistical Classification of Diseases, Injuries, and Causes of Death,* which consists of a detailed list of categories of diseases and injuries. While this system is valuable, it is not totally reliable due to the problems in diagnosing the actual underlying cause of death—something that is especially difficult for some chronic diseases.

Measurement. Mortality rates are reported in ratios such as the **crude death rate (CDR)**. To calculate the CDR, the number of deaths in a designated population during a given year is divided by the population size. This figure is then multiplied by a standard number (usually 1,000 or 100,000). The formula for crude death rate is:

$$\frac{\text{Total number of deaths in specified population in a given year}}{\text{Total population of the group at mid-year}} \times 100,000$$

In 2003, the CDR for the United States was 840 per 100,000 population, though this rate varies considerably among age groups, racial and ethnic groups, and between males and females. A more useful measure for sociologists who are interested in the effects of specific social characteristics on death within a population is an "age-specific" or other "characteristic-specific" rate. To determine the death rate for a particular group, a Specific Rate (SR) is calculated by confining the number of deaths and the population size to that given segment of the population. For example, in 2001 the specific death rate for white males, ages 15 to 24, was 108 per 100,000, while the rate for black males in the same age group was 181. The overall population rate of 117 for this sex/age group does not illuminate the disadvantage young black males experience.

Trends.   The crude death rate in the United States has declined by almost 50 percent since 1900 and continues to drop each year. The largest reduction has been for females, both black and white, while the least reduction has been for black males. In addition, the major causes of death have changed substantially. Today, death is much more likely than ever before to result from a chronic, degenerative disease. Almost three-fourths of deaths in the United States are due to heart disease, cancer, stroke, diabetes, lung disease, and cirrhosis, while in 1900, the major killers were infectious diseases such as influenza and pneumonia, gastrointestinal diseases, and tuberculosis. To an increasing extent, people are now dying of multiple system diseases—being afflicted with more than one fatal disease (see Table 3–2).

TABLE 3–2   The Ten Leading Causes of Death in the United States, 1900 and 2001

1900	2001
1. Influenza and pneumonia	Heart disease
2. Tuberculosis	Cancer
3. Gastroenteritis	Stroke
4. Heart disease	Lung disease
5. Cerebral hemorrhage	Accidents
6. Kidney disease	Diabetes
7. Accidents	Influenza and pneumonia
8. Cancer	Alzheimer's disease
9. Certain diseases of infancy	Kidney disease
10. Diphtheria	Blood poisoning

Source: National Center for Health Statistics, *National Vital Statistics Reports, www.cdc.gov/nchs/fastats/ 1cod.htm, 2004.*

Sociodemographic Variations in Life Expectancy

Social Class.   The upper class has a distinct advantage over the less affluent with regard to life expectancy. On average, people with low incomes live approximately seven years less than the more affluent. Level of education and occupational status—two components of socioeconomic status—have been found to be among the most important predictors of health. Higher levels of education and occupational status are associated with less overall stress, healthier and safer living and working environments, and a more nutritious diet. The more affluent use more preventive health services and are less likely to delay seeking care when sick (Hertz, Hebert, and Landon, 1994).

Race and Ethnicity.   In the United States, whites have a much longer life expectancy than most racial and ethnic minority groups. Life expectancy for African Americans lagged behind that for the total population throughout the twentieth century, but since 1990, the gap has decreased. In 2001, while the overall population was expected to live 77.2 years, life expectancy for whites was 77.7 years and for blacks just 72.2 years—still a difference of 5-1/2 years (see Table 3–3).

The leading causes of death for blacks are the same as for whites (heart disease, cancer, and stroke), but blacks are much more vulnerable to each of these diseases (see Table 3–4). In addition the death rate from AIDS is about five times higher among blacks than whites, and among women and children, the gap is even wider.

What accounts for these differences? One study determined that approximately 38 percent of the racial mortality differential is due to income differences (blacks are three times more likely than whites to be below the poverty level); about 31 percent is due to blacks having more high-risk factors such as cigarette smoking and generally higher incidences of hypertension, high cholesterol levels, and diabetes; and the remaining 31 percent is due to less access to

TABLE 3–3 Life Expectancy by Race, Sex, and Age, 2001

Average Years of Life Remaining	Expectation of Life in Years				
		White		Black	
	Total	Male	Female	Male	Female
At birth	77.2	75.0	80.2	68.6	75.5
65	18.1	16.5	19.5	14.4	17.9

Source: National Center for Health Statistics, *National Vital Statistics Report,* Hyattsville, MD: NCHS, 2003.

health services and differences in social and physical environment (Otten et al., 1990).

Hispanics are the second largest racial/ethnic minority group in the United States, comprising 12 percent of the population. Though Hispanics (a broad term covering several groups with important differences) are more likely than non-Hispanic whites to be below the poverty level and less likely to have health insurance, they have a lower death rate. This is a product of having lower death rates from heart disease, cancer, accidents, and suicide. Efforts are underway to explain the lower death rates from heart disease and cancer, but they may be due to dietary factors or the strong family life and support networks found in many Hispanic families.

Asian and Pacific Islanders, another strikingly diverse population, are the fastest-growing population group in the United States. Included among this group are some well-established Asian-American populations (Japanese, Chinese, and Filipinos) and many recent immigrants and refugees from Southeast Asia. As a

whole, leading causes of death mirror those of other population groups, but, with the exception of very recent immigrant groups, rates are lower. The clearest differences are with respect to heart disease, cancer, and suicide.

Social Class and Race. While some life expectancy and mortality differentials may have a genetic basis (e.g., sickle cell anemia, diabetes, and hypertension in blacks), social-environmental factors play a much larger role and most of these factors are related to higher rates of poverty among minorities. Poverty reduces life expectancy by increasing the chances of infant mortality, acute and chronic diseases, and traumatic death.

Among others, Navarro (1991) has argued that the traditional debate as to whether race or class has more impact misses the most important point—that both race and class impact on mortality. However, in examining data from a 1986 mortality survey, Navarro found that class differentials in mortality (for heart disease and stroke) were larger than race differentials.

TABLE 3–4 Age-Adjusted Death Rates from Selected Diseases, United States, 2001

	Heart Disease	Cancer	Stroke	Suicide	Homicide
	Per 100,000 Population				
Whites	243.5	193.9	55.8	11.7	4.9
Blacks	316.9	243.1	78.8	5.5	21.2
Hispanics	192.2	132.3	44.9	5.7	8.3
American Indians	159.9	131.0	41.3	10.5	6.8
Asians/Pacific Islanders	137.6	119.5	51.2	5.4	4.2

Source: National Center for Health Statistics, *National Vital Statistics Report,* Hyattsville, MD: NCHS, 2003.

The relatively greater impact of class was also discovered in analyses of data from the Charleston (SC) Heart Study. This study focused on a random sample of black and white men who were 35 years of age or older when recruited into the Heart Study in 1960. Education level and occupational status of the subjects were collected so that mortality rates over the 28-year period to 1988 could be analyzed. Researchers reported that in no instance were black-white differences in all-cause or coronary disease mortality rates significantly different when socioeconomic status (SES) was controlled. In this study, class was the more powerful predictor of mortality; when class was controlled, the effects of race decreased (Keil et al., 1992).

Gender. Females have a longer life expectancy than males. At birth, female infants can expect to live about 80 years compared to just 74 years for male infants. Within racial groups, white female infants are expected to live about 5 years longer than their white male counterparts, and black females more than 7 years longer than black male infants. Mortality rates for all three leading causes of death in the United States—heart disease, cancer, and stroke—are higher for men than for women.

Females have a biological advantage over males from the beginning of life, as demonstrated by lower mortality rates at both the prenatal and neonatal (i.e., first 28 days) stages of life. However, the sizable gap in expected years of life between men and women is traceable to an interrelationship among several biological and sociocultural influences. A discussion of these factors is provided in the box, "Why Do Women Live Longer Than Men?"

INFANT MORTALITY

Measurement

Infant mortality is defined as the number of infant deaths for every 1,000 babies born. The formula for the **infant mortality rate** is:

$$\frac{\begin{array}{c}\text{Total number of deaths in} \\ \text{specified population} \\ \text{of persons under age 1} \\ \text{in a given year}\end{array}}{\begin{array}{c}\text{Total number of live} \\ \text{births during the year}\end{array}} \times 1,000$$

Epidemiologists divide infant mortality rate into two components: the **neonatal mortality rate** (deaths among infants in the first 28 days of life) and the **postneonatal mortality rate** (deaths between 29 days and 1 year of life). While infant mortality rates are sometimes used as an indicator of the quality of health care within a country, the postneonatal mortality rate is actually a better indicator for two reasons. First, deaths in the first 28 days of life are often a direct consequence of genetic problems or difficulties in the birthing process. Second, using the neonatal rate to assess quality or delivery of care creates an illogical situation. The better health care technology gets at sustaining an early life, but one that it cannot sustain over the long term, the higher the neonatal mortality rate and the lower the evaluation of the health care system (i.e., babies who die during birth are not counted in infant mortality rates; babies who are sustained and given a chance at life but die in the first 28 days are). The postneonatal mortality rate is a better reflection of babies who die due to socioenvironmental conditions.

Trends

Since the turn of the century, the infant mortality rate in the United States has steadily declined. Between 1950 and 2001, the mortality rate for infants dropped from 29.2 per 1,000 live births to a rate of 6.8. Most of this improvement is due to socioenvironmental factors such as improved socioeconomic status, housing, and nutrition; clean water; and pasteurized milk. However, medical discoveries such as antibiotics and immunizations, better prenatal care and delivery, and technological breakthroughs in infant care (such as neonatal intensive care and new surgical techniques) have also been important. In spite of the decline in mortality among infants, the United States still ranks far below

---

IN THE FIELD

WHY DO WOMEN LIVE LONGER THAN MEN?

In the United States, women live approximately five years longer than men. Is this an inescapable sex-based feature? No. In the early part of this century, there was little difference in life expectancy between men and women, and by 1920, women lived only about two years longer than men. Although women live longer than men in all industrialized countries, in some agriculturally based societies, men live longer than women. These patterns reflect the importance of social and cultural influences—not genetic determination. Systematic analyses of sex differentials in mortality point to two primary reasons: (1) differences in health-related behaviors and circumstances and (2) differences in the manner in which health services are used.

In the United States, women are more likely to experience acute illnesses such as upper respiratory infections and gastroenteritis and have higher rates of certain chronic, debilitating (but usually not life-threatening) conditions such as anemia, thyroid conditions, colitis, and arthritis. Men are more likely to have life-threatening chronic conditions such as cancer, stroke, and liver disease (Rieker and Bird, 2000).

This pattern can be traced to behavioral differences. Over most of the age span, males are more likely than females to die of cancer. This is traced to a greater likelihood of cigarette smoking by men; to men's greater propensity to drink alcohol excessively; and to men being more likely to be exposed to cancer-causing agents in the workplace. Sex differences in reproductive anatomy and effects of sex hormones also play a role and help explain the greater likelihood of women dying from certain types of cancer, such as breast cancer.

Men are more likely to die in automobile accidents (studies show men drive more miles but also drive faster, less cautiously, and violate more traffic regulations); are more likely to die in on-the-job accidents; and are more likely to commit suicide and to be a victim of homicide. Whether or not male sex hormones create a predisposition to more aggressive behavior, socialization experiences relative to alcohol consumption, use of guns, physical risk-taking, and assumption of risky jobs sets the pattern (Stillion and McDowell, 2002).

In addition, women are more likely than men to seek medical care. Women perceive more symptoms, take them more seriously, and are more willing to see a physician about them. They are more likely to have a regular source of medical care, to use more preventive care, to see physicians more often, to be prescribed medications, and to be hospitalized (Rieker and Bird, 2000). Often, men would benefit from earlier and increased medical attention as a means of earlier diagnosis and intervention into diseases that become life threatening.

---

most nations of comparable (or even lesser) resources (see Table 3–5).

Causes

By far, the single most hazardous condition for infants is low birth weight. About 7 percent of all live births are considered to be low birth weight (less than 2,500 grams—about 5-1/2 pounds); about 1 percent of all births are very low birth weight (less than 1,500 grams). Low birth weight is the primary determinant of approximately 75 percent of all deaths in the first month and 60 percent of all infant deaths. Low-weight babies are also at risk of congenital anomalies such as malformations of the brain and spine, heart defects, and long-term disabilities such as cerebral palsy, autism, mental retardation, and vision and hearing impairments.

What factors increase the likelihood of a baby being low birth weight? At a micro level, low birth weight has been linked to age of the mother (younger females have a more difficult time sustaining a healthy pregnancy); maternal smoking and use of alcohol or other drugs; and

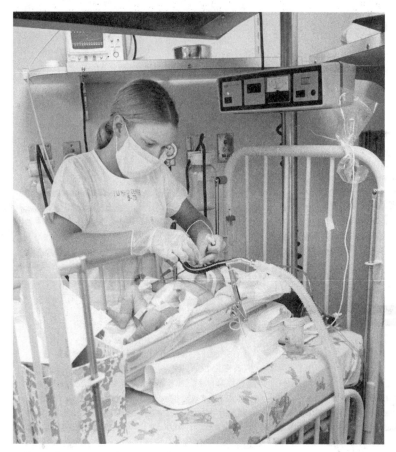

Despite the existence of sophisticated, high-technology care for newborns, the infant mortality rate in the United States lags behind that of most other modern countries.

inadequate prenatal care. Estimates suggest that half of the infant deaths due to low birth weight would be preventable with adequate prenatal care (most women at risk for delivering a low birth weight baby can be identified at an initial visit and monitored for factors such as inadequate nutrition, substance use, hypertension, urinary tract infections, and other potential risks to the fetus). Many European countries attribute their lower infant mortality rate to the provision of adequate prenatal care to all women, yet up to one-third of pregnant women in the United States fail to get adequate prenatal care.

At a macro level, several social structural (social, economic, and political) factors directly impinge on infant mortality rate. A strong relationship exists between economic status and all of the micro factors which increase the likelihood of a low birth weight baby. Poor women experience more health problems during pregnancy and are much less likely to receive adequate (if any) prenatal care. One recent study of state infant mortality levels compared the influence of social structural factors (such as percentage of persons in poverty, percentage of blacks and Hispanics in the population, amount of residential segregation, and political voting patterns) and health services variables (such as number of physicians relative to population and proportion of state expenditures on health care). The researchers found that the social structural factors were much more strongly related to the rate of infant mortality (Bird and Bauman, 1995). Despite the appeal of focusing only on individual level explanatory factors, it is very important also to consider the influence of social structural factors as determinants of infant mortality.

TABLE 3–5   Infant Mortality Rates in 2003
in Countries with 5+ Million
Persons

Country	Number of Deaths Under 1 Year/1,000 Live Births
Sweden	2.8
Japan	3.3
Finland	3.6
Czech Republic	4.0
Germany	4.2
France	4.3
Switzerland	4.4
Spain	4.5
Denmark	4.6
Austria	4.7
Australia	4.8
Belgium	4.8
Canada	4.8
Netherlands	5.1
United Kingdom	5.2
Ireland	5.5
Greece	5.6
Italy	6.1
Cuba	6.5
Taiwan	6.5
United States	6.6 (21st)

Highest 10:

Angola	192.5
Afghanistan	166.0
Sierra Leone	145.2
Mozambique	137.1
Niger	122.7
Somalia	118.5
Mali	118.0
Tajikistan	112.1
Malawi	104.2
Tanzania	102.1

Source: United States Bureau of the Census,
Population Division, International Programs Center,
*International Data Base, www.census.gov/ipc/www/
idbnew.html,* 2003.

Variations by Race and Social Class

The overall infant mortality rate masks a significant discrepancy that exists between white and
black infants and between babies born into poor
and more affluent homes. The infant mortality
rate is one to one-and-one-half times higher in
families below the poverty level, and black babies
are more than twice as likely as white babies to be
low birth weight and to die before the age of one.
This relates to general maternal health (Hummer,
1993) and a higher likelihood of contracting dis-

ease during pregnancy, a much greater propensity
for child-bearing while still in the teenage years,
and being less likely to receive adequate prenatal
care. Schoendorf et al. (1992:1525) tie the greater
likelihood of low birth weight babies to the ele-
vated risk of prematurity due to:

> poor maternal health prior to pregnancy, increased
> physiologic risks associated with psychosocial
> risks, poor health habits during pregnancy,
> insufficient access to health care services, sub-
> standard health care (from physicians or other
> health care personnel), or standard medical care
> that does not adequately address the needs of
> pregnant black women.

Several excellent studies have emphasized the
importance of social structural factors as explanations for the differences in black and white infant
mortality rates. LaVeist (1993) has documented
the effects of poverty (the fact that blacks are
more likely to be below the poverty level), racial
segregation (segregated black urban communities
being more likely to be toxic environments lacking in city services and medical services and having an inflated cost of living), and political
empowerment (the black infant mortality rate is
lower in cities with greater black political power,
perhaps due to reduced feelings of hopelessness
and greater availability and inclination to use
appropriate health services). Table 3–6 shows the
relationship between infant mortality and race/
ethnic background of the mother.

TABLE 3–6   Infant Deaths per 1,000
Live Births by Race of
Mother, 1999

Race/Ethnic Origin	Percentage
Japanese	3.5
Cuban	3.6
Chinese	4.0
Mexican	5.6
White	6.0
Filipino	6.2
Puerto Rican	7.8
American Indian or Alaskan Native	9.3
Black	13.8

Source: National Center for Health Statistics, *Health,
United States, 2003,* United States Department of
Health and Human Services, Hyattsville, MD, 2003.

MATERNAL MORTALITY

The **maternal mortality rate** is defined as the number of women who die in the process of giving birth for every 100,000 live births. Most modern countries have reduced the maternal mortality rate to a low level. In 2001, the rate in the United States was 8.8. This is a low rate, but it does still translate into two or three women dying each day from complications related to pregnancy or delivery.

Significant variations in this rate continue among population subgroups: black women are four times more likely than white women to die, and unmarried women have nearly three times the maternal mortality rate as married women. The risk of death decreases as level of education increases, with women under 20 years of age who have not graduated from high school at highest risk.

Lack of prenatal care is the major risk factor for maternal mortality. Because about one out of four pregnant women in the United States experiences a major complication, such as high blood pressure, diabetes, or a hemorrhage, prenatal care can be of as much benefit to a pregnant woman as to her fetus.

MORBIDITY

Morbidity refers to the amount of disease, impairment, and accident in a population—for several reasons, a concept more difficult to measure than mortality. As we discuss in Chapter 7, the definition of illness varies considerably from one individual to another and one group to another. Some people have a disease and do not realize it; others think they have a disease though there is no clinical confirmation. Even if one is sick, home care may be used instead of professional care so the illness is never officially reported. In cases where a physician is consulted, the results of the examination may or may not be reported since the law does not require the reporting of all diseases. While certain communicable diseases such as tuberculosis, polio, measles, mumps, and chicken pox are reportable, others such as cancer and heart disease are not.

If written records (such as hospital records) are used, only the professionally treated cases are counted—resulting in an underestimation of the number of cases. Much of the morbidity data we rely on is gathered through health surveys such as the National Health Interview Survey. While sampling techniques are now very successful in representing a population, accurate data still depend upon respondents' memories, and reporting still reflects individual perceptions of illness.

Measurement

Two epidemiological techniques are used extensively to determine the social and ecological distribution of disease and illness: incidence and prevalence.

Incidence and Prevalence.   The **incidence** of disease, impairment, or accident refers to the number of new cases added to the population within a given period. For example, one could report on the incidence of AIDS in the United States during the last year—that would be interpreted as the number of people newly diagnosed with AIDS in the last 12 months. **Prevalence** refers to the total number of cases of a condition present at a given time. For example, the prevalence of AIDS in the United States today would be the total number of living people who have been diagnosed with AIDS. Together, incidence and prevalence help identify disease patterns.

Patterns and Sociodemographic Variations in Morbidity

Because there is no systematic reporting of illness and injury, the best way to determine their incidence and prevalence in the population is through health interview surveys. One aggregate approach for summarizing the extent to which illness and injury exist is by collecting information on **restricted-activity days**, which are defined as days in which a person cuts down on his or her activities for more than half of the day because of illness or injury. In the United

IN COMPARATIVE FOCUS

MORTALITY PATTERNS IN DEVELOPING COUNTRIES

Worldwide, life expectancy increased more in the twentieth century than in all prior human history, and the biggest increases were in the second half of the century. Average life expectancy in the world increased from just 48 years of age in 1955 to 66 years of age at the turn of the century and is expected to increase to about 73 years of age by the year 2025.

These data, of course, camouflage continuing disparities between the world's wealthiest and poorest nations. In 1996, 76 percent of the deaths reported in Africa were people younger than 50 years of age; the corresponding figure in Europe was just 15 percent. By 2025, the percent in Africa is predicted to diminish to 57 percent while the figure for Europe should decrease to 7 percent—both marked improvements but a continuing large disparity (Hager, 1998).

Maternal mortality rates remain at a very high level in many developing countries. The United Nations Children's Fund estimates that as many as 600,000 women die during pregnancy and childbirth each year. As many as 99 percent of these deaths occur in the Third World—95 percent of maternal deaths occur in sub-Saharan Africa, where nearly 1,400 women die for every 100,000 who give birth. It is estimated that 30 percent of births worldwide occur without any trained person in attendance, and maternal mortality is especially high in these situations (LaVeist, 1998).

Although still at a high level, infant mortality rates have been slowly decreasing throughout the developing world. In many developing countries, focus is more on "child mortality" (death in the first five years of life) than just on infant mortality. This is because children ages 2 through 5 are at continued high risk in these

countries—a situation unlike that in industrialized countries.

The experience of Pakistan, the world's seventh largest country, illustrates the influence of economic and social development on infant mortality rates. Despite having a high infant mortality rate, little progress has been made in reducing the number of infant deaths. Concerned about this pattern, Sohail Agha studied national, community, and household data and two national surveys and identified two primary factors that accounted for the lack of progress.

First, Pakistan has considerable socioeconomic inequality that has resulted in the concentration of political power in a powerful rural elite. Throughout the 1980s and early 1990s, economic planning was built around the "trickle-down theory" by which efforts were made to promote economic flourishing of the upper classes with an expectation that their success would filter down to the lower classes. The failure of this policy resulted in substantial disparities in income, education, nutrition, and access to quality housing, sanitary conditions, and clean water—all factors implicated in infant mortality rates.

Second, Agha identified gender inequity as contributing to the high infant mortality rate. Relative to Pakistani men, women tend to be poor, illiterate, less educated, and have low social and legal status. This may contribute to a lack of priority being placed on women's and children's health. In addition more highly educated women generally prefer having fewer children, stopping procreation at an earlier age, and having more birth spacing—again, all factors that have an effect on the health and sustainability of newborns (Agha, 2000).

States, in 1996, the average person experienced 14.5 restricted activity days. As summarized in Table 3–7, illness and injury were much higher for those age 65 and older than for younger persons, much higher for the poor than the wealthy, and higher for blacks than whites and for females than males.

Among the important sociodemographic factors influencing morbidity rates are age, socioeconomic status, race and ethnicity, and gender.

Age.   The health of children in the United States has changed dramatically in the past four

TABLE 3–7   Number of Restricted Activity Days by Selected Characteristics, 1996

Characteristic	Average Number of Restricted Activity Days
Total population	14.5
Male	12.3
Female	16.5
White	14.3
Black	16.4
Under age 65	12.3
Age 65 and older	30.5
Family income	
Under $10,000	27.9
$10,000 to $19,999	21.1
$20,000 to $34,999	13.0
$35,000 and more	9.9

Source: United States Bureau of the Census, *Statistical Abstract of the United States, 2000.* Washington, DC: USGPO, 2000.

decades. One by one, the major infectious diseases that used to imperil children have been eliminated or significantly reduced by widespread immunization. Smallpox has been eliminated and polio will be soon. Diphtheria, scarlet fever, cholera, tetanus, pneumonia, measles, mumps, and whooping cough are increasingly uncommon in this country (though many of these diseases continue to plague children in developing countries). Though a substantial percentage of children in the United States get all of their immunizations by their third birthday (78 percent of children had received all of their diphtheria-tetanus-pertussis, polio, meningitis, and measles-mumps-rubella shots by age 3 in 2002), some children, especially in inner-city and rural areas, do not. Many epidemiologists emphasize that the country needs to remain vigilant in ensuring that children are immunized against these diseases.

As the prevalence of these infectious diseases has decreased, epidemiologists have increased attention on four other conditions that contribute to morbidity among children and adolescents:

1. *Poor diet and lack of exercise.* Poor nutrition, lack of exercise, and resulting obesity among adolescents have become a major problem. Estimates are that as many as 20 percent of adolescents are overweight, and the percentage has been increasing. This pattern has been created by twin conditions: an increasing percentage of adolescents eating less nutritious, high-fat, high-sugar diets (as with most fast-food) and a decreasing percentage getting the recommended amount of exercise. While these same patterns characterize adults, patterns set in adolescence are especially difficult to break.

2. *Use of tobacco, alcohol, and other drugs.* Cigarette smoking among youth increased substantially during the 1990s among whites, Hispanics, and especially among African Americans. By the year 2000, almost half of all male teenagers and over one-third of female teenagers smoked cigarettes or cigars or used smokeless tobacco. Alcohol use has remained at about the same level of use in recent years— just over 20 percent. The use of illicit drugs among youths declined during the 1970s, 1980s, and 1990s. In 1995, use of marijuana, cocaine, inhalants, hallucinogens, stimulants, sedatives, tranquilizers, and analgesics were all at lower levels among 12- to 17-year-olds than 10 years previously. However, data from the early 2000s suggest that drug use may again be on the upswing. While use of certain drugs (e.g., LSD) continues to decline, use of other drugs (e.g., marijuana, cocaine, ecstasy) has increased.

3. *Sexual activity and pregnancy.* In the last five years, teen sexual activity has declined. However, about 50 percent of teens are sexually active, about one in seven has had at least four sexual partners, and about 40 percent do not routinely use a condom. This means that a substantial percentage of teens are susceptible to sexually transmitted infections. In the early 2000s, the incidences of both gonorrhea and the human papilloma virus (HPV) are increasing—and they are increasing most rapidly among young people.

After years of increase, the birth rate for teenage women is also declining. However, in 2001, more than 1.3 million infants were born to unmarried mothers, accounting for one-third of all infants (28 percent of whites, 68 percent of blacks, and 42 percent of Hispanics). About one-fourth of these babies were born to mothers in their teen years. While blacks continue to have a substantially higher rate of teen pregnancy, the gap between whites and blacks has narrowed in recent years. Teenage mothers are more likely not to finish school, to be unemployed, and to have low-birth-weight babies.

4. *Violence.* Physical abuse is an increasingly recognized problem, as are emotional and sexual abuse. Substantial increases in reported physical and sexual abuse cases have occurred since 1980, although the increase is partially due to improved reporting. Suicide and homicide are increasing dangers for children and adolescents with victimization increasingly likely to occur in school facilities. Homicide is the second leading cause of death for persons age 15 to 34.

At the other end of the age spectrum, the level of health among the elderly has improved in recent years as a result of better diet, more exercise, and more advanced and accessible health care. Despite the fact that health problems increase in the later years, older people now tend to rate their own health status as good. This assessment is consistent with physician evaluations and seems realistic relative to the elderly's reduced requirements for active levels of functioning, since most are no longer parenting or working.

Many believe that the human life span is relatively finite and fixed, at about 85 years on average, and that improvements in health will compress the onset of morbidity and disability into the later years of life. This will result in an improved quality of life and a reduced need for medical care. Others argue that life expectancy is rising more rapidly than the onset of morbidity is being postponed. They predict that gains in life expectancy will be accompanied by additional years of chronic illness and disability.

Socioeconomic Status. Nearly one in every eight Americans lives in a family with an income below the federal poverty level, and more than 20 percent of children under 18 years of age are in such families. House, Kessler, and Herzog (1990) have investigated the relationship between socioeconomic status and level of health (measured by number of chronic conditions, functional status, and limitation of daily activities) at various ages. They discovered a vast amount of preventable morbidity and functional limitations in the lower socioeconomic strata of American society and that the discrepancy between the poor and nonpoor was especially great for those between the ages of 35 and 75.

The disadvantages in health status at middle and early old age is explained by the vulnerability of this group to a number of psychosocial and environmental risk factors. These include greater exposure to physical, chemical, biological, and psychosocial hazards; increased stress due to employment insecurity and inadequate financial resources; and greater participation rates in various harmful behaviors such as smoking and alcohol consumption as well as poorer eating habits and lack of exercise. Variation among socioeconomic groups in these risk factors appears to be relatively small in early adulthood, greater during middle and early old age, and then small again in older age (House, Kessler, and Herzog, 1990).

Figure 3–1 is a representation of one model of how poverty influences morbidity and mortality. Persons in the lower social class are more likely to live and work in areas with hazardous chemicophysical conditions and are less likely to be involved in supportive social networks (e.g., the unemployed). These conditions lead to higher levels of psychological stress. The poor are more likely to engage in certain health-damaging behaviors (e.g., cigarette smoking), in part due to the high level of stress. The harmful lifestyle behaviors, the high levels of stress, and the lack of support networks all contribute to increased morbidity and greater likelihood of mortality. Because the poor often cannot afford preventive or therapeutic care, health problems

Figure 3–1 The Cycle of Poverty and Pathology

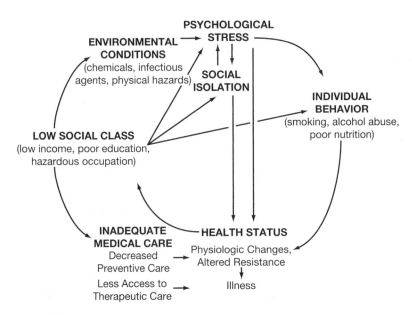

Source: Diana B. Dutton, "Social Class, Health, and Illness," pp. 31–62 in *Applications of Social Science to Clinical Medicine and Health Policy,* Linda H. Aiken and David Mechanic (eds.). New Brunswick, NJ: Rutgers University Press, 1986. Adapted from, Barbara Starfield, "Social Factors in Child Health," pp. 12–18 in *Ambulatory Pediatrics III,* Morris Green and Robert J. Haggerty (eds.). Philadelphia: W. B. Saunders, 1984.

frequently do not receive immediate attention; therefore serious conditions worsen.

Race and Ethnicity.   One of the most discouraging health-related trends in the United States in the 1990s was the worsening state of health of African Americans. Rates of morbidity are higher for blacks than whites for most diseases, including heart disease, cancer, diabetes, pneumonia and influenza, liver disease and cirrhosis, accidental injuries, and AIDS. Blacks experience more health problems than whites early in life, and their health deteriorates more rapidly. Much, but not all, of this health disadvantage is due to the lower economic standing of blacks. But, at all ages and at all levels of socioeconomic standing, blacks have more health problems than whites (Ferraro and Farmer, 1996).

Hypertension or high blood pressure is an especially prevalent health problem for blacks and one that can be used to illustrate reasons for morbidity differentials. Blacks have an almost one-third greater chance than whites of having

hypertension, and black females and those in the lower class are at especially high risk. Cockerham (2001:49) has summarized six plausible explanations for these higher rates of hypertension:

1. A *genetic hypothesis* argues that blacks are genetically different from whites in ways that predispose them to hypertension. (Recent research has identified that many blacks at high risk of stroke share a gene mutation that helps to control blood pressure. Many whites also have this mutation, but early research suggests that it increases the stroke risk only for blacks).

2. A *physical exertion hypothesis* postulates that blacks are more likely than whites to be engaged in manual labor, and that greater physical exertion leads to higher mortality from hypertension.

3. An *associated disorder hypothesis* asserts that blacks are more prone to diseases such as pyelonephritis and syphilis that may result in secondary hypertension.

4. A *psychological stress hypothesis* theorizes that blacks are severely frustrated by racial discrimination, and that this stress and the repressed aggression associated with it lead to a higher prevalence of hypertension.

5. A *diet hypothesis* emphasizes that blacks may have dietary patterns that increase their susceptibility to hypertension.

6. A *medical care hypothesis* argues that blacks receive poorer medical care than whites and that this results in greater morbidity and mortality from hypertensive disease and perhaps a higher prevalence of secondary hypertension.

All of these factors have received some empirical support, although which factor is most important in explaining the high rate of hypertension experienced by blacks or their greater propensity than whites to be hypertensive is yet to be clarified.

The health of Asians and Pacific Islanders is as varied as the people are diverse. Those born within the United States and established in the culture are very similar in their level of health to that of the population as a whole, but on most major indicators, Asians and Pacific Islanders are the healthiest of all racial/ethnic groups in the country.

On the other hand, most Hispanic groups—but especially Puerto Ricans—fare less well than whites on indicators of morbidity. Rates of diabetes, tuberculosis, hypertension, and AIDS are all especially high in Hispanic communities. As with other groups, Hispanics below the poverty level are at special risk.

The Mexican Americans most at risk of morbidity are the approximately one million farm workers who do exhausting work, have high rates of accidents, and limited access to health care providers. Groups on both sides of the U.S.-Mexico border contend with serious air and water pollution, poor sanitation, considerable overcrowding, and illegally dumped hazardous wastes.

For Puerto Ricans, who are more likely than Cuban Americans or Mexican Americans to be under the poverty level, health problems common to metropolitan inner-city areas are the main concern, and their morbidity rates tend to be highest of the Hispanic groups.

Gender. Although men have a higher prevalence of fatal conditions and thus higher mortality rates, women have higher morbidity rates for most acute illnesses (including infectious and respiratory diseases) and for most chronic conditions. For men and women age 45 and older, arthritis and high blood pressure are very common problems, but beyond age 75, hearing impairment and heart disease become more prevalent (both bigger problems for males).

Five reasons have been offered to account for gender differences in morbidity:

1. *Biological risks.* These result from differences in genes or hormones. Males are at some disadvantage because of women's intrinsic protection. Reproductive conditions (pregnancy, childbirth, disorders of puerperium) account for a substantial amount—but not all—of the morbidity differential even at ages 17 to 44.

2. *Acquired risks due to differences in social factors such as work and leisure activities, lifestyle and health habits, and psychological distress.* Acquired risks are different for men and women. Some lifestyle behaviors, such as smoking, alcohol consumption, and occupational hazards, are more common among men. Others, such as less active leisure activities, being overweight, stress and unhappiness, and role pressures (e.g., women being more likely than men to feel tension between work and family commitments), are associated more with females. Most analysts perceive this to be the most important explanation for gender differences in mortality and an important part of the explanation for gender differences in morbidity.

3. *Psychosocial aspects of symptoms and care.* This refers to the way people perceive symptoms, assess their severity, and decide what to do to relieve or cure health problems. Gender differences in responding to illness may stem from childhood or adult socialization that it is more acceptable for women to reflect upon and discuss symptoms and concerns. The presence of physiological conditions such as menstruation, pregnancy, breast-feeding, and menopause may encourage women to pay more attention to their bodies and to be more observant of physiological changes. Much research has confirmed that women place higher value on health and have more of a preventive orientation toward health. This may be the other most important explanatory factor in morbidity differentials.

4. *Health reporting behavior.* Females are more willing to acknowledge symptoms and illness and to seek care. In one study, women were discovered to be significantly more likely than men to report headache-related disability and to seek health care services for their headaches—even after controlling for severity of the headache (Celetano, Linet, and Stewart, 1990). Depending on the source of the data, part of these differences may relate to continuing differences in the socioeconomic position of men and women. Women are less likely than men to be employed, so they can more easily arrange a medical visit. If a family member is ill, it is more likely that the woman calls in sick, since women on average earn less than men, and in many families it is the wife's "duty" to take care of sick children or to be at home on school holidays.

5. *Prior experience with health care and caretakers.* Males use fewer health care services. As a result of their greater participation in self-care and greater attentiveness to health status, women may derive more benefit from seeing a health care provider and receive more positive reinforcement for their attentiveness (Verbrugge, 1990).

DISABILITY

The United States Bureau of the Census defines **disability** as, "a reduced ability to perform tasks one would normally do at a given stage in life"

(United States Bureau of the Census, 1992:70–33). Disability is the gap between what the body is capable of doing and the demands made on the body by the environment and is the result of a complex process that involves disease, changes in physiological and physical functioning, and medical and personal intervention. Disabilities may be physical or mental and they may include motor or sensory limitations.

Health status and disability status are often related because many health problems arise from or are related to the main cause of disability. These secondary conditions often are linked to living conditions. For example, pressure sores and musculoskeletal disorders are common among those who are confined to a

TABLE 3–8   Percentage of the United States Population (Age 18 and Older) with Specified Difficulties in Physical Functioning, Age-Adjusted, 2002

Characteristic	Percentage of Distribution
With any physical difficulty	14.0
Male	10.9
Female	16.7
18–44	5.2
45–64	17.5
65–74	26.8
75 and older	44.4
Less than $20,000	23.8
$20,000–34,999	16.2
$35,000–54,999	13.1
$55,000–74,999	11.1
$75,000 and more	9.2
Walking a quarter mile	6.5
Climbing 10 steps without resting	4.9
Standing for 2 hours	8.5
Sitting for 2 hours	3.1
Stooping, bending, kneeling	8.2
Reaching over head	2.4
Grasping small objects	1.7
Lifting 10 pounds	4.0

Source: United States Bureau of the Census, *Current Population Reports,* Washington, DC: USGPO 2004.

As the number of persons with chronic illnesses and disabilities increases, home health care and home health equipment have become booming businesses.

wheelchair or bed. Not only can these complicating medical conditions arise from immobility or inactivity, they may also be a result of the progression of the original disabling condition, such as visual impairment among diabetics. Of course, it is possible for a person to be disabled and yet be in good health (e.g., someone who is blind), while another may have a chronic condition (e.g., a heart condition) but have adequate capacities to function in his or her roles and therefore not be disabled.

In 2002 approximately 50 million people had a chronic, significant disability (almost one adult in four). About two-thirds of these disabilities were considered to be severe and to involve major activity limitation. Table 3–8 identifies some major forms of physical functioning difficulty and the percentage of the population age 18 and older with that condition.

Blacks are slightly more likely than whites to have a disability, and Hispanics are slightly less likely. Females report more disabilities than males and lose more days from school and from work and have more days confined to bed than males. Persons in the lowest income groups average almost three times the number of disabilities as people in higher income groups. Their lack of financial means often results in not getting access to needed services. This in turn often hinders the successful management of a chronic medical condition and makes it more difficult to live successfully in the community (Allen and More, 1997).

Disability is very much related to age—persons 65 years of age and older are about three times more likely than younger persons to have a disability. However, disability among seniors has been declining rapidly for the last decade. Better nutrition, higher levels of education, improved economic status, and medical advances have all contributed to this important change.

SUMMARY

Prior to urbanization and migration, the threat of infectious disease and epidemics was minimal. However, diseases and epidemics began to spread with the emergence of cities and easier modes of travel. With the development of the germ theory of disease and other advances in medicine, as well as greater understanding of the importance of social factors in the transmission of diseases, the threat of epidemic diseases has been reduced. In modern societies, chronic, degenerative diseases have replaced acute, infectious diseases as the most frequent cause of death.

The average number of years of life to be expected from birth—life expectancy—has increased dramatically in the United States during this century but still lags behind many other countries. Significant improvements have also been made in the overall mortality rate, the infant mortality rate, and the maternal mortality rate, though the United States still has higher rates than those in most other modern countries.

Sociodemographic characteristics are significant determinants of life expectancy, mortality, morbidity, and disability within the population. In general, the poor and African Americans are most vulnerable to illness, disability, and death. Men have a significantly higher mortality rate than women, though women consistently experience more morbidity.

HEALTH ON THE INTERNET

A good way to stay abreast of mortality and morbidity data is to check the Centers for Disease Control and Prevention's *Morbidity and Mortality Weekly Report* on the Internet. After you enter the Web site, click on "Youth Violence."

http://cdc.gov/ncipc/dvp/dvp.htm

What are some important patterns and trends in youth violence? What are the key individual, family, peer/school, and neighborhood/community risk factors? What are some of the ways that CDC is attempting to reduce youth violence? What is the significance of violence being included in the Web site of a center for "disease control"?

KEY CONCEPTS AND TERMS

acute, infectious disease
chronic, degenerative disease
crude death rate (CDR)
epidemiological transition
epidemiology
disability
incidence
infant mortality rate
life expectancy

maternal mortality rate
morbidity
mortality
neonatal mortality rate
postneonatal mortality rate
prevalence
restricted activity days
social epidemiology

DISCUSSION CASE

This chapter demonstrates how much valuable information epidemiologists provide for understanding and controlling diseases. However, data gathering can conflict with the rights of individuals. It is therefore extremely important that the responsibilities of epidemiologists be carried out while adhering to ethical principles of respect, justice, and equity. As Nakajime (1991:169) reminds us:

Surveillance and control of communicable disease can infringe autonomy, by the identification and reporting to public health authorities of persons who suffer from or have been in contact with communicable diseases. There can sometimes be severe stigma and loss of liberty if cases or contacts are isolated or quarantined. In cases of sexually transmitted diseases, public health workers attempt to trace and treat contacts as well as cases. In many nations and local jurisdictions, these procedures are enforced by law.

Discuss these issues as they relate to the following case:

CASE #1: Thomas Hoskins is a 21-year-old full-time college student who is also employed 30 hours per week. The pressures of school, work, and a marriage on the rocks have been adding up for him. Three weeks ago, he went out with a few friends, had too much to drink, and ended up sleeping with a woman he met at the bar. Tests confirm that he now has gonorrhea. While giving him an injection, his physician tells him that all sexually transmitted diseases must be reported to the state health department.

Thomas is panic-stricken. He fears that his wife will somehow find out (she has friends who work for the health department), and that if she does, their marriage will be over. He pleads with the physician to make an exception to his duty to report. This is his first extramarital sexual contact, and he assures the physician it will be his last.

Should the physician make an exception in this case and not comply with the state manda-tory reporting law? Or should physicians always report regardless of the circumstances?

CASE #2: Life expectancy in the United States has increased to about 77 years and is continuing to increase. Many respected demographers anticipate that life expectancy will top out around 88 years for females and 82 years for males. But Donald Loria, a professor at the New Jersey Medical School believes that the average could reach 100 by the end of the century just with continued gradual increases and could reach 110 or 120 with revolutionary advances in health and medicine (Curtis, 2004). Some others do not see this as being likely or possible.

But what if this happened? What if average life expectancy reached 100 or 110 by mid-century? Identify the changes that would occur in social institutions if 30 or 40 percent of the population was age 65 or older (up from today's 12.5 percent). If we knew this change was going to occur within the next five decades, what social planning could be done to try facilitate it?

REFERENCES

Agha, Sohail. 2000 "The Determinants of Infant Mortality in Pakistan." *Social Science and Medicine,* 51:199–208.

Allen Susan M., and Vincent More. 1997 "The Prevalence and Consequences of Unmet Need." *Medical Care,* 35:1132–1148.

Bird, Sheryl T., and Karl E. Bauman. 1995 "The Relationship Between Structural and Health Services Variables and State-Level Infant Mortality in the United States." *American Journal of Public Health,* 85:26–29.

Celetano, David D., Martha S. Linet, and Walter F. Stewart. 1990 "Gender Differences in the Experience of Headache." *Social Science and Medicine,* 30:1289–1295.

Cockerham, William C. 2001 *Medical Sociology* (8th ed.). Upper Saddle River, NJ: Prentice Hall.

Coe, Rodney. 1970 *Sociology of Medicine.* New York: McGraw-Hill.

Curtis, Wayne. 2004 "The Methuselah Report," *AARP Bulletin,* 43:5–7.

Dutton, Diana B. 1986 "Social Class, Health, and Illness," pp. 31–62 in *Applications of Social Science to Clinical Medicine and Health Policy,* Linda H. Aiken and David Mechanic (eds.). New Brunswick, NJ: Rutgers University Press.

Ferraro, Kenneth F., and Melissa Farmer. 1996 "Double Jeopardy to Health Hypothesis for African-Americans: Analysis and Critique." *Journal of Health and Social Behavior,* 37:27–43.

Hager, Mary. 1998 "The World Health Organization Has Seen the Future, and It's Full of Good Health." *Newsweek,* June 1, p. 10.

Henley, Eric. 2003 "SARS: Lessons Learned Thus Far." *The Journal of Family Practice,* 52:528–530.

Hertz, Erica, James R. Hebert, and Joan Landon. 1994 "Social and Environmental Factors and Life Expectancy, Infant Mortality, and Maternal Mortality Rates: Results of a Cross-National Comparison." *Social Science and Medicine,* 39:105–114.

House, James S., Ronald Kessler, and A. Regula Herzog. 1990 "Age, Socioeconomic Status, and Health." *The Milbank Quarterly,* 68:383–411.

Hummer, Robert A. 1993 "Racial Differentials in Infant Mortality in the U.S.: An Examination of Social and Health Determinants." *Social Forces,* 72:529–554.

Keil, Julian E., Susan E. Sutherland, Rebecca G. Knapp, and Herman A. Tyroler. 1992 "Does Equal Socioeconomic Status in Black and White Men

Mean Equal Risk of Mortality?" *American Journal of Public Health,* 82:1133–1136.

Lappe, Marc. 1994 *Evolutionary Medicine.* San Francisco: Sierra Club Books.

LaVeist, Thomas A. 1993 "Segregation, Poverty, and Empowerment: Health Consequences for African Americans." *The Milbank Quarterly,* 71:41–64.

———. 1998 "Maternal Mortality Mars Women's Progress Worldwide." *World Population News Service Pipeline,* 20:3.

McKinlay, John B. 1996 "Some Contributions from the Social System to Gender Inequalities in Heart Disease." *Journal of Health and Social Behavior,* 37:1–26.

Nakajime, Hiroshi. 1991 "The Responsibilities of the Epidemiologist." *Law, Medicine and Health Care,* 19:164–174.

National Center for Health Statistics. 2003 *Health, United States, 2003.* Washington, DC: USGPO.

National Center for Health Statistics. 2003 *National Vital Statistics Reports.* Washington, DC: USGPO.

National Center for Health Statistics. 2004 *National Vital Statistics Reports,* www.cdc.gov/nchs/fastats/1cod.htm.

Navarro, Vicente. 1991 "Race or Class or Race and Class: Growing Mortality Differentials in the United States." *International Journal of Health Services,* 21:229–235.

Olshansky, S. Jay, and A. Brian Ault. 1986 "The Fourth State of the Epidemiologic Transition: The Age of Delayed Degenerative Diseases." *The Milbank Quarterly,* 64:355–391.

Omran, A. R. 1971 "The Epidemiologic Transition: A Theory of the Epidemiology of Population Change." *Milbank Memorial Fund Quarterly,* 49:309–338.

Otten, Mac W., Steven M. Teutsch, David F. Williamson, and James F. Marks. 1990 "The Effect of Known Risk Factors on the Excess Mortality of Black Adults in the United States." *Journal of the American Medical Association,* 263:845–850.

Rieker, Patricia P., and Chloe E. Bird. 2000 "Sociological Explanations of Gender Differences in Mental and Physical Health," pp. 98–113 in *Handbook of Medical Sociology* (5th ed.), Chloe E. Bird, Peter Conrad, and Allen M. Fremont (eds.). Upper Saddle River, NJ: Prentice Hall.

Schoendorf, Kenneth C., Carol J. R. Hogue, Joel C. Kleinman, and Diane Rowley. 1992 "Mortality Among Infants of Black as Compared with White College Educated Parents." *New England Journal of Medicine,* 326:1522–1526.

Stillion, Judith M., and Eugene E. McDowell. 2002 "The Early Demise of the 'Stronger' Sex: Gender-Related Causes of Sex Differences in Longevity." *Omega,* 44:301–318.

Susser, Mervyn, and Ezra Susser. 1996 "Choosing a Future for Epidemiology: I. Eras and Paradigms." *American Journal of Public Health,* 86:668–673.

Thacker, Paul D. 2003 "An Ebola Epidemic Simmers in Africa." *Journal of the American Medical Association,* 290:317–319.

United States Bureau of the Census. 1992 *Current Population Reports,* Washington, DC: USGPO.

United States Bureau of the Census. 2004 *Current Population Reports.* Washington, DC: USGPO.

United States Bureau of the Census. 2000 *Statistical Abstract of the United States, 2000.* Washington, DC: USGPO.

United States Bureau of the Census. 2003 International Data Base, *www.census.gov/ipc/www/idbnew.html.*

Verbrugge, Lois M. 1990 "Pathways of Health and Death," pp. 41–79 in *Women, Health and Medicine—A Historical Handbook,* Rima D. Apple (ed.). New York: Garland Publishing, Inc.

4

SOCIETY, DISEASE, AND ILLNESS

As we discussed in Chapter 3, the types of diseases that are most common within a society are determined by a wide range of factors that include the presence of disease agents; characteristics of the social, economic, physical, and biological environment; and demographic characteristics and lifestyles of the people. However, even within countries, diseases are not randomly distributed in the population. In every society some groups are more vulnerable to disease than others and are more likely to contract specific diseases.

ETIOLOGY OF DISEASE

Explaining the reasons for disease patterns requires identification of the **etiology** (that is, causes) of disease. To fully understand disease causation and distribution, it is important to consider both *fundamental causes* and *proximate risk factors*.

Link and Phelan (1995, 2000) stress the importance of understanding the *fundamental causes* of disease and illness. These causes include socioeconomic status and social inequality, race, gender, community and neighborhood, exposure to stressful life events of a social nature (e.g., the death of a loved one or crime victimization), and access to a supportive social network. They point out that recent epidemiological studies have focused more on proximate risk factors of diseases, such as diet and exercise, and have given insufficient attention to basic social conditions that impact on health. Social factors such as socioeconomic status and social support are viewed as "fundamental causes" of disease because they influence exposure to multiple risk factors (like drug-taking) which can affect the onset of many diseases, and they provide access to important resources (like money and social connectedness) that can bolster health or lead to therapeutic treatment. Moreover, social conditions provide a necessary context in which to consider individual risk-taking behaviors. They help us determine what factors put people at "risk of risks"—for example, affecting the likelihood of abusing drugs.

It is equally important to consider the *proximate risk factors* of disease and illness.

These factors typically are located within individual behaviors and include diet, exercise, use of tobacco and alcohol, control of stress, and other behaviors related to health protection. Epidemiologists have amassed volumes of research that link these factors to the onset of specific diseases and illnesses. Ultimately, the most complete understanding of disease causation and distribution comes when the interplay between underlying social conditions and proximate risk factors is considered.

An example of an underlying social condition that has a significant impact on disease and illness, both directly and indirectly through an influence on proximate risk factors, is education. The fact that more highly educated people are healthier has been well documented. Recently, Ross and Wu (1995) used national data sets to identify three pathways through which this influence occurs. First, well educated persons are more likely to be employed, to work full-time and at a fulfilling job, and to have a high income with little economic hardship—all of which impact positively on health. Second, the well educated have a greater sense of control over their lives and their health and have higher levels of social support—both associated with good health. Third, well educated persons are less likely to smoke and are more likely to get adequate exercise and to drink in moderation—all positively impacting health.

Recently, economist Robert Evans, epidemiologist Morris Barer, and political scientist Theodore Marmor focused on patterns of disease distribution in their book, *Why Are Some People Healthy and Others Not? The Determinants of Health of Populations* (1994). In writing the book, they synthesized the research done in several disciplines and included studies conducted in the United States and in other countries. While not discounting the influence of heredity in disease causation, they concluded that the primary determinants of the health of people and of the distribution of diseases within society are embedded in the social structure of society.

In one of the chapters in their book, Hertzman, Frank, and Evans (1994) identify six possible causal pathways through which one's position in the social structure could determine health status or the likelihood of disease:

1. *Reverse causality.* In this pathway, one's health status influences position in the social structure rather than the commonly assumed other way around. For example, the relationship between income and sickness might occur because the sick become poor rather than because the poor become sick. However, with the exception of chronic mental illness, the authors find little empirical support for this pathway.

2. *Differential susceptibility.* The opportunities that individuals have for occupational success and/or upward social mobility are influenced by physical traits (e.g., appearance or height). A tall person with an attractive appearance may gain some occupational advantages over a shorter person with a more disheveled appearance. These advantages may ultimately translate into circumstances (e.g., higher and more secure income) that lead to health benefits.

3. *Individual lifestyle.* This pathway describes differences in health habits and behaviors. But something more than completely unconstrained free choice is at work here because individual lifestyle does not explain differences in average lifestyle patterns between large groups. For example, why are highly educated people or those with high incomes consistently healthier than others?

4. *Physical environment.* Some persons are more likely than others to be exposed to the potentially harmful effects of physical, chemical, and biological agents. The presence of harmful substances in the workplace (e.g., hydrocarbons in coal), or in the home (e.g., lead pain chipping from the walls), or in the neighborhood (e.g., the proximity to a landfill) serve as a pathway to ill health.

5. *Social environment (and psychological Response).* Included in this pathway are the effects of living a stressful versus less stressful lifestyle and the influence of having or not having significant social support.

IN THE FIELD

DETERMINING DISEASE ETIOLOGY

Although identification of the causes of acute, infectious diseases may be a complicated matter, tracing the origin of most chronic, degenerative diseases is far more difficult. Among the most important reasons for this greater challenge are the following:

1. Most chronic, degenerative diseases, like cancer and coronary heart disease, have multiple causes. Rather than being traceable to the presence of a particular bacterium, factors related to diet, exercise, personality type, smoking and drinking behavior, stress, social support and other factors interrelate in countless configurations. Measuring the amount, duration, and effects of each factor on an individual is very difficult.

2. With many chronic, degenerative diseases, there is a long latency period between the influence and the consequence. The appearance of cancer often comes 20 to 30 or more years after exposure to the carcinogenic substance, making it difficult to determine cause-and-effect relationships. Moreover, not everyone who is exposed to a harmful lifestyle or a carcinogenic substance will contract degenerative disease (e.g., some lifetime smokers never get lung cancer).

3. It is very difficult to determine how much of a behavior or how much of a substance is necessary to trigger a disease. Some researchers point out that almost any substance taken in sufficiently large quantities can be health damaging. Many regulations of substances in society are based on the idea that there is a threshold of exposure below which there is no danger to health. Others disagree, saying that there are only lower levels of danger.

4. The validity of generalizations from animal testing to humans is an unresolved question. For example, the amount of a substance required to cause cancer in an animal may not realistically indicate the amount to which humans can safely be exposed. There are many toxicologists on both sides of this issue. Some years ago, when limits on human consumption of saccharin were contemplated based on laboratory tests on rats, one wag suggested that diet soft drinks should contain the following: "Warning: Extensive use of this product has been shown by scientists to be dangerous to your rat's health."

6. *Differential access to/response to health care services.* Differences in health status may result from systematic differences in access to health care services, in differential propensity to use services, and in differential benefit (possibly, in some cases, for genetic reasons) of services received. A recent study in California found that those with less education were least likely to make positive health changes in response to a five-year comprehensive program of community organization and health education (Winkleby, Flora, and Kraemer, 1994).

The process of sorting through all of these factors and determining disease etiology, especially for chronic degenerative diseases, is a challenging task, as the box, "Determining Disease Etiology," explains.

THE INTERRELATIONSHIP OF FUNDAMENTAL CAUSES AND PROXIMATE RISK FACTORS: THE CASE OF DEVELOPING COUNTRIES

In Chapter 3, we used the epidemiological transition to explain the general shift from acute, infectious diseases to chronic, degenerative diseases within societies as they modernize. Because the pace of this transition has accelerated in recent years, developing countries in the world today are confronted with a double burden. While they are continuing to have to deal with infectious, parasitic diseases (such as malaria and tuberculosis), they are already facing increased rates of the chronic, degenerative diseases (such as heart disease and cancer) that predominate in industrialized countries. For example, China and India, the world's two largest countries, have huge populations today with diabetes and high blood pressure, a sign that increased rates of heart disease are likely in the near future.

To assist in handling this critical situation in developing countries, a broad program for research and empowerment called the **health transition (HT)** has been developed (Caldwell, 1993). The program consists of three elements (Gallagher, Stewart, and Stratton, 2000):

1. *The importance of public and community health.* It is commonly accepted that the decline in the death rate in industrialized countries resulted more from public health measures than from advances in clinical medicine. Therefore, developing countries are being urged to invest in social policies that emphasize improvements in food and water supply, sanitation, access to primary health care, community development, and greater opportunities for women in education, employment, and public life. Countries are being discouraged from investing available funds in high-technology medicine with much more limited impact.
2. *The importance of equitable distribution of income and wealth.* Health progress occurs more rapidly in countries without huge disparities in wealth. Some countries that are relatively poor but do not have sharp divisions in wealth (e.g., China and Cuba) have made more headway in reducing death rates than some relatively wealthier countries with greater inequality (e.g., Iran).
3. *The importance of lifestyle and behavioral factors.* While proximate risk factors such as diet, tobacco, and sexual behavior are especially important in industrialized countries because of their link to chronic diseases, they

are especially important in developing countries because of their link to infectious diseases. Thus, emphasis is encouraged on such behaviors as drinking only safe water (which might necessitate considerable travel and inconvenience), limiting family size to a number that can be economically supported, and using a condom for nonmonogamous sex.

THE INFLUENCE OF GENETIC TRANSMISSION ON DISEASE AND ILLNESS

Given the importance of underlying social conditions and proximate risk factors in affecting disease and illness, what role is played by genetic transmission? Essentially, genes affect disease and illness in two primary ways:

1. *As the specific cause of approximately 4,000 "genetic diseases," including Down syndrome, cystic fibrosis, Tay-Sachs disease, Huntington's disease, and sickle-cell Anemia.* Some diseases are monogenic in that they can be traced to a single gene. For example, chromosome 21 is the site of genes for Down syndrome, Lou Gehrig's disease, and epilepsy. More diseases are polygenic in that they result from several genes acting together. Polygenic diseases have more complicated causal relationships about which much more needs to be known.

   While genetic diseases represent a small component of all diseases, they are especially apparent early in life. About one-fourth of all admissions to U.S. hospitals for persons under the age of 18 is for genetic diseases and conditions, and they are the second leading cause of death for children between the ages of 1 and 4.
2. *As a factor that increases the likelihood of occurrence of many other diseases, including heart disease, some types of cancer, Alzheimer's disease, and diabetes.* In these cases an individual's genetic makeup provides or denies an opportunity for environmental factors to trigger its occurrence. An even greater

number of diseases follow this multifactorial path in which the genes and the environment interact in causing a disease to occur.

Knowledge about genetic diseases has increased substantially in the last few years with the successful mapping of the approximately 40,000 genes within each human. The **Human Genome Project** began in 1990 with the goal of assigning each gene to its proper location on a chromosome. The work, which was conducted in the United States (about 60 percent) and in England (30 percent) and elsewhere was completed in 2000. This knowledge could eventually contribute to an elimination of genetic diseases.

Ultimately, efforts to eliminate genetic diseases will focus both on prevention and repair of defective genes. Already, some couples are turning to *preimplantation genetic diagnosis* to attempt to ensure that an offspring does not carry a defective gene. In this process parents who carry the gene for a particular genetic disease use in vitro fertilization (a process described in Chapter 16) for procreation. The resulting embryo can be genetically analyzed for disease and implanted only if determined to be disease-free. However, this is a very expensive procedure (the in vitro process often is around $10,000, and the analytical test is now about $2,000).

A more common approach may be to do the analytical test prenatally and then to repair any identified defective genes. Technology for gene repair is only now being perfected, but the process may well become commonplace in the foreseeable future. Additional discussion of ethical questions created by the use of advanced genetic knowledge is presented in Chapter 16.

In the remainder of this chapter, five significant but very different diseases and conditions in American society are examined. Cardiovascular diseases and cancer are the two leading causes of death in the United States; mortality from the former has decreased in recent years while mortality from the latter has levelled off. HIV/AIDS is a relatively recently identified disease which

has quickly become a worldwide epidemic, while Alzheimer's disease was first identified in the early 1900s as a disease of mental deterioration in mid and late adult life. Scientists continue to search for effective cures for both. Mental illness and severe mental disorders have long been studied and a considerable body of research has developed around their etiology.

CARDIOVASCULAR DISEASES

The Cardiovascular System

The body's cardiovascular system transports necessary nutrients, oxygen, and water to all of the body's tissues; carries substances like disease-fighting antibodies to wherever they are needed in the body; and removes carbon dioxide and other waste products. The pumping of the heart stimulates the flow of blood, which acts as the transportation system. For the heart to function properly (it beats about 100,000 times a day, pumping about 1,800 gallons of blood), it must receive an adequate supply of blood from the three main coronary arteries and their smaller branches. Heart disease occurs when this system is disrupted.

Cardiovascular Disease (CVD)

The inner surface (or inner layers) of any artery may become thickened, resulting in a narrowing and hardening of the artery (atherosclerosis) that decreases the amount of blood that can flow through it. If this occurs to one or more of the coronary arteries (usually caused by a buildup of plaques of cholesterol and other fatty substances or by a blood clot), the result is **coronary heart disease (CHD)**—often called ischemic heart disease. If the blood flow is severely restricted, the heart may not receive enough blood to meet its needs (this often happens during exercise). The person may feel a tightening sensation or squeezing feeling in the chest that may radiate into the left arm and elsewhere. This is the most common form of cardiovascular disease.

If a coronary artery becomes completely blocked because of a blood clot, the heart may not receive enough blood to fulfill its normal workload. In only a few hours, the heart undergoes irreversible damage. This is a heart attack—also called a **myocardial infarction**, which is the sudden death of part of the heart muscle. There are many other forms of heart disease that can occur with the heart valves, the veins, or the heart muscle itself.

Two other cardiovascular diseases are discussed in this chapter. High blood pressure—also called **hypertension**—is the name given to the condition when an abnormally large amount of force is exerted against the arterial walls by the flow of blood; it is a sign that the heart is pumping harder than it should to circulate the blood and that the arteries are under a strain. If untreated, the heart may begin working harder and harder and may eventually become enlarged and not be able to function properly. In addition, the arteries may not be able to deliver blood properly, thus endangering other body organs.

A **stroke** is a condition that occurs when part of the brain does not receive the amount of blood it requires to sustain normal activity. If a blood vessel bringing oxygen and other nutrients to the brain gets clogged or bursts, the brain's nerve cells will be deprived of oxygen, and within minutes, they die. This eliminates their ability to send messages to other parts of the body and may result in partial paralysis; speech, language, or memory loss; changes in behavior; and spatial and perceptual deficits.

THIS YEAR 250,000

WOMEN

will die of a

MAN'S DISEASE.

Most people associate heart disease with men. Truth is, it's the number one killer of American women, claiming more lives than all cancers combined. One reason for the toll is that women aren't aware of the danger, or how to reduce their risk through exercise and a heart-healthy diet. Help save yourself and others by taking charge of your health and spreading the word. Call 1-888-MYHEART for a free packet of information. Or visit www.women.amhrt.org to learn more.

American Heart Association®
Fighting Heart Disease and Stroke

This space provided as a public service. © 1997, American Heart Association

At times, public misperceptions of disease and illness discourage necessary policy and individual action. This American Heart Association poster is designed to convince policy makers and the public that heart disease is a significant problem among women as well as men. (Reproduced with permission. American Heart Association Advertisement © 2000. Copyright American Heart Association.)

Incidence and Mortality

In 2001, more than 64 million Americans had one or more forms of cardiovascular disease, including high blood pressure (50 million), coronary heart disease (13.2 million) and stroke (4.8 million). About one male in five and about one female in five has some form of cardiovascular disease, but because there are more women in the U.S. population, more women than men have heart disease.

CVD is the number one killer in the United States, claiming just under 40 percent of all deaths. Approximately 930,000 Americans—about one-sixth under the age of 65—die of heart and blood vessel diseases each year, almost as many as from cancer, accidents, pneumonia, influenza, and all other causes of death combined. If all major forms of CVD were eliminated, life expectancy would rise by about seven years. Death rates for CVD are much higher for black males than for white males and for black females than for white females, but heart disease is the leading cause of death for both women and men and for both blacks and whites (American Heart Association, 2003).

Etiology

The major proximate risk factors for CVD are cigarette smoking, high cholesterol levels in the blood, obesity and lack of exercise, the aggressive Type A personality, high blood pressure (both a disease and a risk factor for other diseases), and other factors including family history.

Cigarette Smoking. The World Health Organization has called tobacco the single biggest cause of premature adult death throughout the world—it kills about 3 million people annually. About one person in five living in the world's industrialized countries will die from a tobacco-related cause. Studies in the United States have determined that cigarette smoking is the biggest risk factor for sudden cardiac death and that smokers have two to four times greater risk than nonsmokers of having a heart attack.

Smokers are approximately 30 percent more likely than nonsmokers to experience fatal coronary heart disease.

Moreover, a recent review of nine epidemiologic studies confirms extensive danger in breathing in **environmental tobacco smoke (ETS)**—that is, other people's tobacco smoke. Never-smokers living with smokers had a 1 percent to 3 percent greater chance of developing heart disease than never-smokers living with nonsmokers. Nationally, this equates to 35,000 to 40,000 deaths from coronary heart disease annually as a result of breathing ETS.

High Cholesterol. Cholesterol is a type of fat (lipid) that can build up in the bloodstream. It is transported in the bloodstream via little packages called lipoproteins. Most blood cholesterol is carried into the circulatory system by low-density lipoproteins (LDL) where it may be deposited and accumulate on the arterial walls causing restriction of blood flow. Cholesterol is also carried on high-density lipoproteins (HDL), which actually help to remove the plaque from the arteries. The greater the ratio of LDL to HDL, the more likely is cholesterol plaque buildup.

Though the relative weight of factors that contribute to a high LDL/HDL ratio is yet to be understood, the main determinants are recognized to be genes (causing the liver to produce excessive levels of cholesterol) and diet. Diets rich in saturated fats and cholesterol (meats high in animal fat; organ meats—liver, kidney, and brains; and dairy products (milk, cheese, and egg yolks) contribute to higher levels of LDL.

The risk of heart disease rises as blood cholesterol levels increase. Combined with cigarette smoking or high blood pressure, the risk is even greater. Efforts to lower the LDL/HDL ratio center mostly on drugs designed to retard the liver's production of cholesterol; reductions of high cholesterol foods; increases of cholesterol-balancing foods (unsaturated fats, dietary fiber, and vegetable protein); weight reduction; and exercise (which helps build the beneficial HDL level).

High Blood Pressure.   Approximately one-third of American adults have high blood pressure (defined as a pressure of 140/90 mmHg or higher or taking antihypertensive drugs), which is the major cause of strokes and deaths from strokes and one of the major causes of heart attacks and heart attack deaths. Several factors are associated with high blood pressure. Generally, the older people get, the more likely they are to develop high blood pressure. People whose parents have high blood pressure are more likely to develop it, and blacks are more likely than whites to suffer from the disease (see Chapter 3). When high blood pressure exists with obesity, smoking, high blood cholesterol levels, or diabetes, the risk of stroke or heart attack increases substantially.

Type A Behavior Pattern.   In the 1950s, two cardiologists, Meyer Friedman and Ray Rosenman, observed that many of their patients had similar personality characteristics: impatience, competitiveness, aggressiveness, exaggerated sense of time urgency, tension, and a strong achievement orientation. They called this package of traits the **Type A Behavior Pattern**. Of course, they could not tell whether these characteristics led to heart troubles or were a consequence of them.

Thus, they designed a prospective study and tested the personalities of thousands of men without any history of coronary heart disease. They followed these men for more than two decades, recording incidence of CHD. They discovered that the men who had exhibited Type A behaviors were much more likely to develop heart disease than were those with opposite personality traits—these men were more able to relax, were less time-oriented, and were less concerned with accomplishment. They were said to exhibit the Type B Behavior Pattern. Subsequent research, however, has tended to identify a single personality trait of the Type A Pattern—feelings of hostility/anger—as most strongly predictive of heart disease.

How does the Type A Behavior Pattern lead to CHD? Suls and Sanders (1989) suggest three possible behavioral routes:

Adequate exercise is one of the most important means of preventing heart disease, but most Americans get far too little.

1. The Type A Pattern may be a marker of some underlying inborn structural weakness that makes CHD more likely (e.g., arterial walls may be physiologically more susceptible to lesions and this preexisting abnormality is really the key);

2. Type As have a kind of **hyperresponsivity**— an exaggerated psychophysiological reactivity to certain situations (e.g., more reactive sympathetic nervous systems that cause increased production of hormones, leading to physiological changes related to CHD). This is the best supported explanation thus far;

3. Type As are exposed to or expose themselves to inherently more risky circumstances that are dangerous to cardiovascular health (e.g., they may delay seeing a physician after chest pains).

An offshoot of this third route is supported by recent studies that suggest that at least part of the Type A effect on CHD occurs indirectly by increasing participation in other risk factors. Garrity and colleagues (1990) conducted a longitudinal study of 375 white and black males and females from 1978–1979 through 1985–1988 to determine association between Type A behavior and coronary risk factors. During the eight-year study period, those with the Type A pattern experienced a steeper increase in blood pressure and were more likely to increase cigarette consumption. Therefore, Type As may experience more CHD due to their greater involvement in other risk factors.

Other Factors.   Other factors that contribute to the risk of heart disease include family history, diabetes, physical inactivity and lack of exercise, and stress. Having a family history of heart disease—especially in one's parents or siblings and at an early age—elevates personal risk for the disease. Diabetes significantly increases the risk of developing CHD, partly because of the effects the disease has on cholesterol and triglyceride (blood sugars) levels. More than 80 percent of people with diabetes die of some form of heart or blood vessel disease. Sedentary life styles contribute to obesity and increased blood cholesterol levels, thus increasing one's chance for heart disease. Unmediated stress is also an important contributing factor (and is examined in Chapter 5). Recently, compelling research has discovered a link between poor dental health, such as chronic gum disease, and heart disease.

Trends

The death rate from cardiovascular diseases has declined steadily and dramatically over the past several decades—by approximately 50 percent in the last 50 years (and by about nine percent between 1991 and 2001). The percent of deaths due to heart disease has declined and heart failure typically now occurs much later in life (usually past the age of 70). This decline is primarily the consequence of disease-prevention efforts aimed at changing individual behaviors.

Cigarette smoking is down significantly, changes in diet have brought cholesterol levels down, and blood pressure levels are lower than a decade ago. On the other hand, research is less clear about the contributions of technological advances (e.g., new antiarrhythmic drugs, coronary artery bypass surgery, the Coronary Care Unit) to the reduced mortality level. While some studies have concluded that medical interventions have played a significant role in the lowered mortality levels, others have concluded that there have been only limited effects.

CANCER

Normally the body's cells reproduce themselves in an orderly manner. As the body grows, worn-out tissues are replaced and injuries are repaired. Occasionally, however, some abnormal cells develop and may begin to spread throughout the body. These abnormal or cancer cells are usually defeated and eliminated by the body's immune system—a specialized group of cells that guard against the invasion of foreign cells in the body. The term **cancer** refers to a group of diseases that are characterized by an uncontrolled growth (often into masses of tissue called tumors) and spread of abnormal cells. "Benign" tumors are noncancerous (these do not spread and are not typically a threat to life); "malignant" tumors are cancerous. When the cancer cells remain at their original site, the disease is said to be localized; when they spread and invade other organs or tissue, the disease is said to have metastasized, or **metastasis** has occurred.

Cancer often creates considerable pain. This occurs as various tubes within the body (e.g., esophageal, intestinal, urinary bladder) become obstructed or as the expanding tumor destroys additional healthy tissue. Infections often occur. A cancerous tumor unsuccessfully removed or destroyed eventually causes death.

Incidence and Mortality

Current estimates are that 9.6 million Americans alive now have been diagnosed with cancer, that

IN THE FIELD

THE HISTORICAL UNDERREPRESENTATION OF WOMEN AND RACIAL AND ETHNIC MINORITIES IN BIOMEDICAL RESEARCH

Because the physiology and social position of women and men and blacks and whites differ in ways that may relate to disease and illness; because gender and racial/ethnic groups show different propensities to different diseases; and because therapeutic and pharmacological agents affect people differently biomedical research must be conducted on samples reflecting population differences (within or among studies). Until the 1990s, this was often not the case. Dresser summarized the issue in 1992.

> The failure to include women in research populations is ubiquitous. An NIH-sponsored study showing that heart attacks were reduced when subjects took one aspirin every other day was conducted on men, and the relationship between low cholesterol diets and cardiovascular disease has been almost exclusively studied in men. Yet coronary heart disease is the leading cause of death in women. Similarly, the first twenty years of a major federal study on health and aging included only men. Yet two-thirds of the elderly population are women. The recent announcement that aspirin can help prevent migraine headaches is based on data from males only, even though women suffer from migraines up to three times as often as men.
>
> The list goes on: studies on AIDS treatment frequently omit women, the fastest growing infected population. An investigation of the possible relationship between caffeine and heart disease involved 45,589 male research subjects . . . Moreover, the customary research subject not only is male, but is a white male. African Americans, Latinos, and other racial and ethnic groups have typically been excluded. . . . (Dresser, 1992:24)

What is the outcome of this bias? Of the ten prescription drugs that were withdrawn from the market between 1997 and 2000, eight had a more adverse reaction on women than men. Two of the drugs caused a rare but dangerous form of heart arrhythmia in some women who took them. These unanticipated reactions occurred because the drugs had not been adequately tested on women.

In addition, several studies identified the absence or inadequate representation of racial and ethnic minority group members in biomedical research. Despite recognized differences in drug response and metabolism among members of various racial/ethnic groups, they have been routinely underrepresented in clinical drug trials (Thomas et al., 1994; Beech and Goodman 2004).

How has this exclusionary policy been justified? Some cited the benefits of studies with homogenous samples: the more alike the samples, the more that variation can be attributed to the intervention under study. Some argued that women would complicate studies by their hormonal changes during the menstrual cycle; that research could be jeopardized by women who become pregnant during the research; and that women are more difficult to obtain as volunteers.

None of these reasons is adequate. Critics pointed out that comparable studies could be conducted on groups other than white males or statistical controls could be used within heterogenous samples. Hormonal changes during the menstrual cycle are part of reality; rather than being viewed as somehow distorting results, efforts needed to be made to understand the influence of personality type on heart disease and the influence of aspirin on migraine headaches and so forth in women given their particular physiology. It was argued that, logically, it would make just as much sense to say that the absence of a menstrual cycle ought to disqualify males for fear of skewed results (Dresser, 1992; Merton, 1993).

Criticism of previous protocols has had some effect. A major research initiative—the Women's Health Initiative—was started in 1991 to study heart disease and stroke, cancer, and osteoporosis in women of all races and all socioeconomic strata. Medical researchers who receive federal grants are now prohibited from studying only men. Spending for women's health research is at an all-time high. The successful effort to bring this issue to public attention and to enlist Congress in making change was directed by a number of important groups including many sociologists (Auerbach and Figert, 1995). However, some recent research has found that heart failure clinical trials still over-represent younger, white, males in their study populations, suggesting that more attention needs to be paid to this area (Heiat, Gross, and Krumholz, 2002).

an additional 1.4 million persons will be diagnosed with cancer each year, and that about one male in two and one female in three will be diagnosed with cancer at some point in his or her lifetime. These figures do not include the estimated 1 million cases of skin cancer (which are discussed later in this chapter) diagnosed annually (American Cancer Society, 2004).

Cancer is the second leading cause of death in the United States, claiming more than 560,000 lives each year. One death in four is due to cancer. The national death rate from cancer has increased steadily during the last 50 years. The age-adjusted rate has gone from 143 per 100,000 in 1930 to 152 in 1940, to 158 in 1950, and has been about 170–175 since 1984. The largest portion of this increase is due to lung cancer, with nearly 175,000 new cases identified each year with almost 160,000 annual deaths. In fact, if lung cancer deaths were excluded, the mortality rate from cancer would have actually declined between 1950 and 2000.

Figure 4–1 portrays the most common sites of cancer, by incidence and by mortality, for males and females. For males, the prostate, the lungs, and the colon/rectum are the most common cancer sites, but lung cancer is by far the most lethal cancer, accounting for one-third of all male cancer deaths. The breast, the lungs, and the colon/rectum are the most common cancer sites for females, and lung cancer is the most common fatal site, accounting for one-fourth of female cancer deaths.

Cancer incidence and mortality rates at almost all body sites are higher for blacks than for whites—cancer incidence is 25 percent higher and cancer mortality is 40 percent higher. The five-year survival rate for cancer is more than ten percentage points higher in whites. Studies of racial disparities in cancer all point to socioeco-

nomic explanations. African Americans are more likely to be in poverty, have less education, and are less likely to have health insurance. One result of the lack of insurance is the later stage at which cancer is detected in blacks. Most Hispanic and Asian groups have somewhat lower rates than whites of cancer incidence and mortality. Because lifestyle relates so closely to cancer risk, many of these groups are being studied to determine reasons for their lower susceptibility.

Table 4–1 shows the five-year survival rates for whites and blacks for selected cancer sites. Note the considerable improvement overall from 1974–76 to 1992–99.

Etiology

The World Health Organization estimates that up to 90 percent of all cancers are environmentally induced or related. Environmental cancer-producing substances or **carcinogens** are found in the food and drugs we ingest, the water we drink, the air we breathe, the occupations we pursue, and the substances with which we come into contact.

Cigarette Smoking. The strong relationship between cigarette smoking and heart disease is duplicated for cancer. Smoking is associated with high rates of lung cancer as well as cancer of the mouth, pharynx, larynx, esophagus, pancreas, uterine cervix, kidney, and bladder. The American Cancer Society estimates that cigarette smoking is responsible for almost one-third of all cancer deaths and for almost 90 percent of all lung cancer deaths. Lung cancer mortality rates are more than 22 times higher for current male smokers and more than 12 times higher for current females smokers compared to lifetime never-smokers. Alone, smoking greatly

Figure 4–1 Most Common Sites of New Cancer Cases and Deaths, 2004

Estimated New Cases*		Estimated Deaths	
Male	Female	Male	Female
Prostate 230,110 (33%)	Breast 215,990 (32%)	Lung & bronchus 91,930 (32%)	Lung & bronchus 68,510 (25%)
Lung & bronchus 93,110 (13%)	Lung & bronchus 80,660 (12%)	Prostate 29,500 (10%)	Breast 40,110 (15%)
Colon & rectum 73,620 (11%)	Colon & rectum 73,320 (11%)	Colon & rectum 28,320 (10%)	Colon & rectum 28,410 (10%)
Urinary bladder 44,640 (6%)	Uterine corpus 40,320 (6%)	Pancreas 15,440 (5%)	Ovary 16,090 (6%)
Melanoma of the skin 29,900 (4%)	Ovary 25,580 (4%)	Leukemia 12,990 (5%)	Pancreas 15,830 (6%)
Non-Hodgkin lymphoma 28,850 (4%)	Non-Hodgkin lymphoma 25,520 (4%)	Non-Hodgkin lymphoma 10,390 (4%)	Leukemia 10,310 (4%)
Kidney 22,080 (3%)	Melanoma of the skin 25,200 (4%)	Esophagus 10,250 (4%)	Non-Hodgkin lymphoma 9,020 (3%)
Leukemia 19,020 (3%)	Thyroid 17,640 (3%)	Liver 9,450 (3%)	Uterine corpus 7,090 (3%)
Oral cavity 18,550 (3%)	Pancreas 16,120 (2%)	Urinary bladder 8,780 (3%)	Multiple myeloma 5,640 (2%)
Pancreas 15,740 (2%)	Urinary bladder 15,600 (2%)	Kidney 7,870 (3%)	Brain 5,490 (2%)
All sites 699,560 (100%)	All sites 668,470 (100%)	All sites 290,890 (100%)	All sites 272,810 (100%)

*Excludes basal and squamous cell skin cancers and in situ carcinoma except urinary bladder.
Note: Percentages may not total 100% due to rounding.

©2004, American Cancer Society, Inc., Surveillance Research

Source: American Cancer Society. *Cancer Facts and Figures—2004.* Reprinted with permission. www.cancer.org.

increases risk, but with other carcinogens (e.g., exposure to asbestos), the risk is multiplied even more.

Environmental tobacco smoke also has been identified as a cause of cancer in nonsmokers with an estimated 3,000 lung cancer deaths per year and 35,000 to 40,000 heart disease deaths per year attributable to ETS. Secondary smoke may have especially serious effects on fetuses and young children. A mother who smokes is more likely than a nonsmoker to have a spontaneous abortion and much more likely to produce a low-birth-weight infant (with a greater chance of dying in the first year of life). Infants born to women who smoked during pregnancy are also more likely to die from sudden infant death syndrome. In addition, children of parents who smoke have a higher incidence of impaired lung function, bronchitis, pneumonia, and middle ear infections than children of nonsmokers (American Cancer Society, 2004).

Diet. Research has demonstrated a clear link between diet and the incidence of cancer. Experts have concluded that diet may be related to as many as 35 percent of all cancer deaths.

TABLE 4–1   Five Year Survival Rates for Selected Cancer Sites

Site	All Races (%)		Whites (%)	Blacks (%)
	1974–76	1992–99	1992–99	1992–99
All sites	50	63	64	53
Prostate	67	98	98	93
Melanoma	80	90	90	64
Female breast	75	87	88	74
Cervix uterus	69	71	73	61
Kidney	52	63	63	61
Colon	51	62	63	53
Rectum	49	62	62	53
Oral	54	57	60	36
Ovary	37	53	52	52
Lung	12	15	15	12
Pancreas	3	4	4	4

Source: American Cancer Society. *Cancer Facts and Figures—2004*. Reprinted with permission. www.cancer.org.

This evidence is based partly on studies that reveal international variations in cancer mortality. For example, higher rates of cancers of the colon, rectum, breast and prostate are found in Western countries in which diets are relatively high in meat and fat but low in fruits, vegetables, and whole grains. On the other hand, stomach cancer rates are higher in countries in which diets are relatively high in starch, contain small amounts of meats and fats, and frequently use pickled, salted, smoked, or other preserved foods.

Evidence of a link between diet and cancer also comes from (1) studies of migrants who experience cancer rates at levels between those of their countries of origin and those of their adopted countries, (2) studies comparing the diets of patients with newly diagnosed cases of cancer relative to individuals in control groups (a retrospective approach), and (3) longitudinal studies of dietary habits and the likelihood of developing cancer (a prospective approach) that confirm that diets high in fruits and green and yellow vegetables offer some protection against cancer and diets high in fats increase cancer risks.

Obese people are at increased risk for cancer of the colon, breast, and uterus; and people who eat diets high in fat are more likely to develop breast, colon, and prostate cancer. On the other hand, high fiber foods lower the risk of colon cancer, and diets rich in vitamins A and C reduce risk for cancers of the larynx, esophagus, stomach, and lung.

Sunlight. Almost all of the 1 million cases of nonmelanoma skin cancer diagnosed each year in the United States are considered to be sun-related. If detected early, these cancers are fairly routine to remove. Much more dangerous is malignant **melanoma** skin cancer, which is not so much related to amount of sun exposure over a lifetime but rather to one or a couple of intense episodes of sunburn (often early in life).

The incidence of health problems from an excessive amount of the sun's harmful ultraviolet rays may well increase significantly in the next decade. As humankind continues to pour ozone-depleting chemicals into the atmosphere, the earth's protective barrier against ultraviolet rays will continue to be destroyed. The United Nations Environmental Program predicts significant increases in the incidence of both cataracts and skin cancer in the coming years.

Alcohol. Excessive alcohol consumption is the primary cause of cirrhosis of the liver, a very grave disease resulting in serious malfunction. In turn, people with longstanding liver cirrhosis are at high risk for developing liver cancer, a type of cancer with generally poor prognosis. Cancer of the mouth, larynx, throat, and esophagus all have been linked to excessive drinking of alcoholic beverages, especially in combination with the use of tobacco products.

Radiation.   The link between ionizing radiation and cancer has long been recognized. The major source of radiation in the United States is the natural cosmic background, which accounts for about half of the typical individual's total environmental exposure to ionizing radiation. Other major sources of radiation are diagnostic medical procedures, occupations in which there is exposure to substantial amounts of radiation or radioactive materials, and exposure to radon within the home.

Occupational Hazards.   Individuals who work in industries that involve hazardous substances have increased risks of cancer. For example, exposure to the hydrocarbons found in petroleum and coal is associated with increased risk of cancer of the lung, skin, and bladder; exposure to benzine can induce leukemia; mustard gas exposure is related to a higher incidence of lung cancer; and exposure to asbestos is clearly associated with increased risk for several types of cancer (especially in conjunction with cigarette smoking).

Environmental Pollution.   Determining direct cause-effect links between environmental pollution and cancer risk is problematic because of the large number and diversity of industrial chemicals being released into the environment today. In addition, the fact that most cancers have multiple causes presents researchers with the challenge of isolating specific effects of individual chemicals. Complicating the issue even more is the difficulty in assessing the amount of past exposure an individual has had to a particular pollutant that may have taken decades to adversely affect the individual. Finally, the number of people exposed to a particular carcinogen is usually quite small. Thus, a negative effect may either go undetected or be difficult to prove.

Despite these difficulties, it is widely recognized that human biological defenses are having great difficulty protecting against pollutants and that they are a cause of cancer today. These include petroleum products, synthetic organic chemicals, and insecticides, as well as sometimes seemingly uncontrolled toxic waste dumps. Phil Brown (1987) coined the term **popular epidemiology** to describe the processes by which laypersons take the lead in gathering statistics and other information to understand the epidemiology of particular diseases. This type of action is now occurring throughout the country as communities are fighting corporate pollution and improperly handled toxic waste dumps that have been linked to higher rates of cancer in nearby residents.

Heredity.   Though most cancers are not inherited, heredity does play a role in the etiology of some cancers. In the early 1990s, researchers identified genes that increased susceptibility to breast and ovarian cancers. These researchers now estimate that between 5 and 10 percent of these two cancers is linked to inheritance of a gene that confers high risk. In the next decade, research should be better able to identify the contribution of heredity to cancer.

Trends

Data reported in the late 1990s showed that the number of cancer cases nationwide dropped between 1990 and 2001. This was the first reported drop in cancer rates since a brief downturn in the 1930s. The primary reason for the decrease is reduced lung cancer in men as cigarette smoking has declined. However, lung cancer due to cigarette smoking continued to increase for women through the 1990s and has only recently leveled off (Patel, Bach, and Kris, 2004).

A second key trend is the changing site at which cancer occurs. Perhaps the most important points of Figure 4–2 are (1) the sharp

Figure 4–2 Cancer Death Rates by Site, Males and Females, 1930–2000

Age-Adjusted Cancer Death Rates,* Males by Site, US, 1930–2000

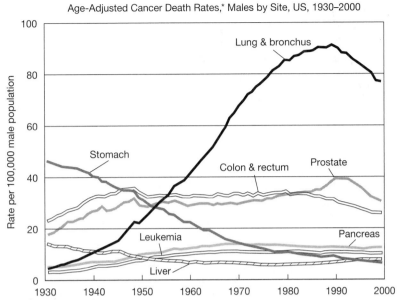

*Per 100,000, age-adjusted to the 2000 US standard population.
Note: Due to changes in ICD coding, numerator information has changed over time. Rates for cancers of the liver, lung & bronchus, and colon & rectum are affected by these coding changes.

Source: US Mortality Public Use Data Tapes 1960-2000, US Mortality Volumes 1930-1959.
National Center for Health Statistics, Centers for Disease Control and Prevention, 2003.   American Cancer Society, Surveillance Research, 2004

Age-Adjusted Cancer Death Rates,* Females by Site, US, 1930–2000

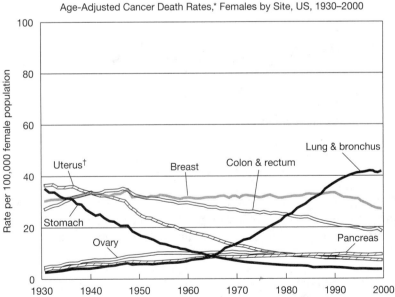

*Per 100,000, age-adjusted to the 2000 US standard population. †Uterus cancer death rates are for uterine cervix and uterine corpus combined.
Note: Due to changes in ICD coding, numerator information has changed over time. Rates for cancers of the liver, lung & bronchus, colon & rectum, and ovary are affected by these coding changes.

Source: US Mortality Public Use Data Tapes 1960-2000, US Mortality Volumes 1930-1959.
National Center for Health Statistics, Centers for Disease Control and Prevention, 2003.   American Cancer Society, Surveillance Research, 2004

Source: American Cancer Society. *Cancer Facts and Figures—2004*. Reprinted with permission. www.cancer.org.

increase in the death rate from lung cancer for both males and females between 1930 and 2000, and (2) the declining cancer death rates at several sites for both males and females.

A third trend is the increasing rate of survival for persons diagnosed with cancer. In the early part of this century, few persons diagnosed with cancer had any likelihood of long-term survival. By the 1930s, about 20 percent of cancer patients survived at least five years. This percentage increased to about 25 percent in the 1940s, to 50 percent in the 1970s, and to about 60 percent in the 1990s, and is now approaching 65 percent. If persons who die from other causes are taken into consideration, more than half of those diagnosed with cancer today will survive at least five years.

Improved survival rates are due both to earlier detection of cancer and to improved treatment effectiveness. The probability of early detection and survival varies considerably according to the cancer's anatomic location. However, when cancer is still localized when detected, the survival rate for most types of cancer jumps to over 80 percent (American Cancer Society, 2004).

HIV/AIDS

Acquired Immunodeficiency Syndrome (AIDS) is an infectious disease caused by the **human immunodeficiency virus (HIV)**. HIV disables the immune system and enables normally controllable infections to overcome the body and ultimately kill the person.

Persons who have contracted the HIV virus typically remain in a latent (asymptomatic) stage for up to ten years and sometimes much longer. During this time, the person may show no symptoms but is capable of transmitting the virus to others. In fact, studies indicate that the virus may be 100 to 1,000 times more contagious during the first two months after infection. Because tests to identify the presence of antibodies in the body to HIV—the means by which exposure to the virus is determined—are

not reliable for up to two months following exposure, these months represent a critical time for transmission.

The transition to AIDS itself occurs when significant suppression of the body's immune system begins to lead to other medical conditions or diseases. Common among these are chronic, unexplained weight loss, chronic fevers, night sweats, constant diarrhea, swollen glands, and thrush (a thick, white coating on the tongue). As AIDS progresses, the patient typically experiences debilitating bouts of pneumonia, chronic herpes infections, seizures, and dementia, and ultimately death.

Prevalence, Incidence and Mortality

A Global Pandemic.   In the late 1970s, HIV spread silently around the world, unrecognized and unnoticed. Though the first case was officially recognized in the United States in 1981, the vast scope of the infection was not realized until the mid-1980s. It is now considered to be a worldwide pandemic or plague. Although an accurate prevalence rate is difficult to determine, it is estimated that in 2003 approximately 40 million persons in the world were infected with HIV with 5 million more being infected each year. More than 20 million persons have died from AIDS-related diseases (globally, AIDS is the fourth most common cause of death). Figure 4–3 portrays the global AIDS situation.

HIV/AIDS in the United States.   Because AIDS has such a long latency period, and because most Americans have never been tested for exposure to the HIV virus, it is very difficult to calculate the number of persons who are HIV-positive. Epidemiologists use two estimation methods. The first method involves *back calculation,* taking into consideration the information available on incubation times and the change in trends of AIDS incidence (all states are required to report AIDS cases to the CDC) to estimate the number of persons already exposed to the virus. The second method uses *seroprevalence* data (confirming the presence of antibodies to the

Figure 4–3 A Geographical Distribution of HIV/AIDS Cases, 2003

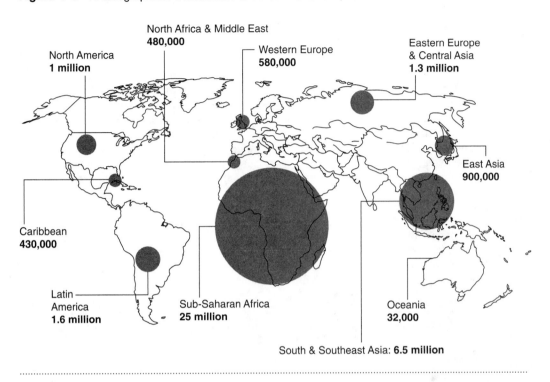

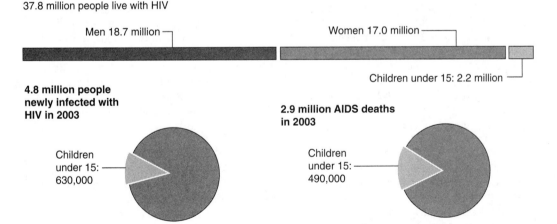

Source: United Nations Program on HIV/AIDS. 2003 *Newly Infected AIDS Cases Highest Yet.* New York: United Nations.

virus) from CDC surveys of specific groups such as blood donors, civilian applicants for military service, childbearing women, ambulatory patients, and federal prisoners. By using both methods, the CDC estimates that approxi- mately 900,000–1,000,000 Americans are currently infected with HIV (with as many as 300,000 not knowing it). By the end of 2000, nearly 500,000 persons in the United States had died from AIDS and more than 225,000 persons

IN COMPARATIVE FOCUS

AIDS: THE KILLING FIELDS IN AFRICA

The devastating effects of HIV/AIDS are taking the greatest toll on the world's less developed countries. While HIV rates have stabilized in most developed countries, they continue to escalate in some developing countries. Today, 95 percent of persons infected with the HIV virus live in a developing country.

Africa is experiencing the most severe problem. In 16 countries in the world—all in sub-Saharan Africa—more than 10 percent of persons ages 15 to 49 are infected with HIV. In South Africa and Zimbabwe, where more than 20 percent of the population is infected, it is estimated that half of today's 15-year-olds will die from AIDS. In Botswana, where one in three adults is already infected, two-thirds of 15-year-olds will die of AIDS.

In addition to the human toll, AIDS is wreaking havoc on the entire social fabric. Because the primary mode of transmission in these countries is through unprotected heterosexual sex (about 80 percent of transmittals), most of the infected people acquire HIV by their twenties and thirties. This has led to a significant shortfall of workers and an increase in the number of people unable to financially support themselves. Life expectancy is dropping sharply. Millions of children are being left without parents (more than 13 million children worldwide have lost one or both parents to AIDS). In some countries there are more persons in their 60s and 70s than in their 30s and 40s, meaning that there is inadequate support for the elders. Some countries anticipate a 15 to 20 percent decrease in their national wealth just in the next decade.

Why has HIV/AIDS spread so rapidly in sub-Saharan Africa? Several circumstances have had an effect. Many African men in rural villages form a migrant labor pool that migrates to large cities or mining areas or large commercial farming areas. Their wives typically remain at home to take care of the home and children. These long absences from home make common the use of prostitutes (most of whom are infected) or multiple sexual partners—thus increasing the opportunity for the virus to be spread. The desire to have a large family leads many men to be reluctant to use a condom when back home, which means that wives then become vulnerable to infection.

In addition, health education and promotion programs have frequently been unsuccessful. There are many rural areas where knowledge of HIV/AIDS is still lacking and where there is inadequate or incorrect information about the manner by which the virus is transmitted.

Finally, there is simply not enough money to provide necessary care. The United States currently spends almost $900 million fighting about 40,000 new AIDS cases a year. All of Africa spends about $150 million fighting 4 million new cases a year. This means there is insufficient medicine in most of the countries and stark inability to pay for AIDS treatment. In 2003 and 2004, new efforts were initiated in the United States and around the world to commit more money to battling HIV/AIDS in the developing world. The United States pledged increased contributions (up to $3 billion in 2004); the World Health Organization and the United Nations started a new program to bring antiretroviral drugs to people; the United Nations, the World Bank, the Global Fund to Fight AIDS, Tuberculosis, and Malaria, and former President Clinton created a joint plan to buy and distribute inexpensive, generic AIDS drugs in poor countries; and actor Richard Gere, with MTV and VH1 and two of India's largest entertainment networks, began creating AIDS awareness programs. Still, estimates were that more money and more programs would be needed to successfully combat the pandemic.

IN THE FIELD

SHOULD WE GIVE CLEAN NEEDLES TO DRUG USERS?

In 1998, the Clinton administration refused to fund programs that allow drug users to trade dirty needles for clean ones even though they acknowledged evidence that such exchanges reduce the spread of HIV and do not encourage drug abuse. The surgeon general had supported needle-exchange programs based on research that showed that they do not increase drug abuse and that they are effective in getting drug abusers into treatment. The administration stated that such programs are better designed at the local level than if imposed by the federal government. But, critics charged that the statement was designed to dodge a threatened block of funds by congressional Republicans had the administration proceeded. The Presidential Advisory Council on HIV/AIDS rebuked the president for not funding the programs.

Many Republicans joined the administration's drug czar, Barry McCaffrey, in saying that needle exchange programs send the wrong message to children. McCaffrey asked rhetorically if people would want one of these programs in their neighborhood if they were parents fighting to bring their children up right and to protect them from drugs.

What ought to be the decisive factor in policy debates of this type?

were living with the disease. New HIV infections peaked at about 150,000 a year in the mid-1980s and then dropped to about 40,000 per year throughout the 1990s. In the early 2000s, the number of new cases began to increase once again, and there was concern that commitment to safer sexual behaviors was diminishing.

The two population groups in the United States most likely to contract AIDS are gay/bisexual men and injectable drug users. Of the new cases of AIDS reported in 1999, just over half acquired the disease through male same-sex intercourse and 22 percent from sharing needles. The proportion of cases attributed to heterosexual contact was 10 to 15 percent.

Blacks and Hispanics constitute a disproportionate number of persons with HIV/AIDS, although there is no evidence that race per se is a biological risk factor for vulnerability to the disease. Blacks account for more than half of the new HIV cases diagnosed each year. The death rate from AIDS is about 3 times higher for black males than for white males and more than 20 times higher for black females than for white females. Rates for Hispanic males and females were about 2 times and about 3.5 times

the rates for their white counterparts. High rates of unemployment and despair in inner-city areas and associated drug use, and less accurate knowledge about AIDS help to account for the higher rates among blacks and Hispanics.

Etiology

HIV is transmitted in the same basic way throughout the world: through the exchange of bodily fluids. This exchange may occur through coital, oral, or anal sex (the latter being a common means of transmission for gay men because the tissue of the rectal wall is very thin and easily penetrated by the virus); through the passing of HIV-contaminated blood (e.g., via a blood transfusion, a sharing of needles by intravenous drug users, or reuse of contaminated needles for medical injections); and from an infected mother to a child (either prenatally or through breastfeeding).

Trends

By the early 2000s, AIDS was spreading more quickly among women and children. Research

This is the way many people deal with HIV.

A lot of people don't think they have to worry about HIV. But the truth is, anyone can get HIV infection if they are sharing drug needles and syringes, or having sex with an infected person. Call your State or local AIDS hotline. Or call the National AIDS Hotline at 1-800-342-AIDS. Call 1-800-243-7889 (TTY) for deaf access.

HIV is the virus that causes AIDS.   AMERICA RESPONDS TO AIDS

Many AIDS educational campaigns have designed creative messages and visuals to catch the attention of young persons.

has determined that HIV is more easily transmitted from men to women than the reverse, in part because the vagina is a more receptive contact surface than a man's penis. AIDS among children can be considered as two separate subepidemics because of differing modes of transmission: (1) pediatric AIDS affects children from birth to 13 years of age, most of whom are infected through perinatal transmission of the virus from their mothers during pregnancy or birth (although transmission does not occur in most cases); and (2) teenage youth through age 19 are generally infected through the same transmission modes as adults. Beginning in the late 1990s, the number of perinatally acquired AIDS cases decreased significantly—a result largely of prevention interventions.

Predictions for the future of the HIV/AIDS epidemic in the United States are difficult both because it is too early to determine how effective the current educational strategy to change personal behavior will be on a long-term basis (there is some evidence of a reversal in the precautions used during sex by those at high-risk), and because of the continuing development of new medical discoveries. While a vaccine to prevent AIDS does not seem imminent, significant progress in understanding the disease has occurred in recent years. Scientists are now studying people—perhaps as many as 5 percent of those with HIV—who show little or no signs of damage despite having had the virus for 12 or more years. Their source of resistance may point to clues in battling the disease. In addition the discovery of the potential of new drugs and increased understanding of the benefits of drug combinations have extended the lives of those already having AIDS. There is hope that techniques will be found to turn AIDS from a fatal to a controllable, chronic disease.

ALZHEIMER'S DISEASE

Alzheimer's disease (AD) is a chronic, degenerative, dementing illness of the central nervous system. It is the most common cause of dementia—a condition that involves personality change, emotional instability, disorientation, memory loss, loss of verbal abilities, and an inability to care for oneself. Other specific symptoms of AD include intellectual impairment, depression, agitation, and delusions.

To diagnose AD, an extensive evaluation is necessary which includes a complete medical history, interviews with the patient and family members, mental status examination, physical and neurological examination, and formal neuropsychological testing. Work is under way to diagnose AD through a simple observation of the dilation of the pupils in the eyes after being given ordinary eye drops.

Prevalence, Incidence, and Mortality

It is difficult to determine the prevalence of AD for a number of reasons. Because the onset of the disease is often extremely slow and the symptoms may go unnoticed or misinterpreted and because there is no cure for the disease, many persons with Alzheimer's may not have sought medical attention. That notwithstanding, it is commonly estimated that about 4.5 million persons in the United States have AD (one in five of persons age 75 to 84, and nearly half of those age 85 and older) and that about 100,000 die from it each year.

Projections indicate that, without an effective cure or preventive mechanism, the prevalence of AD will grow substantially in the next 50 years as the number of persons in the oldest age groups increases. By the year 2050, it is estimated that more than 14 million persons will have AD. The progression of AD varies from person to person. On average, a person afflicted with AD lives for more than 8 years before dying, though some persons have lived up to 25 years. Alzheimer's is now the eighth leading cause of death for persons age 65 and older.

Etiology

In 1998, scientists confirmed that Alzheimer's is caused by a protein (beta amyloid) that forms plaque on brain cells. The protein typically is a harmless substance found throughout the body. But, for unknown reasons, it can change and form toxic strands that build up on brain cells. Part of the explanation for this is in the genes. Researchers have now identified three genes that, when mutated, cause our cells to overproduce part of the amyloid plaque. These mutations are inheritable, and virtually everyone who inherits one develops Alzheimer's by age 60. But later-onset Alzheimer's also has a large genetic component with individuals with one affected parent three times more likely to get AD, and those with two affected parents being five times

more likely. However, it appears that the genes are not causative of AD; they simply make one more susceptible to it when exposed to certain environmental triggers. Much current research is focused on understanding these triggers, and researchers are making headway in finding a drug that could melt away the plaque.

Trends

Awareness of AD has increased dramatically over the past decade. This new awareness among members of the medical community and the public is largely a result of the efforts of a small number of dedicated neuroscientists, the National Institute on Aging (NIA), and the Alzheimer's Disease and Related Disorders Association (ADRDA) advocacy group. Sociologists have helped to understand the tremendous demands made on caregivers, the importance of support groups for families, and the reformulation of roles that occurs after the death of a spouse.

MENTAL ILLNESS

Neither mental health nor **mental illness** is an easy term to define. In part, this is due to the sociocultural basis for determining what orientations or behaviors are indicative of mental illness. Some conditions (e.g., homosexuality) that were once considered to be mental illness no longer are. Some conditions (e.g., having visions) that are considered as evidence of mental illness in some cultures are considered perfectly natural in others. Research even indicates that members of different cultures manifest very different symptoms in response to the same clinical psychopathology; for example, schizophrenics in some cultures are loud and aggressive, whereas in other cultures, they are quiet and withdrawn.

The most widely used classification system for mental disorders is the **Diagnostic and Statistical Manual of Mental Disorders, Text**

Revised (2000) (DSM-IV-TR), prepared by the Task Force on Nomenclature and Statistics of the American Psychiatric Association. It is the system used by mental health professionals, many social workers, the courts, and insurance providers. The DSM-IV-TR assesses each disorder on the basis of the nature and severity of clinical symptoms, relevant history, related physical illnesses, and recent adaptive functioning especially with regard to the quality of social relations.

However, the DSM-IV-TR is a controversial document. Critics charge that its definitions of disorders and the ability of clinicians to apply the definitions lack validity (Does it measure what it intends to measure?) because they are subjectively based. An example is the fact that homosexuality was listed as a mental disorder through the first two editions of the book. When a large number of members of the American Psychiatric Association challenged this perspective in the 1970s, the APA voted to delete homosexuality from the list of disorders. Critics of the biomedical approach charge that nothing "objective" about homosexuality changed, only its subjective interpretation.

Moreover, the DSM-IV-TR has been criticized for lacking reliability (is it used consistently by different clinicians?). Studies have shown that clinicians often disagree about diagnosis and do not apply defined conditions uniformly (Mirowsky and Ross, 1989). Studies that show that the race or gender of a patient influence the diagnosis of clinicians offer further evidence of a lack of reliability. The DSM-IV-TR is widely used and has some utility but carries with it some serious problems.

Prevalence

Everyone has impairments in functioning or "problems in living" from time to time, and many people consult with mental health professionals such as psychiatrists, clinical psychologists, social workers, and marriage and family counselors about these problems. Most are seeking help with marital or other family relationships, work-related problems, stress, or a lack of self-confidence. Some conditions are more intense, persist longer, and require more significant treatment.

Among the commonly used categories of mental disorders are:

1. **Anxiety disorders** include phobias (abnormally intense fears or dislikes), panic disorders (sudden feelings of terror), and obsessive-compulsive disorders (behaviors that must be performed to avoid anxiety).

2. **Depression** (sometimes referred to as affective disorder) is a mental disorder with a lasting altered mood (excessive sadness or hopelessness) for no obvious external cause.

3. Abuse or dependence on alcohol or drugs.

4. **Schizophrenia** is a mental disorder characterized by delusions, hallucinations, thought disturbances, and possibly withdrawal from social relationships. The severity of schizophrenia varies considerably.

5. **Antisocial personality disorders** are manifested in superficial charm, refusal to accept guilt, substance abuse, and inability to accept responsibility.

There are two major sources of prevalence data on these more serious mental disorders in the United States. The first is a general population survey of persons age 18 and older—the Baltimore Epidemiologic Catchment Area (ECA) program—that was conducted in five localities in the United States. It was conducted by the National Institute of Mental Health in the early 1980s and has been supplemented by a series of additional national surveys in the years since then. The other study is the National Comorbidity Survey (NCS) which was a nationally representative household survey conducted in the early 1990s. It focused on persons ages 15 to 54.

Estimates of the prevalence of mental illness in the population were similar in the two studies. Both estimated between 2 and 4 percent of the population had a severe mental illness and an additional 5 to 8 percent had a serious (but less severe) mental illness in 1990. Between 20 and 25 percent of the population experienced at least one mental disorder listed in DSM (not counting substance abuse) in that year. More recent estimates are that about one in five Americans experiences some type of mental disorder each year, and that about 40 percent of these disorders can be considered serious. Most of these disorders are treatable, but estimates are that—because of potential stigma and financial concerns—nearly half do not seek treatment.

Social Class and Race. With the possible exception of anxiety and mood disorders, the highest rates of mental illness are among members of the lowest socioeconomic class. This inverse relationship is consistent for schizophrenia and personality disorders characterized mainly by antisocial behavior and substance abuse. Lower-class members are also more likely to be depressed although this may be true only for women (Link and Dohrenwend, 1989).

There are three possible explanations for the high prevalence of mental disorders among the poor. The *genetic* explanation asserts that genetic inheritance predisposes members of the lower class to mental disorders. This theory has not received research support. The *social selection/drift* explanation maintains that mentally ill persons may drift downward in the social structure or that mentally healthy individuals tend to be upwardly mobile, thus leaving a "residue" of mentally ill persons. However, although research indicates that mental problems tend to prevent upward social mobility, it has not found that it leads to downward mobility. A third explanation—*social causation*—posits that people in lower socioeconomic groups live in a social environment that is more stressful and that they are more vulnerable to the effects of this stress because they lack the personal and financial resources to get needed help. None of these three explanations is totally satisfactory; each may make some contribution to an overall

explanation. It does not appear that race per se is directly related to incidence of mental illness. While blacks are much more likely than whites to report symptoms of depression, this is due primarily to their being poor (Tausig, Michello, and Subedi, 1999).

Gender. Most studies examining the relationship between mental disorder and gender have found that (1) there are no consistent differences between men and women with regard to rates of schizophrenia; (2) rates of mood and anxiety disorders are higher for women; and (3) rates of personality disorders are higher for men. These differences are due both to biological and sociocultural factors. Some research has focused on hormonal differences and chromosomal differences between women and men as explanatory factors for differential mental health, but evidence is insufficient to draw conclusions (Cockerham, 2000).

On the other hand, it is known that differences in behavior are at least partially the result of socialization into prescribed roles for males and females. Men are at an advantage in terms of self-direction and employment opportunities, but they are in turn more susceptible to personality disorders, whereas women are more vulnerable to depression and anxiety. These patterns are discussed in detail in Chapter 5.

Urban-Rural Differences. The overall rate of mental illness is higher in urban than in rural areas, but the differences are not great. Though rates tend to be especially high in central city areas (Link and Dohrenwend, 1989), rural life does not protect one completely from the risk of mental illness. In fact, manic-depressive disorders are more common among rural residents than among those living in urban areas—possibly due to greater social isolation. On the other hand, schizophrenia, anxiety, and personality disorders are more prevalent among city residents. Schizophrenia is especially prevalent in inner cities, suggesting a link with social class. Other possible explanations may be the negative consequences of crowding, and the stressful and competitive environment of urban areas (Cockerham, 2000).

Marital Status.   Research consistently finds that married people experience better mental health than unmarried people and that married men are even healthier mentally than married women. This is partially due to the social and emotional support received from stable, supportive relationships that can serve to protect one from psychological consequences of difficult life situations. However, it may also reflect the fact that the mentally ill are less likely to be married, and thus the differences between level of mental health are a result of a selection process rather than of marriage itself (Turner and Gartrell, 1978).

Etiology

There are three primary approaches for understanding the etiology of mental illness: the *biogenic or physiological approach* (also called the medical model), the *environmental or social approach*, and a combination of the two, the *gene-environment approach.*

The traditional biogenic view of mental illness is that it is an observable and measurable condition, stemming from individual psychological or biological pathology, and that is amenable to proper treatment. Many sociologists have challenged this way of thinking and support a social approach. They argue that definitions of mental illness rely more on subjective social judgments than objective facts. Thoits (1985) believes that the mental illness label is applied when a behavior is inconsistent with: (a) *cognitive norms* (one's thinking is at odds with norms), (b) *performance norms* (one's behavior is at odds with norms), or (c) *feeling norms* (one's feelings are at odds with the range, intensity, and duration of feeling expected in a given situation). She believes that violations of feeling norms are the most common basis for labeling someone mentally ill.

Finally, a third school of thought advocates for a combination of the two approaches. Those supporting the gene-environment approach contend that neither biogenic nor social factors can be dismissed and that a comprehensive explanation requires both.

Trends

Some sociologists who focus on the sociology of mental health have challenged the desirability of thinking in terms of clinical diagnoses at all and suggest that we focus on measurements that reflect the true range of human feelings and emotions. Mirowsky and Ross (2002:152) encourage a "human science" that centers on life "as people feel it, sense it, and understand it" and that includes consideration of human suffering even if it does not fall within preformulated diagnostic categories. Kessler (2002) also sees greater value in thinking in terms of dimensional assessments (placing each individual on a continuum of psychological distress without identifying a specific point at which a mental illness is established) rather than the traditional procedure of making categorical assessments (each individual either has or does not have a mental illness). These ideas have genuine potential for reshaping our whole approach to understanding human suffering and mental distress.

A positive development is that public discourse about mental health and mental illness is perhaps more open than ever before, and more people than ever seek treatment. Nevertheless, mental disorders continue to receive less public attention than physical ailments despite the very large percentage of people who experience some mental disorder each year. In the political arena, coverage of mental health services was one of the most controversial provisions in the failed health care reform package proposed in the early 1990s by the Clinton administration. For some, providing for mental health needs lacked the legitimacy of providing coverage for other diseases. Perhaps the biggest battle yet to be won in treating mental disorders is convincing politicians and others of the vast importance of making these services available.

SUMMARY

Understanding the causes and distribution of disease and illness requires attention be given both to fundamental causes (underlying social conditions) and to proximate risk factors.

Cardiovascular disease and cancer account for over 1.5 million deaths annually in the United States. Although the rate of CVD has decreased substantially in recent decades, it remains the number one killer of Americans. On the other hand, overall cancer rates continued to increase until the 1990s when a slight reduction occurred.

Both diseases are influenced by lifestyle. Cigarette smoking and diet are major risk factors for both diseases. High serum blood cholesterol, high blood pressure, and the Type A Behavior Pattern are major risk factors for CVD, whereas excessive consumption of alcohol and overexposure to the sun, radiation, and environmental pollutants, as well as occupational hazards, are key risk factors for cancer.

AIDS begins with HIV infection and is transmitted by body fluids through sexual activity, unsterile needles, infected blood supplies, and the placenta. AIDS is a major health problem around the world and will become increasingly so in the next decade. To date, no cures exist for the disease although progress continues to be made in combining drugs to slow the progression of the disease. Alzheimer's disease—a disease of mental deterioration that begins in mid to late life—also affects millions of persons in the United States. Recent significant advances in understanding the cause of AD have increased hopes that a successful treatment may be found in the next several years.

Approximately one American in five experiences some form of mental disorder each year. Most types of mental illness are more common in the lower classes. This is most likely due to conditions of poverty, including higher levels of stress and less access to necessary support.

HEALTH ON THE INTERNET

If you would like to find out information about a particular disease, there are many good Web sites such as that sponsored by the American Cancer Society at:

http://cancer.org

At their home page, click on "Health Information Seekers" and check out "Who Is at Risk?" "Prevention & Early Detection," and "Myths and Half-Truths About Cancer." What personal behaviors increase the chances of getting cancer? What social etiology (e.g., social circumstances or social policies) affects the likelihood of these cancers occurring?

KEY CONCEPTS AND TERMS

Acquired Immunodeficiency Syndrome (AIDS)
Alzheimer's Disease (AD)
antisocial personality disorders
anxiety disorders
cancer
carcinogen

cardiovascular disease
cholesterol
coronary heart disease (CHD)
depression
Diagnostic and Statistical Manual of Mental Disorders, Text Revised (DSM-IV-TR)

environmental tobacco smoke (ETS)
etiology
health transition (HT)
Human Genome Project
Human Immunodeficiency Virus (HIV)
hyperresponsivity
hypertension
melanoma

mental illness
metastasis
myocardial infarction
popular epidemiology
schizophrenia
stroke
Type A Behavior Pattern

DISCUSSION CASE

Some of the documented health dangers of cigarette smoking are reported in this chapter. The link to cardiovascular diseases and to cancer (especially lung cancer) has consistently been confirmed in research, is well accepted within the medical community, and has now been acknowledged by the tobacco industry (after years of lack of forthrightness).

But what can society legitimately do to discourage cigarette smoking? Recently, a major development has occurred. The tobacco industry has entered into negotiated settlements with states that sued them to recover expenses for treating Medicaid beneficiaries with smoking-related illnesses. The combined total of the settlement was approximately $250 billion over the next 25 years. The federal government has also sued the tobacco companies charging a long-running conspiracy to deceive the public; the status of this suit is now pending. In addition, juries are now frequently finding for individual smokers or groups of individual smokers in suits against the tobacco industry. A Florida jury returned a $145 billion judgment against the tobacco industry in the state for 700,000 sick smokers in the state.

The following are three additional issues that are being considered. What would you anticipate to be the consequences of the enactment of each of the following strategies?

1. *Prohibiting all advertising related to tobacco products.* Tobacco companies argue that would constitute an impingement on free speech and on their right to conduct their business. They state that their advertis-

ing attempts to get current smokers to change brands. Even if someone opposes use of tobacco products, they contend, because they are legal, advertising should be permitted.

Critics respond that tobacco ads are almost entirely focused on persuading nonsmokers to begin smoking and are targeted at adolescents. Ads contain "images and symbols of success, elegance, power, sexual conquests, the macho role, and an enhanced ability to be sociable, self-assured, confident, daring, adventurous, and mature" (Tuckson, 1989). Rarely, do they include any discussion of the relative merits of one brand versus any others. Since nearly 90 percent of smokers become regular smokers before the age of 21 (the average starting age is 18 for males, 19 for females), and about 3,000 young people begin smoking each day, advertisements are constructed to appeal to this age group. To halt the creation of new smokers, some people argue for elimination of all tobacco advertising. What would be the consequences of enacting this type of prohibition? Would you favor or oppose such a prohibition?

2. *Adding a very steep tax on cigarettes to discourage use.* Critics of the tobacco industry have suggested that tobacco companies ought to be responsible for covering the costs associated with their participation in the marketplace. The cost to the health care system of treating smoking-related diseases could be calculated and then a surcharge sufficient to cover these costs added to the price

of each pack of cigarettes. Estimates are that this might be as much as $3.00 or $4.00 added per pack. The rationale is that the higher price would discourage use and that the social costs of cigarette smoking would be paid for by tobacco companies. What would be the consequences of adding a surcharge to the price of cigarettes? Would you favor or oppose a steep surcharge on cigarettes?

3. *Allowing the Food and Drug Administration to regulate tobacco as a drug and giving it authority to ban nicotine after a specified number of years.* What would be the consequences of this regulatory power? Would you favor or oppose this possibility?

REFERENCES

American Cancer Society. 2004 *Cancer Facts and Figures—2004*. Atlanta: American Cancer Society.

American Heart Association. 2003 *Heart and Stroke Statistical Update*. Dallas: American Heart Association.

Auerbach, Judith D., and Anne E. Figert. 1995 "Women's Health Research: Public Policy and Sociology." *Journal of Health and Social Behavior,* Extra Issue:115–131.

Beech, Bettina, and Maurine Goodman. 2004 *Race and Research: Perspectives on Minority Participation in Health Studies.* Washington, DC: American Public Health Association.

Brown, Phil. 1987 "Popular Epidemiology: Community Response to Toxic Waste-Induced Disease in Woburn, Massachusetts." *Science, Technology, and Human Values,* 12:76–85.

Caldwell, John C. 1993 "Health Transition: The Cultural, Social, and Behavioural Determinants of Health in the Third World." *Social Science and Medicine,* 36:125–135.

Cockerham, William C. 2000 *Sociology of Mental Disorders,* 5th ed. Upper Saddle River, NJ: Prentice Hall.

Dresser, Rebecca. 1992 "Wanted: Single, White Male for Medical Research." *Hastings Center Report,* 22:24–29.

Evans, Robert G., Morris L. Barer, and Theodore R. Marmor. 1994 *Why Are Some People Healthy and Others Not? The Determinants of Health of Populations.* New York: Aldine de Gruyter.

Gallagher, Eugene B., Thomas J. Stewart, and Terry D. Stratton. 2000 "The Sociology of Health in Developing Countries," pp. 389–397 in *Handbook of Medical Sociology,* 5th ed., Chloe E. Bird, Peter Conrad, and Allen M. Fremont (eds.). Upper Saddle River, NJ: Prentice Hall.

Garrity, Thomas F., Morley Kotchen, Harlley E. McKean, Diana Gurley, and Molly McFadden. 1990 "The Association Between Type A Behavior and Change in Coronary Risk Factors Among Young Adults." *American Journal of Public Health,* 80:1354–1357.

Heiat, Asefeh, Cary P. Gross, and Harlan M. Krumholz. 2002 "Representation of the Elderly, Women, and Minorities in Heart Failure Clinic Studies." *Archives of Internal Medicine,* 162:1682–1688.

Hertzman, C., J. Frank, and R. G. Evans. 1994 "Heterogeneities in Health Status and the Determinants of Population Health," pp. 67–92 in *Why Are Some People Healthy and Others Not? The Determinants of Health of Populations,* Robert G. Evans, Morris L. Barer, and Theodore R. Marmor (eds.). New York: Aldine de Gruyter.

Kessler, Ronald C. 2002 "The Categorical Versus Dimensional Assessment Controversy in the Sociology of Mental Illness." *Journal of Health and Social Behavior,* 43:171–188.

Link, Bruce G., and Bruce P. Dohrenwend. 1989 "The Epidemiology of Mental Disorders," pp. 102–127 in *Handbook of Medical Sociology,* 4th ed., Howard E. Freeman and Sol Levine (eds.). Upper Saddle River, NJ: Prentice Hall.

Link, Bruce G., and Jo Phelan. 1995 "Social Conditions as Fundamental Causes of Disease." *Journal of Health and Social Behavior,* Extra Issue:80–94.

———. 2000 "Evaluating the Fundamental Cause Explanation for Social Disparities in Health," pp. 33–46 in *Handbook of Medical Sociology,* 5th ed., Chloe E. Bird, Peter Conrad, and Allen M. Fremont (eds.). Upper Saddle River, NJ: Prentice Hall.

Merton, Vanessa. 1993 "The Exclusion of Pregnant, Pregnable, and Once-Pregnable People (a.k.a. Women) from Biomedical Research." *American Journal of Law and Medicine,* 19:379–445.

Mirowsky, John, and Catherine E. Ross. 1989 "Psychiatric Diagnosis as Reified Measurement." *Journal of Health and Social Behavior,* 30:11–25.

———. 2002 "Measurement for a Human Science." *Journal of Health and Social Behavior,* 43:152–170.

Patel, Jyoti D., Peter B. Bach, and Mark G. Kris. 2004 "Lung Cancer in U.S. Women: A Contemporary Epidemic." *Journal of the American Medical Association,* 291:1763–1768.

Ross, Catherine E., and Chia-ling Wu. 1995 "The Links Between Education and Health." *American Sociological Review,* 60:719–745.

Suls, Jerry, and Glenn S. Sanders. 1989 "Why Do Some Behavioral Styles Place People at Coronary Risk?" pp. 1–20 in *Search of Coronary Prone Behavior: Beyond Type A,* Aron W. Siegman and Theodore M. Dembroski (eds.). Hillsdale, NJ: Lawrence Erlbaum Associates.

Tausig, Mark, Janet Michello, and Sree Subedi. 1999 *A Sociology of Mental Illness.* Upper Saddle River, NJ: Prentice Hall.

Thoits, Peggy A. 1985 "Self-Labeling Processes in Mental Illness: The Role of Emotional Deviance." *American Journal of Sociology,* 91:221–249.

Thomas, Charles R., Harlan A. Pinto, Mack Roach, and Clarence B. Vaughn. 1994 "Participation in Clinical Trials: Is It State-of-the-Art Treatment for African Americans and Other People of Color?" *Journal of the National Medical Association,* 86:177–182.

Tuckson, Reed V. 1989 "Race, Sex, Economics, and Tobacco Advertising." *Journal of the National Medical Association,* 81:1119–1124.

Turner, R. Jay, and John W. Gartrell. 1978 "Social Factors in Psychiatric Outcome: Toward the Resolution of Interpretive Controversies." *American Sociological Review,* 43:368–82.

United Nations Program on HIV/AIDS. 2004 "Newly Infected AIDS Cases Highest Yet." New York: United Nations.

Winkleby, Marilyn A., June A. Flora, and Helena C. Kraemer. 1994 "A Community-Based Heart Disease Intervention: Predictors of Change." *American Journal of Public Health,* 84:767–772.

5

SOCIAL STRESS

There may be few health-related concepts that have captured both the research interest of scientific investigators and the popular imagination as much as "social stress." This reflects both the substantive appeal of the concept for researchers in medicine and the biological and behavioral sciences and attempts by individuals to understand and take responsibility for their own health.

This chapter presents a brief description of the historical development of the concept, an introduction to the various ways that stress is conceptualized, and a model of social stress that attempts to capture its causes, mediating effects, and outcomes. Current research into stress as it is related to social class, race, and gender is also presented.

DEFINITION OF STRESS

The term **stress** is used in almost countless ways. It can refer to events or circumstances, such as an examination, that cause us unease; to the general unease we feel during such events; to the specific bodily responses to such events, such as rapid heartbeat; or to the mind's and

body's attempts to deal with the unease in order to recapture a sense of wellness.

Most researchers include in the concept of stress some reference to the resulting state in an individual who has experienced various demands. Stoklos (1986:35) defines stress as "a state of imbalance within a person, elicited by an actual or perceived disparity between environmental demands and the person's capacity to cope with these demands." Stress occurs in response to "strainful and threatening circumstances in the environment" and has clearer boundaries than states such as anxiety or depression, which are more global and more diffuse and may exist "even in the absence of specific threats" (Pearlin and Schooler, 1978:4).

HISTORICAL DEVELOPMENT OF THE STRESS CONCEPT

The idea of stress has existed for centuries. As discussed in Chapter 2, such historical luminaries as Hippocrates believed in the humoral theory of illness—that positive health results from a mind and body in harmony—perhaps the earliest characterization of an individual who is not "stressed out." Hippocrates' belief in the self-healing powers of the body also is consistent with an understanding of the body's adaptation to stress.

Historical records indicate that in the fourteenth century the term was equated with hardship and affliction, and in nineteenth-century medicine, stress was cited as a cause of ill health, as many diseases were attributed by physicians to conditions of "melancholia," "grief," or "despair." Clearly, by the 1800s, there was widespread recognition of the link between mind and body.

Ironically, Pasteur's demonstration that bacteria cause disease (the germ theory of disease) led many physicians and medical researchers to confine their attention to such germ-caused disease in the hopes of finding specific disease etiology and appropriate "magic bullets." In doing so, many researchers abandoned interest in the less concrete areas of attitudes and emotions.

Walter Cannon and Hans Selye

Early in this century, Walter Cannon, an American physiologist, used the term **homeostasis** to describe a state in which the body's physiologic processes are in balance and are properly coordinated. He identified many highly specific physiologic (adaptive) changes made by the body in response to hunger, thirst, extreme cold, pain, and intense emotions.

Cannon described a "fight or flight" reaction: When circumstances offered opportunity for success (or there was no choice), humans would fight; in the face of overwhelming odds, humans sought flight. Physiologic changes such as sugar entering the bloodstream to provide quick energy, heavy breathing to provide more oxygen, and acceleration of the heart to provide more fuel and oxygen occur to enhance the individual's reaction.

However, Cannon noted that while this resource mobilization was quite functional for early humans, it is often activated today when it is not really useful—a first date, for example—and may be harmful as it exhausts the individual.

Hans Selye, an endocrinologist at McGill University, often is cited as the classic figure in stress research. Hoping to discover a new sex hormone, Selye experimentally injected laboratory rats with hormones. Typical reactions were enlarged adrenal glands, shrunken immune systems, and bleeding ulcers. To confirm these effects, he injected nonhormonal substances into a control group of rats and surprisingly found a similar reaction. He realized the response was a general reaction rather than a substance-specific reaction. The physiological reaction was termed *stress*, and the trio of responses (alarm, adaptation, and exhaustion) was called the **general adaptation syndrome**.

Based on this work, Selye eventually pinpointed a truth with which people could immediately identify: In our daily lives we all experience stressful situations. These situations upset our body's equilibrium—our homeostasis—and make us more susceptible to mild diseases and illnesses. If stressful situations persist over an extended period of time, the body's resources become depleted, and more severe disease or illnesses—or even death—may result.

A MODEL OF SOCIAL STRESS

Several researchers have developed models to describe the effects of stress on individuals. The model presented in Figure 5–1 is influenced by several of these models but especially that by Morton Lieberman (1982) and Pearlin and Aneshensel (1986). Although stress is a broad intellectual concept, this model highlights the importance of using the sociological perspective to understand the following areas:

1. The nature and dynamics of how social forces and circumstances (stressors) create stressful situations.
2. How the perception or appraisal of stressors affects the manner in which they are handled.
3. How the appraisal of stressors affects the enactment of social roles (and strain created in these roles).
4. How social resources influence the likelihood of stressful circumstances occurring, the appraisal of these circumstances, the

Figure 5–1   A Model of the Stress Process

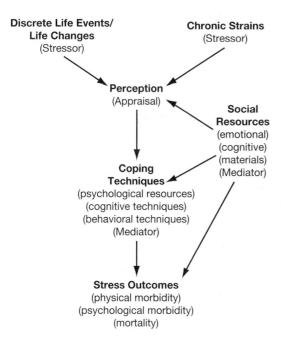

**Discrete Life Events/
Life Changes**
(Stressor)

Chronic Strains
(Stressor)

Perception
(Appraisal)

**Social
Resources**
(emotional)
(cognitive)
(materials)
(Mediator)

**Coping
Techniques**
(psychological resources)
(cognitive techniques)
(behavioral techniques)
(Mediator)

Stress Outcomes
(physical morbidity)
(psychological morbidity)
(mortality)

extent to which role enactment is problematic, the ability of individuals to cope and the coping mechanisms they use, and the extent to which the stressful circumstances result in negative stress outcomes.

STRESSORS

A primary concern of many sociologists is the identification of **stressors**—social factors or social forces that contribute to stress. Cataloging these forces is a difficult task, however, as they range from the broadest of social forces and large-scale social organization (a macro perspective), on the one hand, to the personal social environments in which people function on a day-to-day basis (a micro perspective), on the other hand.

Stressors and the Sociological Perspective

Attempts to understand human behavior must, of course, consider the importance of broader social forces and social organization. A key insight of

sociology is that all human behavior, even that which seems to be individualistic, is shaped by larger forces in the social environment.

The French sociologist Emile Durkheim (1858–1917) helped stimulate interest in identifying ways that individual behaviors are shaped by larger social forces. In his book *Suicide,* first published in 1897 (trans. 1951), Durkheim focused on what might seem the most individual of human behaviors and described how it is influenced by social forces. Durkheim asked these questions: If suicide is an entirely personal, individual behavior, why do rates of suicide vary from social group to social group? Why are suicide rates higher among men than women, higher among the unmarried than the married, and higher among Protestants than Catholics? And why do patterns in suicide rates persist over time?

While acknowledging the many possible motivations for suicide, Durkheim emphasized that suicide rates exhibit clear patterns among social groups. Apparently, he reasoned, there must be something about the social organization of groups that has an influence on the individual behavior of their members. Durkheim hypothesized that the extent to which an individual is integrated within a group affects the likelihood of suicide. On this basis, he identified three primary types of suicide:

1. *Egoistic suicide,* which occurs when an individual is insufficiently integrated within a group and has few social bonds (e.g., an elderly person whose lifetime partner dies and who feels as if there is little reason to go on living).
2. *Altruistic suicide,* which occurs when an individual so identifies with a social group that he or she is willing to sacrifice life for the group (e.g., a kamikaze pilot).
3. *Anomic suicide,* which occurs during times when society's norms and values are undergoing upheaval or rapid change so that individual society members may feel a sense of **anomie**—normlessness—and society's constraints against suicide weaken (e.g., Durkheim detected that suicide rates increase during times of economic prosperity as well as economic downturn—both periods of upheaval).

Durkheim's analysis is an excellent example of the **sociological imagination** (see Chapter 1). It is an ability to see how personal troubles (thoughts of suicide) are influenced by wider social forces (changes in the state of the economy or extent of social integration). Although it is tempting to look only at what is going on inside a person experiencing high levels of stress, it is essential also to examine the influence of the social context.

Types of Stressors

In recent years sociologists have distinguished between two major types of stressors: specific **life events** and more enduring life problems called **chronic strains**.

Life Events.   Life events are important specific events or experiences that interrupt an individual's usual activities and require some adjustment. A distinction is now made between anticipated (or scheduled) life events (e.g., marriage, divorce, beginning or ending of a school year) and unanticipated (unscheduled) life events (e.g., death of a loved one, a sudden failure, sudden loss of a job, learning of a terminal illness).

To determine the effects of these specific life events on stress level, researchers have employed three kinds of techniques: (1) studies of the psychiatric effects of specific events such as reactions to combat and natural and human disasters, (2) comparison of the number and types of life events experienced by psychiatric patients prior to their hospital admission to those for a nonpatient control group, and (3) general population surveys examining the relationship between life events, stress, and illness. One commonly used scale to measure life events—the *Social Readjustment Rating Scale*—is presented in Table 5–1. It contains a list of 43 events that were evaluated by a panel of judges as to the level of readjustment (converted to life-change units) that each required. The events range from 100 LCUs for the death of a spouse to 11 LCUs for minor violations of the law.

Efforts continue to strengthen life events scales. For example, it is increasingly common to omit positive life events from the

TABLE 5–1   The Social Readjustment Rating Scale

Rank	Life Event	Mean Value
1	Death of spouse	100
2	Divorce	73
3	Marital separation	65
4	Jail term	63
5	Death of close family member	63
6	Personal injury or illness	53
7	Marriage	50
8	Fired at work	47
9	Marital reconciliation	45
10	Retirement	45
11	Change in health of family member	44
12	Pregnancy	39
13	Sex difficulties	39
14	Gain of new family member	39
15	Business readjustment	39
16	Change in financial state	38
17	Death of close friend	37
18	Change to different line of work	36
19	Change in number of arguments with spouse	35
20	Mortgage over $10,000	31
21	Foreclosure of mortgage or loan	30
22	Change in responsibilities at work	29
23	Son or daughter leaving home	29
24	Trouble with in-laws	29
25	Outstanding personal achievement	28
26	Wife begin or stop work	26
27	Begin or end school	26
28	Change in living conditions	25
29	Revision of personal habits	24
30	Trouble with boss	23
31	Change in work hours or conditions	20
32	Change in residence	20
33	Change in schools	20
34	Change in recreation	19
35	Change in church activities	19
36	Change in social activities	18
37	Mortgage or loan less than $10,000	17
38	Change in sleeping habits	16
39	Change in number of family get-togethers	15
40	Change in eating habits	15
41	Vacation	13
42	Christmas	12
43	Minor violations of the law	11

Reprinted from *Journal of Psychosomatic Research*, Vol. 11, Thomas Holmes and Richard Rahe, "The Social Readjustment Rating Scale," pp. 213–218, © 1967, with permission from Elsevier.

scale. Pearlin (1989) has called into question the notion that *all* life changes are potentially harmful because of the readjustment required. Some research has determined that desirable life changes were linked to illness only among subjects with low self-esteem; among subjects with higher self-esteem, desirable life changes correlated with better health.

Does experiencing undesirable life events negatively impact health? Yes, and sometimes the event is traumatizing, but often the effect is not large and, in most cases, it does not persist over a long period of time. Researchers do continue to detect a relationship between adverse life events and certain depressive disorders (Dohrenwend, 2000), but the effects are not large and generally dissipate within three months (Avison and Turner, 1988).

Chronic Strains. The second major type of stressor—now often referred to as chronic strains—has been defined by Pearlin (1989) as "the relatively enduring problems, conflicts, and threats that many people face in their daily lives." The most common bases for these types of stressors are family problems with spouse, parents, or children; love or sex problems; problems on the job or in school; and problems in any site that involve competition.

Pearlin (1989:245) has recommended that focus be placed on "problems that arise within the boundaries of major social roles and role sets." These are likely to be important problems because the relationships that exist in role sets usually are enduring. Because they also tend to be extremely important relationships (e.g., spouse, child, boss, teacher), strains that develop are likely to be of great significance to the individual.

Pearlin (1989:245) uses the concept of "role strain" to refer to "the hardships, challenges, and conflicts or other problems that people come to experience as they engage over time in normal social roles." The five most common types of role strain are discussed next.

1. **Role overload** occurs when the combination of all the role demands placed on an individual exceed that individual's ability to meet them. Within the workplace, evidence exists that work overload is most likely to be felt by those at opposite ends of the spectrum: salaried, white-collar workers and the least-skilled blue-collar workers. For different reasons, both may feel little control over work demands—an important predictor of job stress. Excessive workload may also be experienced by the homemaker in overseeing house maintenance, food preparation, and child-rearing functions, as well as increasingly playing the caregiver role for parents unable to live independently. Primary caregivers and those caring for elders with significant needs often must resort to taking unpaid leave, reducing work hours, rearranging their work schedule, or even leaving the work force altogether. As women add the caregiver role to their other obligations, psychological distress increases (Pavalko and Woodbury, 2000).

Role overload—too much to do in the available time—is a very common type of chronic strain.

Perception of role overload also is influenced by the level of economic return on one's labors. Brenner (1973) has shown that both the absolute level of economic reward and the perceived fairness with changes in the amount of reward influence level of stress. Teaching and nursing are good illustrations of careers that pay more than the national average, but are stressful, in part, because the level of training required and the amount and intensity of work demanded are not always commensurately rewarded. Likewise, a frustration of many homemakers is that the value of their contributions often is not rewarded at all—either in monetary fashion or in terms of genuine appreciation.

2. **Interpersonal conflicts within role sets** includes problems and difficulties that arise within complementary role sets, such as wife-husband, parent-child, and worker-supervisor and is the type of strain that often touches people most deeply. Marriage is typically the center of our most intimate relationships, the context of many of our most far-reaching decisions (e.g., children, major purchases, degree of equalitarianism), and the role set in which many spend the most time. Therefore, it has the potential for great bliss as well as for significant interpersonal conflict. Rates of separation and divorce, emotional and physical abuse within families, and reported levels of marital dissatisfaction all reflect high levels of stress. Pearlin (1983:10) pinpointed one aspect of this conflict:

One of the more common elements of discord— and one of the more stressful—involves a breakdown in reciprocity. By reciprocity and its failure, I mean the sense of inequity people have about their marriages . . . people see themselves in marital relationships where . . . they invest more than their partner in the relationship, and are more considerate of their partners than they think their partners are of them.

Pearlin (1983) identifies other common sources of strain in marriages: (1) a perception that the spouse does not recognize or accept "quintessential" elements of one's self—that the spouse fails to authenticate what is judged to be an especially prized aspect of the self-image; (2) a belief that the spouse is failing to fulfill basic marital expectations such as wage earning or housekeeping; and (3) a feeling that the spouse is failing to provide even minimal levels of affection or that sexual relations are insufficiently satisfying. The lack of physical as well as emotional intimacy clearly relates to marital stress.

3. **Interrole conflict** occurs when the demands of two or more roles held by a person are incompatible, and the demands cannot simultaneously be met. On a small scale, genuine conflict occurs whenever any health care worker is "on call" and gets called in to the hospital just as he or she is about to participate in a family function (let's say a one-showing only of a play or dance for which the youngest child has earnestly practiced for months). Being a responsible health care worker and being a loving parent are both very important roles, but on the night in question, the child will be disappointed. In a marriage of two persons equally dedicated to careers, an elderly parent or young child who requires significant attention during the day will force some resolution of an interrole conflict.

4. **Role captivity** is the term used by Pearlin to describe situations in which an individual is in an unwanted role—he or she feels an obligation to do one thing but prefers to do something else (Pearlin, 1983). A retired person who wishes to continue working and a person working who wishes to retire are both held in role captivity. A college student forced to attend college by parents and a college-age person who wants to go to college but cannot afford it are role captives. Anyone hating his or her job and longing for another is a role captive.

The captive situation can also occur within families. Feeling trapped in an unhappy

IN THE FIELD

THE DAILY STRESS INVENTORY

The Daily Stress Inventory (DSI) was developed by Brantley et al. (1987) to measure the sources and impact of relatively minor stressful events.

Below are listed a variety of events that may be viewed as stressful or unpleasant. Read each item carefully and decide whether or not that event occurred within the past 24 hours. If the event did not occur, place an "X" in the space next to the item. If the event did occur, indicate the amount of stress that it caused you by placing a number from 1 to 7 in the space next to that item (see numbers below). Please answer as honestly as you can so that we may obtain accurate information.

X = did not occur
1 = occurred but was not stressful
2 = caused very little stress
3 = caused a little stress
4 = caused some stress
5 = caused much stress
6 = caused very much stress
7 = caused me to panic

1 performed poorly at task
2 performed poorly due to others
3 thought about unfinished work
4 hurried to meet deadline
5 interrupted during task/activity
6 someone spoiled your completed task
7 did something you are unskilled at
8 unable to complete a task
9 was unorganized
10 criticized or verbally attacked
11 ignored by others
12 spoke or performed in public
13 dealt with rude waiter/waitress/salesperson
14 interrupted while talking
15 was forced to socialize
16 someone broke a promise/appointment
17 competed with someone
18 was stared at
19 did not hear from someone you expected to hear from
20 experienced unwanted physical contact (crowded, pushed)

21 was misunderstood
22 was embarrassed
23 had your sleep disturbed
24 forgot something
25 feared illness/pregnancy
26 experienced illness/physical discomfort
27 someone borrowed something without your permission
28 your property was damaged
29 had minor accident (broke something, tore clothing)
30 thought about the future
31 ran out of food/personal article
32 argued with spouse/boyfriend/girlfriend
33 argued with another person
34 waited longer than you wanted
35 interrupted while thinking/relaxing
36 someone "cut" ahead of you in line
37 performed poorly at sport/game
38 did something that you did not want to do
39 unable to complete all plans for today
40 had car trouble
41 had difficulty in traffic
42 money problems
43 store lacked a desired item
44 misplaced something
45 bad weather
46 unexpected expenses (fines, traffic ticket, etc.)
47 had confrontation with an authority figure
48 heard some bad news
49 concerned over personal appearance
50 exposed to feared situation or object
51 exposed to upsetting TV show, movie, book
52 "pet peeve" violated (someone fails to knock, etc.)
53 failed to understand something
54 worried about another's problems
55 experienced narrow escape from danger
56 stopped unwanted personal habit (overeating, smoking, nailbiting)
57 had problem with kid(s)
58 was late for work/appointment

Take the inventory. How many of the items have you experienced in the previous 24 hours? What is the total sum of the weights you applied to the experienced items? What is the average weight you attached to the experienced items?

After testing a slightly larger pilot scale, Brantley et al. administered this inventory to 433 residents of their community. They calculated the following averages:

	Number of Items	Sum of Weights	Average Weight
Males	17.56	42.47	2.36
Females	16.99	48.00	2.68

marriage can be an extremely stressful situation. Sometimes children in families can be role captives as is illustrated by recent research by Fischer et al. (2000) on the stressfulness of growing up in a family with parental alcoholism.

5. **Role Restructuring** occurs in situations in which long established patterns or expectations undergo considerable restructuring. Pearlin (1989) offers such examples as a rebellious adolescent who desires more independence; an apprentice who grows frustrated with his or her mentor as the craft is learned; and adult children who must take on increased responsibilities for aging parents. He notes that the transition can be more difficult when it is forced by circumstances (rather than voluntary effort) and when the transition involves some redistribution of status, privilege, or influence over others. Stress in the workplace seems to be increasing, and part of the explanation for this is anxiety over the possible loss of job (as businesses downsize) and rearranged job responsibilities (to make up for the reduced staff size).

Three final points about chronic strains deserve attention:

1. Chronic strains are a more powerful determinant of depressive disorders and other health problems than are discrete life events. Their persistence, emergence in important areas such as marriage and work, and presence throughout the course of each day gives them powerful force within our lives.
2. Valid and reliable measurement of chronic strains (like life events) is complicated. For example, it may be difficult to determine the actual "chronicity" of a strain. Interpersonal conflict within a marriage rarely can be represented as a linear phenomenon—it often ebbs and flows, sometimes swinging back and forth between bliss and misery, and does so with uneven degrees of intensity. How then does one accurately measure the length of time for which discord has occurred? What may seem rather straightforward actually is quite complex (Kessler, Price, and Wortman, 1985).
3. Life events and chronic strains often may overlap. The occurrence of specific life events may alter the existence or meaning of chronic strains. An example is the effect of sudden job loss (a discrete life event) on division of labor within the household (possibly a chronic strain). Moreover, life events may create new strains or magnify existing strains, as might occur if the sudden job loss created marital discord (Kessler, Price, and Wortman, 1985; Pearlin, 1989).

Multidimensional Consideration of Stressors. In recent years stress researchers have begun to expand their consideration of types of stressors beyond discrete life events and chronic strains. An increasingly common approach is to consider measures of stressors that include life events and chronic strains and additional indicators such as lifetime accumulation of major life events and perceived discrimination. Analyses of stress and negative health outcomes associated with stress using a multidimensional approach has significantly added to understanding of how stress differs for women than men and for members of racial and ethnic minority groups versus whites (Turner and Avison, 2003).

APPRAISAL OF STRESSORS

Appraisal and the Sociological Perspective

Within sociology, **symbolic interactionism** is a micro-level perspective that focuses on small-scale, everyday patterns of social interaction. Symbolic interactionists believe that social life is composed of myriad episodes of daily social interactions in which people communicate verbally and nonverbally and engage in a constant process of interpreting others' messages and responding to these interpretations. According to symbolic interactionism, the world is not so much imposed on the individual, dictating or strongly influencing behavior, as it is created by the individual through the exchange of these verbal and nonverbal symbols. Berger and Luckmann (1967) assigned the term **social construction of reality** to identify this pattern.

A classic example of the symbolic interactionist perspective is found in the work of W. I. Thomas (1863–1947). Thomas recognized that individuals are affected by events only to the extent to which they are perceived. In other words, neither life events nor chronic strains are in and of themselves stressful. They are simply situations or occurrences in which the likelihood of a stressful response is increased. It is the perception of these events and their interpretation—what an individual believes the implications of the events/strains to be—that is stressful. The **Thomas Theorem** is often summarized as: "if situations are defined as real, they are real in their consequences." It is the perceived world, whether it is perceived accurately or not, that becomes the basis for response.

The Appraisal Process.   Whenever any potentially stressful life event or chronic strain occurs, we immediately evaluate or **appraise** its significance for us. We may attempt to recreate the circumstances that surrounded some similar event in the past and recall how it affected us then or attempt to systematically remember anything that we have heard or read about the event. We may ask ourselves: Have I ever handled anything like this before? If so, what happened? Can I get through this on my own? Do I need help? Who can help?

This is done in order to determine whether the current situation is irrelevant to our personal well-being, is benign in its implications, or is stressful. If it is stressful, we likely will calculate how much damage has already occurred and what threat for additional damage remains. We may assess the availability of resources to help deal with the event. We will calculate the stressfulness of the event in absolute terms but also relative to whatever helping resources are available.

The appraisal process does not involve the "real" event, but the individual's *perception* of the real event. To the extent that perceptions differ, individuals will respond differently to the same "real" circumstances. Being laid off from the job may be perceived by some as a tragic event; others may view it as an unsolicited step in searching for a better job.

MEDIATORS OF STRESS: COPING AND SOCIAL SUPPORT

The same stressful circumstances do not lead to the same **stress outcomes** in all people. Other factors exist that modify the stressor/stress outcome relationship. These additional factors are referred to as **mediators** of stress; they are so identified because research has demonstrated their potential to influence or modify (i.e., mediate) the effects of stressors. This section concentrates on coping and social support, the two types of mediators that have received the most attention.

Mediators and the Sociological Perspective

Several sociological concepts and perspectives contribute to an understanding of the mediating role of coping and social support. A classic illustration of the way the social environment influences our self-image (and, thus, our feelings of confidence in dealing with social stress) is Charles Horton Cooley's (1864–1929) theory of the **looking-glass self**. Cooley illustrated the way that reality is socially constructed by describing the process by which each person develops a self-image. According to this theory, we come to see ourselves as we believe other people see us. Consciously or subconsciously, we attempt to interpret how we are viewed by others (and the judgment being placed on that view), and we gradually develop a self-image consistent with what we perceive (Cooley, 1964). If I believe people with whom I interact see me as a very humorous person, I will likely see myself that way. However, if others never laugh at my jokes and convey to me that I need a sense-of-humor transplant, I'm not likely to see myself as being very funny.

Coping

Most people develop a repertoire of personal responses that can be activated when stressful circumstances arise. This repertoire consists of responses which have been learned through socialization experiences and evolve over time as particular techniques work or fail to work to mediate stress.

Coping refers to things people do to prevent, avoid, or control emotional distress (Pearlin and Schooler, 1978) and includes efforts (1) to eliminate or modify the stressful situation so that it will not be a continuing problem, (2) to control the meaning of the problem, by "cognitively neutralizing" the situation, and (3) to control the stress created by the situation (e.g., through stress management techniques).

Specific Coping Techniques.   There are three types of specific coping techniques: psychological resources, cognitive techniques, and behavioral techniques.

1. *Psychological resources* are "the personality characteristics that people draw upon to help them withstand threats posed by events and objects in their environment" (Pearlin and Schooler, 1978:5). Three such characteristics have received the most attention:
   a. Individuals with positive feelings about self—*positive self-esteem*—have been shown to cope better with stressful situations. This may be due to greater self-

confidence, a feeling that one is held in high regard by others (recall Cooley's looking-glass self), and a real or perceived assessment of one's previous ability to handle the stressful situation (DeLongis, Folkman, and Lazarus, 1988).
   b. Individuals with a feeling of being in control, of controlling their own destiny, of being able to master situations (i.e., *internal control*) have been shown to cope better with stressors than individuals who see themselves as being less competent and who believe that their life is controlled by luck, fate, or outside others (i.e., *external control*).
   c. Individuals characterized by a trait referred to by Kobasa (1979) as **hardiness** are better able to handle stress. Hardy individuals exhibit a strong commitment to work, family, friends, and other causes and interests; accept change as a challenge rather than as a foe; and have a feeling of personal control over life (internal control).

2. *Cognitive techniques* involve the assignment of specific interpretations to a stressful event in order to control its meaning (i.e., to neutralize its stressfulness). In light of some potentially stressful event, one might respond by denying that the event is happening, or by telling herself or himself that the event is not as crucial as it might seem, that it will be over soon, that it might even be a good challenge, or that other people have been in this situation and survived. Many people rely on their spiritual beliefs or participation in religious activities to help find meaning in uncontrollable life events.

3. *Behavioral techniques* also can be used to help cope with a stressful event. Individuals might focus on developing and implementing a plan to reduce or eliminate the stressor. Some individuals use biofeedback, yoga, or other meditative techniques to help reduce stressfulness (research supports the health value of these techniques). Many persons try to get their mind off the object of despair by engaging in some alternative, distracting activity, such as listening to music, engaging in

some physical activity, or using alcohol or some other drug. More than one of our students has resorted to the old adage, "When the going gets tough, the tough go shopping."

Are all coping techniques equally effective in all situations? No. Research has shown that different coping techniques are most effective in different situations. In fact most people use different coping techniques in different situations (e.g., in parental versus marital situations) and different people effectively use different coping techniques in the same situation. Accordingly, the larger and more varied the coping repertoire, the more likely it is that an individual can cope with any stressful situation (Kessler, Price, and Wortman, 1985). In general, however, problem-focused strategies (that deal directly with the stressor) are associated with more positive health outcomes than strategies that include mentally distancing oneself from the stressor, wishful thinking, self-blame, and simply emphasizing the positive (Penley, Tomaka, and Wiebe, 2002).

Several interesting studies have been conducted of the specific kinds of coping techniques used in specific circumstances. For example, Schwab (1990) identified five primary coping strategies used by married couples who had experienced the death of a child: (1) seeking a release of tension through talking, crying, exercising, and writing about the death; (2) concentrating on avoiding painful thoughts and feelings by engaging in diversionary activities such as work around the house; (3) cognitively dealing with the situation by reading materials on loss and grief; (4) helping others and/or contributing to a cause; and (5) relying on religiously based beliefs that their child is in a better place and that the family will someday be reunited.

Social Support

Most people do not deal with stressful situations on their own but rather receive assistance from others. Although the extent to which persons are integrated into families, friendship networks,

---

IN COMPARATIVE FOCUS

NURSING AND STRESS IN SINGAPORE

Much research has focused on stress among nurses in the United States. Vivien Lim and Edith Yuen (1998) sought to extend knowledge about the general relationship between nursing and stress by focusing on a non-Western setting, Singapore. They posited that different cultures might vary in the degree of prestige that is assigned to various career paths and that employees might reflect these differences in how they perceive and feel about their careers.

Two aspects of health care and nursing in Singapore are similar to aspects in the United States: the health care system has recently undergone significant changes, including an increase in health care costs that has created greater public expectations for quality health care; and a severe shortage of nurses exists. To combat the nursing shortage, the government has increased salaries for nurses and instituted flexible and part-time work schedules.

Despite the changes, nursing remains a less-preferred vocational choice among young job seekers, and nurses routinely report high levels of stress.

Lim and Yuen focused their research on identifying the relative effect on nurses' stress of the increasing demands made by patients, the increasing demands made by physicians (also responding to public and patient expectations), and the perceived job image of nurses. The researchers found that all three of these factors had an effect on job satisfaction, on organizational commitment to their hospital-employer, to job-induced tension, and to intention to quit. Which factor had the largest influence on job-induced stress? The demands from patients created the most tension, perhaps reflecting that nurses were committed more to patient care than to pleasing the physicians or the hospital.

occupational or school groups, and religious and civic groups varies, research confirms that **social support** is an extremely important mediator of the effects of stress.

Social Support as a Concept

Pearlin and Aneshensel (1986:418) consider social support as the "social resources one is able to call upon in dealing with . . . problematic conditions of life," particularly those that overwhelm the individual's own coping ability. Social support includes (Jacobson, 1986): (1) *emotional support* (feelings of comfort, respect, love, caring, and concern); (2) *cognitive support* (information, knowledge, and advice); and (3) *materials support* (products or services to assist in handling specific problems).

The Effect of Social Support on Stress and Stress Outcomes.   People with positive social support tend to have better physical and mental health and are better able to adjust to such events as loss of spouse, unemployment, serious illness, and criminal victimization. Two primary models have been developed to explain this relationship.

The **main effects model of social support** asserts that social support contributes directly to well-being and positive health and that these beneficial effects occur even in the absence of stress. The overall sense of well-being that social support provides, the feeling of being accepted, the knowledge that others care and are available, and the degree of comfort within one's social environment may contribute to inner feelings of contentment and outer expressions of good health.

The alternative model, the **buffering effects model of social support**, asserts that the beneficial effects of social support occur only in the presence of stress. By acting as a buffer, social support may decrease the likelihood of negative stress outcomes occurring as a response to high stress levels. The support offered by others, according to this model, provides some sense of security and confidence that stressful circumstances can be handled and, perhaps, even that

specific assistance in handling the situation will be available.

Although research findings are not completely consistent, the wealth of evidence shows that both types of effects occur—that social support does contribute directly to positive health, and it serves an important buffering effect in times of high stress.

How Social Support Affects Health

There are three specific mechanisms through which social support directly or indirectly affects health: (1) *behavioral mediators* (which encourage an individual to engage in or to change behaviors, such as quitting cigarette smoking); (2) *psychological mediators* (which attempt to restore a person's self-esteem and to provide a satisfying shared interaction); and (3) *physiological mediators* (which help relax the fight-or-flight response or strengthen the immune system). Although it has not been empirically confirmed, social support may be an adequate stimulus for the release of certain bodily hormones (certain neuropeptides) that bolster the immune system.

As is true with specific coping mechanisms, the most effective means of social support are situationally determined. Wellman and Wortley (1990) have shown that most relationships provide specialized forms of support. For example, friends are more likely than parents to provide companionship but less likely to offer financial assistance, and women are more likely than men to provide emotional support.

Finally, the complexity of the relationship between social support and stress must be emphasized. Often, it is impossible to disentangle stressors and their mediators. This is something of a "double whammy"—certain circumstances both add to the stressfulness of life and detract from available social support at the same time. For example, much research has confirmed the stressfulness of unemployment and its relationship to depression. However, research has demonstrated that unemployment carries an extra burden: Following job loss, social support from spouse and from fellow workers often diminishes. At the very instant when social support is especially needed, it becomes less readily offered. Thus, the psychological distress traditionally tied to job loss may actually be due both to job loss and the reduction in social support that often accompanies it (Atkinson, Liem, and Liem, 1986).

STRESS OUTCOMES

In one sense, identification of specific "outcomes" or "ills" of stress is remarkably simple: All of us can relate various ailments we have suffered with stress. In another sense, however, making specific linkages can be quite difficult because stress leads to a wide variety of outcomes through a wide variety of pathways. In any case it is clear that when one's level of stress cannot successfully be mediated through coping and social support, negative stress outcomes are likely to occur.

In attempting to bring some order to the variety of ills produced by stress, Brown (1984) suggested the following categorization:

1. *Bona fide emotional disturbances* include anxiety, insomnia, tension headaches, neuroses, phobias, hysterias, and hypochondriasis and are major factors in aging, sexual impotency, alcoholism, drug abuse, sleep disorders, and learning problems.
2. *Abnormal behaviors* such as compulsive behaviors, aggression, withdrawal, criminal activities, battered child/spouse/parent syndrome, and sexual deviation. Some research is now beginning to examine "road rage" and other types of rage as a response to accumulated stress.
3. *Psychosomatic illnesses* such as hypertension, coronary heart disease, ulcers, and colitis.
4. *Worsening of genuine organic illnesses* such as epilepsy, migraine, herpes zoster, coronary thrombosis, and rheumatic arthritis.

Grouped somewhat differently, we might say that unchecked stress increases the likelihood of psychological morbidity (e.g., anxiety and depression); physical morbidity (e.g., coronary heart disease and cancer); and mortality (Pearlin and Aneshensel, 1986).

Pathways Between Stress and Disease

Stress responses may be produced voluntarily or involuntarily (see Figure 5–2). A sudden noise or other unanticipated event works through the hypothalamus in the brain (the center of primitive and automatic responses), which stimulates the sympathetic nervous system (and the larger brain system) which arouses the body for action. The cerebral cortex then evaluates the genuine danger presented by the stressor and determines whether the state of arousal is necessary.

The pathway for voluntary responses begins in the cerebral cortex, which assesses and interprets the stressor, and then moves through the limbic system (the center of emotions) and the hypothalamus to the pituitary gland, which activates the adrenal glands and thyroid gland to secrete hormones to trigger the body's stress response (if that is judged to be appropriate by the cerebral cortex).

The specific responses made by the body include a sharp increase in blood pressure and increased respiration (to increase the availability of oxygen), an increase in blood sugar (to provide energy for muscles), increased muscle tension (to enable quick applications of strength), a release of thyroid hormone (to speed up metabolism for energy), a release of cholesterol in the blood (for endurance fuel), and a release of endorphins (the natural painkillers of the body). Ultimately, stress may lead to disease through the wearing down of bodily organs, through a weakening of the body's immune system, or through the development of health-impairing behaviors (e.g., increased cigarette smoking or alcohol consumption) in reaction to stress.

THE ROLE OF SOCIAL CLASS, RACE, AND GENDER IN SOCIAL STRESS

Social Class

People in the lower social classes have higher rates of psychological distress and mental health problems (Turner, Wheaton, and Lloyd, 1995)

Figure 5–2   The Physiological Pathways of the Stress Response

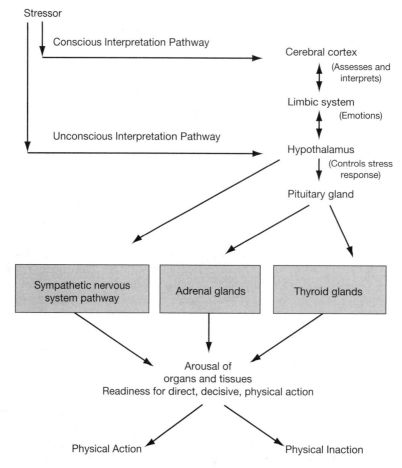

Source: Clint Bruess and Glenn Richardson. *Decisions for Health* (4th Ed.). Dubuque, IA: Brown & Benchmark Publishers, 1995.

than the more affluent. Two explanations for this pattern have been advanced. The first, the **exposure hypothesis**, states that lower-class people are exposed to more stressful life experiences than those in the middle or upper classes, and that higher rates of distress are a logical result of this exposure. Research has confirmed that stressful life experiences are more common in lower SES groups. When multidimensional measures of stressors are used (as described earlier in this chapter), the higher level of reported stress in lower SES groups is shown to be partly explained by this factor.

Research also has supported an alternative explanation, the **vulnerability hypothesis**, which states that stressful life experiences have a greater impact on those in the lower class and a greater capacity to lead to negative stress outcomes (Turner and Lloyd, 1999). This greater vulnerability has been traced to three factors: inadequate financial resources, greater use of ineffective coping strategies, and less access to social support networks (McLeod and Kessler, 1990).

First, lower-SES persons not only experience more of several stressful life events (e.g., job instability and loss, chronic health problems, and poorer quality of housing), but by definition have fewer financial resources available to deal with these problems. For example, purchasing health insurance might be recognized as a partial solution to health care worries, but financial limitations may eliminate this option.

Second, people from the lower social classes are less likely to have psychological traits, such as high self-esteem, internal control, and confidence in dealing with stressors, that buffer stress, and they are more likely to use ineffective coping strategies, such as avoidance, in responding to stressful situations. These patterns may be linked to socialization experiences. For example, growing up in a family unable to secure needed health care may encourage feelings of powerlessness and external control.

Finally, aspects of living in the lower class may reduce the likelihood of establishing or maintaining supportive social resources. While evidence is mixed on this point, it does appear, for example, that lower-SES persons are less likely to have a confidant in whom they can rely.

Race

For more than 30 years, research has demonstrated that African Americans have higher rates than whites of psychological distress. A key question is whether this difference can solely or largely be attributed to an economic disparity or whether race exhibits an independent effect on stress level. In other words, do low economic status and racial discrimination contribute individually to stress levels?

Beginning in the 1970s and, in part, continuing today, much research on racial differences has supported the position that the higher rates of distress in blacks are due entirely, or almost entirely, to economic differences. These studies have concluded that when social class is controlled, the racial disparity in distress is eliminated.

However, Ronald Kessler and Harold Neighbors (1986) have challenged this view. Offering theoretical justification in the fact that the effects of social class on many outcomes (e.g., educational attainment and financial achievement) vary depending on one's race, they have contended that class and race are interactive factors. They posited that racial differences in distress might be largest in the lower class (especially with competent blacks whose aspirations have been thwarted by discrimination) or in the upper class (especially with financially successful blacks feeling status inconsistency). Their analysis of eight studies (a pooled sample of 22,000 respondents) determined that race continues to be an important predictor of distress even when class is controlled, and that blacks experience more distress than whites at all levels of income. Considerable recent research has shown that perceiving racial discrimination is highly stressful, and that the heightened stress does increase the likelihood of negative health outcomes (Sellers et al., 2003; Turner and Avison, 2003).

Research by Ulbrich, Warheit, and Zimmerman (1989) supports the Kessler-Neighbors thesis. Using epidemiological data on 2,115 adults in Florida, they found that lower-SES blacks are more vulnerable than middle-SES blacks to both discrete life events and economic problems and more vulnerable than lower-SES whites to the impact of discrete life events (though less so in response to economic problems). These results reflect an interactive pattern for class and race and indicate that the effects of race do not dissipate when class is controlled.

Furthermore, some research continues to find that blacks respond differently than whites to stressful situations. For example, research continues to show that black women are more likely than white women to encounter unfair treatment in their everyday life (Schulz et al., 2000) and to experience hypertension as a result.

On the other hand, there is evidence to support the pattern that blacks are more likely than whites to have access to social support. The group solidarity that often exists among members of minority groups may have important stress-buffering effects (Lincoln et al., 2003). In addition, having a strong sense of ethnic identity (e.g., strong group pride, cultural commitment to the group) can be a buffer to the stress of racial and ethnic discrimination and help to prevent negative health outcomes (Mossakowski, 2003).

This may help explain the pattern that blacks often evidence higher levels of stress than whites but not higher levels of mental disorder.

Gender

Women have higher rates (perhaps double) than men of psychological distress and depression. As Rosenfield (1989:77) summarized, these differences are found "across cultures, over time, in different age groups, in rural as well as urban areas, and in treated as well as untreated populations." Consistently, these differences are greater among the married than the unmarried, though distress is greater in women regardless of marital status.

As important as this pattern is in sociological analysis and clinical application, only recently has significant attention been focused on women as subjects in stress research. This lack of attention has been especially obvious in the area of occupational health research, where early research on women was often conducted primarily to secure a better understanding of men's stress. The consequence of this inattention is that much remains to be learned about the bases of the high rates of distress in women.

A wide variety of plausible explanations for the gender disparity in stress have been advanced and tested:

1. Women are exposed to more discrete, stressful life events than are men. This differential exposure hypothesis has not been supported in most research. However, some research has highlighted the importance of the fact that women are much more likely than men to fill the caregiver role and to be affected by it, and Keith (1993) found that the higher levels of distress in older women than older men are due to their greater likelihood of having financial problems.

2. Women include more people in their social network, care more about these people, and are more emotionally involved in the lives of people around them. As such, they are more apt to feel stress when others in their network are

feeling stress (Kessler and McLeod, 1984). Women are more likely than men to be both providers and recipients of support, though both men and women rely more on women for support during stressful times. Whereas married women use both spouse and friends as confidants, married men tend to rely on their wives (Edwards, Nazroo, and Brown, 1998).

3. Women are more vulnerable to stress than men due to their socialization to respond more passively, to introject rather than to express anger, and to use less effective coping skills (Kessler and McLeod, 1984). There is some research to support this notion. In a study of coping techniques used by college students, male students used more problem-focused coping (cognitive and behavioral attempts to control the meaning of the situation) while female students were more likely to use emotion-focused coping (attempting to regulate emotional responses elicited by the situation). Both male and female students rated the problem-focused techniques as being more effective (Ptacek, Smith, and Zanas, 1992). Countering this research is the fact that women appear to cope with many crises as well as or better than men (e.g., women typically deal better with the death of a spouse, with financial difficulties, and with marital separation and divorce).

4. Continuing power differences between women and men in society and within families lead to the gender disparity in distress. Rosenfield (1989, 1992), focusing on married couples, has argued that women's relative lack of decision-making power within the family and the lesser resources and decreased prestige attached to the conventional feminine role of housewife cause and reflect this power differential. How does this affect psychological state?

Low power implies less actual control over the environment and thus lower perceptions of personal control. With diminished assessments of their ability to act on and affect their social world, individuals experience greater psychological distress. Thus . . . women have higher rates of anxious and depressive symptoms because their positions of lower power produce lower actual control and thus lower perceived control than those of men. (Rosenfield, 1989:77-78)

5. A final perspective on this issue asserts that the size of the gender disparity in social stress has been exaggerated and misinterpreted. Aneshensel, Rutter, and Lachenbruch (1991) argue that most stress research has focused on a single disorder or stress outcome and then has assumed that those who have this disorder are victims of stress and those without the disorder are not. For example, much of the research that has found that women report higher rates of depression than men has concluded that women experience more stress. However, they argue that most research has focused on outcomes that are more common in women and neglected to study antisocial personality and alcohol abuse-dependence disorders that are more common among men. If the full gamut of stress outcomes is considered, women and men may be found to experience comparable levels of stress.

Gender, Work, and Psychological Distress. An important implication of these explanations is that women's different levels and types of participation in the workplace create conditions that lead to the gender disparity in distress. This suggests an avenue for study: comparing women who are full-time workers outside the home (both married and unmarried) with women who are employed part-time and with women not employed outside the home. If it is simply a matter of "social roles," then the benefits and liabilities of working should be the same for men and women. If, on the other hand, the effects of employment are conditional on gender (a sex-role perspective), then other factors related to expectations for men and women must be involved (Gore and Mangione, 1983).

Studies addressing these questions have not always produced a coherent picture. Some research has found a reduced disparity in gender distress when the wife is employed, but other research has not. Moreover, some of the research that identifies smaller differences trace

them to increased distress in males rather than a decrease in females. Most research has pointed to positive effects for women who work outside the home, but other research has failed to find differences between employed women and housewives. Even when such a difference is discovered, both groups of women have higher distress scores than employed men.

Efforts to sort through these research findings have produced three primary perspectives: role overload, role enhancement, and role context. The role overload perspective is based on the proposition that there is only so much time and energy in the day. When women couple homemaking, child-rearing, and full-time employment responsibilities, there is role overload—too much work and too many responsibilities—an obviously stressful situation. The same combination of activities may not overload males since they engage in considerably fewer homemaking and child-rearing activities—even when their spouse is employed. Because many women feel primary responsibility for household obligations, and many men do not, it can be more psychologically distressing for women to occupy the multiple roles of spouse, parent, and worker. A recent study of dual career couples in the United States, Sweden, and the Netherlands found that working women in all three countries do more household chores and childcare and make more compromises with their job than do their husbands (Gjerdingen et al., 2000).

The **role enhancement perspective** asserts that the more roles any person fulfills, the greater are the opportunities for social contacts, satisfactions, and self-esteem, and consequently, better health and psychological well-being (Hong and Seltzer, 1995). According to this theory, feelings of anxiety or depression ought to be inversely related to the number of role involvements. This may occur directly or indirectly as contacts made through employment often become the most important nonkin source of social support for women who work outside the home.

The third perspective, **role context** asserts that employment outside the home has neither inherently positive nor negative consequences on stress level but rather is dependent on particular factors within the personal, family, and work environments and on the meaning that is attached to work and familial roles (Simon, 1997). What are these additional factors?

1. *The woman's desire to work outside the home.* Waldron and Herold (1986) have demonstrated the importance of attitude towards the effects of employment. Based on a national sample of middle-aged women, they found that for women who desired to work outside the home, employment had beneficial effects and nonemployment had detrimental effects. No specific effects were noted for women who were unfavorable or neutral toward outside employment.

2. *The woman's perception of the balance of benefits and liabilities in outside employment.* The greater the "role integration"—the balance of role satisfaction and role stress within and between roles—the greater is the sense of well-being. This is related to number of roles. Thoits (1986) posits a curvilinear relationship between number of role involvements and well-being; that is, there is role enhancement up to a certain threshold whereupon role overload begins. Well-being is also affected by the compatibility of the work role with other roles (e.g., child care), the extent to which each can be handled, and the amount of spousal support received for the work career. Spousal support is jeopardized, however, if husbands are distressed by their wives' outside employment—something that often happens when the husband's relative share of the household income decreases or demands that his contribution to household domestic labor increase (Rosenfield, 1992).

Bird (1999) discovered that inequity in the division of household labor creates more stress than does the actual amount of labor performed. Her research confirmed that women continue to do a greater percentage of household chores, that husbands' contributions were about what they desired, but that wives' contributions went beyond the point of maximum psychological benefit.

3. *Qualities of the work environment itself.* Because women, on average, continue to occupy more lower level positions than men, they are subject to greater stress relative to work conditions, sexual harassment, and job instability (Lennon, 1987). Workplaces in which gender discrimination is perceived add another important source of stress for women that has been linked with negative health outcomes (Pavalko et al. 2003).

Two aspects of the working environment that are particularly important are autonomy/control and work complexity. Much research confirms that women are more likely than men to occupy positions with little autonomy or control and that lack of control on the job is related to psychological distress. Work complexity involves the amount of variability on the job and is an indicator of its degree of challenge, its level of interest, the extent to which it is psychologically gratifying, and the likelihood that it will contribute to the individual's self-esteem (Pugliesi, 1995). To the extent that men are more likely than women to hold positions higher in the occupational hierarchy, they have access to these greater rewards.

It is clear that employment affects women differently and in more complicated ways in situations in which women are expected to be the primary household managers and child rearers. According to Rosenfield (1989), women's employment does provide them greater power and a greater sense of personal control. These are health enhancers. However, something else occurs simultaneously—something that occurs with lesser intensity for men—and that is the likelihood of role overload when work responsibilities are added to being the primary household/child caretaker. This role overload decreases feelings of personal control—a health negater. The complex maze of possibilities within this configuration of roles will require substantial additional research to be fully understood.

SUMMARY

Stress has been defined as "a state of imbalance within a person, elicited by an actual or perceived disparity between environmental demands and the person's capacity to cope with these demands." The configuration of the stress process can be stated in this way: various stressful situations (or stressors) occur and are appraised by the individual as to their degree of threat. Individuals are forced to cope with those situations involving some threat; stressors that are unsuccessfully resolved lead to negative stress outcomes. Throughout the process, social support can help mediate the stress-stress outcome relationship.

Stressors are of two basic types: specific life events and chronic strains (the latter being more enduring problems in everyday life). Pearlin has classified chronic strains according to problems created in discharging our role obligations: (1) role overload, (2) interpersonal problems within role sets, (3) interrole conflict, (4) role captivity, and (5) role restructuring.

Interpretation and appraisal of stressors are key aspects of the stress process. It is the perceived threat, rather than the actual threat, to which a person responds. If a threat is perceived, the individual may activate certain coping responses (psychological, cognitive, and behavioral techniques) from his or her repertoire, and also use social support. Negative stress outcomes occur through the individual's taking on certain health-impairing behaviors, such as cigarette smoking, or through specific psychophysiological changes including a weakening of the immune system.

Certain groups have higher rates of psychological distress: those with less income (who are exposed to more stressful life events and have fewer resources to combat them); African Americans (though the issue of whether this can simply be attributed to economics or whether race constitutes an added factor in creating stress is unresolved); and females (possibly due to women being exposed to more stressful life events, caring more about others' problems, being especially vulnerable to stress due to the effects of socialization, and responding to having less access to power within families and within society). Employment affects stress level differently for women than men; this may be due to the fact that women often maintain primary responsibility for household tasks and child rearing, even when they are in the labor force.

HEALTH ON THE INTERNET

A significant trend in the United States is the rapidly increasing number of households that are caring for elderly relatives (often taking them into their home). More than 20 million households provide this caregiving today, and the number is expected to jump to almost 40 million in the next five years. This trend is a consequence of the increasing number of people who are living into their 80s and 90s, often with limitation on their ability to care for themselves, *and* the very high cost of assisted living and nursing home care.

To learn more about the relationship between caregiving and social stress, check out the following Web site:

http://www.4woman.gov/faq/caregiver.htm

Answer the following questions: What activities do caregivers often provide? What is caregiver stress? What can caregivers do to prevent stress and burnout?

KEY CONCEPTS AND TERMS

anomie
appraise
buffering effects model of social support

caregiver stress
chronic strains
coping

exposure hypothesis
general adaptation syndrome
hardiness
homeostasis
interpersonal problems within role sets
interrole conflict
life events
looking-glass self
main effects model of social support
mediator
role captivity
role context perspective

role enhancement perspective
role overload
role restructuring
social construction of reality
social support
sociological imagination
stress
stressor
stress outcomes
symbolic interactionism
Thomas Theorem
vulnerability hypothesis

DISCUSSION CASE

The stress process as it relates to racial and ethnic minorities and to women was discussed in this chapter. Think about social stress as it relates to racial and ethnic minorities and female students at your college or university. Are racial and ethnic minority students and female students more likely (or less likely) to face any particular stressful discrete life events than those faced by all students? Are racial and ethnic minority students and female students more likely (or less likely) to face any of the five sources of chronic strain (role overload, interpersonal conflicts within role sets, interrole conflict, role captivity, and role restructuring) than those faced by all students?

Do racial and ethnic minority students cope with stress or use social support differently than other students? Do female students cope with stress or use social support differently than male students?

REFERENCES

Aneshensel, Carol S., Carolyn M. Rutter, and Peter A. Lachenbruch. 1991 "Social Structure, Stress, and Mental Health: Competing Conceptual and Analytic Models." *American Sociological Review,* 56:166–178.

Atkinson, Thomas, Ramsay Liem, and Joan H. Liem. 1986 "The Social Costs of Unemployment: Implications for Social Support." *Journal of Health and Social Behavior,* 27:317–331.

Avison, William R., and R. Jay Turner. 1988 "Stressful Life Events and Depressive Symptoms: Disaggregating the Effects of Acute Stressors and Chronic Strains." *Journal of Health and Social Behavior,* 29:253–264.

Berger, Peter L., and Thomas Luckmann. 1967 *The Social Construction of Reality: A Treatise in the Sociology of Knowledge.* Garden City, NY: Anchor Books.

Bird, Chloe E. 1999 "Gender, Household Labor, and Psychological Distress: The Impact of the Amount and Division of Housework." *Journal of Health and Social Behavior,* 40:32–45.

Brantley, Philip J., Craig D. Waggoner, Glenn N. Jones, and Neil B. Rappaport. 1987 "A Daily Stress Inventory: Development, Reliability." *Journal of Behavioral Medicine,* 10:61–74.

Brenner, Harvey M. 1973 *Mental Illness and the Economy.* Cambridge, MA: Harvard University Press.

Brown, Barbara B. 1984 *Between Health and Illness.* New York: Bantam Books.

Bruess, Clint, and Glenn Richardson. 1995 *Decisions for Health* (4th Ed.). Dubuque, IA: Brown & Benchmark Publishers.

Cooley, Charles H. 1964 *Human Nature and the Social Order.* New York: Schocken.

DeLongis, Anita, Susan Folkman, and Richard S. Lazarus. 1988 "The Impact of Daily Stress on Health and Mood: Psychological and Social Resources as Mediators." *Journal of Personality and Social Psychology,* 54:486–495.

Dohrenwend, Bruce P. 2000 "The Role of Adversity and Stress in Psychopathology: Some Evidence and Its Implications for Theory and

Research." *Journal of Health and Social Behavior,* 41:1–19.

Durkheim, Emile. trans., 1951 *Suicide: A Study in Sociology.* New York: The Free Press.

Edwards, Angela C., James Y. Nazroo, and George W. Brown. 1998 "Gender Differences in Marital Support Following a Shared Life Event." *Social Science and Medicine,* 46:1077–1085.

Fischer, Kathy E., Mark Kittleson, Roberta Ogletree, Kathleen Welshimer, Paula Woehlke, and John Benshoff. 2000 "The Relationship of Parental Alcoholism and Family Dysfunction to Stress Among College Students." *Journal of American College Health,* 48:151–156.

Gjerdingen, Dwenda, Patricia McGovern, Marrie Bekker, Ulf Lundberg, and Tineke Willemsen. 2000 "Women's Work Roles and Their Impact on Health, Well-Being, and Career: Comparisons Between the United States, Sweden, and the Netherlands." *Women and Health,* 31:1–20.

Gore, Susan, and Thomas W. Mangione. 1983 "Social Roles, Sex Roles and Psychological Distress: Additive and Interactive Models of Sex Differences." *Journal of Health and Social Behavior,* 24:300–312.

Holmes, Thomas H., and Richard H. Rahe. 1967 "The Social Readjustment Rating Scale." *Journal of Psychosomatic Research,* 11:213–218.

Hong, Jinkuk, and Marsha M. Seltzer. 1995 "The Psychological Consequences of Multiple Roles: The Nonnormative Case." *Journal of Health and Social Behavior,* 36:386–398.

Jacobson, David E. 1986 "Types and Timing of Social Support." *Journal of Health and Social Behavior,* 27:250–264.

Keith, Verna M. 1993 "Gender, Financial Strain, and Psychological Distress Among Older Adults." *Research on Aging,* 15:123–147.

Kessler, Ronald C., and Harold W. Neighbors. 1986 "A New Perspective on the Relationships Among Race, Social Class, and Psychological Distress." *Journal of Health and Social Behavior,* 27:107–115.

Kessler, Ronald C., and Jane D. McLeod. 1984 "Sex Differences in Vulnerability to Undesirable Life Events." *American Sociological Review,* 49:620–631.

Kessler, Ronald C., Richard H. Price, and Camille B. Wortman. 1985 "Social Factors in Psychopathology: Stress, Social Support, and Coping Processes." *Annual Review of Psychology,* 36:531–572.

Kobasa, Suzanne C. 1979 "Stressful Life Events, Personality, and Health: An Inquiry into Hardiness." *Journal of Personality and Social Psychology,* 37:1–11.

Lennon, Mary C. 1987 "Sex Differences in Distress: The Impact of Gender and Work Roles." *Journal of Health and Social Behavior,* 28:290–305.

Lieberman, Morton A. 1982 "The Effects of Social Supports on Responses to Stress," pp. 764–783 in *Handbook of Stress: Theoretical and Clinical Aspects,* Leo Goldberger and Shlomo Breznitz (eds.). New York: The Free Press.

Lim, Vivien K.G., and Edith C. Yuen. 1998 "Doctors, Patients, and Perceived Job Image: Am Empirical Study of Stress and Nurses in Singapore." *Journal of Behavioral Medicine,* 21:269–282.

Lincoln, Karen D., Linda M. Chatters, and Robert J. Taylor. 2003 "Psychological Distress Among Black and White Americans: Differential Effects of Social Support, Negative Interaction, and Personal Control." *Journal of Health and Social Behavior,* 44:390–407.

McLeod, Jane D., and Ronald C. Kessler. 1990 "Socioeconomic Status Differences in Vulnerability to Undesirable Life Events." *Journal of Health and Social Behavior,* 31:162–172.

Mossakowski, Krysia N. 2003 "Coping With Perceived Discrimination: Does Ethnic Identity Protect Mental Health?" *Journal of Health and Social Behavior,* 44:318–331.

Pavalko, Eliza K., Krysia N. Mossakowski, and Vanessa J. Hamilton. 2003 "Does Perceived Discrimination Affect Health? Longitudinal Relationships Between Work Discrimination and Women's Physical and Emotional Health." *Journal of Health and Social Behavior,* 43:18–33.

Pavalko, Eliza K., and Shari Woodbury. 2000 "Social Roles as Process: Caregiving Careers and Women's Health." *Journal of Health and Social Behavior,* 41:91–105.

Pearlin, Leonard I. 1983 "Role Strains and Personal Stress," pp. 3–32 in *Psychosocial Stress: Trends in Theory and Research,* Howard B. Kaplan (ed.). New York: Academic Press.

———. 1989 "The Sociological Study of Stress." *Journal of Health and Social Behavior,* 30:241–256.

Pearlin, Leonard I., and Carol S. Aneshensel. 1986 "Coping and Social Supports: Their Functions and Applications," pp. 417–437 in *Application of Social Science to Clinical Medicine and Health Policy,* Linda H. Aiken and David Mechanic (eds.). New Brunswick, N.J.: Rutgers University Press.

Pearlin, Leonard I., and Carmi Schooler. 1978 "The Structure of Coping." *Journal of Health and Social Behavior,* 19:2–21.

Penley, Julie A., Joe Tamaka, and John S. Wiebe. 2002 "The Association of Coping to Physical and Psychological Health Outcomes: A Meta-Analytic Review." *Journal of Behavioral Medicine,* 25:551–603.

Ptacek, J. T., Ronald E. Smith, and John Zanas. 1992 "Gender, Appraisal, and Coping: A Longitudinal Analysis." *Journal of Personality,* 60:747–770.

Pugliesi, Karen. 1995 "Work and Well-Being: Gender Differences in the Psychological Consequences of Employment." *Journal of Health and Social Behavior,* 36:57–71.

Rosenfield, Sarah. 1989 "The Effects of Women's Employment: Personal Control and Sex Differences in Mental Health." *Journal of Health and Social Behavior,* 30:77–91.

———. 1992 "The Costs of Sharing: Wives' Employment and Husbands' Mental Health." *Journal of Health and Social Behavior,* 33:213–225.

Schulz, A., B. Israel, D. Williams, E. Parker, A. Becker, and S. James. 2000 "Social Inequalities, Stressors and Self-Reported Health Status Among African American and White Women in the Detroit Metropolitan Area." *Social Science and Medicine,* 51:1639–1653.

Schwab, Reiko. 1990 "Paternal and Maternal Coping With the Death of a Child." *Death Studies.* 14:407–422.

Sellers, Robert M., Cleopatra H. Caldwell, Karen H. Schmeelk-Cone, and Marc A. Zimmerman. 2003 "Racial Identity, Racial Discrimination, Perceived Stress, and Psychological Distress Among African-American Young Adults." *Journal of Health and Social Behavior,* 43:302–317.

Simon, Robin W. 1997 "The Meanings Individuals Attach to Role Identities and Their Implications for Mental Health." *Journal of Health and Social Behavior,* 38:256–274.

Stoklos, D. 1986 "A Congruence Analysis of Human Stress," pp. 35–64 in *Stress and Anxiety: A Sourcebook of Theory and Research,* C. D. Spielberger and I. G. Sarason (eds.). Washington, DC: Hemisphere.

Thoits, Peggy A. 1986 "Multiple Identities: Examining Gender and Marital Status Differences in Distress." *American Sociological Review,* 51:259–272.

Turner, R. Jay, and Donald A. Lloyd. 1999 "The Stress Process and the Social Distribution of Depression." *Journal of Health and Social Behavior,* 40:374–404.

Turner, R. Jay, Blair Wheaton, and Donald A. Lloyd. 1995 "The Epidemiology of Social Stress." *American Sociological Review,* 60:104–125.

Turner, R. Jay, and William R. Avison. 2003 "Status Variations in Stress Exposure Among Young Adults: Implications for the Interpretation of Prior Research." *Journal of Health and Social Behavior,* 44:488–505.

Ulbrich, Patricia M., George J. Warheit, and Rick S. Zimmerman. 1989 "Race, Socioeconomic Status, and Psychological Distress: An Examination of Differential Vulnerability." *Journal of Health and Social Behavior,* 30:131–146.

Waldron, Ingrid, and Joan Herold. 1986 "Employment, Attitudes Toward Employment, and Women's Health." *Women and Health,* 11:79–98.

Wellman, Barry, and Scot Wortley. 1990 "Different Strokes from Different Folks: Community Ties and Social Support." *American Journal of Sociology,* 96:558–588.

6

HEALTH BEHAVIOR

Through much of its history, medical sociology has directed far more attention to disease and illness than to health and wellness. Today, medical sociologists, as well as the medical profession and society in general, are seeking more balance in their focus and are studying health more closely.

This expanded focus has produced some important questions. What does it mean to be "healthy" or "well"? How does society encourage healthy lifestyles? To what extent do people engage in behaviors that promote health—or, at least, to what extent do they not engage in health-damaging behaviors? And, what are the strongest influences on participation in these positive and negative health behaviors?

THE CONCEPT OF HEALTH

There is no consensus about what traits constitute a genuinely "healthy" person, and researchers operationalize the concept of health in many ways. John Ware (1986) reviewed the literature of studies on health and identified six primary orientations (or dimensions) used by researchers:

1. *Physical functioning*—focuses on physical limitations regarding ability to take care of self, being mobile, and participating in physical activities; ability to perform everyday activities; and number of days confined to bed.
2. *Mental health*—focuses on feelings of anxiety and depression, psychological well-being, and control of emotions and behaviors.
3. *Social well-being*—focuses on visiting with or speaking on the telephone with friends and family and the number of close friends and acquaintances.
4. *Role functioning*—focuses on freedom of limitations in discharging usual role activities such as work or school.
5. *General health perceptions*—focuses on self-assessment of current health status and amount of pain being experienced.
6. *Symptoms*—focuses on reports of physical and psychophysiologic symptoms.

The Biomedical Focus

The traditional **biomedical definition of health** focuses solely on the individual's physiological state and the presence or absence of symptoms of sickness. *Health* is defined simply as the absence of disease or physiological malfunction; it is not a positive state, but the absence of a negative state—if you're not sick, you're well. According to Wolinsky (1988), the biomedical model makes four primary assumptions that limit its utility for completely understanding health and illness:

1. The presence of disease, its diagnosis, and its treatment are all completely objective phenomena: symptoms and signs provide accurate and unbiased information from which valid diagnosis can unfailingly be made. However, this assumption is faulty. For example, studies have found that individuals' cultural backgrounds affect not only reaction to symptoms but also how these symptoms are reported to physicians and that the presentation of symptoms can influence diagnosis (Zola, 1966; Mechanic, 1980).

2. Only medical professionals are capable of defining health and illness. In reality, however, both the patient and her or his significant others are involved in the process. While one must not discount the power that society has granted to physicians for defining health and illness, a great deal of diagnosing and treatment occur outside the physician's office.

3. Health and illness should be defined solely in terms of physiological malfunction. In fact, people are not merely biological beings; they are also psychological and social creatures, and the state of health is affected by all three aspects.

4. Health is defined as merely the absence of disease. This focuses attention on the malfunctioning part of the organism but excludes the rest of the positively functioning being. Thus, much may be learned about disease, but little is known about health.

The Sociological (Sociocultural) Approach

The **sociological definition of health** typically considers all of the six dimensions in defining health and emphasize the social and cultural aspects of health and illness. This approach focuses on the individual's capacity to perform roles and tasks in everyday living and acknowledges that there are social differences in defining health.

Capacity to Perform Roles and Tasks. Objecting to the biomedical definition, Talcott Parsons suggested that health be viewed as the ability to comply with social norms. He defined health as, "the state of optimum capacity of an individual for the effective performance of the roles and tasks for which he has been socialized" (Parsons, 1972:123). Note the almost completely opposite orientation of this definition to the biomedical approach: No assumption is made that disease can be objectified; the focus is much broader (and more socially relevant) than mere physiological malfunctioning; the individual's own definition of his or her health is given centrality (rather than the physician's definition); and the definition is stated in positive terms. According to this approach, health is not just the lack of something—it is a positive capacity to fulfill one's roles; it is not just a physiological condition—it includes all the dimensions of individuals that impact on social participation.

Social Differences in Defining Health. Twaddle (1974) sees health as being defined more by social than physical criteria. He views health and illness as being on a continuum between the perfect state of health and the perfect state of illness (death). While "normal" health and illness fall somewhere between the two extremes, what may be considered a healthy state for one person may be considered unhealthy by another. Perception of health is relative to one's culture (e.g., being ten pounds overweight is suggestive of ill health in some cultures but is socially approved in others) and one's position in the social structure (e.g., back pain that may cause a salaried worker to miss a day of work might be ignored by an hourly wage worker) and is influenced by social criteria.

Research has demonstrated that social factors do influence how individuals define personal health status. For example, data from the Health and Lifestyle Survey, a national survey of men and women living in England, Wales, and Scotland, show that personal definitions of health vary by age, gender, and perceived level of health. Younger men conceptualize health in terms of physical strength and fitness, whereas their female counterparts are more focused on energy, vitality, and the ability to cope. Older men and women consider health in terms of function as well as a state of contentment and happiness. Women of all ages often include social relationships in their definitions while men rarely do so (Blaxter, 1990).

The World Health Organization Definition

The World Health Organization takes an inclusive approach by defining health as a state of complete physical, social, and mental well being. This definition suggests that health relates to one's ability to cope with everyday activities and to being a fully functioning human being— physically, socially, and emotionally. In this sense, health is a resource for everyday life. It is a positive concept emphasizing social and personal resources as well as physical capacities (World Health Organization, 1986).

HEALTH BEHAVIOR

When medical sociologists first began to study **health behavior**, they conceptualized it as activity undertaken by an individual believing himself or herself to be healthy for the purpose of preventing health problems (Kasl and Cobb, 1966). In recent years, sociologists have recognized that health behavior actually consists of several dimensions and types of activities. Alonzo (1993) has identified four separate dimensions:

1. *Prevention.* The goal of preventive health behavior (**prevention**) is to minimize the risk of disease, injury, and disability. These "health-protective behaviors" include participating in regular exercise, maintaining a favorable weight and healthy diet, not smoking, and obtaining immunizations against communicable diseases.

2. *Detection.* **Detection** involves activities to detect disease, injury, or disability before symptoms appear and includes medical examinations (such as taking the blood pressure) or screenings for specific diseases.

3. *Promotion.* **Health promotion activities** consist of efforts to encourage and persuade individuals to engage in health-promoting behaviors and to avoid or disengage health-harming behaviors.

4. *Protection.* **Health protection activities** occur at the societal rather than the individual level and include efforts to make the environment in which people live as healthy as possible. Doing this involves monitoring the physical and social environments in which people live; physical structures and infrastructures; systems of transportation; available food, air, and water; places of work; and developing social and economic policies that permit and encourage good health.

DESCRIBING INDIVIDUAL HEALTH BEHAVIORS

Prevention

Health-protective behaviors (HPBs) are individual actions taken to protect, promote, or maintain health. These actions are both prescriptive in nature (e.g., eat a nutritious diet, wear a seat belt when in a car, get adequate exercise) and proscriptive (e.g., avoid unsafe driving, smoking, and excessive alcohol consumption).

Through much of the 1980s and 1990s, *Prevention Magazine* teamed with a polling/survey research organization to conduct an annual survey of participation in health-protective behaviors. Beginning in 1983 (which became the 1984 **Prevention Index**), a random sample of Americans was surveyed regarding participation in 21 key HPBs. To facilitate longitudinal comparisons, all research procedures were identical each year. Results of the survey were published in *Prevention Magazine* and in a separate document entitled *Summary Report—The Prevention Index: A Report Card on the Nation's Health*. Both the validity and reliability of the Index were demonstrated, but responses must be interpreted with some caution because this type of behavioral research has the potential to produce socially favorable responses (respondents giving answers that they believe are more socially acceptable).

Table 6–1 reports results of the 1995 Prevention Index. The 21 HPBs are listed in order from the most to the least participation. The composite score—the Prevention Index—ranges from zero (if no one participated in any of the HPBs) to 100 (if everyone participated in all 21 behaviors). Roughly, it can also be interpreted as the mean percentage of the 21 behaviors engaged in by respondents. The overall score for the Prevention Index for 1995 was 65.6, meaning that the average respondent engaged in about two-thirds of the 21 behaviors. Ultimately, the survey was discontinued because the index score changed very little from year to year.

The behaviors that inspire the highest participation rate include avoiding smoking in bed (93 percent do not smoke in bed); having a smoke detector in the home (93 percent do); drinking alcohol moderately (89 percent drink moderately); and socializing on a regular basis (86 percent do so). By far, the behavior with the lowest reported rate of participation is maintaining the proper weight (only 18 percent do). Other low rates of participation are for getting frequent strenuous exercise (37 percent do); limiting sugar in the diet (40 percent do); limiting cholesterol in the diet (45 percent do); and limiting sodium in the diet (47 percent do).

Blaxter's (1990) national study of individual lifestyles reports findings consistent with the Prevention Index. Her research revealed that few individuals' lifestyles are totally healthy or totally unhealthy. Only 15 percent of those she surveyed had healthy habits in all four areas she investigated (smoking, alcohol consumption,

TABLE 6–1   The 1995 Prevention Index

Health-Protective Behavior	Percentage of Adults Practicing
Avoid smoking in bed	93
Smoke detector in home	93
Drink alcohol moderately	89
Socialize regularly	86
Avoid driving after drinking	85
Annual blood pressure test	84
Avoid home accidents	75
Do not smoke	74
Wear seat belt	73
Annual dental examination	73
Control stress	70
Adequate vitamins/minerals	59
7–8 hours sleep per night	59
Consume fiber	54
Limit fat in diet	53
Obey speed limit	48
Limit sodium in diet	47
Limit cholesterol in diet	45
Limit sugar in diet	40
Frequent strenuous exercise	37
Maintain proper weight	18

Source: *Summary Report: The Prevention Index, 1995: A Report Card on the Nation's Health*. Emmaus, PA: *Prevention Magazine*, 1995.

exercise, and diet), and just 5 percent had unhealthy habits in all areas.

What is the summary picture in the three key areas of cigarette smoking, diet and exercise, and excessive alcohol consumption? It is widely agreed that cigarette smoking is the single most damaging behavior in which we can engage. According to studies that have traced deaths back to the actual cause, tobacco is responsible for more deaths (an estimated 19 percent of deaths in the United States each year) than any other factor (McGinnis and Foege, 1993). Nevertheless, about one-fourth of American adults smoke cigarettes. Though that fraction is down from one-half who smoked 40 years ago, it still represents more than 50 million smokers. Approximately half of all smokers today began before the age of 18, and more than 3,000 teenagers become regular smokers each day in the United States.

Poor diet (especially being high in sugar and fat) and inadequate exercise combine to lead to

IN THE FIELD

THE INCREASING PROBLEM OF OBESITY IN AMERICA

In the United States, 65 percent of the adult population is at least ten pounds over their recommended weight (compared to only 25 percent in 1960). Recent statistics show that 34 percent of adults are *overweight*—from 10 to 30 pounds over a healthy weight—and 31 percent of adults are *obese*—more than 30 pounds over a healthy weight. Of those in the latter category, 2 percent (about 4 million people) are *extremely obese*—more than 100 pounds over a healthy weight. On average, individual weight in the United States is increasing by 1 to 2 pounds per year. Between 1986 and 2000, there was a 216 percent increase in the number of obese individuals and a 389 percent increase in the number of extremely obese individuals. Obesity is becoming a worldwide problem, but the United States has the largest percentage of its population that is obese. Obesity increases dramatically in the late teens and 20s, but an alarmingly high percentage of children and adolescents are overweight. The percentage of 12- to 19-year-olds who are obese tripled between 1976 and 2000.

The consequences of this pattern are clear. Obesity increases the likelihood of heart disease, diabetes, cancer, high blood pressure, arthritis, and premature death (Fontaine et al. 2003). Estimates are that overweight nonsmokers lose three years of life, that obese nonsmokers lost 7 years of life, and that obese smokers lose 13 years of life.

What has caused this dramatic shift towards weight gain? There is some genetic predisposition to obesity (e.g., genes that influence appetite control) and there are physiological influences on hunger. For some individuals, these factors are the primary culprit. But, these factors have not changed over time and do not explain the escalating figures. The primary reason for weight gain is a high calorie, low physical activity lifestyle. People are eating more and more, the foods we eat are larger in portion size and contain more calories and more fat, and we consume many more calories per day than are required. The average adult American ate 140 more pounds of food in the year 2000 than in 1990. In addition fewer than half of adults get the recommended amount of exercise: 20 to 30 minutes per day on most days of the week.

obesity and to be the second most dangerous lifestyle pattern. Together, dietary factors and inadequate exercise are estimated to account for about 14 percent of deaths annually in the United States (McGinnis and Foege, 1993). Between 1984 and 1995, Americans became slightly more likely to engage in almost all of the 21 HPBs included in the Prevention Index. However, participation dropped by at least ten points during the survey years for each of three items: driving below the speed limit, avoiding too much sugar in the diet, and not being overweight.

Excessive alcohol consumption is the behavior that contributes to the third largest number of deaths in the United States (about 5 of every 100 deaths) and is a problem for 10 to 15 percent of adult Americans (McGinnis and Foege, 1993). Unlike the percentage of smokers (which is going down) or the percentage of persons considered to be obese (which is going up), the percentage of persons who drink excessively has remained at about the same level for at least the last decade.

The Multidimensional Basis of HPBs. Almost all research has discovered individual HPBs to have very small intercorrelations. This means that individual behaviors are often not related—engaging in one particular HPB (e.g., drinking in moderation) does not automatically mean (or even increase the chances of) engaging in another HPB (e.g., getting adequate exercise). For example, men are much more likely than women to get more exercise and to drink immoderately (perhaps both reflecting a traditional male ethic).

IN THE FIELD

BINGE DRINKING ON COLLEGE CAMPUSES

In response to several binge drinking-related deaths among college students in the early 1990s, the Harvard School of Public Health conducted a national survey in 1993 to accurately describe the prevalence of binge drinking on campus. They defined binge drinking as the consumption of at least five drinks in a row for males or four drinks in a row for females during the two weeks prior to the survey. Based on this definition, they determined that 44 percent of students were binge drinkers.

Prompted by the publicity surrounding the deaths and the widely disseminated findings of the study, many institutions decided to challenge the traditional notion that binge drinking is simply part of the college experience. Drinking awareness and education courses were developed, alcohol counselors were employed, and more stringent college rules were established. However, follow-up surveys conducted in 1997 and 1999 found that the percentage of binge drinkers on campus was essentially unchanged. What happened? Why did all of the interventions basically not make a dent in the rate of binge drinking?

Close analysis of the data discovered that at least two significant changes did occur during the 1990s. Reflecting some increasing polarization on campus, both the rate of abstention (19 percent in 1999) and the rate of *frequent* binge drinking—three or more binges in the previous two weeks (23 percent in 1999) increased during the decade. Further, while binge drinking among dormitory residents actually declined in the 1990s, it increased among students living off campus—especially among those living in fraternity and sorority houses. Thus, the gaps between nondrinkers/light drinkers and intensive drinkers and between Greeks and non-Greeks widened. The study found that, while binging occurs among all campus subgroups, the rate is especially high among white male fraternity members.

To what extent are students aware of binge drinking on their campus and to what extent do they view it as a problem? The Harvard survey discovered that half of students underestimated the binge drinking rate on their campus (29 percent overestimated it, and only 13 percent were on target). Binge drinkers were especially likely to *overestimate* the campus rate. Researchers found little of a healthy alcohol-related social norm among fraternity members. They view their level of consumption as being the same as their close friends (positive reinforcement) and do not see binging as a negative health behavior (Keeling 2002).

At this point, many institutions are undertaking systematic research projects to test the effectiveness of various types of interventions. The negative effects of binge drinking on personal health, classroom performance, and civic behavior have been well documented. But, the best means for addressing the prevalence of binging are yet to be understood (Keeling, 2000; Wechsler et al., 2000).

Nevertheless, some consistent relationships between HPBs do exist. Some studies have found a positive relationship between smoking and alcohol consumption and between alcohol consumption and poor dietary habits. While level of exercise is highly dependent on age, in general, those who eat nutritiously are more likely to exercise than those who eat poorly. In fact, among those over age 60, smokers and drinkers with a good diet are more than twice as likely to exercise vigorously as nonsmokers and nondrinkers with a poor diet (Blaxter, 1990).

Correlates of Participation in HPBs. Participation in many of the health-protective behaviors is related to such sociodemographic characteristics as age, gender, race, education, and income. For example, studies have consistently found that females are more likely than males to engage in health-protective behaviors. Women are more likely to wear seat belts, less likely to smoke cigarettes and to be heavy smokers, and less likely to drink alcohol excessively (men are three to four times more likely to be classified as problem drinkers). However, a much higher percentage of men than women get adequate exercise. Overall, however, women, especially young women, are more likely to lead a healthy lifestyle.

Level of education, occupation, and income also affect participation in HPBs. Blaxter (1990) found that those having high incomes were more likely to have a healthy lifestyle, especially among older people. People working in occupations requiring higher levels of education practiced more healthy lifestyles than those working in jobs requiring less education. Lower levels of education are strongly associated with smoking and are related to obesity and lack of exercise. People with lower incomes are more likely to smoke, less likely to exercise, and less likely to wear a seat belt.

Black women are more likely to be obese and less likely to be physically active than white women, though these differences may be explained by differences in education, income, social networks, and life events. On the other hand, smoking rates of black and white women are nearly identical, and about the same percentage of blacks and whites use seat belts.

Table 6–2 reports correlates for one of the key health-protective behaviors, exercising. Males, younger persons, those with more education and earning higher incomes, and those with self-described excellent health are most likely to exercise strenuously three or more times per week.

Detection

Today, a wide range of health screening procedures are available, including periodic physical examinations, eye and dental examinations, blood pressure and cholesterol readings, prenatal and well-baby care, and screenings to detect cancer. These procedures are designed to identify and monitor health problems. Much research has

TABLE 6–2   Strenuous Exercise by Background Characteristics

Total	Percentage Who Exercise Strenuously Three or More Times per Week
All Adults	37
Region	
East	34
South	35
Midwest	33
West	49
Gender	
Male	45
Female	30
Age	
18 to 29	48
30 to 39	44
40 to 49	30
50 to 64	33
65 or over	26
Education	
Not high school graduate	29
High school graduate	37
Some college	43
College graduate	38
Income	
$7,500 or less	32
$7,501 to $15,000	31
$15,001 to $25,000	37
$25,001 to $35,000	39
$35,001 to $50,000	37
Over $50,000	45
Self-assessed Health Status	
Excellent	51
Very good/good	35
Fair/poor	30

Source: *Summary Report: The Prevention Index, 1995: A Report Card on the Nation's Health.* Emmaus, PA: *Prevention Magazine,* 1995.

demonstrated considerable health and cost benefits of participation in these services.

Correlates of Participation in Detection Services. Because these detection services are so effective, the question becomes why more people do not use them. One important reason is that the cost of some of these services discourages participation by people with low incomes and inadequate or no health insurance (Faulkner, 1997). In the United States, low-income women receive one-third less prenatal care, and children from poor families are only one-fourth as likely as children in nonpoor families to have a routine physical examination.

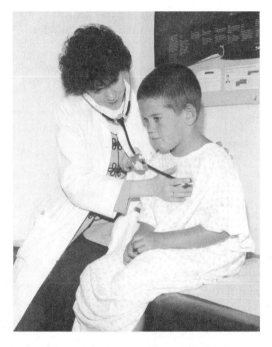

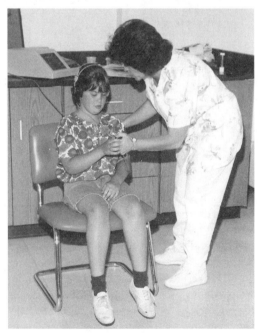

Detection activities, such as health screenings, eye and dental examinations, and blood pressure readings, represent one aspect of the four dimensions of health behavior.

Table 6–3, based on the 1992 Prevention Index (these data were not reported in later surveys), displays the relationship between several types of preventive health measures and health insurance status. For five of the measures, those with health insurance have significantly higher rates of participation than those without insurance coverage. The one exception? Conducting a monthly breast self-exam by women—the only activity of the six that could always be done at no charge. This study suggests that people without health insurance in this survey did not lack motivation for preventive health action—they lacked financial or physical resources to obtain it. Other studies have found that individuals who prepay for their health care services and do not incur any expense in using preventive care services are more likely than those who pay out-of-pocket to receive a breast exam, a Pap smear, a digital rectal exam, a blood stool test, and a mammogram.

Cost of services can be calculated in ways other than not having enough money or not having insurance coverage. It also includes not having access to a physician, not being able to get off work (without losing wages) to visit a physician, and ultimately, becoming accustomed to going without care. When funds are unavailable or physicians inaccessible, some families forego detection services hoping to stay well without them.

Similarly, many poor parents forego any medical contacts for themselves so that whatever funds are available can be used for their children. Research on families who receive services at free health clinics—where services typically are offered at no charge by volunteer physicians and dentists—has found that many parents bring children to the clinic for preventive or therapeutic care but do not ask to be seen themselves. Often, when staff inquire, the parent acknowledges having some medical problems that could be addressed by clinic staff personnel. But, the parent has become so accustomed to doing without medical care that no request for personal services is made (Weiss, 1984).

IN COMPARATIVE FOCUS

PROVIDING PRENATAL CARE IN WESTERN EUROPE

The fact that many countries in the world have a lower infant mortality rate than the United States was documented in Chapter 3. A key part of the explanation for this pattern is that a higher percentage of babies born in the United States have low birth weight. Epidemiologists state that the most effective means for reducing the number of low-birth-weight babies is increasing access to prenatal care for all pregnant women.

Why do other countries do better than the United States? McQuide, Delvaux, and Buekens (2000) examined the situation in 17 Western European nations and determined that all provide comprehensive and accessible prenatal care at no charge to all women. Unlike the United States, no woman is ever turned aside due to inability to pay or lack of available services. All of these countries offer universal coverage for health services, readily available prenatal clinics, and special outreach programs for high-risk pregnant women and for postpartum care. In some countries, there are additional pregnancy (financial) allowances and the provision of prenatal care at work sites.

How do these countries afford this? The irony is that they save money by guaranteeing prenatal care to all women. Studies conducted in the United States have determined that the average hospital delivery charge is almost twice as much for women who have not received prenatal care as for those who have (because of the greater likelihood of problem births) and that significantly greater expenses are incurred at least through childhood and adolescence (Henderson, 1994). Those who advocate guaranteeing prenatal care in the United States cite economic reasons as well as moral reasons for their rationale.

If the United States guaranteed adequate prenatal care, would the infant mortality differential between the poor and the nonpoor disappear? Much of it would, but probably not all of it. Continuing differences in such areas as nutrition, general health of the mother, and health knowledge may mean some differential would remain (as it has in other countries), but the social class difference is much smaller in other countries than in the United States.

TABLE 6–3   Use of Detection Services by Insurance Coverage

Detection Service	Percentage with Health Insurance Using	Percentage Without Health Insurance Using
At least annual blood pressure reading	88	68
At least annual cholesterol test	59	38
At least annual dental check-up	79	62
(Women Only)		
Pap smear at least every one or two years	83	72
Monthly breast self-exam	46	61
Mammogram at least every two years	49	32

Source: *Summary Report: The Prevention Index, 1992: A Report Card on the Nation's Health.* Emmaus, PA: *Prevention Magazine,* 1992.

TABLE 6–4   Use of Preventive Care in the Last Year

	Percentage of Those Who Used Detection Service in the Last Year
All Adults	42
Gender	
Male	34
Female	50
Race	
White	46
Black	28
Hispanic	32
Age	
18–29 years	31
30–39 years	37
40–49 years	50
50–64 years	46
65 and over	58
Education	
Not high school graduate	32
High school graduate	37
Some college	44
College graduate	55
Income	
$7,500 or less	29
$7,501 to $15,000	46
$15,001 to $25,000	39
$25,001 to $35,000	44
$35,001 to $50,000	38
Over $50,000	54

Source: *Summary Report: The Prevention Index, 1992: A Report Card on the Nation's Health.* Emmaus, PA: *Prevention Magazine,* 1992.

Additional Research on Correlates. Research has also discovered that use of detection services varies by racial or ethnic group and by level of education. For example, studies show that blacks and those with less education are less likely to be screened for cervical cancer. These patterns were explained by differences in knowledge and attitudes toward cancer and to less access to health care. However, recent educational and free screening programs may be having an effect. Research indicates that black women are now more likely than white women to have a Pap test and breast exam (Duelberg, 1992).

These patterns are reflected in Table 6–4, which portrays data collected for the 1992 Prevention Index. In the prior year, females, whites, older respondents, and those with more education and higher incomes were most likely to have used some type of detection services.

Healthy People 2010

Every ten years, the Department of Health and Human Services publishes a document containing broad national health goals and very specific targeted objectives for the following decade. *Healthy People 2010* was published in January 2000 and is designed to serve as the basis for the development of similar plans in communities and states across the country. Like previous documents published in 1980 and 1990, the document called upon the best scientific knowledge and a broad cross section of individuals from around the country (U.S. Department of Health and Human Services, 2000).

The two overarching goals established for the first decade of the millennium are (1) to increase the quality and years of healthy life (i.e., to increase life expectancy and improve quality of life), and (2) to eliminate health disparities among population subgroups. Identified in the document are the ten leading health indicators for the nation: (1) physical activity, (2) overweight and obesity, (3) tobacco use, (4) substance abuse, (5) responsible sexual behavior, (6) mental health, (7) injury and violence, (8) environmental quality, (9) immunization, and (10) access to health care.

EXPLAINING HEALTH BEHAVIOR

In the late nineteenth century, Max Weber identified both *macro* factors (social-structural conditions) and *micro* factors (personal choices) as being important influences on the formation of lifestyle. He referred to the impact of social-structural conditions as "life chances" and the impact of personal choices as "life conduct" and argued that they are interlinked and interdependent. This interdependence of life chances and life conduct is particularly insightful in relation to health and illness. After all, certain life chances (e.g., income) influence individual health behaviors, and certain behaviors (e.g., substance abuse) are health-damaging and can harm

An increasing, but still low, percentage of American adults have incorporated exercise into their daily activities.

one's life chances (Cockerham, 2000). In the United States, without question, more attention has been directed to examining participation in health behaviors from the micro perspective. This section of the chapter reviews contributions from both approaches.

The Macro Approach

Several medical sociologists have criticized the almost exclusive focus that policy makers and the general public have given to personal choices and individual behaviors in considering health behaviors. They seek a more **macro explanatory approach to health behavior**. The late Irving Zola creatively captured this criticism in an oft-quoted metaphor:

> "You know, sometimes it feels like this. There I am standing by the shore of a swiftly flowing river and I hear the cry of a drowning man. So I jump into the river, put my arms around him, pull him to shore and apply artificial respiration. Just when he begins to breathe, there is another cry for help. So I jump into the river, reach him, pull him to shore, apply artificial respiration, and then just as he begins to breathe, another cry for help. So back in the river again, reaching, pulling, applying, breathing and then another yell. Again and again,

without end, goes the sequence. You know, I am so busy jumping in, pulling them to shore, applying artificial respiration, that I have no time to see who the hell is upstream pushing them all in. (Zola in McKinlay, 1974)

What are the upstream factors? Cohen, Scribner, and Farley (2000) identify four types of health-related macro-level factors that have a direct impact on individual behaviors. These include:

1. *The availability of protective or harmful consumer products* (e.g., tobacco, high-fat foods, sterile needles, condoms).
2. *Physical structures/physical characteristics of products* (e.g., childproof medical containers, seat belts, well-lit neighborhood streets).
3. *Social structures and policies* (e.g., enforcement of fines for selling tobacco to those who are under-age, provision of community day-care services).
4. *Media and cultural messages* (e.g., advertisements for alcohol products).

John McKinlay (1974) cogently argues that with regard to preventive health actions, we have spent most of our time downstream being

Fitness centers have become very popular around the country. They enable vigorous exercise throughout the year and can add a social dimension to physical conditioning.

preoccupied with encouraging people to avoid risky behaviors, while we have neglected the consumer products, physical structures, social structures, and media messages upstream that create the options of risky behaviors. He states that significantly greater impact on health occurs with legislative acts that raise taxes or restrict advertising on cigarette manufacturers than a multitude of efforts to persuade individual smokers to quit. Yet most efforts are directed downstream at the individual smokers rather than upstream at the tobacco industry.

In concurring with McKinlay, Nancy Milio (1981) states that the paramount factor in shaping the overall health status of society is the range of available health choices rather than the personal choices made by individuals at any given time. Moreover, the range of choices is largely shaped by policy decisions in both government and private organizations. To really affect the health of the people, she argues, it is national-level policy that must be affected.

The Prevention Index testifies to the importance of laws and social policies in changing risky behaviors. By far, the most dramatic change that occurred in HPBs during the survey years pertained to seat belt use. A significant increase in seat belt usage occurred in the mid-1980s, when states began requiring their use. These legislative acts had far more effect on seat belt usage than all of the public education

"Buckle Up" campaigns combined. The authors of the *Summary Report* (*Prevention Magazine,* 1992:6) concluded that "the most dramatic areas of improvement have been brought about not by lifestyle changes, but by technology and legislation."

A second example pertains to the treatment of tobacco. Efforts in the United States have concentrated on encouraging smokers to quit. But these efforts have occurred against a backdrop of formal and informal social policies that subsidize the tobacco industry and prevent measures that would discourage tobacco use. First, since the 1930s, there has been a government program that stabilizes the price of tobacco and encourages small farmers to stick with tobacco as their primary crop. In 2004 legislation was signed to end this program (over a ten-year period); part of the program termination is a $10.1 billion payout to tobacco farmers. Contrary to the wishes of public health advocates, the price of tobacco in the United States should decrease under the new program. Second, the federal government and most state governments continue to tax tobacco products at a low level—especially relative to other countries like the United Kingdom, Canada, Norway, and Denmark, where the cigarette tax is several times higher per pack. Research indicates that as the price of cigarettes increases, the number of people—especially teenagers—able and willing to purchase them decreases. Taxes on cigarettes have increased in the last five years, and the percentage of teenagers smoking has correspondingly decreased. Third, there continues to be lax enforcement in many localities of the ban on cigarette sales to teenagers. If the primary concern is a reduction in the number of smokers, then legislative action "upstream" is likely to have far more effect than continued appeals to personal choice "downstream."

Reasons for Lack of Attention to Macro Factors.   Why is so little attention devoted to macro-level factors? At least three factors seem important. First, using social policy and the force of laws to regulate individual behavior is viewed by some as contradicting the cultural value of individualism. Alonzo (1993) points out that people are willing to cede to the government prevention activities that they cannot do for themselves; for example, inspecting the safety of each bridge. But, people are more reluctant to empower the government to protect us from our own behaviors. Many believe that allowing the government to go too far upstream oversteps its legitimate role in a free society.

Second, the value of individualism carries over into the political economy. Donahue and McGuire (1995) use the term *marketplace strategy* to describe the view that the government's primary obligation is to stay out of the marketplace so that individual consumers can exercise their own judgment about what to purchase and how to live. Of course, the view that the medical marketplace is completely open is inaccurate. Corporations and the government itself greatly influence health (e.g., through the location of toxic dumps), and corporations contribute sizable amounts of money to political candidates each year hoping to influence the political process. For example, in recent years the tobacco industry has contributed millions of dollars each year to members of Congress. Whether these contributions have influenced Congress' refusal to increase the cigarette tax—a measure with broad public support—can only be surmised, but the more money a member received, the less likely he or she was to support tobacco control legislation (Moore et al., 1994).

Third, the absence of attention to macro-level factors enables society to forego dealing with the wealth of research that establishes a direct relationship between individuals' social and physical environment and their health status. Studies have shown that even a small increase in years of education for an individual—or in average years of education for a population—have a greater impact on health status than the available quantity of health resources. But, by focusing on the individual, and solely affixing responsibility for health behavior at that level, the important effects of poverty and unemployment, racism, and lack of educational opportunity can be ignored (Becker, 1993). In writing about the significance of these social structural conditions relative to personal choices, Carlyon (1984:29) wryly made the following observation about jogging: "I'm not sure how well it works for the unemployed, the unskilled, inner-city welfare mothers, Asian-Pacific refugees, the poor, the handicapped, and the dispossessed among us."

The Micro Approach

The importance of macro-level factors does not negate the importance of understanding the factors that influence individual decisions about health behaviors. Several **micro explanatory approaches to health behavior** have been developed to explain health behavior; this section of the chapter describes two that have received significant attention.

The Health Belief Model (HBM).   The **Health Belief Model** provides a paradigm for understanding why some individuals engage in health-protective behaviors, whereas others behave in knowingly unhealthy ways. The model recognizes that, in making health decisions, individuals consider both health-related and non-health-related consequences of behavior.

Development of the Health Belief Model was sparked by the concern of many public health researchers in the 1950s and 1960s that few people were altering their behavior (e.g., ceasing

Figure 6–1 The Health Belief Model

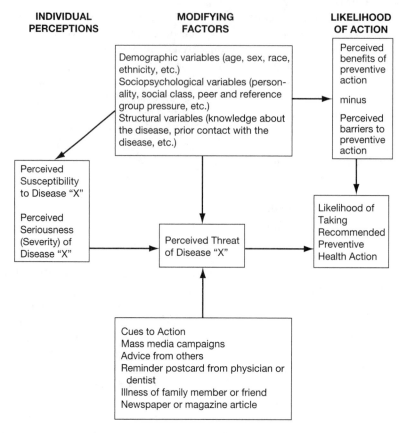

Source: Marshall H. Becker (ed.) *The Health Belief Model and Personal Health Behavior*. San Francisco: Society for Public Health Education, Inc., 1974.

to smoke) *despite* public health warnings. Developed by a group of social psychologists, the basic premise of the HBM is that the likelihood of engaging in preventive health behavior is influenced by certain beliefs about a given condition, such as developing cancer, rather than by objective facts. As shown in Figure 6–1, the HBM asserts that individuals will take preventive health action only when the following four conditions exist: (1) the individual feels susceptible or vulnerable to a certain disease or condition; (2) the individual feels that contracting the disease would have serious consequences; (3) the individual believes that taking the preventive action would effectively reduce susceptibility to the disease (or at least reduce its seriousness if contracted), and that the action

would not involve serious barriers (e.g., inconvenience, expense, pain, or trauma); and (4) one or more cues or triggers for action (e.g., media attention, advice from others, a physician reminder, or an illness of a family member or friend) occurs (Chen and Land, 1986).

All of these perceptions can be influenced by several nonhealth factors including demographic (age, gender, social class, race/ethnicity), sociopsychological (personality, peer, and reference group pressure), and structural (knowledge about the disease, prior contact with the disease) factors.

The Health Belief Model has been shown to be an effective predictor of preventive health action in studies focusing on such behaviors as breast self-examination, patient compliance with regimens, getting an influenza vaccination, seeking dental care, dietary compliance among obese children, keeping follow-up appointments, and cigarette abandonment. These studies have shown that taking preventive health action is more likely when perceived vulnerability to a serious disease or illness is high and when a preventive health action is perceived to be effective in avoiding a negative outcome (Mullen, Hersey, and Iverson, 1987).

However, limitations of the HBM have also been identified. A key limitation is that the model is structured to focus on preventive health action relative to a particular disease or illness. To use the model, one must assess perceptions of a particular disease and perceptions of the efficacy of taking action to prevent that disease. Although the model has been helpful in examining these disease-specific behaviors, it is less applicable to understanding preventive health actions in general or in predicting the likelihood of engaging in general health-promoting behavior unrelated to fear of a particular disease.

The Health Belief Model and AIDS Risk and Reduction Among Young People. The Health Belief Model has been used to explain why some young people voluntarily protect themselves against the deadly HIV infection while others remain knowingly vulnerable. Without question, many young people are at risk for AIDS. More than three-fourths of males and females have engaged in sexual intercourse by the age of 19. The high rate of pregnancy among teenagers (more than a million pregnancies per year) and the very high rates of sexually transmitted diseases (especially gonorrhea, syphilis, and chlamydia) among the young testify to the lack of safe sex practices. In addition, about one-third of diagnosed cases of AIDS are people between the ages of 20 and 29. Given the long incubation period, most of these people were infected during their teen years.

According to the HBM, individuals have differing perceptions regarding their susceptibility to infection as well as the seriousness of HIV/AIDS. For example, a gay male may feel particularly vulnerable due to the high incidence of AIDS in this group and may recognize its

seriousness if he has witnessed the illness and death of friends. These perceptions must be complemented by information about the methods of transmission and the precautions that must be taken to avoid transmission.

However, individuals may still fail to take precautions. Some trust that medical technology will find a solution to the problem (which may be a reflection of incorrect information as well as a form of denial of individual risk); others may not have been exposed to a triggering event (e.g., the death of a friend); and others may calculate that perceived barriers (e.g., sacrificing sexual pleasure) outweigh perceived benefits of preventive action. One must also feel capable of making the recommended behavioral changes and believe that those changes will actually make a difference. In high-prevalence areas, some may continue to engage in unsafe practices because they believe they are already exposed.

A study of more than 300 introductory psychology students in California postulated that three factors (perceptions of personal vulnerability, sexual behavior history, and homophobia) would predict levels of worry about contracting a sexually transmitted disease, and in turn, that worry would predict behavioral change to safer sex practices. These predictions were supported in the research, although somewhat different patterns were found for female and male students. For both females and males, worry was a strong predictor of risk reduction behaviors. However, only females were influenced by sexual behavior history (e.g., number of partners and having had a STD), and only males were influenced by perceived vulnerability and homophobia. Thus, gender was identified as a key influence on the processes within the HBM (Cochran and Peplau, 1991).

The Theory of Reasoned Action (TRA). Developed by Azjen and Fishbein (1973), the central premise of the **Theory of Reasoned Action** is that intention or motivation to perform a behavior precedes actual performance of the behavior. The intention to behave in a particular way is influenced by attitude toward the behavior (How enjoyable or unenjoyable is this behavior?), social norms (Is this an expected behavior in society?), messages conveyed by significant others (Do others want me to engage in this behavior?), and the importance to the individual of complying with the relevant social norms and wishes of others.

Actual participation in a preventive health action would be preceded by beliefs, attitudes, and norms that encourage the action and an intention to engage in it. Similar to the HBM, background characteristics of the individual and certain personality and other social-psychological traits can be important influences. Unlike the HBM, TRA is almost entirely rational and does not include a significant emotional component (like perceived susceptibility to disease). In addition, TRA includes much more explicit consideration of social influences by incorporating the wishes of significant others for the individual and the desire of the individual to comply with these wishes (Mullen, Hersey, and Iverson, 1987). Vanlandingham and others (1995) determined that TRA was a better predictor than HBM of using safe sex practices precisely because it places more emphasis on peer group influence.

The Theory of Reasoned Action and the Cessation of Smoking.   Though TRA has not in general been as successful as the HBM in predicting preventive health actions, it has been more effective in predicting smokers who would attempt to stop smoking. One study that was based on a general household survey determined that behavioral intention was a critical precursor to actual attempts to cease smoking and that it was a more powerful predictor than any of the individual items in the HBM (which was also tested). Although the researchers preferred the HBM for other reasons, they concluded that the intention to engage in a preventive health action is an important influence of the action (Mullen, Hersey, and Iverson, 1987).

Other Social-Psychological and Social-Structural Influences.   Three additional variables with potential explanatory power for health behavior have been studied. The underlying the-

ory of **health locus of control (HLC)** is that healthy behaviors are selected by individuals based on the expectation that they will actually lead to positively valued health outcomes. That is, those who feel they have control over their own health (internal locus of control) are more likely to engage in health-protective behavior than those who feel powerless to control their own health and believe health to be determined by luck, chance, or fate (external locus of control).

Some research shows that persons with an internal locus of control are less likely to smoke and use alcohol and other drugs (Clarke, Macpherson, and Holmes, 1982) and are more likely to engage in personal health screening activities, but many studies have failed to find locus of control to be an important predictor of health behaviors (e.g., Cockerham et al., 1986).

Several studies have shown that the value that individuals attach to their health helps to predict participation in health behaviors—those who prioritize good health are more likely to lead a healthy lifestyle. In some recent studies, researchers have examined health locus of control in conjunction with a measure of *value of health.* Theoretically, behaviors followed by reinforcements high in value are more likely to be learned and repeated (Rotter, 1954). Therefore, it is reasonable to expect that internal health locus of control beliefs would predict HPBs only for people who place a high value on their health.

Some studies have found that internally controlled individuals who place a high value on health are more likely than others to quit smoking and to have good eating habits, but other studies have not detected this relationship. Thus, though HLC and health value are intuitively appealing, research thus far has found that they have only modest ability to predict health behavior.

Several studies have shown that individuals engaged in ongoing interpersonal relationships with family members, friends, and co-workers *(social support)* are more likely to participate in health-protective behaviors. Among adults, this often occurs as significant others attempt to influence and persuade the individual to practice a healthy lifestyle. For example, among a group of employees enrolled in a worksite health promotion program, friends, relatives and co-workers were positive influences in changing health-related behaviors initially, and in encouraging subjects to maintain these changes over time (Zimmerman and Conner, 1989). This pattern of influence also occurs within marriages, though wives are more likely to try to influence husbands' behavior than the other way around. This may help explain why there is a significant health benefit for males in getting married though not for females. Broman (1993) has further established this relationship in his research showing that disengagement from social relationships is often accompanied by an increase in health-harming behaviors.

The influence of other persons is particularly strong among adolescents. Research has identified both perceived peer and parental approval of alcohol use to be important determinants of drinking behavior among teenagers. Adolescents who reported high parental approval of alcohol use also reported high levels of alcohol use by their friends. In a study of health care practices during the first three years of college, both parents and peers were found to have a significant influence on students' alcohol consumption, diet, exercise, and seat belt use. The researchers concluded that the direct modeling of behavior was the most important avenue of influence by both parents and peers (Lau, Quadrel, and Hartman, 1990).

SUMMARY

The World Health Organization defines health as a state of complete physical, social, and mental well-being. Sociological approaches to understanding health emphasize the social and cultural aspects of health and illness and an ability to function in various social roles.

In general, Americans have made slight improvements in healthy lifestyle in the last two decades. On average, people engage in about two-thirds of health-protective behaviors, and many also receive recommended screenings. However, since these often involve direct or indirect costs, low-income persons receive less preventive care. The most worrisome lifestyle indicators for Americans are the continuing high rate of smokers (though the percentage of smokers is down) and the high (and increasing) rate of individuals who are overweight.

Explanations for participation in healthy lifestyles follow both a macro and micro orientation. Macro approaches focus on the important influence of the social structure (including poverty, unemployment, and racism) on ill health and on the potential of social policy to influence participation in health-protective behaviors. Micro approaches, like the Health Belief Model and the Theory of Reasoned Action, focus on individual decision making and the process of determining whether or not to participate in specific preventive health actions. Both perspectives are important in understanding health behavior.

HEALTH ON THE INTERNET

The chapter discusses an effort by the Department of Health and Human Services to identify objectives for health and health-related behaviors for the next decade. Connect to the Web site for *Healthy People 2010* at:

http://www.health.gov/healthypeople

Enter the document through the "Publications"

link, and review the 28 categories in which objectives have been developed. Examine *HIV, Nutrition and Overweight,* and *Tobacco Use* more closely. How specific are the objectives? In which of these three areas has the most progress been made during this decade? In which area has the least progress been made?

KEY CONCEPTS AND TERMS

biomedical definition of health
detection
health
health behavior
Health Belief Model (HBM)
health locus of control (HLC)
health promotion activities
health protection activities
health-protective behavior (HPB)

macro explanatory approach to health
  behavior
micro explanatory approach to health
  behavior
obesity
prevention
Prevention Index
sociological definition of health
Theory of Reasoned Action (TRA)

DISCUSSION CASES

American businesses are becoming more active in monitoring the lifestyle of employees. Business leaders argue that these regulatory activities are justified in order to maintain a high level of on-the-job performance and to hold down cost increases for health insurance by having a healthier workforce with fewer costly episodes of disease and illness. Critics of the increased monitoring activities contend that employers have no right to interfere in the private lives of workers. While job performance can and should be evaluated, they argue, attempting to control lifestyle decisions in off-the-job hours is inappropriate and an invasion of privacy.

Businesses are now using several types of monitoring activities, including:

1. *Drug screening of all employees.* The Occupational Safety and Health Administration (OSHA) estimates that 65 percent of all work-related accidents are traceable to substance abuse. Metropolitan Insurance Company estimates that substance abuse costs employers $85 billion annually. In response, many companies (more than one-quarter of Fortune 500 companies) have instituted urine drug testing for all employees—white collar and blue collar. Tests can show the presence of such substances as amphetamines, barbiturates, cocaine, marijuana, and opiates. Companies have a variety of policies for dealing with those identified as drug users,

including first-time warnings, drug education classes, job suspension or termination, and in the case of work situations related to public safety (e.g., firefighters and railroad engineers), prosecution.

2. *Programs of incentives and mandates for specific lifestyles.* Some businesses have established financial reward/penalty systems for worker lifestyles. For example, workers who maintain a certain level of fitness or who do not smoke or who have a cholesterol count below a designated level are given cash bonuses (or the company pays more of the premium for health benefits). Workers who do not meet these lifestyle standards pay a financial penalty (or pay more of the health insurance premium).

Other businesses have developed even more stringent plans. Some employers refuse to hire people (or they fire current employees) who smoke cigarettes, are overweight, have high cholesterol readings, or in at least one case, ride a motorcycle. Thus far, courts have sent mixed signals on the legality of such provisions.

What are the social implications of programs of drug screening and lifestyle incentives and mandates? What would be the consequences if every company established plans like these? Are these programs an invasion of worker privacy? Are there any significant differences in these two types of programs?

REFERENCES

Alonzo, Angelo A. 1993 "Health Behavior: Issues, Contradictions, and Dilemmas." *Social Science and Medicine,* 37:1019–1034.

Azjen, I., and M. Fishbein. 1973 *Belief, Attitude, Intention, and Behavior.* Reading, MA.: Addison-Wesley.

Becker, Marshall H. (ed.). 1974 *The Health Belief Model and Personal Health Behavior.* San Francisco: Society for Public Health Education, Inc.

———. 1993 "A Medical Sociologist Looks at Health Promotion." *Journal of Health and Social Behavior,* 34:1–6.

Blaxter, Mildred. 1990 *Health and Lifestyles.* New York: Tavistock/Routledge.

Broman, Clifford L. 1993 "Social Relationships and Health-Related Behavior." *Journal of Behavioral Medicine,* 16:335–350.

Carlyon, William H. 1984 "Disease Prevention/Health Promotion—Bridging the Gap to Wellness." *Health Values,* 8:27–30.

Chen, Meei-Shia, and Kenneth C. Land. 1986 "Testing the Health Belief Model: LISREL Analysis of Alternative Models of Causal Relationships Between Health Beliefs and Preventive Dental Behavior." *Social Psychology Quarterly,* 49:45–60.

Clarke, John H., Brian V. Macpherson, and David R. Holmes. 1982 "Cigarette Smoking and External Locus of Control Among Young Adolescents." *Journal of Health and Social Behavior,* 23:253–259.

Cochran, Susan D., and Letitia A. Peplau. 1991 "Sexual Risk Reduction Behaviors Among Young Heterosexual Adults." *Social Science and Medicine,* 33:25–36.

Cockerham, William C. 2000 "The Sociology of Health Behavior and Health Lifestyles," pp. 159–172 in the *Handbook of Medical Sociology,* (5th ed.). Chloe E. Bird, Peter Conrad, and Allen M. Fremont (eds.), Upper Saddle River, NJ: Prentice Hall.

Cockerham, William C., Guenther Leuschen, Gerhard Kunz, and Joe L. Spaeth. 1986 "Stratification and Self-Management of Health." *Journal of Health and Social Behavior,* 27:1–14.

Cohen, Deborah A., Richard A. Scribner, and Thomas A. Farley. 2000 "A Structural Model of Health Behavior: A Pragmatic Approach to Explain and Influence Health Behaviors at the Population Level." *Preventive Medicine,* 30:146–154.

Donahue, John M., and Meredith B. McGuire. 1995 "The Political Economy of Responsibility in Health and Illness." *Social Science and Medicine,* 40:47–53.

Duelberg, Sonja I. 1992 "Preventive Health Behavior Among Black and White Women in Urban and Rural areas." *Social Science and Medicine,* 34:191–198.

Faulkner, Lisa A. 1997 "The Effect of Health Insurance Coverage on the Appropriate Use of Recommended Clinical Preventive Services." *American Journal of Preventive Medicine,* 13:453–458.

Fontaine, Kevin R., David T. Redden, Chenxi Wang, Andrew O. Westfall, and David B. Allison. 2003 "Years of Life Lost to Obesity." *Journal of the American Medical Association,* 289:187–193.

Henderson, James W. 1994 "The Cost Effectiveness of Prenatal Care." *Health Care Financing Review,* 15:21–32.

Kasl, Stanley, and Sidney Cobb. 1966 "Health Behavior, Illness Behavior, and Sick Role Behavior." *Archives of Environmental Health,* 12:246–266.

Keeling, Richard P. 2000 "The Political, Social, and Public Health Problems of Binge Drinking in College." *Journal of American College Health,* 48:195–198.

———. 2002 "Binge Drinking and the College Environment." *Journal of American College Health,* 50:197–201.

Lau, Richard R., Marilyn J. Quadrel, and Karen A. Hartman. 1990 "Development and Change of Young Adults' Preventive Health Beliefs and Behavior: Influence from Parents and Peers." *Journal of Health and Social Behavior,* 31:240–259.

McGinnis, J. Michael, and William H. Foege. 1993 "Actual Causes of Death in the United States." *Journal of the American Medical Association,* 270:2207–2212.

McKinlay, John B. 1974 "A Case for Refocussing Upstream: The Political Economy of Illness," pp. 502–516 in *Sociology of Health and Illness: Critical Perspectives,* Peter Conrad and Rochelle Kern (eds.). New York: St. Martin's Press.

McQuide, Pamela A., Therese Delvaux, and Pierre Buekens. 2000 "Prenatal Care Incentives in Europe." *Journal of Public Health Policy,* 19:331–349.

Mechanic, David. 1980 "The Experience and Reporting of Common Physical Complaints." *Journal of Health and Social Behavior,* 21:146–55.

Milio, Nancy. 1981 *Promoting Health Through Public Policy.* Philadelphia: F. A. Davis.

Moore, Stephen, Sidney M. Wolfe, Deborah Lindes, and Clifford E. Douglas. 1994 "Epidemiology of

Failed Tobacco Control Legislation." *Journal of the American Medical Association,* 272:1171–1175.

Mullen, Patricia D., James C. Hersey, and Donald C. Iverson. 1987 "Health Behavior Models Compared." *Social Science and Medicine,* 24:973–981.

Parsons, Talcott. 1972 "Definitions of Health and Illness in Light of American Values and Social Structure," pp. 165–187 in *Patients, Physicians and Illness,* 2nd ed., E. Gartly Jaco (ed.). New York: Free Press.

Prevention Magazine. 1992 Summary Report: The 1992 Prevention Index: A Report Card on the Nation's Health. Emmaus, PA: *Prevention Magazine.*

———. *1995 Summary Report: The 1995 Prevention Index: A Report Card on the Nation's Health.* Emmaus, PA: *Prevention Magazine.*

Rotter, Julius B. 1954 *Social Learning and Clinical Psychology.* Upper Saddle River, NJ: Prentice Hall.

Twaddle, Andrew. 1974 "The Concept of Health Status." *Social Science and Medicine,* 8:29–38.

United States Department of Health and Human Services. 2000 *Healthy People 2010.* Washington, DC: DHHS.

Vanlandingham, Mark J., Somboon Suprasert, Nancy Grandjean, and Werasit Sittitrai. 1995 "Two Views of Risky Sexual Practices Among Northern Thai Males: The Health Belief Model and the Theory of Reasoned Action." *Journal of Health and Social Behavior,* 36:195–212.

Ware, John E. 1986 "The Assessment of Health Status," pp. 204–228 in *Applications of Social Science to Clinical Medicine and Health Policy,* Linda H. Aiken and David Mechanic (eds.). New Brunswick, NJ: Rutgers University Press.

Wechsler, Henry, Jae E. Lee, Meichun Kup, and Hang Lee. 2000 "College Binge Drinking in the 1990s: A Continuing Problem." *Journal of American College Health,* 48:199–210.

Weiss, Gregory L. 1984 "Adaptability and Change in Alternative Institutions: An Analysis of Free Health Clinics in the Southeastern United States." *Virginia Social Science Journal,* 19:22–29.

Wolinsky, Fredric D. 1988 *The Sociology of Health—Principles, Practitioners, and Issues,* 2nd ed. Belmont, CA: Wadsworth Publishing Company.

World Health Organization. 1986 "Ottawa Charter for Health Promotion." *Health Promotion,* 1:iii–v.

Zimmerman, Rick S., and Catherine Conner. 1989 "Health Promotion in Context: The Effects of Significant Others on Health Behavior Change." *Health Education Quarterly,* 16:57–75.

Zola, Irving K. 1966 "Culture and Symptoms: An Analysis of Patients' Presenting Complaints." *American Sociological Review,* 31:615–630.

7

EXPERIENCING ILLNESS AND DISABILITY

Medical sociologists have a natural interest in how people respond to illness. The concept, **illness behavior**, refers to "the way in which symptoms are perceived, evaluated, and acted upon by a person who recognizes some pain, discomfort, or other signs of organic malfunction (Mechanic and Volkart, 1961:52). On the surface, it may seem that the nature and severity of an illness would be the sole determinants of an individual's response, and for very severe illnesses, this often is true. But many people fail to see a physician or go very late in the disease process despite the presence of serious symptoms, while many other people see physicians routinely for trivial or very minor complaints. These patterns suggest that illness behavior is influenced by social and cultural factors in addition to (and sometimes instead of) physiological condition.

STAGES OF ILLNESS EXPERIENCE

Edward Suchman (1965) devised an orderly approach for studying illness behavior with his elaboration of the five key **stages of illness experience:** (1) symptom experience; (2) assumption of the sick role; (3) medical care contact; (4) dependent patient role; and (5) recovery and rehabilitation (see Figure 7–1). Each stage involves major decisions that must be made by the individual that determine whether the sequence of stages continues or the process is discontinued. While some elaboration of the model is necessary (for example, see the section near the end of this chapter on living with chronic illness and disability), Suchman's schema is used for organizing the beginning part of the chapter.

STAGE 1: SYMPTOM EXPERIENCE

The illness experience is initiated when an individual first senses that something is wrong—a perception of pain, discomfort, general unease, or some disruption in bodily functioning. Suchman states that three distinct processes occur at this time: (1) the physical pain or discomfort, (2) the cognitive recognition that physical symptoms

Figure 7–1 Suchman's Stages of Illness Experience

	I Symptom Experience	II Assumption of the Sick Role	III Medical Care Contact	IV Dependent-Patient Role	V Recovery and Rehabilitation
Decision	Something is wrong	Relinquish normal roles	Seek professional advice	Accept professional treatment	Relinquish sick role
Behaviors	Application of folk medicine, self-medication	Request provisional validation for sick role from members of lay-referral system—continue lay remedies	Seek authoritative legitimation for sick role—negotiate treatment procedures	Undergo treatment procedures for illness—follow regimen	Resume normal roles
Outcomes	Denial (flight into health) → Delay → Acceptance	Denial → Acceptance	Denial → Shopping → Confirmation	Rejection → Secondary gain → Acceptance	Refusal (chronic sick role) → Malingerer → Acceptance

Source: Edward A. Suchman, "Stages of Illness and Medical Care" *Journal of Health and social Behavior*, 6:114–128, 1965.

of an illness are present, and (3) an emotional response of concern about the social implications of the illness, including a possible disruption in ability to function.

Assessment of Symptoms

David Mechanic (1968) developed a **theory of help-seeking behavior** to facilitate an understanding of this assessment process and how individuals act prior to (or instead of) seeking a health care provider. Mechanic traces the extreme variations in how people respond to illness to differences in how they define the illness situation and to differences in their ability to cope with the situation. The process of definition and the ability to cope are both culturally and socially determined. As individuals mature through life stages, they are socialized within families and within communities to respond to illness in particular ways. Part of this socialization is observing how others within the group respond to illness and noting the positive or negative reaction their behaviors elicit. Sociologists refer to this process as the **social construction of illness**. Mechanic identifies ten (sometimes overlapping) factors that determine how individuals respond to symptoms of illness.

1. *The visibility, recognizability, or perceptual salience of symptoms.* "Many symptoms present themselves in a striking fashion, such as in the case of a sharp abdominal pain, an intense headache, and a high fever. Other symptoms have such little visibility (as in the early stages of cancer and tuberculosis) that they require special checkups to be detected in their early stages" (p. 143).

2. *The perceived seriousness of symptoms.* "If the symptom is familiar, and the person understands why he has the symptom and what its probable course will be, he is less likely to seek care than if the symptom is unusual, strange, threatening, and unpredictable" (p. 144).

3. *The extent to which symptoms disrupt family, work, and other social activities.* "Symptoms that are disruptive, and which cause incon-venience, social difficulties, pain, and annoyance are more likely to be defined and responded to than those that do not" (p. 146).

4. *The frequency of the appearance of symptoms, their persistence, or frequency of recurrence.* "The more persistently ill a person feels, other factors remaining constant, the more likely he is to seek help, and frequent or persistent symptoms are more likely to influence a person to seek help than occasional recurring symptoms" (p. 146).

5. *The tolerance threshold of those who are exposed to and evaluate the deviant signs and symptoms.* "An individual's tolerance for pain and discomfort and his values about stoicism and independence, may also affect how he responds to symptoms and what he does about them. Persons vary a great deal in how much discomfort they are willing to tolerate and the attention they give to bodily troubles" (p. 148).

6. *Available information, knowledge, and cultural assumptions and understandings of the evaluator.* "The sophistication of patients about medical matters varies from those who are aware of the latest new therapeutic developments even before their doctor to those who cannot identify the basic body organs and who have only very naive notions of bodily functioning. Such differences in medical knowledge and understanding have considerable influence in how people recognize, define, and respond to symptoms" (p. 150).

7. *Perceptual needs which lead to autistic psychological processes.* Anxiety and fear may impact on symptom recognition and the decision to seek care in complex ways. Anxiety about illness may prompt quicker care seeking, but fear of particular diagnoses may delay seeking help.

8. *Needs competing with illness response.* People assign varying degrees of priority to health. While illness symptoms might be a central focus for some, family and work-related activities are more important to others.

9. *Competing possible interpretations that can be assigned to the symptoms once they*

are recognized. "People who work long hours expect to be tired, and are therefore less likely to see tiredness as indicative of an illness. People who do heavy physical work are more likely to attribute such symptoms as backache to the nature of their lives and work rather than to an illness condition" (p. 153).

10. *Availability of treatment resources, physical proximity, and psychological and monetary costs of taking action.* The cost of treatment, convenience of treatment, and the cultural and social accessibility of the provider all impact on the care-seeking decision.

Research on Symptom Assessment

There are significant social and cultural influences on the way people interpret and respond to medical symptoms such as pain. For example, variations in response to pain are based on differing levels of pain tolerance that are culturally prescribed in different ways for women than for men or for members of different ethnic groups.

Zborowski (1969) found that Protestants of British descent tended to respond in a matter-of-fact way to pain, which enabled them to adapt to illness more quickly than other groups. Patients of Irish heritage often repressed their suffering and tended to deny pain. Both Jewish and Italian patients responded to pain with more open emotionality; however, Jewish patients were primarily concerned about the long-term consequences of their illness and were not much comforted by the administration of pain-killing medication, while Italian patients were more oriented to the current pain and were at least somewhat satisfied when the pain was relieved.

More recent research focusing on perceived pain in getting one's ears pierced also found significant ethnic differences. Testing both male and female volunteers between the ages of 15 and 25, Thomas and Rose (1991) found that Afro-West Indians reported significantly less pain than Anglo-Saxons, who reported significantly less pain than Asians—all for the same procedure.

What causes these patterns? Both role modeling within families and social conditioning are

important influences. As one grows up in a family, there are countless opportunities to observe reaction to pain and alarm expressed by family members. Children's anxiety about receiving painful medical treatment has been shown to be strongly correlated with parental anxiety.

In response to the assessment of symptoms, the individual may decide to deny that the symptoms need attention, delay making a decision until symptoms become more obvious, or acknowledge the presence of an illness. Should an illness be admitted, the person may enter stage 2—the sick role.

STAGE 2: ASSUMPTION OF THE SICK ROLE; ILLNESS AS DEVIANCE

If the individual accepts that the symptoms are a sign of illness and are sufficiently worrisome, then the transition is made to the sick role, at which time the individual begins to relinquish some or all normal social roles.

Background of the Sick Role Concept

The **sick role**, one of the most fundamental concepts in medical sociology, was first introduced by Talcott Parsons in a 1948 journal article but elaborated upon in his 1951 book, *The Social System*. Parsons emphasized that illness is not simply a biological or psychological condition, and it is not simply an unstructured state free of social norms and regulation. When one is ill, one does not simply exit normal social roles to enter a type of social vacuum; rather, one substitutes a new role—the sick role—for the relinquished, normal roles. The sick role is "also a social role, characterized by certain exemptions, rights, and obligations, and shaped by the society, groups, and cultural tradition to which the sick person belongs" (Fox, 1989:17).

Parsons viewed sickness as a type of deviant behavior in that it is a violation of role expectations. Functionalist theorists (like Parsons) are concerned about the impact of deviant behavior upon society and parts of society. Sickness is assessed as being dysfunctional for the family because when one member is sick and relinquishes normal responsibilities, other members are required to pick up the slack—and may become overburdened in so doing. In addition, sickness is dysfunctional for society. The equilibrium that society maintains can be disrupted when individual members, due to sickness, fail to fulfill routine responsibilities. The "lure" of sickness—the attraction of escaping responsibilities—requires society to exercise some control over the sick person and the sick role so that disruption is minimized.

Sickness is acknowledged to be a special form of deviant behavior; however, **illness as deviance** is not equivalent to other forms of deviance such as crime or sin. Institutions (e.g., law and medicine) are created in society to deal with both behaviors but, while criminals are punished, the sick are provided with therapeutic care so that they become well and return to their normal roles.

Within the context of the social control responsibilities of medicine, society allows two explicit behavioral exemptions for the sick person but also imposes two explicit behavioral requirements. The exemptions are:

1. The sick person is temporarily excused from normal social roles. Depending on the nature and severity of the illness, a physician can legitimize the sick role status and permit the patient to forego normal responsibilities. The physician's endorsement is required so that society can maintain some control and prevent people from lingering in the sick role.
2. The sick person is not held responsible for the illness. Society accepts that cure will require more than the best efforts of the patient and permits the patient to be "taken care of" by health care professionals and others.

In order to be granted these role exemptions, however, the patient must be willing to accept the following two obligations:

1. The sick person must want to get well. The previous two elements of the legitimized sick role are conditional on this requirement. The patient must not get so accustomed to the sick role or so enjoy the lifting of responsibilities that motivation to get well is surrendered.
2. The sick person is expected to seek medical advice and cooperate with medical experts. This requirement introduces another means of social control. The patient who refuses to see a health care professional creates suspicion that the illness is not legitimate. Such a refusal inevitably reduces the patience and sympathy of society and those surrounding the patient.

Criticisms of the Sick Role

Sociologists today are divided on the sick role's current value as an explanatory concept. The four main criticisms of the concept are briefly described here:

1. The sick role does not account for the considerable variability in behavior among sick persons. Variation occurs not only by age, gender, and ethnicity, but also by the certainty and severity of prognosis.
2. The sick role is applicable in describing patient experience with acute illnesses only and is less appropriate in describing persons with chronic illnesses who may not have easily recognizable symptoms (e.g., a build-up of plaque in the coronary arteries) and may not get well no matter how much they want to and how faithful they are in following the physician's instructions.
3. The sick role does not adequately account for the variety of settings in which physicians and patients interact; it is most applicable to a physician-patient relationship that occurs in the physician's office.
4. The sick role is more applicable to middle-class patients and middle-class values than it is for persons in lower socioeconomic groups. Not everyone can follow this pathway; for example, lower income persons have less freedom to curtail their normal responsibilities, especially their jobs, and thus have a more difficult time complying with the model.

Rebuttal to Sick Role Criticism

Talcott Parsons, in a 1975 journal article (he died in 1978), and others have suggested that critics have failed to capture nuances in the sick role concept and have failed to see its flexibility (Fox, 1989). For example, Parsons argued that the sick role can pertain to persons with chronic illness—even though they are not "curable," their condition is often "manageable," and they are able to return to many of their pre-illness role responsibilities—and that, as an ideal type, it is unnecessary for the concept to account for all variations.

Medicalization

Although Parsons described the role of medicine as an instrument of social control, many believe that the powers of the medical institution have now expanded far beyond areas of genuine expertise. This has led to **medicalization,** a concept that has two primary meanings. First, an increasing number of behaviors and conditions are being interpreted in medical terms, giving the medical profession increased powers in determining what is normal and desirable behavior; and second, medical practice is understood to be the proper mechanism for controlling, modifying, and eliminating these "undesirable" deviant behaviors.

Freund and McGuire (1999) argue that, in contemporary society, the power of religious definitions of deviance has declined. Such definitions appear to lack rationality and societywide acceptance in a religiously pluralistic country. In addition, the force of legal definitions of deviance has declined, even though they appear more rational; they often ultimately come down to the subjective decisions of some small number of people on a jury. In their place, society has turned to medical definitions of deviance that appear rational, scientifically based, and dependent upon technical expertise rather than human judgment. People may be comforted by the knowledge that "undesirable" behaviors have a nice, neat medical explanation and can be eradicated when sufficient scientific knowledge is accumulated.

The consequences of this medicalization can be interpreted in various ways. Fox (1989) points out that labeling additional behaviors as sickness and extending sick role exemptions to more people may be less stigmatizing and punitive than relying on religious definitions of sin or legal definitions of crime. Bringing behaviors such as alcoholism, drug addiction, compulsive overeating, and compulsive gambling under a medical rubric introduces a "quality of therapeutic mercy into the way that they are handled" (Fox, 1989:29).

Others argue that defining someone as being sick is ultimately a moral decision in that it requires definition of what is normal or desirable (Freidson, 1970). Medicalizing behaviors leads inevitably to social stigmatization which has occurred today with conditions such as leprosy, AIDS, pelvic inflammatory disease, and cirrhosis of the liver (Freund and McGuire, 1999). According to this view, rather than being benevolent, the process of medicalization places a societally endorsed stamp of disapproval upon certain behaviors and extends the power of the medical profession over people's lives. An example follows.

Attention-Deficit/Hyperactivity Disorder. In 1975, Peter Conrad described the medicalization of deviant behavior as it pertained to hyperkinesis (a concept that has evolved today to attention-deficit/hyperactivity disorder or ADHD). The term refers to a condition that has long been observed in children (about three times more common in males) and is characterized by hyperactivity, short attention span, restlessness, and mood swings—all typically defined as violations of social norms. Prompted by pharmaceutical developments (such as the development and marketing of Ritalin—a drug that has a depressing effect on hyperkinetics) and by parents' groups (who sought medical solutions), the medicalization of ADHD occurred. Today, ADHD is the most commonly diagnosed childhood psychiatric disorder—more than two million children in the United States are considered to have ADHD.

Conrad articulated the "up" side of this transition: Hyperactive children are considered to have an illness rather than to be "bad" kids (research has discovered some biochemical differences in the brains of people with ADHD); there is less condemnation of them (it's not their fault) and less social stigma; and the medical treatment may be a more humanitarian form of control than the criminal justice system. In addition, proper diagnosis increases the chances that ADHD kids will have access to appropriately focused educational programs.

On the "down" side, however, identifying the behavior in medical terms takes it out of the public domain where ordinary people can discuss and attempt to understand it; enables the introduction and use of new and powerful drugs (alternatives to Ritalin that include fewer negative side effects are now available and becoming more common); contributes to an "individualization of social problems" by focusing on the symptoms of the child and diverting attention from family and school and other aspects of the social structure that may be facilitating the problem; and depoliticizes deviant behavior—encouraging the view that deviant behaviors are individual problems rather than results of or challenges to the social system.

Demedicalization

Concern that the medical profession's powers of social control have become too extensive, a counter movement towards **demedicalization** is now underway (Fox, 1989). It includes such elements as the removal of certain behaviors (e.g., homosexuality) from the American Psychiatric Association's list of mental disorders and the de-institutionalization of mental health patients (mental patients who can survive on the outside and are not dangerous are mainstreamed into society). Ironically, both medicalization and demedicalization are occurring simultaneously in society.

Symbolic Interactionism: The Labeling Approach to Illness

Whereas the biomedical approach assumes illness to be an objective state, **labeling theory** views the definition of illness to be a subjective matter

worked out in particular cultural contexts and within particular physician-patient encounters.

Every society has its own particular norms for identifying the behaviors and conditions that are defined and treated as illnesses. These illness definitions are not objective and are not permanently fixed in at least two important ways. First, the definitions differ from culture to culture and change over time within cultures. In the United States, alcoholism was once considered to be a voluntary, criminal act; it is now considered to be a medically treatable illness. On the other hand, homosexuality used to be considered an illness; now it is more often considered to be biologically predetermined or a lifestyle choice.

Second, applications of the illness label are influenced by social position. Many people might be considered mentally ill for engaging in the same kinds of behaviors for which college professors are labeled "eccentric." Cocaine addicts, alcoholics, and people who abuse valium are all medically defined in different ways even though all may be experiencing chemical substance abuse. The stigma (or lack of it) is certainly influenced by the individual's social standing.

Application of the illness label is especially important because of the influence labels have on how a person is treated. Individuals who have received mental health care may always be viewed somewhat differently than people who have not received such care, even after treatment ends and mental health is restored. Likewise, someone who is diagnosed with cancer may forever after be considered fragile even if the cancer is successfully combatted.

The Work of Eliot Freidson

Eliot Freidson (1970) has devised a scheme to illustrate (1) that variations in the sick role do exist depending on one's illness, (2) that how sick people are treated depends upon the imputed seriousness of their disease and whether or not it is stigmatized within the society, and (3) that the illness label is not objective but rather a reflection of societal norms and cultural traditions. Contrary to Parsons's formulation, Freidson asserts that certain conditions are typically considered to be the responsibility of the sick person, and that society often responds negatively to these persons, much as they would respond to one who has broken the law. Examples of these conditions would include AIDS and other sexually transmitted diseases, alcohol-related diseases, and, increasingly, smoking-related diseases.

In part, the likelihood of stigma relates to the perceived seriousness of the disease, that is, the extent to which it deviates from normality. The consequent stigma results from societal definition; diseases that are stigmatized in one society may be relatively accepted in others (e.g., leprosy is highly stigmatized in India but much less so in Sri Lanka and Nigeria) (Freund and McGuire, 1999). A person with a socially stigmatized disease is much more likely to be looked down upon or victimized by discrimination than a person with a disease not so labeled.

Freidson's typology (see Table 7–1) considers both the extent of deviation from normality created by a disease (its "imputed seriousness") and the extent of stigmatization of persons with the disease (its "imputed legitimacy"). Illness states produce one of three types of legitimacy:

1. *Illegitimate (or stigmatized illegitimacy),* which provides some exemption from role responsibilities but few additional privileges and may carry social stigmatization. Freidson considers stammering (Cell 1) to be a minor deviation from social norms, and epilepsy (Cell 4) to be a serious deviation. Because of the stigma attached, both present challenges to persons with either of the conditions. See the Box "Labeling Theory and Stuttering."

2. *Conditional legitimacy,* which provides temporary exemption from role responsibilities with some new privileges—provided that the individual seeks to get well. Cell 2 (a cold) and Cell 5 (pneumonia) are Freidson's examples of a minor and a serious deviation from social norms respectively.

3. *Unconditional legitimacy,* which provides permanent and unconditional exemption from role responsibilities due to the hopelessness of the condition. Cell 3 (pockmarks) is the example of a minor deviation, and Cell 6 (cancer) exemplifies a serious deviation.

TABLE 7–1   Freidson's Model of Types of Illness (Deviance) for Which Individual Is Not Held Responsible

Imputed Seriousness	Illegitimate (Stigmatized)	Conditionally Legitimate	Unconditionally Legitimate
Minor deviation	Cell 1 "Stammer" Partial suspension of some ordinary obligations; few or no new privileges; adoption of a few new obligations.	Cell 2 "A cold" Temporary suspension of few ordinary obligations; temporary enhancement of ordinary privileges. Obligation to get well.	Cell 3 "Pockmarks" No special change in obligations or privileges.
Serious deviation	Cell 4 "Epilepsy" Suspension of some ordinary obligations; adoption of new obligations; few or no new privileges.	Cell 5 "Pneumonia" Temporary release from ordinary obligations; addition to ordinary privileges. Obligation to cooperate and seek help in treatment.	Cell 6 "Cancer" Permanent suspension of many ordinary obligations; marked addition to privileges.

Source: Eliot Freidson, *The Profession of Medicine: A Study in the Sociology of Applied Knowledge,* New York: Harper and Row, 1970.

IN THE FIELD

LABELING THEORY AND STUTTERING

"Since childhood, I have had a stutter that makes a regular appearance in my oral inter-actions and, at one time or another, has af-fected nearly all facets of my life. My frustrated parents and I tried in vain to locate a solution, they hoping that years of speech therapy would pay off, me dreaming for a miracle cure that could instantly remove this painfully humil-iating trait . . . At the end of one school year, some of the other children in my therapy group received certificates of accomplishment. When I questioned the therapist as to why I didn't get one, she explained that, unlike me, the other children had achieved the goal of fluency and were therefore being rewarded. Most likely, she used this as a means of encouraging those of us who "failed" to try harder to suc-ceed the next year, but to me this seemed a di-rect indication that my stutter was *my* fault, and that I was a less adequate person because of it . . . When one is being told repeatedly that stuttering is bad and that one should attempt to eliminate it, any instance of dysfluency will contribute to the individual's sense of despair and hopelessness . . . The definitive labels I received from myself and others only served to more deeply ingrain me in the role of a 'stut-terer'"(Hottle, 1995).

STAGE 3: MEDICAL CARE CONTACT/SELF-CARE

When Suchman's (1965) "stages of illness ex-perience" was devised in the mid-1960s, the third stage was labeled as "medical care con-tact" and described as the point at which an in-dividual sought professional medical care. Today, medical sociologists are much more aware of the variety of options available to per-sons who have entered the sick role, the in-creasingly common practice of self-care, and the importance of the individual's social and cultural environment in shaping the action taken.

How do people decide how to behave in re-sponse to being sick? Borrowing from *rational choice theory,* one common approach has been to view sick individuals as people who have prefer-ences and goals in life, who often meet con-straints in satisfying these preferences, and who must make choices from available options. The rational individual will identify possible options, determine the advantages and disadvantages of each option, and then select the option that will maximize the opportunity to satisfy preferences. A sick individual, for example, might consider the cost, availability, and convenience of seeing a

medical doctor and recall the satisfaction or dis-satisfaction produced in a prior visit.

Bernice Pescosolido (1992) believes that this approach focuses on the individual too much and that it fails to include the important influence of social relationships. She advocates for a **social organization strategy (SOS)** that emphasizes the importance of social interaction and social networks as "the mechanism through which in-dividuals learn about, come to understand, and attempt to handle difficulties" (p. 1096). Viewed this way, the decision about how to respond to sickness is "socially constructed"—it occurs in interaction with and consultation with others (termed by Freidson as a **"lay-referral system"**) and is centered in the routine of daily life.

> In the SOS approach, illness careers start with an event that sets into motion a process of attempting to cope with a physical or emotional problem, given an ongoing structured system of social rela-tions. These attempts at coping are created in negotiation with others and constrained by social structure. (Pescosolido, 1992:1114)

The SOS approach emphasizes that respond-ing to illness is a process—rather than making a single choice, sick persons continue to talk with others, solicit advice, and possibly use a variety

TABLE 7–2   The Range of Choices for Medical Care and Advice

Option	Advisor	Examples
Modern medical practitioners	M.D.'s, osteopaths (general practitioners; specialists), allied health professionals	Physicians, psychiatrists, podfatriete, optometrists, nurses, midwives, opticians, psychologists, druggists, technicians, aides
Alternative medical practitioners	"Traditional" healers	Faith healers, spiritualists, shamans, curanderos, diviners, herbalists acupuncturists, bonesetters, granny midwives
	"Modern" healers	Homeopaths, chiropractors, naturo paths, nutritional consultants, holistic practitioners
Nonmedical professionals	Social workers Legal agents Clergymen Supervisors	Police, lawyers Bosses, teachers
Lay advisors	Family Neighbors Friends Co-workers, classmates	Spouse, parents
Other	Self-care	Nonprescription medicines, self-examination procedures, folk remedies, health foods
None		

Source: Bernice Pescosolido. "Beyond Rational Choice: The Social Dynamics of How People Seek Help." *American Journal of Sociology,* 97:1096–1138, 1992, with permission.

of professional, semiprofessional, and lay advisors until the matter is resolved or until options are exhausted. Table 7–2, condensed from Pescosolido, identifies some of the many medical care options from which people select.

The social construction of illness is demonstrated in research by Hunt, Jordan, and Irwin (1989). They conducted extensive interviews with 23 women about their illness experiences just before seeing a physician and at 2, 6, 10, and 15 weeks post consultation, and they also interviewed their physicians and collected information from their charts. All of the women in the sample reported at least two nonspecific symptoms such as dizziness and fatigue.

How did these women's understanding of their illnesses evolve? The researchers discovered that each woman brought several sources of information into the process, including prior medical history, ongoing experiences, and interaction with others. Each woman had evaluated her problems prior to seeing the physician and, in part, interpreted the physician's diagnosis in light of these prior understandings and thoughts.

In almost all of the cases, the physician's diagnosis was not simply accepted or rejected by patients but rather transformed and incorporated into the illness concepts they had prior to the consultation. The diagnoses were also filtered through previous and current observations of others and comments and advice offered by those in the patient's social world. Over the four-month period, the patients continually adjusted and reworked the construction of their illnesses.

The next two sections in this chapter examine two of the many options for responding to illness: seeking professional medical care and self-care.

The Decision to Seek Professional Care

In the Chapter 6, we emphasized the importance of considering both macro (social structural) and micro (individual decision making) factors as influences on participation in health behaviors. Both factors also are important influences on the decision about seeking professional medical care. Ronald Andersen and Lu Ann Aday, who have helped to guide sociological thinking about the use of medical services, developed a framework for examining access to care that includes both structural and individual factors.

They posit that access to care can best be understood by considering (1) the general physical, political, and economic environment; (2) characteristics of the health care system, including health care policy and the organization and availability of services; and (3) characteristics of the population including those that may *predispose* one to use services (age, gender, attitudes about health care); those that *enable* one to use health services (income and health insurance coverage); and the *need* for health services (Andersen and Newman, 1973; Andersen, 1995).

The ability of this model to predict use of services has been affirmed in much research. Recently, McEwen (2000) used data from a national health survey to determine the predictive ability of the model with respect to postponement of needed medical care and to presence of unmet medical need. She found that the best prediction of these dependent measures occurred when all three of the predisposing, enabling, and need factors were considered.

Concentrating more on the individual level, DiMatteo and Friedman (1982) have specified three factors that influence the decision to seek care:

1. *The background of the patient.* Propensity to see a physician is influenced by such factors as age, gender, race and ethnicity, and social class. For example, men often are more reluctant then women to see a physician, and many married men schedule an appointment only when pressured by their wives to do so (estimates are that women make 70 percent of all health care decisions). Many (especially older) men prefer to "tough it out" and are embarrassed to discuss such matters as sexual dysfunction, prostate enlargement, and depression.

2. *The patient's perception of the illness.* Zola (1973:677–689) has identified five **"social triggers"** that influence the judgment that the symptoms need professional health care:

The decision to seek formal medical care is shaped by many factors, including the patient's age and gender, the perception of the illness, and the social situation. Here, a radiologist explains the results of a set of X-rays to a patient.

(a) perceived interference with vocational or physical activity, especially work-related activity; (b) perceived interference with social or personal relations; (c) an interpersonal crisis; (d) a **temporalizing of symptomatology** (setting a deadline—If I'm not better by Monday, I'll call the physician); and (e) pressure from family and friends.

3. *The social situation.* Even for pain that may relate to a serious condition, situational factors matter. Symptoms that begin during the week, rather than on the weekend, are more likely to motivate prompt contact with a physician, as do symptoms which appear at work, and symptoms which appear when other people are present (DiMatteo and Friedman, 1982).

Use of Medical Care Services

Americans average about five or six physician contacts each year. However, this average camouflages significant differences among population sub-groups. Overall, number of contacts increases significantly with age and is higher for females than males, and is highest among people in the lowest income category.

The following section describes patterns in the utilization of health services among several important population subgroups.

The Poor and the Medically Indigent. People below the poverty level and those just above it often have difficulty gaining access to quality medical care. Since the late 1960s (and largely as a result of Medicaid and Medicare), the poor have averaged as many or more physician contacts each year as the nonpoor. However, relative to their greater medical need, the poor continue to have lower access. And the lowest utilization rates relative to need are found among those just above the poverty level. These persons—often called the *medically indigent* or the *working poor*—earn just enough money to fail to qualify for Medicaid but not enough to afford private medical care.

Most of the medically indigent lack any form of health insurance (about 45 million Americans lack health care coverage). Most are in households with a wage earner who works in a job that does not offer health insurance as a benefit. The other largest groups of people without insurance are unemployed persons and their families who have lost their health insurance along with their jobs and those with major health problems who cannot afford an individual insurance policy (or who have been denied insurance altogether due to their condition).

The use of health care services by the poor differs from the nonpoor in at least three other important respects. First, the poor are much less likely to have a regular source of care—that is, a physician who is routinely seen for health care problems or services (Andersen, Aday, and Lytle, 1987). Often, this is due to the lack of physicians in low-income areas.

Second (as a consequence of the first), the poor are much more likely to use a hospital emergency room (ER) or outpatient department as a routine care site. While this is not an efficient use of services (care in the ER is more expensive), and may be resented by hospital staff, these may be the only available and convenient facilities. These public hospital and clinic sites tend to be larger, busier, colder, and more impersonal than medical offices. Waiting time to see a physician may be long—sometimes most of a day. The staff often are fiercely overworked and have little time for patients. The actual physician-patient encounter may be hurried and abrupt, with little warmth and little investigation of a patient's psychosocial concerns. Often, it is not a satisfying experience for the patient or the physician, and further use is discouraged. Dutton (1986) considered these aspects of care to be a "systems barrier" to use of services by the poor and concluded it was a more potent barrier than either financial considerations or motivational level.

Third (partially as a consequence of the first two), low-income persons are much sicker when they are admitted to a hospital and require longer hospital stays. Due to the higher rates of disease and illness in poor communities, the lack of access to ambulatory care, and the lack of adequate financial resources or health insurance coverage to pay hospital costs, the poor often become very sick before admission occurs.

In order to study this pattern, Epstein, Stern, and Weissman (1990) interviewed almost 17,000 patients admitted to five Massachusetts hospitals in 1987. They collected information on three components of socioeconomic standing (income, occupation, education) and several aspects of the hospital stay. Patients in the lowest socioeconomic group had hospital stays 3 to 30 percent longer than patients of higher status. Hospital charges were from 1 to 18 percent higher reflecting the longer stay and greater number of services provided. These patterns held even when age and severity of illness were controlled. A separate 1987 study of a national sample of hospitals found that patients who were uninsured at time of admission were much sicker and were 1.2 to 3.2 times more likely to die while in the hospital (Hadley, Steinberg, and Feder, 1991).

The Homeless.   The homeless population in the United States is in great need of mental and physical health care services but is not receiving them. Estimates of the prevalence of psychiatric disorders among the homeless range from 25 to 50 percent, and estimates of previous psychiatric hospitalization range from 15 to 42 percent. A study of the New York City homeless revealed a clinically significant level of depression for 53 percent of the population, while only 13 percent had used mental health services in the three months prior to the survey (Padgett, Struening, and Andrews, 1990).

Racial and Ethnic Minorities.   In recent years, the black-white disparity in utilization of health care services has almost disappeared. However, significant differences remain in other aspects of use patterns. Blacks are less likely than whites to have a regular source of health care and are more likely to secure care in hospital outpatient clinics, emergency rooms, or community health centers. Research has documented that racial and ethnic minorities experience more difficulty in getting an initial and follow-up appointments with a physician and wait longer during an appointment. These disparities persisted

even if after health status and socioeconomic status were controlled (Shi, 1999).

In addition to economic reasons, another factor accounting for these patterns is the lack of services in black communities in inner-city areas of large metropolitan cities and in rural areas, especially in the Southeast. These are the two areas of the country most underserved by physicians. This shortage makes it difficult for physicians who are located in these areas and complicates the patients' efforts to find a physician with whom to establish a continuing relationship. Since persons with a regular source of care tend to be more satisfied with their physician, other benefits accrue, including higher compliance rates.

Despite very high levels of mortality and morbidity, Hispanics have the lowest utilization rate of medical services of any racial or ethnic group in the United States. Only about half as many Hispanics as whites have a regular source of medical care; they are twice as likely to use a hospital emergency room as a regular source of care; they are much more likely to be admitted to a hospital through an emergency room; and they are likely to be much sicker at the point of admission (indicating delay in seeking services), resulting in longer and more expensive hospital stays. Hispanics are much less likely to initiate prenatal care in the recommended first trimester and are three times less likely to receive any prenatal care whatsoever.

Several factors are responsible for these differential utilization patterns, including lower family incomes, a greater likelihood of having a job that does not offer health insurance, and a lack of accessible health care services for Mexican American farm workers and those who live in inner-city areas of large cities.

Age.   Older persons are consistently the heaviest users of health care services. Persons over 65 years of age receive more preventive care than do younger people and visit physicians more frequently in response to medical need. Although people over age 65 comprise only about 12 percent of the U.S. population, they account for one-third of all personal health care expenditures.

IN COMPARATIVE FOCUS

GENDER AND THE USE OF MEDICAL SERVICES IN RURAL INDIA

While certain cultural norms in the United States discourage males from seeking professional medical care, the opposite pattern is evident in some parts of rural India. Even in areas where health services are readily available, certain cultural values related to gender ideology and gender-based behavior influence women to under-use medical care. To better understand this pattern, Kumar (1995) spent nine months in a rural village in northern India conducting a general household survey and open-ended interviews with married women.

Married women in the village observe *ghungat* (veiling) which includes covering the face with a veil and complying with a set of restrictions on speech, mobility, and social relationships. The female body is associated with shame for reasons that relate to ideas about cleanliness (menstruation and childbirth add even further restrictions due to the powerful meaning ascribed to blood as a particularly dirty substance), the necessity of maintaining pure patrilineage, and fear of uncontrolled sexuality. Women are financially dependent on men, although men are dependent on women to manage the home and raise the children. *Ghungat* is viewed as a practice that honors both men and women because it is a visual expression of the acceptance of the greater power of males and their control over females.

When sick, wives' access to medical care is limited by the necessity of having the husband's approval to seek care, by not having direct access to financial resources, and by the difficulty of taking time off from household chores. Limitations in movement throughout the village and a requirement of not visiting the health center alone are further discouragements as is the perceived inappropriateness of having a male physician "look at" parts of her unclothed body. These cultural restraints explain the lesser use of medical services by women than men and the fact that women are sometimes not seen until an advanced stage of illness.

Gender.   Consistent differences exist in utilization of health care services between women and men. Women use more physician services, are more likely to have a regular source of care, receive significantly more preventive care, take more medications, are more likely to visit outpatient clinics, and are more likely to be hospitalized. On the other hand, men are more likely to use emergency room services.

Why do women and men have such different utilization patterns? Perhaps the most obvious reason—the extra use of services by women for reproductive care—explains only part of the difference (reproduction accounts for only about 20 percent of women's physician contacts). More important factors are the greater number of illnesses reported by women (need for care being an important predictor of use) and the greater willingness of women to seek professional health care.

Gender roles are clearly implicated with the latter reason. Women are socialized to be more sensitive to medical symptoms, and once symptoms are perceived, to take them more seriously. Once this evaluation has occurred, women find it easier to seek medical assistance; therefore, they show a higher utilization rate. On the other hand, men often exhibit a reluctance to get checkups, required screening tests, and medical attention when warranted. Recent research has traced at least some of this pattern to the traditional men's sex role: a sense of immunity and immortality, difficulty relinquishing control, and a reluctance to seek help (Tudiver and Talbot, 1999).

The Concept of Self-Care

Self-care describes the broad range of behaviors initiated by individuals to promote optimal health, prevent illness, detect symptoms of ill health, heal acute illness, and manage chronic conditions. It includes obtaining information about health and illness, doing self-screening exams, managing one's own illness, including self-medication, and formulating clear goals and preferences regarding end-of-life treatment decisions. Although the term *self-care* implies an individual behavior, these practices occur within a social network and are very much influenced by family, friends, and cultural norms.

However it is defined, it is clear that self-care practices are an extremely common and routine response to illness symptoms and are practices that are pervasive throughout the population. A national study found that more than five in six persons age 55 and older had experienced at least one illness symptom in the previous six months for which they relied on self-care only. Almost 90 percent of these respondents assessed their health care efforts as being good, very good, or excellent (Kart and Engler, 1994).

Self-care is certainly not a new concept. Since the earliest civilizations, people have taken personal measures to protect their safety and well-being and to deal with illnesses. However, the advent of modern scientific medicine shifted primary responsibility for managing health and illness from the individual and family to the physician. Now, there is renewed interest among both the general public and many health care professionals in shifting the overall management of health care from the professional back to the individual.

The Self-Help Movement.   In the 1960s and 1970s a **self-help** movement promoting personal involvement and responsibility in health emerged in the United States. It was part of a larger cultural critique of authority and expertise and a partial contradiction to the prevailing value attached to professionalism. Since that time, personal initiative toward health and the management of illness has continued to grow due to several factors:

1. An expansion of alternative medical philosophies and clinical approaches that place primary responsibility for health on the individual rather than on the professional. These include behavioral approaches, concepts of holistic health, and therapies derived from Eastern philosophies (e.g., yoga, meditation, and biofeedback).

2. As health care costs have continued to climb, there has been increased interest in potential savings from more vigorous health promotion and disease prevention efforts. Studies indicate that persons who use self-care practices reduce both the number of visits to physicians and the number of days in the hospital, and that the commonplace use of self-selected, over-the-counter drugs saves the nation millions of dollars each year in physicians' fees. One study asked a panel of physicians to evaluate the self-care practices of a random sample of people; they judged only 2 percent of their actions to be medically inappropriate (Wilkinson, Darby, and Mant, 1987).

3. Increased recognition that advances in health status and life expectancy will come more from changes in personal patterns of lifestyle than from additional technological or scientific advances in medicine.

4. Encouragement from the women's movement for women to reevaluate the quality of care received in a male-dominated health care system: "Demands for self-care increased because of women's dissatisfaction with biotechnical medicine, as well as better education, the availability of more technical information through the media, increased reliance on personal judgement, and greater isolation of individuals" (Cayleff, 1990:329).

Self-Help Groups.   In recent years, there has been tremendous growth in the number of self-help groups—groups of individuals who experience a common problem and who share their personal stories, knowledge and support to help one another. An estimated 10 million persons annually participate in the nation's half million self-help groups, and more than 25 million persons have participated at some time. Groups have been organized around almost every conceivable

IN THE FIELD

SELECTED SELF-HELP GROUPS

Alcoholics Anonymous
Al-Anon and Alateen
Alliance for the Mentally Ill
Alzheimer's Support Group
Breast Cancer Support Group
Bereavement Support Group
Bulimia, Anorexia Self-Help
Cocaine Anonymous
Co-Dependents Anonymous
Compassionate Friends (Bereaved Parents)
Concerned United Birthparents
Crohn's and Colitis Foundation of America
Diabetes Support Group
Exceptional Cancer Patients
Fathers United Inc.
Gamblers Anonymous
Grief Support Group

Impotence Anonymous
Infertility Support Group
La Leche League
Menopause Support Group
Multiple Sclerosis Support Group
Narcotics Anonymous
Overeaters Anonymous
Parkinson's Support Group
Parents Anonymous
Parents of Children With Asthma
Parents Without Partners
Sex Addicts Anonymous
Shhh (Hard-of-Hearing)
Step-Family Association of America
Suddenly Single
Veterans Outreach Program
Weight Watchers

disease, addiction, and disability. See the box, "Selected Self-Help Groups."

While it is believed that these groups are extremely useful and effective, significant research on specific outcomes is only now being conducted. One study of 232 members in 65 different disease-related groups revealed that most members reported many positive changes in psychosocial well-being (a reduction in emotional stress and a stronger feeling of being safe and sheltered), in feelings of competence (learning new behaviors and more self-confidence), in greater participation in social life (more social activities and more interest in helping other people), and in knowledge and understanding of their disease and its treatment. Less than one-fourth, however, reported improvement in physical symptoms or a reduction in physical impairment. Participants did report making more demands on professional helpers due to their ability to express their needs and their desire to play a more active role in the management of their diseases (Trojan, 1989).

A recent study of self-help groups for parents of children with cancer found that the group increased members' confidence and willingness to work with others for changes in the medical care system that would benefit their children or others with cancer. Thus, members were inspired not only to become more active as individuals or in family units, but also to engage in social activism (Chesney and Chesler, 1993).

STAGE 4: DEPENDENT-PATIENT ROLE

The patient enters the fourth stage, the dependent-patient role, when the recommendation of the health care provider for treatment is accepted. This also creates new role expectations that include increased contact with the provider and altered personal relationships. The patient is expected to make every effort to get well. Some people, of course, enjoy the benefits of this role (e.g., increased attention and escape from work responsibilities) and attempt to malinger. Eventually, however, the acute patient will either get well and move on to stage 5 or terminate the treatment (and perhaps seek alternative treatment).

Support groups now exist in most communities to offer practical assistance and emotional support for people with any of a wide variety of diseases, ailments, and difficult life situations.

STAGE 5: RECOVERY AND REHABILITATION

The final stage of Suchman's schema for patients with acute illnesses occurs as the treatment succeeds and recovery occurs. As that happens, the patient is expected to relinquish the sick role and move back to normal role obligations. For chronic patients, the extent to which prior role obligations may be resumed ranges from those who forsake the sick role to those who will never be able to leave it. An interesting subfield of sociology—animals and society—has developed in recent years. The animal–human bond has important implications for health and rehabilitation (see the box "The Role of Animals in Human Therapy").

EXPERIENCING CHRONIC ILLNESS, IMPAIRMENT, AND DISABILITY

While patients usually survive acute illnesses and recover from them, other conditions continue over time. This section of the chapter focuses on three such conditions. A **chronic illness** is one that is ongoing or recurrent and one that typically persists for as long as the person lives. Diabetes is an example of a chronic illness. While it can be treated with insulin, there is no cure for diabetes, and it never disappears. An **impairment** is the loss of some anatomical or physiological function, such as a limb amputation or paralysis. A **disability** can be said to be the consequence of an impairment, such as an inability to walk or climb stairs (Freund and McGuire, 1999).

Relationships Among Chronic Illness, Impairment, and Disability

Although some individuals with chronic illness become impaired and disabled, this is not inevitable. Many chronically ill persons are neither impaired not disabled, and the impairments and disabilities of many people can be traced to trauma, accidents, injuries, and genetic disorders rather than chronic illness (Bury, 1999).

Often, chronic illnesses have an insidious onset (cancer and coronary heart disease are examples) and are characterized early-on by symptoms that are not immediately detectable. Eventually, most chronic illnesses can be identified by diagnostic laboratory procedures. Likewise, impairment is a relatively objective medical term with specific referents to anatomy or physiological function. On the other hand, disability is more of a relational concept; it is rarely entirely present or absent in any individual, but rather its presence is often a matter of degree. It is a more subjective term in that it can only be understood by considering an individual within cultural context (Bury, 1999).

Traditional definitions of disability tended to draw a firm link between health status and disablement. However, many sociologists believe

IN THE FIELD

THE ROLE OF ANIMALS IN HUMAN THERAPY

Research has begun to document the health benefits for humans who interact positively with animals. Interaction with animals has been shown to have: (1) *preventive benefits for health* (reduced stress, lower blood pressure, and greater happiness), (2) *therapeutic benefits* (Riding horses is helpful in the physical rehabilitation of the developmentally disabled, animals can assist with the emotional recovery of battered women and their children, they assist with loneliness of groups such as the elderly or those with HIV disease, and they are valuable in working with stroke victims and those with orthopedic problems), and (3) *recovery and rehabilitation benefits* (One major study examined the influence of hundreds of physical, social, and economic factors on the long-term survival of patients released from a hospital coronary care unit—the most important influence was the extent of the damage to the heart tissue itself, but the second largest influence was living with a pet. Less than half of the patients had a pet, but they were four times less likely to die. In addition service dogs and guide dogs are trained to help individuals who require physical assistance in order to maintain an independent life).

Why do these benefits occur? Research has identified that companion animals help fulfill: (1) *social-psychological needs* such as contact, comfort, a feeling of being needed, unconditional love, empathy, patience, relaxation, and coping with stress; (2) *physical needs* such as more exercise (dog owners walk much more than non-dog owners); and (3) *help with child socialization* in that children raised with an animal have been found to be more nurturing, have a greater sense of responsibility, and have more social and less self-absorbed behavior (Schoen, 2001).

Animals now assist in a variety of therapeutic procedures, and positive interaction with animals has been found to provide important benefits for human health.

this approach focuses too much on the individual outside of any social context. They prefer a **social model of disability** that posits that restrictions in activities or functions experienced by individuals are the result of a society that has not made appropriate accommodations. According to David Mechanic (1995:1210):

In the older conception, while disability deserved public sympathy and assistance, it was viewed in essence as a personal problem that required considerable withdrawal from usual activities. The contemporary view has had a transformative influence in its implication that persons with almost any impairment can meet most of the demands of everyday living if they adopt appropriate attitudes and if physical, social, and attitudinal barriers are removed.

From this perspective, disability occurs only when there is an absence of "fit" between the capabilities of persons and the physical environment in which they live. This gap can partially be addressed at the individual level (for example, modifying the impairment, increasing patient motivation, and teaching coping strategies) but must also be addressed through social policy and environmental remediation (for example, providing assistive devices, removing unnecessary physical barriers, and ensuring fair treatment).

Living with Chronic Illness and Disability

Experiencing chronic illness and/or disability typically involves a period of assessment, emotional adjustment, and mental and physical accommodation. Research has identified at least five very important concerns shared by many chronically ill and disabled persons.

1. *Impairment of personal cognitive functioning.* Patients may be concerned that their illness will progress to a point that their cognitive functioning ability may be impaired or that medications will have a dulling effect on memory, reasoning ability, and capacity for communication.
2. *Loss of personal independence.* Many people deeply value their independence and appreciate it even more when it is threatened. Reliance on others may be a devastating thought—because of the inconvenience and, in a larger sense, the idea of becoming a burden on others.
3. *Changes in body image.* For patients whose illness creates any dramatic alteration in physical image, a major readjustment may be needed. Many people view themselves as physical as much as or more than mental beings; any change in body image is significant.
4. *Withdrawal from key social roles.* Because so many people derive their identity from their

work, any disruption in work pattern or work accomplishment is very threatening. If remuneration is affected, an extra emotional burden is created. The withdrawal from key family responsibilities may be of paramount concern along with anxiety about creating more work for other family members. This withdrawal and concern about it can jeopardize family cohesiveness.
5. *The future.* Any chronic or disabling condition creates questions about the patient's future and the extent to which there will be further incapacitation or physical or mental limitations, questions about financial indebtedness, and questions about permanent losses in daily activities.

The Impact on Sense of Self

Having a chronic illness or disability challenges the individual's sense of self. Patients may have to get accustomed to significant changes in the body, in lifestyle and interaction, in prolonged regimens of medication, in continuing bureaucratic hassles with the medical care system, and sometimes with disabling pain.

Based on more than 100 interviews with 55 persons, Charmaz (1991) has described how experiencing a progressively deteriorating chronic illness can reshape a person's life and sense of self. People experience chronic illness in three ways: as an *interruption in life,* as an *intrusive illness,* and as an *immersion in illness.*

At first, a person with a chronic illness may notice the disruption in life. There is time spent hoping for the best and trying to convince oneself that things will work out. Difficult times lower hopes and increase fears that important life events will need to be sacrificed. A bargaining process may occur when the person promises to do whatever can be done to feel better. Not fully comprehending chronicity, ill persons seek recovery, and in so doing, maintain the same image of self and keep the illness external, not allowing it to become an essential part of one's being. Only through time and through the words and actions of others do the meanings of disability, dysfunction, and impairment become real.

Chronic illness becomes intrusive when it demands continuous attention, more and more time, and significant accommodations. Intrusion happens when the illness is recognized as a permanent part of life—when symptoms and treatments are expected and planned around. The ill person loses some control over life but may work to maintain some control and to boost self-esteem. Limits may be placed on the illness—e.g., allowing one's self a certain number of bad days. Efforts are made to prevent the illness from occupying more and more of one's time and being.

Immersion occurs as the illness begins to dominate life. Responsibilities are surrendered, and days are dominated by dealing with the illness. "No longer can people add illness to the structure of their lives; instead, they must reconstruct their lives upon illness" (Charmaz 1991:76). They face physical and maybe social and economic dependency; their social world shrinks; more and more of each day is ordered by the routines demanded by the illness. People turn inward, become more socially isolated, and begin challenging their own identity ("How can I continue to be myself while having relentless illness?") (p.101).

The trajectory of self-image for those with traumatic but stable disabilities may differ in some ways. In a study of 35 adults with traumatic spinal cord injury, Yoshiba (1993) found that patients actively sought to "reconstruct" the self, and this process swung back and forth like a pendulum between the nondisabled and the disabled aspects of self. At any one time, these adults had a "predominant identity view" that at one extreme emphasized the former, noninjured self and at the other extreme emphasized the disabled identity as the total self. Between the extremes were several gradations based primarily on the extent of dependence on others. She discovered that the primary identity view is dynamic and shifting and can be very fluid from one day to another and/or one situation to another.

Moreover, with the possible exception of the disabled identity as the total self, Yoshiba's respondents contradicted the popular perception that having a disability is a totally negative experience. Some shared with her examples of activities for which they had never previously had time, and several spoke of their personal maturation in dealing with the situation. These experiences are akin to observations of chronically ill and disabled patients made by Lindsay (1996). She noted a constant striving for "health within illness" among her respondents as many sought to identify or achieve positives from their condition.

The Role of Social Stigma

The adjustment of persons with a chronic illness or disability can be very much influenced by the manner in which they are treated by others. When others view an illness or disability in a demeaning manner, they impose a **stigma** or deeply discrediting label on the individual. The stigmatizing attitudes of others can have a pronounced effect on an individual's sense of self.

People with AIDS in American society are stigmatized when others try to avoid or ostracize them, disparage them or their disease, and label them in negative terms. Weitz (1991) points out that stigma is a central concern during all phases of the illness from before diagnosis (when individuals must be concerned about the consequences of being tested for HIV), to living with the illness (and being differentially treated by family, friends, and health care providers), to the time of death (and being concerned about discriminatory treatment by funeral directors).

Recently, in a study comparing perceived stigma attached to cancer patients and HIV/AIDS patients, Fife and Wright (2000) identified four dimensions of perceived stigma:

1. *Social Rejection*—feelings of being discriminated against at work and in society, including a perception that others do not respect them, want to avoid them, and feel awkward in their presence.

2. *Financial Insecurity*—inadequate job security and inadequate income that result from workplace discrimination.

3. *Internalized Shame*—feelings of being set apart from others who are well, blaming oneself for the illness, and feeling a need to maintain secrecy about the illness.

4. *Social Isolation*—feelings of loneliness, inequality with others, uselessness, detachment.

They found that while stigma was a central force in the lives of both sets of patients, the HIV/AIDS patients did perceive greater stigma on all four dimensions. The more negative self-perception held by both sets of patients came more from the perceived stigma attached to the disease than from the disease itself. For example, both cancer and HIV/AIDS patients had reduced self-esteem. However, their lowered self-esteem stemmed not from having the disease but from the negative stigma that had been attached to them because of the disease. Other research (Turner-Cobb et al., 2002) has confirmed that HIV/AIDS patients who are more satisfied with their relationships and are more securely engaged with others make a better adjustment. These findings well illustrate the dramatic effect of societal response on sense of self.

SUMMARY

Illness behavior refers to activity undertaken by a person who feels ill in order to define the illness and seek relief from it. As outlined by Edward Suchman (1965), the illness experience consists of five stages: (1) symptom experience; (2) assumption of the sick role; (3) medical care contact; (4) dependent patient role; and (5) recovery and rehabilitation. Decisions that are made during these five stages and the behaviors exhibited are culturally and socially determined.

The symptom experience stage occurs in response to physical pain or discomfort and includes cognitive reflection and emotional response. Individuals use many types of cues to determine whether to seek help. If individuals decide to relinquish normal social roles in response to illness, they enter a sick role. Persons used this term to signify that giving up normal roles and the responsibility of caring for self are granted by society only if the individual wants to get well and takes action to do so. Labeling theorists emphasize that the definition of illness is a subjective phenomenon that is socially constructed within society and within particular physician-patient encounters.

Medicine's license to legitimate illness has extended more widely than originally envisioned— a process termed "medicalization." An increasing number of behaviors (e.g., alcoholism, infertility) have come under medicine's domain, and physicians and other health care providers are sought for guidance.

The use of professional medical services in times of illness varies among population groups. Response to symptoms is affected greatly by socioeconomic, cultural, and structural variables. Access to quality medical care is still a problem for a number of disadvantaged population groups, especially the uninsured and many racial and ethnic minority groups.

Self-care is an extremely common and pervasive practice that involves a number of behaviors related to promoting health, preventing illness, and restoring health if illness occurs. Millions of people are helped annually through self-help groups.

Those who experience progressively deteriorating chronic illnesses and those who experience traumatic but stable disabilities undergo transformations in self-image and sometimes experience stigmatization. Whereas the former gradually become "immersed" in the disease, the latter often shift back and forth between a disabled and nondisabled identity.

HEALTH ON THE INTERNET

One of the leading advocacy groups for disability rights in the United States is the Disability Rights Education and Defense Fund. Connect to their Web site at:

http://www.dredf.org

What is the mission of this group? What is the focus of its children and family advocacy program? What recent judicial cases does it consider to be important?

KEY CONCEPTS AND TERMS

Americans with Disabilities Act (ADA)
chronic illness
demedicalization
disability
illness as deviance
illness behavior
impairment
labeling theory
lay referral system
medicalization
self-care

self-help
sick role
social construction of illness
social model of disability
social organization strategy (SOS)
social triggers
stages of illness experience
stigma
temporalizing of symptomology
theory of help-seeking behavior

DISCUSSION QUESTION

Since 1997, the case of Casey Martin has been closely watched both by advocates for basic accommodations for persons with impairments and by professional sports organizations. Martin is a golfer who has had some success on the professional golf tour. However, he suffers from Klippel-Trenauney-Weber Syndrome, a rare and painful circulatory disorder that affects his lower right leg (his right leg has only half the girth of his left) and severely limits his ability to walk a golf course.

The Professional Golf Association (PGA) mandates that participants in its tournaments walk the golf course though they hire others to carry their golf bag. Martin requested an exemption to this rule and asked to be allowed to use a golf cart (the kind most recreational golfers use) to get around the course. The PGA refused on the grounds that walking the course is an integral part of the game.

Martin sued the PGA under the **Americans with Disabilities Act (ADA)**. The ADA, which was passed in 1990, prohibits discrimination on

the basis of disability in jobs, housing, and places of public accommodation. The law requires businesses to make reasonable modifications for people with disabilities unless doing so would fundamentally alter the nature of the activity in question. Martin contended his being allowed to ride a cart would not constitute such a fundamental change, but the PGA argued that it would.

The case ultimately wound its way to the U.S. Supreme Court. In May 2001, by a 7–2 vote, the court ruled that walking was, at most, peripheral to the game of golf and that Martin's use of a cart would not fundamentally alter the activity. Justices Scalia and Thomas, the dissenting judges, argued that the ruling would doom all sports at all levels because anyone with any disability could insist on having the rules of a game changed to accommodate a disability. ADA advocates insisted that the "fundamental change" stipulation would prevent such interpretation.

In your judgment, did the Supreme Court rule properly or improperly in the Casey Martin case?

REFERENCES

Andersen, Ronald M. 1995 "Revisiting the Behavioral Model and Access to Medical Care: Does It Matter?" *Journal of Health and Social Behavior,* 36:1–10.

Andersen, Ronald M., and John F. Newman. 1973 "Societal and Individual Determinants of Medical Care Utilization in the United States." *Milbank Memorial Fund Quarterly,* 51:95–124.

Andersen, Ronald M., Lu Ann Aday, and C.S. Lytle. 1987 *Ambulatory Care and Insurance Coverage in an Era of Constraint.* Chicago: Pluribus.

Bury, Michael. 1999 "On Chronic Illness and Disability," pp. 173–183 in *Handbook of Medical Sociology,* Chloe E. Bird, Peter Conrad, and Allen M. Fremont (eds.). Upper Saddle River, NJ: Prentice Hall.

Cayleff, Susan E. 1990 "Self-Help and the Patent Medicine Business," pp. 311–336 in *Women, Health and Medicine in America—A Historical Handbook,* Rima D. Apple (ed.). New York: Garland Publishing Inc.

Charmaz, Kathy. 1991 *Good Days, Bad Days: The Self in Chronic Illness and Time.* New Brunswick, NJ: Rutgers University Press.

Chesney, Barbara K., and Mark A. Chesler. 1993 "Activism Through Self-Help Group Membership" *Small Group Research,* 24:258–273.

Conrad, Peter. 1975 "The Discovery of Hyperkinesis: Notes on the Medicalization of Deviant Behavior." *Social Problems,* 23:12–21.

DiMatteo, M. Robin, and Howard S. Friedman. 1982 *Social Psychology and Medicine.* Cambridge, MA: Oelgeschlager, Gunn, & Hain.

Dutton, Diana B. 1986 "Social Class, Health, and Illness," pp. 31–62 in *Applications of Social Sciences to Clinical Medicine and Health Policy,* Linda H. Aiken and David Mechanic (eds.). New Brunswick, NJ: Rutgers University Press.

Epstein, Arnold M., Robert S. Stern, and Joel S. Weissman. 1990 "Do the Poor Cost More? A Multihospital Study of Patients' Socioeconomic Status and the Use of Hospital Resources." *New England Journal of Medicine,* 322:122–128.

Fife, Betsy L., and Eric R. Wright. 2000 "The Dimensionality of Stigma: A Comparison of its Impact on the Self of Persons with HIV/AIDS and Cancer." *Journal of Health and Social Behavior,* 41:50–67.

Fox, Renee. 1989 *The Sociology of Medicine.* Upper Saddle River, NJ: Prentice Hall.

Freidson, Eliot. 1970 *The Profession of Medicine: A Study in the Sociology of Applied Knowledge.* New York: Harper and Row.

Freund, Peter E. S., and Meredith McGuire. 1999 *Health, Illness, and the Social Body* (3rd ed.). Upper Saddle River, NJ: Prentice Hall.

Hadley, Jack, Earl P. Steinberg, and Judith Feder. 1991 "Comparison of Uninsured and Privately Insured Hospital Patients." *Journal of the American Medical Association,* 265:374–379.

Hottle, Elizabeth. 1995 "Making Myself Understood: The Labeling Theory of Deviance Applied to Stuttering." Paper presented at the Virginia Social Science Association Annual Meeting, March 25.

Hunt, Linda M., Brigitte Jordan, and Susan Irwin. 1989 "Views of What's Wrong: Diagnosis and Patients' Concepts of Illness." *Social Science and Medicine,* 28:945–956.

Kart, Cary S., and Carol A. Engler. 1994 "Predisposition to Self-Help Care: Who Does What for Themselves and Why?" *Journal of Gerontology,* 49:S301–S308.

Kumar, Anuradha. 1995 "Gender and Health: Theoretical Versus Practical Accessibility of Health Care for Women in North India," pp. 16–32 in *Global Perspectives on Health Care,* Eugene B. Gallagher and Janardan Subedi (eds.). Upper Saddle River, NJ: Prentice Hall.

Lindsay, Elizabeth. 1996 "Health Within Illness: Experiences of Chronically Ill/Disabled People." *Journal of Advanced Nursing,* 24:465–472.

McEwen, Kellie J. 2000 "The Behavioral Model Applied to the Postponement of Needed Healthcare and Unmet Healthcare Need." Paper presented at the annual meeting of the Southern Sociological Society, April.

Mechanic, David. 1968 *Medical Sociology.* New York: The Free Press.

———.1995 "Sociological Dimensions of Illness Behavior." *Social Science and Medicine,* 41:1207–1216.

Mechanic, David, and Edmund H. Volkart. 1961 "Stress, Illness Behavior and the Sick Role." *American Sociological Review,* 26:51–58.

Padgett, Deborah, Elmer L. Struening, and Howard Andrews. 1990 "Factors Affecting the Use of Medical, Mental Health, Alcohol, and Drug Treatment Services by Homeless Adults."*Medical Care,* 28:805–821.

Parsons, Talcott. 1951 *The Social System.* Glencoe, IL: The Free Press.

———. 1975 "The Sick Role and Role of the Physician Reconsidered." *Milbank Memorial Fund Quarterly,* 53:257–278.

Pescosolido, Bernice A. 1992 "Beyond Rational Choice: The Social Dynamics of How People

Seek Help." *American Journal of Sociology,* 97:1096–1138.

Schoen, Allen M. 2001 *Kindred Spirits.* New York: Broadway Books.

Shi, Leiyu. 1999 "Experience of Primary Care by Racial and Ethnic Groups in the United States." *Medical Care,* 37:1068–1077.

Suchman, Edward. 1965 "Social Patterns of Illness and Medical Care." *Journal of Health and Human Behavior,* 6:2–16.

Thomas, V.J., and F.D. Rose. 1991 "Ethnic Differences in the Experience of Pain." *Social Science and Medicine,* 32:1063–1066.

Trojan, Alf. 1989 "Benefits of Self-Help Groups: A Survey of 232 Members from 65 Disease-Related Groups." *Social Science and Medicine,* 29:225–232.

Tudiver, Fred, and Yves Talbot. 1999 "Why Don't Men Seek Help? Family Physicians' Perspectives on Help-Seeking Behavior in Men." *Journal of Family Practice,* 48:47–52.

Turner-Cobb, Julie M., Cheryl Gore-Felton, Feyza Marouf, Cheryl Koopman, Peea Kim, Dennis Israelski, and David Spigel. 2002 "Coping, Social Support, and Attachment Style as Psychosocial Correlates of Adjustment in Men and Women with HIV/AIDS." *Journal of Behavioral Medicine,* 25:337–353.

Weitz, Rose. 1991 *Life With AIDS.* Rutgers, NJ: Rutgers University Press.

Wilkinson, Ian F., David N. Darby, and Andrea Mant. 1987 "Self-Care and Self-Medication." *Medical Care,* 25:965–978.

Yoshiba, Karen K. 1993 "Reshaping of Self: A Pendular Reconstruction of Self and Identity Among Adults With Traumatic Spinal Cord Injury." *Sociology of Health and Illness,* 15:217–245.

Zborowski, Mark. 1969 *People in Pain.* San Francisco: Jossey-Bass.

Zola, Irving K. 1973 "Pathways to the Doctor: From Person to Patient." *Social Science and Medicine,* 7:677–689.

8

PHYSICIANS AND THE PROFESSION OF MEDICINE

As described in Chapter 2, American physicians of the eighteenth and nineteenth centuries were not regarded as professionals. Medical "knowledge" was often inaccurate and sometimes dangerous; credentials were easy to acquire or nonexistent; and there was little prestige associated with the field.

Moreover, families (typically the wife/mother) were the primary locus of healing services, and information was secured from newspapers, almanacs, and domestic guides that discouraged the use of physicians. Apothecaries dispensed medical preparations, sometimes provided medical advice, and even performed amputations; midwives commonly assisted in the birthing process; and enslaved blacks from Africa were the primary healers on Southern plantations.

Furthermore, a variety of countercultural health movements flourished. Most sought to disempower the dangerous techniques and drugs of the regular physicians and to promote a new attitude toward health, based on the improved conditions already brought about by better nutrition and hygiene. "Every man his own doctor" was one of the slogans of the time, and the

"regular" doctors were attacked as members of the "parasitic, nonproducing classes" (Ehrenreich and English, 1973).

By the early 1900s, however, medical doctors had secured virtually total domination of the health care field. They had largely eliminated many of their competitors (e.g., some of the countercultural movements); had subordinated others (e.g., women in nursing); and had obtained state-endorsed legitimation to control medical education. Few occupations in any country have ever enjoyed the dominance that was captured by professional medicine in the United States in the early part of the century (and which reached its peak in the 1950s and 1960s).

THE PROFESSION OF MEDICINE

Characteristics of Professions

There have been many efforts to define the essential traits of **professions**. A classic formulation, offered in 1960 by William Goode, is

IN THE FIELD

ESSENTIAL TRAITS OF A PROFESSION

Pertaining to Autonomy:

1. The profession determines its own standards of education and training.
2. Professional practice is often legally recognized by some form of licensure.
3. Licensing and admission boards are manned by members of the profession.
4. Most legislation concerned with the profession is shaped by that profession.
5. The practitioner is relatively free of lay evaluation and control.

Pertaining to Rigorous Standards:

6. The student professional goes through a more stringent socialization experience than the learner in other occupations.

7. The norms of practice enforced by the profession are more stringent than legal controls.

Pertaining to Prestige and Identification:

8. The occupation gains in income, power, and prestige ranking and can demand high caliber students.
9. Members are more strongly identified and affiliated with the profession than are members of other occupations with theirs.
10. The profession is more likely to be a terminal occupation. Members do not care to leave it, and a higher proportion assert that if they had it to do over again, they would choose that type of work (Goode, 1960).

---

organized (by us) around the three common denominators of autonomy, rigorous standards, and prestige and identification (see the box, "Essential Traits of a Profession").

The Dominance of the Medical Profession

In 1970, Eliot Freidson published two books, *Professional Dominance* and *The Profession of Medicine,* that have dramatically influenced subsequent thinking about the medical profession. He defined a profession as "an occupation which has assumed a dominant position in a division of labor, so that it gains control over the determination of the substance of its own work" (1970a:xvii).

Freidson identified medicine as the epitome of professions, and introduced the term **professional dominance** to refer to the extensive control held by the medical profession over the organization, laws, clinical practice, and financing of medical care and to its ability to promote its own autonomy, prestige, and income. It means, according to Navarro (1988:59) that the medical profession is the "dominant force in medicine."

How is this dominance acquired? First, dominance is achieved by convincing the public that the profession does valuable work, that it requires high standards for entry into the field and has rigorous educational standards, and that it can be trusted to perform its work ethically and to police itself. It is accepted by the public as the most knowledgeable authority on the subject matter.

If public acceptance is acquired, then the second requirement may be achieved: granting of legal autonomy (including the power over licensure of new members) by governing bodies. This is likely to occur only when the public is convinced that the profession is committed to a service orientation—that is, it is committed to the public good and to the welfare of clients rather than to self-interest. This legal conferral of autonomy bestows upon the profession the right to be self-regulating (and to have control over other workers in the same domain)—a significant departure from the status of occupations—and frees the profession from external competition, evaluation, and control (Wolinsky, 1993).

Medical credentials help to convey the amount of training and rigorous standards required to earn a medical degree.

The Decline of Professional Dominance

Has the medical profession remained the dominant force in the health care system? Over the last several years, countless challenges to medicine's dominance have occurred, including the consumer movement, the women's health movement, drives for self-care, the growth of the for-profit industry in health care, increasing government efforts to regulate and bureaucratize medicine, and the managed care revolution (see Chapter 14). Has the collective weight of these and other challenges curtailed the professional dominance of medicine? Has its autonomy been eroded? Is the profession being controlled by forces outside medicine—in much

the same manner as occupations experience outside controls? Two major perspectives have suggested that significant change has occurred.

Deprofessionalization. Primarily developed by Marie Haug of Case Western Reserve University, the **deprofessionalization** theory contends that, over time, patients have become increasingly well-informed about health and illness and increasingly assertive about assuming more control over their own health. Coupled with some loss of confidence in the service orientation of physicians and the medical profession, patients have sought more egalitarian relationships in medicine—more participation in decision making about their own medical treatment and a less authoritarian demeanor in their physician. This had led to a reduction in the medical profession's monopoly over medical knowledge, a reduction in the dominion of physicians over patients, and a decrease in physician autonomy—all elements of reduced professional dominance (Haug, 1973, 1988; Haug and Lavin, 1983).

Proletarianization.   John McKinlay and others also see a reduction in professional dominance, but they trace the stimulus to changes that have occurred in the health care system. For many years during the middle and latter part of the 1900s, professional medicine was largely concerned about losing its autonomy to encroachment by the federal government. The **American Medical Association (AMA)** consistently opposed public health-related government programs out of a fear that they would allow the government to increase its authority over medicine. Efforts to legislate some form of national health insurance were especially heatedly opposed.

Some analysts believe that the attention of medicine was so strongly focused on minimizing government's involvement in health care that the increasing corporate presence in medicine was largely ignored and its potential for reducing medical dominance much underestimated.

By the 1980s, however, **corporatization**, an increasing amount of corporate control of medicine, had clearly occurred and was best illustrated by the tremendous influence over the use of and payment for services by managed care companies. According to this perspective, once corporations were allowed into the medical field—in hospital construction, medical equipment supply, laboratories, and insurance companies—it was only a matter of time until they assumed greater control of medical practice itself. Their control was enhanced by other developments within medicine, such as specialization and increasingly sophisticated technologies that required more organizational complexity, greater bureaucracy, more money, and more managers to run the entire operation (Light and Levine, 1988).

This large-scale entrance of corporations into medicine created no less than a "clash of two cultures" according to McArthur and Moore (1997). They see a threat to the quality and scope of medical care as the culture of medical professionalism (focusing primarily on the patient's welfare) is replaced by a commercial culture that seeks profit from the clinical care of the sick. Corporatized medicine contains the paradox that physicians increasingly must rely on corporate organization and finances while simultaneously realizing that these forces intrude on their work and reduce their credibility with society (Light and Levine, 1988).

For some, this corporatization has led to a **proletarianization** of medicine—that physicians, like all workers in capitalist economies, eventually have their autonomy and self-control stripped and replaced with control by corporate owners and managers. New medical technologies reduce the need for certain traditional skills (possibly diagnosis), make work more routinized (more like a trade than a profession), and create needs for capital and bureaucracy (with the potential for control by those with capital).

As examples, the government can now influence medical school admissions and curricula through the provision of grants and scholarships, and the physician-patient relationship is increasingly influenced by outside parties such as insurance companies. These changes convert the physician into a worker within the system rather than a controller of it (McKinlay and Stoeckle, 1988).

The Decline of the American Medical Association

The American Medical Association was first established as a national society in 1847 "to promote the science and art of medicine and the betterment of public health." It sought control over the profession by determining who entered it, how they were trained, and how they practiced medicine, and it hoped to elevate the public's opinion of the profession by driving out untrained practitioners. Though without power in the beginning (see Chapter 2), the association gained significant status as a result of the power bestowed upon it by the federal government to oversee standards for medical education and medical licensure. Over the next several decades, the AMA grew into the most powerful and effective health care lobbying group in the United States.

Today, although the AMA retains considerable power and prestige (it is one of the best-organized, best-funded, and most effective lobbying agents in Washington, DC), its influence has declined. While almost 80 percent of licensed physicians were members in 1963, only 32 percent were members at the end of 2000 (having approximately 290,000 members, though more than 80,000 of those were medical students or residents who are often lured by deeply discounted dues). Recent aggressive membership recruiting campaigns have largely failed.

Some of the membership decline can be attributed to increasing numbers of physicians who have joined societies within their specialty (e.g., the American College of Surgery) or a medical society based on gender (the American Medical Women's Association for female physicians) or race (the National Medical Association for black physicians) rather than the national organization. Many physicians have joined professional societies that expressly seek to offer an alternative to the traditional conservatism of the AMA, and many physicians have not joined or have dropped out due to a belief that large managed care organizations have become the most effective medical lobbying groups today. In a remarkable sign of its change in status, the AMA has recently dropped its adamant and long-standing opposition to physicians forming or joining unions. See the box, "The Unionization of Physicians," about this issue.

Freidson's Reaction.   Have these perspectives convinced Freidson that professional dominance has declined? No. Freidson (1984, 1985) does not discount the importance of many of these trends, but he does not believe that they have measurably detracted from the professional dominance of medicine. According to Freidson, physicians remain *the* health care

experts, the prestige of physicians has remained relatively stable over the last 50 years (and what reduction has occurred is no greater for physicians than members of other professions), and the institutional authority of physicians remains intact. Freidson concludes that physicians continue as the dominant force within medicine.

Mechanic (1996) places the "erosion of trust" in the medical institution in the context of declining public trust in all social institutions. Though the percentage of Americans who express confidence in medical leaders has decreased from three-in-four in the mid-1960s to one-in-four in the mid-1990s, this is still greater than the percentage who express confidence in education, television, major companies, and Congress.

An Alternative Theory: Countervailing Power.   Donald Light and others have offered an alternative perspective in which to consider professional dominance: the theory of **countervailing power**. Light (1991) agrees that professional dominance was won by medicine decades ago, but he does not see it as having become an entrenched part of the health care system. Rather, when any profession gains extraordinary dominance, it stimulates countervailing powers—efforts by other agents to balance its power.

The relationship between a profession and related institutions within a society is in a constant state of flux—sometimes an imbalance of power occurs with one side or the other clearly gaining a dominant position. Professional dominance describes the time when the powers of the profession are great—even though that circumstance initiates efforts that will eventually diminish the profession's dominant position. In medicine, the use of unnecessary procedures, the unexplained large variations in clinical practice, the lack of attention to cost-effectiveness, and the lack of technological self-restraint inevitably led to increased efforts by countervailing agents. For medicine today, these include (1) the government, (2) other providers of health care services such as nurses and chiropractors, (3) consumers in the form of advocacy groups such as the American Association of Retired Persons,

IN THE FIELD

THE UNIONIZATION OF PHYSICIANS

The year 1999 may be remembered as being pivotal in the alteration of the profession of medicine. In that year, the AMA reversed its long-standing and adamant opposition to medical unions. Responding to members' frustration with declining autonomy and stagnant incomes, the Board of Delegates voted to form a national labor union and to seek federal approval for the country's 300,000+ private practitioners to join a union and to collectively bargain.

Union activity among physicians actually began many years earlier and at least five physicians' unions had been formed by the mid-1990s. In 1997, the largest union of physicians, the 9,000 member New York-based Committee of Interns and Residents affiliated with the 475,000 member Washington-based Service Employees International Union, the country's largest union of nonphysician health-care workers. By the end of the year, approximately 14,000 to 20,000 physicians, about half of whom were medical residents, had joined a union. At that time, the AMA endorsed collective bargaining but steadfastly opposed unions and encouraged members to use their state, county, and specialty medical societies for collective negotiation.

By 1999, however, the tide had turned. The AMA called its newly created labor organization *Physicians for Responsible Negotiations.*

Because federal antitrust laws ban collective bargaining by the self-employed (which is most physicians), only a minority of physicians (e.g., those who are employed by a hospital or a municipality) were eligible to join. In 1999 about 110,000 physicians were eligible to join a union; about 40,000 of these individuals had already joined. Late in 1999, the National Labor Relations Board (NLRB) ruled that the nation's 90,000 medical residents in teaching hospitals were employees rather than students and had a right to join a union. Later that year, residents at Boston Medical Center became the first group to take advantage of this new right by voting 177 to 1 to join the Committee of Interns and Residents.

Growth in union membership has been steady but slow. The unions contend that managed care contracts signed by physicians are the equivalent of employment agreements and should give those physicians a right to join the union. If this interpretation was granted, about half of the nation's physicians would become union-eligible. However, a 2001 U.S. Supreme Court decision that health care workers cannot join a union if their duties include supervising other employees will make this impossible. The decision by the AMA to form a union remains highly controversial within medicine and within society (Thompson, 2000; Romano, 2001).

---

(4) large employers ("corporate purchasers") who purchase health care for their employees, and (5) "corporate sellers" of health care services (such as insurance companies). Each of these agents seeks to exercise influence on the evolution of health care and thus exists in a constant interplay with the medical profession (Hafferty and Light, 1995).

Does this mean that physicians today have been converted into corporatized workers? According to Light—no. Relations between physicians and the corporate sector are very complex. Physicians sometimes own hospitals and facilities and laboratories and, thus, are owners as well as workers. Employers, management companies, and insurance companies enter into contractual arrangements with physicians who sometimes have a voice in the companies. However, it does mean that complete physician control over any aspect of medical practice no longer exists (Light, 2000).

THE SOCIAL CONTROL OF MEDICINE

Sociologically, the term **social control** refers both to the ability of individuals and groups to regulate themselves (internal control) and to measures taken by outsiders to regulate an individual or group (external control). One expression of the autonomy that professional groups so earnestly desire is the license to be self-regulatory and to be allowed to rely on internal control mechanisms. Perhaps more than any other profession in the United States, physicians have emphasized their autonomy and their disapproval of outside efforts at control.

This section offers a brief review of internal control mechanisms within medicine and of an important external mechanism: medical malpractice litigation. Of course, in the last few decades, medicine has had to contend with two other powerful external agents: the federal government and the corporate sector. Medicine's relationship with these agents is touched upon throughout the book, but is examined in detail in Chapter 14 and Chapter 15.

Internal Control Mechanisms

Three types of internal controls are described here: peer review, hospital review committees, and the board of medicine in each state.

Peer Review. The most basic and potentially most pervasive type of control mechanism is **peer review**—the comments, questions, suggestions, and personal conversations that occur on a daily basis as physicians work with or near each other. Obviously, this does not occur for physicians working independently and with little interaction, but most physicians now work in some type of group setting and encounter other physicians while attending patients at the hospital.

Is the peer review process an effective internal control mechanism? What typically happens when one physician observes an error or problematic behavior in a colleague? Based on dozens of insider accounts and a couple of "what if" surveys of physicians, the answer seems clear—little or nothing. Physicians express considerable reluctance about making public judgments about colleagues and provoking a formal or informal hostile response. In situations like these, physicians often consider that medicine is an "art" rather than a "science," and they feel uncomfortable suggesting that they know better than the colleague being observed. Even if a clear error occurs, many physicians express their view that everyone is fallible ("There, but for the grace of God, go I.")

If physicians observe a colleague making repeated errors, then a personal chat may occur; patient referrals might be avoided; and a system of "grayzoning" (overseeing the physician's patient care) may be created, but there is a strong unwritten code of not making an official report. This code explains situations sometimes reported in the media about a physician practicing blatantly incompetent or negligent medicine over a period of years—with the full knowledge of others—but never being reported. Some years ago, a California physician admitted in court that he had needlessly maimed at least 30 surgical patients over a period of seven years and that he had performed many unnecessary procedures simply for financial gain. Despite the fact that others were aware of the situation, he was never once challenged by any other staff member.

Hospital Review Committees. A more formal mechanism occurs with a variety of **hospital review committees**. Some of them are mandated by the federal government or other regulatory groups, and some have been created by hospital initiative. They include credentials committees (especially for new hospital employees), internal quality control committees (usually to guard against overprescribing medication or unnecessary procedures), mortality review committees (for any patient who dies in the hospital), and peer review organizations (PROs; established to ensure that Medicare patients receive high quality care).

Are these effective agents against poor clinical practice? Yes, sometimes; no, at other times. For example, most states require all health care facilities to report to the State Board of Medicine any instance when they question the competence of a physician. But hospitals are reluctant to do this and often do not. Imagine the terrible publicity a hospital would receive if it becomes known that it is questioning the performance of its own physicians. In addition most states require that the board be advised whenever a physician loses hospital privileges (this becomes public knowledge in some states). Attempting to avoid the negative publicity, the hospital may pressure the offending physician to leave on his or her own accord. No formal action is taken; the physician often moves to another community or state; and a possibly dangerous physician is not stopped. One review of the performance of PROs determined that the committee missed two-thirds of the cases that were judged by an independent panel of physicians to have involved substandard care (Rubin et al., 1992).

State Boards of Medicine.   Ultimately, the most severe form of internal control is enacted when a physician is reported to the **State Board of Medicine**. Although states have organized these boards in different fashions, they typically consist of several health care practitioners (sometimes even a consumer or two) with an investigative staff who can conduct informal or formal hearings on charges against physicians. In most states the charges can be brought by anyone—the courts, hospitals, physicians, and patients. The board has various sanctions it can levy including reprimands, continuing education, fines, probation, suspension, and license revocation.

These boards work well in some states, not very well in others, and pursue wrongdoers with widely divergent levels of effort. The total number of actions taken by state medical boards is very small—in 2003, only about 4,600 serious disciplinary actions (involving a punitive measure such as loss of license, limitations on the license, and probation) against physicians were taken. Most agree that the number of physicians sanctioned represents only a small fraction of those guilty of wrongdoing. As an example, about 5 percent of the nation's physicians account for more than half of the medical malpractice suits. Of those physicians who have paid out more than five malpractice claims, only about in seven has ever been professionally disciplined. Common problems among the boards are too few investigators (producing huge backlogs and long delays); the failure to make actions public

(in some states); and an unwillingness to impose and/or maintain penalties. As an example, see the box, "The Slow Disciplinary Process."

The National Practitioner Data Bank. The **National Practitioner Data Bank** was created in September 1990 as a federal repository for specific information on all health care practitioners. Reports of malpractice payments and adverse licensure actions must be reported to the NPDP within 30 days of final action. All health care institutions that grant clinical privileges and medical-staff appointments must request information from the data bank. Ironically, the NPDP is not available to the public. An effort in Congress in 2000 to open it up so that patients could check the records of physicians received little support.

On the other hand, more than 30 states now publish lists of physicians who have been disciplined or have been convicted of medical malpractice, and some have begun to use the Internet to post this information. National repositories of information on physicians are now springing up, though some of these are available only for payment.

Medical Errors: The Failure of Internal Control Mechanisms.   The dominance that the medical profession has held carries with it the presumption that physicians will conscientiously monitor the practice of medicine. It is the most dependable method of ensuring consistently high quality of care and to avoid harmful medical errors. The failure of peer review, hospital review committees, and state medical boards to carefully protect patients from incompetent and negligent physicians and from medical care systems with inadequate quality controls is an indictment of the extent to which responsibilities have been carried out.

This failure makes likely the possibility that serious and repeated medical errors can occur, and considerable research has shown medical errors to be common and devastating. In 1998 the Institute of Medicine issued a report that caught national attention. The report estimated that medical errors are responsible for the deaths of

IN THE FIELD

THE SLOW DISCIPLINARY PROCESS

The following is an actual account of a particular case handled before a State Board of Medicine.

April 26, Year 1: Board of Medicine informs Dr. S. that it will hold a hearing on charges that he knowingly, intentionally, and unlawfully did indiscriminately prescribe amphetamines.

June 26, Year 1: Board committee concludes that Dr. S. was extremely careless in the excessive prescription of amphetamine drugs and issues a reprimand—warning S. not to do so in the future.

May 30, Year 2: Board committee sets up hearing to investigate whether S. has continued to improperly prescribe amphetamines.

June 11, Year 2: Committee concludes that S. was extremely careless in excessive prescribing of amphetamine drugs and restricts S.'s ability to prescribe controlled drugs.

April 22, Year 5: Dr. S.'s local medical society writes the State Board expressing concern about S.'s handling of two cases indicating that S. is a longstanding problem in the community and needs investigation.

May 2, Year 6: The president of the local medical society again writes the Board about S. expressing fear for the safety of the general population.

May 11, Year 6: The Board tells the local medical society that S. is being investigated and that the investigation will be completed in the near future.

November 26, Year 7: The Board informs S. that it has scheduled a formal hearing to decide if S. failed to diagnose or improperly treated 18 patients, including an 11-year-old boy who died of asthma.

January 15, Year 8: The formal hearing for S. is postponed due to legal maneuvering by his attorneys.

May 27, Year 8: S.'s attorneys and the state's Attorney General's office in consultation with a few Board members reach a compromise settlement the day before the formal hearing is scheduled. S.'s license is suspended and he is ordered to take continuing education courses and to work under the supervision of another physician.

November 14, Year 8: Board returns S.'s license and puts him on probation for two years. He is to continue taking education courses and his practice is monitored by a team of physicians.

August 31, Year 12: Board informs S. that it will hold a formal hearing on charges that S. illegally sold and prescribed weight control drugs and failed to maintain proper records for drugs kept in his office. S. retires before hearing is held (Hite and Pardue, 1984).

between 44,000 and 98,000 hospital patients in the United States each year. Two types of errors were discussed. Front-line errors include such problems as a failure to promptly and correctly diagnose an illness, the administration of substandard or faulty treatment, and the administration of the wrong medication or the wrong dosage of the correct medication. Such common and obvious problems as the poor handwriting of physicians (so that pharmacists misread important information) and the failure of health workers to wash their hands between patients contribute to these errors. Second-line (less conspicuous) errors are those that are removed from the physician or nurse and include inadequate staffing to offer proper care, shortcomings in practitioner licensing and credentialing, a faulty medical malpractice system, fragmented delivery systems, and a failure to implement new technologies to help physicians avoid errors. *The Journal of the American Medical Association* describes these medical errors as being real and common.

External Control: Medical Malpractice

Patients may attempt to exert several kinds of control over the practice of medicine. If they are sufficiently assertive and are working with a communicative physician, they may discuss desired parameters of their interaction, including amount of communication, the right to ask questions and to receive understandable answers, and how truthful they want the physician to be. If this communication does not occur or the physician is not responsive to requests, the patient may "doctor-shop"—search for a more compatible physician. Patients are always free to encourage others to see or to avoid any physician. In cases where wrongdoing is perceived, a complaint may be filed with the State Board of Medicine. In cases where an adverse event occurs as a result of physician error or negligence, the patient may file a medical malpractice legal suit. The following section of the chapter focuses on trends in the process and use of malpractice and examines the medical malpractice system in the United States.

The Malpractice Concept.   The underlying concept of legal **medical malpractice** is straightforward. Malpractice litigation is intended to compensate patients who have been preventably harmed by the actions (or inactions) of a physician and to discourage such harms from occurring. The injured patient (the plaintiff) must prove that: (1) she or he was injured or damaged; (2) the health care provider (the defendant) was negligent—that is, failed to meet a standard of care expected in the community; and (3) the negligence caused or contributed to the injury or damage. If convicted of the malpractice, the defendant is to pay the plaintiff a sum of money determined by a judge or jury; in reality, almost all providers carry malpractice insurance so the insurance company is the payor in successful suits.

The Incidence and Severity of Malpractice Litigation.   Measurement of malpractice typically is expressed in terms of the number of claims filed per 100 physicians. This ratio increased from only 1 per 100 physicians in 1960 to a high of 17/100 in the mid-1980s and has leveled off in the mid-teens per 100 since the mid-1990s. In recent years there has been a small increase in the number of claims and little change in the number of suits that are successful.

However, the median dollar value of successful suits has increased, and there has been an increase in high-value (more than $1 million) judgments (Mello, Studdert, and Brennan, 2003). About 1 in every 20 or 25 physicians is successfully sued each year. But, of the 6 percent of cases that actually go to court, 70 percent are won by the defendant physician. The most common malpractice claims involve delayed breast cancer diagnosis and infant brain damage. The average malpractice settlement given by juries in 2002 was about 1 million dollars.

Malpractice Versus Actual Negligence. The malpractice system functions best when those who are injured through negligence file and win suits and those who receive no injury or who are injured but not through negligence do not file suits and do not win if they do file. This acknowledges that some injuries occur but are not caused by negligence, and some negligence occurs but does not lead to injury. It is the negligence-caused injury that is the proper object of malpractice.

The **Harvard Medical Practice Study** of malpractice claims and medical records of 31,429 patients hospitalized in New York State in 1984 is the most thorough study done on malpractice. The study identified patients who filed a malpractice claim against physicians and/or hospitals and also examined their medical records to determine the incidence of injuries caused by medical negligence (Localio et al., 1991). See Figure 8–1.

While the patients filed a total of 51 malpractice claims, the audit of medical records revealed 280 actual cases of injury caused by negligence. Were the 51 part of the 280? Not for the most part. Only 8 of the 280 filed a malpractice claim; 272 had a legitimate claim but did not file; 43 did not have a legitimate claim but did file. Thus, most actual cases of negligence-caused injury do not get filed and a large percentage of those that are filed are not justified—the opposite of the way the system is designed to work (Localio et al., 1991). This pattern was affirmed in a similar type of study in Utah and Colorado in the early 1990s (Studdert et al., 2000).

Figure 8–1   How the Malpractice Tort System Should and Does Work

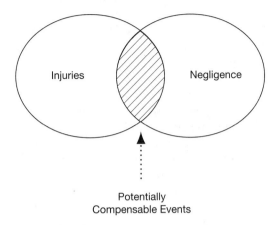

Model 1. How the Tort System *Should* Work

Injuries   Negligence

Potentially
Compensable Events

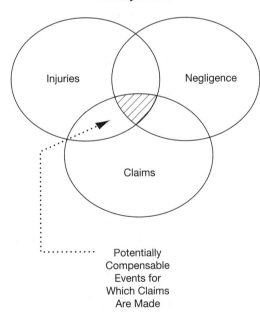

Model 2. How the Tort System *Actually* Works

Injuries   Negligence

Claims

Potentially
Compensable
Events for
Which Claims
Are Made

Source: Robert Wood Johnson Foundation, 1991 *A Bridge.*
Princeton, NJ: Author

Why the Surge in Malpractice Cases?
Several factors help to explain the large increase in the number of malpractice suits filed in the 1970s and 1980s. The consumer movement in health care produced patients who were more sophisticated about health matters and more assertive in defending their rights. Civil-rights based social movements, such as the movements for racial, sexual, and sexual preference equality, stimulated thought about the rights of patients. An increasing number of trial lawyers developed a specialty in medical malpractice and advertised their services. The media picked up on the increase in the number and size of malpractice suits, which undoubtedly stimulated both more legitimate and more frivolous suits to be filed. Finally, all of these circumstances occurred simultaneously with the evolution of increasingly distant relationships between physicians and patients—an important precursor to malpractice litigation.

Consequences of the Malpractice Crisis.
The intended consequences of the medical malpractice system represent only the tip of the iceberg as to the realized effects. Many patients who have received injury through medical negligence have secured compensatory damages, and many physicians who committed injuries by negligence have been found guilty. But the health care system has been affected in other ways.

1. The AMA and individual physicians acknowledge the common practice of **defensive medicine**—physicians prescribe every imaginable test for patients in order to protect themselves from liability in the case of a negative patient outcome. The AMA estimates that defensive medicine adds $15 billion to the nation's health care bill each year.
2. The premiums physicians pay to insurance companies also add to the nation's total health care bill. Ultimately, of course, physicians pass on these costs to patients—further driving up the health care bill.
3. The malpractice crisis has embittered many physicians who are more likely to see every patient as a potential lawsuit, thus creating

strain in the relationship; who believe their profession has been subjected to criticism beyond what is justified; and who see a system that often brings them negative public attention when a suit is filed but little public exoneration when the complaint is unproven. Many physicians who have been charged but not convicted of malpractice are among the most bitter for the trauma created by the experience, as are many physicians who "settle" the case for economic reasons while perceiving themselves not to be liable (Peeples, Harris, and Metzloff, 2000).

4. The high cost of malpractice premiums has caused many physicians to stop offering services. The amount that physicians pay for malpractice can be looked at from several angles and interpreted in different ways. On average, physicians pay about 3 or 4 percent of their revenue for malpractice insurance (as compared to about 12 percent for staff salaries, about 12 percent for office expenses, and about 2 percent for equipment). However, the premium varies widely by specialty, and obstetricians, at about 7 percent, pay the most. Prices tend to be higher in some states and areas than others. For example, Georgia, a state with high premiums, has experienced many obstetricians ceasing to deliver babies in order to lower their malpractice premiums. In January, 2003 more than two dozen physicians at hospitals in Wheeling, West Virginia, took 30-day leaves of absences—causing cancellation of elective surgeries and transfer of some patients to other hospitals—in order to dramatize their malpractice costs.

5. The malpractice crisis has increased acrimony between the medical and legal professions—each of which accuses the other of being the root cause of the crisis. Lawyers argue that malpractice cases are caused by medical errors that physicians commit and that the way to reduce malpractice cases is to reduce malpractice. Physicians argue that malpractice lawyers encourage patients to file suits and to seek large rewards because the lawyer gets a percentage of the award. Doctors believe that the large number of cases is primarily due to

attorney behavior. Some physicians have gone so far as to stop offering services to lawyers and to spouses of lawyers.

Efforts to Reduce the Malpractice Crisis. Attempts to redress these problems are directed along two lines: (1) efforts to improve the physician-patient relationship and (2) efforts to alter the malpractice system.

Research shows that negligence in physician behavior often results from poor physician-patient communication. Patients filing suit often charge that the physician did not provide sufficient information or did not clarify the risks of treatment. Moreover, patients who have rapport with a physician are much less likely to file a malpractice claim than patients in a more distant relationship. In a study of sued and nonsued physicians and suing patients, Shapiro and colleagues (1989) found that, prior to a malpractice claim's being filed, suing patients and their physicians viewed their relationship very differently. Suing patients were much less likely than the physician to believe that theirs was an honest and open relationship.

Given these findings, many physicians have enrolled in workshops and seminars to learn how to better manage relationships with patients. To the extent that these classes are directed at making substantive improvements, real progress may occur; to the extent that these classes are cynical efforts at manipulation, the problems are not likely to be effectively redressed.

Although Congress has spent an enormous amount of time debating malpractice, it has not been able to agree on any actions. However, several states have initiated efforts to modify the malpractice system. Some have placed a maximum cap on the dollar value of awards for "pain and suffering" and for punitive damages (meaning that insurance companies would pay out less when suits are won and would therefore charge physicians lower premiums, resulting in a cost savings that could be passed on to patients). The typical cap amount is $250,000. Physicians and insurance companies strongly endorse this approach, but lawyers and patients who have been victimized strongly oppose it.

Some states have debated a *no-fault insurance system* that would work more quickly and less adversarily than the current system but with smaller payments (physicians could still be penalized by the state medical board). Another option sometimes considered is restricting the amount of money that lawyers can earn from successful malpractice suits. Typically, they receive 30 to 40 percent of the judgment in successful suits.

THE NUMBER, COMPOSITION, AND DISTRIBUTION OF PHYSICIANS IN THE UNITED STATES

Physicians in the United States have never been scrutinized as closely as they have been in the last decade. Three key areas of examination have been the number of physicians (Is the increase in the number of physicians lagging behind or exceeding population growth?); the composition of physicians (What is the representation of women and racial and ethnic minorities in American medicine?); and the distribution of physicians (Are physicians sufficiently dispersed geographically and by specialty?).

The Number of Physicians

In 2000, there were 813,770 physicians in the United States. This is about 32 percent more than in 1990 (an increase of 198,000 physicians) (see Table 8–1). Growth in the number of physicians in the last 30 years has been more than 4 times faster than growth of the U.S. population. This has resulted in a substantial increase in the ratio of physicians per 100,000 population. In 1960, there were 703 persons per physician, compared with 346 persons per physician in 2000.

Has this phenomenal growth in the number of physicians given the United States an adequate supply? There is not a single easy way to answer this question. In fact, the Council on Graduate Medical Education has reversed its position four times in the last three decades on the adequacy of physician supply. As of 2003 (reversing a position held for the previous decade) the position is that (overall) the United States needs to increase its physician supply. This new position results partly from a diminished flow of foreign physicians into the United States since the World Trade Center tragedy on September 11, 2001. Foreign-born physicians account for about one-fourth of all physicians in the United States and an even greater percentage of physicians working in medically underserved areas.

The Composition of Physicians

By Gender. The total number of women physicians in the United States increased from around 54,000 in 1980 to more than 195,000 in 2000—an increase of 278 percent. Women accounted for only 11.6 percent of all physicians in 1980 but 24.0 percent in 2000 (AMA, 2003). Significant increases in medical school

TABLE 8–1   Physicians 1970, 1980, 1990, and 2000

Category	1970	1980	1990	2000
Total	334,028	467,679	615,421	813,770
Male	92.4%	88.4%	83.1%	76.0%
Female	7.6%	11.6%	16.9%	24.0%
Patient care	83.4%	80.5%	81.9%	77.5%
Primary care	41.2%	40.1%	39.7%	40.2%
Graduate of U.S. medical school	81.0%	77.5%	77.2%	74.5%

Source: American Medical Association, Department of Physician Data Sources, Division of Survey and Data Resources, *Physician Characteristics and Distribution in the United States.* Chicago: AMA, 2003.

applications, matriculants, and graduates in the last two decades are reflected in the age distribution of male and female physicians. Older physicians in the United States are predominantly male; younger physicians are more evenly divided.

By Race and Ethnicity.   Due to extensive recruiting efforts, the number of underrepresented racial and ethnic minority students in medical school has increased in the last decade. However, their proportion remains low. While blacks, Hispanics, and Native Americans comprise more than one-fourth of the U.S. population, they represent only about 6 percent of physicians. The medical education of individuals from these groups is particularly important because they are more likely than white physicians to practice in medically underserved areas and to provide medical care for underserved black, Hispanic, and Native American patients (Reede, 2003).

By Geography.   Despite the significant growth in overall physician supply, millions of Americans have inadequate access to health care. In 1999 there were more than 40 million people living in almost 2,000 (mostly rural and inner-city) areas designated as primary care **health professional shortage areas**.

The number of practicing physicians per 100,000 residents is more than twice as high in urban as in rural areas. One-quarter of the United States population—one third of the elderly—live in rural areas, but only 12 percent of active physicians practice there (and many of these are nearing retirement).

Recruitment and Retention of Rural Physicians.   Why are rural areas so undersupplied? Research has discovered three key factors.

1. *Personal factors.* Preference for practice location appears to be dependent on personal desire for rural or urban living rather than on characteristics of specific settings. Considerations include opportunity for personal time, employment opportunities for spouse, quality educational opportunities for children, and the availability of social and cultural activities.
2. *Professional considerations.* These include access to professional colleagues for consultation, medical libraries, and continuing education opportunities.
3. *Economic factors.* As more and more medical students incur large debts, economic factors influence preference for practice location. The widespread poverty in most rural areas results in lower salaries; the percentage of underinsured and uninsured individuals in rural areas is large and growing; and Medicaid eligibility and reimbursement are often more restricted in rural states.

Have the medical profession, medical schools, and governing bodies noticed the physician shortage in rural areas? Yes. The National Health Service Corps (NHSC) was created in 1972 to provide financial assistance to medical students in return for a commitment to practice in an assigned underserved area for a specified number of years. Despite the significant contribution these physicians made to rural health care, studies have discovered that many were unhappy with the area to which they were assigned and with the work conditions that exist in isolated areas. In addition to these efforts, some medical schools have begun to encourage graduates to practice in rural areas, and some states and localities have devised strategies to boost recruitment of physicians in underserved areas. All of these efforts notwithstanding, rural and inner-city areas continue to lack adequate medical resources, and significantly greater effort will be needed to correct the inequity.

By Specialty.   At some point during the medical school years, students decide upon an area of specialization. Although the choice may later change, students apply for residencies in a particular specialty. Specialization choice has been an important issue in the United States as a large percentage of American physicians have opted for a specialty area (e.g., surgery, cardiology, radiology, ophthalmology, psychiatry, and dermatology) rather than entering a primary care field (family practice, internal medicine, and pediatrics—which are specialties themselves).

This pattern is important for two related reasons. First, primary care physicians are the logical entry point into the health care system; if primary care is unavailable, patients are forced to go to a less appropriate first stop—a specialist. Second, the cost of care from a specialist is higher than the cost for primary care—both in terms of standard fees and in the greater number of more expensive tests conducted by specialists.

Early in the twentieth century, the vast majority of physicians were in primary care, but by 2000 almost 80 percent were specialists. The percentage of medical school graduates was low in the late 1980s and early 1990s, increased in the late 1990s, and has now dropped again in the early 2000s (Newton and Grayson, 2003).

What factors have contributed to this drop of interest in primary care? Faculty in many medical schools openly encourage students to pursue specialization and explicitly discourage primary care. Why? The specialties offer more prestige, higher incomes, less frantic work schedules, more research opportunities, and more opportunities to work with high-tech medicine. Despite the recognized need for primary care physicians, most students have found these to be compelling reasons and have opted for a specialty area.

FEMALE PHYSICIANS

Research on physician gender has increased significantly in the last decade. Researchers have especially focused on differences between female and male physicians and on finding explanations for differences. Significantly less research has systematically compared black versus white physicians.

Research in a variety of settings and with a variety of samples has identified three consistent differences between female and male physicians: (1) females and males tend to enter different specialties; (2) females and males have different practice patterns; and (3) females and males interact differently with patients. The first two of these differences are examined here; the third is covered in Chapter 12. A fourth significant difference—the presence of gender-based and sexual harassment—is described in the box, "Gender-based and Sexual Harassment of Female Physicians."

Different Specializations

When female and male fourth-year students are queried about reasons for selecting a particular specialty area for their residency, they offer similar reasons: opportunities for self-fulfillment, positive clinical experiences, and the intellectual

---

IN THE FIELD

GENDER-BASED AND SEXUAL HARASSMENT OF FEMALE PHYSICIANS

Is it possible that widespread gender-based and sexual harassment could exist in medicine and be directed toward female physicians? Emphatically, yes. Based on more than 4,500 responses in a Women Physicians' Health Study, Frank, Brogan, and Schiffman (1998) discovered that almost half of the female physicians (47.7 percent) had experienced gender-based (but not sexual) harassment, and 36.9 percent had experienced sexual harassment.

Where did harassment occur? The most common settings were in medical school and during internship, residency, and fellowship. Younger physicians reported higher rates of harassment. The authors acknowledged that this may reflect a heightened sense of awareness among younger women, but they speculated that harassment actually may be increasing and that female physicians continue to be trained in settings that value power and hierarchy and a legitimation of gender-based and sexual harassment.

challenge of the field. The only key differences are financial advantage, which is somewhat more important to males, and type of patient, which is somewhat more important to females. Despite the similarity in motivation, male and female students systematically choose different specializations (Bowman and Allen, 1985).

The clearest difference in specialization is that women are more likely than men to train in primary care and men are more likely than women to train in surgery. Also, female physicians are less likely than their male counterparts to become board-certified (i.e., to receive certification from a board overseeing each specialty). Over the last few decades, however, specialty choices for women and men have begun to converge. This pattern is even more pronounced among black and Hispanic physicians, who are much more likely than their white counterparts to enter a primary care field.

Different Practice Patterns

Male and female physicians differ in several significant ways in their medical practices:

1. Women are much more likely than men to work in salaried positions in institutional settings (including academic medicine) and are more likely to practice in urban areas. Women are less likely to have an office-based practice.

2. Women work fewer hours per week than men and earn less money. Although differences in both dimensions are narrowing, overall, male physicians still work about 10 to 20 percent more hours per week than female physicians (around 7 to 10 hours per week difference), and males earn considerably more in salary (not all of which can be explained by the difference in hours worked). Differences in number of hours worked per week is also converging—not because women are working more, but because men are working fewer hours.

3. Women are more likely than men to see younger, female, and minority patients. Young black and Hispanic physicians are also much more likely to treat minority patients than are white physicians.

Reasons for the Different Specializations and Practice Patterns.   Analyses of the differences between female and male physicians have suggested two underlying causes: more nonprofessional demands are placed on women (number of family responsibilities relative to career) and influences of professional socialization (especially attitudes of faculty and colleagues).

The difference in number of hours worked per week by male and female physicians occurs almost entirely among physicians who are parents—the difference in hours worked among nonparents is insignificant. At later ages of the life span, when family responsibilities have largely been completed, women work about the same number of hours as men—and are even more likely to be working full time at age 60 (Grant, Simpson, Rong, and Peters-Golden, 1990; Zimmerman, 2000).

This pattern is explained by the different societal expectations regarding emphasis placed on career versus family for males and females. Traditionally, few would even have thought about a male physician altering career commitments (e.g., working fewer hours) upon the birth of a child, but that expectation often is still communicated to female physicians.

In dual-career families with a female physician, as in other dual-career families, the man's career often is still given priority. The woman has primary responsibility for family life and child rearing in addition to her career, while the man often focuses solely on career. Female physicians with a family often continue to do family chores such as house cleaning with little help from the husband or an outside domestic worker. Many female physicians find full dedication to career incompatible with full dedication to family and compromise by temporarily dropping out of the labor force or significantly reducing the number of work hours per week—in essence, sacrificing career advancement for time to raise the children (Grant, Simpson, Rong, and Peters-Golden, 1990).

Females account for one in five primary care physicians but are two in five of today's medical students.

An alternative interpretation for this circumstance has been suggested by some analysts. Some research indicates that child care responsibilities account for only a small part of the work hour differential. Since most female physicians are married to a professional (about 70 percent) and about half are married to a physician, they do not have financial pressures to continue working after the birth of a child.

Thus, upon the arrival of a child, women physicians reduce work hours and reduce workload to the level they most desire. Figure 8–2 documents differences in actual versus ideal work hours by gender and parental status. This explanation, however, does not account for the reason physician-mothers desire a smaller workload than others nor does it account for the fact that female, but not male, physicians reduce work hours after a birth. Whichever explanation prevails, the woman's career (but not her husband's) is put on hold after the birth of a child.

Some of the differences between male and female physicians are traceable to socialization processes in medical school and during internship and residency. Some female students are discouraged by male faculty members from entering certain specialties or in being so dedicated to a career that family interests are subsumed. For

Figure 8–2   Average Weekly Practice Hours of Women and Men Physicians, by Parental Status

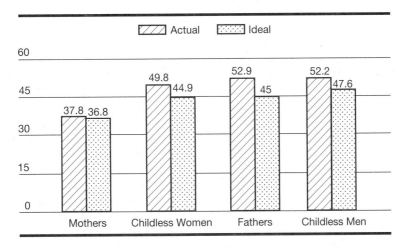

Source: Linda Grant, Layne A. Simpson, Xue L. Rong, and Holly Peters-Golden, "Gender, Parenthood, and Work Hours of Physicians," *Journal of Marriage and the Family,* 52:39–49, 1990, with permission.

IN COMPARATIVE FOCUS

FEMALE PHYSICIANS IN MEXICO

Since the 1970s, social scientists have conducted considerable research on the role of women in economic, social, and political development in developing countries. However, little of this research has focused on the small number of well-educated, middle-class professional women in these countries.

Increased access to medical education has provided many women in Mexico with the opportunity to be physicians. Today, females comprise approximately 30 percent of physicians and 50 percent of medical graduates in Mexico—both figures being higher than the corresponding percent in the United States. However, given the strong emphasis in Mexican culture on the family and on women's central role within family life, the question emerges about the practice patterns of female physicians. Harrison (1998) focused on the extent to which female physicians were as able as male physicians to migrate within Mexico and especially to migrate to areas underserved by physicians. Would female physicians be more influenced by professional opportunities and responsibilities or by expectations for responsibilities to family and home life?

Using both personal interviews and analyses of secondary data sources, Harrison found that female physicians tended to live and work in their native or adopted (often the city in which their medical school is located) states in order to be close to family and friends. This is partially influenced by constraints in the health care system such as availability of specialist training and the medical labor market. However, at virtually every point in the life course, family and household demands strongly influence specialist choice, career development, and migration patterns. Career decisions are viewed as being subordinate to those of the husband, thus conforming to traditional Mexican sociocultural values.

example, faculty often encourage women to enter specialties with limited time commitments and those in which they perceive less competition; male students receive encouragement to enter more competitive specialties that require longer residencies. This problem is exacerbated by the fact that women are still very much underrepresented in leadership positions in academic medicine and are therefore less available as role models and mentors (Yedidia and Bickel, 2001). A recent study based on in-depth interviews with 16 female physicians found that all of them could identify instances of gender bias in their educational careers (Wallace, 1998).

PHYSICIAN SATISFACTION AND DISSATISFACTION

Are today's physicians satisfied with their careers? Some research has found generally positive feelings. Almost three-fourths of physicians in Indianapolis in a recent survey reported satisfaction with their overall practice, though just 59 percent reported satisfaction with their income (Bates et al., 1998). Colby (1997) concludes that, despite reported discontent by physicians, medicine is still an appealing career that draws talented students.

However, much recent research has reported higher levels of dissatisfaction. A 1987 study compared data on young physicians (those under age 40 who had been in practice more than one but fewer than seven years after completing residency and/or fellowship training) with comparable data of an AMA survey among prime physicians (those who were at least age 40 or had been in practice 7 to 24 years) and senior physicians (those in practice 25 years or more). To measure career satisfaction, physicians were asked to respond to the following question: Given what you now know about medicine as a career, if you were in college today, would you go to medical school?

Forty percent of all young physicians reported that they would not or were not sure that they would select a career in medicine (white females were the most dissatisfied of the young physicians). Older physicians reported regret slightly more often than their younger counterparts. Overall satisfaction among the physicians varied by specialty and income: Pediatricians were much more satisfied than anesthesiologists, and physicians with lower incomes were less likely to express regret than higher income physicians. Greater satisfaction was also associated with lower educational debt at graduation and with working in multiple practices (Cohen, Cantor, Barker, and Hughes, 1990).

In addition to this study, medical bulletins, newsletters, letters to editors in journals, newspapers, and conversations at professional meetings give some indication of increasing job dissatisfaction among physicians. Using such anecdotal sources, Stoeckle (1989) identified the chief complaint among physicians to be the bureaucratic and institutional controls that limit discretionary decisions and participation. These controls result from the many external regulations that restrict professional decision making and can reduce power and control over clinical practice. Regulations by third-party payers and amount of paperwork have been the two most frequently cited sources of dissatisfaction found among family practice physicians. Those who are employees of health care facilities also feel they have little control of or participation in practice management. These perceptions have been linked to the likelihood of feeling emotional exhaustion and a sense of burnout (Deckard, Meterko, and Field, 1994).

Many physicians are disturbed that the mission of medicine has changed from one of service to patients to marketing technologies and medical commodities to consumers. The traditional view of provision of care as a civic and/or religious service is viewed as being counter to the newer, secular image of medical work as a "corporate job for the distribution of medical products" (Stoeckle, 1989:85).

Many physicians (especially those in primary care specialties) also express concern about declining incomes relative to purchasing power and report increasing work loads to maintain income levels. As a result of this economic erosion, some physicians perceive a decline in their status. These concerns are accompanied by feelings of vulnerability as a result of quality assurance reviews in hospitals. Physicians often feel under constant scrutiny over the quality of their work and that they are easy targets of criticism and malpractice charges.

In the past, interaction among colleagues was an important source of job satisfaction among physicians. Recently, however, interprofessional communication has declined as competition among providers has increased. This lack of satisfactory contact with fellow physicians is accompanied by less satisfactory encounters with patients. Traditionally, the relationship between physician and patient was considered to be central to medical practice both because of its importance in the diagnosis and treatment of unique individuals and because it inspired and rewarded physicians. The relationship was extremely important because physicians enabled patients to cope with their diseases, disabilities, and death. Today, tests often take the place of patient communication in diagnosis, and advanced technologies deter physicians from encouraging patients to cope with the realities of disability and death. David Mechanic (2003) interprets data in this area to read that most physicians today (about 8 in 10) are satisfied with their medical career, but that they qualify this satisfaction with perceptions of increased time pressures and erosion of autonomy brought on by administrative and regulatory controls.

PHYSICIAN IMPAIRMENT: STRESSES AND STRAINS OF THE PHYSICIAN ROLE

Many people consider physicians to "have it made." They are bright, well-educated, wealthy, prestigious members of the community who typically live in exceptional houses in exceptional neighborhoods with an exceptional number of personal possessions. The image contains a lot of truth—but it misses another side to the career in medicine. Being a physician is a stressful responsibility, and physicians frequently suffer from the accumulation of stressors.

Cultural expectations for physicians certainly are high. Physicians are expected not only to be medical experts but to exercise this expertise without error. Every physician is expected to function at a maximum level of competence all the time. Few patients would be very understanding about a misdiagnosis that occurs because a physician's mind is temporarily diverted. Yet physicians as people experience the same personal traumas as everyone else and sometimes find it difficult to block personal concerns from professional activity.

Traditionally, physicians have been expected to be assertive decision makers in the office or hospital. They have wanted and been given tremendous authority. They are often treated with considerable deference. While these qualities may not always be beneficial in a health care setting, they can be devastating within family relationships. (Many medical auxiliaries swear that physicians believe that the M.D. degree stands for *medical deity*.) When physicians do not make the conversion in their right to give orders from office to home, family relationships can suffer. Moreover, many physicians—especially those in primary care specialties and ob-gyn—are rarely off the job. Knowing that they are only a beep or telephone call away from going back to work, they find it difficult to really relax. Getting out of town is the only solution for many physicians.

Stressors like these sometimes take a serious toll and produce an **impaired physician**—defined by the AMA as "one who is unable to practice medicine with reasonable skill and safety to patients because of physical or mental illness, including deterioration through the aging process or loss of motor skills, or excessive use or abuse of drugs including alcohol" (Shortt, 1979).

One study reported that between 12 and 14 percent of all physicians have had, have now, or will have serious problems with alcohol or other drugs—chemical dependency has been estimated to be 30 to 100 times greater among physicians than the general population. The incidence of mental health problems is higher among practicing physicians than members of similarly educated groups. Physicians end their own lives with greater frequency and earlier in life than other members in the general population, and suicide rates for women physicians are among the highest of any occupational group.

Recognizing the problem, in 1972, the AMA created an "impaired physicians' program" that encouraged physicians to report colleagues in trouble and urged state and local medical societies to initiate treatment programs. All 50 states now have programs in place. The perception is that it is becoming somewhat easier for physicians to seek treatment as the public and physicians have become more enlightened about physician impairment.

SUMMARY

The medical profession in the United States evolved from a poorly regarded, poorly paid, disorganized occupation in the eighteenth and nineteenth centuries to a position of professional dominance by the early twentieth century. Scientific developments had given the public more confidence in medicine and the government extended legal autonomy—the right of self-control.

However, most analysts believe that the medical profession's dominance is waning and being replaced by a variety of agents, including corporations and the federal government. The theory of countervailing power posits that any profession's dominance is a temporary phenomenon existing only till other forces increase their power.

Social control of medicine refers to forces inside and outside medicine that can regulate medical practice. Internal control mechanisms have a mixed record of effectiveness as regulatory processes; patients can exercise some external control through such means as malpractice litigation. While injured patients are sometimes compensated through lawsuits, the American system has many problems including many victims of malpractice who are not compensated and many nonvictims who do file suits.

The number of physicians in the United States has increased to an extent that many believe a surplus exists, but too few physicians have been entering primary care or choosing to practice in medically underserved areas. Female, Hispanic, and black physicians are more likely than white male physicians to enter primary care, and some systematic differences between female and male physicians in practice patterns remain. These are attributable to family responsibilities being differentially defined and to professional socialization.

Recent research has focused on two significant problems among physicians: increasing professional dissatisfaction and high rates of stress-induced physician impairment.

HEALTH ON THE INTERNET

Information is now available on the Internet about individual physicians, hospitals, and other health care providers. Not all states are included yet, but they are likely to come sooner or later. Check out the following Web sites:

> http://www.docboard.org
> http://www.healthgrades.com
> http://www.healthcarechoices.org

What kind of information can you acquire at each of these sites? Why can't you get even more detailed information? How do you think the presence of Internet sites such as these will affect the practice of medicine?

KEY CONCEPTS AND TERMS

American Medical Association (AMA)
corporatization
countervailing power
defensive medicine
deprofessionalization
Harvard Medical Practice Study
Health Professional Shortage Area
hospital review committees
impaired physician

medical malpractice
National Practitioner Data Bank
peer review
profession
professional dominance
proletarianization
social control
State Board of Medicine

DISCUSSION CASE

("When the Doctor is on Drugs," *Hastings Center Report,* Volume 21, September-October, 1991:29.)

You are both personal physician and friend to another physician, Dr. G. He has seemed withdrawn, irritable, and distracted recently. You have heard rumors through the hospital grapevine that not long ago he made a serious error in calculating a medication dosage, but that the error was caught by the pharmacist before the drug was dispensed.

Dr. G. has resisted your gentle explorations and expressions of concern during casual encounters, so you are surprised when he blurts out while seeing you for a routine office visit that he is using cocaine daily. You encourage him to enter a detoxification and addiction treatment program but he declines, saying that he can "handle it" by himself. Unfortunately, his personality changes persist, and even though he assures you that he is now drug free you strongly suspect that Dr. G.'s drug abuse continues. No further obvious medical errors occur, but stories are circulating in the hospital about his abusive responses to late-night telephone calls. When you directly confront him with your suspicions, he cuts off all further contact with you.

You wish to intervene, but are uncertain how to proceed. You believe you should at least raise your concerns to the quality assurance committee of the hospital medical staff or to the impaired physicians' committee of the state medical society, if not to the state licensing board. Are you justified in doing so on the basis of your current information? Won't Dr. G. just deny everything and accuse you of possessing an economic motive? Should his admission of cocaine use to you during a professional contact be kept confidential? What are the moral and legal implications of breaking confidentiality?

If you do not reveal everything that you know, you have no convincing evidence to present. You realize you have no proof that Dr. G. has harmed any patient, but wonder if your social duty extends to protecting his patients from the possibility of future damage. What if you're wrong, and he is no longer using drugs? If being irritable is a crime, the hospital medical staff is going to be decimated! If you intervene, there is a real chance that Dr. G. will end up the victim of rumors in the community and perhaps have his name listed in the National Practitioner Data Bank. How can you sort through your duties to him as friend, as his physician, and as his colleague, while remembering that you have duties to society as well?

REFERENCES

American Medical Association, Department of Physician Data Sources, Division of Survey and Data Resources. 2003 *Physician Characteristics and Distribution in the United States.* Chicago: American Medical Association.

Bates, Ann S., Lisa E. Harris, William M. Tierney, and Frederic D. Wolinsky. 1998 "Dimensions and Correlates of Physician Work Satisfaction in a Midwestern City," *Medical Care,* 36:610–617.

Bowman, Marjorie A., and Deborah I. Allen. 1985 *Stress and Women Physicians.* New York: Springer-Verlag.

Cohen, Alan B., Joel C. Cantor, Dianne C. Barker, and Robert G. Hughes. 1990 "Young Physicians and the Future of the Medical Profession." *Health Affairs,* 9:138–148.

Colby, David C. 1997 "Doctors and Their Discontents." *Health Affairs,* 16:112–114.

Deckard, Gloria, Mark Meterko, and Diane Field. 1994 "Physician Burnout: An Examination of Personal, Professional, and Organizational Relationships." *Medical Care,* 32:745–754.

Ehrenreich, Barbara, and Deirdre English. 1973 *Witches, Midwives, and Nurses—A History of Women Healers.* Old Westbury, NY: The Feminist Press.

Frank, Erica, Donna Brogan, and Melissa Schiffman. 1998 "Prevalence and Correlates of Harassment Among U.S. Women Physicians." *Archives of Internal Medicine,* 158:352–358.

Freidson, Eliot. 1970a *Profession of Medicine: A Study in the Sociology of Applied Knowledge.* New York: Dodd, Mead.

———. 1970b *Professional Dominance: The Social Structure of Medical Care.* New York: Atherton Press.

———. 1984 "The Changing Nature of Professional Control." *Annual Review of Sociology,* 10:1–20.

———. 1985 "The Reorganization of the Medical Profession." *Medical Care Review,* 42:11–35.

Goode, William J. 1960 "Encroachment, Charlatanism, and the Emerging Profession: Psychology, Sociology, and Medicine." *American Sociological Review,* 25:902–914.

Grant, Linda, Layne A. Simpson, Xue L. Rong, and Holly Peters-Golden. 1990 "Gender, Parenthood, and Work Hours of Physicians." *Journal of Marriage and the Family,* 52:39–49.

Hafferty, Frederic W., and Donald W. Light. 1995 "Professional Dynamics and the Changing Nature of Medical Work." *Journal of Health and Social Behavior,* Extra Issue:132–153.

Harrison, Margaret E. 1998 "Female Physicians in Mexico: Migration and Mobility in the Lifecourse." *Social Science and Medicine,* 47:455–468.

Haug, Marie. 1973 "Deprofessionalization: An Alternate Hypothesis for the Future." *Sociological Review Monograph,* 20:195–211.

———. 1988 "A Re-examination of the Hypothesis of Physician Deprofessionalization." *Milbank Quarterly,* 66(Supp. 2):48–56.

Haug, Marie, and Bebe Lavin. 1983 *Consumerism in Medicine: Challenging Physician Authority.* Beverly Hills, CA: Sage.

Hite, Chuck, and Douglas Pardue. 1984 "Despite 'Ignorance, Carelessness,' Doctor Regains License to Practice." *Roanoke Times and World News,* October 7, pp. A1, A14.

Light, Donald W. 1991 "Professionalism as a Countervailing Power." *Journal of Health Politics, Policy, and Law,* 16:499–506.

———. 2000 "The Medical Profession and Organizational Change: From Professional Dominance to Countervailing Power," pp. 201–216 in *Handbook of Medical Sociology* (5th ed.). Chloe E. Bird, Peter Conrad, and Allen M. Fremont (eds.). Upper Saddle River, NJ: Prentice Hall.

Light, Donald W., and Sol Levine. 1988 "The Changing Character of the Medical Profession: A Theoretical Overview." *The Milbank Quarterly,* 66:10–32.

Localio, A. Russell, Ann G. Lawthers, Troyen A. Brennan, Nan M. Laird, Liesi E. Hebert, Lynn M. Peterson, Joseph P. Newhouse, Paul C. Weiler, and Howard H. Hiatt. 1991 "Relation Between Malpractice Claims and Adverse Events Due to Negligence." *New England Journal of Medicine,* 325: 245–251.

McArthur, John H., and Francis D. Moore. 1997 "The Two Cultures and the Health Care Revolution." *Journal of the American Medical Association,* 277:985–989.

McKinlay, John B., and John D. Stoeckle. 1988 "Corporatization and the Social Transformation of Doctoring." *International Journal of Health Services,* 18:191–205.

Mechanic, David. 1996 "Changing Medical Organization and the Erosion of Trust." *The Milbank Quarterly,* 74:171–189.

———. 2003 "Physician Discontent: Challenges and Opportunities." *Journal of the American Medical Association,* 290:941–946.

Mello, Michelle M., David M. Studdert, and Troyen A. Brennan. 2003 "The New Medical Malpractice Crisis." *New England Journal of Medicine,* 348: 2281–2284.

Navarro, Vicente. 1988 "Professional Dominance or Proletarianization?: Neither." *The Milbank Quarterly,* 66:57–75.

Newton, Dale A., and Martha S. Grayson. 2003 "Trends in Career Choice by U.S. Medical School Graduates." *Journal of the American Medical Association,* 290:1179–1182.

Peeples, Ralph, Catherine T. Harris, and Thomas B. Metzloff. 2000 "Settlement Has Many Faces: Physicians, Attorneys, and Medical Malpractice." *Journal of Health and Social Behavior,* 41:333–346.

Reede, Joan Y. 2003 "A Recurring Theme: The Need for Minority Physicians." *Health Affairs,* 22:91–93.

Robert Wood Johnson Foundation. 1991 *A Bridge.* Princeton, NJ: Author.

Romano, Michael. 2001 "AMA Rethinks Unionizing Efforts; Cites Recent Ruling." *Modern Healthcare,* 30:14–16.

Rubin, Haya, William H. Rogers, Katherine L. Kahn, Lisa V. Rubenstein, and Robert H. Brook. 1992 "Watching the Doctor-Watchers: How Well Do Peer Review Organization Methods Detect Hospital Care Quality Problems?" *Journal of the American Medical Association,* 267:2349–2354.

Shapiro, Robyn S., Deborah E. Simpson, Steven L. Lawrence, Anne M. Talsky, Kathleen A. Sococinski, and David L. Schiedermayer. 1989 "A Survey of Sued and Nonsued Physicians and Suing Patients." *Archives of Internal Medicine,* 149:2190–2196.

Shortt, S. E. D. 1979 "Psychiatric Illness in Physicians." *Canadian Medical Association Journal,* 121:283–288.

Stoeckle, John D. 1989 "Reflections on Modern Doctoring." *The Milbank Quarterly,* 66:76–91.

Studdert, David M., Eric J. Thomas, Helen R. Burstin, Brett W. Zbar, E. John Orav, and Troyen A. Brennan. 2000 "Negligent Care and Malpractice Claiming Behavior in Utah and Colorado." *Medical Care,* 38:250–260.

Thompson, Elizabeth. 2001 "Unionization of Physicians a Small But Significant Force as Relationships with Hospitals Change." *Modern Healthcare,* 31:35–40.

Wallace, Susan L. 1998 "Female Physicians' Perspectives on Gender Bias in Education: Negotiating Gender Through Insulation." Paper presented at the Virginia Social Science Association Annual Meeting, Bridgewater, VA, March 27.

"When the Doctor is on Drugs." 1991 *Hastings Center Report,* 21:29.

Wolinsky, Frederic D. 1993 "The Professional Dominance, Deprofessionalization, Proletarianization, and Corporatization Perspectives: An Overview and Synthesis," pp. 11–24 in *The Changing Medical Profession.* Frederic W. Hafferty and John B. McKinlay (eds.). New York: Oxford University Press.

Yedidia, Michael J., and Janet Bickel. 2001 "Why Aren't There More Women Leaders in Academic Medicine? The Views of Clinical Department Chairs." *Academic Medicine,* 76:453–465.

Zimmerman, Mary K. 2000 "Women's Health and Gender Bias in Medical Education," pp.121–138 in *Research in the Sociology of Health Care, 2000.* Jennie J. Kronenfeld (ed.). Stamford, CT: Jai Press.

9

MEDICAL EDUCATION AND THE SOCIALIZATION OF PHYSICIANS

Socialization is the process by which a person becomes a member of a group or society and acquires values, attitudes, beliefs, behavior patterns, and a sense of social identity. It is a lifelong process; as each new role is added, one integrates new expectations with previous behavior.

Physicians undergo both formal and informal socialization into the medical role. The medical school experience is structured to impart knowledge and technique and also certain attitudes and values. Through the process, medical students are consciously and subconsciously converted from laypersons to health care professionals. This chapter traces the development and organization of the formal educational system for physicians and describes the socialization processes that occur.

THE HISTORY OF MEDICAL EDUCATION

Early Medical Education

During the colonial period, the primary mode of medical instruction was the apprenticeship system, but the quality of these apprenticeships varied enormously. A few preceptors provided meaningful experiences in active practice and close supervision of their students, but many others made little effort to provide any systematic instruction. Though a three-year apprenticeship was considered standard, in reality a certificate was routinely issued to any student who merely registered with a physician.

By the year 1800, three formal medical schools (the University of Pennsylvania, Harvard, and King's College) had been established. These schools were eventually joined by an increasing number of proprietary (for-profit) medical schools, which became the dominant vehicle of medical education by the mid-nineteenth century. Ability to pay the fees was the only entrance requirement for white males, and few of the applicants had any college preparation. In fact, most students had completed elementary school only, and many were illiterate (Ludmerer, 1985).

Two four-month terms of lectures made up the standard course of instruction. The curriculum focused on subjects of "practical" value with little attention to scientific subjects.

Written examinations were not required in order to graduate, but the diploma "licensed" the young physician to practice medicine anywhere in the country. Some students opted to supplement their medical education by serving as a "house pupil" in a hospital. These pupils, selected by a competitive examination, would reside in a hospital and assume responsibility for managing cases, much as medical students and house officers do today (Ludmerer, 1985).

An alternative to an apprenticeship or American medical school was European study—most often in France. Between 1820 and 1861, nearly 700 Americans studied medicine in Paris. However, few aspiring doctors had the financial means to study abroad (Ludmerer, 1985).

Medical Education for Women. While the standards for admission were lax for white males, women faced much greater obstacles. By 1880, only a handful of medical schools accepted women on a regular basis. Though **Elizabeth Blackwell** (1821–1910) earned an M.D. degree from the Geneva College of Medicine in upstate New York in 1849 (becoming the first woman in this country to do so), most women were forced to attend independent medical schools created expressly for their training. During the second half of the nineteenth century, 14 of these women's medical colleges were established in the United States.

Some of this gender bias receded during the latter part of the nineteenth century and the first two decades of the twentieth century, and numerous medical societies began admitting women. By 1900, women accounted for more than 10 percent of enrollment at almost 20 medical schools, and 12 of the women's colleges had closed or merged. However, beginning around 1920, a reversal occurred as women's acceptance by professional medicine declined.

Medical Education for Blacks. Medical education was formally denied to blacks throughout the United States prior to the Civil War. After emancipation, would-be black physicians turned to missionary or proprietary medical schools established in the South. The most common motivation for starting these schools was to train black physicians to serve the black population.

The most prestigious black medical college, Howard University, opened in 1869, and it remained the primary source for medical education of blacks for the next century. As late as 1890, however, blacks comprised less than 1 percent of physicians in the United States, and both black and female institutions engaged in constant struggles for survival.

Early Reform Efforts

Early efforts to reform medical education included raising standards for admission, lengthening the training process, revising curricula, and adding clinical instruction. One obstacle to reform was the dependence of medical professors on student fees—thus mandating that students not be discouraged from applying or persisting once admitted. In addition, American physicians distrusted the laboratory and lacked respect for experimental science, and few medical educators had any interest in research (Ludmerer, 1985).

However, by the mid-1880s, many medical schools themselves had initiated reform. Length of training expanded—eventually to four years— and entrance requirements were strengthened. Curricula were revised to stress scientific subjects, and laboratory experiences were included whenever possible. Though these changes were not instituted uniformly—so that the quality of medical education varied greatly—momentum for reform was high (Ludmerer, 1985).

The Flexner Report. Capitalizing on this desire for improvement, The American Medical Association made reform of medical schools a top priority in 1904 by establishing a Council on Medical Education. The Council determined premedical education requirements, developed a standard training period, and constructed a licensing test. In addition, the quality of medical schools was evaluated and many schools were judged to be inferior. The report was distributed to medical schools but was never published because it was considered politically risky for a medical organization to criticize medical schools publicly.

Instead, the Council commissioned the Carnegie Foundation for the Advancement of Teaching to conduct a similar study, to be headed by Abraham Flexner. As discussed in Chapter 2, the **Flexner Report** recognized the diversity of the American medical scene—which included some of the best and some of the worst medical schools in the world. His 1910 report, *Medical Education in the United States and Canada,* strongly attacked the weakest schools, especially the proprietaries. "The result was a classic piece of muckraking journalism that deserves to rank with the other great muckraking treatises of the era. He provided a wealth of details, named names, and devastated the bad schools with humiliating public exposure" (Ludmerer, 1985:179).

The report accomplished its purpose as it aligned medical educators and the public against proprietary schools and in favor of a homogeneous, university-based system of education focused on scientific medicine. The AMA worked closely with philanthropic foundations to provide financial assistance to help embed this model on a national level. Small, proprietary schools, which could not mimic the model approach, were not funded by corporate trusts. Numerous colleges were forced to close, including five of the seven black medical schools and all but one of the women's colleges. As a result, the total number of medical graduates, and especially the number of female and black graduates, declined.

MODERN MEDICAL EDUCATION

The Foundation of a New Curriculum

By the 1920s, a new type of medical education had begun. Advocated by Flexner and embraced by the AMA and the nation's top medical schools, a revised medical school curriculum (sometimes referred to as the Johns Hopkins model) was implemented. Despite some later innovations, the basic principles of the new curriculum remain in place today. They include:

1. A clear separation between the basic sciences (taught in the first two years) and the clinical sciences (taught in the third and fourth years).
2. A heavy reliance on didactic instruction in the form of lectures to large classes (especially in teaching the basic sciences) utilizing the instructor as expert (as opposed to personal investigation).
3. Relatively independent and often uncoordinated courses taught by full-time faculty in many different departments.
4. The clerkship years (often relying on residents as instructors) as an integral part of medical education.

Academic Health Centers and Medical Schools Today

There are 125 medical schools in the United States accredited by the Liaison Committee on Medical Education (LCME), the official accrediting agency for programs leading to the doctor of medicine degree. This marks an increase from 86 schools in 1960–1961 and 103 in 1970–1971 but a decrease of one school (Oral Roberts University) since 1990. U.S. medical schools employ more than 100,000 full-time faculty; in recent years, the number of full-time medical faculty has increased more rapidly than the number of medical students.

Each medical school is part of a large configuration of programs and services called an **academic health center (AHC)**. These centers typically consist of one or more hospitals with comprehensive medical specialties, the latest and most advanced medical technology, and sophisticated research laboratories. Often, they are a dominant part of the university in which they are located; and they may be the institution's largest securer of grant money and its most prestigious component. In many cases the health centers have such extensive facilities and generate so much money that they are largely independent of university control.

IN COMPARATIVE FOCUS

MEDICAL EDUCATION IN CHINA

As the most populated country in the world and one whose population is largely rural, China faces a difficult challenge in having a sufficient number of health care providers. In a model that is partly based on western-style medical education and partly based on its own culture and social circumstances, China provides three levels of education for physicians:

Assistant Doctors are trained for several months to two years and then are able to provide basic primary care in mostly rural villages.

Medical Doctors are trained either at Level 1 (a three-year program that includes condensed basic sciences and clinical subjects in the first two years and hospital practice in the third year and prepares doctors to work in rural communities) or at Level 2 (a five-year curriculum that includes all of the basic sciences in the first three years, general medicine and surgery in the fourth year, and hospital practice in the fifth year and prepares doctors to work in urban areas).

Specialists undergo seven or eight years of training and essentially receive the same

training as Level 2 doctors plus additional training in specialty areas. They then typically work in urban areas and provide specialty care and complex surgeries.

Medical education in China includes both a western style, scientific-based curriculum (including anatomy and physiology) and education in traditional Chinese healing theory and practice (including knowledge of acupuncture). Some schools focus more on Western medicine whereas others focus more on traditional medicine.

The Chinese system for medical education acknowledges that China does not have a sufficient number of fully trained physicians to meet the needs of the total population. By requiring fewer years of preparation for those who will solely provide basic primary care, more individuals can be medically trained and the needs of both the urban and rural populations can be addressed. In addition, health care providers can focus their education on more or less traditional healing practices, thus making both approaches available to patients (Lassey, Lassey, and Jinks, 1997).

Medical Students

The number of applicants to U.S. medical schools declined significantly during the 1980s, rose sharply in the early and mid-90s (there were about 47,000 applicants in 1996), and then dropped very sharply every year from 1997 until 2003 (there were about 33,600 applicants in 2002 and 35,000 in 2003) when there was a slight rebound (see Table 9–1).

At least three factors have contributed to this decrease: (1) many bright male students have become more attracted to the multiple opportunities and potentially larger salaries in business,

TABLE 9–1   Applications to U.S. Medical Schools Over 25-Year Period

Academic Year	Number of Applicants	Total Applications	Number of Accepted Applicants	First-Year Enrollment
1979–1980	36,141	335,141	16,886	17,014
1989–1990	26,915	262,426	16,975	16,749
1999–2000	38,529	454,380	17,445	16,856
2003–2004	34,785	392,118	17,539	16,538

Source: Reprinted with permission from the Association of American Medical Colleges.

TABLE 9–2 Women in U.S. Medical Schools Over 25-Year Period

Academic Year	Number Women Applicants (%)	Number Entering Women (%)	Number Graduates (%)
1979–1980	10,222 (28.3)	4,748 (27.9)	3,497 (23.1)
1989–1990	10,546 (39.2)	6,404 (38.2)	5,197 (33.9)
1999–2000	17,433 (45.2)	7,725 (45.8)	6,712 (42.4)
2003–2004	17,672 (50.8)	8,212 (49.7)	6,909 (44.1)

Source: Reprinted with permission from the Association of American Medical Colleges.

computers, and technology; (2) physician dissatisfaction with managed care has dissuaded some potential medical students from applying; and (3) judicial and legislative decisions that have scaled back affirmative action programs have led to a decrease in the number of racial and ethnic minority applicants.

The mean grade point average for admitted students in 2002 was 3.61. Once admitted, almost all students earn their degree (the attrition rate is only about 1 percent).

Female Medical Students. In 2003, just over 50 percent of applicants and just under 50 percent of matriculants to medical school were women—the highest percentage ever (see Table 9–2), but the percentage of women admit-

tants by school varies widely. In recent years, female applicants and matriculants have a slightly lower grade point average than their male peers in science, but an overall grade point average that is slightly higher. Performance in medical school is indistinguishable by gender (Ramsbottom-Lucier, Johnson, and Elam, 1995).

Racial and Ethnic Minority Medical Students. In 2004, 37.9 percent of first-year medical students were racial and ethnic minority students. Asian-American students (18.6 percent), Hispanic students (7.1 percent), and African-American students (6.5 percent) account for the vast majority of these students (see Table 9–3). The number of applications from members of underrepresented minority groups

TABLE 9–3 Race and Ethnic Background of Medical School Enrollees, 2004–2005

Background	Applicants (%)		First-Year Enrollment (%)	
White	21,023	(58.8)	10,338	(62.1)
African American	2,803	(7.8)	1,086	(6.5)
Hispanic	2,545	(7.1)	1,174	(7.1)
Mexican American	810	(2.3)	377	(2.3)
Puerto Rican	505	(1.4)	282	(1.7)
Cuban American	144	(0.4)	80	(0.5)
Other Hispanic	890	(3.0)	359	(2.2)
Multiple Hispanic	196	(0.5)	76	(0.5)
Asian	6,732	(18.8)	3,093	(18.6)
Native American/ Alaskan Native	106	(0.3)	48	(0.3)
Hawaiian//Pacific Islander	39	(0.1)	11	(0.1)
Other/Unknown	347	(1.0)	172	(1.0)
Multiple Race	1,107	(3.1)	497	(3.0)
Non-U.S.	1,025	(2.9)	219	(1.3)
Total	**35,727**		**16,638**	

Source: Reprinted with permission from the Association of American Medical Colleges.

increased during the 1990s. Acceptance of minority applicants continues to be approximately the same as for other applicants. The landmark civil rights court decisions and the legislation of the 1950s and 1960s served to open the doors of all medical schools to minority candidates. In 1969, the Association of American Medical Colleges (AAMC) established an Office of Minority Affairs in an attempt to encourage more minority students to seek a medical education. The AAMC has established the goal of proportional representation in medicine for all groups and has paid special attention to minorities that have been underrepresented. However, the scaling back of affirmative action programs in the late 1990s and early 2000s has led to a significant decrease in minority applicants (Cohen, 2003). For example, 1,455 black students entered medical school in 1996 while just 1,086 did so in 2004.

The Medical Education Curriculum

Years One and Two.   Most medical schools offer a similar **medical school curriculum**. The first two years are devoted to the basic sciences (e.g., anatomy, biochemistry, microbiology, pathology, pharmacology, and physiology). Largely taught through the traditional lecture format, students are often overwhelmed by the amount of information presented. The units are highly compacted and very intense; students quickly learn that they cannot possibly learn everything, so they quickly search for memorization aides. Classes often are large, and medical faculty tend to be impersonal (a significant change and major disappointment for many students). Most schools require Part I of the National Board of Medical Examiners (NBME) examination to be taken and passed after the second year.

Years Three and Four.   During the third and fourth years—the clinical years—students learn to use their basic medical science to solve actual clinical problems by working with patients (almost always in hospitals). During these two years, students rotate through several (typically about nine) clerkships to learn specialized applications of medical knowledge. Students spend an average of about 6 weeks in family practice, 12 weeks in internal medicine, 8 weeks in general surgery, 8 weeks in pediatrics, 7 weeks in obstetrics and gynecology, and 7 weeks in psychiatry Students often make rounds during these years—accompanied by impersonal faculty and intensive oral exams. Most schools require passage of Part II of the NBME exam after the fourth year.

The Internship and Residency.   After the fourth year, most students enter a medical residency (except for those who intend to do research or work outside medicine). A computerized matching process is used to pair residents looking for a teaching hospital with particular traits (e.g., specialization or location) and for hospitals attempting to secure the best possible residents. The number of years required in residency depends upon the specialty interests of the resident—three is common but several specialties require more. The resident (the first year of the residency is still sometimes referred to as the internship) is legally able to practice medicine under the supervision of a licensed physician.

Significant role identity change from student to physician occurs during these years. The resident has much more authority than the fourth-year student, and that often comes across in relationships with patients and with ancillary staff. This is a learning period for residents, and they often search for—and are most excited to work with—intriguing cases. On the other hand, medical residents are a primary source of cheap labor for hospitals, and they are expected to handle many routine responsibilities. The hours assigned typically are very long; exhaustion is not uncommon (due to medical school debts, many residents even moonlight—taking on additional paid medical responsibilities in the few off-hours they have); and it is often a frustrating and disillusioning time.

The Crisis in Academic Health Centers

The nation's academic health centers are in an extremely perilous state at present, and many have operated in recent years with sizable debt and are now struggling to remain solvent. In a

Despite some reform efforts, most medical students spend much of their first two years in large lecture classes covering the basic sciences.

highly praised book, *Time to Health: American Medical Education from the Turn of the Century to the Era of Managed Care,* Kenneth Ludmerer (1999) describes a wide range of factors that have recently put enormous pressure on the resources of the centers. These forces include the managed care revolution that requires health providers to look for lowest cost options in delivering care (such as doing more services on an outpatient basis) and to collaborate in ways to be more efficient; the increasing costs in providing medical education and in conducting medical research; the substantial provision of care for those unable to pay; and sharp reductions in government reimbursement for care provided. AHCs have been hit particularly hard by these forces because of the ways they traditionally have been configured: prices are typically higher in AHCs than in nonacademic hospitals; staffs are dominated by specialists rather than generalists; emphasis is on expensive high-tech medicine; large research expenses are incurred, and, in most schools, departments have not his-

torically worked closely together—all patterns that are incompatible with recent changes in health care.

Ludmerer contends that part of the problem is the inability and unwillingness of the centers to reconfigure in ways that would enable them to continue providing high quality medical education and high quality medical care. Instead, financial cutbacks have tended to come in areas that directly compromise the quality of programs and services. For example, new clinical faculty are hired but often are not asked to be part of the teaching program. Faculty who do teach spend less time mentoring students. Clinicians are asked to speed up each patient encounter so that more patients can be seen in the day. In this environment, Ludmerer fears that students are increasingly likely to focus on the business and bureaucratic side of medicine while neglecting medicine's core: a Samaritan concern for the care, suffering, and well-being of the sick (Fox, 1999). Hafferty (1999) concurs and encourages the centers to restore the primacy of the teaching

IN THE FIELD

HEALTH CARE REFORM AND MEDICAL EDUCATION

What effects will health care reform have on medical education? These four effects are likely (Iglehart, 1994; Pardes, 1997).

1. Either through personal initiative or government regulation, medical schools will reduce the number of students accepted into their programs in order to reduce the expected oversupply of physicians. (This did occur, but is now being reversed.)
2. Medical schools will devise new programs to encourage students to enter a primary care field. These programs will involve the hiring of additional primary care physicians to the faculty, utilizing more ambulatory care sites for clinical instruction, and adding emphasis in the curriculum on prevention, public health, and effective communication with patients. These plans will supplement the greater financial rewards that managed care plans are investing in primary care.
3. The federal government will offer increased subsidies to provide for the training of

physicians and for clinical research and technological development conducted in AHCs. In the past, health insurers were willing to pay higher prices for care delivered in AHCs. Part of these extra funds subsidized research and development (R&D) activities. Now, price competition and regulation have reduced this surplus so that R&D activities are jeopardized. The government may choose to pick up part of the difference. In the last few years the National Institutes of Health has significantly increased its financial commitment to medical research.
4. AHCs will increasingly seek formal relationships with managed care organizations and will make adjustments in their traditional organization. To remain competitive, the number of faculty, their salaries, and the creation of new programs may be diminished. AHCs will form partnerships with each other to reduce expenses.

of values and professionalism to the core of the curriculum and to focus less on the transmission of esoteric knowledge and core clinical skills.

Specific Criticisms of the Medical Education Curriculum

There is considerable agreement that the traditional medical school curriculum falls short of the ideal. Critics, often from inside academic health centers, have identified at least four important criticisms.

First, too little priority is given to teaching by medical faculty who are hired and promoted based on their record in research, grantsmanship, and clinical practice. As the entire incentive structure focuses on nonteaching activities, dedication to working with medical students often is lacking (Regan-Smith, 1998). As an illustration, despite the fact that the number of

faculty has increased significantly in recent years while the number of students has increased by only a small number, faculty are not spending any additional time in the classroom. In reflecting on the dominance of nonteaching activities in academic centers, David Rogers (1987:38) laments the passing of earlier ways:

> Gone are the leisurely laboratory sessions where students and faculty became acquainted one with another in a problem-solving mode. Gone are the informal after-hours get-togethers with faculty who knew students and vice versa, which I remember with such fondness from my own student days. Gone are the genuine, go-at-your-own pace problem-solving sessions in which students learned to think deductively and gained experience in logical decision making.

Second, an extensive amount of departmental and research specialization prevents integration of the curriculum. Many academic physicians focus on only one aspect of medical education—clinical practice, teaching, research, or administration—and have little interaction with those who have other priorities. Departments (referred to as "fiefdoms" by many faculty themselves) are locked into continuing competition for prestige and for both internal and external funding (e.g., basic science and clinical departments often struggle for power) (Ludmerer, 1985).

> The faculty members from any one discipline are usually unaware of and not interested in the material presented in other courses. As a consequence, students are presented with uncoordinated information from the various biological sciences. The content of any one course is unrelated to the content of other courses and there may be gaps or duplications. Information from the courses taken collectively is unrelated in any explicit manner to clinical application. (Bussigel, Barzansky, and Grenholm, 1988:5)

Third, most medical curricula continue to focus on the presentation of facts and on the ability of students to memorize facts. Especially in the first two years, lecture pedagogy and fact-based exams dominate. Much less time is devoted to the enhancement of students' analytic skills. Given the speed with which new facts become available and the nature of medicine as a question-answering, problem-solving field, the emphasis on passive rather than active learning is difficult to understand.

Moreover, crucial aspects of the actual practice of medicine are sometimes given little or no attention. Understanding the importance of sociocultural influences on patient behavior, the development of interpersonal skills (such as verbal and nonverbal communication and the development of rapport with patients) and reflection on ethical questions rarely are highlighted.

Finally, today's medical school curriculum is out of step with current realities, such as changes in disease patterns and changes in the financing of health care. Despite the fact that chronic disease accounts for approximately 75 percent of deaths in the United States, medical education continues to focus heavily on acute health problems and late intervention therapies and largely ignores the importance of lifestyle education, preventive health care, and the influence of social factors on disease and illness.

Curricular Reform

Over the course of the last three decades, at least four significant efforts at curricular change have occurred.

Problem-based learning (PBL), developed at McMaster and Michigan State Universities in the 1970s and incorporated elsewhere, attempts to overcome the fact-based approach in the traditional curriculum by emphasizing student problem solving. In contrast to traditional lecture-based learning, students studying under PBL are more likely to have actual patient contact from the beginning of medical school and to work routinely with patient case studies and with simulated patients. Emphasis is placed on analytical reasoning and methods for acquiring and applying information. The instructor is not the "answer expert" but a facilitator assisting students in doing the problem solving.

Is this an effective teaching strategy? Research indicates that it is. Several studies have found that students using PBL outperform students using lecture-based learning on tasks such as retention of factual knowledge, ability to take a history and perform a physical exam, derive a diagnosis, and organize and express information (Richards et al., 1996). Medical school faculty who have worked with PBL rate it highly in the areas clinical preparation, medical reasoning, and student interest but less highly in teaching factual knowledge and efficiency of learning. Faculty most involved with PBL rate it most highly (Vernon and Hosokawa, 1996).

Teaching professional skills and perspectives has long been recommended but only recently seriously developed by a sizable number of medical schools. Though often taken only on an elective basis, courses in physician-patient communication, physical examination, health promotion and disease prevention, working with diverse populations, medical ethics, and medical sociology are now widely available in medical schools and increasingly recognized as being essential in the comprehensive training of physicians. It is likely that these courses will be further integrated into medical school curricula in the future (Makoul, Curry, and Novack, 1998).

Community-based medical education involves the shifting of clinical training from hospital wards to outpatient settings such as physicians' offices and community health centers. Although this shift may reduce the number of opportunities that medical students have to do certain procedures (e.g., insertion of a nasogastric tube), it creates many more opportunities to interact with patients in the type of setting in which most physician-patient interaction actually occurs (Hensel et al., 1996).

Evidence-based medicine (EBM) has become a well-accepted curricular change. Acknowledging that wide disparities in diagnosis and standard treatment exist among and even within communities, EBM is an effort to have physicians' selection of medical therapies rely less on intuition and anecdotal evidence and more on medical therapies that have been tested and determined to be effective in scientific research. It has evolved now to a point at which physicians are asked to integrate evidentiary knowledge with clinical experience and patient preferences. EBM allows individuals to define what "evidence" means in different ways; one study found that some pediatric residents interpreted it to mean consulting the relevant literature, whereas others more critically analyzed the available research. Using EBM did not remove all physician uncertainty about the proper course of action but did strengthen use of available outcomes-based research (Timmermans and Angell, 2001).

Does all of this portray significant reform in medical education? Yes, according to some; no, according to others. In 1988, Sam Bloom, himself a medical school faculty member, expressed criticism of modifications in medical curricula that left the basic teaching and learning experience unchanged. Referring to such modifications as "reform without change," Bloom said that the experience of teachers and students had changed so little "that current medical students are startled by the mirrorlike familiarity of 30 year old accounts of medical student life" (Bloom, 1988:295). In the late 1990s, Bloom's analysis of the meaningfulness of reform efforts had not changed. Perhaps, however, the continued development of problem-based learning, the teaching of professional skills and perspectives, community-based programs, and evidence-based learning offer hope of "reform with change."

The Future of Reform

Are medical schools committed to curricular change? Perhaps. It is clear that the Liaison Committee on Medical Education is encouraging schools to develop more integrated curricula, to promote active and problem-based learning approaches, to increase students' exposure to primary care and community settings, to further develop evidence-based medicine, to place increased emphasis on chronic diseases, to expand focus on women's health, to add emphasis to relief of pain, and to introduce learning of complementary and alternative healing approaches. In schools where these innovations have been introduced, medical students have responded favorably. Although many such programs need to be fine-tuned, students are strong proponents of meaningful change (Ross and Fineberg, 1998).

THE MEDICAL SCHOOL EXPERIENCE: ATTITUDE AND VALUE ACQUISITION

Sociologists are keenly aware of the powerful socializing influence of the medical school experience. The length of time in medical training, the intensity of the experience, and formal and informal interaction with faculty, fellow students, other health care workers, and patients help to shape important attitudes and values of the physician-to-be. This section of the chapter summarizes research on two important attitude and value changes experienced by many medical students: a tolerance for uncertainty and detached concern.

Tolerance for Uncertainty

In studies at Cornell University, researchers identified a clear and explicit effort to train medical students in **tolerance for uncertainty**. As physicians, they would face many kinds of uncertainties. Renee Fox (1957) identified three kinds of uncertainty that confronted the students as they progressed through medical school. Early in the first year, a type of uncertainty was created when students became aware that they could not possibly master all of the concepts and facts covered in their classes and textbooks. For students accustomed to mastery of course materials, the enormity of the field of medicine can be a threatening and disheartening realization.

> In college, I didn't always do all the work, but I was good at managing my time, and I was happy with the work I was doing and satisfied with what I was achieving. But somehow here, it's Pass/Fail . . . it should be easy, [but] the pressure is so much greater . . . I think part of it is the sense that what you learn now may make the difference in someone's life. The material begins to impress you over and over again; this is serious. You need to know it to treat people. (Good and Good, 1989:304)

Second, and more gradually, students became aware that the knowledge base of medicine is incomplete. There is much about the human being—genetically, physiologically, emotionally, socioculturally—that is yet to be fully understood, and important gaps in information exist in understanding disease and illness and their treatment. Students come to realize that even if they could somehow know all that is known about medicine, there is much they would not know.

The third type of uncertainty was created when students attempted to distinguish between the first two types. When they ran into a question in the process of making a patient diagnosis, students would need to determine whether it was a limitation in their own knowledge or something not yet comprehended in medicine. As clinical work increased, students often were concerned that their own lack of knowledge might jeopardize a patient's health or recovery.

Aware of this rite of passage, medical faculties and upper-level students socialize newer students to accept that some uncertainty is inevitable in medicine, that it has some fortunate consequences (e.g., stimulating new medical knowledge), and that it is best dealt with by openly acknowledging its existence (Fox, 1989).

However, students also realize the dysfunctions of being too candid about their own uncertainties. Desiring to come across as knowledgeable and competent future physicians, and not wishing to jeopardize the confidence of the patient (or their instructors) in them, they often present themselves as more certain about a matter than they really are. Light (1979) suggests that the real socialization that occurs is "training for control." This is accomplished through mastery of course materials and clinical experience, but also through "psyching out instructors" (e.g., finding out what instructors want and giving it to them, using impression management techniques) and becoming more authoritarian with patients. Katz (1984) has referred to this process not as tolerating but "disregarding" uncertainty.

Do these efforts to control uncertainty carry over into clinical practice? It has been suggested that some of the excessive diagnostic testing that is a concern today is due to physicians seeking diagnostic certainty and pursuing every test that might offer it (Allison, Kiefe, and Cook, 1998).

When diagnostic certainty does not exist, however, physicians often become and portray themselves to patients as being supremely confident about their conclusions ("micro-certainty")—even when there is considerable dissensus with other health care professionals about the diagnosis ("macro-uncertainty"). This pattern was recently identified in treatment choices made by physicians working with breast cancer patients and in the rapid decision making of nurses in an intensive care unit (Baumann, Deber, and Thompson, 1991).

Detached Concern

Concern for one's patients is certainly an accepted ideal in medical education, but students are encouraged to develop **detached concern**—concern about the patient without excessive emotional involvement or overidentification. It is a "supple balance" of "objectivity and empathy" and "equanimity and compassion" that are combined to enable the "delivery of competent, sagacious, and humane patient care" (Fox, 1989:85). The danger of becoming too emotionally involved with a patient is that diagnostic proficiency or treatment recommendations might be compromised by personal involvement. The death of a patient often is difficult for physicians, but if there is extensive emotional involvement, the death may so affect the physician that the care of other patients would be compromised—not a desirable circumstance. These are reasons many physicians prefer not to treat family members.

Students learn specific techniques to facilitate this detachment. They learn to "intellectualize" and "technicalize" the cadavers they work with in anatomy laboratory and to engage in "gallows humor" as a means of venting personal emotions. In their clinical years, they repeatedly perform certain tests (e.g., urinalyses) so that they become accustomed to them and feel less awkward about doing them. As actual patient care begins, many students feel uncomfortable about certain questions that need to be asked (e.g., sexual history) and certain procedures that must be done (e.g., a rectal examination). Students often are still thinking of the patient as an individual person—making these tasks more difficult. Often, they consciously seek more detachment (Fox, 1989).

At some point during the third year, many students become aware that their efforts to detach have been too successful. They have made a transition by depersonalizing the patient and by focusing on diseases and procedures and tasks that are becoming second nature—rather than focusing on the person. Some refer to this as a type of "emotional numbness" (Fox, 1989). Rather than having learned to walk the fine line between concern and detachment, students often master detachment at the expense of genuine concern, become increasingly doctor-centered and less patient-centered (Haidet et al., 2002), and sometimes develop disinterested or even hostile attitudes toward patients.

Curing Rather Than Caring.   Critics charge that these attitudes are more than an unfortunate byproduct of learning to maintain objectivity. Rather, it is posited that medical schools are so devoted to teaching students how to "cure" patients that they offer little guidance or training or encouragement in ways to "care" for patients. Conrad (1988) analyzed four separate book-length accounts ("insider reports") of the medical school years written by medical students. The accounts portrayed an educational experience clearly oriented toward curing—understanding disease, technical procedures, and high-tech medicine—with little attempt to focus on caring for patients. An "ideology of caring" was sometimes voiced but not often demonstrated.

> Perhaps the most consistent theme that recurred in these accounts was the scarcity of humane and caring encounters between doctors and patients . . . Doctors' clinical perspectives focused almost entirely on the disease rather than on the illness. Virtually all teaching emphasized the technical aspects of doctoring: diagnosis, treatment, and intervention. Too often this approach caused patients to become the disease: "the lymphoma in Room 304." A fascination with technological intervention pervades medicine, from neonatal intensive care to neurosurgery to cardiac catheterization. These are the frontiers of medicine . . . and are seductive to medical students. (Conrad, 1988:328)

The physician-patient interaction that is observed often devalues the importance of caring behaviors. During rounds in a hospital, physicians often talk to residents or medical students about a patient as if the patient is not even present. When talking to the patient, many doctors do not make eye contact, are not attentive, and are very abrupt—these are the behaviors students observe.

Renee Anspach (1988) also investigated the way that physicians talk to each other about patients. She conducted a 16-month field study of life and death decision making in two newborn intensive care units and spent an additional three months in a hospital ob-gyn department. She closely studied "case presentations"—formal and informal case histories presented at formal conferences, during daily rounds, in consultations with specialists, and at various points on the case record—made by interns, residents, and fellows. She observed that the terminology used often "de-personalized" the patient (e.g., using a very impersonal vocabulary); that the passive voice was used to omit reference to the physician or nurse or other health care worker who attended the patient or that a technology was identified as the agent (e.g., "the arteriogram showed"); and that skepticism was often expressed about patients' self-reports.

Medical students also have developed special terms that they use among themselves to identify patients they perceive to be undesirable: "gomers" (get out of my emergency room—often used to describe patients with poor hygiene, incontinence, habitual malingering, and having a tendency to pull out intravenous lines), "crocks," "dirtballs," and "brain stem preparations" (Liederman and Grisso, 1985). Terry Mizrahi's fascinating 1986 book, *Getting Rid of Patients,* describes a whole process of enculturation for interns and residents that often results in a GROP (getting rid of patients) perspective.

It is little wonder that when medical students begin their own interaction with patients, they are often ill-equipped to offer a caring manner. A nurse's letter to the editor of the *Journal of the American Medical Association (JAMA)* summarizes her observations:

> Most medical students examine patients like laboratory specimens. They do not consider introducing themselves or explaining the examination, much less whether the patient is uncomfortable, frightened, or in pain. Such social and emotional concerns are often perceived by the medical student as frustrating obstacles to "treating the case," rather than manifestations of the vulnerability of an individual with a debilitating illness in an often dehumanizing environment . . . No effort is made

to accustom medical students to being with people who are ill, so they wear the defensive mask of "omnipotent clinician" rather than genuinely relating to patients. (Rawlins, 1990:1658)

Exceptions. Are there physicians who disavow these patterns and genuinely encourage and demonstrate positive and caring interaction techniques with patients? Absolutely—and students often express admiration for them. Are there medical students and interns and residents who are disappointed at the lack of emphasis on patients as people? Absolutely—and they often express concern that their own caring attitudes and behaviors will be threatened or lost due to the inhospitable environment. Are things changing? As described earlier in this chapter, some medical schools are attempting now to develop more humane settings for their students and to offer more encouragement for caring physician-patient interaction.

THE MEDICAL SCHOOL EXPERIENCE: STRESS

Without question, the four years of medical school and the three or more years of internship/residency are an extremely stressful time. Some have chosen to ignore this stress as simply a rite of passage. Recently, however, systematic attention has been given to this issue.

Stressors in the First Four Years

Based on clinical reports (case studies of medical students who seek psychiatric or counseling support), intervention studies that measure the impact of stress-reduction programs on medical students, and social surveys that measure self-reports of stress by medical students, three primary categories of stressors in the medical school experience have been identified (Carmel and Bernstein, 1987): (1) current academic stressors, including examinations and hours required for study; (2) anticipated medical career stressors, including various aspects of patient contact; and (3) social stressors, including especially finding time for and relationships with friends and family.

In a study of students at an Israeli medical school, the "death of a child under your care" and "death of a young adult under your care," were identified as the largest sources of stress. The other most commonly identified stressors in this study were: "error in diagnosis or treatment," "lacking time for family and friends," and "death of an old person under your care." The student's gender, marital status, and year of study did not influence perceptions, though older students were most likely to be troubled by the death of a child or young adult (Carmel and Bernstein, 1987).

Stressors During Internship and Residency

Considerable research has focused on the stressful position and lifestyle of medical interns and residents. These stresses usually occur at a point in life when other stressful life events also often happen: marriage and children, altered relationships with parents, financial worries, and postschool emotional let-down. Piled onto these activities are responsibilities that often are physically and emotionally draining. Three aspects of this role that are especially stressful are reviewed here:

1. *The grueling schedule.* The tradition of residencies calls for extended work shifts (often 36 consecutive hours on) with work weeks of 100 hours or more. The long shifts may include some time for sleep (in the hospital) but the resident remains on call and could conceivably not get any sleep during this time. The long hours are justified in various ways—as important socialization for the long hours physicians work, an opportunity to learn more, and a way to staff hospitals—but the dangers of sleep deprivation (e.g., fatigue, lack of time for family and personal interests, errors) are also well known.

   These dangers were dramatized in the 1984 hospital death of Libby Zion—an 18-year-old woman who was brought to the emergency room of New York Hospital at 11:30 P.M. on March 4 and died (needlessly) seven hours later of bilateral bronchopneumonia. Although no criminal indictments were ever handed down, Zion was treated only by an intern and a junior resident, each of whom had been at work for 18 hours. The grand jury criticized five specific aspects of the care Zion received as contributing to her death. Its report was viewed as an indictment of the traditional system of graduate medical education (Asch and Parker, 1988). However, most of the medical residents studied in the early 1990s reported sleep deprivation to be a problem, 10 percent said it was almost a daily problem, and 70 percent reported having observed a colleague working in an impaired condition (with sleep deprivation the most common cause) (Daugherty, Baldwin, and Rowley, 1998). In 2002 the Accreditation Council for Graduate Medical Education approved the first set of national limits on the number of hours that medical residents can work (a limit of 80 hours, at least 10 hours rest between shifts, and not longer than 24 consecutive hours at a time).

2. *Worries about medical school debts.* Although medical school tuition comprises a very small percentage of the medical school budget (4 to 5 percent on average), it has been increasing rapidly in both private and public medical schools. Approximately 90 percent of medical students receive financial assistance, but increasingly this is in the form of loans (now about 80 percent is loan assistance). Today, more than 80 percent of graduating medical students accrue some debt, and the average amount owed now exceeds $100,000. Repayment of the loan is a major worry for many medical students and often colors their perception of the entire medical school experience.

3. *Feelings of mistreatment.* Although it is difficult for students to speak up, many develop feelings of being abused by the medical school process. Both empirical research and widely shared personal anecdotes are beginning to portray the extent of these feelings. A recent study of 431 students at a medical school discovered that almost half felt that they had received some abuse in medical school, and by the fourth year, more than

80 percent reported personal abuse. The kinds of abuse reported included verbal abuse— insulting, humiliating, unjust statements; academic abuse—excessive workload, unnecessary scut work, unfair grade; sexual abuse—solicitation, harassment, sexism, discrimination; physical abuse—threatened or actual; and intentional neglect or lack of communication. Who did the abusing? For juniors and seniors, physician clinical faculty were most often cited; for freshmen, PhD faculty were cited most (Silver and Glicken, 1990)—in both cases, the medical school faculty with whom they had most interaction.

This comes as no surprise to Howard Stein (1990), a leading critic of medical education. According to Stein, students often arrive at medical school with idealism, a concern for others, and general communication skills but leave narrowly focused on biological factors and without the desire and ability to listen to and talk with others.

Medical students often use **excremental symbolism** to describe themselves, their work, their status, their clinical experiences and their patients. They feel treated like "shit"; they are often asked to do "shit work"; they learn who is entitled to "shit on" whom; one learns how much "shit" one must take and for how long. In effect, "one learns how to be a physician and how to occupy one of the highest of American social statuses by beginning as one of the lowest of the low" (Stein, 1990:201).

The Toll of Stress

While some medical students handle stress better than others, the high level of stressors frequently results in high levels of distress (Collier et al., 2002). Studies document significant dysfunctional behaviors among medical residents. About one in eight residents increases alcohol or other drug use during residency (though residents use fewer drugs than demographically matched nonphysician groups); one in five fears that a current relationship will not survive the residency years; one in three suffers a significant

depression sometime during the residency, and studies report between 27 and 58 percent of medical students engage in some form of cheating during medical school (Levey, 2001).

THE MEDICAL SCHOOL EXPERIENCE: CAREER CHOICES

During medical school, students make several important decisions about their medical career. Among these decisions are the size and type of community in which to practice, the specific type of setting desired, and the field in which to specialize. Research has attempted to understand factors that influence these choices.

Relatively little research has focused on the community and setting decisions. An intriguing study was conducted of a medical school cohort in 1981 (during their third year) and again in 1983 (at graduation) on these choices. During this two-year period, there was a clear shift in interest away from practice in small towns and communities toward locations in larger cities; away from office-based practice toward clinical practice in a university medical center; and away from primary care practice toward the surgical specialties (in all three cases, away from areas that are more needed to areas where physicians are well supplied). What motivated these interest changes? Exposure to (and being intrigued by) the research careers of faculty members and exposure to (and appreciation of) high-tech medicine stimulated students to consider settings and specialties where research and sophisticated technologies would be part of their careers (Brooks, 1991), as well as the potential remuneration associated with the choices.

Specialization

The fact that many of the students shifted their choice of a specialty is not uncommon. In fact, one study found that 80 percent of all U.S. medical school graduates in 1983 and 1987 changed their minds regarding specialty during their educational experience (Babbott et al., 1989) with as many as 40 to 60 percent shifting in the last two years.

A study at the University of Washington School of Medicine reported a 70 percent no-change rate, but students were able to identify several potential areas of interest in the first time point. The researchers suggested that students entering medical school may be considering a variety of specialties and later opt for one of these, although it may not originally have been the first choice (Carline and Greer, 1991).

Reasons for Specialty Choice. Several factors influence the selection of a specialty. These include the content of the specialty; having a role model in a particular specialty; and the prestige, opportunities for cognitive performance, and future financial remuneration of the specialty. In recent years, medical students have begun to assign increased importance to a concept called **controllable lifestyle (CL)**—the extent to which particular specialties allow for some control over the hours worked (Dorsey, Jarjoura, and Rutecki, 2003). Even some young physicians practicing in primary care and surgical specialties are switching to CL specialties. Students choosing specialties having a noncontrollable lifestyle (e.g., internal medicine, family practice, pediatrics, obstetrics-gynecology) rated altruism as being a more important motivator than did those selecting CL specialties (Schwartz et al., 1990).

The desire for a controllable lifestyle has been identified in other studies on specialty choice. In one study, respondents were first interviewed in 1975–1976 to determine their motivations for entering medicine and their specialty and practice plans. Data were collected a second time in 1985–1986 after the majority had been in practice two to five years. Female medical students were more likely than male students to be strongly interested in having an ob-gyn career but often entered another specialty instead—often explaining the changed plans as being due to a concern about the difficulty of having a "manageable life" as an ob-gyn physician. Men, however, entered ob-gyn without having been strongly interested in the field as medical students but were attracted by its surgical dimension (Kutner and Brogan, 1990).

Choosing Primary Care. What motivates a choice for **primary care**? In a study at eight New England medical schools, students selecting primary care rather than high-tech specialties were more likely to be motivated by opportunities to provide direct patient care and care in an ambulatory setting and the opportunity to be involved in the psychological aspects of medical care. The opportunity to do research and to perform procedures and a desire for a high income and a favorable lifestyle were more important factors in the decisions of those of their peers who selected high-tech specialties (Kassler, Wartman, and Silliman, 1991).

Does the formal and informal structure of medical schools influence these motivations for type of practice? Yes. A mission of the institution that is consistent with community service and the presence of a primary care-oriented curriculum and physician role models in primary care do influence students to pursue primary care training.

Are these aspects of the program the chief influence on those seeking a career in primary care? No. According to several studies, the most important factors are admissions criteria and the selection of students into the medical school. Applicants who have a high *service index* reflective of a strong orientation to community service, who have taken a generous number of nonscience courses as an undergraduate (and who take several nonscience electives in medical school), and who come from a lower socioeconomic family background and rural areas are those who later are most likely to pursue a career in primary care. Because all of these factors are determined by the time of admission, medical schools could consciously choose those most likely to pursue primary care (Xu et al., 1999).

FUTURE DIRECTIONS IN U.S. MEDICAL EDUCATION

Abraham Flexner advocated a strong scientific foundation for medicine, but not at the expense of humanism. He envisioned the ideal physician as one in whom science and humanity were united. While medical education is strongly grounded in science, many question the degree to which humanism has been maintained as a key element. Research that has discovered that fourth-year, male medical students are much less favorably inclined than first-year students toward caring for the medically indigent highlights this concern (Crandall, Volk, and Loemker, 1993).

Edmund Pellegrino (1987), a distinguished university and health center administrator, has encouraged medical education to follow a path of medical humanism by emphasizing humanitarianism—humaneness and sensitivity to the patient's needs as a person. Although it is possible to heal in the strictest sense without compassion, he views healing as being more complex than simply applying the correct medical method. This is true because illness and disease affect the whole life of a person and because effective clinical decisions should be "morally good" as well as technically correct. This requires the physician to have some sense of what the illness means and does to the life of a particular patient.

Pellegrino suggests four specific avenues for fostering compassionate attitudes in future physicians:

1. *Selecting humanistic students*—considering such qualities as independence and critical capacity, character and integrity, breadth of knowledge, evidence of leadership, work habits and motivation to study, personality and attitude, service orientation, altruism, personal effectiveness, and cultural sensitivity.

2. *Teaching the behavioral and social sciences* — to increase physicians' knowledge about American society, culture, and subcultures; the role of human values in illness and healing; the importance of social structures and social roles for both patient and practitioner; and about health care financing, including costs and resource allocation.

3. *Teaching human values, ethics, and the humanities*—to teach skills of ethical analysis and moral choices, to increase awareness of ethical issues in clinical decisions, and to help the student understand the structure and origins of his or her own value system.

4. *Providing positive faculty role models*—including treating students and patients with compassion, perhaps the most important change possible (Pellegrino, 1987). It is this final point with which Sam Bloom would most strongly agree. Behavior is formed in the cultural norms of the professional environment, and neither by adding courses in the humanities nor by making any other curriculum revision will significant changes occur in teaching and learning unless matching changes occur in the structure of the educational environment . . . within schools' service and research programs. . . . (Bloom, 1995:908)

SUMMARY

Until the early 1900s, formal medical education in the United States was often poorly organized, lacking in academic rigor, and discriminatory against women and racial and ethnic minorities. The Flexner Report issued in 1910 strongly recommended a science-focused, university-based curriculum with significant clinical practice. Though several schools have and are experimenting with innovations, the model Flexner advocated continues to dominate medical education. However, critics contend that current circumstances prohibit medical education from achieving many of its most important objectives.

Applications to the 125 U.S. medical schools increased in the early and mid-1990s but has been dropping since then. Females account for an increasing percentage of students (now about half) though the percentage of traditionally underrepresented minorities has remained level or dropped in recent years.

The medical school years have a profound influence on students. The structured, highly intense first two years in the basic sciences and the clinical experiences of the second two years not only are very stressful experiences but also help mold students' attitudes and values and career choices (especially away from interest in primary care fields in smaller towns and communities).

Among the most important value orientations to which students are socialized are a tolerance for uncertainty (learning to identify and accept what they do not know and what science does not know—and to distinguish between the two) and detached concern (learning to be concerned about the patient without being overly involved emotionally). Critics believe that formal and informal socialization often leads students to depersonalize and dehumanize patients.

HEALTH ON THE INTERNET

To find out what is happening in medical education or to learn about a particular medical school, you can gather information at the Web site of the American Association of Medical Colleges:

http://aamc.org

Click on "Focus on Issues" to identify what the AAMC identifies as top issues affecting medical students and medical schools today. Given what you have read in this chapter and in the preceding one, do you think that medical residents should unionize? How would joining a union affect their socialization process? What would be the primary arguments in favor of and opposed to the unionization of medical residents?

KEY CONCEPTS AND TERMS

academic health center (AHC)
Elizabeth Blackwell
controllable lifestyle (CL)
detached concern
evidence-based medicine
excremental symbolism

Flexner Report
medical school curriculum
primary care
problem-based learning
socialization
tolerance for uncertainty

DISCUSSION CASE

At a recent (hypothetical) meeting of government and education leaders in your state, the usual litany of problems in medical education and health care delivery were being discussed. Those present were sensitive to the large debts that most medical students incur and understanding of the pressure they felt upon graduation to enter specialties and move to locations where their earning capacity would be greater than if they practiced primary care in inner-city or rural areas—where needs are the greatest. Concern was also expressed about the lack of access many people have to health care at the same time the country seems to have a physician surplus.

One of the leaders at the meeting proposed an idea to try to resolve both problems. Beginning with the next academic year, the state would initiate a mandatory program—it would pay the complete education costs for all students attending one of the state's medical schools; in return, students would be obligated to spend the first four years of their career in a location assigned by the state—presumably an inner-city or rural area in need of physicians. The idea is similar to the National Health Service Corps—an underfunded federal government program—and the Armed Forces Health Professions Scholarships but differs in that it is a mandatory program.

If a state referendum were held on this proposal, how would you vote? Is this a creative response to the problems of large debts of medical students and the lack of health care services in certain areas? Or, is the mandatory nature of the program unfair to medical students? Does the government have a right to dictate practice site to physicians even if it does pay their medical education expenses? Might other students—in law, engineering, business, education, and sociology for example—demand a comparable program? The state government could not afford all of these programs: Is medical education and the delivery of care qualitatively different?

REFERENCES

Allison, Jeroan J., Catarine I. Kiefe, and E. Francis Cook. 1998 "The Association of Physician Attitudes About Uncertainty and Risk Taking with Resource Use in a Medicare HMO." *Medical Decision Making,* 18:320–329.

Anspach, Renee. 1988 "Notes on the Sociology of Medical Discourse: The Language of Case Presentation." *Journal of Health and Social Behavior,* 29:357–375.

Asch, David A., and Ruth M. Parker. 1988 "The Libby Zion Case: One Step Forward or Two Steps Backward?" *New England Journal of Medicine,* 318:771–775.

Association of American Medical Colleges. 2003 *www.aamc.org/data/facts/2003/2003summary.htm.*

Babbott, D., D. C. Baldwin, Jr., C. D. Killian, and S. O' Leary-Weaver. 1989 "Trends in Evolution in Specialty Choice: Comparison of U.S. Medical School Graduates in 1983 and 1987." *Journal of the American Medical Association,* 261:2367–2373.

Baumann, Andrea O., Raisa B. Deber, and Gail G. Thompson. 1991 "Overconfidence Among Physicians and Nurses: The 'Micro–Certainty, Macro-Uncertainty' Phenomenon." *Social Science and Medicine,* 32:167–174.

Bloom, Samuel W. 1988 "Structure and Ideology in Medical Education: An Analysis of Resistance to Change." *Journal of Health and Social Behavior,* 29:294–306.

———. 1995 "Reform Without Change? Look Beyond the Curriculum." *American Journal of Public Health,* 85:907–908.

Brooks, Charles H. 1991 "The Influence of Medical School Clinical Experiences on Career Preferences: A Multidimensional Perspective." *Social Science and Medicine,* 32:327–332.

Bussigel, Margaret N., Barbara Barzansky, and Gary G. Grenholm. 1988 *Innovation Process in Medical Education.* New York: Praeger.

Carline, Jan D., and Thomas Greer. 1991 "Comparing Physicians' Specialty Interests upon Entering Medical School with Their Eventual Practice Specialties." *Academic Medicine,* 6:44–46.

Carmel, Sara, and Judith Bernstein. 1987 "Perceptions of Medical School Stressors: Their Relationship to Age, Year of Study, and Trait Anxiety." *Journal of Human Stress,* 13:39–44.

Cohen, Jordan J. 2003 "The Consequences of Premature Abandonment of Affirmative Action in Medical School Admissions." *Journal of the American Medical Association,* 289:1143–1149.

Collier, Virginia U., Jack D. McCue, Allan Markus, and Lawrence Smith. 2002 "Stress in Medical Residency: Status Quo After a Decade of Reform?" *Annals of Internal Medicine,* 136:384–390.

Conrad, Peter. 1988 "Learning to Doctor: Reflections on Recent Accounts of the Medical School Years." *Journal of Health and Social Behavior,* 29:323–332.

Crandall, Sonia J. S., Robert J. Volk, and Vicki Loemker. 1993 "Medical Students' Attitudes Toward Providing Care for the Underserved." *Journal of the American Medical Association,* 269:2519–2523.

Daugherty, Steven R., DeWitt C. Baldwin, and Beverley D. Rowley. 1998 "Learning, Satisfaction, and Mistreatment During Medical Internship." *Journal of the American Medical Association,* 279:1194–1199.

Dorsey, E. Ray, David Jarjoura, and Gregory W. Rutecki. 2003 "Influence of Controllable Lifestyle on Recent Trends in Specialty Choice by U.S. Medical Students." *Journal of the American Medical Association,* 290:1173–1178.

Fox, Renee C. 1957 "Training for Uncertainty," pp. 207–241 in *The Student-Physician,* Robert K. Merton, George G. Reader, and Patricia Kendall (eds.). Cambridge, MA: Harvard University Press.

———. 1989 *The Sociology of Medicine: A Participant Observer's View.* Upper Saddle River, NJ: Prentice Hall.

———. 1999 "Time to Heal Medical Education?" *Academic Medicine,* 74:1072–1075.

Good, Mary-Jo D., and Byron J. Good. 1989 "Disabling Practitioners: Hazards of Learning to be a Doctor in American Medical Education."

American Journal of Orthopsychiatry, 59:303–309.

Hafferty, Frederic W. 1999 "Managed Medical Education?" *Academic Medicine,* 74:972–979.

Haidet, Paul, Joyce E. Dains, Debora A. Paterniti, Laura Hechtel, Tai Chang, Ellen Tseng, and John C. Rogers. 2002 "Medical Student Attitudes Toward the Doctor-Patient Relationship." *Medical Education,* 36:568–574.

Hensel, William A., Donald D. Smith, Dennis R. Barry, and Robert Foreman. 1996 "Changes in Medical Education: The Community Perspective." *Academic Medicine,* 71:441–446.

Iglehart, John K. 1994 "Health Care Reform and Graduate Medical Education." *New England Journal of Medicine,* 330:1167–1171.

Kassler, William J., Steven A. Wartman, and Rebecca A. Silliman. 1991 "Why Medical Students Choose Primary Care Careers." *Academic Medicine,* 66:41–43.

Katz, Jay. 1984 *The Silent World of Doctor and Patient.* New York: The Free Press.

Kutner, Nancy G., and Donna Brogan. 1990 "Gender Roles, Medical Practice Roles, and Ob-Gyn Career Choice: A Longitudinal Study." *Women and Health,* 16:99–117.

Lassey, Marie L., William R. Lassey, and Martin J. Jinks. 1997 *Health Care Systems Around the World,* Upper Saddle River, NJ: Prentice Hall.

Levey, Robert E. 2001 "Sources of Stress for Residents and Recommendations for Programs to Assist Them." *Academic Medicine,* 76:142–150.

Liederman, Deborah B., and Jean-Anne Grisso. 1985 "The Gomer Phenomenon." *Journal of Health and Social Behavior,* 26: 222–232.

Light, Donald W. 1979 "Uncertainty and Control in Professional Training." *Journal of Health and Social Behavior,* 20:310–322.

Ludmerer, Kenneth M. 1985 *Learning to Heal: The Development of American Medical Education.* New York: Basic Books, Inc.

———. 1999 *Time to Heal: American Medical Education from the Turn of the Century to the Era of Managed Care.* New York: Oxford University Press.

Makoul, Gregory, Raymond H. Curry, and Dennis H. Novack. 1998 "The Future of Medical School Courses in Professional Skills and Perspectives." *Academic Medicine,* 73:48–51.

Mizrahi, Terry. 1986 *Getting Rid of Patients.* New Brunswick, NJ: Rutgers University Press.

Pardes, Herbert. 1997 "The Future of Medical Schools and Teaching Hospitals in the Era of Managed Care." *Academic Medicine,* 72:97–102.

Pellegrino, Edmund D. 1987 "The Reconciliation of Technology and Humanism: A Flexnerian Task 75 Years Later," pp. 77–111 in *Flexner: 75 Years Later: Current Commentary on Medical*

Education, Charles Vevier (ed.). Lanham, MD: University Press of America.

Ramsbottom-Lucier, Mary, Mitzi M. S. Johnson, and Carol L. Elam. 1995 "Age and Gender Differences in Students' Preadmission Qualifications and Medical School Performances." *Academic Medicine,* 70:236–239.

Rawlins, Kathleen. 1990 "Letter to the Editor." *Journal of the American Medical Association,* 264:1658–1659.

Regan-Smith, Martha G. 1998. "Reform Without Change: Update, 1998," *Academic Medicine,* 73:505–507.

Richards, Boyd F., K. Patrick Ober, Liza Cariaga-Lo, Martha G. Camp, James Philip, Mary McFarlane, Randall Rupp, and Daniel J. Zaccaro. 1996 "Ratings of Students' Performances in a Third-Year Internal Medicine Clerkship: A Comparison Between Problem-based and Lecture-based Curricula." *Academic Medicine,* 71:187–189.

Rogers, David E. 1987 "Medical Education: Its Purpose and Its Problems," pp. 35–45 in *Flexner: 75 Years Later: Current Commentary on Medical Education,* Charles Vevier (ed.). Lanham, MD: University Press of America.

Ross, Robert H., and Harvey V. Fineberg. 1998 "Medical Students' Evaluations of Curriculum Innovations at Ten North American Medical Schools." *Academic Medicine,* 73:258–265.

Schwartz, R. W., J. V. Haley, C. Williams, R. K. Jarecky, W. E. Strodel, A. B. Young, and W. O. Griffen. 1990 "The Controllable Lifestyle Factor and Students' Attitudes about Specialty Election." *Academic Medicine,* 65:207–210.

Silver, Henry K., and Anita D. Glicken. 1990 "Medical Student Abuse: Incidence, Severity, and Significance." *Journal of the American Medical Association,* 263:527–532.

Stein, Howard F. 1990 *American Medicine as Culture.* Boulder, CO: Westview Press.

Timmermans, Stefan, and Alison Angell. 2001 "Evidence-Based Medicine, Clinical Uncertainty, and Learning to Doctor." *Journal of Health and Social Behavior,* 42:342–359.

Vernon, David T. A., and Michael C. Hosokawa. 1996 "Faculty Attitudes and Opinions about Problem-based Learning." *Academic Medicine,* 71:1233–1238.

Xu, Gang, Mohammadreza Hojat, Timothy P. Brigham, and J. Jon Veloski. 1999 "Factors Associated with Changing Levels of Interest in Primary Care During Medical School." *Academic Medicine,* 74:1011–1015.

10

NURSES, MID-LEVEL HEALTH CARE PRACTITIONERS, AND ALLIED HEALTH WORKERS

As disease patterns have shifted from acute to chronic conditions and as modern medicine increasingly utilizes a multitude of technologies, a growing array of specialized practitioners has emerged. To understand the delivery of health care, it is necessary to describe the full range of health care providers and the relationships that develop within and among them. This chapter focuses on nurses and the field of nursing, mid-level practitioners, and allied health personnel.

EVOLUTION OF NONPHYSICIAN HEALTH CARE PRACTITIONERS

Early America

As described in Chapter 8, families rather than physicians were the most important health care providers in colonial America. Most families relied on their female members to provide for health care, and when additional help was necessary, they employed medically knowledgeable females from other families. Duties of these formally untrained, but typically wise and benevolent "nurses," generally focused on child care, surrogate breast feeding, birthing, and care of the ill.

Early Midwifery. Midwifery was a vital source of care for women in colonial times. Most midwives came from England where the Church of England granted licenses to practice. They were generally held in high esteem and were often paid for their services, even though they were sometimes suspected of practicing witchcraft (e.g., in the case of an impaired baby). Many midwives served on Southern plantations; some were enslaved women, others were white women who were paid in kind for their services. Though formal training was not available in the United States, some manuals were in print so that any woman who had borne children herself and had assisted in a few births could be designated a midwife.

With the development of the obstetric forceps and the subsequent acceptance of midwifery as a science, male physicians assumed greater responsibility for the birthing process. This transition was enabled by a general belief that women were incapable of understanding and performing obstetric techniques. As formal medical education in the United States became available and was routinely restricted to men, physicians gained even further advantage over midwives and attempted to monopolize the birthing field.

Early Nursing.   The increased dominance of males in the birthing process led many women to the field of nursing. Many became private duty nurses whose responsibilities were to tend to the sick at their bedside and to provide both caring and curing services. Most of these nurses were relatively uneducated and lacked any formal nursing training, but they provided a valuable service (Reverby, 1987).

Whereas private duty nursing was regarded as an acceptable occupation, hospital nursing—given the marginal nature of hospitals at this time—was perceived to be less desirable. Many hospital nurses both lived and worked in the hospital (and often were recovering patients themselves). Their qualifications and the quality of their work were uneven. The job was marked by long hours, physically demanding responsibilities, and frequent friction with physicians and hospital managers over the content and pace of their work.

The importance and visibility of nursing increased during the Civil War. Thousands of women on both sides of the conflict established hospitals and worked in them as volunteers and as paid nurses. Many were working-class women who were accustomed to hard labor as domestics and nurses, though others were middle-class women who had not worked previously for wages outside the home. In addition to patient care, some worked through the Sanitary Commission, which implemented several innovative public health measures, while others attempted to create a role for women in the army's medical system.

Post-Civil War to 1920: Professional Medicine and Separate Domains

Growth of Health Care Institutions. With the end of the Civil War and the beginning of accelerated urbanization and industrialization, many families were separated geographically. Increasingly, nonfamily members were needed to provide care for the sick and injured and in places other than the home. It was particularly important to the growing "middling class" that the caretakers in institutions be as "reliable, respectable and clean (in all senses) as the mothers or sisters . . . formerly charged with the responsibility" (Baer, 1990:460).

As a result, a custodial role of "nurse" was established in these institutions. "Religious sisters managed Roman Catholic, Lutheran, and Episcopal hospitals. Community women worked for wages in hospitals for the working poor. In big city almshouses, the progression from inmate to keeper to assistant nurse to nurse comprised a sort of job ladder" (Baer, 1990:461). None of these "nurses" had any formal training.

Advent of Nursing Education.   As more and more hospitals demanded public assistance in caring for the ill, demands for formal training of nurses accelerated. Programs were developed around the philosophy of **Florence Nightingale** (1820–1910), an upper-class British reformer, who believed that the proper moral, environmental, and physical order was necessary for the restoration of health. She accepted a gender division of labor as a given and believed that women's characteristics made them naturals for creating the conditions needed for care of the ill.

Despite the fact that nursing was known for its drudgery, it attracted both white and black women who regarded it as a way to serve fellow human beings as well as an opportunity for personal autonomy and geographic mobility. However, employment opportunities for trained nurses were few. After completion of training, the nurse often had neither a place in the hospital (which depended upon cheap student labor) nor in private duty (where cheaper, untrained nurses typically were used). Many physicians and families were unconvinced that the training offered any significant benefit (Reverby, 1987).

Maternity Care.   By the late 1800s, the American medical profession had taken specific steps to ensure a place for obstetrics. In 1859, practical medicine and obstetrics was designated as one of four scientific sections of the American Medical Association and in 1868, the *American Journal of Obstetrics* became the first specialized medical journal published in the United States. In 1876 the American Gynecological Society was formed, followed by establishment of the American Association of Obstetricians and Gynecologists in 1888.

In spite of these developments, at least half of all births were still attended by midwives at the beginning of the twentieth century. Midwives were especially important for Southern black families, immigrant families, and families living in rural areas. On the other hand, middle- and upper-class women were more likely to have physician-assisted deliveries. There was a general belief, however, that lack of adequate maternity care was a problem.

Home Nursing Care. An important source of employment for nurses at the turn of the century was in agencies that provided home nursing care. These agencies were primarily located in northeastern cities which had large concentrations of immigrants and were characterized by poverty, disease, and unsanitary conditions. In the beginning, a few wealthy women hired nurses to visit the poor sick in their homes, but visiting nurses soon became popular in other settings. All types of groups began to hire these public health nurses including Metropolitan Life, an insurance company, which discovered that it could reduce the number of death benefits it had to pay by offering home nursing to policyholders.

1920s Through the 1950s: The Advent of Scientific Medicine

Midwifery. Debate concerning the regulation of midwifery reached its height between 1910 and 1920. In 1921 the Sheppard-Tower Maternity and Infancy Protection Act provided funds in several states for midwife education and registration. By 1930, all but 10 states required midwives to be registered. These regulations were partly responsible for the decline in midwifery, but other factors such as declining birth rates, restricted immigration, an increase in the

number of hospital beds available for maternity cases, and a growing anxiety about the danger of birth also contributed to the decline. However, midwifery was kept from extinction by the needs of the urban and rural poor (DeVries, 1985).

The first *nurse-midwives* to practice in the United States were brought from England in 1925 by Mary Breckinridge as part of her plan to provide health care for the rural people in Kentucky. As a consequence of these midwives' services, comprehensive health care services were made available to the rural population and the maternal death rate declined dramatically. Eventually some states passed laws granting legal recognition to midwives and several midwifery schools were established as a result.

Emergence of Staff Nursing. During the Depression years of the 1930s, the emphasis on nursing shifted back from private duty nursing to hospital staffing. Although there was an oversupply of nurses in the 1920s and 1930s, a shortage developed during World War II. This was due in part to the fact that women had opportunities for better paying jobs in war-related industries. This shortage led to the creation of "practical nurses" and nursing assistants. These new occupations initially provided a temporary solution to a short-term problem, but their contributions to health care were evident and they eventually became permanent health care occupations.

The New Allied Health Workers. The emergence of **allied health workers** (e.g., physical therapists, medical technologists) occurred during the second quarter of the twentieth century. The development of these positions was encouraged by the complexity of new methods of diagnosis and treatment that required a specialist, and primary care physicians were in short supply to handle the additional workload.

Beginning in the 1930s and continuing into the 1940s, the Committee on Allied Health Education and Accreditation (CAHEA), sponsored by the AMA, began to accredit a variety of allied health occupational areas. "Essentials" (nationally accepted minimum standards for an educational program) were first adopted for occupational therapy programs in 1935 and for most other allied health fields in the late 1930s and 1940s.

Nursing Moves Away from Patient Care. During World War II and its aftermath, nursing moved away from direct patient care. Other than distributing medication, nurses spent much of the war years in the nurses' station, coordinating other staff, making notes on charts, and keeping records. In response, new categories of nurse-related workers emerged to provide direct patient care: the **licensed practical nurse (LPN)** or vocational nurse and the nurse's aid (Reverby, 1987).

Meanwhile, nurse-midwifery struggled to establish standards for education, legal recognition, and a professional identity. In 1955, the American College of Nurse-Midwifery was founded; it subsequently joined the Kentucky-based American Association of Nurse-Midwives in 1969 and formed the American College of Nurse-Midwives. But, legal recognition continued to be a problem. By 1959, just two states, New Mexico and New York, formally recognized the nurse-midwife despite the positive impact of nurse-midwifery on maternal and infant morality rates.

NURSES AND THE FIELD OF NURSING

Overview

In the United States, regulation of the field of nursing is a state responsibility. Under a state board of nursing, each state licenses nurses and defines the boundaries of the practice. All states require that prospective nurses attend an approved training program and take a national licensing examination. Certification is administered by the **American Nurses Association (ANA)** and its various specialty organizations.

Types of Nurses.   There are three main types of nurses:

1. *Licensed practical nurses* typically are high school graduates who have completed a short vocational program leading to the LPN certification.

2. *Registered nurses (RNs)* have obtained a diploma or degree in nursing; they are distinguished by the type of nursing education they have completed.

   a. *Diploma nurses* have completed a (typically) three year program in a hospital-based school of nursing; until the early 1970s, most registered nurses graduated from a diploma school though now only a small percentage of RNs (less than 10 percent) graduate from these programs.

   b. *Associate degree* nurses have completed a (typically) two to three year program consisting of both academic and nursing courses in a community college or junior college-based program and earn an associate degree and a nursing license. These programs primarily offer a vocational orientation to nursing. In recent years, they have produced more than half of graduating registered nurses.

   c. *Baccalaureate nurses* have completed an undergraduate curriculum of academic courses usually with a nursing major and have earned a BSN (Bachelor of Science in Nursing) degree. With a greater emphasis on theory and broad-based knowledge, these programs offer more of a professional orientation to nursing. Generally speaking, the more education one has completed, the higher status the nurse enjoys. Baccalaureate programs now produce slightly more than one-third of nursing graduates but are becoming more common. In addition, many colleges that already offer the BSN degree have begun to offer "RN to BA" programs in which nurses with an associate degree can add additional courses to earn the baccalaureate degree.

3. *Advanced practice nurses (APN)* are registered nurses who have acquired additional certification in one or more of about 20 nursing specialties either in primary care (e.g., nurse practitioners, nurse-midwives) or in acute care (e.g., clinical nurse specialists). These nurses often have a Master's degree;

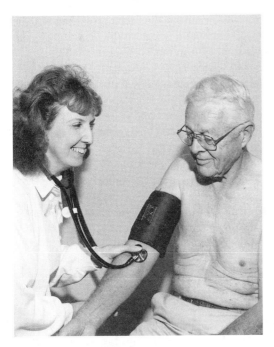

Despite continually expanding work responsibilities, nurses often are still the primary "carers" in the health care setting.

they must pass a certifying examination; and they handle many responsibilities that have traditionally been handled by physicians. There are now more than 200,000 APNs in the United States.

Key Roles of Nurses. McClure (1991) identifies the two key roles held by nurses today as being the caregiver and the integrator. As a caregiver, the nurse functions to meet patients' needs: dependency (hygiene, nutrition, safety, etc.); comfort (physical and psychological); therapy (medications and other treatments); monitoring (collecting, interpreting, and acting on patient data); and education. As an integrator, the nurse coordinates the contributions of separate medical units in the hospital or clinic to provide total and effective patient treatment and care.

Viewed from another perspective, Chambliss (1996) identifies three difficult and sometimes contradictory roles that hospital nurses must fulfill. First, nurses must be caring individuals who interact directly with patients and work with them as "whole people." Second, nurses are professionals who have an important job that requires special competence and deserves special status and respect. Finally, within the hospital hierarchy, nurses are subordinate workers often under the direction of physicians. The contrasting expectations created by these disparate roles place nurses in an awkward position where the practical requirements of the job may explicitly conflict with the moral expectations of the professional role.

Nurse Supply and Demand

In 2003, approximately 2.3 million nurses held RN licenses and were employed in the nursing field— a 75 percent increase over the 1.3 million active RNs in 1980. Nursing school enrollments have fluctuated during the last two decades—reaching a high point of about 270,000 in 1994, declining over the next six years, and increasing since 2001.

An almost constant shortage of registered nurses existed throughout the 1900s, but during the 1980s and 1990s, demand for nurses reached a high level. Hospitals routinely reported nurse vacancy rates above 10 percent and many community-based nursing jobs (e.g., in home health care) went unfilled. Several factors converged to create this demand, including the increased number of elderly people seeking care; the heavy time demands of patients with chronic diseases; delays in seeking treatment by the medically uninsured (which thereby increases the severity of illness); the expansion of home health care; and increased use of a wide variety of health care technologies (for which nurses must have at least sufficient knowledge to coordinate care).

There are many signs that the shortage of nurses today is severe and may get worse before it gets better. In 2003, hospitals reported that about one nursing position in eight was unfilled—a shortage of more than 125,000 nurses (about 75 percent of all job openings in hospitals are for nurses), and estimates are that the vacancy rate could be as high as 1 in 5 by 2020 (a shortage of 500,000 nurses in 2015 and 800,000 by 2020). The number of graduates from nursing schools has increased somewhat in the early 2000s, although the average age of nurses continues to get higher (from 37 in 1983 to 45 in 2000). This is despite the fact that nursing is routinely advertised as a high-growth field (which ought to attract interest in the career); despite recent, sometimes sizable increases in nursing salaries (the median salary now exceeds $48,000 per year); and despite the move by many hospitals to reorganize staff responsibilities (hiring less well-educated individuals to do traditional nursing tasks) in order to downsize the number of nurses who are needed (Aiken, Sochalski, and Anderson, 1996). This latter effort is a contentious issue in medicine and is discussed in more detail later in this chapter.

An added problem is a nursing faculty shortage. Nursing programs indicate that they turn away several thousand qualified applicants each year because of an insufficient number of nurse instructors. Many of those with the educational credentials to serve on the faculty are now taking advantage of increased opportunities in health care management and leaving education. The average age of nursing instructors is over

50, which means that a large cohort will be reaching retirement age in the next decade, and the shortage could become even greater.

One response that hospitals and health systems in the United States is making is to heavily recruit nurses from other countries. This practice has raised some important ethical questions that are addressed in the box, "Recruiting Nurses form Abroad."

Recruitment and Socialization

Background of Nursing Students. Although the nursing field remains female-dominant (94 percent of nurses are female), the number of men entering nursing is increasing. In 1998, males accounted for about 15 percent of registered nursing students and about 6 percent of advanced practice nursing students. Unlike medical students, nursing students have traditionally been drawn from working- and lower-middle-class families whose parents are less likely to be college educated than are those of comparable nonnursing students. In part, they have been drawn to nursing

---

IN THE FIELD

RECRUITING NURSES FROM ABROAD

Faced with a sizable and chronic shortage of nurses and an inability to adequately address the problem, hospitals and health care systems in the United States have begun intense recruiting of nurses from other countries. Recruiting has been most successful in the Philippines, India, Canada, Nigeria, Korea, the United Kingdom, and Russia, and is now intensifying in Mexico. The National Council of State Boards of Nursing began in 2004 to offer the mandatory U.S. licensing nursing exam in other countries to make it easier to get licensed. Hospitals frequently employ recruiting companies (and pay as much as $15,000 to $20,000 per hire) to secure nurses to come to this country.

The interest of nurses in other countries—especially very poor countries—is understandable. The average monthly take-home salary

for nurses in Mexico is $300 or $400, and in India, less than $100, compared to about $4,000 in the United States. However, there can be drastic consequences for the health care system in the countries from which the United States is recruiting. Joyce Thompson (2003:20), a professor of community health nursing at Western Michigan University, says that the practice is "clearly devastating the health care infrastructure" in several of these countries which have been forced to close hospitals due to a lack of nurses. Thompson personally witnessed the exodus of nurses from Africa during her work on a program promoting women's health in Uganda and Malawi. Her reaction: "It's always difficult (to see) a resource-rich country that hasn't planned appropriately depend on lesser-developed countries to meet their needs."

because of the security of employment and the opportunity to move into the middle class.

Moreover, nursing students have traditionally reflected some value differences from other students. Over the years, several studies have found nursing students to be more likely to place value on "helping others," "altruism," and being "nurturant" and less likely than others to endorse "doing well financially" and "personal power" as important life goals.

In recent years, some important shifts have occurred. Today's nursing students tend to be older (often in their thirties and forties) than students in the past, they are more likely to come from a middle-class background, they frequently work part-time in addition to going to school, and many are parents (often single parents). For many, nursing is a second career—one to which they have been drawn later in life and one which is attractive at least as much for its socioeconomic rewards as for the opportunity to enter a helping career.

Socialization of Nursing Students.   The socialization of nursing students has received much less systematic study than that of medical students. One of the best studies of nursing socialization was conducted at a West Coast school of nursing by Fred Davis (1972). He discovered a six-step socialization experience not unlike that experienced by medical students.

Students enter nursing school with an *initial innocence,* seeking to become mother surrogates by engaging in nurturant and helping behaviors. The failure of nursing instructors to endorse or model this image, however, creates frustration and anxiety. Students spend their time learning technical, and seemingly inconsequential, skills. Later during the first semester, students enter a *labeled recognition of incongruity* stage. This includes open statements of disillusionment and despair over the incongruity between their anticipated view of nursing school and their actual experience. Many question their career choice, and many drop out of nursing school during this time.

Students who remain enter a *psyching out* the faculty stage (just as medical students do, as described in Chapter 9). They attempt to determine what part of course materials and training the faculty thinks is most important so that they can concentrate on that. Typically, they realize that the faculty places high value on professionalism, and like it or not, the students collectively begin to mold their behavior in that direction. This is the *role simulation* stage, which usually occurs around the end of the first year. Students engage in a type of role playing in which they consciously attempt to exhibit the professional demeanor toward patients desired by the faculty. However, as their behaviors become more convincing, the students gain confidence in themselves.

As the students enter the second half of their training (the *provisional internalization* and *stable internalization* stages), they increasingly accept a professional identity and get accustomed to it until, by graduation, it is typically fully accepted and internalized.

However, even by the fourth year of school, substantial value differences may exist between students and their nurse instructors. Eddy et al. (1994) discovered that faculty placed significantly more value than students on freedom (e.g., honoring patients' right to refuse treatment), equality (basing care on patients' needs and not their background characteristics), and human dignity (e.g., maintaining confidentiality), whereas students placed more emphasis than faculty on esthetics (creating a pleasing environment for patients and creating a pleasant work environment for self and others). The study suggested that responses reflected students' idealism about work settings and lack of experience in actual settings.

Occupational Status

Although it is common to speak of "the nursing profession," the lack of genuine professional autonomy among nurses means that "paraprofessional" or "semi-professional" may be more accurate descriptors. Most nursing responsibilities are under the direction of physicians, and this external control is a primary barrier to a genuinely professional status. At the same time, however, nurses have gained greater autonomy in recent years. This is largely a result of the strengthening of nursing education and the professionalization of nursing socialization so that nurses are capable of exercising more independence in patient care decisions and have the desire to do so.

In addition nursing associations have developed a larger advocacy voice. The most prominent nursing associations are the National League for Nursing (NLN) and the American Nurses Association (ANA). The membership of the NLN is composed primarily of nursing educators and agencies associated with nurse education; their primary goal is to promote quality standards for nursing education. The majority of ANA members are registered nurses with practice-related concerns. The ANA has experienced considerable tension in recent years over the best way to lobby for nursing's role in the changing health care system. In 1995, the 20,000 member California Nurses Association broke from the ANA in order to emphasize a collective bargaining strategy to exert influence on hospital staffing reorganization.

Issues in Nursing Today

Education and Image.   Throughout its history, nursing has struggled internally to define its primary goals and purposes. In essence, one faction has attempted to maintain an image of a nurturer/caregiver whereas another faction has worked to professionalize nursing by emphasizing education and a scientific-based nursing curriculum.

This controversy over image centers on educational preparation. At one time, most practicing nurses were diploma-trained, and they actively resisted increased emphasis on training in academic institutions and curricular changes that would make science rather than technique the primary focus of nursing education. Today, however, in spite of this resistance, nearly all training occurs in academic institutions and with science increasingly at the core of the curriculum.

Some friction remains between graduates of associate degree and four-year programs. Because associate-level and bachelor-level programs prepare students for the same state

licensing examination, it is assumed by many that they can perform at the same skill level. Advocates of bachelor-level programs are concerned that two-year programs do not adequately prepare students for the rapid changes in modern technology that nurses now encounter. Advocates of associate-level programs dismiss the need for an undergraduate degree and prefer the technique-focused curriculum. Because hospitals do not typically differentiate training background when determining salary and responsibilities, advocates of baccalaureate training feel this devalues the bachelor's degree.

Since 1965, the ANA has tried unsuccessfully to make a bachelor's degree the minimum educational requirement for licensure of registered nurses. In 1985, the ANA revised its stance to recommend two levels of nursing based on educational preparation: the professional nurse with a baccalaureate degree and the technical nurse with an associate degree.

This is consistent with the concept of **differentiated practice.** A differentiated practice model bases the roles and functions of registered nurses on education, experience, and competence. It clarifies which type of registered nurse is appropriately accountable for which aspects of nursing by separating technical and professional practice. Proponents of the model believe that it will lead to more effective and efficient patient care, increased job satisfaction among nurses, and greater organizational viability. A sizable number of hospitals across the nation are now using some type of differentiated practice model.

Specific Job Responsibilities.   Without question, nurses have taken on additional responsibilities in recent years. Some of these involve direct patient care though others simply comply with bureaucratic requirements. An investigative medical journalist recently summarized his conversation with a retired nurse about nursing's additional patient care responsibilities:

> She is amazed that nurses now routinely make assessments of what patients need and write plans to take care of those needs. When she was in training, nurses wouldn't presume to say what should be done for a patient . . . Nurses didn't do patient

assessments. Nurses weren't taught to read electrocardiograms. They weren't trained to know if lab results were abnormal. They rarely put in an intravenous line and would never have dreamed of removing arterial catheters or inserting feeding tubes. Now nurses are expected to check a patient's heart and lungs, to listen for abnormal bowel sounds, to check the reaction of their eyes to light as a sign for neurologic problems, to look for any skin lesions that may point to a particular problem, to monitor blood pressure and to watch lab values for abnormalities. (Hite, 1990a)

However, studies have found that between 25 and 50 percent of what registered nurses do in the hospital, "has nothing to do with nursing, and instead involves running errands, doing paperwork, delivering and retrieving laboratory specimens, and so forth" (Friedman, 1990:2977). The excessive workload created by these routinized tasks, the perceived lack of input into decisions, and poor internal communication are among the factors that have been demonstrated to influence nurse morale and voluntary turnover (Davidson et al., 1997). The box, "The Bureaucratization of Nursing," shows many nurses' frustration with the amount of paperwork now required.

The increased responsibilities taken on by nurses have occurred simultaneously with other significant changes related to nursing practice—a dramatic increase in involvement in ethical questions (e.g., in the treatment of impaired newborns or in handling do-not-resuscitate decisions); the emotional and physical demands of working with AIDS patients; and the ever-increasing numbers of very ill, geriatric patients. Many believe that nurses are simply being assigned too many different responsibilities within the hospital setting.

Downsizing Nursing Staffs.   In the mid-1990s, hospitals throughout the country began to reduce their nursing staffs. Responding to pressures to become more cost effective, hospitals have cut back on nurses and reassigned some of their job responsibilities to a new category of health care worker, variously referred to as "nurses' aides" "patient care technicians," "unlicensed assistive personnel," and "care associates." These workers, who sometimes receive only a month or two of training, typically assist with such tasks as changing linen, bathing patients, and assisting physicians with routine procedures but are also involved in EKG testing, drawing blood, and respiratory therapy (Norrish and Rundall, 2001). An ad that was posted on commuter trains and in bus-stop shelters in New York City and carried in *New York* magazine read "BABY CARE TECHNICIAN WANTED—Work with newborns and preemies in NY hospitals. Regulate incubators, draw blood, insert feeding tubes, give medications. On-the-job training. NO EXPERIENCE NECESSARY/NO EDUCATION NECESSARY" (Moore, 1995:3).

The ANA and other groups have charged that this "reconfiguration" is threatening quality patient care (see the box, "Replacing Nurses with Unskilled Assistants"). An impressive array of studies have linked longer hospital stays, higher patient mortality rates, and higher rates of adverse outcomes with lower RN-to-patient ratios. To make up for a nursing shortage, hospitals often direct nurses to work extended shifts (sometimes even 12 hours or more) and extra shifts. Research now documents that the risks of making a medical error increase for nurses working these long hours (Rogers et al., 2004). A 1994 survey of nurses conducted by the Boston College School of Nursing (reported in *Modern Healthcare*) found that 43 percent of nurses employed in Massachusetts hospitals felt that unsafe staffing levels were in existence in their own hospital (Burda, 1994). This issue is likely to be at the forefront for the next several years.

Level of Political Activism.   The frustrations that many nurses feel with their working conditions have fostered increased political activism. In recent years, some state nursing associations have disaffiliated with the American Nurses' Association (which is both a professional association and union) believing it to be too moderate. Nurses in California in 1995 and in Maine and Massachusetts in 2001 broke with the ANA so that they could more aggressively try to combat issues such as staff shortages and mandatory overtime. Some state nurses' associations have affiliated with other unions without

IN THE FIELD

THE BUREAUCRATIZATION OF NURSING

"This is just such a waste." Helen is standing at her medication cart, writing on a clipboard with a patient's room number at the top. There are several clipboards piled beside the one she is writing on. "All this writing. I don't know why we do it," she says.

It is just after 2 p.m. The nurses on the next shift will be coming in soon, and Helen is nowhere caught up with her paperwork. She will stay until after 4—more than an hour after her shift ends—to complete it. It is not an unusual occurrence.

Helen and the other nurses on Five East know the rationale for the paperwork. When asked, they all give a variation of this answer: "If it's not documented, you didn't do it." It is a refrain prompted by an era of lawsuits and insurance.

If a patient sues and says something wasn't done, the hospital needs a written record to prove it was. It won't do any good to have a nurse simply say she did it. Likewise, if an insurance company questions whether a patient actually got a treatment on the bill, it doesn't do the hospital any good to have the nurse say it was done. It must be in black and white.

The hospital has all kinds of forms to help nurses prove they did things. The clipboards, for instance, hold a four-page form called "Nurse's Progress Notes." Every two hours, the nurse must record the status of her patient. The form also has a checklist—also filled out every two hours—that tells such things as whether the patient has had a bath, needs turning, is in traction, or is wearing an abdominal binder.

That's not all. There's another section of this form entitled "Nursing Assessment" where the nurse evaluates a patient's organ systems: such things as motor skills, heart sounds, and respiratory patterns. Each patient also has a "Nursing Care Plan" that must be filled out by the nurse on each shift. Each care plan actually consists of several individual plans. The number of plans depends largely on how sick the patient is.

One plan focuses on a patient's "impaired physical mobility." It states why the patient has the problem, what the nurse can do to overcome the problem, and what the patient can do. Other plans might focus on controlling infection, pain control, psychosocial concerns, or overcoming a patient's "knowledge deficit."

"The patients would be much better off if we could get through this and have more time to take care of them," Helen says, glancing at a pile of paperwork. The nursing assessments and care plans are only part of the story. Each time a patient gets medication, that must be recorded and signed on a form at the nurse's cart. That can mean an awful lot of writing for several patients. During one shift, Helen had seven patients. One was to get 16 medications, another 15, and another 12. The total for all seven was 72.

. . . The nurses on Five East had no quarrel with a national study that estimated the average hospital floor nurse spends about 40 percent of her time doing paperwork. "The sad part is, it keeps you from spending time with your patients," Dietrich says. "It's frustrating. You are here until five o'clock so you can finish your paperwork." Dietrich says a colleague put it best when she said, "The nursing has gone out of nursing" (Hite, 1990b).

formally breaking away from the ANA. In 2001 the 100,000-member union arm of the ANA formally joined the AFL-CIO to strengthen its collective bargaining position.

The more activist approach includes extensive lobbying, marches, and demonstrations in Washington and around the country. A prime objective has been to get state legislatures to adopt nurse-staffing laws that require hospitals to maintain at least a minimum ratio of nurses to patients. California was the first state to pass such legislation. In specifying the minimum ratio, California nurses recommended it be one nurse per three patients; California hospitals recommended that it be one nurse per ten patients.

IN THE FIELD

REPLACING NURSES WITH UNSKILLED ASSISTANTS

In the mid-1990s, the downsizing of nursing staffs and the hiring of unskilled assistants to take over some of their work became a controversial issue. In 1995, the following exchange (excerpts presented here) occurred on the Commentary page of *Modern Healthcare* (see Marullo and Mayer and Booth, 1995).

"It was only 10 short years ago that the media alerted the general public and policymakers to the nursing shortage. This shortage was as much of a public scandal as Wall Street insider trading. At that time, the thought of substituting registered nurses with minimally skilled personnel in an acute-care setting was unconscionable. It's ironic that the same industry that raced to end the nursing shortage a few years ago now may be willing to sacrifice high-quality nursing care in the name of short-term profit margins . . . It is impossible to conclude a rational and meaningful reason for this trend of destroying the essential nursing infrastructure needed to provide safe care to patients. Perhaps it boils down to a difference in opinion about exactly how quality care is prioritized in relation to profit margins."

Geraldine Marullo
Executive Director
American Nurses Association

"It would behoove organized nursing to stop whining and abandon the 'poor me' syndrome. For the past 25 years (my tenure as a nurse), organized nursing has been complaining about the same things—not enough staffing, cutting staff, substituting nonnursing staff, not enough pay and 'we just don't get any respect' in general . . . We need nurses and other healthcare professionals who are innovative, caring, able to meet patients' complex needs in a rapidly changing environment and who are not wedded to the way things used to be. We need to slay a sacred cow every day, something organized nursing finds difficult to do."

Gloria G. Mayer
President and CEO
Friendly Hills HealthCare Network

"Instead of writing revisionist history that cites organized nursing as whining about the status quo, Mayer would do better to openly acknowledge the innovative and positive changes in healthcare delivery that nursing organizations have been pressing for, developing, and instituting for years."

Rachel Z. Booth
President
American Association of Colleges of Nursing

In recent years when nurses have determined that their grievances have received insufficient response, they have engaged in labor strikes. In 2000 alone, there were ten strikes by nurses in communities around the country.

MID-LEVEL HEALTH CARE PRACTITIONERS

Two key problems in health care today are high health care costs and a shortage of primary care physicians, especially in many rural and inner-city areas. One response to these critical problems has been the creation of several **mid-level practitioner** positions jointly referred to as **physician extenders (PEs)**. These positions include several advanced practice nursing positions—the **nurse practitioner (NP)**, the **certified nurse midwife (CNM)**, and the **certified registered nurse anesthetist (CRNA)**—and the **physician assistant (PA)**. These physician extenders offer several benefits to the health care system: They provide extensive services to patients in rural and inner-city areas that have a shortage of physicians; they enable physicians with whom they work to see from 20 to 50 percent more patients; they are cost-efficient because they earn considerably less than physicians; and many research studies have found that they offer high quality services that are appreciated by patients.

IN COMPARATIVE FOCUS

DISCONTENT AMONG NURSES: A REPORT ON HOSPITAL CARE IN FIVE COUNTRIES

In one of the largest studies of its kind ever done, a 2001 survey by Aiken and others of more than 43,000 nurses in 711 hospitals in the United States, Canada, Germany, England, and Scotland found widespread discontent. Though the countries have very different types of health care systems, nurses reported similar shortcomings in their work environments and in the quality of hospital care. Five sources of discontent emerged in the study.

1. A large majority of the nurses in all five countries indicated that there are not enough registered nurses in their hospital to provide high-quality care, that there is not enough support staff, and that hospital management is nonresponsive to their needs.
2. Nurses in most countries reported that their workload increased in the last year while nursing managerial staff were eliminated or decreased.
3. Nurses in the United States, Canada, and Germany reported that they often spend

considerable time on non-nursing-skill duties (e.g., cleaning rooms, transporting food trays), whereas many tasks that are markers of good patient care (e.g., oral hygiene, skin care) get left undone.
4. Nurses reported concerns with the quality of patient care being delivered. Only one German nurse in nine, and one in three nurses in the other countries, rated the quality of nursing care on their unit as being excellent. Nurses in the United States and Canada were most likely to report that the quality of care provided had deteriorated in the last year.
5. Many of the nurses are dissatisfied, burned out, and intent on leaving nursing.

Interestingly, the nurses reported positive feelings about the quality of the physicians and nurses with whom they work and about physician-nurse interaction. Their complaints focused on problematic working conditions and the negative effects of those conditions on the quality of patient care.

Advanced Practice Nurses

Nurse Practitioners. A nurse practitioner is a registered nurse with additional training; about 90 percent complete a two-year master's degree beyond the RN. NPs are able to do about 70 to 80 percent of the basic primary and preventive care offered by physicians. They do social and medical histories; conduct physical examinations, including breast and pelvic exams; do pregnancy testing, Pap smears, and tests for sexually transmitted diseases; provide or prescribe contraceptive devices; and order laboratory tests and X-rays. They engage in patient counseling and provide health education. There are more than 100,000 NPs working today, and more than 80 percent of them work in primary care (most often in hospital inpatient and outpatient settings, in

private practice, in primary care settings, and in school settings).

The practice of the NP is governed by state nurse practice acts. States require collaboration with or some form of supervision by a physician but specific terms and conditions vary. However, in all states NPs can and do practice without direct physician supervision. More than half of NPs in freestanding primary care settings, HMOs, school and college health clinics, and hospital outpatient clinics reported that physicians saw less than 10 percent of their patients. All states allow some form of prescriptive privileges, but only 18 allow NPs to prescribe medication without any cosigning or approval by a physician.

Several studies have concluded that NPs typically give care that is equivalent to that provided by physicians and that they are especially good at caring for patients with chronic health problems. Other studies have found that NPs have better communication, counseling, and interviewing skills (especially helpful with chronic patients), are more likely to be familiar with community resources such as self-help groups, are more likely than physicians to adapt medical regimens to patients' family situations and environments (Mundinger, 1994), and spend more time dealing with psychosocial issues (Campbell et al., 1990).

One recent study (Mundinger et al., 2000) was based on a randomized trial in which patients were randomly assigned to either a nurse practitioner or a physician and in which nurse practitioners had the same authority, responsibilities, productivity, administrative requirements, and patient population as the primary care physicians. No significant differences were found in patient outcomes at either six months or one year. In part due to the extensive amount of personal interaction that occurs, patient acceptance of NPs (and other physician extenders) will likely remain at a high level.

Certified Nurse-Midwives. A certified nurse-midwife is a registered nurse who has additional nationally accredited training (usually 18 months to two years) in midwifery and who possesses certification by the American College of Nurse-Midwives. CNMs receive extensive training in gynecological care, especially as it relates to pregnancy and childbirth, as well as in other areas. Restrictive practice acts limit autonomous CNM practice in some states, but 47 states and the District of Columbia provide statutory prescriptive authority for CNMs. Most states now require private health insurers to reimburse nurse-midwives, and all states provide for reimbursement for treating Medicaid patients.

There are approximately 7,000 certified nurse-midwives who have been certified by the American College of Nurse-Midwives. Many CNMs are employed by hospitals, by physicians, by other CNMs, by managed care networks, or are in private practice. They are more likely to work in inner-city areas than in any other location. Average annual salary ranges from $40,000 to $50,000.

After considerable disagreement between lay-midwives and nurse-midwives, and debate over home versus hospital deliveries, nurse-midwifery experienced significant growth and success in the 1980s and 1990s. In 1985, the Institute of Medicine recommended that programs serving high-risk mothers use more certified nurse midwives and that state laws support nurse-midwifery practice.

In 1986 the Congressional Office of Technology Assessment concluded that CNMs manage routine pregnancies safely, noting that CNMs are more likely than physicians to test for urinary tract infections and diabetes, but less inclined to prescribe drugs; that CNMs are less likely to rely on technology, but communicate and interact more with their patients; and that patients of CNMs spend less time waiting for visits, have shorter hospitalizations and are more likely to feel satisfied with their care. (Rooks, 1990:34)

Despite serving mothers who are younger, more likely to be unmarried, more likely to be foreign-born, more likely to be minorities, but less likely to have received prenatal care than the average mother in the United States, midwife-attended births have better than average outcomes (Gabay and Wolfe, 1997). Altogether, CNMs deliver about 10 percent (more than 300,000 babies) of U.S. births each year; worldwide, midwives deliver more than two-thirds of all births.

Certified Registered Nurse Anesthetists. A CRNA is a registered nurse with an additional 2 or 3 years training for certification. They are fully qualified to perform anesthesiology in all 50 states. CRNAs administer 65 percent of all anesthetics given in the United States and are the sole anesthesiology providers in 85 percent of rural hospitals. There are more than 28,000 Certified Registered Nurse Anesthetists in the United States; their average salary is about $100,000.

Physician Assistants. Under the direct or indirect supervision of a physician, a PA can perform most of the basic care provided by the physician, including giving physical exams, monitoring and treating minor ailments, counseling, and prescribing some medications. The role of

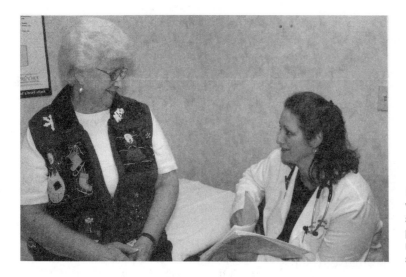

Physician assistants work under the supervision of a physician and provide most primary care services.

PA was created to handle routine patient care tasks so that physicians could spend their time on more complicated patient problems. In addition to primary care physicians, PAs may also assist specialists such as surgeons, anesthesiologists, pathologists, and radiologists.

Applicants for PA programs must have completed at least two years of college (most have a baccalaureate degree) and have a minimum of two years experience in the health care field. Programs are located in medical schools and generally require two years. A national certification exam must be passed before a PA can be licensed.

There are approximately 50,000 PAs licensed to practice in the United States as of the year 2000. About one-third work in primary care and half in a specialty area (general surgery and emergency medicine being most common). While nurse practitioners are primarily female, slightly more than half of all physician assistants are male. The median salary of PAs is about $65,000.

The professional autonomy of PAs is much more limited than that of NPs. Virtually all states and Washington, DC, allow PAs to provide medical services but only under physician supervision (some states allow PAs to practice with off-site physician supervision). PAs are allowed to prescribe some medications in 47 states and Washington, DC.

Research indicates that PAs could handle more than 80 percent of all office visits with minimal physician supervision. Analysts have concluded that they are competent in taking social and medical histories and in performing physical examinations and that quality of care is not decreased when they provide these services. Several studies have found high levels of satisfaction with the care offered by PAs. With the average cost of PA care ranging from one-quarter to one-half that of physicians, obvious potential exists for expanding PA care within the health care system.

ALLIED HEALTH WORKERS

A majority of the health care work force is referred to as allied health personnel. These providers work in all types of care, including primary, acute, tertiary, and chronic, and in all settings including physicians' and dentists' offices, health maintenance organizations, laboratories, clinics, ambulance services, home care, and hospitals. Allied health practitioners require varying amounts of education and training and they work with widely differing degrees of autonomy, dependence on technology, and regulation.

Table 10–1 lists the allied health fields that are accredited by the CAHEA, the prerequisites for entry into training, and the length of training. Many of the occupations have several levels of certification so that the prerequisites and length of training vary considerably, even within some fields.

TABLE 10–1   Allied Health Fields

Field	Prerequisite	Length of Training
Anesthesiologist's Assistant	Bachelor's degree	2 years
Blood Bank Technology	Bachelor's degree	1 year
Cardiovascular Technology	High school diploma	1–4 years
Cytotechnology	High school diploma; science background	varies
Electroneurodiagnostic Technology	High school diploma	1 year+
Emergency Medical Services	EMT-ambulance certification	600–1000 hours
Medical Assisting	High school diploma	1–2 years
Medical Illustration	Bachelor's degree	2–3 years
Medical Laboratory Technology	High school diploma	1–4 years
Medical Record Administration	High school diploma or bachelor's degree	1–4 years
Nuclear Medicine Technology	High school diploma; science background	1–4 years
Occupational Therapy	High school diploma	4 years
Ophthalmic Medical Technology	High school diploma	1–2 years
Perfusion	High school diploma; science background	1–2 years
Physician Assistant	Two-year undergraduate	2 years
Radiologic Technology	High school diploma; science background	1–4 years
Respiratory Therapy	High school diploma	2 years
Sonography	High school diploma	1–4 years
Surgical Technology	High school diploma	9–24 months

Source: *AMA Young Physician Survey;* reported in Alan B. Cohen, Joel C. Cantor, Dianne C. Barker, and Robert G. Hughes, "Young Physicians and the Future of the Medical Profession." *Health Affairs,* 9:138–148, 1990.

Many allied health fields have developed around particular technologies or techniques that require specialized knowledge and training. Although physicians continue to do some of these procedures themselves, it is more efficient to employ specialized workers. Many of these workers (e.g., nuclear medicine technologists) perform diagnostic tests, which are then interpreted by physicians.

Nuclear medicine is one of several high-technology imaging fields that offers enhanced diagnostic abilities.

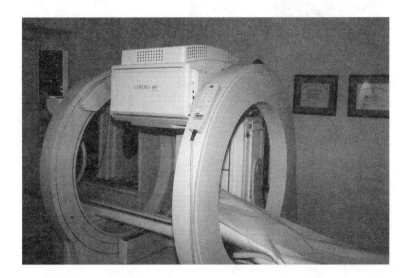

THE HEALTH CARE TEAM

The Concept of a Health Care Team

During the last several decades, the **health care team** approach has become commonplace in health care institutions. In reality, the concept of "team" is used in many different ways: (1) to describe a group of highly competent technical specialists, sub-specialists, and supporting personnel who join together to execute some dramatic, intense, and usually short-term activity (e.g., a neurosurgery team); (2) to refer to the cooperation of technically oriented providers (e.g., physician specialists) with socially, and/or behaviorally oriented providers (e.g., social workers); and (3) to simply refer to a less hierarchic and more egalitarian mode of health care organization and decision making (especially among physician and nonphysician providers).

The primary objectives of team care over traditional care are to avoid duplication and fragmentation of services and to develop better and more comprehensive health plans by including more perspectives. Ideally, this occurs through a group process involving cooperation and coordination. Research has documented that the existence of a "teamwork culture" in a hospital is related to greater feelings of patient satisfaction (Meterko, Mohr, and Young, 2004).

In many health care settings, a "team" of health care professionals work together to offer comprehensive care.

Perceptions of the Team Approach

Although enthusiasm for the team approach remains high among many health care workers and among many patients, some recent reexamination of the concept has occurred. Recent studies have shown that the approach is viewed differently among providers. For example, Temkin-Greener (1983) conducted interviews with 12 senior faculty members who were department heads in a large medical center/teaching hospital to explore ways in which leaders in nursing and medicine understand and define the team concept, its purposes, and its goals. She found that the physicians and nurses differed on their views of health care teams. Physicians often viewed teamwork as "a nursing concept, beneficial primarily to nursing and used to 'usurp' the traditional authority of medicine in health care provision" (p. 647), while the nurses imputed considerable value to the team approach but believed medicine to be closed to the concept unless it was imposed from outside (e.g., by the Joint Commission for Accreditation of Hospitals). Tempkin-Greener interprets these divergent attitudes as evidence of two different cultures, one in which medicine "emphasizes the status quo of its traditional authority and inherently hierarchical mode of organization and function" and one in which nursing "stresses a more egalitarian vision of power relations with collaboration and peer cooperation as prerequisites for team care provision" (p. 647). These varying perceptions indicate that the team approach is still evolving and has certain difficulties to resolve. However, it is expected to remain a part of health care delivery.

RELATIONSHIPS AMONG HEALTH CARE WORKERS

The delivery of health care services involves an extensive and interdependent network of personnel. Each position carries with it certain expectations for the practitioners themselves as well as for those with whom they interact. Furthermore, these positions are arranged in a hierarchy of status based on prestige and power. These occupational expectations and status arrangements significantly affect the dynamics of interaction among personnel throughout health care. The following section examines the relationship among physicians and the nonphysician practitioners discussed earlier in this chapter.

The Relationship Among Physicians and Nurses

Of all the interactions among health care workers, the relationship between the nurse and the physician has received the most attention. To better understand this relationship historically, Keddy and colleagues (1986) interviewed 34 older nurses who had worked and/or trained in the 1920s and 1930s about their interactions with physicians. They recalled that 50 years ago, physicians were primarily in control of nursing education, giving many of the lectures and examinations, serving on registration boards, and controlling the hiring of nurses. The role of the nurse was defined in terms of efficient compliance with the physician's orders rather than patient care responsibilities. Early in training, student nurses were taught the hierarchy of the hospital personnel and proper conduct in the presence of physicians. They were expected to show respect to physicians by standing at attention when physicians were present, and they were taught never to make direct recommendations regarding patient care and never to suggest diagnoses to the physician. Although nurses had ideas, they did not voice them. For carrying out this role, these nurses believed that the doctors admired and respected them. One interviewee recalled, "The physician signs and he'd write this long order, and then he'd look at you over his glasses and say 'Now it's up to you whether she gets better or not.' They didn't all say it, but . . . it was implied" (Keddy et al., 1986:749).

Dynamics such as these persisted, and in 1967 Leonard Stein coined the phrase "the doctor–nurse game" to describe these relationships. According to this game, physicians and nurses agree that their relationship is hierarchical, that physicians are superordinate and that this structure must be maintained. While nurses can make recommendations to physicians, the suggestions must appear to be initiated by the physician and open disagreements are to be avoided at all costs.

In 1990, Stein and two colleagues revisited the doctor–nurse game in an article in the *New England Journal of Medicine*. They described a changing milieu that encouraged a new type of physician–nurse relationship. Changes that had occurred included a deterioration in public esteem for physicians, increased questioning of the profession's devotion to altruistic concerns, and a greater recognition of physicians' fallibilities. By 1990, physicians were increasingly likely to be female, and although female medical graduates are trained to play the same game as their male counterparts, "the elements of the game that reflect stereotypical roles of male dominance and female submissiveness are missing" (p. 546). The critical nursing shortage at the time also restructured nurse–physician interaction by focusing attention on the value of nurses, especially as they became more highly trained and specialized. Stein et al. perceived the possibility that a feeling of colleagueship between the two might replace the typical hierarchical relationship between superior and subordinate.

For all of these reasons, and partly in response to the women's movement, nurses now seek greater equality with physicians as well as autonomy in defining their own roles. In addition, nursing education, increasingly located in academic settings, is socializing nursing students to relate to physicians differently than they did in the past. Most nurses are no longer willing to stand aside as subordinates. This has provoked a mixed reaction among physicians—whereas some physicians are supportive of nurses' attempts to become more professional and autonomous, others believe that nurses are no longer doing their jobs.

The "Revisited" piece aroused considerable discussion in the editorial section of the *New England Journal of Medicine* (July 19, 1990).

Much resistance was expressed by physicians who tended to defend an ongoing status differential between themselves and nurses. The letter writers stated that nurses are not equal partners with physicians because they are less well-educated and less technically proficient, and they are not autonomous because they lack ultimate responsibility for patient treatment.

Two nurses responded that as physicians' control over medical practice shrinks, physicians "are beginning to appreciate what it is like to provide care for patients when one has little or no control over one's work" (Lewis, 1990:201) and that nurses are still unappreciated for what they offer to health care.

Campbell-Heider and Pollock (1987:423) caution that nurses' expectations that their status will be enhanced through increased knowledge and skills fail to consider the deeply rooted gender hierarchy in medical care: "It is clear that the social control of nurses (and women) has enabled physicians to increase their own status and that the maintenance of female stereotypes has increased the power differentials between gender groups."

One of the most extensive studies regarding the dynamics within the physician–nurse relationship was conducted by Prescott and Bowen (1985). Contrary to a number of studies documenting significant problems in the relationship between nurses and physicians, they found considerable satisfaction among both groups, although they differed in their descriptions of the elements of a good relationship and in the factors that contribute to positive relationships.

Sixty-nine percent of nurses and 70 percent of physicians described their relationships as essentially positive. Nurses emphasized mutual respect and trust as the most important elements of a good relationship and considered it important that physicians regard them as intelligent resources who should be involved in the planning and decision making related to patient care. For physicians, the most important elements of a good relationship with nurses were how well the nurse communicated with the physician, the nurse's willingness to help the physician, and the nurse's competency.

Areas of disagreement between physicians and nurses were also examined. Nurses disagreed most often with physicians concerning general plan of care, specific orders, and patient movement (from unit to unit and timing of discharge). On the other hand, physicians were concerned about nurses taking actions they considered outside the nursing domain, making poor clinical decisions, and not following specific physician orders. Approximately half of the physicians and one-third of the nurses reported that disagreements were handled in the organization through the medical chain of command, but final authority almost always rested with the physician.

The Relationship Among Physicians and Mid-Level Practitioners

There are many situations in which physicians and mid-level practitioners work cooperatively and with mutual respect. There are also many situations in which the interests and goals of the groups differ and conflict prevails. In general, physicians are most comfortable with practitioners who clearly supplement their own work and who are restricted from practicing without physician supervision. For this reason, physicians have had the most amicable relationships with physician assistants (who typically work for physicians and under their supervision), with certified registered nurse anesthetists (as long as they work under and are paid by anesthesiologists), and with certified nurse midwives (as long as they work for and are paid by hospitals or an obstetrician, as most are). There is more tension in the relationship with nurse practitioners, who are sometimes seen as more of a competitor for patients seeking primary care, and with CRNAs and CNMs who work independently and are reimbursed directly.

The most heated point of contention today is the extent to which advanced practice nurses should be able to practice independently. The American Nurses Association contends that the two to four years of training beyond the nurses' degree should qualify APNs to serve as primary care providers without physician supervision. In addition, the ANA believes that, where necessary, state laws should be changed to enable

APNs to receive direct reimbursement from public and private insurance programs and to have extensive—if not complete—legal authority to write prescriptions.

The American Medical Association vehemently opposes these changes. The AMA contends that the additional training required of physicians makes them the most effective providers of health care services and the only group sufficiently knowledgeable about pharmacology to have full prescription writing authority. An AMA report issued in late 1993 stated, "Substitution for, rather than extension of, physician care by nonphysicians raises questions of patient safety, competence of therapeutic decision, fragmentation of care and delays to patients in need of medical care" (reported in Burda, 1993:6).

Several studies have documented communication problems between physicians and mid-level practitioners. An intriguing study by Susan B. Graham (1991), an anthropologist and physician, analyzed interaction patterns of physicians and midwives working in an obstetrical training program at a major medical center. Midwives were added to the Department of Obstetrics and Gynecology at the center to help provide additional coverage for an increased workload. All of the 20 midwives were CNMs and all of the physicians were residents in obstetrics/gynecology.

The CNMs were to provide prenatal care to low-risk patients and to do normal vaginal deliveries of those patients. Residents would have responsibility for high-risk patients and difficult labors and deliveries. The faculty and administration envisioned two separate but equal services and they expected little friction between the two groups of providers. In fact, what emerged were competing and often conflicting systems that potentially jeopardized patient care.

Because 70 percent of the residents and all of the CNMs were female, Graham concluded that differences between the two groups could not be attributed to gender. Instead, the primary problems were the absence of a formally articulated structure for interaction and differing perceptions concerning group status. The CNMs saw themselves as professionals who had already completed their training and had acquired many years of experience; they regarded residents as inexperienced apprentices. On the other hand, residents regarded themselves as "doctors" and the midwives as "nurses," stressing their own extended training, abilities to do procedures that the CNMs could not, and longer working hours. Differing treatment philosophies also contributed to the problem. The midwives considered their emphasis on the individual and the use of noninterventionism to be superior to what they regarded as the impersonal, interventionist philosophy of the residents.

THE CHANGING ENVIRONMENT AMONG HEALTH CARE WORKERS

Relationships among physicians, nurses, mid-level practitioners, and allied health personnel must be viewed as a constantly evolving and dynamic process. This process is governed not only by factors internal to each field—such as changing education requirements and a search for autonomy—but also by changes in the wider health care system (such as managed care), the economy, and society (Hartley, 1999).

SUMMARY

The numbers and types of health care workers in the United States have changed significantly in the past 200 years. With these changes has come a complex bureaucracy to regulate and control millions of providers working in numerous health care settings.

The field of nursing is undergoing significant change. No longer content to be silent and obedient assistants to physicians, nurses have sought to professionalize the field through increased educational requirements and greater assertiveness. While nursing does not offer genuine autonomy—an important prerequisite for a profession—the field does have much in common with professions. There is now general acknowledgment that nurses have become more centrally involved in the direct provision of health care.

Several important mid-level practitioners—nurse practitioners, physician assistants, certified

nurse-midwives, and certified registered nurse anesthetists—now occupy an important niche in the health care system. While their ability to practice independent of physician supervision varies, all perform services once provided by physicians and at lower cost. Research confirms that these practitioners offer high-quality services with which patients are satisfied. Relationships with physicians vary, but physicians' attitudes are more positive when the mid-level provider has less autonomy.

Extremely important scientific developments during the 1920s, 1930s, and 1940s led to the development of a wide variety of allied health positions that have become essential parts of the overall health care system. These personnel perform diagnostic work that is interpreted by physicians, and they provide certain therapeutic modalities and types of rehabilitative care.

HEALTH ON THE INTERNET

A Web site that contains a wealth of information on nursing, including nursing case studies and other trends and issues related to nursing, is the nursing research site of the National Institutes of Health:

   http://www.nih.gov/ninr

Click on "News and Information," then click on "Science Advances." What are some of the recent scientific advances related to nursing?

KEY CONCEPTS AND TERMS

advanced practice nurse (APN)
allied health workers
American Nurses Association (ANA)
certified nurse midwife (CNM)
certified registered nurse anesthetist
   (CRNA)
differentiated practice
Florence Nightingale

health care team
licensed practical nurse (LPN)
mid-level practitioner
midwifery
nurse practitioner (NP)
physician assistant (PA)
physician extender (PE)

DISCUSSION QUESTION

In some areas of the country, groups of health care workers (most often nurses and allied health workers) have unionized. Ostensibly, the unions will help provide a bargaining force for increased salaries and benefits, job security, and greater say in management decisions. Unions derive much of their power from the willingness of members to go on strike if they feel they have not been treated fairly by management.

Suppose you heard that all of the hospital-based nurses in your community had presented a list of grievances (lower-than-average salaries, inadequate benefits, little workplace autonomy, reduction in staff, patient care being compromised) to the administrative officers of the hospitals who have refused to consider them. In response, efforts are underway to form a nurses'

union to establish stronger bargaining power. The nurses have indicated that they will consider a general strike if their requests (demands?) are not met.

Should health care workers have the same rights as other workers to unionize and, if they deem it necessary, to go on strike? Are health care occupations qualitatively different than other occupations because of their role in working in life-and-death situations? If nurses cannot unionize and strike, what options do they have in bargaining for better job conditions?

Is your position the same or different regarding the right of physicians to unionize, to collectively bargain, and if deemed necessary, to strike? What are the conditions, if any, in which you think that a physician strike would be justifiable?

REFERENCES

Aiken, Linda H., Julie Sochalski, and Gerard F. Anderson. 1996 "Downsizing the Hospital Nursing Workforce." *Health Affairs,* 15:88–92.

Aiken, Linda H., Sean P. Clarke, Douglas M. Stoane, Julie A. Stochalski, Reinhard Busse, Heath Clarke, Phyllis Giovannetti, Jennifer Hunt, Anne Marie Rafferty, and Judith Shamian. 2001 "Nurses' Reports on Hospital Care in Five Countries." *Health Affairs,* 20:43–53.

Baer, Ellen D. 1990 "Nurses," pp. 459–475 in *Women, Health, and Medicine in America: A Historical Handbook,* Rima D. Apple (ed.). New York: Garland Publishing, Inc.

Booth, Rachel Z. 1995 "Letter to the Editor." *Modern Healthcare,* 25:24.

Burda, David. 1993 "AMA Report Slams Practice of Using Nurses, Not Doctors, as Primary-Care Providers." *Modern Healthcare,* 23:6.

———. 1994 "Massachusetts Nurse Survey Ignites Battle." *Modern Healthcare,* 24:38–40.

Campbell, James D., Hans O. Mauksch, Helen J. Neikirk, and Michael C. Hosokawa. 1990 "Collaborative Practice and Provider Styles of Delivering Health Care." *Social Science and Medicine,* 30:1359–1365.

Campbell-Heider, Nancy, and Donald Pollock. 1987 "Barriers to Physician-Nurse Collegiality: An Anthropological Perspective." *Social Science and Medicine,* 25:421–425.

Chambliss, Daniel. 1996 *Beyond Caring: Hospitals, Nurses, and the Social Organization of Ethics.* Chicago: University of Chicago Press.

Cohen, Alan B., Joel C. Cantor, Dianne C. Barker, and Robert G. Hughes. 1990 "Young Physicians and the Future of the Medical Profession." *Health Affairs,* 9:138–148.

Davidson, Harriet, Patricia H. Folcarelli, Sybil Crawford, Laura J. Duprat, and Joyce C. Clifford. 1997 "The Effects of Health Care Reforms on Job Satisfaction and Voluntary Turnover Among Hospital-based Nurses." *Medical Care,* 35:634–645.

Davis, Fred. 1972 *Illness, Interaction, and the Self.* Belmont, CA: Wadsworth.

DeVries, Raymond G. 1985 *Regulating Birth: Midwives, Medicine, and the Law.* Philadelphia: Temple University Press.

Eddy, Diane M., Victoria Elfrink, Darlene Weis, and Mary J. Schank. 1994 "Importance of Professional Nursing Values: A National Study of Baccalaureate Programs." *Journal of Nursing Education,* 33:257–262.

Friedman, Emily. 1990 "Nursing: New Power, Old Problems." *Journal of the American Medical Association,* 264:2977–2962.

Gabay, Mary, and Sidney M. Wolfe. 1997 "Nurse-Midwifery: The Beneficial Alternative." *Public Health Reports,* 112:386–394.

Graham, Susan B. 1991 "A Structural Analysis of Physician-Midwife Interaction in an Obstetrical Training Program." *Social Science and Medicine,* 32:931–942.

Hartley, Heather. 1999 "The Influence of Managed Care on Supply of Certified Nurse-Midwives: An Evaluation of the Physician Dominance Thesis." *Journal of Health and Social Behavior,* 40:87–101.

Hite, Charles. 1990a "Caring to the Limits: Nursing's New Obligations." *Roanoke Times & World News,* October 14, pp. A1, A6-A7.

———. 1990b "Caring to the Limits: Juggling Tougher Tasks." *Roanoke Times & World News,* October 16, pp. A1, A4, A6.

Keddy, Barbara, Margaret J. Gillis, Pat Jacobs, Heather Burton, Maureen Rogers. 1986 "The Doctor-Nurse Relationship: An Historical Perspective." *Journal of Advanced Nursing,* 11:745–753.

Lewis, Mary Ann. 1990 "The Doctor-Nurse Game Revisited." *New England Journal of Medicine,* 323:201.

Marullo, Geraldine. 1995 "Hospitals Putting Profit Margins Ahead of High-Quality Nursing Care." *Modern Healthcare,* 25:32.

Mayer, Gloria G. 1995 "It's Time for Nursing to Drop 'Poor Me' Attitude and Take Leadership Role in Healthcare." *Modern Healthcare,* 25:38.

McClure, Margaret L. 1991 "Differentiated Nursing Practice: Concepts and Considerations." *Nursing Outlook,* 39:106–110.

Meterko, Mark, David C. Mohr, and Gary J. Young. 2004 "Teamwork Culture and Patient Satisfaction in Hospitals." *Medical Care,* 42:492–498.

Moore, J. Duncan. 1995 "Nurses Nationwide Air Gripes Against Hospitals." *Modern Healthcare,* 25:3.

Mundinger, Mary O. 1994 "Advanced Practice Nursing—Good Medicine for Physicians?" *New England Journal of Medicine,* 330:211–214.

Mundinger, Mary O., Robert L. Kane, Elizabeth R. Lenz, Annette M. Totten, Wei-Yann Tsai, Paul D. Cleary, William T. Friedewald, Albert L. Siu, and Michael L. Shelanski. 2000 "Primary Care Outcomes in Patients Treated by Nurse Practitioners or Physicians." *Journal of the American Medical Association,* 283:59–68.

Norrish, Barbara R., and Thomas G. Rundall. 2001 "Hospital Restructuring and the Work of Registered Nurses." *The Milbank Quarterly,* 79:55–79.

Prescott, Patricia A., and Sally A. Bowen. 1985 "Physician-Nurse Relationships." *Annals of Internal Medicine,* 103:127–133.

Reverby, Susan M. 1987 *Ordered to Care—The Dilemma of American Nursing,* 1850–1945. Cambridge: Cambridge University Press.

Rogers, Ann E., Wei-Ting Hwang, Linda D. Scott, Linda H. Aiken, David F. Dinges. 2004 "The Working Hours of Hospital Staff Nurses and Patient Safety." *Health Affairs,* 23:202–212.

Rooks, Judith P. 1990 "Nurse-Midwifery: The Window Is Wide Open." *American Journal of Nursing,* 90:30–36.

Stein, Leonard I. 1967 "The Doctor-Nurse Game." *Archives of General Psychiatry,* 16:699–703.

Stein, Leonard I., David T. Watts, and Timothy Howell. 1990 "The Doctor-Nurse Game Revisited." *The New England Journal of Medicine,* 322:546–549.

Temkin-Greener, Helena. 1983 "Interprofessional Perspectives on Teamwork in Health Care: A Case Study." *Milbank Memorial Fund Quarterly,* 61:641–657.

Thompson, Joyce. 2003 Quoted in Patrick Reilly, "Importing Controversy." *Modern Healthcare,* 33:20–24.

11

COMPLEMENTARY AND ALTERNATIVE MEDICINE

Through much of the twentieth century, the scientific medicine paradigm (as described in Chapter 2) was so dominant in the United States that it was referred to as *orthodox* or *conventional* medicine. Although alternatives to medical doctors—everything from home remedies to prayer to chiropractors—were frequently used, they were considered to be unorthodox or unconventional medicine. Scientific medicine has been taught almost exclusively in health courses in schools, has been the subject of public health campaigns, and has been the dominant perspective in the medical school curriculum.

THE MEANING OF COMPLEMENTARY AND ALTERNATIVE MEDICINE (CAM)

Although scientific medicine has been given this societal endorsement, it is rather remarkable that **complementary and alternative medicine (CAM)**—"a group of diverse medical and health care systems, practices, and products that are not presently considered to be part of

conventional medicine" (National Center for Complementary and Alternative Medicine, 2002:1)—has flourished and is today more popular than ever before. Goldstein (1999) has extracted five core elements from the wide variety of CAM healing practices:

1. *Holism*—This practice involves treating the patient holistically; that is, considering the entire physical, mental, spiritual, and social make-up of the patient in diagnosing illness and providing therapeutic care.
2. *The interpenetration of mind, body, and spirit*—While most physicians today recognize the importance of the mind-body connection, CAM places great emphasis on their relationship and generally never treats one without the other.
3. *The possibility of high-level wellness*—Health is viewed as being a very positive physical-emotional state and not just as the absence of symptoms or clinical disease.
4. *Vitalism: life suffused by the flow of energy*—Life is viewed as a type of ecosystem in which the various elements of mind, body, and

spirit are united by a force or flow of energy throughout the body.

5. *The healing process*—In most forms of CAM, unlike much of conventional medicine, healing is viewed as a cooperative, active process that involves both healer and patient. The healer is a caring and nurturant individual who works "with" instead of "on" patients.

Given the disdain that organized medicine has historically had for CAM (and in many cases the disdain that CAM has had for scientific medicine), the popularity of the alternatives makes an important statement about many people's understanding of health and healing. In fact, Goldner (1999) argues that one of the reasons that many patients choose a CAM technique is precisely because they feel alienated by the impersonality of conventional medicine and prefer a more holistic approach.

SCIENTIFIC MEDICINE AND ALTERNATIVE HEALING

Orthodox Medicine's View of Alternative Healers

Historically, physicians justified their traditional opposition to alternative healing practices in two ways. First, many medical doctors have considered any form of "nonscientific" healing to be quackery—a medically worthless practice—or a danger to public health (if a harmful substance is administered or if people delay seeking conventional care). Their criticism of CAM was viewed as being part of a duty to protect the public's health. Physician-critics acknowledge that some alternative healers make a professional appearance and seem to base their practice on well-articulated (though nonscientific) principles. But, by virtue of offering a healing practice that has not undergone rigorous scientific testing, they are viewed as deluding the public and risking people's health (Angell and Kassirer, 1998).

Second, physicians have expressed concern that some people are fooled into believing the claims of alternative healers. Whether it is due to effective advertising or to appeals made to people who have not been helped by orthodox medicine, users of CAM have sometimes been seen as being unable to distinguish between legitimate and illegitimate medical care (Beyerstein, 2001).

An alternative view suggests that organized medicine's opposition to alternative healers has been based on perceived self-interest. By persuading the public (and politicians) that it is the only legitimate healing practice, scientific medicine's cultural authority (as described in Chapter 2) is protected. This in turn restricts competition for patients, and for private and public money spent on health care. How has this been done?

> One way to do so was through an educational campaign, using the vast public relations resources of the AMA and other organizations to expose the dangers and errors of these cults. Another approach was to employ political leverage and legal muscle. Organized medicine excluded from its ranks those who espoused such systems; denied such practitioners the privilege of consultation; refused to see patients when such healers were assisting in the case; prevented such practitioners from working in or otherwise using public hospitals; went to court to prosecute them for violating existing medical practice acts; and actively opposed legislative protection for them or, when that failed, opposed allowing them any additional privileges. (Gevitz, 1988:16–17)

CAM's View of Conventional Healers

Practitioners and proponents of complementary and alternative healing practices view their work in a completely different way. Many have argued that their goal is the same as that of conventional medicine: to offer effective healing therapies. Their belief is that orthodox medicine has helped some people but has failed to help many others and, in fact, often harms them (e.g., negative drug reactions or drug dependency).

CAM healers contend that the many people who have been helped by their practices, the high levels of satisfaction in their patients, and the high percentage of people who see them on a continuing basis testify to the efficacy of their treatments. They believe patients should have an unencumbered right to choose their healing practice from a variety of options, just as they

IN THE FIELD

A SHORT HISTORY OF MEDICINE

"Doctor, I have an earache."

2000 B.C. "Here, eat this root."

1000 B.C. "That root is heathen, say this prayer."

1850 A.D. "That prayer is superstition, drink this potion."

1940 A.D. "That potion is snake oil, swallow this pill."

1985 A.D. "That pill is ineffective, take this antibiotic."

2000 A.D. "That antibiotic is artificial. Here, eat this root."

have a right to choose their religion. If a particular type of healing practice is worthless, patients will soon discover that, and the demand for that service will diminish. Alternative healers often have asked for the right to practice without attack from organized medicine.

COMPLEMENTARY AND ALTERNATIVE HEALERS

Use of Complementary and Alternative Healers

It is now recognized that millions of people use complementary and alternative healers every year. The 2002 National Health Interview Survey found that 36 percent of adults in the United States use some form of CAM, and when megavitamin therapy and prayer specifically for health reasons are included, the number rises to 62 percent. Each year, Americans pay more visits to CAM healers than to primary care physicians. When Oxford Health Plans included use of CAM in its benefit package, between 40 and 50 percent of members saw a CAM provider in the first year (Kilgore, 1998). Many health maintenance organizations around the country have now begun including coverage for CAM.

Use of CAM is common by both men and women (females slightly more likely), both blacks and whites (whites somewhat more likely), and people at all levels of education (with use highest among the best educated) and in all socioeconomic groups (where use is highest among those with the most income) (Astin, 1998).

The most common problems for which CAM therapies are used are back problems, allergies, and arthritis. Table 11–1 identifies the 10 most frequently cited reasons for using CAM. The therapies most frequently used are herbal therapy, chiropractic, and massage therapy. The rates of utilization for 11 therapies are presented in Table 11–2.

The Dual Model of Care

Are all or most of the people who use CAM completely dissatisfied with conventional medical care? No. Researchers have discovered that many

TABLE 11–1 Ten Most Common Reasons to See an Alternative Healer

Condition	Reporting Condition (%)	Used Alternative Healer* (%)
Back problems	20	36
Allergies	16	9
Arthritis	16	18
Insomnia	14	20
Sprains, strains	13	22
Headache	13	27
High blood pressure	11	11
Digestive problems	10	13
Anxiety	10	28
Depression	8	20
All 10 combined	73	25

*Percentages are of those who reported the condition

Source: David M. Eisenberg, Ronald C. Kessler, Cindy Foster, Frances E. Norlock, David R. Calkins, and Thomas L. Delbanco. 1993 "Unconventional Medicine in the United States." *New England Journal of Medicine,* 328:246–252. Copyright © 1993 Massachusetts Medical Society. All rights reserved.

TABLE 11–2   Use of 11 Unconventional Therapies in 1997

Type of Therapy	Used Therapy (%)
Herbal therapy	17
Chiropractic	16
Massage	14
Vitamin therapy	13
Homeopathy	5
Yoga	5
Acupressure	5
Biofeedback	2
Acupuncture	2
Hypnotherapy	1
Naturopathy	1

Source: "Landmark Healthcare 1997 Poll on Use of Alternative Care," in Christine Kilgore, "Alternative Medicine: Probing Its Core," *Health Measures,* 3:26–30, 1998.

people follow a "dual model of medical care," making use of an alternative healer at the same time as they receive care from a medical doctor.

Although some people have become disillusioned with conventional care and have made a cognitive commitment to complementary and alternative practices, the more common pattern is that individuals use different healers for different problems. For example, many patients consult with chiropractors about chronic low back pain but continue to rely on medical doctors for other problems. Their selection of a healer is made on very pragmatic grounds: They continue to see medical doctors for most ailments because that has been helpful in the past; but if their back pain has received little relief from the family doctor, they will seek relief from a chiropractor. If that works, they will maintain allegiance to both practitioners—each in a specified domain (Kronenfeld and Wasner, 1982; Kelner and Wellman, 1997). In a 1985 study of asthma patients using an alternative healer, more than three-fourths reported that they were satisfied with *both* their medical doctor and the alternative healer (Donnelly, Spykerboer, and Thong, 1985). However, several studies have discovered that most persons who follow the dual model of care do not inform their medical doctor that they are also seeing a CAM healer, even if it is for the same complaint.

The Efficacy of Complementary and Alternative Healers

Is this information a valid and reliable indication that at least some CAM healers offer efficacious treatment? Possibly, but not necessarily. Determining the efficacy of any medical treatment, conventional or unconventional, is more complicated than it might seem at first. Rodney Coe (1970) has identified three reasons why the use of magic in primitive medicine is (or seems to be) effective. These reasons can be generalized to any form of medical treatment whatever the level of scientific sophistication in the society.

First, in all societies, most patients most of the time will recover regardless of the form of treatment received or even whether any treatment is provided. The amazing recuperative powers of the human body are only now being recognized. The same point is made by the old adage about seeing a physician for a cold: If you do, you'll be well in a week; if you don't, it will take seven days. Thus, whether one receives muscle relaxants from a medical doctor or spinal manipulation from a chiropractor, one's back pain will usually diminish eventually. Typically, we give credit to whatever treatment was received though we would often have healed without treatment.

Second, when patients believe strongly in the medical care they receive, it has great psychotherapeutic value, whatever its direct effects. The determination to get well and the confidence that recovery will occur are relevant factors in the healing process. Believing in the cure offered by your family physician can contribute to its success, just as believing in the efficacy of being needled by an acupuncturist or sharing prayer with a Christian Science practitioner can.

Finally, some medical practices are empirically correct even though there is not a clear explanation. Coe uses the example of a medicine man treating a snakebite victim. He might open the wound further and suck out the evil spirit that had entered. In so doing, he is actually sucking out the poisonous venom from the wound, thus accomplishing what orthodox medicine would recommend but basing it on an entirely different underlying theory.

Furthermore, every medical treatment must be considered within the context of the practitioner–patient relationship. It is now well recognized that the quality of this relationship may influence the course of treatment and the healing process.

Treatments offered by alternative healers often are enhanced by the greater rapport that develops with patients. Alternative healers often are more sympathetic than medical doctors to minor but nagging conditions that can trouble an individual. Most of the alternative healing practices involve more talking and more touching, both tremendously reassuring processes, than are often involved in treatment by the medical doctor. Alternative healers also are viewed as giving more time (more than four times as much time as MDs give per patient); doing a better job of avoiding medical jargon; and providing warmer, more relaxed treatment settings.

All this is not to say that we do not make individual judgments about the efficacy of medical care received. We do. And it is not to say that patterns of efficacy cannot be studied. They can. But, it is to say that drawing firm conclusions about the efficacy of any form of medical care must be done carefully.

Mainstream Interest in Complementary and Alternative Healing Practices

In recent years interest in complementary and alternative healing practices has increased among policymakers. In 1992 the United States Senate established the Office of Alternative Medicine (OAM) within the National Institutes of Health to evaluate the effectiveness of unconventional medical practices. Now called the National Center for Complementary and Alternative Medicine, the first-year budget of $2 million has grown more than 50-fold to over $100 million in 2003. Much of the money has been allocated to research projects on various practices and to public education.

Concurrently, many medical schools have started or are developing courses on alternative therapies—two-thirds of medical schools in the United States offered at least one CAM course in 2000. Health insurance policies now routinely cover care from at least some types of alternative healers, and Washington has become the first state to pass an "any-willing-provider" law that requires ensurers to cover the services of every licensed or certified healthcare provider in the state.

The general attitude of medical doctors toward CAM practices has certainly softened. Although some remain skeptical of approaches that have not undergone rigorous scientific testing (although many CAMs have been so tested), many physicians now accept the value of at least some of the practices and routinely refer patients who they are unable to help to CAM practitioners.

In this chapter we examine four CAM practices: chiropractic, acupuncture, religious healing (particularly Christian Science), and ethnic folk healing (curanderismos and Navajo healers).

CHIROPRACTIC

The field of **chiropractic** contains many contradictions. Millions of people in the United States enthusiastically support chiropractic, whereas many continue to see it as nothing more than successful quackery. (A former president of the American Chiropractic Association was fond of saying, "People either swear by us or at us.") Without altering its basic philosophy or practice, it has achieved increased acceptance by many physicians yet is condemned by many others. There is even dissensus among chiropractors themselves as to the appropriate boundaries of the field.

Nevertheless, certain facts are clear. Chiropractic is a licensed health profession in all 50 states, and chiropractors are recognized and reimbursed by federal, state, and most commercial insurance companies. There are more than 70,000 licensed doctors of chiropractic in the United States. An estimated 15 to 20 million people are treated by chiropractors each year. Chiropractic represents an important component of the health care system.

Origin

The field of chiropractic was founded by Canadian–born Daniel David Palmer (1845–1913), a healer living in Davenport, Iowa. Palmer

IN THE FIELD

LEGALIZING MEDICAL MARIJUANA?

In 1996, California voters approved Proposition 215, which permitted physicians to *recommend* marijuana for their patients. Because it would violate federal law, physicians were prohibited from *prescribing* it. Within four years, eight additional states (Alaska, Arizona, Colorado, Hawaii, Maine, Nevada, Oregon, and Washington) had endorsed or enacted medical marijuana laws, and 35 states went on record acknowledging marijuana's medical value. However, the U.S. Justice Department has maintained that federal law prohibits any use of marijuana and indicated that it would use its authority under the Controlled Substances Act to revoke the license to prescribe drugs of any physician who *recommended* marijuana to a patient. In May 2001, the United States Supreme Court ruled that the federal law prohibiting the manufacture and distribution of marijuana means that it cannot be sold or used for medicinal purposes.

Can marijuana be medicinal? Yes. Research has shown four beneficial medical effects: (1) it reduces the nausea associated with cancer chemotherapy; (2) it reduces "wasting syndrome"—the deadly loss of appetite and consequent weight loss that many AIDS patients feel near the end of life; (3) it reduces the painful muscle spasms and tremors experienced by many people with spinal cord injuries and multiple sclerosis; and (4) it reduces pressure inside the eye for persons with glaucoma (though another drug is now more effective). There is experimental evidence that it may be helpful in treating other conditions such as depression.

Are there any demonstrated negative side effects of marijuana use? Yes. Two such effects are: (1) it impairs cognitive functioning, negatively affecting coordination and short-term memory (studies have been inconsistent on whether there is any long-term cognitive impairments); and (2) it leads to respiratory damage (studies have found that smoking marijuana is even harder on the lungs than smoking tobacco).

Proponents of medical marijuana argue that individuals should have the right to decide for themselves whether the benefits outweigh the dangers. Because many of the users would be light users and would only be using marijuana on a temporary basis, they argue that the dangers are overstated. Besides, it is well known that many persons with cancer and with AIDS are already using marijuana for relief but are being forced to do so surreptitiously. Opponents argue that liberalizing use of the drug might lead to increased use of marijuana and/or other drugs and that the dangers of the drug justify its continued ban.

In 1997, the *New England Journal of Medicine* endorsed the legalization of medical marijuana, arguing that it has clearly brought relief from pain for many people. Later that year, the American Medical Association, though rejecting endorsement of legalization, called for the right of physicians to discuss any treatment alternatives with patients without possibility of criminal sanction.

---

credited his vision of the field to two successful experiences he had in 1895: By realigning displaced vertebrae, he restored hearing to one man who had become deaf 17 years earlier when something had "given way" in his back, and he relieved another patient's heart problems. He reasoned that if two such disparate conditions could be treated through manipulation of the vertebrae, potential existed for curing all ailments in this fashion. His research findings, published in 1910, served as the foundation for this new healing practice and the basis for a chiropractic school, which he established in 1897 (Wardwell, 1988).

Basic Principles

Coulehan (1985) describes the two basic tenets of chiropractic:

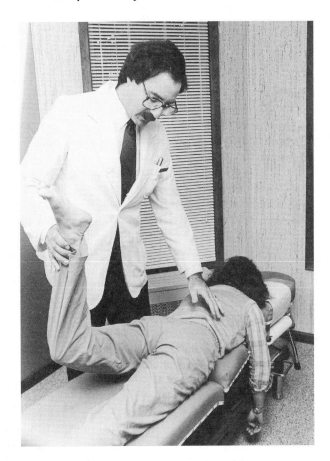

Chiropractors believe that health problems are expressions of underlying problems including blockages of the flow of vital energy caused by malalignments of the vertebrae.

1. Illness results from a failure of the positive homeostatic drive toward health. Health problems or symptoms are general expressions of underlying problems rather than indicators of some specific problem. Maintenance of homeostasis occurs through good nutrition, good posture, exercise, stress management, creative meditation, and natural (nonpharmacological) healing. Serious disease is viewed as the end result of a process that could have been avoided through this holistic approach.

2. Vital energy flows throughout the body's nerves during a homeostatic state. However, this energy can be blocked by subtle malalignments of the vertebrae called **subluxations**. These vertebral subluxations are the origin of most human illness. By correct-

ing the spinal malfunction, the chiropractor expects the specific problem to disappear and the patient's general health to improve.

Caplan (1984) explicates the three main ways that this philosophy of healing contrasts with orthodox medicine.

1. Medical doctors typically equate symptoms with particular diseases and identify health as the absence of symptoms. Disease is discovered when symptoms appear and is usually judged to have ended when the symptoms disappear. Chiropractic does not make this equation. A body is assumed to be diseased for some period of time before symptoms appear. Rather than focusing on symptoms, chiropractors focus on the subluxation.

2. Orthodox medicine considers microorganisms to be the underlying cause of many disorders. The medical profession considers this to have been scientifically proven and disdains any healing philosophy that does not subscribe to it. The task of the physician is to diagnose what microorganisms are present and to offer treatment to reduce their presence in order to restore health.

   Chiropractic's adherence to the belief that subluxations cause disease is in seeming contradiction to scientific medicine. Chiropractors believe that microorganisms are a necessary condition for many diseases but not a sufficient one. For a disease to occur, the host must have been made susceptible to the disease by factors such as poor nutrition, stress, heredity, and vertebral subluxations.

3. While chiropractors see themselves as holistic healers specializing in preventive care, many physicians believe the field should be restricted to musculoskeletal conditions or eliminated altogether.

Historical Developments

Early on, the field of chiropractic split into camps. The first camp maintained that chiropractic was not the practice of medicine and ought to offer spinal adjustment solely as a therapeutic modality. An alternative view developed among many of the MDs who were also doctors of chiropractic that chiropractors ought to offer a wide variety of treatment techniques in addition to spinal adjustment. The former school became known as "straights," while the latter group became known as "mixers." Eventually, each group began its own national association: the American Chiropractic Association (ACA) for the straights and the International Chiropractors Association (ICA) for the mixers. For most people, however, the similarities between the groups were more telling than their differences.

The field of chiropractic struggled through its early years. The Flexner Report of 1910 condemned existing chiropractic schools for failure to develop ties with universities and for the absence of demanding training programs. The Great Depression significantly reduced philanthropic contributions and cut back applications for schooling.

However, the most important early battle for chiropractic was to gain state–sanctioned licensure. It was not an easy battle as chiropractors were often jailed for practicing medicine without a license. Ultimately, being jailed became a successful strategy used to win public support for the field as a reaction to its persecution. Kansas passed the first chiropractic licensing law in 1913; 39 states gave some form of legal recognition by 1931; and, in 1974, when Louisiana began licensure for chiropractors, acceptance had been won in every state.

Wardwell (1992) has suggested that 1974 was the turning point for chiropractic. In addition to Louisiana's accepting licensure, the U.S. Office of Education gave the Chiropractic Commission on Education the right to accredit schools of chiropractic; the federal government determined that chiropractors' fees were reimbursable under Medicare; and Congress authorized spending $2 million for a study of the merits and efficacy of chiropractic treatment by the National Institute of Neurological Disorders and Stroke (NINDS) of the National Institutes of Health. The NINDS Conference concluded that spinal manipulation does provide relief from pain, particularly back pain, and sometimes even cures.

Organized Medicine and Chiropractic

For decades, the American Medical Association attempted to drive chiropractic out of existence. As early as 1922, AMA officials adopted the slogan, "Chiropractic must die" (Reed, 1932). In 1963, the AMA's Committee on Quackery referred to the elimination of chiropractic as its ultimate mission and engaged in such activities as "producing and distributing anti–chiropractic literature, communicating with medical boards and other medical associations, fighting chiropractic–sponsored legislation, and seeking to discourage colleges, universities, and faculty members from cooperating with chiropractic schools" (Gevitz, 1989:292).

In 1965, the AMA declared it a violation of medical ethics for MDs to have any professional association with chiropractors. Presumably, this proscription included making or accepting referrals of patients; providing diagnostic, laboratory, or radiology services; teaching in chiropractic schools; or practicing jointly in any form.

What was the motivation for such strong action? Organized medicine defended its actions on the grounds that it was attempting to eliminate a practice it considered to be detrimental to patient welfare. Believing the vertebral subluxation concept to be grossly inaccurate and denigrating the low standards of chiropractic education, orthodox medicine defined chiropractic as having little or no therapeutic value and as being potentially dangerous. The AMA viewed these efforts as being consistent with its responsibility to guard the public against medical quacks and charlatans.

On the other hand, chiropractic contended that the AMA's actions were motivated by professional elitism (not wanting to share the prestige of the medical profession) and an effort to restrict economic competition. In fact, these contentions became part of a lawsuit brought by chiropractors in 1976 against the AMA for violating the Sherman Antitrust Act.

Whether motivated by sincere change in ideology or fear of an expensive defeat in the courts, the AMA instituted changes in policy during the decade–plus that the case was bogged down in court. In 1978, the AMA adopted the position that medical doctors could accept referrals from and make referrals to chiropractors; and in 1980, the Principles of Medical Ethics were revised to eliminate the professional association prohibition.

Nevertheless, in August 1987, U.S. District Judge Susan Getzendanner found the AMA, the American College of Radiology, and the American College of Surgeons guilty of violating the Sherman Antitrust Act. She judged the three associations had acted conspiratorially in instituting a boycott of chiropractic and had failed to justify it by its "patient care defense." She required that the actions cease.

Current and Future Status

Chiropractic clearly has established a very important place in the health care system (Cooper and McKee, 2003). The educational preparation for chiropractors has continued to be upgraded. The curriculum is now comparable to that in medical schools with respect to study of the basic sciences; the major difference is that chiropractic students take courses in spinal analysis and manipulation and nutrition rather than in surgery and pharmacology (chiropractors are prohibited from doing surgery or prescribing drugs). Chiropractors must pass a national examination administered by the National Board of Chiropractic Examiners and must be licensed by a state board. Unlike many medical doctors, chiropractors are required to continue their education in order to retain their license (Wardwell, 1992).

Unquestionably, many people believe strongly in the value of chiropractic treatment. Several studies have reported benefits of chiropractic care. A 1982 New York study found that almost 3 in 10 (28 percent) persons had been examined by a chiropractor at some time, that 72 percent of recent users found it to be very effective, and that 92 percent would definitely or probably see a chiropractor again should a need arise. Numerous other studies confirm that an increasing percentage and genuine cross-section of the population visits chiropractors, that patient satisfaction is quite high, and that the general prestige of the field is on the upswing (Meeker and Haldeman, 2002).

Has all this changed the attitudes of physicians toward chiropractic? Apparently, it has to some extent. An increased number of medical doctors now recognize the benefit that chiropracty has for some patients, and medical doctors and chiropractors are increasingly likely to make and accept referrals from each other.

What will be the future status of chiropractic in American society? Aside from a continuation of the status quo, Wardwell (1988) suggests four possibilities:

1. Chiropractic could be absorbed by orthodox medicine as a routine part of medical practice, and it could be taught to all medical doctors (especially those in appropriate specialties) as part of their medical education. Although chiropractors fear this eventuality, it is not likely

that orthodox medicine could easily absorb the practice or that there would be sufficient MDs to provide all the required treatments.

2. Chiropractic could become a profession but be subordinate to physician supervision. Although organized medicine may prefer that manipulative therapy be done by physical therapists (or chiropractors serving as physical therapists), this option is not appealing to chiropractors who would have to surrender the autonomy of having patients come directly to them.

3. Chiropractic could practice in a limited domain but be independent of supervision or regulation by organized medicine. Achieving this status would require chiropractic to modify its underlying theory, but Wardwell believes that this is possible and is the most likely future direction for the field.

4. Chiropractic could become a parallel profession (like osteopathic medicine) by elevating its standards of medical training, reducing the gulf in underlying theory, and continuing to gain greater acceptance in the eyes of the public and organized medicine. Clearly, many young chiropractors prefer this possibility and would like to be seen as appropriate family care providers. However, some skepticism in organized medicine remains, and many chiropractors are determined not to compromise their basic practice modality.

ACUPUNCTURE

Chinese understanding of health and illness has evolved over nearly 3,000 years and is recorded in more than 6,000 texts. Traditional Chinese medicine is a holistic system in which health is understood only in the context of the relationship between the human body and nature.

Medical theory rests on the belief that each object in nature is both a unified whole and a whole composed of two parts with opposing qualities: **yin and yang**. They are constantly in a dynamic interplay, shifting from being opposites to becoming each other. Yin is "negative, dark, cold, feminine and Yang [is] positive, light, warm, masculine. Later additional important meanings were contractive and downward flowing (Yin) and expansive and flowing upward and outward (Yang). All things in the universe could be categorized as Yin or Yang" (Chow, 1984:116). Health is a fluctuating but balanced harmony of yin and yang. If an imbalance is created within the body (if one or both become deficient or in excess), then disease results.

The other most important concept in Chinese medical thinking is **chi** (written *qi* in Chinese), or vital energy, which is conceptualized as the key material substance. It is considered to be the primary force of nourishment and bodily protection. Though there is nothing exactly comparable in Western thought, it is sometimes viewed as the "will to live." Chi flows through the body through 12 main channels (or meridians), activating energy in the circulatory system as it flows. The exact location of these channels has been charted and diagrammed, and each is thought to represent (and be connected with) an internal organ. Some of the exercises and martial arts performed by Chinese people stimulate the flow of this vital energy in the channels (Chow, 1984).

The harmony and balance within the body may be disrupted either by endogenous factors, which originate from some serious internal imbalance, or by exogenous factors, which come from the external environment and may be physical (e.g., climactic conditions) or biological (e.g., bacteria, viruses). In performing diagnosis, traditional Chinese medicine follows the principle, "anything inside is bound to manifest outwardly." An implication of this principle is that even localized symptoms (e.g., a headache) are not viewed as local disturbances but rather as a sign of abnormality within bodily organs and the body's channel system. Therefore, a headache does not necessarily mean an imbalance in or near the head.

The primary goal of Chinese medicine is to restore the internal balance of the body and the harmony between the environment and the human being. Since the body's internal balance is constantly fluctuating, specific treatment must be tailored to the situation at the time.

Although much of Western attention has focused on acupuncture as a treatment technique, it is actually only one of many options in traditional Chinese medicine. Other important treatment techniques include acupressure (significant pressure applied to the body via the fingertips), herbology (the use of natural herbs), moxibustion (placing ignited moxa wool on certain points of the body to create heat), various breathing exercises, physical activity, massage, and cupping (placing a small jar with a partial vacuum created by a flame over a selected part of the body producing an inflammatory response) (Chow, 1984). Due to acupuncture's unique history in the United States, this section will focus on it as a healing practice.

Origin of Acupuncture in the United States

Even though it has been used in China for more than 3,000 years and was often practiced by Chinese immigrants in the states, acupuncture gained broad popular attention in the United States only in the early 1970s. This discovery of acupuncture can be traced to two events that occurred in 1971: the lifting of the "bamboo curtain" with China, which opened relations between the countries, and an attack of appendicitis suffered by famed *New York Times* columnist James Reston while he was visiting China—acupuncture was used the day after surgery to eliminate significant pain. Reston wrote of his experience in the *Times*, thus drawing widespread interest to the subject. A select group of American physicians (including a delegation from the AMA) visited China in the ensuing months, and their glowing reports of the efficacy of acupuncture ensured further popular and professional attention (Wolpe, 1985).

Basic Principles

Acupuncture is the insertion of fine needles into one or more acupuncture "points" charted on the body. Today, there are more than 700 points that have been identified, though only 40 or 50 are commonly used. The needles used vary in length, width, and type of metal, and treatments vary in the depth to which needles are inserted, the duration of insertion, and the needle rotation.

The insertion of the needles is performed to stimulate chi in the body and to redirect it so that imbalances are corrected. The needles are inserted in those points that correspond to the particular internal organs where the imbalance exists.

Historical Developments

Though American physicians largely focused on the anesthetic value of acupuncture, and ignored its therapeutic utility, the popular press offered vivid descriptions of acupuncture as a miracle process. The federal government encouraged research into acupuncture, and scientific journals published scores of articles. The Internal Revenue Service decided that payments for acupuncture service qualified as a medical expense, and the Food and Drug Administration developed quality control regulations for acupuncture needles. An American Society of Chinese Medicine was formed (Wolpe, 1985).

In July 1972, the first acupuncture clinic opened in New York City. When it was shut down a week later for practicing medicine without a license, it had already served 500 patients and was booked solid for several months. Acupuncture had captured America by storm. Although the manner in which it would be incorporated remained to be determined, acupuncture seemed on the verge of becoming a major healing practice in the United States.

Organized Medicine and Acupuncture

However, the medical establishment quickly reined in the enthusiasm. One can understand the professional embarrassment created by a healing practice based on a theory that seemed completely contradictory to "scientific" medicine. The tremendous media and lay interest in acupuncture:

> . . . quickly became anathema to most of organized medicine. Physicians had no expertise in acupuncture and no knowledge of physiological mechanisms that could account for it. Indeed, it seemed

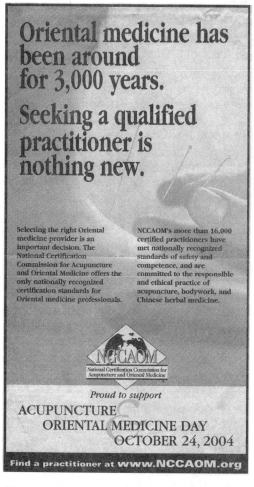

Oriental medicine has been around for 3,000 years.

Seeking a qualified practitioner is nothing new.

Selecting the right Oriental medicine provider is an important decision. The National Certification Commission for Acupuncture and Oriental Medicine offers the only nationally recognized certification standards for Oriental medicine professionals.

NCCAOM's more than 16,000 certified practitioners have met nationally recognized standards of safety and competence, and are committed to the responsible and ethical practice of acupuncture, bodywork, and Chinese herbal medicine.

NCCAOM
National Certification Commission for
Acupuncture and Oriental Medicine

Proud to support
ACUPUNCTURE
ORIENTAL MEDICINE DAY
OCTOBER 24, 2004

Find a practitioner at www.NCCAOM.org

After many years of severe restriction in the United States, traditional Oriental approaches to healing are now available in much of the country.

to violate laws of anatomy and neurophysiology. Acupuncture was an alien treatment with an alien philosophical basis imported as a package from the East; it was not an indigenous alternative modality that reacted to (and thus was informed by) the biomedical model. (Wolpe, 1985:413)

Negative and often hostile physician reactions escalated. The therapeutic effects of acupuncture were dismissed as being nothing more than placebo, and its effectiveness as an anesthetic was dismissed as being a type of hypnosis or form of suggestibility, or even that "Chinese stoicism" or patriotic zeal enabled patients to undergo excruci-

atingly painful surgery without other anesthetics (Wolpe, 1985). One physician referred to acupuncturists as "nonscientific weirdos" and attempted to portray the entire acupuncture practice as modern-day quackery (Goldstein, 1972).

Wolpe (1985) contends that in order to protect its cultural authority over medicine, the medical establishment employed two additional strategies. The first was to sponsor and conduct research that would explain acupuncture in terms of the traditional biomedical model. While Chinese practitioners strongly believe that the practice cannot be separated from its underlying theory, and therefore cannot be studied by traditional scientific methods, much research has been conducted to find a conventional explanation for its anesthetic effects.

For example, Melzack and Wall (1965) developed the "gate control theory" based on research that shows that the insertion of needles excites certain nerve fibers that enter the spinal column and inhibit the onward transmission of pain to the brain. Stimulating these nerve fibers effectively "closes the gate" to pain. An alternative theory, also consistent with traditional neurophysiology, is that the needle insertion stimulates the release of certain pain-reducing hormones (endorphins and enkephalins), which create the anesthetic or analgesic effects. Some recent research has found that needle insertion reduces the flow of blood to the areas of the brain that control pain.

The second strategy was to arrange for the practice of acupuncture to be placed under the jurisdiction of medical doctors. After all, if acupuncture was beneficial only for pain relief, and if the explanation for that could be provided in conventional terms, then it could be argued that Oriental practitioners were not as able as Western practitioners to provide safe and effective treatment. Regulations governing the practice of acupuncture were quickly established in many states (either by the legislature or the State Medical Board).

Current and Future Status

Today, there are more than 50 accredited programs in acupuncture, and more than 16,000 licensed (by the National Certification Commission for Acupuncture and Oriental Medicine) practitioners. Regulation is provided by states but with different requirements. In some states, only medical doctors trained in acupuncture can provide it; in other states non-MD acupuncturists under the supervision of licensed physicians are also able to practice. It is estimated that about 12 million Americans visit acupuncturists each year. Many private insurers and the Medicaid programs in some states now cover the cost of acupuncture treatment.

Is acupuncture an effective anesthetic or therapeutic healing practice? Considerable research has reported favorable findings. In late 1997 a panel of scientists at the National Institutes of Health (including some who practice acupuncture and some skeptics of it) concluded that acupuncture clearly works in treating many conditions including nausea and vomiting after chemotherapy and surgery, the nausea of pregnancy, and post-operative dental pain. Though less data were available, they concluded that acupuncture may help stroke rehabilitation and relieve addictions, headaches, menstrual camps, a variety of muscle pains, carpal tunnel syndrome, and asthma. They acknowledged that these benefits occur while acupuncture has fewer side effects and is less invasive than conventional treatment. The World Health Organization now recognizes more than 40 conditions as being treatable by acupuncture. Acupuncture is a fully accepted and practiced therapy in countries around the world.

SPIRITUAL HEALING AND CHRISTIAN SCIENCE

A belief in "psychic healing" has been present in early and modern times, and in Western and non-Western cultures. Psychic healing "refers to the beneficial influence of a person on another living thing by mechanisms which are beyond those recognized by conventional medicine. These mechanisms may include focused wishes, meditation, prayers, ritual practices, and the laying-on-of-hands" (Benor, 1984:166).

Psychic healers use one of four approaches: (1) activating innate recuperative forces within the healee, (2) transferring her or his own healing energy to the healee, (3) serving as a conduit through which universally available cosmic energy is transferred to the healee, or (4) serving as a conduit through which the healing powers of spirits or God are transferred to the healee. This final channel also is referred to as **spiritual healing** or "faith healing" (Benor, 1984). Spiritual healers do not claim any personal ability to heal but rather an ability to convey the power of some transcendent being to the sick. Spiritual healers may or may not be affiliated with a particular church and may or may not be full-time healers.

Efficacy of Spiritual Healing

Determining the efficacy of spiritual healing is difficult. Most of the evidence supporting positive effects is anecdotal and comes from people strongly predisposed to its benefits. Other, more systematic research has been done but in ways that allow alternative explanations of the findings.

Many people accept that there are at least some cases where a subject's health status has improved following a spiritual healing encounter. These cases are interpreted in different ways. Those involved in the healing process typically contend that God has intervened and in a miraculous way effected a cure. Others believe that the health improvement or cure has occurred through psychological processes, for example, marshalling the healee's mental powers and determination to combat the ailment and/or convincing the healee that a cure will occur (akin to the placebo effect).

In a study of spiritual healing groups in Baltimore in the early 1980s, Glik (1988) discovered that most of the reported illnesses were chronic and mild to moderate in severity, with "nonspecific" diagnosis (but related to psychosomatic, stress, or mental health problems). Less than 10 percent of the reported conditions were life threatening or serious. Many of the symbols and rituals used in the groups (as well as the supportive social context) would be likely to affect the psyche of those present.

Public Perceptions of Spiritual Healing

Many people do relate religion and illness experience. Although the perception that disease and illness are caused by God is less common today than earlier in the century, many people continue to rely on religion as a coping mechanism when they are sick.

A recent study of older adults discovered many who were unclear about God's role in health and illness but nevertheless turned to prayer when sick. For most of these illnesses, care had also been sought from a medical doctor. Rather than viewing prayer and conventional medical treatment as being mutually exclusive, most of these respondents saw them as complementary (Bearon and Koenig, 1990).

Most of the increasing number of studies conducted thus far have found that religion positively influences health. Compelling evidence has accumulated that individuals who attend a religious service on a regular basis have longer life expectancy than non-church-goers. Other research has found that regular church-goers average lower blood pressure and cope better with illness. The findings may be interpreted in different ways. One national survey found that about one-third of Americans use prayer for health concerns, and that about 7 in 10 of these individuals considered it to be very helpful (McCaffrey et al., 2004). Several studies have found that individuals who regularly attend church are less likely to engage in unhealthy lifestyles. Some research has found that prayer or meditation has a calming effect on individuals, which would help explain patterns like lower blood pressure (Koenig, McCullough, and Larson, 2001). Many analysts are concerned that these studies might be misinterpreted as providing evidence that faith-based practices may be used in lieu of medical treatment. All agree that more research is needed to understand the basis for these patterns.

The high level of religious commitment among many patients and the potentially positive effects of religious participation on health are acknowledged by most physicians. Even physicians who are themselves religiously skeptical must walk a thin line on this issue for fear of alienating devout patients. Koenig, Bearon, and Dayringer (1989) found that about two-thirds of a sample of family physicians and general practitioners believe that strong religious beliefs and frequent involvement in religious activities have a positive impact on mental health, and four in ten believe there is a positive effect on physical health. Many of the physicians were unclear about the extent to which they should become involved in religious discussions with patients; most would in some circumstances, but few preferred this as a standard course of action. Almost one-fourth expressed a belief that faith healers divinely heal some people whom physicians cannot help.

However, skepticism about spiritual healing remains at a high level. Spiritual healers do not have (nor have they created) any licensure process; there are no formal associations per se; and they may even be arrested for practicing medicine without a license. Even though it is careful in its language, the AMA is disdainful of spiritual healing and sees the practice as an attempt to take advantage of vulnerable people.

Public opinion surveys reveal that many in the general public share this suspicion of spiritual healing. A recent survey in rural North Carolina, an area where one might expect to find above-average participation in spiritual healing, found that 58 percent of respondents considered faith healers to be quacks (King et al., 1988).

Christian Science as an Example of Spiritual Healing

Of all the specific spiritual healing philosophies, that of **Christian Science** has received the most professional study.

Origin. To understand the many dimensions of Christian Science, it is necessary to understand its founder, Mary Baker Eddy (1821–1910). During her youth, Mary Baker suffered frequent bouts of illness that prompted her to devote her life to finding a cure for disease. Failing to be helped by medical doctors, she experimented with a variety of alternative healing philosophies (Schoepflin, 1988).

At the age of 45, Mary slipped on an icy street, causing very painful head, neck, and back problems. When she received little help from local physicians, she turned to the Bible for comfort. While reading the account of the healings of Jesus, she discovered the "Healing Truth" and experienced a complete recovery. She initiated work as a healer, and in 1875 wrote *Science and Health,* which became the textbook of Christian Science (Schoepflin, 1988).

The next few years were not easy. While alternately gaining followers and losing them (because of charges of temper tantrums, love of money, and hypocrisy), Mary Baker, her third husband, Asa Eddy, and a small group of devotees moved to Boston and founded the First Church of Christ, Scientist in 1879. Although criticized by some, the church grew rapidly, branching out to additional churches, local societies, and schools. However, concerned about the bureaucratization of the church, Eddy dismantled much of its organizational structure and substituted a highly centralized structure with herself and the mother church in key positions (Schoepflin, 1988).

Basic Principles.   Gottschalk (1988) summarizes the basic principle of Christian Science healing as follows:

> Christian Scientists hold that behind all diseases are mental factors rooted in the human mind's blindness to God's presence and our authentic relation to God, revealed in the life of Christ. They hold that treatment is a form of prayer or communion with God in which God's reality and power, admitted and witnessed to, become so real as to eclipse the temporal "reality" of disease and pain. (p. 603)

In other words, illness and pain are not real but only illusions of the mind; since people are reflections of God, and God cannot be sick, people cannot be sick. A person feels ill only when the underlying spiritual condition is in disrepair. This causes the mind to think illness is present.

The only appropriate curative techniques are prayer and spiritual rediscovery. Through prayer, a deeper understanding of one's own spirituality is achieved. Christian Scientists believe that they have the power within to heal themselves, though the assistance of a Christian Science practitioner is frequently used.

Unlike many alternative healing practices. Christian Science healing is believed to be incompatible with orthodox medicine. Medical doctors are viewed as adding pain and illness to the world as a consequence of their lack of understanding of the mind's role. In fact, even obtaining a medical diagnosis is thought likely to worsen any condition.

Historical Developments.   The key issues during this century have pertained to the standardization of Scientist healing practices and external negotiation regarding their legality. Issues such as the appropriateness of Christian Science healing for emotional disorders and the extent to which Scientists should be commanded to live a "healthy lifestyle" have been debated.

Organized Medicine and Christian Science. Two chief points of contention continue to exist between the medical establishment and Christian Scientists. The first is the extent to which Christian Science healing should be acknowledged by the government and commercial health insurance companies as a legitimate form of health care. While this issue continues to be debated, it is clear that Christian Science has largely prevailed.

Several states have written legislation that provides recognition for Christian Science healing as the equivalent of conventional medical care (e.g., Christian Science practitioners can sign certificates for sick leave and disability claims). Hundreds of commercial insurance companies reimburse charges for Christian Science practitioners as they would for medical doctors. Christian Science prayer treatment typically is covered by insurance plans for government employees, and Medicaid and Medicare also provide coverage (Skolnick, 1990b).

The second continuing issue is the status of **religious exemption laws,** which permit legal violation of other laws based on religious grounds. For example, some states have religious exemptions for premarital blood tests for adults, for prophylactic eye drops for newborns, for required physical examinations for schoolchildren, and for instruction about diseases and health in school. Some states provide for exemption to required immunizations (e.g., for measles).

Following a widely reported case in Massachusetts in 1967, in which a Christian Scientist was convicted of manslaughter after her five-year-old daughter died of medically untreated pneumonia, Christian Scientists have conducted a massive lobbying campaign for exemption from child neglect laws. Today, almost every state provides for some type of exemption for religious groups relative to these laws. Still in dispute, however, is whether these laws extend to situations where forgoing likely effective orthodox medical treatment results in the death of a child.

Christian Scientists argue that religious exemption laws are required to enable adherents to practice their religion. What meaning is there in "freedom of religion," they ask, if society compels its members to violate important tenets of the faith? Christian Science healing "is part of a whole religious way of life and is, in fact, the natural outcome of the theology that underlies it. This theology . . . is both biblically based and deeply reasoned" (Talbot, 1983:1641).

In addition, a second line of reasoning has been adopted: Christian Science treatment is at least as efficacious as orthodox medicine. In a widely quoted passage, a senior official in the First Church of Christ, Scientist, Nathan Talbot, said:

> Christian Scientists are caring and responsible people who love their children and want only the best possible care for them. They would not have relied on Christian Science for healing—sometimes over four and even five generations in the same family—if this healing were only a myth. (Talbot, 1983:1641)

The church now disseminates data from research it has conducted to demonstrate that Christian Science children are healthier than their peers and that there are lifetime health benefits in relying solely on Christian Science treatment. This line of reasoning has recently been incorporated in statutes in some states that permit reliance on healing practices that have a "proven record of success" or a "generally accepted record of efficacy" (Skolnick, 1990a).

Opponents of religious exemption laws contend that they violate the antiestablishment clause of the First Amendment, which prohibits special privileges for any religious group. Since Christian Science is singled out in some of these statutes, it is argued that they are given special license or endorsement by the government. For instance, in several states Christian Science nursing homes do not have to meet required minimums for staffing or daily care provided to patients.

Religious exemptions to health laws are said to have harmful public health consequences. For example, a schoolteacher in Van Nuys, California, died in 1954 of tuberculosis after exposing hundreds of children to the disease. As a Christian Scientist, she had been exempted from the routinely required chest examination. Other reported disease epidemics include 11 children paralyzed by polio at a Christian Science boarding school in 1972; a 1985 outbreak of measles at an Illinois college for Christian Scientists; and a second outbreak of measles in 1985 at a Colorado camp attended by Christian Scientists.

Opponents of these laws are especially displeased when the care provided to children is affected. The argument is that children are unable to make fully informed and competent decisions about their religious preference and should not be placed in a life-threatening situation by the religious beliefs of their parents. An analogy often cited is the medical treatment given to Jehovah's Witness children. While most courts today routinely allow adult Jehovah's Witnesses to forgo blood transfusions (an important proscription of the faith), children are routinely transfused over the wishes of the parents. Only at the age of competence does the scale tip in favor of the patient's wishes. The American Academy of Pediatricians has recently been leading an effort to remove religious exemptions to child neglect laws, and a couple of states have made this change in the law.

Current and Future Status. Specialized training for Christian Science practitioners remains minimal. Typically, people who have demonstrated special interest and knowledge in Christian Science healing are selected for training. The primary course lasts only about two weeks and focuses on Christian Science theology. At the conclusion of the class, one is listed as a practitioner in the *Christian Science Journal*. After three years of full-time successful healing, practitioners may apply to the Board of Education to take a six-day course. Graduates of the class are given a C.S.B. (Bachelor of Christian Science) degree.

Is Christian Science healing efficacious? Beyond the highly favorable data published by the church itself, two scientific studies by researchers outside the church have been conducted. An early study (based on data from 1935 to 1955 in the state of Washington) found lower life expectancy among Christian Scientists, a much higher than average rate of cancer, and about 6 percent of deaths medically preventable (Skolnick, 1990b).

A more recent study (Simpson, 1989) comparing the longevity of graduates of a Christian Science college with a neighboring university found a much higher death rate among Christian Scientists. This pattern was discovered despite the fact that Christian Scientists neither smoke nor drink, factors that should have prompted a lower death rate.

The efficaciousness of Christian Science treatment is at least somewhat amenable to scientific study. To resolve the contradictory patterns reported by the church and the two studies cited above, Christian Science practitioners and patients may need to make themselves available for study by impartial outsiders.

IN COMPARATIVE FOCUS

ALTERNATIVE MEDICINE IN THE NETHERLANDS

In 1993 the Dutch parliament passed a rather astonishing piece of legislation: a formal end to the monopoly of the medical profession on medical practice and an end to the ban on alternative medical healers.

As early as 1818, the Netherlands enacted a law that granted a monopoly on the practice of medicine to a heterogenous group of qualified healers including medical doctors, surgeons, and male midwives (whether or not they had been university trained). In 1865, a succeeding law provided for a self-regulated and exclusionary medical profession with university training mandated. Parallel to the United States, the medical profession guarded its authority very carefully and conducted ongoing attempts (both in the courts and the media) to drive out unorthodox "quacks." In the years following World War II, pressure against alternative healers subsided to the point that they were prosecuted only in the case of harm to a patient.

What was the rationale for the 1993 legislation? The main argument relied on freedom of choice of consumers/patients. An increasing number of patients was growing frustrated with the failure of physicians to provide whole-person care, and they sought alternatives. A second argument was that the restrictive law was being violated so often (more and more patients were already seeing alternative healers) that it was unenforceable. Finally, there was a widespread feeling that the entire legal foundation underlying medicine needed to be modernized.

The change in law shifted the Netherlands from one European point of view to the other. Many northern and western European countries allow anyone who wishes to practice medicine but reserves certain procedures (e.g., surgery) to licensed medical doctors. Southern and eastern European countries (plus France, Belgium, and Luxembourg) continue to hold very restrictive laws regarding alternative healers and require that almost all medical practice be conducted by orthodox medical doctors (Schepers and Hermans, 1999).

ETHNIC FOLK HEALING

Folk understandings of disease and illness are typically interwoven into the beliefs and practices of cultural groups. In the United States, folk understandings of the causes and cures of disease occur most often in low-income racial and ethnic minority groups. Some of the common denominators in folk healing systems have been identified and illustrated by Snow (1993) in her studies of black folk healers and their patients in Chicago. She found that her subjects' views of disease and illness were part and parcel of their religious beliefs—that illness may result from natural factors, but also might be the result of sorcery, a temptation from Satan, or a punishment from God. Although traditional herbal remedies and prayer might be sufficient for some conditions, others were perceived to be beyond the scope of either self-care or care by medical doctors and required a special healer from within the group. The folk healers practiced holistic medicine—they treated the whole person rather than just the particular malady and were more concerned about the cause of illness than its symptoms.

These patterns also appear in the two most widely studied systems of folk healing—curanderismo, the Mexican and Mexican-American form of folk healing, and traditional Native American folk healing—that are covered in this section.

Curanderismo

Although many people use the term **curanderismo** to refer only to Mexican-American folk healing, the term is used throughout the Hispanic world (especially in Mexico, Latin America, and the southwestern United States) to describe a unique system of health care beliefs and practices that differ significantly from modern, scientific medicine.

Origin and Historical Developments.

Curanderismo developed out of three primary sources: (1) the humoral theory of Western Europe (brought to the New World by the conquistadores); (2) herbal medicine as practiced by the Aztecs, Mayans, and other Native American groups; and (3) religious belief systems, including both Spanish Catholicism and various witchcraft belief systems (Kiev, 1968). Over time, curanderismo has taken on important cultural meaning in Hispanic communities above and beyond its therapeutic value.

Basic Principles. First, good health is associated with "a strong body, the ability to maintain a high level of normal physical activity, and the absence of persistent pain and discomfort" (Krajewski-Jaime, 1991:160–161). Good health is viewed as a reward for those who have kept God's commandments.

> Even when a curandero uncovers specific causes of illness, he is still likely to focus on sin and the will of God as critical factors which have affected the susceptibility of the patient and predisposed him to illness. When illness occurs in a religious and pious person, it is rationalized by the belief that God allows men to suffer in order to learn. (Kiev, 1968:34)

Second, diseases are classified according to their underlying cause. Krajewski-Jaime (1991) traces disease etiology along three lines: (1) natural and supernatural forces (diseases believed to be caused by natural forces, such as moonlight, eclipses, cold, heat, air, wind, sun, and water or traced to the supernatural and magic); (2) imbalances of heat and cold (drawing directly from the ancient humoral theory, which identified positive health as occurring when the hot and cold forces within the body are in balance); and (3) emotion-based diseases (often resulting from a frightening or traumatic experience).

Third, like all healing systems, curanderismo healing logically follows the nature of disease etiology. Because disease is traced through several lines, the curandero (or curandera) must have several types of healing treatments available. Two examples (the first pertaining to hot-cold diseases and the second to emotion-based diseases) are used as illustration. First,

> Some diseases are hot and some are cold. Foods and herbs are also classified into hot or cold for treatments. Sickness that enhances the cold within the body requires a hot treatment to restore the balance, and vice versa. To avoid a hot sickness,

the person must not become cold; therefore, the individual must not walk barefoot on cold tiles for fear of catching tonsillitis. . . . People are given chili, a hot food, or chicken soup, for a cold disease such as pneumonia or a common cold, and lard, having cold properties, is used on burns. (Krajewski-Jaime, 1991:162)

The second example is a healing treatment used for a person suffering from *espanto*—a form of fright thought to be caused by the spirit's being so frightened that it leaves the body.

Treatment by the folk healer includes having the patient lie down on the floor with arms outstretched in the position of a cross. Sweeping the body with branches, herbs, and prayers, she coaxes the lost spirit to reenter the victim's body. (Krajewski-Jaime, 1991:162)

Finally, the curandero–patient relationship is very close. Curanderos typically live in the same community as their patients, share the same basic values, and recognize the importance of personal involvement and rapport. Patients expect, and receive, extensive time with the curandero. The culture within which this relationship occurs supports the therapeutic value of the curandero's healing practices.

Organized Medicine and Curanderismo. Due to the cultural importance of folk healing in the Chicano community, the extent to which it is intertwined with religious beliefs, and its location primarily in just one region of the United States (though it exists in Hispanic communities around the country), organized medicine has been reluctant to aggressively comment on or act against curanderos. Research indicates that they are paid very little (sometimes with food or other goods) and are not viewed as representing a generalized or serious threat to the medical establishment. Moreover, there is evidence that use of curanderos has declined during the last few decades (Rivera, 1988).

Current and Future Status. Research has found that many Hispanics follow the "dual model of medical care" in that they seek care from both medical doctors and curanderos.

Padilla et al. (2001), found that almost all of the Hispanic patients receiving conventional care at a public hospital in Denver knew what a curandero was and 29 percent had been to a curandero at some time in their lives. Visits were most commonly of treatment of Mexican folk illnesses such as espanto and *empacho* (gastrointestinal obstruction). Research (Hunt, Arar, and Akana, 2000) on Hispanic patients with diabetes found two-thirds who used some form of alternative medicine (mostly herbs and prayer) but none who used a curandero.

Native American Healing

Traditional Native American healing continues to be commonly used among the 2 million Native Americans in the United States. Although a general understanding of the causes of health and illness and healing practices is shared by all Native American peoples, there are, in effect, as many different healing systems as tribes. This section focuses on healers and healing among the Dineh—the Navajo people— the largest (with approximately 250,000 members) Native American group today.

Origin and Historical Developments. Navajo healing practices can only be appreciated within the context of Navajo culture. Understandings of disease and illness emanate from and are consistent with Navajo legends about the creation of earth and how the Navajo people came to be located where they are—on Dinetah (mostly northern Arizona).

Navajo healing is completely intermeshed with the religious belief system. Many of the Navajo's religious rituals are focused on maintaining good health—or on wellness—and eliminating the root causes of illness. To maintain good health, one must live according to prescribed lifeways that were identified at the time of creation.

Basic Principles. First, Navajo philosophy rests on the belief that "everything in the world has life; all things breathe and live and have a spirit and power . . . all of these beings are interrelated and influence the workings of

A traditional Navajo hogan in which diagnostic and healing ceremonies occur. Navajos believe that wellness exists when one is in harmony with nature.

the universe; each has a role and responsibility for maintaining order in the universe" (Avery, 1991:2271). This philosophy contributes to a love and respect for "mother earth" and "father sky" and the wonders of the natural environment and a feeling of oneness with animals. Navajos do not attempt to "master" nature but to be one with it.

Wellness exists when one is in harmony with nature. Ursula Knoki-Wilson, a Navajo nurse-midwife, interpreter, and teacher, defines health holistically as "the synergistic interaction of all the dimensions (physical, mental, and spiritual) of a person at full potential," and wellness as the "way that positive thought influences feeling so that the nature of a person's life experience includes growth, renewal, and miracles" (Knoki-Wilson, 1992).

Second, when imbalance or disharmony develops, illness results. Illness occurs "when the free flow of spiritual energy to the mind, body, and soul is decreased by factors inside or outside the person" (Knoki-Wilson, 1992). Internal factors include such things as violence, destructiveness, anger, stubbornness, guilt, shame, and participation in any Navajo taboos (e.g., wasting natural resources). Outside factors include being a victim of witchcraft, disease or object intrusion

(i.e., invasion of the body by a worm, snake, or insect); and soul loss (which usually occurs during a dream when the soul departs the body). All of these occurrences may have supernatural origin (Knoki-Wilson, 1983).

Third, restoration to health occurs when the disharmony or imbalances are resolved or eliminated. Healing is enacted in physical, mental, and spiritual dimensions. Practitioners of Western medicine often emphasize the mental and spiritual dimensions of Navajo healing but only because they often are given so little prominence in their own techniques. Navajos emphasize that healing can only occur when all dimensions are involved. The ultimate goal of the healing practice is a return to oneness or harmony with nature. Figure 11–1 displays the ingredients necessary for successful Navajo healing.

Finally, at least four separate medical persons (all of whom can be female or male) are used in Navajo healing. One sees a **diagnostician** to learn the cause of illness and to obtain a prescription for the appropriate healing practice. The diagnostician, who is believed to have a special gift, may be a hand-trembler (who diagnoses by passing her or his hands over the patient's body and receiving messages from the

Figure 11–1 Ingredients of Navajo Healing

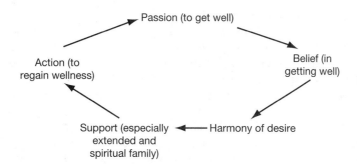

spirits), a star-gazer (who reads messages in the stars), or a crystal-gazer (who looks through crystals to "X-ray" the body in order to locate problems).

The primary healer is called a **medicine person** or **singer** and has received a divine calling as someone with special qualities through whom the spirits can work: "Medicine persons are gifted with extrasensory perception that allows them to make mythological associations and identify the causes and remedies for illnesses" (Knoki- Wilson, 1983:279). Healing practices include prayer, participation in rituals, use of herbal medicines, chants, physical manipulations, and ceremonial observances (Avery, 1991). Elaborate ceremonies lasting from a few hours to nine days (with only brief respites)—for example, the Yeibeichei Dance—are used to effect cures. Because the ceremonies are very structured and elaborate and must be followed precisely, medicine persons often study and apprentice for years to be able to conduct just one or two types.

The **herbalist** has practical knowledge about treatment of minor illnesses and has expertise in the preparation and use of herbal remedies.

Rather than utilizing the complex, traditional healing ceremonies, some Navajos will use religious rituals of the Native American Church and practitioners known as **roadmen.** These ceremonies typically use peyote as the healing herb and last only a single night, but they combine elements of the philosophy of the Navajos, the Plains Indians, and Christianity.

Organized Medicine and Native American Healing. Today, scientific medicine and Native American healing practices peacefully coexist on the Navajo reservation. Although scientific medicine is practiced in the hospitals and clinics of the Indian Health Service, provisions are made within the hospitals for patients to bring in medicine persons, and space is provided for traditional healing ceremonies. Many Navajos, including those who live on the reservation and those who live in urban areas, use both conventional and traditional types of medicine (Kim and Kwok, 1998; Buchwald, Beals, and Manson, 2000). Navajos often will use scientific medicine to treat the symptoms of illness but rely on traditional healing practices to treat the illness cause. This enables access to modern medical knowledge and technology without sacrificing the many benefits of the holistic approach and the community support provided by traditional healing practices.

Current and Future Status. It is hoped the beauty of the Navajo culture and the benefits of traditional Native American healing practices will be preserved. A main challenge will be to continue to find young Navajo women and men who have been called to be healers and who are willing to make the commitment to learning the healing ceremonies.

SUMMARY

While scientific medicine is firmly established in the United States, millions of people use and are satisfied with complementary and alternative healing practices. Organized medicine contends that many CAM practices are ineffective and potentially harmful to users' health (if only because they divert contact from conventional sources). CAM healers argue that, like conventional healers, they seek to provide efficacious care, and they counter that orthodox healing practices have proven ineffective or even harmful for some. Many people follow a "dual model of medical care"—using both orthodox and CAM healers.

Although chiropractic may still be a "marginal" profession, it has also gained significant legitimacy. It is licensed in all 50 states, accepted by insurance companies, and is increasingly being accepted by many medical doctors.

In the early 1970s, acupuncture took America by storm. Though it quickly became very popular with patients, orthodox medicine did not accept its theoretical foundation and acted to restrict its practice. Recently, there has been substantial scientific endorsement of acupuncture so that its use may become more common.

Many physicians and laypersons perceive religious practices to have beneficial effects on health, but much skepticism exists about the general efficacy of spiritual healing. Although the relative health of the Christian Science population is in dispute, Christian Scientists have had much recent success in having their healers recognized as legitimate and in getting religious exemption laws passed in states.

Curanderismo and Native American healing represent two types of folk healing practices. Both are very much a part of their respective cultures and religious belief systems. Although there are differences between the systems, both are more holistic than orthodox medicine and are more concerned with the causes of illness than with merely treating symptoms.

HEALTH ON THE INTERNET

You can learn more about complementary and alternative medicine by visiting the Web site of the National Center for Complementary and Alternative Medicine at

http://nccam.nih.gov

What is the purpose of this site? Click on "Health Information," then click on "What is Complementary and Alternative Medicine." Read through all of the information provided. What are the five major types of complementary and alternative medicine? How many of these types have been used by you or members of your family?

KEY CONCEPTS AND TERMS

acupuncture
chi
chiropractic
Christian Science
complementary and alternative
    medicine (CAM)
curanderismo
diagnostician

herbalist
medicine person (singer)
religious exemption laws
roadmen
spiritual healing
subluxation
yin and yang

DISCUSSION CASE

In June 1990, a jury in Boston, Massachusetts, found David and Ginger Twitchell guilty of the negligent homicide (involuntary manslaughter) of their two-and-a-half-year-old son, Robyn. The Twitchells were sentenced to 10 years' probation for failing to provide medical care that could have saved the life of their son, who died of an untreated bowel obstruction. The parents had contacted a Christian Science practitioner, but not a medical doctor. Massachusetts law does recognize spiritual healing as a form of medicine, but it requires parents to seek orthodox medical care for seriously ill children.

Testimony at their trial revealed that Robyn had suffered excruciating pain during the last five days of his life. A large section of his colon, scrotum, and other tissues had become necrotic and even the pressure of a diaper on his abdomen caused him to scream in pain. Before becoming comatose, he began vomiting fecal material. The Twitchells consulted a Christian Science practitioner and nurse whose treatment consisted of "heartfelt yet disciplined prayer." A medical doctor was not consulted.

The jury was said to be affected by testimony that, while forbidding medical care for children with critical illnesses, Christian Science does permit orthodox obstetric care (Mrs. Twitchell had received anesthesia when Robyn was born) and orthodox dental care (Mr. Twitchell had received treatment from a dentist for a root canal and impacted wisdom teeth).

What should be the legal responsibility of parents with critically ill children? Should society legally obligate all parents, regardless of their religious convictions, to utilize orthodox medical care? Would this, as Christian Scientists claim, interfere with the First Amendment right to religious freedom? Do judges and juries have a right to state that prayer is inadequate medical treatment? Based on the histories of alternative healing practices presented in this chapter, what dangers would there be from this type of regulation?

On the other hand, there are many laws in the United States governing parental behavior toward children and prohibiting child abuse and neglect. Shouldn't the failure to get medical care that would probably have eliminated their son's pain and saved his life be considered the ultimate act of child abuse? Even if adults have a right to use whatever type of healing practice they choose, shouldn't society require orthodox medical care for children (after all, wasn't Robyn too young to adopt Christian Science as his own religious philosophy)?

REFERENCES

Angell, Marcia, and Jerome P. Kassirer. 1998 "Alternative Medicine: The Risks of Untested and Unregulated Remedies." *New England Journal of Medicine*, 339:839–841.

Astin, John A. 1998 "Why Patients Use Alternative Medicine." *Journal of the American Medical Association*, 279:1548–1553.

Avery, Charlene. 1991 "Native American Medicine: Traditional Healing." *Journal of the American Medical Association*, 265:2271, 2273.

Bearon, Lucille B., and Harold G. Koenig. 1990 "Religious Cognitions and Use of Prayer in Health and Illness." *The Gerontologist*, 30:249–253.

Benor, Daniel J. 1984 "Psychic Healing," pp. 165–190 in *Alternative Medicines: Popular and Policy Perspectives*, J. Warren Salmon (ed.). New York: Tavistock.

Beyerstein, Barry L. 2001 "Alternative Medicine and Common Errors of Reasoning." *Academic Medicine*, 76:230–237.

Buchwald, Dedra, Janette Beals, and Spero M. Manson. 2000 "Use of Traditional Health Practices Among Native Americans in a Primary Care Setting." *Medical Care*, 38:1191–1199.

Caplan, Ronald L. 1984 "Chiropractic," pp. 80–113 in *Alternative Medicines: Popular and Policy Perspectives*, J. Warren Salmon (ed.). New York: Tavistock.

Chow, Effie P.Y. 1984 "Traditional Chinese Medicine: A Holistic System," pp. 114–137 in *Alternative Medicines: Popular and Policy Perspectives*, J. Warren Salmon (ed.). New York: Tavistock.

Coe, Rodney M. 1970 *Sociology of Medicine*. New York: McGraw-Hill.

Cooper, Richard A., and Heather J. McKee. 2003 "Chiropractic in the United States: Trends and Issues." *The Milbank Quarterly,* 81:107–138.

Coulehan, John L. 1985 "Chiropractic and the Clinical Art." *Social Science and Medicine,* 21:383–390.

Donnelly, William J., J. Elisabeth Spykerboer, and Y. H. Thong. 1985 "Are Patients Who Use Alternative Medicine Dissatisfied with Orthodox Medicine?" *The Medical Journal of Australia,* 142:539–541.

Eisenberg, David M., Ronald C. Kessler, Cindy Foster, Frances E. Norlock, David R. Calkins, and Thomas L. Delbanco. 1993 "Unconventional Medicine in the United States." *New England Journal of Medicine,* 328:246–252.

Gevitz, Norman. 1988 *Other Healers: Unorthodox Medicine in America.* Baltimore, MD: The Johns Hopkins University Press.

———. 1989 "The Chiropractors and the AMA: Reflections on the History of the Consultation Clause." *Perspectives in Biology and Medicine,* 32:281–299.

Glik, Deborah C. 1988 "Symbolic, Ritual, and Social Dynamics of Spiritual Healing." *Social Science and Medicine,* 27:1197–1206.

Goldner, Melinda. 1999 "How Alternative Medicine Is Changing the Way Consumers and Practitioners Look at Quality, Planning of Services, and Access in the United States," pp. 55–74 in *Research in the Sociology of Health Care,* Vol. 16, Jennie J. Kronenfeld (ed.). Stamford, CT: JAI Press.

Goldstein, David N. 1972 "The Cult of Acupuncture." *Wisconsin Medical Journal,* 71:14–16.

Goldstein, Michael S. 1999 *Alternative Health Care.* Philadelphia: Temple University Press.

Gottschalk, Stephen. 1988 "Spiritual Healing on Trial: A Christian Scientist Reports." *The Christian Century,* 105:602–605.

Hunt, Linda M., Nedal H. Arar, and Laurie L. Akana. 2000 "Herbs, Prayer, and Insulin: Use of Medical and Alternative Treatments by a Group of Mexican American Diabetes Patients." *Journal of Family Practice,* 49:216–223.

Kelner, Merrijoy, and Beverly Wellman. 1997 "Health Care and Consumer Choice: Medical and Alternative Therapies." *Social Science and Medicine,* 45:203–212.

Kiev, Ari. 1968 *Curanderismo: Mexican-American Folk Psychiatry.* New York: Free Press.

Kilgore, Christine. 1998 "Alternative Medicine: Probing Its Core." *Health Measures,* 3:26–30.

Kim, Catherine, and Yeong Kwok. 1998 "Navajo Use of Native Healers." *Archives of Internal Medicine,* 158:2245–2249.

King, Dara E., Jeffrey Sobol, and Bruce R. DeForge. 1988 "Family Practice Patients' Experiences and Beliefs in Faith Healing," *Journal of Family Practice,* 27:505–508.

Knoki-Wilson, Ursula M. 1983 "Nursing Care of American Indian Patients," pp. 271–295 in *Ethnic Nursing Care,* Modesta S. Orque, Bobbie Bloch, and Lidia S. Monroy (eds.). St. Louis, MO: C. V. Mosby.

———. 1992 "Lecture: Navajo Traditional Healing," Chinle, Arizona, June 23.

Koenig, Harold G., Lucille B. Bearon, and Richard Dayringer. 1989 "Physician Perspectives on the Role of Religion in the Physician-Older Patient Relationship." *Journal of Family Practice,* 28:441–448.

Koenig, Harold G., Michael E. McCullough, and David B. Larson. 2001 *Handbook of Religion and Health.* New York: Oxford University Press.

Krajewski-Jaime, Elvia R. 1991 "Folk-Healing Among Mexican American Families as a Consideration in the Delivery of Child Welfare and Child Health Care Services." *Child Welfare,* 70:157–167.

Kronenfeld, Jennie J., and Cody Wasner. 1982 "The Use of Unorthodox Therapies and Marginal Practitioners." *Social Science and Medicine,* 16:1119–1125.

McCaffrey, Anne M., David M. Eisenberg, Anna T.R. Legedza, Roger B. Davis, and Russell S. Phillips. 2004 "Prayer for Health Concerns." *Archives of Internal Medicine,* 164:858–862.

Meeker, William C., and Scott Haldeman. 2002 "Chiropractic: A Profession at the Crossroads of Mainstream and Alternative Medicine." *Annals of Internal Medicine,* 136:216–227.

Melzack, Ronald, and Patrick Wall. 1965 "Pain Mechanisms: A New Theory." *Science,* 150: 971–979.

National Center for Complementary and Alternative Medicine, 2002 "What is Complementary and Alternative Medicine (CAM)?" nccam.nih.gov/ health/whatiscam/#sup2:1.

Padilla, Ricardo, Veronica Gomez, Stacy L. Biggerstaff, and Phillip S. Mehler. 2001 "Use of Curanderismo in a Public Health Care System." *Archives of Internal Medicine,* 161: 1336–1340.

Reed, Louis. 1932 *The Healing Cults.* Chicago: University of Chicago Press.

Rivera, George Jr. 1988 "Hispanic Folk Medicine Utilization in Urban Colorado." *Sociology and Social Research,* 72:237–241.

Schepers, R.M.J., and H.E.G.M. Hermans. 1999 "The Medical Profession and Alternative Medicine in the Netherlands: Its History and Recent Developments," *Social Science and Medicine,* 48:343–351.

Schoepflin, Rennie B. 1988 "Christian Science Healing in America," pp. 192–214 in *Other Healers: Unorthodox Medicine in America,* Norman Gevitz (ed.). Baltimore, MD: The John Hopkins University Press.

Simpson, William F. 1989 "Comparative Longevity in a College Cohort of Christian Scientists." *Journal of the American Medical Association,* 262:1657–1658.

Skolnick, Andrew. 1990a "Religious Exemptions to Child Neglect Laws Still Being Passed Despite Convictions of Parents." *Journal of the American Medical Association,* 264:1226, 1229, 1233.

———. 1990b "Christian Scientists Claim Healing Efficacy Equal if Not Superior to That of Medicine." *Journal of the American Medical Association,* 264:1379–1381.

Snow, Loudell F. 1993 *Walkin' over Medicine: Traditional Health Practices in African-American Life.* Boulder, CO: Westview Press.

Talbot, Nathan A. 1983 "The Position of the Christian Science Church." *New England Journal of Medicine,* 309:1641–1644.

Wardwell, Walter I. 1988 "Chiropractors: Evolution to Acceptance," pp. 157–191 in *Other Healers: Unorthodox Medicine in America,* Norman Gevitz (ed.). Baltimore, MD: The Johns Hopkins University Press.

———. 1992 Chiropractic: History and Evolution of a New Profession, St. Louis, MO: Mosby Year Book.

Wolpe, Paul R. 1985 "The Maintenance of Professional Authority: Acupuncture and the American Physician." *Social Problems,* 32:409–424.

12

THE PHYSICIAN-PATIENT RELATIONSHIP: BACKGROUND AND MODELS

Despite the increasing complexity of the health care system and the wide variety of healers and healing techniques that exist, the actual encounter between physician and patient remains an important element. Many people have an idealized picture of this relationship: a sick patient seeks comfort from a benevolent physician; the sincere and helpful patient places trust in the concerned and caring physician; both do whatever is necessary to restore health to the patient.

In fact, neither patients nor physicians are so uncomplicated or behave in such a uniform manner, and the relationship between the two can be an elusive phenomenon to diagram. As sociologists, our goal is to help clarify the relationships that actually develop between physicians and patients and to identify important influences on the relationship.

MODELS OF THE PHYSICIAN-PATIENT RELATIONSHIP

The Parsonian Model

Nature of the Relationship. Within sociology, Talcott Parsons (1951) pioneered efforts

at explaining the sociocultural foundation of health care. He viewed the physician–patient relationship as a subsystem of the larger social system. The key values in this subsystem reflected key values in society; they were shared by physicians and patients as they entered a relationship.

According to Parsons, the physician–patient relationship is inevitably (and fortunately) an asymmetrical one. Parsons believed that three circumstances dictated that physicians play the key, powerful role within the dyad and govern the relationship with patients:

1. **Professional prestige**—this is based on the physician's medical expertise, years of training, and the societal legitimation of the physician as the ultimate authority on health matters.
2. **Situational authority**—it is the physician who has established the medical practice and is offering her or his services to patients who have admitted their own inadequacies by soliciting the physician.
3. **Situational dependency**—it is the patient who has assumed the role of supplicant by seeking out service, scheduling an appointment, often

waiting past the scheduled time, answering the physician's questions, and allowing an examination to occur.

Throughout each encounter, the "competency gap" between physician and patient is highlighted as the patient is dependent on the physician and the resources of the physician's office. However, Parsons expected that physicians would use their power wisely in promoting patients' best interests, and that patients would accept this arrangement as being the most efficient means to enact cure.

Freidson's Criticisms of the Parsonian Model. Perhaps the most important criticism of Parsons's model is that it overstates the "mutuality of interests" between physician and patient and does not provide for the considerable variation that now exists in physician–patient encounters. Conflict theorists dispute the notion that physicians and patients interact harmoniously and develop mutually satisfactory relationships through cooperation and consensus. Eliot Freidson (1970) has been a leading critic of the Parsonian model and an advocate for a conflict approach. He contends that conflict and dissensus are inevitable in any relationship in which the parties have such different backgrounds and power is so unequally distributed.

The Szasz-Hollender Model

An early (and now classic) effort to modify the Parsonian model was developed by two MDs, Thomas Szasz and Marc Hollender (1956). Arguing that Parsons gave too little attention to the important influence of physiological symptoms, they developed their own typology of the physician–patient relationship, which includes three models (see Table 12–1):

The Activity-Passivity Model. This model closely parallels the asymmetrical relationship described by Parsons. The physician represents medical expertise, controls the communication flow between the two parties, and makes all important decisions. The patient is the supplicant, regarded as lacking in important information and necessarily relying on the knowledge and judgment of the physician.

The Guidance-Cooperation Model. Szasz and Hollender view this form of interaction as typical of most medical encounters. The patient is acknowledged to have feelings, may be alarmed by the medical problem, and has certain hopes and aspirations for the outcome of the medical encounter. Compared to the activity-passivity model, the patient has increased involvement in providing information and making decisions with

TABLE 12–1   Three Basic Models of the Physician-Patient Relationship

	Model		
	Activity-Passivity	**Guidance-Cooperation**	**Mutual Participation**
Physician's Role	Does something to patient	Tells patient what to do	Helps patient to help self
Patient's Role	Recipient (unable to respond or inert)	Cooperator (obeys)	Participant in partnership (uses expert help)
Clinical Application of Model	Anesthesia, acute trauma, coma, delirium, etc.	Acute infectious processes, etc.	Most chronic illnesses, psychoanalysis, etc.
Prototype of Model	Parent–infant	Parent–child (adolescent)	Adult–adult

Source: Thomas S. Szasz and Marc H. Hollender, "The Basic Models of the Doctor-Patient Relationship," *Archives of Internal Medicine,* 97:585–592, 1956, with permission.

regard to treatment. Although the physician is still in charge and has responsibility for guiding the encounter, the cooperation of the patient is sought. The physician is less autocratic in the sense that some explanation is provided to the patient and the patient's assent to decisions is desired, but the physician retains the dominant position.

The Mutual Participation Model.   Based on a view that equalitarian relationships are to be preferred in medicine, this model elevates the patient to full participant. In this case, both physician and patient acknowledge that the patient must be a central player for the medical encounter to be successful. The patient knows more about her or his own situation—medical history, symptoms, other relevant events—than does the physician. While the physician attempts to ask the proper questions to elicit key information, it is assumed that the patient also has an obligation to ensure that relevant information is disclosed.

In order for this type of relationship to work, Szasz and Hollender identify three essential traits that must be present. First, both participants must have approximately equal power; second, there must be some feeling of mutual interdependence (that is, a need for each other); and finally, they must engage in interaction that will in some ways be satisfying to both parties.

Because this model "requires" more from the patient, Szasz and Hollender suggest it may be less appropriate for children or those who are mentally deficient, poorly educated, or immature. On the other hand, those who are more intelligent or sophisticated, have broader experiences, and are more eager to take care of themselves may find this to be the only satisfying relationship.

The Veatch Model

Robert Veatch (1972), a professor of medical ethics at the Kennedy Institute for Bioethics at Georgetown University, has emphasized the importance of also capturing the "moral relationship" between physicians and patients. Veatch has identified four possible relationships that may occur:

1. An **engineering model** in which the physician assumes medicine to be a value-free enterprise whose primary task is the presentation of all relevant facts to the patient without involvement in actual decision making. Veatch sees this model as impractical and wrong in excluding physician involvement with ethical concerns.

2. A **priestly model** in which the physician is viewed as a quasi-religious figure who is an "expert" on ethical and on all other matters that emerge in the relationship. Veatch opposes this because the patient's individual autonomy is erased.

3. A **collegial model** in which the physician and patient see themselves as colleagues pursuing a common goal of restoring the patient to good health. Veatch likes this model but perceives it to be unrealistic due to ethnic, class, and value differences between physician and patient.

4. A **contractual model** in which the physician and patient interact with the understanding that there are obligations and expected benefits for both parties though no necessary mutuality of interests: "With the contractual relationship there is a sharing in which the physician recognizes that the patient must maintain freedom of control over his own life and destiny when significant choices are made" (Veatch, 1972:7).

KEY DIMENSIONS OF THE PHYSICIAN-PATIENT RELATIONSHIP

An appropriate model of the physician–patient relationship must acknowledge the considerable differences that exist among physicians and patients of what should occur within the relationship. The following three dimensions of the relationship are key:

1. The appropriate model of health (a belief in the biomedical or biopsychosocial model of health).

2. The primary ethical obligation of the physician (patient autonomy or beneficence).

3. The extent of commitment to and realization of genuine therapeutic communication.

The actual relationship that develops between a given physician and a given patient is determined by the orientations held by both parties. This is not to deny that the physician is in the more powerful position. For the reasons enumerated by Parsons and elaborated upon by many others, physicians have the potential to command the decisive voice. But many physicians now reject this position, and many patients have been socialized not to let them assume it.

The Appropriate Model of Health

The Biomedical Model. As scientific discoveries produced meaningful explanations of diseases and effective medical treatments, the biomedical model of health became the dominant therapeutic orientation—a position it held for most of the last century. Biomedical medicine is essentially disease-oriented or illness-oriented rather than patient-oriented. The key to effective medical care is believed to be correct diagnosis of some physiological aberration followed by proper application of the curative agent. Physicians seek to learn all they can about symptoms and abnormalities so that they can provide the appropriate "magic bullet." Consideration of social, psychological, and behavioral dimensions of illness has little place in this framework because it appears unnecessary. Engel (1977:129) cited one health authority speaking at a Rockefeller Foundation seminar who urged that "medicine concentrate on the 'real' diseases and not get lost in the psychosociological underbrush. The physician should not be saddled with problems that have arisen from the abdication of the theologian and the philosopher." Another speaker cited by Engel had advocated "a disentanglement of the organic elements of disease from the psychosocial elements of human malfunction" (Engel, 1977:129).

This biomedical focus has been reflected in medical education, which has surely helped to sustain it. Both coursework and clinical experience have emphasized the biological basis of disease and illness, whereas psychological and social factors traditionally have received little attention.

The Biopsychosocial Model. While there have always been individuals who lobbied for a broader based approach to health care (George Engel, a professor of psychiatry and medicine at the University of Rochester Medical School has been a key figure for much of his career), it was not until the 1970s that the campaign flourished. Engel argued that the benefits of the biomedical approach need not be sacrificed while incorporating psychosocial matters and that both are needed to provide optimal health care.

> To provide a basis for understanding the determinants of disease and arriving at rational treatments and patterns of health care, a medical model must also take into account the patient, the social context in which he lives, and the complementary system devised by society to deal with the disruptive effects of illness, that is, the physician role and the health care system. This requires a biopsychosocial model. (Engel, 1977:132)

This model calls for physicians to be "patient-centered." In discussing the development of primary care as a medical specialty, Quill (1982) emphasized its potential for applying the biopsychosocial approach. He suggested that four principles distinguish broad-based primary care from the traditional disease-dependent care. In primary care:

1. The patient is addressed as a whole person, whether or not she or he has a disease.
2. The doctor–patient relationship is continuous, at all stages of the patient's life, through sickness and health, until either the physician or the patient dies, moves, or decides to terminate the relationship.
3. The physician uses both biotechnical skills and interpersonal skills to help the patient.
4. Both the patient and the physician make explicit, and then negotiate, their respective needs and expectations (Quill, 1982).

Current Assessment. The extent to which physicians employ the biomedical or biopsychosocial approach can be analyzed by their

TABLE 12–2   Psychosocial Concern Index Taxonomy for Provider Behavior

Current Life Situation	Health Beliefs and Behavior
Home environment and activity	Beliefs
Current household composition	Self-care practices
Household division of labor	Nutritional patterns
Interpersonal relationships	Personal habits
Family relationships	
Socioeconomic status	Mental Health History and Examination
Community commitments and resources	
Work environment and activities	Counseling on Psychosocial Issues
Psychological and personal adjustment	
Sexual activity	Therapeutic Listening to Psychosocial Issues
Past Development	
Childhood development	
Educational, military, occupational history	
Family history (social)	

Source: James D. Campbell, Helen J. Neikirk, Michael C. Hosokawa, "Development of a Psychosocial Concern Index from Videotaped Interviews of Nurse Practitioners and Family Physicians," *The Journal of Family Practice,* 30:321–326, 1990.

efforts to identify psychosocial concerns of patients. Three empirical questions can be posed: Do many patients have specific psychosocial concerns? Do patients want their physicians to consider these concerns? Do physicians attempt to do so?

Most researchers have chosen to operationally define "psychosocial concerns" through a designated list of social or psychological matters that may affect health status. Among the best of these lists is the "Psychosocial Concern Index Taxonomy for Provider Behavior" by Campbell, Neikirk, and Hosokawa (1990) (see Table 12–2).

Research shows that as many as half of patient visits to primary care providers include psychosocial complaints (Robinson and Roter, 1999). Most patients presenting themselves to a physician do not have a serious physical disorder; in general medical practice, estimates are that two-thirds or more are without a serious physical ailment.

What then is the motivation for so many physician contacts being initiated for nonbiomedical reasons? Barsky (1981) summarized the major reasons as being life stress and emotional distress (normal anxiety, grief, frustration, and fear); diagnosable psychiatric disorders (for which general medical physicians are seen more

often than specialists); social isolation (people seeking advice, interpersonal stimulation, and a sense of belonging and sustenance that can be provided by a social support system); and informational needs (which are perhaps even greater than the need for treatment of symptoms).

Are patients genuinely interested in discussing these psychosocial concerns with their physician? Do these discussions actually occur? In one study, questionnaires were administered to 530 patients of a family practice medical center. Some (281) of the questionnaires solicited information on what psychosocial concerns respondents would want their physician to address, while the remaining questionnaires (249) asked which concerns they would expect their physician to address. Overall, results show that patients do want involvement across a wide range of psychosocial issues but typically do not expect it to happen (Frowick, Shank, Doherty, and Powell, 1986).

A study conducted in 23 primary care practices found that more than 70 percent of the patients believed it was appropriate to seek help from primary care physicians for psychosocial problems, but fewer than one-third of those who had experienced such problems had discussed them with their physician. Providers frequently failed to recognize emotional distress and family difficulties (Good, Good, and Cleary, 1987).

These results are consistent with studies that have found that family physicians are unaware of most of what is happening in their patients' lives and that less than 10 percent of the conversation in average medical visits centered on patient psychosocial concerns (Roter, Hall, and Katz, 1988). Some commonly cited reasons physicians give to explain their avoidance of psychosocial issues are detailed in the box, "Physician Avoidance of Psychosocial Aspects of Health Care."

Primary Ethical Obligation

Perhaps the most important ethical orientation of physicians relative to patient care is whether priority is given to patient autonomy or beneficence.

The Principle of Autonomy. **Autonomy** is a term derived from the Greek words for "self" and "rule, governance, or law." When applied to individuals, it refers to the concept of self-determination. Autonomous individuals are able to make their own choices and decisions and have them respected by others. The concept of autonomy makes three key assumptions:

IN THE FIELD

PHYSICIAN AVOIDANCE OF PSYCHOSOCIAL ASPECTS OF HEALTH CARE

Given the importance of tending to psychosocial concerns, why don't more physicians do it? Inadequate exposure in medical school to its importance is one answer, but there are more. Williamson, Beitman, and Katon (1981) wrote of their experience in teaching the biopsychosocial approach to family practice residents. They were confronted with a set of beliefs that inhibited the residents from thinking psychosocially about their patients. They grouped these beliefs into three categories.

A. Beliefs About the Physician's Role

1. I must rule out organic disease. After I do that, then I can focus on psychosocial problems.
2. If I do not completely rule out the organic possibilities, then the patient might die and/or my colleagues might laugh at me, I may get sued.
3. Psychosocial issues have nothing to do with medical problems.
4. I am too pressed for time. I cannot go into everything.
5. I focus on organic disease because I cannot treat the psychosocial. If I open up this area, I will be compelled to treat this person for these problems.
6. If I deal with psychosocial problems with all my patients, I will be overwhelmed and will

soon burn out because more will be asked than I can give.

B. Misconceptions About Patients

1. My patients want me to rule out organic problems.
2. I have no right to inquire into psychosocial areas. It is an invasion of privacy.
3. Talking about psychosocial issues will inevitably inflict pain on the patient and me. I will feel guilty for having done this, and the patient might blame me.
4. If I address psychosocial issues, patients will reject me and never return.
5. If I define a psychosocial problem, patients will find a psychological treatment unacceptable.
6. Patients will become totally dependent on me if I open up psychosocial concerns.

C. Beliefs Concerning Physicians' Reactions to Their Patients as People

1. If the patient has the same problem I do, how can I help if I have not helped myself?
2. If the patient is having a problem beyond my experience, how can I help?
3. It is painful to face the emotional problems of others.

1. An autonomous person is able to make rational and competent decisions following some contemplative thought. People who are incapable of acting autonomously include those who are too young; who are severely mentally retarded or have some significant mental disability; or who are coerced or unduly pressured into a decision by physicians or other health care professionals or, more commonly, by family members—"You have the surgery, or the kids and I are leaving."

2. A second assumption is that an action does not cause harm to others. The freedom of any individual to act stops short of causing harm to another; a decision to harm another incurs no obligation of respect.

3. Patients do not have the right to demand that physicians or other health care professionals violate a personal or professional moral code. For example, patients cannot make an unrestricted claim on some scarce resource, such as demanding a liver transplant. This assumption was clearly described in the Elizabeth Bouvia case described in the box, "The Case of Elizabeth Bouvia."

Application of the principle of autonomy involves physicians ensuring that patients are able to make fully informed decisions and that those decisions are then respected. This does not limit professional expertise in diagnosis, in developing a prognosis, in making recommendations for treatment, or in carrying out agreed-upon treatment. It does limit physicians in selection and pursuit of treatment without the patient's fully informed consent.

Informed Consent. The informed consent requirement is a key mechanism to protect patient autonomy. Legally and ethically, patients able to exercise autonomy must be given all relevant information regarding their condition and

---

IN THE FIELD

THE CASE OF ELIZABETH BOUVIA

In the summer of 1983, Elizabeth Bouvia, a 26-year-old woman with physically incapacitating cerebral palsy, checked into Riverside (California) Hospital and stated her intention to starve herself to death. She said that her deteriorating condition (an inability to feed or care for herself in any way, increasingly painful arthritis, and physical incontinence) made life not worth living. She said that she was unable to take her own life and wished the hospital to provide hygienic care and pain relief while she starved herself to death.

The hospital refused her request and made plans to force feed her should she not eat on her own. The chief of psychiatry at the hospital was quoted as saying, "The court cannot order me to be a murderer nor to conspire with my staff and employees to murder Elizabeth." The story became public, and the American Civil Liberties Union decided to represent Elizabeth's wishes in court.

Eventually, the court ruled against Elizabeth Bouvia. The judge acknowledged prior court decisions (and the ethical principle) that competent, informed patients have the right to refuse medical care, even if their refusal contradicts medical advice or might shorten their life. However, he concluded that Elizabeth's plan not to take food and water in the hospital involved more than a refusal of treatment. Because she desired care while she died of malnutrition and dehydration, she was, in essence, asking hospital staff to assist in a suicide or direct killing that was morally and professionally unacceptable to them.

Although the Bouvia decision carried several ramifications, it has been interpreted to support the principle that neither physicians nor hospital staff may be forced to act in ways they interpret to violate a professional or personal moral code.

IN COMPARATIVE FOCUS

AUTONOMY AND PATERNALISM IN ISRAEL

In 1991, the United States Congress passed the Patient Self-Determination Act (PSDA) as a means to protect and highlight patient autonomy. The PSDA requires hospitals and other institutional providers to inform patients that they have a legal right to make their own health care decisions (through the process of informed consent), to prepare an advance directive to indicate how they would like to be treated if they are unable to make their own decisions at some future time, and to refuse unwanted medical treatment. It is a clear expression of the importance of patient autonomy in the United States.

In 1996, Israel passed the Israeli Patient Rights Act (IPRA) to address some of the same issues. The IPRA guarantees that Israel will provide universal health care coverage (which, of course, is not provided in the United States) and embraces the concept of informed consent. However, Israelis were not provided a right to refuse unwanted medical treatment, and physicians were not obligated to respect the wishes of any patient making an informed refusal of treatment. In those cases, the matter is submitted to an ethics committee, which typically requires that the treatment be given so long as it is expected to help the patient's condition, and there is some expectation that the patient will give a consent *after* the procedure.

The U.S. law is rooted in the importance of the individual and in the right of individuals to determine their own courses of action without paternalistic intervention by the health care provider. Israel is a communitarian society with a high level of collective consciousness, mutual concern, and interdependence. In communitarian societies individual rights are often subservient to collectively defined ideals and goals. Ensuring that health care is available to all citizens is one aspect of the collective ideal, and ensuring that individuals receive lifesaving treatment, with or without their consent, is another aspect (Gross, 1999).

---

alternative treatments, including possible benefits, risks, costs, and other consequences and implications. For a genuine informed consent to occur, the patient must be competent, be given all information that might affect decision making, comprehend this information, and make a voluntary choice. For surgery, other invasive procedures, or procedures with any significant risk, patients typically are required to sign an official informed consent form. However, the spirit of informed consent is no less applicable—though often less followed—in the medical office.

The Principle of Beneficence.   An alternative guiding principle for physicians is beneficence—doing good for the patient. Although the general meaning of the concept is to promote goodness, kindness, or charity, in the medical context it refers to physicians taking whatever actions—for example, surgery or prescribing a medication—that are considered to be in the patient's best interest.

Prioritizing Autonomy and Beneficence. An ethical dilemma arises when doing good for the patient (beneficence) conflicts with an informed patient's wishes (patient autonomy). It often occurs that a rational and competent patient chooses to take an action that a physician believes is not in the patient's best interest. At this point, physicians decide whether it is more important to allow the patient to make her or his own choice or to act in a manner believed to be in the patient's best interest. A physician is said to be showing **paternalism** when she or he overrides a patient's wishes and takes action presumed to be in the patient's best interest but action unwanted by the patient. This situation also creates a choice for the patient. If a patient desires self-determination, and the physician refuses to grant it, the patient can try to be persuasive, can accede to the physician's wishes, or can shop for another physician. Of course, in many cases, patients would not be aware of physician behavior that is molding or limiting their choices.

Current Assessment.   Traditionally, most physicians have automatically made decisions for patients, and neither physicians nor patients gave much thought to the importance of patient self-determination. However, the principle of autonomy gained significant stature in the 1980s and 1990s.

Researchers have attempted to study desire for autonomy by studying patients' requests for information from physicians and their desired participation in actual decision making. In a study of 106 rehabilitation medicine patients, Beisecker and Beisecker (1990) found that patients overwhelmingly want as much information as possible. However, there is ambivalence regarding the proper decision maker. While few subjects believe that the patient should make decisions singly excluding the physician, many believe it should be a shared process, and many are most comfortable with the physician being the primary decision maker. A more recent study of 300 patients undergoing angiogram also found extensive desire for information and discussion of options but reluctance to make the final decision (Deber, Kraetschmer, and Irvine, 1996).

The percentage of patients wanting to participate in actual decision making increased during the 1990s. Research has found that when patients are provided instruction in ways to be more effective participants in their own care, their desire for detailed information and participation in decision making increases (Hack, Degner, and Dyck, 1994). The situation today with living wills (see Chapter 16) illustrates this pattern. Research has shown that the vast majority of people want to have candid discussions with their physician about their options and preferences regarding end-of-life treatments and want to have their wishes followed. Many physicians, however, do not engage their patients in conversations about this subject, are sometimes unaware that particular patients have written a living will, and are often unable to accurately predict end-of-life treatment wishes of their patients (Virmani, Schneiderman, and Kaplan, 1994).

Braddock and colleagues (1999) audiotaped more than 1,000 encounters between patients and primary care physicians or orthopedists in order to determine the extent to which the patients were genuinely informed decision makers. The criteria they used included discussion of the nature of the decision and asking the patient to voice a preference. They judged that only 9 percent of all decisions made fulfilled their criteria for informed decision making. Routinely, the physicians failed to appropriately inform and involve the patient.

Moreover, even on occasions when it may appear that physicians are seeking to involve the patient in decision making, they sometimes conduct themselves in such a way as to offer patients only an "illusion" of choice. In these situations, the physicians have essentially predetermined a course of action and then present options in such a way as to steer the patient toward the physician's preferred course (Zussman, 1992).

Establishment of Therapeutic Communication

It may seem obvious that effective and meaningful communication between physician and patient is to be desired. But this commonsense understanding understates the therapeutic importance of good communication and would certainly not predict its lack of attention in medical education. This section addresses four questions: What is meant by "therapeutic communication"? Does it routinely develop? What barriers prevent it from developing more often? How can it be facilitated?

Therapeutic Communication.   There are three components of **therapeutic communication:** (1) The physician engages in full and open communication with the patient and feels free to ask questions about psychosocial as well as physical conditions; (2) the patient provides full and open information to the physician and feels free to ask questions and seek clarifications; and (3) a genuine rapport develops between physician and patient.

The Frequent Absence of Therapeutic Communication.   Although many physicians place high value on developing therapeutic communication with patients and routinely do

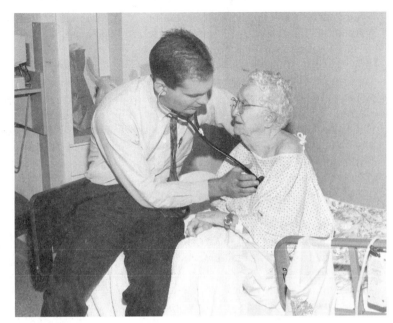

Providing ample time for patients, engaging in full and open communication, and establishing rapport are ways that physicians encourage genuine therapeutic communication.

so, therapeutic communication does not exist in many physician–patient dyads. Patients do not feel comfortable with the physician, do not feel free to talk openly about their worries and concerns (and sometimes even symptoms), have questions that go unasked or unanswered, and do not understand information that is provided. These are not satisfying encounters for most patients.

Barriers to Therapeutic Communication. Development of genuine therapeutic communication requires considerable effort, even for those committed to it as an ideal. This is due to the fact that there are several inherent obstacles to open communication in the medical setting.

1. *Setting of the medical encounter.* Most physician–patient contacts occur in the physician's office or in a hospital—settings that are not conducive to making the patient feel at ease. The unpleasant odors, the many sick people who seem to be invading each other's space, and the paperwork requirements all contribute to discomfort. There are few ways to relax except reading current editions of esoteric magazines or news magazines that were timely in some other year.

2. *Length of the medical encounter.* Genuine therapeutic communication cannot be developed in brief, abbreviated segments of time. The average length of an office visit with a physician in 1998 was calculated in various studies to be between 18 and 22 minutes, representing a slight increase in the previous decade (Mechanic, McAlpine, and Rosenthal, 2001). Because some patients require more than 18 to 22 minutes, some receive less time. Of course, only a fraction of this time is spent discussing the patient's illness.

3. *The mental state of the patient.* It would be a rare person who could communicate best when feeling worst. Most patients are feeling ill, are uncomfortable, may be anxious about their health and fearful of what will be learned, and are in awe of the physician. Not surprisingly, many do not think, speak, or hear clearly.

4. *Mismatched expectations of physicians and patients.* Patients go to a physician with

symptoms, with feelings of discomfort, and with an inability to carry on normal activities. They seek clarification and information, and they want to know something to do to get better. Physicians, on the other hand, have been trained to convert patient complaints into medical diagnoses. Uncomfortable dealing with psychosocial issues, they evade discussions of anxieties and fears and focus on the "medical facts." What the patient may need most is what the physician is least prepared to offer. These contrary expectations make therapeutic communication unlikely.

5. *Physician communication style.* Research on physician–patient communication conducted over the last three decades has demonstrated remarkable consistency regarding two key patterns. First, physicians often "talk down" to patients, are abrupt with them, and discourage open communication. Some physicians offer little greeting to patients as they enter the room. Going after "just the facts," they provide no opening for patients to talk about their concerns or how they perceive current problems relate to other events in their lives. They may interrupt patients or otherwise signal a lack of interest in what is being said. They maintain spatial distance when not conducting a physical examination and do everything possible to reinforce social distance. Buller and Buller (1987) refer to this as the *control* style of communication and the net result is predictable—almost no therapeutic communication occurs. In one study, physicians did not allow patients to complete their opening statement in 69 percent of the visits (they interrupted patients after an average of only 18 seconds) (Beckman and Frankel, 1984), and in another study, physicians directly responded to only 20 percent of patient statements of anxiety (Baker, Yoels, and Clair, 1996). The second or alternative style, *affiliation*, includes such behaviors as friendliness, empathy, genuineness, candor, an openness to conversation, and a nonjudgmental attitude, and is designed to

establish a positive relationship with the patient.

Candace West, in an intriguing book, *Routine Complications: Troubles with Talk Between Doctors and Patients* (1984), confirms this asymmetrical communication process. West transcribed 532 pages of physician/patient encounters in a family practice center in the southern United States. She examined such matters as the number of times each party interrupted the other (male physicians were most likely to interrupt); who asks the questions and who answers (physicians ask almost all the questions); and who invokes laughter (patients invite laughter more often, but there is often no response). However, some encounters did display a symmetrical communication pattern.

Second, patients often do not understand the terminology used by physicians. People who have learned a particular subject's or profession's jargon often forget that most others have not. Even terms that are familiar to most college students are not at all familiar to many patients. One study discovered that many patients had little understanding of such terms as *eating disorder, schizophrenia,* and *depression* (Hadlow and Pitts, 1991). Even such terms as *abdomen* and *stroke* are not understood by many patients. These are commonly used terms in the medical setting; yet when they are used, many patients misunderstand the message being communicated. Not surprisingly, many physicians underestimate their own use of medical jargon.

Physician Frustration with the Communication Process.   Physicians also report frequent feelings of frustration with patient interaction. What do they report as the most common sources of this frustration for themselves? Recent research identified the most common factors to be (1) patients' lack of adherence (not accepting responsibility for their own health and not following through on recommended therapies); (2) patients with a large number of complaints requiring an extensive amount of time; (3) patients being demanding, controlling, and complaining; and

(4) patients with problems associated with alcohol, other drugs, and chronic pain. In more than half of the self-identified frustrating patient visits, the physician perceived the patient to be the source of the problem (Levinson et al., 1993).

THE INFLUENCE OF SOCIAL CLASS, RACE, AND SYMPTOMOLOGY ON THE PHYSICIAN-PATIENT RELATIONSHIP

Ideally, physicians offer their best professional efforts to every patient. This does not mean that every patient will be treated in exactly the same manner—that is unrealistic. College professors do not treat all students the same; clergy do not treat all parishioners the same; physicians do not treat all patients the same. But a reasonable objective is that physicians impartially deliver their best efforts to every patient. Yet, considerable empirical research and anecdotal evidence document that physicians have a more difficult time working with some patients than others.

Medical Symptoms

Among the patients considered to be most difficult are those with certain types of medical symptoms, such as those that offer little hope for cure (e.g., emphysema, chronic back pain, arthritis, obesity), those that are associated with devalued lifestyles (e.g., alcoholism and other substance abuses, prostitution, homelessness, attempted suicides, lack of hygienic care), those that are vague and difficult to describe, and those that have a psychosocial basis.

In many of these cases, it may be the deviation from the sick role that is most frustrating. Physicians who take little personal interest in patients may be least likely to have an emotional response. They patch them up, get paid, and that's the end of it. More patient-oriented physicians, who earnestly want to help restore people to health (or to get them to restore themselves), may be most troubled by the inability or, in some patients, seeming lack of desire to get well.

Patients with lifestyle-related illnesses (e.g., substance abusers) are especially frustrating for physicians. They may present themselves for care on a routine basis, suffering from the same or an advanced stage of the same problem, yet resist efforts to discuss behavior modification. Their worsening condition, use of expensive health care resources, and frequent rejection of physician offers of help often create frustration in physicians.

Personal Characteristics

Several studies have investigated whether personal characteristics of patients influence physician behavior. Some research has discovered that physicians feel higher levels of anxiety and frustration when working with lower class patients and are less interested in the patient encounter. Although there is little research on white physician–black patient relationships, a study of 139 first-year medical students found that they expected to be significantly less comfortable when working with black patients, and they believed that black and Latino patients would be less likely to comply with medical regimens (Gregory, Wells, and Leake, 1987). These expectations can translate into different modes of care. African-American patients rate their visits with physicians as being less participatory than whites, but both black and white patients report feeling more involved in their care when the physician is of the same race (Cooper-Patrick et al., 1999).

The Implications of Labeling. Does this labeling of patients make any difference in the care provided to them? Yes. Hospital staff told Mizrahi (1986) that patients labeled as undesirable were afforded less thorough care, and, in a review of studies of mental health care (an area where race has been systematically studied), cultural insensitivity and bias have been shown to lead to mistaken psychiatric diagnoses for black patients (Neighbors et al., 1989).

Several studies have reported evidence of disparities in treatment for heart disease received by blacks and whites. For example, data from the National Hospital Discharge Survey showed that blacks were less likely than whites to receive cardiac catheterization, coronary angioplasty, and coronary artery bypass surgery even after controlling for age, health insurance, hospital, and condition. The authors concluded that race of the patient influenced the likelihood of receiving these procedures (Giles et al., 1995). In a study of more than 5,000 Medicare recipients, Epstein et al. (2003) found that whites were more likely than blacks to receive clinically indicated revascularization procedures, and that the underuse by black patients was linked to higher mortality rates. Other research has determined that the lower survival rate of black than white patients with early-stage lung cancer is largely explained by lower rates of surgery for blacks (Bach et al., 1999). The AMA's Council on Ethical and Judicial Affairs (1990) has acknowledged racial differences in the provision of care and has called for efforts to eliminate them.

THE INFLUENCE OF GENDER ON THE PHYSICIAN-PATIENT RELATIONSHIP

Gender of the Physician

The influence of physician and patient gender on the physician–patient relationship has received considerable research attention. In 1985, Weisman and Teitelbaum suggested that gender could influence the physician–patient relationship in three ways:

1. *Systematic differences between male and female physicians in personality, attitudes, or interpersonal skills.* Weisman and Teitelbaum speculated that early sex-role socialization might result in female physicians being more nurturant and expressive whereas male physicians might be more reserved and less able to develop empathic relationships. On the other hand, females who have been sufficiently assertive to break through the traditional male stranglehold in medicine might be less likely to have been socialized to traditional sex roles, and/or the

professional socialization that occurs in medical school might dissipate earlier socialization experiences.

2. *Alteration of the expectations that patients bring to the encounter.* This influence could occur in two ways. Patients expecting female physicians to be more nurturant and empathic may convey more information to them, allowing them greater opportunity to actually engage in a more caring relationship (a self-fulfilling prophecy), or patients may simply see what they expect to see—a more nurturant and empathic female physician— even if actual practice style does not differ by gender.

3. *Alteration of the "status relationship" between physician and patient.* The key to this is the match or lack of match in gender between physician and patient. For example, a female patient seeing a female physician is more likely to have status congruence than when seeing a male physician. This status congruence could contribute to openness in the relationship, extended rapport, and increased patient participation. This pattern was partially demonstrated in one study that found that female patients tended to be more satisfied with female than male physicians but that satisfaction of male patients was unrelated to physician gender (Derose et al., 2001).

The following sections examine the first two of these mechanisms of influence in light of recent research.

Systematic Differences Between Female and Male Physicians. Several studies have identified aspects of practice style that are unaffected by physician gender. Female and male family practice physicians evaluate common medical problems in a similar manner; there are few differences in diagnoses, prescriptions of psychotropic medications, or frequency in hospitalizing patients among female and male psychiatrists; and female and male physicians react to patient deaths similarly and offer similar amounts of personal contact,

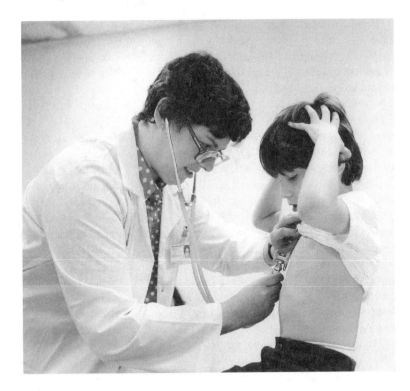

Research indicates that female physicians spend more time with each patient, provide more opportunities for patients to talk, and make more empathic statements than male physicians do.

availability, and follow-up with families after a loved one's death.

These similar practice styles are influenced by the professional socialization process. First-year female medical students do differ from their male counterparts in being more patient-oriented and placing higher value on patient contact. But these differences dissipate during medical school and the residency process. The increased interest first-year women medical students have over men in valuing the interpersonal, psychosocial, and preventive aspects of medicine diminishes by the end of medical school.

However, consistent differences between female and male physicians have been documented in two areas. First, female physicians demonstrate superior communication skills. Research indicates that female physicians spend more time with each patient, provide more opportunities for patients to talk, make more empathic statements, ask more questions, smile and nod more frequently, and are more

egalitarian in the patient relationship (Hall et al., 1994).

Second, female physicians express more sensitivity than male physicians to health-related "women's issues," including contraception, abortion, and discrimination against female physicians and patients. These gender differences exist in medical school, throughout residency, and into practice and may be a key indicator to women of overall physician sensitivity. Moreover, research has shown that female physicians are more likely than male physicians to conduct mammograms and Pap smears and that this difference holds even when health status and background characteristics are controlled (Lurie et al., 1997).

Patient Expectations for Female and Male Physicians.   Do patients have a preference for physician gender? Are the expectations of patients influenced by the gender of the physician? The answer to both questions is yes.

Between one-third and one-half of patients have a preference for the gender of their own physician. In a study of 196 patients in Spokane, 35 percent of the men expressed a preference for physician gender (every one preferred a male physician); 36 percent of the women expressed a preference (25 percent of these preferred a male physician and 75 percent preferred a female physician) (Weyrauch, Boiko, and Alvin, 1990). A study of patients at four family practice centers found 52 percent of female patients and 43 percent of male patients had a gender preference, and clear majorities desired a physician of the same gender (Fennema, Meyer, and Owen, 1990).

Why are there gender-based physician preferences? Fennema et al. (1990) found having a preference was not related to patient age, income, or education but was related to two other factors.

First, having a preference was related to the clinical problem for which the physician was being seen. Preferences were uncommon for strictly medical problems but were customary for problems involving genital or anal examination (strong preference for same-sex physician) and for depression and family problems (strong preference for female physician by both male and female patients).

This finding is consistent with that of several studies that have found that women's strongest preference for a female physician occurs with women's health problems—including cervical screening, breast screening by physical examination, breast screening by mammography, and instruction in breast self-examination. Moreover, while female physicians spend more time than male physicians with each patient, the greatest differential is in obstetrics and gynecology. Women increasingly express preference for a female ob-gyn, and almost three-fourths of ob-gyn medical residents now are female.

Second, several perceived behavioral traits were related to preference. Patients who preferred a male physician associated competence with males and viewed humaneness as a male physician trait. Patients preferring a female physician viewed technical competence neutrally, but considered humaneness to be a female physician trait and felt that female physicians tended to be less hurried (Fennema et al., 1990).

Gender of the Patient

Gender Stereotyping. Although there is considerable anecdotal evidence of sexist ideology among physicians, research has produced an inconclusive picture of the extent to which **gender stereotyping** of patients still occurs. Among the frequently cited health-related stereotypes of women are that they express higher levels of emotional illness and emotional instability, exaggerate claims of the severity of medical symptoms, and are more demanding patients. To what extent are these views held by physicians?

Bernstein and Kane (1981) presented eight hypothetical cases to primary care physicians. Did the gender of the patient (which was rotated) influence physician interpretation? Yes. Female patients were more likely than male patients to be seen as demanding excessive physician time, being influenced by emotional factors, and suffering from psychosomatic illness.

In another study, primary care physicians were presented with hypothetical patients (with gender rotated) with either headache or abdominal pain complaints. The physicians did judge the female patients to be more emotional even though nothing in the two cases varied except gender, but they did not judge their complaints to be less authentic or the patients to be less ill (Colameco, Becker, and Simpson, 1983).

Level of Health Care. Does gender stereotyping lead to differential treatment? In one widely cited study conducted in San Diego, the answer was yes. Five medical complaints (back pain, headache, dizziness, chest pain, and fatigue) were studied in married couples who had been seen for at least five years by one or more male family practice physicians. The researchers found that the physicians had conducted more extensive workups for the male patients and concluded that gender stereotyping had impacted care (Armitage, Schneiderman, and Bass, 1979).

Other studies, however, have failed to detect treatment differences. Greer and colleagues (1986) attempted to replicate the Armitage study (using the same five medical complaints) in examining the medical charts of 100 married couples who had been seen for a minimum of two years by one or more of 20 physicians (10 male and 10 female) in a prepaid health maintenance organization. They found no significant differences in the extent of the workup based on the gender of the patient. The different organizational circumstances (prepaid setting, half of the physicians female) might help explain the different findings.

The largest study yet conducted utilized data on 46,000 adults collected in the 1975 National Ambulatory Medical Care Survey. Verbrugge and Steiner (1981) focused on the extent to which significant differences in care occurred between males and females and whether they were attributable to medically relevant factors or not. They considered diagnostic services, therapeutic services, and dispositions for follow-up in all visits, visits associated with 15 major groups of complaints, and five specific complaints (the same ones used in the aforementioned studies).

The data reflect that health care was often similar for females and males, but that significant gender differences occurred in 30 to 40 percent of the services and dispositions studied—with women receiving more services (including laboratory tests, blood pressure checks, drug prescriptions, and return appointments). These differences persisted even after controlling for medically relevant factors (e.g., patient age, seriousness of problem, reasons for visit) (Verbrugge and Steiner, 1981). The additional services provided to women could be interpreted in either a favorable or unfavorable light, but they are not consistent with a view that female patients are generally deprived of services offered to male patients.

Yet another study (Waitzkin, 1984) attempted to identify biases that occur in the actual communication process between female patients and their physicians. Using audiotapes of 336 interactions between male internists and their male and female patients, evidence of withholding information or "talking down" to female patients more often than to male patients was sought. Contrary to expectations, female patients received more physician time, asked more questions, and received more technical explanations and more clarifications of the technical explanations.

On the other hand, research now seems conclusive that gender bias does exist in the management of coronary heart disease. In a study of adults presenting to an emergency room with acute chest pain, women were less likely to be admitted to the hospital, less likely to undergo a stress test in the next month, and less likely to undergo cardiac catheterization—even after controlling for clinical and nonclinical factors (Johnson et al., 1996). Other studies have found that women receive less aggressive treatment than men following a heart attack—even after controlling for relevant factors. While more needs to be learned about gender differences in clinical decision making, the wealth of evidence of gender bias in treatment of heart disease requires immediate attention and remediation.

PATIENT SATISFACTION WITH PHYSICIANS

Even if there were no instrumental value attached to patient satisfaction, it would be a highly desirable end product of the physician-patient encounter. However, research has confirmed that patient satisfaction is linked with several other desirable outcomes: Satisfied patients are more likely to comply fully with medical regimens, more likely to return for scheduled follow-up visits and to maintain continuity of care (seeing the same physician), more likely to seek physician care when sick, and less likely to initiate a medical malpractice suit. Recognition is increasing that positive health outcomes are more likely when the patient is satisfied with care received.

Level of Satisfaction

Are most patients satisfied with the primary health care they receive from a physician? Yes. Research over the last few decades shows a consistent pattern: Patients have significant misgivings about physicians in general (see Table 12–3)

Research indicates that patients want and appreciate physicians who take time with them and establish genuine rapport.

but are very satisfied with their own physician (see Table 12–4). On most surveys, satisfaction level is high, though perhaps not as high as in some other countries.

Do patients make distinctions among various aspects of physician-patient interaction? Yes. Most researchers have concluded that patients distinguish between the technical competence of the physician (which they have difficulty judging) and the socioemotional aspects of the encounter (which, therefore, become more important in their evaluation).

Factors Related to Patient Satisfaction

Based on dozens of studies, four conclusions can be drawn about factors that influence patient satisfaction.

TABLE 12–3   The Public Image of Physicians

Statement	Percentage Agreeing
Doctors keep patients waiting too long.	75
Doctors are too interested in making money.	67
Doctors are usually up to date on the latest advances in medicine.	61
Doctors don't care about people as much as they used to.	57
Doctors usually explain things well to their patients.	43
Most doctors spend enough time with their patients.	29

Source: Gina Kolata, "Wariness Is Replacing Trust Between Healer and Patient." *The New York Times,* February 20, 1990, pp. 1, 10, with permission.

TABLE 12–4   Satisfaction with Physician Care in Three Countries

Satisfaction Level	Satisfaction with Last Physician Visit (%)		
	U.S.	Canada	U.K.
Very satisfied	54	73	63
Somewhat satisfied	32	21	26
Somewhat dissatisfied	7	4	7
Very dissatisfied	6	2	3

Source: Robert J. Blendon and Humphrey Taylor, "Views on Health Care: Public Opinion in Three Nations," *Health Affairs* 8:149–157, 1989, with permission.

1. When other relevant factors are controlled, most patient background characteristics have little effect on satisfaction. The relationship between race and patient satisfaction has been especially difficult to pin down. Some studies have found no racial gap, while others have reported satisfaction to be higher among blacks or higher among whites. However, in a review of the literature on this subject, Malat (2001a) traced the inconsistent findings to weaknesses in the methodology of many of the studies. She concluded that satisfaction with medical care is lower among blacks than whites and identified both structural (e.g., lower incomes, less likelihood of health insurance, less likelihood of continuity of care) and micro-level (e.g., racial discrimination, social distance) factors as contributing to the pattern.

   Several recent studies have found that, among all race/ethnic groups, patient satisfaction is higher when the race of the provider and the patient is the same (LaVeist and Nuru-Jeter, 2002). Audiotaped physician-patient encounters have documented that race-concordant visits are longer and are characterized by more positive patient affect (Cooper et al., 2003), and that African-American patients perceive that they are treated more respectfully by black than white physicians (Malat, 2001b).

2. Most patients feel ill-equipped to assess the technical competence of their physician. In most cases patients simply assume the physician is competent and base their evaluation on other factors. However, the consumerist movement has stimulated many patients to become more knowledgeable about health matters and has encouraged patients to solicit second opinions; this may provide patients more information to make informed assessments of the technical competence of their physician.

3. The level of satisfaction or dissatisfaction patients have about their health care is significantly influenced by the quality of the communication process that occurs. Patients are much more likely to be satisfied with their health care when they establish an ongoing relationship with a physician (Love et al., 2000); when they establish rapport with the physician; when they are given (and retain) more information about their symptoms and the treatments prescribed (Bertakis, Callahan, and Helms, 1998); and when they are able to ask questions and to discuss their ideas and the ideas of the physician. Not surprisingly, patient satisfaction is lower in situations in which there are language differences between physician and patient (Morales et al., 1999).

4. Patient satisfaction is significantly affected by efforts of the physician to talk about psychosocial concerns and preventive health care. Despite some physicians' reluctance to delve into these areas or their belief that patients might prefer not to talk about them, patients want these matters discussed and are more satisfied with the care received when they are (Bertakis, Callahan, and Helms, 1998).

PATIENT COMPLIANCE WITH MEDICAL REGIMENS

Compliance with medical regimens refers to the extent to which patients follow the instructions given them by physicians. These instructions include requests for follow-up visits, the taking of medications, and changes in lifestyle (either temporary—get plenty of rest this week—or long term—stop smoking cigarettes). Research indicates that between one-third and one-half (and perhaps more) of all patients fail to comply with these regimens. Understanding the reasons for this noncompliance has become an important area of research.

Studies show that physicians tend to see **noncompliance** in terms of noncooperative patients. Most physicians believe they provide sufficient information and rationale for patients to fully comply with their instructions and see noncompliance as an irrational response centered in the patient. Physicians tend to underestimate the percentage of their patients who are noncompliers.

Factors Related to Compliance

Research on factors that relate to compliance behavior has identified several clear patterns:

IN THE FIELD

HEALTH CARE REFORM AND THE PHYSICIAN–PATIENT RELATIONSHIP

Health care reform efforts already underway are having important influences on the physician–patient relationship. Three of these influences are described below.

1. Patients have less choice in selecting their physician. An increasing number of persons are being insured through large managed care organizations like health maintenance organizations and preferred provider organizations that have contracted with a limited number of physicians in the area. Patients pay the least for their care when they see one of the contracted providers. In many cases patients are surrendering physicians with whom they have had a long-standing relationship because that physician is not part of the contracted group.

2. Health insurance companies strongly influence the length of time a patient will stay in the hospital. They determine the number of days of hospitalization that are appropriate for each insured patient, given the relevant medical circumstances, and communicate this information to physicians as they are deciding whether to discharge the patient from the hospital. In this way, the physician serves the role of a "gatekeeper" who makes decisions about what additional services will be recommended or provided to the patient. Typically, in these situations, physicians are reluctant to keep patients

longer than that which will be covered by the insurer. So, patients are discharged at whatever time the insurer refuses to cover additional days. If the physician's compensation from the managed care organization is not affected by the amount of services used by the patient, this entire arrangement would be a major source of frustration. However, if the contractual relationship between the physician and the managed care organization leads to physicians making more money when patients use fewer services, then the physician's role seems more of a "double agent"—ostensibly serving as the patient advocate, but in reality protecting personal and company financial interest (Waitzkin, 1999).

3. Given societal concerns about the high cost of care and some subtle and not-so-subtle encouragement from managed care organizations, many physicians today are giving more consideration to the cost of services in determining whether or not to provide them. Productivity requirements from managed care organizations may pressure physicians to have shorter office visits, reduced access by telephone, and other barriers to patient contact. This "bedside rationing" is controversial and will continue to be an important debate in the coming years (Emanuel and Dubler, 1995).

---

1. Sociodemographic characteristics of patients, such as age, gender, education, and social class, are not reliable predictors of compliance behavior.

2. Patient knowledge of the disease or illness that has prompted the instructions does not accurately predict compliance. For many years, clinicians and social scientists believed that compliance rates could be increased by creating better informed, more knowledgeable patients. However, many

noncompliers are very knowledgeable about their condition but still choose not to follow instructions.

3. The seriousness of the patient's disease or illness is not strongly related to compliance behavior; that is, more seriously ill patients are not more likely to be compliers.

4. The complexity of the medical regimen does influence compliance behavior. More complex regimens (e.g., medications that must be taken several times per day in restricted

situations for a long period of time) are less likely to be fully followed than simpler, more short-term medication orders.

5. The most important factor affecting compliance is the extent of change required in the patient's life. Regimens that require significant life change (e.g., a major change in diet, a significant increase in exercise, a significant reduction or elimination of alcohol or tobacco products)—especially those that require giving something up as opposed to adding something—are least likely to be followed.

Sociological Explanations for Compliance Behavior

Sociologists have tested three plausible explanations for noncompliance; each of these explanations has received some empirical support. One explanation locates the problem within the communication process between physicians and patients—that is, noncompliance results from inadequate or poorly communicated information from physician to patient about the nature or rationale of the regimen (in particular) or in the lack of physician–patient rapport (in general). Research has confirmed that compliance is more likely when physicians give more explicit and complete instructions and make decisions *with* rather than *for* patients (Belgrave, Wykle, and Cogan, 1997).

A second explanation traces noncompliance to the health beliefs of the patient. Some research has found that compliance is more likely when the patient feels heightened susceptibility to the disease or illness; when the condition is believed to negatively affect daily functioning; and when the medical regimen is considered to be an efficacious method of deterring or eliminating the health problem.

Third, Peter Conrad (1987) has suggested that noncompliance be viewed as a matter of patient self-regulation. Rather than viewing noncompliance as a matter of deviance needing correction, this view sees noncompliance as a matter of patients tailoring their medical regimens to their lifestyles and life responsibilities. An in-depth study of 19 women who had been assigned one or more regimens found that they assigned greater priority to normal life routines and modified treatment regimens to fit into their preexisting lifestyles. Rather than seeing themselves as being noncompliant, they perceived that they were complying as much as possible given other life responsibilities (Hunt, Jordan, Irwin, and Browner, 1989).

SUMMARY

More than any other sociologist, Talcott Parsons laid the foundation for understanding physician–patient interaction. He perceived that the physician–patient relationship is asymmetrical, with power residing in the physician. This asymmetry is inherent in the relationship due to the professional prestige of the physician, the authority of the physician on health matters, and the situational dependency of the patient.

To incorporate more variation in the relationship, Szasz and Hollender constructed a model that includes three prototypes: an activity-passivity model (much like Parsons's asymmetry), a guidance-cooperation model (with the physician in charge but the patient being more active), and the mutual participation model (physician and patient are both active agents).

Three key dimensions define the physician–patient relationship: the patient treatment approach (biomedical or biopsychosocial), the primary ethical obligation of physicians (patient autonomy or beneficence), and the extent to which genuine therapeutic communication develops within the relationship. Patients do go to physicians with many psychosocial concerns that they want physicians to address, but many physicians do not do so. Patients want to be well-informed, but many still prefer the physician to be the chief decision maker. Research shows that many physicians talk down to patients and use terminology with which patients are not familiar.

Despite many similarities between female and male physicians, female physicians have better communication skills and convey more interest to patients regarding women's issues. Approximately one-third to one-half of patients have a preference for gender of their physician, but the most apparent difference is that many female patients prefer a female obstetrician-gynecologist. Patients are more likely to reveal personal information or to discuss mental health issues with a physician of the same gender.

Most patients are satisfied with primary health care received. The quality of communication between physician and patient and the physician's interest in patient psychosocial concerns are the major determinants of patient satisfaction level. At least one-third to one-half of all patients fail to comply fully with medical regimens. The more complex the regimen and the more invasive it is in one's life, the less likely is compliance. Noncompliance can occur when there is a breakdown in physician–patient communication, when the patient does not feel especially alarmed by the condition or confident in the regimen, and when the patient modifies the regimen to fit with other life responsibilities.

HEALTH ON THE INTERNET

An interesting medical school-based Web site that deals with issues in the physician–patient relationship is sponsored by the University of Washington. Connect to this site at:

http://depts.washington.edu/bioethx/
topics/index.html

What kinds of topics are covered? Click on "The Physician–Patient Relationship." What are the main values underlying the various questions/answers in this section? Click on each of the case studies. How would you respond in each of these circumstances? What values would underlie your responses?

KEY CONCEPTS AND TERMS

activity-passivity model
autonomy
beneficence
biomedical model
biopsychosocial model
collegial model
contractual model
engineering model
gender stereotyping
guidance-cooperation model

informed consent
mutual participation model
noncompliance
paternalism
priestly model
professional prestige
situational authority
situational dependency
therapeutic communication

DISCUSSION CASE

A complex situation occurs in medicine when a patient's religious beliefs dictate a medical decision that could be life-threatening. Attending physicians are caught between respect for the patient's personal religious values and the First Amendment right to privacy, on the one hand, and their commitment to engaging in all reasonable medical efforts to save the lives of patients, on the other.

A specific illustration of this dilemma occurs when a member of the Jehovah's Witnesses sect needs a blood transfusion in order to live. Jehovah's Witnesses adamantly refuse this procedure based on their interpretation of biblical scripture forbidding the "eating" or "taking in" of blood. Voluntary or involuntary receipt of blood results in the loss of eternal life. For both adults and children, blood transfusions are rejected. For discussion purposes, three cases involving Jehovah's Witnesses (modified from Tierney et al., 1984) are presented.

Scenario 1: A 45-year-old bachelor visits his private physician after regurgitating large quantities of blood in the preceding two hours. He is taken to the hospital where examination reveals a continued slow oozing of blood in the patient's stomach. He is fully alert and informs his physician that, as a Jehovah's Witness, he will not accept a blood transfusion. His condition worsens, and the physician determines that a transfusion may be necessary to save his life.

Scenario 2: A 26-year-old married woman with two small children is in an automobile accident. It is determined that immediate removal of the spleen and a blood transfusion are necessary to save her life. The woman protests that she is a devout Jehovah's Witness and would sacrifice the chance to be with her family eternally if she is transfused.

Scenario 3: An otherwise healthy infant is suffering from Rh incompatibility and is in need of an immediate life-saving blood transfusion. The parents are Jehovah's Witnesses, however, and refuse transfusion of any blood products to their child. The parents consult with the deacon at their church and then state they would rather have their child die (and gain eternal life) than be transfused and continue life on earth but sacrifice eternal life.

What do you think should be done in each of these three situations? Should the blood transfusions be given? What are the implications of your position for the medical profession? For the rights of patients?

REFERENCES

Armitage, Karen J., Lawrence J. Schneiderman, and Robert A. Bass. 1979 "Response of Physicians to Medical Complaints in Men and Women." *Journal of the American Medical Association,* 241:2186–2187.

Bach, Peter B., Laura D. Cramer, Joan L. Warren, and Colin B. Begg. 1999 "Racial Differences in the Treatment of Early-Stage Lung Cancer." *New England Journal of Medicine,* 341:1198–1205.

Baker, Patricia S., William C. Yoels, and Jeffrey M. Clair. 1996 "Emotional Expression During Medical Encounters: Social Disease and the Medical Gaze," pp. 173–199 in *Health and the Sociology of Emotions,* Veronica James and Jonathan Gabe (eds.). Oxford: Blackwell Publishers.

Barsky, Arthur J. 1981 "Hidden Reasons Some Patients Visit Doctors." *Annals of Internal Medicine,* 94:492–498.

Beckman, H. B., and R. M. Frankel. 1984 "The Effect of Physician Behavior on the Collection of Data." *Annals of Internal Medicine,* 101: 692–696.

Beisecker, Analee E., and Thomas D. Beisecker. 1990 "Patient Information-Seeking Behaviors When Communicating with Doctors." *Medical Care,* 28:19–28.

Belgrave, Linda L., May L. Wykle, and David Cogan. 1997 "Medical Self-Care: Compliance with Recommended Treatment Regimens Among Chronically Ill Middle-Aged and Elderly Persons," pp. 99–117 in *Research in the Sociology of Health Care,* Jennie J. Kronenfeld (ed.). Greenwich, CT: Jai Press.

Bernstein, Barbara, and Robert Kane. 1981 "Physicians' Attitudes Toward Female Patients." *Medical Care,* 19:600–608.

Bertakis, Klea D., Edward J. Callahan, and L. Jay Helms. 1998 "Physician Practice Styles and Patient Outcomes: Differences Between Family Practice and General Internal Medicine." *Medical Care,* 36:879–891.

Blendon, Robert J., and Humphrey Taylor. 1989 "Views on Health Care: Public Opinion in Three Nations." *Health Affairs,* 8:149–157.

Braddock, Clarence H., Kelly A. Edwards, Nicole M. Hasenberg, Tracy L. Laidley, and Wendy Levinson. 1999 "Informed Decision Making in Outpatient Practice." *Journal of the American Medical Association,* 282:2313–2320.

Buller, Mary K., and David B. Buller. 1987 "Physicians' Communication Style and Patient Satisfaction." *Journal of Health and Social Behavior,* 28:375–388.

Campbell, James D., Helen J. Neikirk, and Michael C. Hosokawa. 1990 "Development of a Psychosocial Concern Index from Videotaped Interviews of Nurse Practitioners and Family Physicians." *The Journal of Family Practice,* 30:321–326.

Colameco, Stephen, Lorne A. Becker, and Michael Simpson. 1983 "Sex Bias in the Assessment of Patient Complaints." *The Journal of Family Practice,* 16:1117–1121.

Conrad, Peter. 1987 "The Noncompliant Patient in Search of Autonomy." *Hastings Center Report,* 17:15–17.

Cooper, Lisa A., Debra L. Roter, Rachel L. Johnson, Daniel E. Ford, Donald M. Steinwachs, and Neil R. Powe. 2003 "Patient-Centered Communication, Ratings of Care, and Concordance of Patient and Physician Race." *Annals of Internal Medicine,* 139:907–915.

Cooper-Patrick, Lisa, Joseph J. Gallo, J. J. Gonzales, Vu H. Thi, Neil R. Powe, Christine Nelson, and Daniel E. Ford. 1999 "Race, Gender, and Partnership in the Physician-Patient Relationship." *Journal of the American Medical Association,* 282:583–589.

Council on Ethical and Judicial Affairs, American Medical Association. 1990 "Black-White Disparities in Health Care." *Journal of the American Medical Association,* 263:2344–2346.

Deber, Raisa B., Nancy Kraetschmer, and Jane Irvine. 1996 "What Role Do Patients Wish to Play in Treatment Decision Making?" *Archives of Internal Medicine,* 156:1414–1420.

Derose, Kathryn P., Ron D. Hays, Daniel F. McCaffrey, and David W. Baker. 2001 "Does Physician Gender Affect Satisfaction of Men and Women Visiting the Emergency Department?" *Journal of General Internal Medicine,* 16:218–226.

Emanuel, Ezekiel J., and Nancy N. Dubler. 1995 "Preserving the Physician-Patient Relationship in the Era of Managed Care." *Journal of the American Medical Association,* 273:323–329.

Engel, George L. 1977 "The Need for a New Medical Model: A Challenge for Biomedicine." *Science,* 196:129–136.

Epstein, Arnold M., Joel S. Weissman, Eric C. Schneider, Constantine Gatsonis, Lucian L. Leape, and Robert N. Piana. 2003 "Race and Gender Disparities in Rates of Cardiac Revascularization." *Medical Care,* 41:1240–1255.

Fennema, Karen, Daniel L. Meyer, and Natalie Owen. 1990 "Sex of Physician: Patients' Preferences and Stereotypes." *The Journal of Family Practice,* 30:441–446.

Freidson, Eliot. 1970 *Professional Dominance: The Social Structure of Medical Care.* New York: Atherton Press.

Frowick, Bonnie, J. Christopher Shank, William J. Doherty, and Tracy A. Powell. 1986 "What Do Patients Really Want? Redefining a Behavioral Science Curriculum for Family Physicians." *The Journal of Family Practice,* 23:141–146.

Giles, Wayne H., Robert F. Anda, Michele L. Casper, Luis G. Escobedo, and Herman A. Taylor. 1995 "Race and Sex Differences in Rates of Invasive Cardiac Procedures in United States Hospitals." *Archives of Internal Medicine,* 155:318–324.

Good, Mary-Jo D., Byron J. Good, and Paul D. Cleary. 1987 "Do Patient Attitudes Influence Physician Recognition of Psychosocial Problems in Primary Care?" *The Journal of Family Practice,* 25:53–59.

Greer, Steven, Vivian Dickerson, Lawrence J. Schneiderman, Cathie Atkins, and Robert Bass. 1986 "Responses of Male and Female Physicians to Medical Complaints in Male and Female Patients." *The Journal of Family Practice,* 23:49–53.

Gregory, Kimberly, Kenneth B. Wells, and Barbara Leake. 1987 "Medical Students' Expectations for Encounters with Minority and Nonminority Students." *Journal of the National Medical Association,* 79:403–408.

Gross, Michael L. 1999 "Autonomy and Paternalism in Communitarian Society: Patient Rights in Israel." *Hastings Center Report,* 29:13–20.

Hack, Thomas F., Lesley F. Degner, and Dennis G. Dyck. 1994 "Relationship Between Preferences for Decisional Control and Illness Information Among Women with Breast Cancer: A Quantitative and Qualitative Analysis." *Social Science and Medicine,* 39:279–289.

Hadlow, Jan, and Marian Pitts. 1991 "The Understanding of Common Health Terms by Doctors, Nurses, and Patients." *Social Science and Medicine,* 32:193–196.

Hall, Judith A., Debra L. Roter, and Nancy R. Katz. 1988 "Meta-Analysis of Correlates of Provider Behavior in Medical Encounters." *Medical Care,* 26:657–675.

Hall, Judith A., Julie T. Irish, Debra L. Roter, Carol M. Ehrlich, and Lucy H. Miller. 1994 "Gender in Medical Encounters: An Analysis of Physician and Patient Communication in a Primary Care Setting." *Health Psychology,* 13:384–392.

Hunt, Linda M., Brigitte Jordan, Susan Irwin, and C. H. Browner. 1989 "Compliance and the Patient's Perspective: Controlling Symptoms in Everyday Life." *Culture, Medicine and Psychiatry,* 13: 315–334.

Johnson, Paula A., Lee Goldman, E. John Orav, Li Zhou, Tomas Garcia, Steven D. Pearson, and Thomas H. Lee. 1996 "Gender Differences in the Management of Acute Chest Pain." *Journal of General Internal Medicine,* 11:209–217.

Kolata, Gina. 1990 "Wariness Is Replacing Trust Between Healer and Patient." *The New York Times,* February 20, 1990, pp. 1, 10.

LaVeist, Thomas A., and Amani Nuru-Jeter. 2002 "Is Doctor-Patient Race Concordance Associated with Greater Satisfaction with Care?" *Journal of Health and Social Behavior,* 43:296–306.

Levinson, Wendy, William B. Stiles, Thomas S. Inui, and Robert Engle. 1993 "Physician Frustration in Communicating with Patients." *Medical Care,* 31:285–295.

Linn, Lawrence S., Dennis W. Cope, and Barbara Leake. 1984 "The Effect of Gender and Training of Residents on Satisfaction Ratings by Patients." *Journal of Medical Education,* 59:964–966.

Love, Margaret M., Arch G. Mainous, Jeffrey C. Talbert, and Gregory L. Hager. 2000 "Continuity of Care and the Physician-Patient Relationship." *Journal of Family Practice,* 49:998–1004.

Lurie, Nicole, Karen L. Margolis, Paul G. McGovern, Pamela J. Mink, and Jonathan S. Slater. 1997 "Why Do Patients of Female Physicians Have Higher Rates of Breast and Cervical Cancer Screening?" *Journal of General Internal Medicine,* 12:34–43.

Malat, Jennifer. 2001a "Race and Satisfaction with Medical Care: What Do We Know?" Paper presented at the Annual Meeting of the Southern Sociological Society, Atlanta, Georgia.

———. 2001b "Social Distance and Patients' Rating of Healthcare Providers." *Journal of Health and Social Behavior,* 42:360–372.

Mechanic, David, Donna D. McAlpine, and Marsha Rosenthal. 2001 "Are Patients' Office Visits with Physicians Getting Shorter?" *New England Journal of Medicine,* 344:198–204.

Mizrahi, Terry. 1986 *Getting Rid of Patients: Contradictions in the Socialization of Physicians.* New Brunswick, NJ: Rutgers University Press.

Morales, Leo S., William E. Cunningham, Julie A. Brown, Honghu Liu, and Ron D. Hays. 1999 "Are Latinos Less Satisfied with Communication by Health Care Providers?" *Journal of General Internal Medicine,* 14:409–417.

Neighbors, Harold W., James S. Jackson, Linn Campbell, and Donald Williams. 1989 "The Influence of Racial Factors on Psychiatric Diagnosis: A Review and Suggestions for Research." *Community Mental Health Journal,* 25:301–311.

Parsons, Talcott. 1951 *The Social System.* Glencoe, IL: Free Press.

Quill, Timothy E. 1982 "How Special Is Medicine's Nonspecialty?" *The Pharos,* 45:25–30.

Robinson, John W., and Debra L. Roter. 1999 "Psychosocial Problem Disclosure by Primary Care Patients." *Social Science and Medicine,* 48:1353–1362.

Roter, Debra L., Judith K. Hall, and Nancy R. Katz. 1988 "Patient-Physician Communication: A Descriptive Summary of the Literature." *Patient Education and Counseling,* 12:99–119.

Szasz, Thomas S., and Marc H. Hollender. 1956 "The Basic Models of the Doctor-Patient Relationship." *Archives of Internal Medicine,* 97:585–592.

Tierney, William M., Morris Weinberger, James Y. Greene, and P. Albert Studdard. 1984 "Jehovah's Witnesses and Blood Transfusion: Physician's Attitudes and Legal Precedents." *Southern Medical Journal,* 77:473–478.

Veatch, Robert M. 1972 "Models for Ethical Medicine in a Revolutionary Age." *Hastings Center Report,* 2:5–7.

Verbrugge, Lois M., and Richard P. Steiner. 1981 "Physician Treatment of Men and Women Patients: Sex Bias or Appropriate Care?" *Medical Care,* 19:609–632.

Virmani, Jaya, Lawrence J. Schneiderman, and Robert M. Kaplan. 1994 "Relationship of Advance Directives to Physician-Patient Communication." *Archives of Internal Medicine,* 154, 909–913.

Waitzkin, Howard. 1984 "Doctor-Patient Communication: Clinical Implications of Social Scientific Research." *Journal of the American Medical Association,* 252:2441–2446.

———. 1999 "Changing Patient-Physician Relationships in the Changing Health Policy Environment," pp. 271–283 in *Handbook of Medical Sociology* (5th ed.), Chloe E. Bird, Peter Conrad, and Allen M. Fremont (eds.). Upper Saddle River, NJ: Prentice Hall.

Weisman, Carol S., and Martha A. Teitelbaum. 1985 "Physician Gender and the Physician-Patient Relationship: Recent Evidence and Relevant Questions." *Social Science and Medicine,* 20:1119–1127.

West, Candace. 1984 *Routine Complications: Troubles with Talk Between Doctors and Patients.* Bloomington, IN: Indiana University Press.

Weyrauch, Karl F., Patricia E. Boiko, and Barbara Alvin. 1990 "Patient Sex Role and Preference for a Male or Female Physician." *The Journal of Family Practice,* 30:559–562.

Williamson, Penny, Bernard D. Beitman, and Wayne Katon. 1981 "Beliefs That Foster Physician Avoidance of Psychosocial Aspects of Health Care." *The Journal of Family Practice,* 13: 999–1003.

Zussman, Robert. 1992 *Intensive Care: Medical Ethics and the Medical Profession.* Chicago: The University of Chicago Press.

13

PROFESSIONAL AND ETHICAL OBLIGATIONS OF PHYSICIANS IN THE PHYSICIAN-PATIENT RELATIONSHIP

An important strategy for delving into the dynamics of the physician–patient relationship is consideration of the "rights" of patients versus the professional obligations of physicians. Three such issues (truth-telling, confidentiality, and the obligation to treat AIDS patients) have received significant attention from social scientists and medical ethicists as well as those in the health care field.

For sociologists, these issues are important for many reasons: They are closely related to the nature of the medical profession, to the status of patients, and to interactions between physicians and patients; they are creating new role demands for physicians and patients; and they are increasingly becoming part of the formal and informal socialization process for health care professionals.

Moreover, the sociological perspective is essential for understanding the social context of these issues. In the Preface to *Bioethics and Society* (1998:xiv), DeVries and Subedi articulate sociology's contribution to understanding these issues as "getting the whole picture," "looking beyond the taken for granted," scrutinizing "existing arrangements of power," and

raising "questions about the social bases of morality"—"classic sociological concerns."

TRUTH-TELLING AS AN ISSUE

An important gauge of the relative status of patients in the physician–patient relationship is the discretion felt by physicians to lie to or in some manner intentionally deceive patients. This issue commonly occurs when a physician learns some distressing news about a patient, such as a diagnosis of terminal cancer or some other life-threatening or chronic disease. The following brief case study illustrates one kind of situation in which the issue of truth-telling might arise:

A physician determines that a male patient is suffering from an advanced stage of lung cancer. It is too late for benefit from surgery, chemotherapy, or radiation. She feels that communicating this diagnosis to the patient will so depress and traumatize him that he will simply give up and die. In order to try to provide even a few weeks of additional time, she tells him the tests are inconclusive and asks him to return in a couple of weeks for the tests to be performed again.

Are Lying and Deception Acceptable Professional Behaviors?

Medical Codes. Most existing codes of ethical behavior for physicians are silent about the issue of lying and deception. While the Hippocratic Oath includes numerous pledges by physicians to patients, including confidentiality, nothing is said about truth-telling. There is no reference to truth-telling in the Declaration of Geneva, written in 1948 by the World Medical Association as a response to Nazi atrocities performed in World War II under the name of medical science or in the AMA's Code of Ethics up to 1980 (Beauchamp and Childress, 1983).

Other prominent ethical codes in medicine have addressed truth-telling and have occasionally made a strong statement on its behalf. Both the American Hospital Association's Patient's Bill of Rights and the American Medical Association's Code of Medical Ethics now clearly state that patients have a right to complete current information regarding diagnosis, treatment options, and prognosis. Moreover, the President's Commission for the Study of Ethical Problems in Medicine and Biomedical and Behavioral Research (1983) supports full disclosure of information to patients as a way of increasing patient participation in actual decision making.

Arguments Used to Justify Lying and Deception. The most often cited justification for lying and deception by physicians is referred to as **benevolent deception.** Many physicians believe that they have a professional duty to lie to patients if that is perceived to be in the patient's best interest. This argument is supported by the rationale that physicians are employed by patients to provide the best possible diagnosis and treatment. Since physicians are not automatons, they cannot and should not be expected simply to report the "facts." Instead, as persons with extensive training in the practice of medicine, they should be given license to make judgments about what information would be beneficial for a patient to have and what infor-

mation would do harm to the patient, and to act on these perceptions.

Guiora (1980) suggests that too much has been made of "freedom of information" whereas too little consideration has been given to the idea of **freedom from information.**

> Information is medicine, very potent medicine indeed, that has to be titrated, properly dosaged based on proper diagnosis. Diagnosis, of course, in this context means an assessment of how information will affect the course of illness, how much and what kind of information is the most therapeutic in face of the patient's preferred modes of coping. (Guiora, 1980:32)

A second argument used to justify lying is that patients typically are unable to comprehend the "whole truth" of a matter, and physicians, therefore, cannot be expected to try to provide it. This situation is said to occur because most patients have limited medical knowledge and may incorrectly (or at least incompletely) interpret terminology used by the physician. Conveying a diagnosis of cancer exemplifies the point. Despite the tremendous progress made in the treatment of cancer and the steadily increasing rate of cure for many cancers, the "C" word continues to carry frightening implications. Since patients lack understanding of the disease and its treatment, the argument goes, it would make little sense to obligate physicians to communicate this diagnosis fully.

Mack Lipkin, an M.D. and frequent essayist on medical matters, elaborates on this argument.

> How many patients understand that "heart trouble" may refer to literally hundreds of different abnormalities ranging in severity from the trivial to the instantly fatal? How many know that the term "arthritis" may refer to dozens of different types of joint involvement? Arthritis may raise a vision of the appalling disease that made Aunt Eulalee a helpless invalid until her death years later; the next patient remembers Grandpa grumbling about the damned arthritis as he got up from his chair. Unfortunately, but understandably, most people's ideas about the implications of medical terms are based on what they have heard about a few cases. (Lipkin, 1979:13)

Finally, many physicians believe that some patients prefer not to hear the whole truth. Discounting surveys that show that a large majority of patients want full information, many physicians believe patients subtly communicate otherwise to them. Although patients sometimes make explicit their desire to have the truth couched in gentle language or withheld altogether, more often they communicate this preference through body language, tone of voice, or a message that requires the physician to "read between the lines." If this is the message being communicated, many physicians argue, it would be unethical for them to reveal the truth.

Arguments Used to Oppose Lying and Deception. An alternative view is that truth-telling is an unconditional duty—that physicians are morally required always to provide full information to patients and never to lie or attempt to deceive them. Four primary arguments buttress this position. The first is that telling the truth is part of the respect owed to all people. To lie to or intentionally deceive another is to denigrate that person's worthiness and to treat that person as undeserving of a full and honest account. The legal requirement for informed consent from patients or research subjects implies a decision maker who is fully informed and has complete access to the truth. A physician who fails to provide honest information to a patient has usurped the possibility for a genuine informed consent to occur.

Second, veracity is consistent with the ideas of fidelity and keeping promises. When a patient solicits a physician, he or she is entering an implied contract. In exchange for payment, the patient seeks the best possible diagnosis, recommendations for treatment, and (if agreed upon) the provision of treatment. Accordingly, any information learned by the physician about the patient should be provided to the patient. After all, who can be said to "own" that information? Does the physician own it and have a right to parcel it out according to his or her discretion? Or, does the patient own this information? Those arguing from this position believe

the contract established between the patient and physician requires that a full and honest account always be provided.

A third argument used to support unconditional truth-telling is that lying or deception undermines a trusting relationship between patient and physician. If it is assumed that patient trust in a physician is a desirable goal, and that this trust facilitates a therapeutic relationship, then physicians must act in such a way as to maintain this trust. A patient who learns that he or she has been intentionally deceived by a physician may never again be able to trust fully information provided by that physician.

Finally, those taking this position claim that it offers certain clear benefits to the patient. It is argued that no one, including the physician, knows a patient better than the patient himself or herself. For a physician to determine that a given patient would be better off being deceived than hearing the truth, at the least, would require intimate familiarity with the patient's life history, important values, perceived obligations to self and significant others, and decisions the patient would make in light of truthful information. Rarely, if ever, could a physician claim to have access to such matters or to know more about patients than they know about themselves.

Sissela Bok, a prominent medical ethicist at Brandeis University, summarizes this point.

> The damages associated with the disclosure of sad news or risks are rarer than physicians believe; and the benefits which result from being informed are more substantial, even measurably so. Pain is tolerated more easily, recovery from surgery is quicker, and cooperation with therapy is greatly improved. The attitude that "what you don't know won't hurt you" is proving unrealistic; it is what patients do not know but vaguely suspect that causes them corrosive worry. (Bok, 1991:78)

A recent study of terminally ill cancer patients (Weeks, 1998) revealed dangers associated with being given false hope. Those who had an overly optimistic view about their survival chances were much more likely to choose aggressive therapies that made them sick but did not extend their life. Those with realistic views were more likely to opt for treatments designed simply to make them comfortable. The patients utilizing the aggressive therapies did not live longer, but their final months were more likely to be spent in a hospital, and they were more likely to die while still connected to a ventilator— costs attached to the provision of unrealistic expectations.

The Current Situation Regarding Truth-Telling

Do Patients Want to Know the Truth? Social science surveys have found that most respondents express a desire for truthfulness from physicians. In an important early study, 89 percent of cancer patients, 82 percent of patients without cancer, and 98 percent of patients participating in a cancer detection program expressed a desire for honesty in a cancer diagnosis (Kelly and Friesen, 1950). An early 1980s telephone survey of 1,250 persons in the United States found that more than 9 of every 10 respondents (94 percent) wanted all available information about a medical condition and treatment, even if it was unfavorable. This preference for candor crossed all population subgroups; it was not specific to any age, sex, race, or social class (President's Commission, 1983).

Are Physicians Truthful with Patients? Over the last five decades, several studies have been conducted on physicians' attitudes regarding full disclosure of information to patients. In studies of the 1950s and 1960s, large majorities of physicians reported that they sometimes withheld the truth from patients. Some change began to appear in studies conducted in the early 1970s, and by the late 1970s, one study found that 98 percent of physicians reported that their general policy was to inform a cancer patient accurately, and two-thirds of these said they never or very rarely deviated from the policy. What factors most influenced the behavior of the physicians? Patients most likely to be given the truth were those who had expressly asked for the truth, those judged to be high in emotional maturity, the older patients, and those thought to be highest in intelligence (Novack et al., 1979).

Studies conducted in the 1980s and 1990s reflect both an increased propensity to tell the truth and a continued willingness to deceive. Dickinson and Tournier (1994) examined attitudes toward death and terminally ill patients of physicians soon after they graduated from medical school in 1976 and a decade later. Physicians were much more likely in 1986 to express the belief that dying patients should be told their prognosis. In a study conducted by the President's Commission, 86 percent of the physicians acknowledged that most patients want accurate information about diagnosis and prognosis, and most reported a tendency to provide it. But, when given a scenario of a sick patient with a fully confirmed diagnosis of advanced lung cancer, only 13 percent said they would "give a straight statistical prognosis" to the patient for this class of disease (President's Commission, 1983). Physicians expressing a willingness to deceive were found, by Novack and others (1989), to place greater emphasis on the consequences (or outcomes) of a medical encounter than adherence to a principle of unconditional truth-telling.

This pattern is consistent with an important study by Naoko Miyaji (1993) who discovered that American physicians seem to value ethical principles that support disclosure of information to patients—through both truth-telling and informed consent—and these physicians give the impression that patients have control over obtaining information. But, in reality, physicians continue to manage the information-giving process. They interpret the principle of disclosure selectively and in such a way that they share with patients only as much information as they wish them to have. In the case of a patient with a newly diagnosed terminal illness, physicians emphasize possible treatments and decision-making options and give extensive information about them, but give much less information and play down grim prognosis information, citing

IN COMPARATIVE PERSPECTIVE

TRUTH-TELLING AND CANCER PATIENTS IN JAPAN

Most countries in the world continue to struggle with the moral issues involved in disclosing or failing to disclose a terminal prognosis. Japan is a country in which physicians have traditionally refused to disclose terminal illness. In the United States the right of autonomous individuals to be informed is now commonly respected (at least to a degree). In Japan, however, individuals are viewed primarily as being a part of a family and a community. The Confucian emphases on *kyokan* (the feeling of togetherness) and *ningen* (the human person in relationship to others) are prioritized over individual autonomy.

Given these emphases, Japanese physicians typically lie to or deceive patients who are terminally ill (e.g., pretending the cancer is just an ulcer) and instead reveal the prognosis to family members and consult with them. Family members are strongly encouraged not to inform the patient of the real circumstances. Consultation with members occurs both in face-to-face interaction and through written communication.

In recent years the tradition has begun to give way to greater respect for the autonomy of the individual. Although young persons still respect the role of the family in decision making and care, there is now a greater call for open disclosure to the patient. Still, fewer than half of Japanese physicians today provide full disclosure of a terminal illness (Elwyn et al., 1998; Brannigan and Boss, 2001).

---

uncertainty and lack of relevance to future actions.

This communication pattern is justified by physicians as showing compassion and respect for the patient and the principle of disclosure while preserving as much hope as possible for the patient. These physicians could well respond to survey questions that they provide truthful diagnoses to patients; this may explain some of the high percentages of physicians who now report themselves to be unconditional truth tellers. But, in closer examination, they are still in control of the information-giving process, and they are not sharing as much information as they have about the patient's condition. Miyaji (1993:250) concludes that this pattern:

> shows the ambiguity and tension which define the doctor's new role as a partner of the patient. Preservation of their image (and self-image) as compassionate and caring physicians helps them to manage patient care in emotionally-laden situations like truth-telling as a healer. However, this humanistic model of the physician serves also to maintain the power of the profession, enhancing its "cultural authority" over patients.

CONFIDENTIALITY AS AN ISSUE

The *Tarasoff* Case

On July 1, 1976, the California Supreme Court handed down a decision in the **Tarasoff case**—*Tarasoff v. Regents of the University of California*, one of the most important judicial cases to affect medical practice in U.S. history. The facts of the case were basically undisputed. In 1969, a student at the University of California at Berkeley, Prosenjit Poddar, confided to his psychologist, Dr. Lawrence Moore, who was on the staff at Cowell Memorial Hospital on the Berkeley campus, that he intended to kill Tatiana Tarasoff, a young female who lived in Berkeley but was at that time on a trip to Brazil.

Dr. Moore, with the concurrence of a colleague and the assistant director of the Department of Psychiatry, reported the threat to the campus police and asked them to detain Poddar and commit him to a mental hospital for observation. The campus police questioned Poddar, but satisfied that he was rational and based on his promise to stay away from Tarasoff, they released him. They reported their action to Dr. Harvey Powelson, the director of the psychiatry department.

Dr. Powelson requested no further action to detain Poddar or to follow up on the threats. Two months later, shortly after Tarasoff returned from her Brazil visit, Poddar went to her home and killed her. Later, when Tatiana's parents learned that university officials had known about the threat to their daughter's life but had failed to detain Poddar or warn them or their daughter, they brought a negligence suit against the therapists involved, the campus police, and the university and sought additional punitive damages.

The original court hearing the case dismissed all charges against all defendants. However, the California Supreme Court partially reversed the lower court's judgment when a majority ruled that general damages against the therapists and the university were in order for their failure to warn the girl or her family (punitive damages were dismissed) (Tobriner, 1976). (Due to a technical error, Poddar's second degree murder conviction was overturned; because more than five years had elapsed since the murder, he was not retried under an agreement that he would return to his native India, which he did.)

What are the implications of this ruling? Should the therapists have been morally and legally required to warn Tatiana Tarasoff? If so, what other circumstances would justify breaching confidentiality? Or, should physicians maintain absolute confidentiality regarding information shared with them by all patients in all circumstances?

The Meaning of Confidentiality

The term **confidentiality** is often used interchangeably with "privacy" and with the concept of privileged communication. But the terms mean different things. **Privacy** refers to freedom from unauthorized intrusions into one's life. As applied to medical matters, it largely refers to the control that an individual has over information about himself or herself (Wasserstrom, 1986).

Clearly, there are some things—one's thoughts or hopes or fears—about which no one else will know unless that individual chooses to disclose them. As individuals, we are permitted to retain full custody of our private thoughts, and we cannot be compelled to compromise this sense of privacy. There are some occasions when we reveal our private thoughts to others, but we still hold dominion over them. For example, when we share information with certain professionals, such as physicians or the clergy, we do so with an understanding that this other person will respect our privacy and not reveal what has been said. This is the notion of "professional secrecy" (Wasserstrom, 1986).

Once information is revealed to another person, it is never again as private. At this point, the individual must rely on the professionalism or good will of the other person not to reveal the information. This is the meaning of confidentiality. In the medical encounter, an individual patient who reveals information to a physician must now count on the physician not to share the information with others. Maintaining confidentiality means that the information goes no further.

The idea of **privileged communication** comes from the legal system, which operates on the basis of *testimonial compulsion*— individuals with pertinent information can be required to present that information in a court of law. However, our legal system recognizes the value of professional secrecy. To foster a close and trusting relationship between individuals and selected professionals, information shared with these professionals may be exempt from testimonial compulsion. The information or communication is said to be "privileged" in this sense.

The Laws Pertaining to Confidentiality

Contrary to common perception, there are no constitutional provisions covering confidentiality of information shared with a physician. While the Fourth Amendment deals with the issue of privacy, its relevance to medical confidentiality has been left up to judicial interpretation. There is no common law that obliges physicians to hold confidential information shared by a patient. Such law does exist between lawyers and clients and the clergy and parishioners.

In December 2000, shortly before leaving office, President Clinton issued sweeping regulations that sought to protect medical privacy. The most important component of the rules (the entire set of rules occupied 1,500 pages) required that patients must give special permission for any nonroutine uses of medical information about them. "Nonroutine uses" was defined to include employers seeking information on job candidates and product marketers seeking a list of individuals with specific conditions. However, a paperwork mix-up prevented the rules from going into effect before Clinton left office, and they are now being reviewed by the Bush administration. If they go into effect, they would be the first federal laws pertaining to medical confidentiality.

To fill this void, individual states have developed privileged communication statutes. About two-thirds of the states now have these statutes, which state that physicians cannot be compelled to reveal in a court of law information received from a patient. However, states have also identified certain types of information that physicians are legally obligated to share with proper authorities. This information includes certain health conditions (primarily communicable diseases such as tuberculosis and sexually transmitted diseases), gunshot wounds, and suspected or clear physical or sexual abuse of children.

Does a patient who feels that her or his physician has wrongfully breached confidentiality have any recourse in the law? Yes. Physicians may be sued for malpractice for wrongfully disclosing patient information under one or more of three legal theories: (1) an unauthorized disclosure of confidential information, (2) an invasion of privacy, and (3) a violation of an implied contract between the physician and patient (Roth, 1981).

Medical Codes

The principle of confidentiality has been firmly rooted in codes of medical ethics. The classic reference to the importance of confidentiality occurs in the Hippocratic Oath (see Chapter 2): "What I may see or hear in the course of the treatment or even outside of the treatment in regard to the life of men, which on no account one must spread abroad, I will keep to myself holding such things shameful to be spoken about."

This statement is credited with influencing all subsequent efforts to note the ethical responsibilities of physicians. Today, the ethical code for nearly every medical group includes some reference to confidentiality. The AMA's Code of Medical Ethics states that "The physician should not reveal confidential communications or information without the express consent of the patient, unless required to do so by law (1992:25)."

When Confidentiality Becomes an Issue

Today, we generally think of three kinds of situations in which medical confidentiality may be an issue. The first are accidental or not so accidental "slips of the tongue" that physicians commit when chatting with family, friends, or colleagues. Fortunately, most health care professionals are careful not to let information about patients slip, though these "irresponsible" breaches do occur—often when inhibitions have been lowered by exhaustion or alcohol.

The second type results from the increasingly large number of persons who have access to patient information and data. More and more allied health workers have access to patients and patient records; and more and more agencies, including public health agencies, third-party payers, medical peer review committees, employers, credit investigation agencies, social welfare agencies, and medical researchers have a legal right to patient data. The plan announced in 1995 to connect the computers of all physicians, hospitals, labs, pharmacies, nursing homes, and insurance companies in the United States almost guarantees uncontrolled and uncontrollable access by hundreds of thousands of people to medical records. Etzioni (1999) has referred to these breaches of confidentiality as "authorized abuse." They occur on a daily basis and raise serious ethical questions but are currently perfectly legal.

Finally, another set of intriguing ethical questions occurs in situations in which physicians must make a conscious decision about whether or not to violate confidentiality. Cases like *Tarasoff* dramatize the issue. The remainder of this section of the chapter focuses on these issues.

Justifications for the Principle of Confidentiality

Sissela Bok, in *Lying: Moral Choice in Public and Private Life* (1978), summarizes four justifications for physicians to protect the privacy of information shared by patients: (1) protection of the patient's autonomy over personal information; (2) enhancement of the physician–patient relationship; (3) respect for the patient; and (4) opportunity for individuals to communicate more freely with the physician.

This final rationale was used by the justices writing the dissenting opinion in the *Tarasoff* case. Writing for the minority, Justice William P. Clark (1976) described three specific reasons that confidentiality ought not be broken. First, individuals needing treatment will be more likely to seek help. Second, individuals seeking assistance will be more likely to provide full disclosure. Finally, trust in the psychotherapist will be enhanced. Though distressed with situations like the *Tarasoff* case, the justices contended that maintaining confidentiality, rather than breaking it, will minimize tragedies in the long run because those needing help will not be dissuaded from seeking it.

Grounds for Breaking Confidentiality

Few persons dismiss the importance of confidentiality. But where some people see confidentiality as an unconditional duty (never to be broken), others believe it to be a prima facie

responsibility—justifiably broken for very compelling reasons. Three such reasons are cited.

The first is benefit to the patient himself or herself—the principle of beneficence. An example by which this rationale might apply would be a temporarily depressed or traumatized individual who threatens to commit suicide or to engage in some disreputable, out-of-character behavior. In order to secure assistance to prevent the action, the physician may need to break confidentiality and disclose the stated intention of the person. However, physicians must be sure that an action contemplated by a patient really is a product of an irrational mind. Many people are too quick to assume that any decision made by another that is inconsistent with one's own values is not a rational decision.

A second possible justification for violating medical confidentiality is that it may conflict with the rights of an innocent third party. As a society, we must determine whether we prefer that innocent third parties be warned of impending danger, even though that means a breach of confidentiality, or that confidentiality not be broken.

The *Tarasoff* case is an example of this justification, but it may occur in less extreme circumstances. For example, suppose a physician has as a patient a young man engaged to be married. He knows the young man is concealing his permanent impotence from his fiancée. The question arises whether the physician should break confidentiality with this young male patient and reveal the information to the fiancée or place priority on maintaining confidentiality and letting the chips fall where they may.

A third possible rationale for violating the principle of confidentiality is danger or threat to the rights or interests of society in general. As previously mentioned, various states require physicians to report certain specified diseases or conditions to proper authorities. But not all such situations are governed by law. For example, how should a physician respond when he or she detects a serious medical problem in a patient whose occupation influences the safety or lives of countless other people? What should be done in the case of a railroad signaller who is discovered to be subject to attacks of epilepsy or an airline pilot with failing eyesight? Cases such as these force physicians to determine their primary obligation. Is it to protect the confidentiality of the diagnosis, recognizing all the accompanying benefits, or is there a greater obligation to the unknown others whose lives may be jeopardized by the medical condition of the patient (Allmark, 1995)?

Right Versus Duty to Breach Confidentiality

If, in certain situations, we decide that physicians have a "right" to break confidentiality, would we take the next step and conclude they have a "duty" to do so? That is, does the physician who diagnoses the epileptic railroad signaller not only have a right to disclose the information but also a moral responsibility? Should society morally and legally insist that proper authorities be notified?

Where serious harm is likely to occur, Bok (1991) argues that the duty to warn is overriding. She contends that patients have no right to entrust information of this type to physicians and expect them to remain silent. And physicians have no right to promise confidentiality about such information. Of course, this is also the position taken by the majority in the *Tarasoff* case when the judges argued that the university psychotherapists had a duty to warn Tatiana of the threat that had been made.

Others, including many psychotherapists, were unhappy (to say the least) with the *Tarasoff* decision. Even those who could abide with the idea that physicians *may* disclose a threat objected to the requirement that physicians *must* disclose. For many, that compromised professional autonomy. The difficulties in determining which patients are serious about stated threats and the questions about the required severity of threat (is a broken arm sufficiently serious?) make this requirement an impossibility for them. Some research has shown that predictions of dangerousness are unreliable and that mental health professionals are more likely to be incorrect than correct in making such predictions and usually err in overpredicting dangerousness (Oppenheimer and Swanson, 1990).

IN THE FIELD

THE INFLUENCE OF PATIENT GENDER, RACE, AND SEXUAL PREFERENCE ON MAINTENANCE OF CONFIDENTIALITY

Physicians may consider a variety of factors in determining whether to break a confidence with a patient. Schwartzbaum, Wheat, and Norton (1990) attempted to determine if physician behavior was at all influenced by the gender, race, or sexual preference of the patient—factors that would not seem relevant. A sample of white, male primary care physicians were given a case study in which an HIV-infected patient presented a risk to a third party. Eight different descriptions of the gender, race, and sexual preference of the patient were distributed randomly among the physicians—one description to each. Each physician was asked to select his own likely behavior from a list of five choices reflecting a range of confidentiality breaches.

The physician-respondents were more likely to report black homosexual and heterosexual men to the health department and black heterosexual men to their partners than hypothetical patients in other categories. Were these physicians influenced by the greater use blacks make of public health departments (thus informing the health department seemed logical)? Were these physicians influenced by the perception that black HIV-positive men are more likely to be IV-drug users and thus less likely to be conscientious about informing their partners (thus implying that informing partners seemed logical)? Or, was there an explicit or implicit racial bias that influenced behavior?

OBLIGATION TO TREAT AIDS PATIENTS

In the relatively short time that HIV/AIDS has been a catastrophic health problem, much attention has been devoted to the complex ethical questions related to the disease. The "rights" and the "moral duties" of patients with HIV/AIDS, of the physicians and other health care providers who treat them, and of the companies who insure them all contain important issues. One of the most basic questions is whether physicians have a professional obligation to treat patients with AIDS.

Physicians' Perceptions Regarding the Obligation to Treat

There is considerable evidence that a sizable percentage of physicians do not wish to treat AIDS patients and do not believe that they have a professional obligation to do so. Link and others (1988) surveyed medical and pediatric interns and residents in seven New York City hospitals with large AIDS-patient populations. While only 11 percent of respondents were moderately or extremely resentful of having to care for AIDS patients, 25 percent would not continue to care for them if given a choice. Moreover, 24 percent believed that refusing to care for AIDS patients was not unethical; 34 percent believed that house officers should be allowed to decide for themselves whether to treat AIDS patients; and 53 percent believed medical students should be offered treatment choice. In a national survey of family physicians, 62.9 percent stated that physicians have a right to refuse to care for a patient solely because he or she is infected with the AIDS virus (Bredfeldt et al., 1991).

Historical Perspectives on the Obligation to Treat

Does history offer a clear picture as to how physicians in earlier times viewed the issue of obligation to treat contagious diseases? Yes, but a consistent tradition does not exist. Zuger and Miles (1987) found no such tradition in earlier epidemics such as the Black Death (Europe, thirteenth century), the Great Plague of London (seventeenth century), and yellow fever (United States, eighteenth century). Many physicians fled from patients with contagious disease and cities with a large disease population, but many others, often at considerable personal risk, remained to care for these patients.

Laws Pertaining to the Obligation to Treat

Several legal principles do pertain to the issue of treatment obligation. George Annas (1988:26) summarizes the basic concept of legal obligation to treat.

> American common law is firmly grounded on notions of individual liberty and economic freedom that support the proposition that absent some special relationship, no citizen owes any other citizen anything. As applied to the practice of medicine, the general rule, sometimes denoted the "no duty rule," is that a physician is not obligated to treat any particular patient in the absence of a consensual doctor-patient relationship. In the absence of a prior agreement or a statutory or regulatory prohibition, physicians (like other citizens) can, in deciding whether to accept patients, discriminate among them on the basis of all sorts of irrelevant and invidious criteria; from race to religion, to personal appearance and wealth, or by specific disease, like AIDS.

The "special relationship" referred to in the quotation pertains to the obligation to treat of emergency room physicians, physicians in a consensual doctor–patient relationship, and physicians with a contractual obligation (e.g., through a health care institution or insurance plan).

Medical Codes

Hippocratic Oath. It is unclear as to whether the Hippocratic Oath specifies any legal obligation to treat. A line in the oath, "into whatsoever houses I enter, I will enter to help the sick," has been interpreted by many to be stating a prescribed duty of physicians, one "neither abrogated or attenuated by incapacitating or terminal disease, nor by the assumption of personal risk" (Kim and Perfect, 1988:136). On the other hand, some contend the line attaches only very loosely to "obligation to treat" and does not offer sufficient detail to clarify a complex matter like treating AIDS patients.

The AMA's Code of Medical Ethics. The official position of the American Medical Association on obligation to treat has evolved through the years and has undergone important transformations. In constructing its first code of medical ethics in 1847, the AMA broke from existing medical codes by establishing a duty to treat: "... and when pestilence prevails, it is the [physician's] duty to face the danger, and to continue their labors for the alleviation of the suffering, even at the jeopardy of their own lives" (Jonsen, 1990:161).

This phrase notwithstanding, a revision of the Code of Ethics in 1912 included the addition of the statement that: "A physician shall, in the provision of appropriate patient care, except in emergencies, be free to choose whom to serve" (Judicial Council of the AMA, 1986).

Over the last fifty years, the AMA code has been revised on several occasions, sometimes emphasizing the **"duty to face danger"** phrase and sometimes the **"free to choose"** phrase. A 1986 attempt to reaffirm the profession's long-standing role in treating contagious patients while simultaneously offering physicians a method of exemption (e.g., if they were not emotionally able to care for AIDS patients) satisfied some but also engendered some backlash. In critical response, the American College of Physicians and the Infectious Disease Society of America issued a joint statement that proclaimed that "denying appropriate care to sick and dying patients for any reason is unethical" (Health and Public Policy Committee of the ACP and IDS, 1986). A year later, in December 1987, the AMA issued another position paper, clearly shifting its emphasis toward the duty to treat AIDS patients.

The AMA leadership appears to be caught in a dilemma. On the one hand, there seems to be recognition that it is inappropriate for physicians to refuse treatment to AIDS patients simply on the basis of that diagnosis and that an obligation to treat represents a more respectable professional standard. Criticism, especially from inside medicine, has not gone unnoticed. On the other hand, the free-to-choose tenet also has a long tradition in medicine and is clearly very important to many physician-members of the AMA.

This dilemma may explain the frequency of revised statements and even the current situation. For although the current statement offers emphatic support for treatment, AMA leaders have made it clear that any physician who wishes not to treat AIDS patients can label himself or herself incompetent to treat, and the AMA will pro forma accept the excuse. George Annas, a professor of health law, concluded that "In effect, this reduces the AMA's position to a statement that a doctor *must* treat an AIDS patient if the doctor *wants* to treat an AIDS patient" (Annas, 1988:S30).

Rationale for No Obligation to Treat

A key aspect of the philosophical underpinning of the "no-obligation" position is that physicians ought to be free to select their patients. Part of the traditional autonomy of a career in medicine (which has been seriously weakened under managed care) lies in not being told which patients must be seen. Many physicians explicitly state that they wish to exercise this freedom of selection by excluding AIDS patients.

On what grounds are AIDS patients sometimes excluded? Ezekiel Emanuel (1988), an M.D. in Harvard's Program in Ethics and the Professions, has identified four factors that are used as specific justifications for no obligation to AIDS patients.

Excessive Risks. Unquestionably, many physicians are fearful of contracting HIV from patients. Almost half of the physicians surveyed

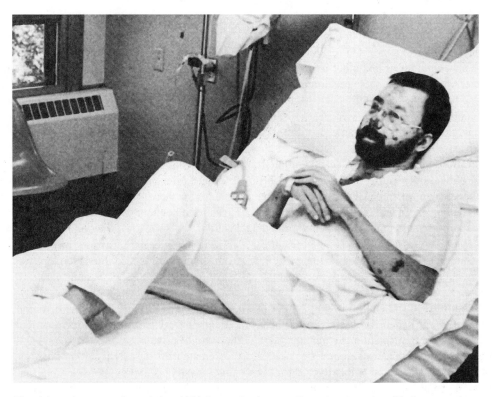

Physicians in general, and the AMA in particular, continue to struggle with the question of whether there is a professional duty to treat AIDS patients.

by Taylor and others (1990) said they were more frightened of contracting AIDS than any other disease. Those who perceived the greatest risk were most likely to believe in the no-obligation position. In a separate study, 30 percent of pediatric residents and 48 percent of medical residents in New York City hospitals reported a moderate to major amount of concern about contracting AIDS from patients (Link et al., 1988). Response to treating AIDS patients is influenced by the physician's stage of career and setting. Medical residents—who provide a significant amount of care for AIDS patients but without having any choice—are more likely than medical faculty and medical students to report fear of exposure to AIDS and an unwillingness to treat AIDS patients (Yedidia, Barr, and Berry, 1993).

These results assess subjective state—the fear of or concern with contracting AIDS. These perceptions are crucial because physicians, as well as others, behave on the basis of what they perceive to be real. Based on experimental studies, the Centers for Disease Control and Prevention estimate that the risk of HIV infection and AIDS after a single accidental exposure to HIV at work (most likely through an accidental puncture wound) is 0.5 percent (1 in 200) or less (Centers for Disease Control and Prevention, 1988).

Are the concerns and fears expressed by physicians unreasonable given these documented levels of risk? Many suggest that physicians have overreacted to the possibility of risk and should recognize that their own behavior (e.g., extreme carefulness in avoiding punctures) can diminish further the likelihood of transmission. However, a commentary in the *Journal of the American Medical Association* took the opposite point of view and condemned efforts to reduce the perceived risks of infection by emphasizing "low" transmission rates. Gerbert and others (1988) ask what is meant by "low" when discussing a condition that is always fatal, and one that can be contracted regardless of the physician's carefulness and other infection control measures. Among their recommendations for dealing with the fear felt by many health care professionals is acknowledgment that risk does exist and that concern is warranted.

Questionable Benefits.   A second rationale for no-obligation pertains to the lack of long-term benefits in treating AIDS patients: "After all, he (she) is going to die anyway, why bother?" Physicians are not obligated to provide unnecessary, useless care, and some procedures (e.g., cosmetic surgery on a dying patient) hardly could be said to be ethically obligatory.

Obligations to Other Patients.   Third, obligation to other patients is used as a rationale for the no obligation position. By treating AIDS patients, the physician risks contracting AIDS, which would make it impossible to care for her or his other patients. Moreover, other patients might discontinue their relationship with the physician when they learn he or she is seeing AIDS patients. One survey reported that 40 percent of a sample of family practice physicians feared that they would lose some patients if they found out that AIDS patients were also being seen in the office (Bredfeldt et al., 1991).

Obligations to Self and Family.   Refusing to treat an AIDS patient on the grounds that his or her medical care is not worth jeopardizing the physician's life or health is a perception held by some physicians. Some critics have asked whether this position is bolstered by an implicit (or explicit) judgmental process about the relative value of the individuals involved. That is, are physicians more likely to feel this way because many of their patients are gay or injectable drug users?

Recent research indicates that the answer is yes. A study of matriculating medical students in Chicago found that 92 percent would welcome HIV patients into their practice, but that homophobia and fear of infection were the most common explanations for those who would not (Carter, Lantos, and Hughes, 1996). Research on preclinical medical students also found largely favorable attitudes toward treatment, but found that students uncomfortable with homosexual behavior and feeling awkward about taking a sexual history from gays were least willing to treat (McDaniel et al., 1995). Finally, a study that compared attitudes of students in their fourth year of medical school and again as third-year residents determined the strongest predictors of change in attitudes for those whose willingness to treat declined were homophobic attitudes and aversion to IV-drug users (Yedidia, Berry, and Barr, 1996).

Two other considerations have emerged from studies in this area. First, some physicians worry that treating AIDS patients carries financial liability. Physicians not treating AIDS patients are more likely to believe that AIDS patients are a financial risk to a practice, that they would drive away other patients, and that they create considerable legal liability. Second, some physicians express considerable fear that they might unknowingly contract HIV and transmit it to their own spouse and/or children. Consideration of this rationale may come down to two questions: Do physicians' spouses and families need to expect to share in some risks of the profession? Are the risks so great as to overcome whatever professional rationale exists for treating AIDS patients?

Rationale for Obligation to Treat

While historical traditions, laws, and medical codes offer a perspective on the obligation to treat position, often they do not articulate the underlying philosophical principles on which it is based. Recently, medical practitioners, philosophers and ethicists, lawmakers, and social scientists have reflected on reasons why there may be an obligation-to-treat. Three such principles are described here.

The Nature of the Profession.   Perhaps the firmest principle on which to base an obligation to treat is the inherent nature of the profession of medicine. Professions represent special statuses;

typically, they involve more training and greater commitment than other careers and are rooted in a special ideal of service to others (as described in Chapter 8). Emanuel (1988:1686) traces a duty to treat to the nature of the profession.

> The objective of the medical profession is devotion to a moral ideal—in particular, healing the sick and rendering the ill healthy and well. The physician is committed to the help and betterment of other people—"selflessly caring for the sick," as the president of the American College of Physicians has put it. When a person joins the profession, he or she professes a commitment to these ideals and accepts the obligation to serve the sick. It is the profession that is chosen. The obligation is neither chosen nor transferable: it is constitutive of the professional activity.

According to this viewpoint, making distinctions among the sick based on the type or nature of the disease is contrary to the ideal of the profession. The noble dimension of this professional duty is treating all patients—especially the most vulnerable—without making these distinctions.

It is largely this factor that has led the U.S. Supreme Court to rule that health care workers cannot refuse treatment to individuals with HIV/AIDS. The justices have contended that the objective and reasonable view of health care professionals is that there is minimal risk in treating AIDS patients and that a contrasting judgment of an individual physician is not sufficient to override the obligation not to discriminate by nontreatment.

The Social Contract.   The second principle used to support obligatory treatment rests on the implicit **social contract** made between society and the medical profession. This rationale states that physicians have an obligation to treat the sick and vulnerable in exchange for the near monopolistic powers they have been given over the clinical practice of medicine. Potential danger in doing so does not exempt the physician from fulfilling this obligation any more than it exempts a police officer or fire fighter (Arras, 1988).

Fulfillment of this reciprocal obligation, however, can be viewed in two ways. One interpretation is that it creates an obligation on the part of each physician to treat those in medical need and not to shun those with particular diseases. After all, the argument goes, every physician benefits from the control physicians have over medical practice. For any physician to treat only those individuals he or she has selected would be a failure to perform the expected reciprocal obligation.

A second view posits that the obligation to care for the sick is attached to physicians in general but not necessarily to individual physicians. According to this view, the reciprocal obligation is fulfilled as long as there are a sufficient number of physicians to care for the sick—specifically, here, to treat AIDS patient—seven if not every individual physician participates (Arras, 1988).

This latter interpretation is consistent with a voluntaristic system in which only willing physicians treat people with AIDS. The idea is appealing in the sense that AIDS patients might expect the most compassionate care from those freely choosing to offer treatment. But the downside is that it could place an unfair burden (in terms of risk, stress, etc.) on those willing to offer treatment (Arras, 1988).

The Dependent Patient.   A third justification is that physicians are linked to patients in ways that extend beyond an explicit or implicit contract. According to this view, there is something unique about the physician–patient relationship. It takes on a moral dimension especially in cases of a **dependent patient** in need of the professional's services.

This responsibility is even more compelling given the physical and emotional suffering endured by AIDS patients. Peter Conrad (1990) and others have written about the "marginal" place in which society often places AIDS patients and the severe stigma still attached to the disease. Although it is now clear that AIDS knows no sexual preference boundaries, the fact that the disease was first reported to be a disease of homosexuals (the "gay plague") created a lack of empathy, and sometimes even blatant hostility and disregard, for those with the virus.

Siegel and Krauss (1991) studied the major challenges of daily living experienced by

55 HIV-positive gay males. One of the three major adaptive challenges they reported was dealing with reactions to a stigmatizing illness. They talked openly in focused interviews of their feelings of shame and contamination based on the way others interacted with them. Even deciding who to tell of their infected status was a difficult decision, knowing that many would respond negatively. Those who speak of a special relationship between physician and "dependent" patient find no better example than that of a physician working with AIDS patients. Many physicians who care for HIV-infected individuals do find their work rewarding and stimulating. In one study, 60 percent of physician-respondents noted patient gratitude for their work; 57 percent mentioned the intellectual challenge of dealing with the disease and well-informed patients; and 30 percent identified a desire to serve the underserved (Epstein, Christie, and Frankel, 1993).

SUMMARY

Much can be learned about the dynamics of the physician–patient relationship by examining the manner in which the issues of truth-telling, confidentiality, and the obligation to treat AIDS patients are handled. Surveys consistently show that the vast majority of people want physicians unconditionally to tell the truth, but many physicians (though fewer than in the past) still use their discretion in deciding whether or not to tell the truth to individual patients.

Those who support unconditional truth-telling justify their position by stating that only truth-telling displays real respect for the patient; that it is necessary to keep promises; that lying would undermine the patient's trust in the physician; and that patients need to know the truth to be able to make decisions on an informed basis. Those who believe that physicians should use their discretion argue that it might be in the patient's best interest; that it is impossible to communicate the "full truth" to a medical layperson; and that many patients really do not want to know the truth about a serious illness.

While most medical codes emphasize the importance of protecting confidentiality, some justify breaking confidentiality in order to protect the patient or an innocent third party (such as in the case of Tatiana Tarasoff) or society in general. Others believe that confidentiality ought always to be maintained to protect the patient's autonomy, to legitimate secrets, to keep faith with a patient, and to encourage people who need help to feel free to seek it.

Research clearly shows that many physicians prefer not to treat AIDS patients. Although neither history nor medical codes offer a decisive position on the existence of a "duty to treat," many believe that physicians should not be compelled to offer care to AIDS patients for four reasons: (1) excessive risks, (2) questionable benefits of treatment, (3) obligations to other patients, and (4) obligations to self and family.

Those who believe there is a treatment obligation cite three reasons: (1) it is an inherent part of the nature of the profession, (2) it is part of a social contract between society and medicine, and (3) the "special" physician–patient relationship calls for physicians to offer care to dependent patients.

HEALTH ON THE INTERNET

You can research the latest ethical policies of the American Medical Association on issues covered in this chapter by accessing the Code of Medical Ethics at:

http://ama-assn.org/ama

Type Medical Ethics in the search box. Explore the site. What are the AMA's basic "Principles of Medical Ethics"? What are a physician's obligations with respect to the Hippocratic Oath? (Look through "Frequently Asked Questions.")

KEY CONCEPTS AND TERMS

benevolent deception
confidentiality
dependent patient
"duty to face danger" phrase
freedom from information

"free to choose" phrase
privacy
privileged communication
social contract
Tarasoff case

DISCUSSION CASES

CASE #1: *Scenario 1:* A 35-year-old female, unmarried and without children but with parents and three sisters in a neighboring state, is diagnosed as having cancer. By the time of diagnosis, the cancer has already spread throughout her body. It is too late to perform surgery, and her physician determines that neither chemotherapy nor radiation can be successful at this advanced stage. Patients diagnosed with cancer at this stage rarely live more than a year.

The physician knows that the patient has been working on her first novel for two years and that it has been the major interest in her life. The patient expects to have it completed in the next three or four months. The physician believes he can stall giving the correct diagnosis and prognosis, through deception and evasive answers, until the patient has completed her novel. He fears that providing the honest diagnosis at this point will so depress the patient that she will not be able to finish the book. The physician and patient have never discussed how a situation like this should be handled.

How would the physician–patient relationship be affected by a general expectation of unconditional truth-telling versus an expectation that physicians ought to use their discretion in revealing information to patients? How do these two expectations affect the physician's role in the encounter, and how do they affect the patient's role? In this case, do you believe the physician ought to provide this patient with the correct diagnosis and prognosis or attempt to deceive her until her novel is completed?

Scenario 2: Alter the preceding scenario in this manner: On the day before the patient is to

return to the office to hear the test results, her parents call the physician long distance. They explain that they are calling out of love and concern for their daughter and due to a fear that she has cancer or some other life-threatening disease. If that is the case, they plead for the physician not to reveal the diagnosis. Their understanding of their daughter leads them to believe that hearing the correct diagnosis will so traumatize her that she would quickly give up the will to live.

Should the physician be influenced by the wishes of the family and attempt to deceive the patient, or should he be sympathetic with the family but make it clear he must be honest with their daughter? What does his decision imply about the role of significant others in the care of patients?

Scenario 3: Same case as before, but omit the information in scenario 2. Add the following circumstance: On the day of her return visit, the patient initiates conversation with the physician. She expresses her fear that she has a life-threatening disease. If that is the case, she says, she would rather not know it. She states that she would rather avoid hard and fast reality, believing that would give her the best opportunity to complete her novel and carry on as normally as possible for as long as possible.

What does the physician do? Do patients have a right to make this request of physicians? If they do, ought physicians comply with the expressed wishes of the patients or explain that the physicians' responsibility is to convey as accurately as possible what has been learned?

CASE #2: The State Medical Board in your home state is considering a new regulation that would strictly forbid any physician to refuse to accept a patient or to refuse to continue seeing a patient (whom he or she is qualified to treat) solely on the basis that the patient is HIV-positive or has AIDS. Suspected violations of this policy would be investigated by the State Medical Board, and a hearing would be held. If convicted of violating this regulation, a physician would lose his or her medical license for six months for a first offense, one year for a second offense, and permanently for a third offense.

Knowing that you have taken a course in medical sociology and have a keen interest in this subject, the board has called you to testify about this proposed regulation. Would you testify in favor of or against this proposal? What is the rationale for your testimony?

REFERENCES

Allmark, Peter. 1995 "HIV and the Bounds of Confidentiality." *Journal of Advanced Nursing,* 21:158–163.

American Medical Association. 1992 *Code of Medical Ethics.* Chicago: Author.

Annas, George J. 1988 "Legal Risks and Responsibilities of Physicians in the AIDS Epidemic." *Hastings Center Report,* 18:S26–S32.

Arras, John D. 1988 "The Fragile Web of Responsibility: AIDS and the Duty to Treat." *Hastings Center Report,* 18:S10–S20.

Beauchamp, Tom L., and James F. Childress. 1983 *Principles of Biomedical Ethics.* New York: Oxford University Press.

Bok, Sissela. 1978 *Lying: Moral Choice in Public and Private Life.* New York: Pantheon Books.

———. 1991 "Lies to the Sick and Dying," pp. 74–81 in *Biomedical Ethics,* 3rd ed., Thomas A. Mappes and Jane S. Zembaty (eds.). New York: McGraw-Hill.

Brannigan, Michael C., and Judith A. Boss. 2001 *Healthcare Ethics in a Diverse Society.* Mountain View, CA: Mayfield Publishing Company.

Bredfeldt, Raymond C., Felicia M. Dardeau, Robert M. Wesley, Beth C. Vaughn-Wrobel, and Linda Markland. 1991 "AIDS: Family Physicians' Attitudes and Experiences." *The Journal of Family Practice,* 32:71–75.

Carter, Darren, John Lantos, and J. Hughes. 1996 "Reassessing Medical Students' Willingness to Treat HIV-Infected Patients." *Academic Medicine,* 71:1250–1252.

Centers for Disease Control and Prevention. 1988 "Update: Acquired Immunodeficiency Syndrome and Human Immunodeficiency Virus Infection Among Health Care Workers." *Medical and Mortality Weekly Review,* 37:229–239.

Clark, William P. 1976 "Dissenting Opinion in *Tarasoff v. Regents of the University of California,*" pp. 160–162 in *Taking Sides: Clashing Views on Controversial Bioethical Issues,* 2nd ed., Carol Levine (ed.). Guilford, CT: The Dushkin Publishing Group.

Conrad, Peter. 1990 "The Social Meaning of AIDS," pp. 285–294 in *The Sociology of Health and Illness: Critical Perspectives,* 3rd ed., Peter Conrad and Rochelle Kern (eds.). New York: St. Martin's Press.

DeVries, Raymond, and Janardan Subedi. 1998 *Bioethics and Society.* Upper Saddle River, NJ: Prentice Hall.

Dickinson, George E., and Robert E. Tournier. 1994 "A Decade Beyond Medical School: A Longitudinal Study of Physicians' Attitudes Toward Death and Terminally Ill Patients." *Social Science and Medicine,* 38:1397–1400.

Elwyn, Todd S., Michael D. Fetters, Daniel W. Gorenflo, and Tsukasa Tsuda. 1998 "Cancer Disclosure in Japan: Historical Comparisons, Current Practices." *Social Science and Medicine,* 46:1151–1163.

Emanuel, Ezekiel J. 1988 "Do Physicians Have an Obligation to Treat Patients with AIDS?" *The New England Journal of Medicine,* 318:1686–1690.

Epstein, Ronald M., Michael Christie, and Richard Frankel. 1993 "Primary Care of Patients with Human Immunodeficiency Virus Infection: The Physician's Perspective." *Archives of Family Medicine,* 2:159–167.

Etzioni, Amitai. 1999 "Medical Records: Enhancing Privacy, Preserving the Common Good." *Hastings Center Report,* 29:14–23.

Gerbert, Barbara, Bryan Maguire, Victor Badner, David Altman, and George Stone. 1988 "Why Fear Persists: Health Care Professionals and AIDS." *Journal of the American Medical Association,* 260:3481–3483.

Guiora, Alexander Z. 1980 "Freedom of Information Versus Freedom From Information," pp. 31–34 in *Ethics, Humanism, and Medicine,* Marc D. Basson (ed.). New York: Alan R. Liss.

Health and Public Policy Committee, American College of Physicians, and the Infectious Diseases

Society of America. 1986 "Position Paper: Acquired Immunodeficiency Syndrome." *Annals of Internal Medicine,* 104:575–581.

Jonsen, Albert R. 1990 "The Duty to Treat Patients with AIDS and HIV Infection," pp 155–168 in *AIDS and the Health Care System,* Lawrence O. Gostin (ed.). New Haven CT: Yale University Press.

Judicial Council of the American Medical Association. 1986 *Current Opinions-1986.* Chicago: American Medical Association.

Kelly, William D., and Stanley R. Friesen. 1950 "Do Cancer Patients Want to Be Told?" *Surgery,* 27:822–826.

Kim, Jerome H., and John R. Perfect. 1988 "To Help the Sick: An Historical and Ethical Essay Concerning the Refusal to Care for Patients with AIDS," *The American Journal of Medicine,* 84:135–137.

Link, Nathan R., Anat R. Feingold, Mitchell H. Charap, Katherine Freeman, and Steven P. Shelov. 1988 "Concerns of Medical and Pediatric House Officers About Acquiring AIDS from Their Patients." *American Journal of Public Health,* 78:455–459.

Lipkin, Mack. 1979 "On Lying to Patients." *Newsweek,* p. 13, June 4.

McDaniel, J. Stephen, Lisa M. Carlson, Nancy J. Thompson, and David W. Purcell. 1995 "A Survey of Knowledge and Attitudes About HIV and AIDS Among Medical Students." *Journal of American College Health,* 44:11–14.

Miyaji, Naoko. 1993 "The Power of Compassion: Truth-Telling Among American Doctors in the Care of Dying Patients." *Social Science and Medicine,* 36:249–264.

Novack, Dennis H., Barbara J. Deterling, Robert Arnold, Lachlan Forrow, Morissa Ladinsky, and John C. Pezzullo. 1989 "Physicians' Attitudes Toward Using Deception to Resolve Difficult Problems." *Journal of the American Medical Association,* 261:2980–2985.

Novack, Dennis H., Robin Plumer, Raymond L. Smith, Herbert Ochitill, Gary R. Morrow, and John M. Bennett. 1979 "Changes in Physicians' Attitudes Toward Telling the Cancer Patient." *Journal of the American Medical Association,* 241:897–900.

Oppenheimer, Kim, and Greg Swanson. 1990 "Duty to Warn: When Should Confidentiality Be Breached?" *The Journal of Family Practice,* 30:179–184.

President's Commission for the Study of Ethical Problems in Medicine and Biomedical and Behavioral Research. 1983 *The Ethical and Legal Problems in Medicine and Biomedical and Behavioral Research.* Washington, DC: Government Printing Office.

Roth, Michael D. 1981 "*Tarasoff.* Patient Privacy vs. Public Protection." *Maryland State Medical Journal,* 30:40–50.

Schwartzbaum, Judith A., John R. Wheat, and Robert W. Norton. 1990 "Physician Breach of Patient Confidentiality Among Individuals with HIV Infection: Patterns of Decision." *American Journal of Public Health,* 80:829–834.

Siegel, Karolynn, and Beatrice J. Krauss. 1991 "Living with HIV Infection: Adaptive Tasks of Seropositive Gay Men." *Journal of Health and Social Behavior,* 32:17–32.

Taylor, Kathryn M., Joan M. Eakin, Harvey A. Skinner, Merrijoy Kelner, and Marla Shapiro. 1990 "Physicians' Perception of Personal Risk of HIV Infection and AIDS Through Occupational Exposure." *Canadian Medical Association Journal,* 143: 493–500.

Tobriner, Mathew O. 1976 "Majority Opinion in *Tarasoff v. Regents of the University of California,*" pp. 154–159 in *Taking Sides: Clashing Views on Controversial Bioethical Issues,* 2nd ed., Carol Levine (ed.). Guilford, CT: The Dushkin Publishing Group.

Wasserstrom, Richard. 1986 "The Legal and Philosophical Foundations of the Right to Privacy," pp. 140–147 in *Biomedical Ethics,* 2nd ed., Thomas A. Mappes and Jane S. Zembaty (eds.). New York: McGraw-Hill.

Weeks, Jane C. 1998 "Relationship Between Cancer Patients' Predictions of Prognosis and Their Treatment Preferences." *Journal of the American Medical Association,* 279:1709–1714.

Yedidia, Michael J., Carolyn A. Berry, and Judith K. Barr. 1996 "Changes in Physicians' Attitudes Toward AIDS During Residency Training: A Longitudinal Study of Medical School Graduates." *Journal of Health and Social Behavior,* 37:179–191.

Yedidia, Michael J., Judith K. Barr, and Carolyn A. Berry. 1993 "Physicians' Attitudes Toward AIDS at Different Career Stages: A Comparison of Internists and Surgeons." *Journal of Health and Social Behavior,* 34:272–284.

Zuger, Abigail, and Steven H. Miles. 1987 "Physicians, AIDS, and Occupational Risk: Historical Traditions and Ethical Obligations." *Journal of the American Medical Association,* 258:1924–1928.

14

THE HEALTH CARE SYSTEM OF THE UNITED STATES

America's health care system is in a profound state of transition. Health care policy debates of the 1990s and 2000s have focused attention on both the strengths and the weaknesses of the health care system and on possible ways to address the weaknesses. Most analysts agree that the U.S. health care system, at its best, provides effective, high-technology care that is among the world's finest. At the same time, the health care system is generally recognized as being expensive, inefficient, and fragmented, and tens of millions of Americans lack the resources to obtain basic care. This chapter describes the continuing fiscal crisis of America's health care system and its inability to provide care for all in need. Reasons for the crisis are examined, and proposed solutions to the problems are analyzed.

HEALTH CARE EXPENDITURES

National Health Expenditures

The United States has the most expensive health care system in the world, and it is getting more expensive. During the last four decades, health care spending has grown more rapidly than any other sector of the economy. **National health expenditures (NHE)**—the total amount of spending for personal health care and for administration, construction, research, and other expenses not directly related to patient care—reached $1.553 trillion (over one thousand billion) in 2002—or more than 6 times the amount spent in 1980.

The 2002 figure accounts for about 14.9 percent of the gross domestic product (GDP)—the nation's total economic output (as depicted in Figure 14–1 and Table 14–1). The percentage of GDP spent on health care is much higher in the United States than in any other country—even those that provide universal health care coverage. On average, Americans spent $5,440 per person on health care in 2002—twice as much as people in any other country.

The annual rates of increase in NHE in the 1980s and early 1990s were among the highest ever—sometimes more than 10 percent per year. In the late 1990s, however, the rate of increase was about 4 to 6 percent per year—still higher

Figure 14–1   Percent of Gross Domestic Product Spent on Health

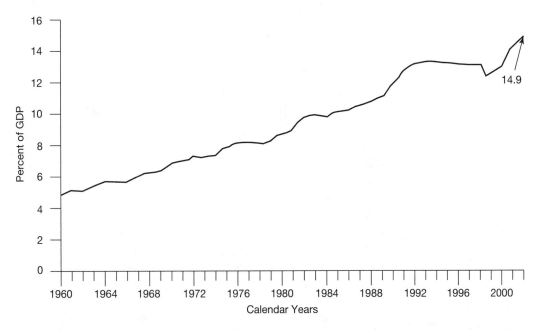

Source: Centers for Medicare and Medicaid Services. *Health Care Indicators.* Office of the Actuary, National Health Statistics Group, Baltimore, Maryland, 2004.

than the increase in the overall Consumer Price Index. By the early 2000s, however, annual increases were back in the 10 percent range. Many analysts believe that the smaller increases in the late 1990s were only a temporary response to changes in the system (changing to managed care created a one-time savings) and that large increases are again the pattern.

TABLE 14–1   National Health Expenditures

Year	Amount (in billions)	Percentage of Domestic Product	Amount Per Capita
1960	$ 26.9	5.1	$ 141
1970	73.2	7.1	341
1980	247.2	8.9	1,051
1990	699.5	12.2	2,689
2000	1,309.4	13.3	4,670
2002	1,553.0	14.9	5,440

Source: Centers for Medicare and Medicaid Services. *Health Care Indicators.* Office of the Actuary, Office of National Health Statistics, Baltimore, Maryland, 2004.

Who are the recipients of health care dollars? For many years, about 40 percent of all health care dollars spent in the United States went to hospitals, but this figure has been dropping, and in 2002, it was about 31 percent. About 20 percent of health care dollars goes to physicians. The lower half of Figure 14–2 identifies the percentage of health care dollars going to particular recipients in 2002.

Personal Health Expenditures

Personal health care expenditures (PHE) include all spending for such health services as hospital care; physician, dental and other professional medical services; home health care; nursing home care; and drugs and over-the-counter products purchased in retail outlets. In 2002, PHE amounted to $1.340 billion. What kinds of health care did these expenditures

Figure 14–2   National Health Expenditures, 2002

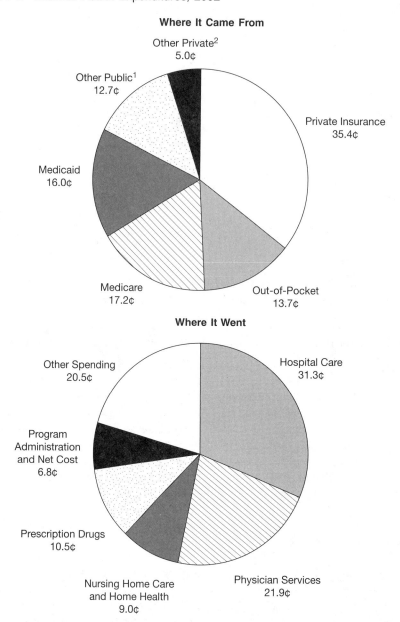

Where It Came From

Other Private[2]
5.0¢

Other Public[1]
12.7¢

Private Insurance
35.4¢

Medicaid
16.0¢

Medicare
17.2¢

Out-of-Pocket
13.7¢

Where It Went

Other Spending
20.5¢

Hospital Care
31.3¢

Program
Administration
and Net Cost
6.8¢

Prescription Drugs
10.5¢

Nursing Home Care
and Home Health
9.0¢

Physician Services
21.9¢

[1]Other Public includes programs such as workers' compensation, public health activity, Department of Defense, Department of Veterans Affairs, Indian Health Service, and State and local hospital and school health.

[2]Other Private includes industrial in-plant, privately funded construction, and nonpatient revenues, including philanthropy.

NOTE: Other Spending includes dentist services, other professional services, home health care, durable medical products, over-the-counter medicines and sundries, public health, research, and construction.

NOTE: Numbers shown do not add to 100.0 because of rounding.

Source: Centers for Medicare and Medicaid Services. *Health Care Indicators.* Office of the Actuary, National Health Statistics Group, Baltimore, Maryland, 2004.

purchase? The four largest items (listed by dollars spent) were:

1. *Hospital care* ($486.5 billion—36.3 percent of PHE). Hospitals remain the largest recipient of dollars, but their share of PHE has been declining for the last several years. Cost-containment efforts that accelerated in the 1990s have reduced admissions to hospitals and led to shorter lengths of hospital stay.
2. *Physician services* ($339.5 billion—25.3 percent of PHE). While expenditures for physician services continue to increase each year, the growth rate is now the slowest since the early 1960s. The lower growth rate is primarily due to more tightly controlled reimbursement levels used by the government and managed care organizations.
3. *Drugs and other medical nondurables* ($194.1 billion—14.5 percent of PHE). This category includes only those drugs and over-the-counter products purchased from retail outlets and excludes drugs dispensed in hospitals, nursing homes, and physicians' offices. Retail sales of prescription drugs account for nearly 65 percent of this category.

   Escalating drug prices in the last decade have pushed the affordability of medications beyond the reach of millions of Americans. For some heart conditions and chronic impairments, prescription medicines can cost upwards of several hundred dollars a month. Few lower- or middle-class families can easily, if at all, absorb such bills. Staff members in low-cost community health clinics often find themselves in the frustrating position of providing basic care but being unable to subsidize the cost of recommended medications.
4. *Nursing home care and home health care* ($139.3 billion—10.4 percent of PHE). While the growth rate for nursing home care dollars is decelerating, the increasing number of elderly persons and the high charges per day of care make this the fourth largest category of expenditures. The home health care

industry continues to expend—it now accounts for almost $40 billion per year.

The ability to pay for long-term care has become a significant societal problem. An increasing number of persons unable to live independently are moving in with adult children—a pattern that sometimes works nicely but often necessitates sizable family adjustments and feelings of guilt on the part of the dependent elders. Others are spending down—that is, spending life savings and giving up assets—in order to qualify for Medicaid assistance with nursing home bills. This pattern creates much resentment in those forced to do so and adds to the fiscal problems of Medicaid. Because the number of elderly persons will continue to expand, paying for long-term care is a problem that will become increasingly widespread.

FINANCING HEALTH CARE

Health care in the United States is financed by a complex mix of private purchasers (employers, individuals, and families) and public purchasers (the federal, state, and local governments) who pay health care providers directly for services and products or who channel payment through private or public health insurance (Levit et al., 2004).

From Private Sources

In 2002 over half (54.1 percent) of all health services were paid for by private sources. Most of these payments—and the single largest source of payments for health care—came from private health insurance companies, and most of the remainder was paid out-of-pocket by individual patients and their families (See Table 14–2). Over the last four decades, the relative contribution of private insurance has increased (from 1/5 of all payments in 1960 to more than 1/3 in 2002), whereas the relative contribution paid out-of-pocket has decreased (from 1/2 of all payments in 1960 to 1/7 in 2002).

TABLE 14–2   Source of Payments for Health Services, 2002

Item	Amount of Expenditures in Billions (%)
National health expenditures	$ 1,553.0
Paid by private sources	839.6 (54.1)
Private insurance	549.6 (35.4)
Out-of-pocket	212.5 (13.7)
Other	77.5 (5.0)
Paid by the government	713.4 (45.9)
Medicare	267.1 (17.2)
Medicaid	249.1 (16.0)
Other	197.2 (12.7)

Source: Centers for Medicare and Medicaid Services. *Health Care Indicators*. Office of the Actuary, Office of National Health Statistics, Baltimore, Maryland, 2004.

Payment for health insurance policies comes both from employers (who pay for all or part of a policy for employees and their families as a fringe benefit) and from individuals and families (who typically pay for part of the employer-provided policy or who purchase a policy directly from a private health insurance company).

Employers.   Health insurance policies are expensive regardless of who pays. In 2003, employers paid more than $9,000 per worker to provide the company's share of health insurance for the worker and covered dependents (and employees contributed more than $2,400). Businesses derive funds to pay for these policies largely by increasing the price of goods or services that they sell.

Rapid increases in insurance premiums in the last two decades have prodded many companies to revise the health insurance benefit provided to employees. Four changes have been especially dramatic. First, some employers (especially small businesses which are hardest hit by providing insurance) have discontinued employee coverage. Only about three in five workers today is covered by an employer-provided plan. Second, most employers have increased the percentage of the health insurance plan that must be paid by employees. Whereas many companies formerly paid 100 percent of costs, the average today

has dropped to 73 percent. In addition, costs for coverage for dependents (many of whom had been largely subsidized) have been decreased. Third, employers have reduced the types and amount of health care covered by the policy. Fourth, policies have increased the deductible, increased the coinsurance, and increased the copayment for those covered. All of these changes have the same effect: employees and dependents pay more out-of-pocket for health care. The announcement of these greater costs often has been met with anger and feelings of betrayal (and not infrequently, labor strikes) by employees. The upper half of Figure 14–2 identifies the source of health care dollars in the United States in 2002.

Individuals and Families.   The changes in the provision of employer-provided health insurance mean that individuals and families pay for health care in a variety of ways: (1) by paying a portion of the cost of a health insurance policy that is largely paid for by the employer or by paying the entire cost if the employer does not provide insurance coverage; (2) paying out-of-pocket health care expenses not covered by an insurance policy (deductibles, coinsurance, copayments, and for uncovered services); and (3) through various taxes such as the Medicare tax (employees have 1.45 percent of salary or wages deducted to subsidize Medicare; employers match this amount).

From the Government

Over the last 40 years, one of the most important changes in the way that we pay for health care is a shift from a reliance on private sources to increased government funding. From 1960 to 2002, the percentage of health care financing that comes from the government increased from 24.9 percent to 45.9 percent. This increase is largely attributable to the implementation of the Medicare and Medicaid programs in 1966 (both are described later in this chapter) and to periodic expansions in them in the intervening years (e.g., expanding coverage to the disabled population in 1972).

The Health Insurance System

Private Health Insurance.   There are over 1,500 **private (commercial) health insurance companies** in the United States. Some of these companies offer only health insurance while others also offer life, homeowners, renters, and automobile insurance. These are profit-making companies whose intention is to set premiums at a level that will allow them to pay out all claims; pay for all administrative, salary, and overhead expenses; and have money left over for profit for investors. Health insurance policies are sold to individuals, families, and groups (usually businesses). It is often said that no two health insurance policies are exactly alike—they cover whatever the buyer negotiates. They may include basic health benefits, major medical benefits (for very large bills), income replacement during disability, and benefits for dental care, eye care, drugs, and so forth. In addition to the basic premium, policies usually have a *deductible* provision (the policy owner pays a set amount of money before the insurance kicks in) and *co-insurance* provision (the policy owner pays a set percentage of all costs beyond the deductible).

Through much of the twentieth century, the health insurance field was dominated by Blue Cross-Blue Shield (BC-BS). BC-BS was established in 1929 to be a nonprofit health insurance company. In exchange for its nonprofit status (and exemption from paying taxes), the BC-BS plans offered comprehensive policies to a wide range of individuals at prices often below commercial companies. However, in the 1990s, the "Blues" determined that their nonprofit status did not serve them well in the changed health care system, and most plans around the country are now for-profit.

Increasingly today, payments to provide coverage for health care services are being channeled through managed care organizations (MCOs) such as health maintenance organizations and preferred provider organizations. These organizations combine the traditional insurance function of private insurance companies with a delivery system of health care providers. This very significant development is described in detail later in this chapter and in the next chapter.

Government-Sponsored Health Insurance. In many respects, the public sector serves as the insurer of last resort. In health care as in other areas, public programs often are created to serve those whose needs are not being met by the private sector. Among the many health programs that are today supported by public dollars are those for the members of the armed forces, veterans, mothers and children, Native Americans, schoolchildren, and the disabled. However, Medicare (the federal government's health insurance program for the elderly) and Medicaid (a federal-state-local health insurance program for the poor) represent the primary vehicles through which governments are involved in the health care sector.

Medicare is a federal insurance program created by Title XVIII of the Social Security Act of 1965. It was originally designed to protect people 65 years of age and older from the rising costs of health care. In 1972, permanently disabled workers, their dependents, and people with end-stage renal disease were added to the program.

There are two parts to the program: The hospital insurance program (HI or Part A) covers inpatient hospital services, posthospital skilled nursing services, home health care services, and hospice care; the supplementary medical insurance program (SMI or Part B) covers physician services, outpatient hospital services, and therapy. All persons 65 years of age and older can be eligible for Part A simply by enrolling, although there are deductible and co-insurance provisions. A premium must be paid for participation in Part B, which also includes a deductible and co-insurance. Medicare is financed by a combination of general tax revenues and payroll taxes levied on employers and employees in addition to the enrollee payments.

Historically, Medicare has not contained any prescription drug benefit. The consequence has been that many seniors (perhaps as many as one-fourth of those age 65 and older) have not been able to purchase needed medications. The extent of the unnecessary suffering and early death expanded in the last decade with the rapidly escalating cost of prescriptive medicine. In 2003 Congress added a hotly debated and very narrowly passed prescription drug benefit to Medicare. Using a complex formula, enrollees in the drug benefit have a deductible ($250), a monthly premium ($35), a copayment (25 percent up to $2,250); pay all costs between $2,250 and $3,600; and then pay a different, smaller copayment as the Medicare primarily foots the bill. Interestingly, the opponents of the bill were primarily those who felt the bill did not go far enough, did nothing to control drug price increases and did nothing to prevent employers from dropping retired workers from their plan. The bill is so widely regarded as being problematic that even most Medicare enrollees view it as a bad law. In 2002, Medicare covered 40.5 million people (about 14 percent of the U.S. population) at a cost of more than $259 billion. Medicare alone accounts for almost one-fifth of all health dollars spent in the United States.

Medicaid is a jointly funded federal-state-local program designed to make health care more available to the poor. Eligibility requirements for Medicaid and program benefits vary (sometimes greatly) from state to state, even though the federal government requires that people receiving Supplementary Security Income (SSI) and families qualifying for Aid to Families with Dependent Children (AFDC) as well as pregnant women, children under age 6, Medicare enrollees, and recipients of foster care and adoption assistance who do not qualify for SSI or AFDC cash benefits be covered by the program.

Federal and state funds paid through Medicaid for personal health care amounted to more than $232 billion for 41.4 million recipients (about 14 percent of the U.S. population) in 2002. Persons who are elderly, blind, and disabled accounted for nearly three-fourths of the funds, even though they represent less than one-third of recipients. On the other hand, more than two-thirds of Medicaid recipients were members of a family receiving public assistance, but they used only one-fourth of program benefits. More than 14 percent of all health dollars spent in the United States come from Medicaid.

The Medicare and Medicaid programs are examples of "entitlement" programs. This means that people receive benefits automatically when they qualify for the programs (in the case of Medicare-Part B, qualifying includes payment of a premium). The number of people covered is determined primarily by the number of people 65 years of age and older for Medicare and by the number of people below a designated income/assets line for Medicaid. The government thus has little control over the number of participants and can restrain the costs of the programs only by tightening eligibility requirements (which are already very tight) or by withdrawing benefits (from already near-minimal or less-than-minimal coverage in most states), or reducing already meager reimbursements to health care providers (which angers them and has led many to decline to see enrollees). As the population ages and as more and more people fall into financial straits, more people have qualified for the programs and their costs have skyrocketed.

Both Medicare and Medicaid are in serious financial difficulty. Without significant revision, the trust fund that contains money for Medicare Part A is predicted to go bankrupt within the next several years. Most states are having a difficult time balancing their budgets due, in part, to their Medicaid expenditures. This cost squeeze notwithstanding, both Medicare and Medicaid leave huge gaps in covered services. By 2000, elderly Americans spent about one-fifth of their disposable income on health care, and almost half of the income of the poor elderly not also covered by Medicaid went for health care. With skyrocketing costs for nursing homes and drugs, two items particularly relevant to seniors, their out-of-pocket expenses will continue to increase rapidly. An additional look at Medicaid's problems is provided in the box, "Medicaid: Problems on All Sides."

AMERICA'S UNINSURED POPULATION

The public sector programs are not an effective safety net for people who do not have private health insurance. By 2004, on any given day, an estimated 45 million Americans (one-quarter of them under the age of 18) did not have any

IN THE FIELD

MEDICAID: PROBLEMS ON ALL SIDES

Medicaid is an expensive program. In 2002, $232 billion of federal and state monies were channeled through Medicaid to assist the poor in paying for medical care. The federal government and most state governments feel besieged by the difficult-to-restrain costs. Does Medicaid do any good? Of course. Many low-income persons across the country receive health care that they would have gone without were it not for Medicaid. Health outcomes for Medicaid enrollees are almost the same as for those with private insurance.

But Medicaid has problems beyond its very high price tag. Among its serious problems are that it does not cover many of the country's poor, and it provides inadequate reimbursement for providers.

More than half of all persons under age 65 who are below the poverty level in the United States are not covered by Medicaid. How can this happen? Some states, especially those in the deep South, have enacted such stringent requirements to qualify for Medicaid that many families below the poverty level do not qualify.

Recent rule changes help somewhat: Children under age 6 with income up to 133 percent of the poverty line and children age 6 to 18 up to 100 percent of the poverty line must now be covered. But millions of low-income people remain uncovered.

Is Medicaid such a spendthrift because it is overcompensating providers? No. There are constant complaints that Medicare inadequately reimburses physicians, and Medicaid reimbursement is less than three-fourths that of Medicare. Almost every state in the country now has some problem (and some states have major problems) with physicians refusing to see Medicaid patients because reimbursement is inadequate. Average reimbursement for pediatricians, family practice physicians, and general practitioners is routinely less than two-thirds of prevailing market rates. The sad irony created is that even persons with Medicaid can have a difficult time seeing a physician (Hoffman, Klees, and Curtis, 2000).

---

private or public health insurance coverage. During the two-year period of 2002–2003, more than 80 million Americans had no health insurance at some time and about two-thirds of these individuals lacked insurance for at least six months. In addition, millions more Americans are *underinsured*—they have an insurance policy that contains major loopholes (important services that are not covered) or requires large out-of-pocket payments for services or both.

Contrary to a popular stereotype, more than half of the uninsured are in families with a full-time worker, and an additional 30 percent are in families with a part-time worker (States Health Access Data Assistance Center, 2004). One study based on a national survey found that the working poor are only one-third as likely as the nonpoor to receive health insurance from their employer, and they are more than five times as

likely not to have any health insurance whatsoever (only 10.2 percent were receiving public health insurance) (Seccombe and Amey, 1995). Typically, these people work for small companies that do not provide health insurance benefits for employees. An increasing number work for employers who offer a partially subsidized health insurance option to employees, but they are unable to afford the employee share. Many of the uninsured have tried to secure health insurance coverage but have been turned away due to preexisting medical conditions such as heart problems, diabetes, and other chronic illnesses (even hay fever, for example).

Research indicates that the uninsured are less likely to have a regular source of care; have fewer physician visits per year (especially by the chronically ill or for preventive care); are less likely to have a hospital stay; if hospitalized, average a shorter stay; and receive fewer procedures in the hospital (even after controlling for condition and need)—especially very costly procedures (Ayanian et al., 2000). Analyzing discharge abstracts for almost 600,000 patients hospitalized in 1987, Hadley, Steinberg, and Feder (1991) found that the uninsured had, at the time of admission, a 44 to 124 percent higher risk of in-hospital mortality and, after controlling for this difference, a 1.2 to 3.2 times greater chance of dying in the hospital. The uninsured were less likely to receive several high-cost, high-discretion procedures. See the box, "The Failure of Health Care."

This difference in services even appears at the beginning of life. A study of almost 30,000 newborns discovered that sick newborns without insurance coverage received fewer inpatient services than comparable newborns with insurance—even after controlling for medical need (Braverman et al., 1991).

Are there any safety valves for the uninsured? Yes, but only in limited cases. Although they receive little recognition for it, many physicians do treat some patients who lack the financial means to pay for care. In 1994, two-thirds of physicians provided some amount of care (an average of 7-plus hours per week) to patients without charge or at reduced fees; however, one-third of physicians provided no "charity care" (Moore, 1995). Public health departments offer care on a sliding scale and free health clinics (described in Chapter 15) do provide care at no or minimal charge to those unable to pay for private care. Most hospitals accept a certain percentage of nonpaying patients each year. But these resources fall far short of meeting the need.

Moreover, it has become clear that one's risk of a health care catastrophe does not end even when one is insured. In 1992, the U.S. Supreme Court allowed to stand a lower court ruling that allows employers to reduce benefits for employees who develop any illness with large medical costs. The case was brought on behalf of a man whose Houston employer reduced AIDS coverage in the company health insurance policy from $1 million to $5,000 after learning that he had the disease. The company argued that it would not be able to afford health insurance for any of its employees if its insuring company

---

IN THE FIELD

THE FAILURE OF HEALTH CARE

Have you ever looked into the eyes of a child after telling his desperately ill mother that you couldn't help her? I have. It was the worst experience of my life, and it's made me feel that I am part of a health care system so fundamentally flawed and unfair that we as Americans should be ashamed.

We should be ashamed that in a country of unmatched wealth and prosperity we simply allow people to suffer and die if they don't have the money to pay for our vast array of medical technologies and services.

We should be ashamed that, with everything we have to offer, people who work hard to support their families frequently find that there is nothing for them when they are sick. Why? Because they can't afford health insurance.

That is why my patient, a 36-year old mother of five whose husband earns about $30,000 a year, may not live to see 37.

Susan Garrett, a nurse in a community health center in Maryland, opened a guest editorial in *The Washington Post* (which was reproduced in the *Roanoke Times,* 2000) with those comments while reflecting on her patient. The young woman had noticed a swelling on her neck, but as the uninsured often do, failed to get prompt medical attention. By the time that she was evaluated, the swelling was very large . . . and the cancer very advanced. The only hope for cure was a bone marrow transplant. At $100,000, a transplant was obviously unaffordable for the patient and her family.

IN THE FIELD

PUBLIC ATTITUDES ABOUT THE UNINSURED

To what extent do Americans understand the problem of the uninsured? In a 1999 survey, just half of Americans correctly stated that the number of people without health insurance was increasing, and only 34 percent realized that the uninsured could not get the care that they need.

Despite the widespread lack of knowledge about the uninsured, a substantial percentage of Americans are sufficiently concerned to desire significant government action. When asked what the government should do about the uninsured, 49 percent preferred a major government effort, 32 percent preferred a more limited effort, and 14 percent were satisfied with the status quo. What was the most common reason for opposing a major effort? Opposition to expected tax increases that would be necessary to provide needed care (Blendon, Young, and DesRoches, 1999).

---

raised premiums because of one employee with AIDS. Although many health insurance policies exclude or limit coverage for specified conditions, the fact that the exclusion happened *retroactively* in this case raised a new issue. After paying premiums for years, a person may be left with few or no benefits at the very time they are needed. See the accompanying box, "Public Attitudes About the Uninsured."

EXPLAINING THE HIGH COST OF HEALTH CARE

One of the most important questions asked of the health care system in the United States is how the country manages to spend more money and a higher percentage of its GDP than any other modern country while being the only modern country that fails to provide universal health care coverage. Traditionally, the United States has relied on a **market-driven health care** strategy to restrain costs. The philosophy underlying this strategy is that health care providers, who compete with each other for private and public health care dollars, are motivated to offer the best possible service at the lowest possible price. Proponents contend that this competitive basis has stimulated the drive for the development of superior medical schools, new medical technologies, and the highest quality of health care possible.

Critics charge, however, that health care does not have the characteristics of a competitive market in at least three ways. First, the traditional lack of cost controls employed by large payers of health care—the government and private insurers—has historically enabled providers to charge whatever they desire.

Second, the law of supply and demand works ineffectively in health care. Since most people are covered by health insurance and pay little out-of-pocket, they have little incentive to be cost-conscious—they buy at whatever price is charged. Some studies have even found that hospital charges are higher in areas where there is more competition. Two Cal-Berkeley health economists examined data from 5,732 hospitals and discovered that costs per admission were 26 percent higher in hospitals that had more than nine competitors within a 15-mile radius ("Wasted Health Care Dollars," 1992).

Third, many patients simply depend upon the advice of their physicians to determine what to buy; they do not independently decide on what medical services they need. It is estimated that 70 percent of all expenditures for personal health care are the result of physicians' decisions and advice. Indeed, few patients even know the price of tests and procedures about to be performed upon them.

The high cost of health care can also be traced to several complex, interrelated aspects of the health care system. Three of these key factors are discussed elsewhere in this text: the effects of sicker and older patients (Chapter 3 and Chapter 4), the effects of having too many specialists and not enough primary care physicians (Chapter 8), and the effects of new health care technologies (Chapter 16). The next section of this chapter focuses on two major systemic explanations for the high cost of health care: (1) high administrative costs, and (2) incentives within the system, including provider reimbursement policies, the medical-industrial complex, and the provision of unnecessary services.

High Administrative Costs

Economist Robert J. Samuelson (1989) contends that health care systems are governed by one or more of three main goals: (1) to provide good care regardless of ability to pay; (2) to allow free choice (patients of physicians, physicians of patients, both of technology); and (3) to keep costs down. However, he contends that no health care system can simultaneously accomplish all three. If a system provides high-quality care to all persons and protects free choice, it cannot control costs. If a system wishes to protect free choice and control costs, it cannot provide universal health care coverage. And if a system provides high-quality care to all persons and wishes to keep costs down, it cannot maintain freedom of choice.

Most modern countries have opted for goals one and three. They provide universal coverage for health care services and work to control costs but have done so by restricting some areas of free choice (e.g., slower incorporation of new technologies or price controls on physician fees). The U.S. system traditionally has prioritized the second goal: considerable patient and provider autonomy and has failed to offer universal coverage or control costs. This has led to an inefficient and fragmented health care system.

> Chaotic? You can't describe our system, let alone control it. It's not socialized medicine. It's not private medicine. We want the security of welfare without the invasiveness of government control. Our health care system is a jumble of groups (doctors, hospitals, government agencies, health maintenance organizations, private insurers) working

under a bewildering array of regulations and pursuing different objectives. No one is in charge. Power is fragmented. (Samuelson, 1989:52)

How much does this chaotic system cost in unnecessary administrative expenditures? Woolhandler, Himmelstein, and Lewontin (1993) examined 1990 fiscal expenses for 6,400 U.S. hospitals. They determined that hospital administrative costs in the United States averaged 24.8 percent. This percentage is more than double the hospital administrative costs in Canada (generally reported at about 9 to 11 percent). Although this comparison may be influenced by several variables, they concluded that if the United States trimmed its hospital bureaucracy to the Canadian level, approximately $50 billion annually could be saved (today, the figure would be more than $200 billion annually). In addition, a similar amount could be saved on overhead expenses of insurance companies and physicians' paperwork. (The AMA estimates that physicians spend an average of 17 hours per week on administrative duties—completing patient charts, ordering tests, justifying procedures to insurers, and seeking reimbursement.)

System Incentives

Protecting the autonomy of physicians to select patients, set fees, choose a practice setting and location, make clinical decisions including the use of technology, protecting patient choice of physician, initial contact within the system, and use of certain technologies (e.g., life-sustaining equipment) has been an important, if not the most important, objective of the U.S. health care system. It is an objective consistent with Americans' belief in individualism and individual rights and in the appropriate discretionary powers of professions. Unfortunately, this objective helped to produce a health care system that historically has included multiple incentives to overuse services. Overuse occurred through several mechanisms and contributed to the high cost of America's health care.

Provider Reimbursement Policies. Until recent years, the reimbursement of health care providers was straightforward. Physicians, hospitals, and other providers could freely order and use whatever tests and procedures they desired and they were then reimbursed for whatever they charged. In earlier times, when patients paid out-of-pocket for health care, many physicians were sensitive to the cost of care being provided—they did not want to gouge patients, and they did not want to drive them to another provider. The establishment of private and public third-party payers (for example, health insurance companies and the government) created large, impersonal, amorphous funding agents. Physicians could order as many tests and procedures as they wished—and charge what they desired for them—knowing that the bill would be paid and that the patient would be obligated to pay little or nothing.

This was a system almost devoid of cost controls. A key support for this system occurred with the passage of Medicare in 1965 and the decision to reimburse physicians on the basis of their "usual and customary fees" for any service. Other insurers adopted this same practice so physicians were largely able to set whatever fees they desired for services rendered. Not surprisingly, physicians' fees began a quick upward spiral. Hospitals also benefitted from Medicare's reimbursement procedures. In addition to paying a daily room charge and fees for other tests, supplies, and procedures, Medicare allowed hospitals to build in the cost of capital improvements. This provision facilitated significant and expensive growth in health care facilities.

Shortly after the passage of Medicare and Medicaid, the costs of American health care began to escalate. Few analysts charge that the programs fail to provide needed assistance for the elderly and those with low incomes, but many believe the policies and procedures of the programs have contributed significantly to runaway health care costs.

The Medical-Industrial Complex. In 1980, Arnold Relman, then editor of the *New England Journal of Medicine,* used the term **medical-industrial complex** to describe a huge and rapidly growing industry that supplied health care services for profit. It included "proprietary hospitals and nursing homes, diagnostic laboratories, home care and emergency room services, renal dialysis units, and a wide variety of other medical care services that had formerly been provided largely by public or private not-for-profit community based institutions or by private physicians in their offices" (Relman, 1991:854).

An example of these services is rehabilitative care. In *The Disability Business: Rehabilitation in America* (1992), Gary Albrecht describes how the provision of rehabilitative products and services has been transformed into an expanding profit-making industry that at times is directed more by the needs of health care professionals, business managers, and shareholders than the needs of those with disabilities. Profits, cash flow management, and domain control explain as much about rehabilitation services as medical need and technological advances (Albrecht, 1992:137).

By the beginning of the 1980s, the medical-industrial complex accounted for between 17 and 19 percent of health care expenditures. What was the problem? Relman expressed concern that the marketing and advertising techniques of the companies and their drive for profit would encourage unnecessary use, inappropriate use, and overuse of health care resources that would push up health care costs; that expensive technologies and procedures would be preferred to less costly efforts; that attention would become riveted on patients able to pay, leaving the poor and uninsured to an overburdened not-for-profit sector; and that physicians' allegiance to patients could be usurped by their involvement in health-related profit-making ventures (Relman, 1980).

Did these problems actually develop during the 1980s and 1990s? Relman says yes and that they included a new **medical entrepreneuralism**, which involved physicians referring patients to diagnostic laboratory facilities or for-profit ambulatory surgery facilities in which the physicians had a financial interest, and deals with pharmaceutical companies or health care suppliers that enable physicians to make money by using particular drugs or supplies (Relman, 1991).

A major controversy now exists over **self-referral**—physicians referring patients to other health care facilities in which they have a financial interest—a practice that became very common in the 1980s and early 1990s. A 1991 Florida study discovered that 40 percent of the physicians in Florida had investments in medical businesses to which they could refer patients. At that time, 40 percent of physical therapy centers, 60 percent of clinical labs, 80 percent of radiation therapy centers, and 93 percent of diagnostic imaging centers in Florida were owned by physicians. The physician-owned facilities did more procedures per patient and charged higher fees. An estimated $500 million per year was being added to Florida's health care costs by overutilization and higher charges at these facilities (Mason, 1992). Eventually, the Florida legislature halted self-referrals.

Other studies affirm this pattern. Hillman and colleagues (1990) studied the use of diagnostic imaging tests among primary physicians who did the tests in their own office (with financial benefit) and primary physicians who referred to radiologists (with no financial benefit). They analyzed more than 65,000 insurance claims for patients with acute upper respiratory symptoms, pregnancy, low back pain, and difficulty in urinating (for men). For all four conditions, self-referring physicians obtained 4 to 4.5 times more imaging examinations than the radiologist-referring physicians, and the charges were higher per exam for those self-referring.

Defenders of self-referring practices counter that these studies do not prove that the higher use of services is inappropriate. They argue that having physician-owned facilities increases the likelihood of needed services being available in communities and that the ease of self-referring may enable physicians to get more appropriate tests performed for their patients. Nevertheless, the AMA has declared self-referring to be unethical and has encouraged physicians to abstain from it, and Congress has established a limited ban on the referral of Medicare and Medicaid patients to labs and facilities in which the referring physician has a financial stake.

Various practices of *pharmaceutical companies* are also under attack as part of the medical-industrial complex. In recent years, drug making has been the most profitable industry in the United States (an average annual return on investments of 25 percent in the last decade). Most drugs cost significantly more in the United States than in other countries. While overall health care costs have been growing much faster than the rate of inflation, drug costs have been growing faster than overall health care costs.

The marketing practices of pharmaceutical companies have been the subject of much criticism. Part of the reason that drugs cost so much is that drug makers spend billions of dollars each year on advertising in attempts to persuade physicians to use their products rather than those of a competitor. By 2000, pharmaceutical companies were spending more than $10 billion annually on advertising and marketing. Part of this sum goes to provide physicians with all-expenses-paid trips ("educational symposia") to plush resorts for self and spouse (sometimes an honorarium is thrown in) and financial incentives to physicians who prescribe specified levels of certain drugs. More than one-third of the price of the average prescription goes to pay for marketing, advertising, and drug-manufacturer profits, while 15 percent goes toward research and development.

The pharmaceutical industry responds that its responsibility is to inform the medical community and the general public about developments in drugs. A high advertising budget and extensive marketing techniques have been successful in capturing physicians' attention. In addition, the industry contends that significant price increases are justified by overall price inflation in society and because of the heavy investment necessary in drug research. Those in the drug industry strongly defend their practices.

Nevertheless, criticism of the pharmaceutical industry ("Big Pharma") is at an extremely high level. Reports that pharmaceutical companies return more money to investors each year as profit than they spend on research and development has undermined the rationale for the very high costs of drugs. In recent years some of the largest companies have paid fines for such crimes as marketing drugs for diseases for which they were not approved, for overcharging the Medicaid program, and for inducing physicians to bill the government for some drugs that the company gave them for free (fraud). The companies spend millions in fees to lobby the government for a variety of protections (e.g., opposing importation of drugs from other countries).

Provision of Unnecessary Services.   By the early 1980s, compelling evidence had been uncovered that many health care services being provided in the United States were unnecessary. Academic researchers and policy analysts had determined that as many as one-sixth to one-fifth of all operations were unnecessary, that the annual cost for these unnecessary operations was in the billions of dollars, and that as many as 12,000 patients per year died in the course of an unnecessary procedure.

The most intensive study of surgical necessity was conducted by the Rand Corporation, a think tank in Santa Monica, California. Based on input from medical experts, they developed a list of indicators of the need for four specific procedures. Then they applied this list to the records of 5,000 recent Medicare patients. They found that 65 percent of carotid endarterectomies (removal of blockages from one or both arteries carrying blood to the brain) were unnecessary—so were 17 percent of coronary angiographies (an X-ray technique in which dye is injected into the coronary arteries to diagnose blockages), 17 percent of upper gastrointestinal tract endoscopies (examining the digestive organs with a fiberoptic tube), and 14 percent of coronary bypass surgeries (helping or replacing blocked arteries by adding or rerouting other blood vessels). Other studies consistently reported high rates of unnecessary surgery for other procedures such as Caesarean birth, hysterectomy, laminectomy, and tonsillectomy.

COST CONTAINMENT: DRGs, RATIONING, AND MANAGED CARE

For the last 20 years, both experts and laypersons have identified the two most serious weaknesses of the United States health care system as being: (1) the inadequate access that many persons have

to the system and (2) the very high cost of health care. During most of this time, considerably more attention has been directed to solving the cost problem than the access problem. Some argue that every major change initiated in the U.S. health care system in the last two decades has been motivated by a desire to contain costs—that is, to reduce the rate of increase in health care costs.

Several specific cost-containment strategies have been discussed, and several have been implemented. These include:

1. *Programs that control the amount that health care providers are reimbursed for services rendered.* The implementation of Medicare cost reimbursement strategies is an example.
2. *Programs that control (and attempt to limit) the utilization of health care services.* The initiation in Oregon of explicit rationing of services for Medicaid enrollees and the hotly debated idea of limiting services to older persons are examples.
3. *Programs and organizations that control both utilization of services and reimbursement for health care providers.* The "managed care revolution"—whether through traditional insurance plans or with managed care organizations such as HMOs and PPOs—has been the dominant event in American health care in the last two decades.

Each of these strategies is briefly described below. Managed care is then described more thoroughly in Chapter 15.

Controlling Reimbursement: Medicare's Diagnostic-Related Groups

Background.   In 1983, Congress passed legislation which established a prospective payment system by which the federal government pays for the hospital care of Medicare beneficiaries. This system relies on **diagnostic-related groups (DRGs)**: a set of 467 categories intended to include all of the ailments or conditions that might be experienced by a Medicare enrollee. Per case payments are prospectively determined for each DRG by criteria related to initial diagnosis, surgical versus medical treatment, complications, and patient's age. Hospitals receive the predetermined amount for each DRG-type patient, regardless of actual costs associated with the patient's treatment. If actual costs are less than the allotted amount, the hospital keeps the difference. If the cost exceeds the allotment, the hospital must absorb the loss. Thus, if the reimbursement level for a particular category is $8,000 and the hospital treats that patient for $6,500, the hospital keeps the $1,500 difference. However, if that patient's care costs $10,000, then the hospital is responsible for the extra $2,000, and it will need to find some other way of recovering that money.

DRGs were designed to give hospitals a financial incentive to keep costs per patient episode down as much as possible. Hospitals are encouraged to become DRG-efficient, that is, to manage patient care in such a way that costs do not exceed the reimbursement level. Many hospitals and physicians view DRGs as an infringement on their autonomy and have reacted to them with considerable disdain and anger.

Actual Effects of the DRG System.   Have DRGs actually changed the hospital experience of patients covered by Medicare? Has money been saved? Based on almost two decades of experience, two key effects of DRGs have been documented:

First, as predicted, the average length of stay in the hospital has substantially declined (thus controlling costs). According to one study, the number of in-patient days for Medicare patients decreased by more than 40 percent between 1982 and 1988 (a couple of days per person per episode).

Second, episodes of hospital care per person have increased. Many critics charge that patients are now being exited from hospitals too early and at a time when they could still easily benefit from continued inpatient care. A possible consequence is that patients who have not fully recovered have relapses or repeated bouts of the same problem that lead to return episodes of care.

The basic approach of the DRG system is now being extended. Most state Medicaid programs have now adopted similar prospective payment financing mechanisms (much of this

movement occurred shortly after the implementation of DRGs), and since 1992, Medicare's prospective payment mechanism has covered reimbursement for physicians as well as hospitals.

Rationing

The dramatic increases in health care costs in the last two decades have increased recognition that it is not possible to provide every potentially helpful health care service to every person who could benefit from it. This has inspired discussion of various rationing plans.

Rationing has two distinct meanings. First, market-based economies ration implicitly by denying goods and services to people who cannot afford them. Health care, like other marketable commodities is, in this sense, rationed to the poor and the medically indigent. Second, rationing can occur explicitly through a specific program to deny commodities to people who have adequate resources to purchase them. The rationing of sugar and gasoline during World War II is an example. Many people in the United States are now asking whether health care ought to be rationed in the latter rather than the former sense, by offering the same basic level of services to everyone (regardless of their ability to pay), even though that might mean discontinuing to provide certain services or increasing waiting time to access services (Ubel and Goold, 1998).

However, Daniel Callahan of The Hastings Center has argued that Americans subscribe to many deeply held and cherished values that make unlikely any explicit form of rationing of health care services. He states that we "prize autonomy and freedom of choice" for patients, providers, and health care administrators, which leads to opposition to governmental control and planning; we "cherish the idea of limitless medical progress," which leads to a belief that every disease should be conquered; and we "long for quality in medicine and health care," which leads to an insistence on ever-improving technological innovations being available promptly when we need them (Callahan, 1990:1811).

In this section of the chapter, two explicit rationing proposals that have received the most attention in the United States (Oregon's rationing plan for Medicaid and a policy of rationing services by age) are examined.

Oregon's Rationing Plan.   The most aggressive rationing proposal to date is Oregon's plan for Medicaid recipients. When the plan was devised in the late 1980s, the goal was to provide basic health care benefits for the 120,000 people below the poverty threshold who were not then covered (more than 200,000 were already covered), while controlling health expenditures by limiting the number of covered services. The proposal was prompted by the realization that some of Oregon's poor were being denied access to basic services whereas others had access to very expensive, sometimes unproven procedures.

Through dozens of community meetings held throughout the state, a prioritized list of services was established based on cost of treatment, length of benefit, and quality of well-being after treatment. Conditions for which treatment can best restore health and quality of life per dollar of investment, such as bacterial pneumonia, tuberculosis, and appendicitis, are given high priority, whereas conditions that offer small improvement per dollar spent, such as treating an extremely low birth weight newborn, aggressive treatment of terminal cancer, infertility therapy, and treatment of the common cold are at the bottom of the list (Jecker, 1992). Proponents argue that this process is based on community values, guarantees a basic package of health services for all Medicaid recipients, and is the most efficient and humane way of spending limited health care dollars.

Although the plan is considered to be a step toward curbing the escalation of health care costs, it has been criticized because it applies to only one segment of the population—the poor. It allows for a lower standard of care for Medicaid patients than for others. Services are rationed to mothers and children, who make up 75 percent of Medicaid recipients but receive only 30 percent of the benefits, while recipients who are aged, blind, and disabled are exempt. Moreover, the level of care can rise and fall with budgetary pressures because the cutoff point of services is financial rather than medical. Some physicians have criticized the list for excluding some services that are standard treatment for everyday medical problems rather than expensive, high-tech procedures. The program was contested in the courts for years but is now fully functional.

Rationing Care Services for the Elderly. Daniel Callahan (1987) has recommended an alternative rationing proposal—rationing health care services for the elderly. Callahan points out that persons 65 years of age and older comprise only about 12 percent of the population but account for one-third of all personal health care expenditures and constitute 70 percent of those who die. In the last year of life, the last six months, the last month, the last week, an enormous amount of health care resources are spent simply trying to extend life. It has been estimated that 1 percent of the gross domestic product is spent on people in the last year of life. As the number of elderly continues to increase (doubling to 65 million in 2030), this pattern of resource consumption will become an increasingly significant problem.

Callahan contends that the relief of suffering rather than the extension of life should be the proper medical goal for persons who have lived a natural life span (not a maximum *biological* life, but a full *biographical* life). He does not advocate setting an absolute age cutoff point, but by the late seventies or early eighties, most people's biographies—that is, their years of maturation, work career, reproduction, and major life accomplishments—are largely completed. At this point, medical care should no longer be focused on resisting death—death would not be premature.

Callahan identifies two perceived fears of elderly persons: (1) that they will be abandoned or neglected if they become critically ill, and (2) conversely, that they will be excessively treated and their lives painfully extended. His proposal would ensure that neither of these fears would be realized.

Several rationales have been offered by Callahan and others in support of age-based rationing. From society's vantage point, it may be the most effective means of reducing health care costs while subtracting the least amount of productivity, and concentrating health care resources on younger persons would maximize the return in life-years. From the individual's standpoint, death is more tolerable once the natural life span has been reached. An orientation of living as well as possible for as long as possible rather than maximizing days of life might be a healthier, more productive philosophy. Finally, it is not a discriminatory policy in that all of us will have full access to health care resources when we are young and less access when we are older (Jecker and Pearlman, 1989).

Those who oppose age-based rationing contend that society's greatest obligation may be to the elderly—to show appreciation for past contributions, to honor the network of family and friendship relationships within which they may be enmeshed, and to assist those whose essential needs would be unmet without society's assistance. Opponents argue that the practice would be discriminatory against the elderly and offer a clear message that the elderly are less worthy persons. George Washington University's Amitai Etzioni (1988) has suggested that this might lead to intergenerational conflict and establish a "slippery slope"—making it easier to place restrictions on care for other groups (such as the mentally retarded) in society. Finally, taking aggressive actions to extend life is consistent with the wishes of most elderly persons (Jecker and Pearlman, 1989).

Managed Care

Perhaps the most significant trend within health care is the movement toward **managed care** arrangements. Managed care plans go beyond regulatory cost control systems like DRGs by incorporating a wide range of regulations on patient behavior and structuring the relationship between patients and providers. These components are designed to manage or guide the patient care process, ensuring that appropriate, cost-efficient care is obtained and that inappropriate and unnecessarily expensive care is rejected. Managed care has been incorporated both as a feature within traditional health insurance plans and as the underlying foundation of new delivery systems such as health

TABLE 14–3   Distribution of Employees Across Health Benefit Plans

Type of Plan	1990 (%)	1994 (%)	1999 (%)
Conventional	62	37	11
Health Maintenance Organization	20	23	30
Preferred Provider Organization	13	25	43
Point of service	5	15	16
Total managed care	**38**	**63**	**89**

Source: "The State of Health Care in America, 2000," *Business and Health,* 18 (Supp.):17, 2000.

maintenance organizations and preferred provider organizations.

Managed Care Within Traditional Health Insurance Plans.   In the last decade, conventional health insurance plans have developed extensive managed care features in order to restrain costs. As recently as 1984, an estimated 96 percent of insured employees were covered with conventional health insurance *without* any utilization review. However, as is shown in Table 14–3, by 1999, 86 percent of employees were in managed care systems, and only 11 percent still carried conventional insurance—but almost all of these had some form of utilization management.

The most common utilization management techniques are preadmission review for all elective hospital admissions, mandatory second surgical opinions, continued review of patient care during hospital stays, discharge planning, and alternative benefit coverage (such as ambulatory surgery, home health care, and skilled nursing facility care). Employers or insurers contract with a **utilization management organization (UMO)** to facilitate this process. In the case of preadmission review, a physician (or his or her nurse or assistant) will call the UMO to have a nurse-reviewer verify the admission and report the expectations (e.g., length of stay) of the insurance company. Failure of the physician or hospital to stay within the limits jeopardizes full reimbursement. Renegotiation can occur while the patient is in the hospital.

Managed Care Organizations.   Wholey and Burns (2000:219) define **managed care**

organizations as, "organizations using administrative processes or techniques to influence the quality, accessibility, utilization, costs, and prices or outcomes of health services provided to a defined population by a defined set of providers." Health maintenance organizations and preferred provider organizations are the primary MCO options for the financing and delivery of health care. (This chapter considers HMO and PPO roles in cost-containment; a more comprehensive examination of them is provided in Chapter 15.).

Health Maintenance Organizations (HMOs) are *prepaid* plans in which a group of physicians and hospitals provide health care in return for a fixed premium from enrollees. HMOs are responsible for providing a stated range of health care services (typically, a minimum of ambulatory and hospital care, dental care, medications, and laboratory tests) that must be available 24 hours a day. These services are provided by salaried, full-time physician-employees or a subset of a community's providers who contract with the HMO and accept a lower reimbursement level

and some guidelines to follow in exchange for a promise of patients.

There are two primary differences between HMOs and traditional private insurance plans. First, in a traditional plan, the patient (or the provider) is reimbursed after a service is provided. HMOs require fixed membership fees (and a small fee each time a service is used). Thus, traditional financing arrangements have built-in incentives for providers to do more tests and procedures to maximize income, whereas HMOs have incentives to reduce the use of services. HMOs maximize profit by keeping people healthy (they stress wellness and prevention) and by discouraging inappropriate use of costly physician and hospital services (they stress the use of primary care physician services and home health care). Second, with private health insurance, the patient has complete freedom to select any available provider. HMO enrollees must select from the list of providers who have contracted with the HMO. Although there are other differences, many patients view enrollment in

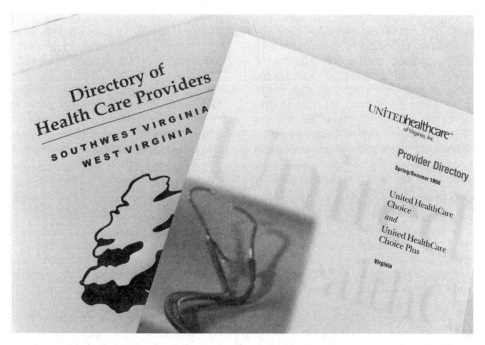

With the emergence and development of HMOs and PPOs comes a new element of the health care system—directories of providers within the system. Patients must select one of these providers or pay out-of-pocket to see another provider.

an HMO as sacrificing some choice in provider in order to pay lower health care costs.

Have these managed care, cost-control mechanisms worked as envisioned? In most respects, yes. Studies indicate that HMO enrollees do pay less each year for health care. Though the cost savings vary widely from community to community (depending upon a host of factors in the local health care system and in the community), employers on average save approximately 10 to 20 percent in insurance costs for employees enrolled in HMOs. Savings in this range would not be expected; however, if HMOs were generalized across the population because more low-income, elderly, and chronically ill persons would be included among the enrollees.

Preferred Provider Organizations (PPOs) are sets of providers that contract with employers or insurers to provide a comprehensive set of health care services on a *fee-for-service* basis at a discounted rate. Subscribers are motivated to join to get the discounted prices. Providers are motivated to join because the patients who enroll will likely be using only resources within the PPO. Although subscribers are not usually limited to these providers, lower deductibles

---

IN COMPARATIVE FOCUS

PHYSICIANS' VIEWS ABOUT QUALITY OF CARE

Despite living in countries with widely divergent cultural norms about health care and with very different types of health care systems, physicians in five countries all express concern about a recent deterioration in the quality of medical care provided. A 2000 survey of physicians in the United States, Australia, Canada, New Zealand, and the United Kingdom—all countries with an aging population, rising health care costs, increasing public expectations, and emerging medical technologies—found some striking similarities. More than half of the physicians in Canada (59 percent), the United States (57 percent), and New Zealand (53 percent) and 46 percent of United Kingdom physicians and 38 percent of Australian physicians believe their ability to deliver high-quality care has deteriorated in the last five years. Similar percentages in each country are concerned about continuing deterioration in the future.

What other specific concerns emerged?

1. Physicians in all five countries reported that hospitals are not good at finding and addressing medical errors. More than 60 percent of physicians in Australia and New Zealand and more than 40 percent of physicians in the United States and Canada say that they are either "discouraged from reporting" or "not encouraged to report" medical errors.

2. Physicians in four of the five countries reported major shortages of important resources. Only in the United States were shortages not reported to be a problem, although an inadequate supply of nurses in hospitals was identified as a significant problem there.

3. Waiting times for specialist referral and for hospital and surgical care were identified as problems in all of the countries except the United States.

4. A much higher percentage of physicians in the United States than in the other four countries reported that their patients cannot afford necessary prescription drugs and that there are restrictions on the drugs that they can prescribe.

5. Physicians in the United States and New Zealand were much more likely to express a concern that patients will not be able to afford the care that they need.

Physicians were asked for their reaction to several possible ways that the health care system in their country could be improved. Generally, the most positive responses were given to "access" items—being able to spend more time with patients; better access to specialized care, preventive care, and patient education; and increased access to new prescription medicines (Blendon et al., 2001).

and copayments encourage the use of the providers included in the plan. Periodic utilization reviews provide incentives for the providers to keep costs down.

PPOs are appealing to providers, insurers, and patients as a way to reduce health care costs quickly without increasing cost-sharing burdens. For the provider, PPOs can provide a means for increasing the volume of patients without the financial risk associated with prepaid financing. For patients, the plan preserves more of the freedom of choice among providers and reduces out-of-pocket expenses compared to traditional insurance plans. On average, cost savings for PPOs relative to traditional fee-for-service arrangements are in the 5 to 15 percent range.

THE POLITICS OF HEALTH CARE REFORM

Efforts to Establish a National Health Program

Efforts to establish a national health program in the United States have a long history. Initiatives began in 1926 when the privately funded Committee on the Costs of Medical Care (CCMC) considered policy changes to address the high costs of, and inadequate access to, health care services. The CCMC proposed that health care be delivered primarily by physicians organized in group practices and that funding come from voluntary insurance plans and subsidies from local governments for low-income persons. However, the AMA and many other groups inside and outside medicine strongly opposed the ideas as threats to private practice and physician autonomy (Waitzkin, 1989).

The Roosevelt administration pushed for National Health Program (NHP) legislation in 1938 as did the Truman administration in 1945, but Congress failed to support either. Despite widespread popular support, the AMA, along with the American Hospital Association and the American Chamber of Commerce, led continuing campaigns against what they labeled "socialized medicine." Coupled with general anticommunist sentiment that mounted during the 1950s, no proposal was ever passed (Waitzkin, 1989).

The turmoil of the 1960s revitalized support for health care reform. As a consequence, Congress considered a number of proposals for a NHP leading to the eventual establishment of Medicaid and Medicare in 1965. These programs brought major changes in public funding for health care but did not create a comprehensive program.

The 1990s and the Clinton Health Initiative

By the late 1980s and early 1990s, public sentiment seemed to be running strongly in favor of a national health program. A 1989 Lou Harris poll of consumers in Great Britain, Canada, and the United States found that U.S. consumers were the *least* satisfied with their own health care system. Only 10 percent of U.S. respondents assessed the health system as working even fairly well, and 9 out of 10 thought that the system was in need of fundamental change in direction and structure (Coddington et al., 1990). Several surveys found that a large plurality, or even a majority, of Americans had a preference for a Canadian-style, single payer system with universal coverage.

Moreover, support for health care reform was expressed by a broader cross-section of the population than in earlier years and included many business leaders and health care providers formerly opposed to significant change. Popular support for a comprehensive program appeared to be so pervasive that a bipartisan effort in Congress seemed possible.

With this backdrop, Bill Clinton made health care reform a major issue in the 1992 Presidential campaign and, after his election, a major commitment of his administration. After many months of fact-finding and deliberation by a task force led by his wife, Hillary Rodham Clinton (now a senator from New York), the Clinton proposal—termed "**managed competition**"—was introduced in November 1993. The proposal attempted to address both the problems of access and cost in a proposal that would be politically acceptable to Congress, key health care constituencies, and the American people.

The proposal called for a system that would guarantee a comprehensive set of health care services be provided for all Americans (universal coverage). Large health alliances (groups of employers) would be created to negotiate for the best financial arrangements with health maintenance organizations and other managed care systems. The plan would largely be funded through taxes applied to employers, with small employers being subsidized. Other cost control mechanisms, such as capping insurance premiums and malpractice reform, were included. The complete proposal—all 1,342 pages of it—contained an enormous amount of detail.

Opposition to the plan emerged within weeks. Small business owners felt that they could not afford to provide health care coverage for their workers. Small insurance companies were alarmed that they would not survive in the new system. Liquor, beer, and cigarette companies decried the extra taxes that would be placed on their products to help pay for the system. The AMA and the AHA opposed limits being placed on physicians' fees and hospital charges. Drug companies opposed mandatory cost controls on drugs. Trial lawyers opposed malpractice reform. Many persons expressed reservations about new forms of bureaucracy (e.g., the health alliances) being created. Some analysts have charged that the Clinton administration made a variety of "strategic errors" (for example, not working closely enough with Congressional leaders) in developing the plan, whereas others cite the continual difficulty of passing any broad-based reforms within the American political system.

In the ensuing months, when the Congressional Budget Office declared that the proposal would cost significantly more than Clinton had estimated, many middle-class families became frightened about the necessity of tax increases. While public opinion polls continued to show support for many of the basic values guiding the proposal (e.g., guaranteeing health care for everyone), controlling costs had become a more important objective for most people than universal coverage. In September 1993, almost 6 in 10 Americans supported the proposal; by July of 1994, almost 6 in 10 opposed. By fall of 1994, it was clear that the proposal lacked majority support in either house of Congress.

The Current Direction of Health Care Reform

There continue to be at least three major positions on health care reform now held by politicians in Congress and by the American people.

Market-oriented Approaches.   Generally favored by Republican politicians, market-oriented approaches favor a pluralistic view of the health care system with a mix of public and private providers and a mix of public and private insurers. For a time, some espousing this position believed that managed care had the potential to effectively contain health care cost increases. Two additional proposals, medical vouchers and medical savings accounts, also have considerable support. A *medical voucher* system would provide people (the elderly? the poor?) with a set amount of money each year to shop for and purchase private health care insurance—instead of having the government pay their medical bills. Presumably, many would buy into managed care systems. *Medical savings accounts* (MSA) would allow individuals and families to set aside pre-tax dollars to pay for health care costs as they arise (and to have this backed up by an insurance policy covering catastrophic situations). Many analysts agree that these programs would have limited effect on the profound problems of lack of access in the U.S. health care system. In the 2004 election, President Bush advocated programs of this type.

Incremental Reforms.   Many of those who supported the Clinton health care reform package now believe that the optimal path is to make as many changes as possible on a one-at-a-time basis and to try to secure as much overall change as possible in this manner. Some of these reforms are: instituting a uniform insurance billing form; prohibiting the denial of insurance because of preexisting conditions and ensuring that insurance coverage is not lost when a person changes jobs (legislation—the Health Insurance Portability and Accountability Act—to accomplish these things was passed in 1996); and extending guaranteed coverage to children and pregnant women (legislation to increase access to services for low-income children was passed in 1997). Many analysts see these programs as having some benefit in the long run for some of the people currently left out of the health care system though not addressing broad health care reform or the needs of all of the uninsured. In the 2004 election Senator John Kerry of Massachusetts advocated programs of this type.

A Single Payer System. The third approach to health care reform—calling for the most drastic change from the current system—is adoption of government-sponsored, single-payer national health insurance (similar to the Canadian system). The core of this plan is universal health insurance coverage under a single plan that would be administered by the federal government or by state governments (which might have some ability to tailor the program but would have to meet federally specified provisions). These plans eliminate existing public financing programs and either eliminate private health insurance companies or significantly reduce their role to that of a provider of supplemental services for the well-to-do. Patients have free choice of provider; physicians' clinical autonomy is maintained though fees may be negotiated with the government; and some form of prospective budgeting would be likely. This approach has a core (but much less than a majority) of supporters in Congress, is increasingly supported by physicians, and has won endorsement from several prominent groups in recent years including the Institute of Medicine, the American Public Health Association, and the Catholic Health Association. But, groups such as the insurance industry, the pharmaceutical industry, and conservative politicians strongly oppose universal care and thus it is not politically feasible in the foreseeable future.

Health Care Reform at the State Level

While the executive and legislative branches of the federal government have been devising, de-

bating, and ultimately rejecting a national health program, several of the states have initiated their own statewide health care system reforms. These reforms typically revolve around modifications to the Medicaid program. Cost containment is a primary goal in almost all of these efforts, though many are also attempting to boost the poor's access to services.

The momentum began in Hawaii where, since 1974, all employers have been required to provide their employees with comprehensive health care benefits. Employees also make a contribution. Combined with Medicare and Medicaid (which is set at the most generous eligibility level in the country), 98 percent of Hawaiians have basic health care coverage. In Tennessee, TennCare replaced the state's Medicaid program in 1994 and has now enrolled former Medicaid recipients and the previously uninsured in 1 of 12 private managed care plans. Washington has approved a comprehensive reform package that includes managed competition, mandatory payments by employers and employees, and caps on insurance premiums. Florida has created a system wherein large groups of patients (health care purchasing cooperatives) bargain for health care policies with providers and insurers. In 2000 Maine adopted a plan to require pharmaceutical companies to provide drug discounts to Medicaid beneficiaries and the uninsured. Then, in 2003 Maine adopted a plan that will lead to all residents having health care coverage by 2009. These programs may well point the way to more comprehensive reforms in the U.S. health care system (Kronenfeld, 1993; Cantor, Long, and Marquis, 1998).

On the other hand, the fiscal problems being experienced in most states is restricting plans to expand health care coverage. In the last few years more than half of the states have reduced Medicaid funding or enacted other restrictions. In 2002 voters in Oregon defeated a ballot initiative to provide universal coverage within the state. So, while there is more commitment to assisting the uninsured in some of the states than in the federal government, there are also limits in what they are able to accomplish.

SUMMARY

Although offering high-quality, high-technology care, the U.S. health care system is not accessible for many people (especially the uninsured and underinsured), it is plagued by inefficiency, and it is very expensive. America spends almost 15 percent of its GDP each year on health care—more than any other country in the world—yet has more than 45 million people without insurance.

The financing of health care is provided by a complex mix of employers, individuals and families, and the government. Over time, third-party payers have paid a greater share of health care costs. The implementation of Medicaid and Medicare has made the federal government the largest single purchaser of health care services.

Several factors contribute to the rapidly escalating costs of health care, including administrative inefficiency and system incentives such as provider reimbursement policies, the medical-industrial complex, and the provision of unnecessary services. In response, numerous cost containment strategies have been implemented or are being considered. Cost control systems have been attached to Medicare and Medicaid.

The state of Oregon now rations care to Medicaid recipients based on type of service, and Daniel Callahan and others suggest that age be used as a rationing consideration. Both proposals seek a way to deliver care equitably within a system that does not offer universal coverage. The managed care revolution has occurred in response to concerns about health care costs. Private insurance companies are using various management techniques in an effort to reduce unnecessary and inappropriate care. Health Maintenance Organizations and Preferred Provider Organizations attempt to provide health care for less money by rewarding physicians for keeping patients healthy and by encouraging enrollees to use specified providers.

Once again, proposals to establish a national health care system—like the Clinton plan of managed competition—have been defeated. More narrow alternatives for controlling costs and expanding access are now being considered in Congress. Meanwhile, several states have taken the initiative in developing their own plans to accomplish increased access to services.

HEALTH ON THE INTERNET

The Centers for Medicare and Medicaid Services is responsible for collecting data about Medicare, Medicaid, and other government-sponsored health care programs. Connect to the CMS Web site at:

http://www.cms.hhs.gov

By clicking on "Medicare" and "Medicaid," you can connect to links with data on each of these programs. What is the trend in enrollments for Medicare? What are the basic eligibility standards for Medicaid? Click on "SCHIP." What is this program?

KEY CONCEPTS AND TERMS

diagnostic-related groups (DRGs)
health maintenance organizations (HMOs)
managed care
managed care organizations
managed competition
market-driven health care
Medicaid
medical entrepreneuralism
medical-industrial complex

Medicare
national health expenditures (NHE)
personal health expenditures (PHE)
preferred provider organizations (PPOs)
private health insurance companies
rationing
self-referral
utilization management organization
  (UMO)

DISCUSSION CASES

CASE #1: The pharmaceutical industry in the United States is under increasingly intense pressure due to the high and rapidly escalating price of drugs, its high profit margins, and its massive lobbying efforts to protect its prices. During the last few years, more and more Americans—and now even some state and city governments—have chosen to purchase drugs from pharmacies in Canada and in other countries. In most countries the price of drugs is controlled to assure their affordability. For example, many drugs sell in Canadian pharmacies for 50 to 80 percent less than they do in U.S. pharmacies.

The federal government has taken efforts (such as the Food and Drug Administration warning cities and states not to import) to reduce or prohibit importation of drugs from other countries. The pharmaceutical industry has argued that foreign pharmacies are not under the control of U.S. regulatory agencies and that they might ship expired, contaminated, or counterfeit drugs. Supporters of importation contend that the Canadian Ministry of Health oversees drug quality (as the FDA does in the U.S.), that there is no evidence of improper drugs being sent, and that unaffordable drug prices in the United States make this process necessary.

What do you see as the key issues in this argument? Is it appropriate for the federal government to forbid individuals and city and state governments from importing drugs?

CASE #2: As described in this chapter, Daniel Callahan and others have advocated that the United States emphasize providing people with a "full biographical life" rather than a "full biological life." He would not have anyone neglected and he would provide as much relief from pain and suffering as possible, but at some point, death would no longer be resisted.

What are the strongest points in favor of this type of "age-based rationing"? What objections might be identified? All things considered, would you advocate or oppose such a policy?

REFERENCES

Albrecht, Gary L. 1992 *The Disability Business: Rehabilitation in America,* Newbury Park, CA: Sage Publications.

Ayanian, John Z., Joel S. Weissman, Eric C. Schneider, Jack A. Ginsburg, and Alan M. Zaslavsky. 2000 "Unmet Health Needs of Uninsured Adults in the United States." *Journal of the American Medical Association,* 284:2061–2069.

Blendon, Robert J., Cathy Schoen, Karen Donelan, Robin Osborn, Catherine M. DesRoches, Kimberly Scoles, Karen Davis, Katherine Binns, and Kinga Zapert. 2001 "Physicians' Views on Quality of Care: A Five-Country Comparison." *Health Affairs,* 20:233–243.

Blendon, Robert J., John T. Young, and Catherine M. DesRoches. 1999 "The Uninsured, the Working Insured, and the Public." *Health Affairs,* 18:203–211.

Braverman, Paula A., Susan Egerter, Trude Bennett, and Jonathan Showstack. 1991 "Differences in Hospital Resource Allocation Among Sick Newborns According to Insurance Coverage." *Journal of the American Medical Association,* 266:3300–3308.

Callahan, Daniel. 1987 *Setting Limits: Medical Goals in an Aging Society.* New York: Simon & Schuster.

———. 1990 "Rationing Medical Progress: The Way to Affordable Health Care." *New England Journal of Medicine,* 322:1810–1813.

Cantor, Joel C., Stephen H. Long, and M. Susan Marquis. 1998 "Challenges of State Health Reform: Variations in Ten States." *Health Affairs,* 17:191–199.

Centers for Medicare and Medicaid Services. 2004 Health Care Indicators. Office of the Actuary, Office of National Health Statistics, Baltimore, Maryland.

Coddington, Dean C., David J. Keen, Keith D. Moore, and Richard L. Clarke. 1990 *The Crisis in Health Care: Costs, Choices, and Strategies.* San Francisco: Jossey-Bass Publishers.

Etzioni, Amitai. 1988 "Spare the Old, Save the Young." *The Nation,* June 11, pp. 818–822.

Garrett, Susan. 2000 "Health Care: How America Has Failed." *The Roanoke Times,* August 27, p. H4.

Hadley, Jack, Earl P. Steinberg, and Judith Feder. 1991 "Comparison of Uninsured and Privately

Insured Hospital Patients." *Journal of the American Medical Association,* 265:374–379.

Hillman, Bruce J., Catherine A. Joseph, Michael R. Mabry, Jonathan H. Sunshine, Stephen D. Kennedy, and Monica Noether. 1990 "Frequency and Costs of Diagnostic Imaging in Office Practice—A Comparison of Self-Referring and Radiologist-Referring Physicians." *New England Journal of Medicine,* 323:1604–1608.

Hoffman, Earl D., Barbara S. Klees, and Catherine A. Curtis. 2000 "Overview of the Medicare and Medicaid Programs." *Health Care Financing Review,* 22:175–193.

Jecker, Nancy S. 1992 "Futility and Rationing." *The American Journal of Medicine,* 92:189–196.

Jecker, Nancy S., and Robert A. Pearlman. 1989 "Ethical Constraints on Rationing Medical Care by Age." *Journal of the American Geriatrics Society,* 37:1067–1075.

Kronenfeld, Jennie J. 1993 *Controversial Issues in Health Care Policy.* Newbury Park, CA.: Sage Publications.

Levit, Katharine, Cynthia Smith, Cathy Cowan, Art Sensenig, Aaron Catlin, and the Health Accounts Team. 2004 "Health Spending Rebound Continues in 2002." *Health Affairs,* 23:147–159.

Mason, Michael. 1992 "A Little Clinic on the Side: Self-Referral by Physicians to Facilities in Which They Have Part Ownership." *Newsweek,* March 30, p. 71.

Moore, J. Duncan. 1995 "Physicians Are Providing More Charity Care, But 32 Percent Do None, AMA Survey Finds." *Modern Healthcare,* 25:26.

"Palliation in the Age of Chronic Disease." 1992 *Hastings Center Report,* 22:41.

Relman, Arnold S. 1980 "The New Medical-Industrial Complex." *New England Journal of Medicine,* 303:963–970.

———. 1991 "The Health Care Industry: Where Is It Taking Us?" *New England Journal of Medicine,* 325:854–859.

Samuelson, Robert J. 1989 "The Cost of Chaos." *Newsweek,* October 2, p. 52.

Seccombe, Karen, and Cheryl Amey. 1995 "Playing By the Rules and Losing: Health Insurance and the Working Poor." *Journal of Health and Social Behavior,* 36:168–181.

"The State of Health Care in America, 2000." *Business and Health,* 18 (Supp.):17.

States Health Access Data Assistance Center, University of Minnesota. 2004 *Characteristics of the Uninsured: A View from the States.* Princeton, NJ: Robert Wood Johnson Foundation.

Ubel, Peter A., and Susan D. Goold. 1998 "Rationing Health Care: Not All Definitions Are Created Equal." *Archives of Internal Medicine,* 158: 209–214.

Waitzkin, Howard. 1989 "Health Policy in the United States: Problems and Alternatives," pp. 475–491 in Howard E. Freeman and Sol Levine (eds.). *Handbook of Medical Sociology,* 4th ed. Upper Saddle River, NJ: Prentice Hall.

"Wasted Health Care Dollars." 1992 *Consumer Reports,* July, pp. 435–448.

Wholey, Douglas R., and Lawton R. Burns. 2000 "Tides of Change: The Evolution of Managed Care in the United States," pp. 217–239 in *Handbook of Medical Sociology,* (5th ed.). Chloe E. Bird, Peter Conrad, and Allen M. Fremont (eds.). Upper Saddle River, NJ: Prentice Hall.

Woolhandler, Steffie, David U. Himmelstein, and James P. Lewontin. 1993 "Administrative Costs in U.S. Hospitals." *New England Journal of Medicine,* 329:400–403.

15

HEALTH CARE DELIVERY

Through much of the twentieth century, the private physician's office—for primary care—and the hospital—for emergency, life-threatening, and surgical care—were almost the only medical treatment sites available. However, in the last few decades, the health care delivery system has undergone a significant transformation, and now a wide array of care sites are available. This chapter describes four key changes (the emergence of freestanding ambulatory care sites, the flourishing of managed care organizations, the changing structure of hospitals and the services they offer, and the reemergence of home health care) and analyzes the reasons for these developments.

THE EMERGENCE OF FREESTANDING AMBULATORY CARE SITES

Ambulatory care is personal health care provided to an individual who is not an inpatient in a health care facility. Ambulatory care services include preventive care, acute primary care, minor emergencies, and many surgical procedures,

and they are provided today in an increasing variety of facilities.

The Traditional Setting

The traditional and still most common means for delivering ambulatory care is by a private physician (working alone, with a partner, or in a group) in an office or clinic setting. About 9 in 10 active U.S. physicians are involved in patient care, and three-fourths of these physicians had an office-based practice (the other one-fourth were full-time staff, residents, or clinical fellows in hospitals).

Of physicians working in patient care, the long-term shift has been from solo practice (a physician practicing alone) to **group practice** (three or more physicians formally organized and practicing together). Group practice began in the late nineteenth century in the United States with the establishment of the Mayo Clinic. The clinic started in the 1880s as a small but busy for-profit surgery practice involving a father and his two sons and grew into a mammoth clinic (that was converted to not-for-profit) with enough staff to handle not only surgery but extensive diagnostic and preventive services as well (Starr, 1982).

With the growing awareness of the successful Mayo Clinic, the increasing specialization of medicine, and the positive experience physicians had with group practice during World War I, interest grew rapidly. By the 1930s, approximately 300 group practices existed with a median size of five or six physicians (Starr, 1982).

Many physicians, however, expressed reservations about group practice. Some considered groups to be a threat to physician autonomy and to the sanctity of the physician–patient relationship; many solo practitioners considered group practices to be a threat to their very existence; and many objected that the group format opened the door to corporate control of medical practice and erosion of clinical autonomy. Nevertheless, expansion of group practices has continued. Today, most physicians practice in a group setting, and those that do overwhelmingly prefer it as a practice style.

Emerging Ambulatory Care Sites

The number of both independently owned and hospital-affiliated **freestanding ambulatory care centers** has increased dramatically in the last several years. Services offered in these settings include primary/urgent care, diagnostic imaging, rehabilitation, sports medicine, dialysis, and minor surgery. Some of the most important of these care sites are described in this section of the chapter.

Urgent-Care Centers (Walk-In Centers). **Urgent-care (or walk-in) centers** provide services, without an appointment, for minor medical problems such as a sore throat or a cut needing stitches. Developed in the early 1980s to attract patients needing acute episodic care, they are now often viewed as an alternative to the family physician because they offer a stable professional staff, and many are open for extended hours seven days a week.

Patients of walk-in centers tend to be young to middle-aged adults who are attracted to these

Developed in the early 1980s to offer acute, episodic care, walk-in centers are sometimes viewed as an alternative to the family physician.

facilities by their convenience and flexibility. This group experiences a higher incidence of acute episodic rather than chronic health problems so that continuity of care may be of less importance, and they are less likely to have established a relationship with a regular health care provider.

Ambulatory Surgical Centers (Surgicenters or ASCs). Surgicenters, or **ambulatory surgical centers,** offer minor, low-risk outpatient surgery. Only a few years ago, the vast majority of surgical procedures were performed in hospital operating rooms on an inpatient basis. Today, an increasing proportion of surgery is done on an outpatient basis, much of it in facilities other than the hospital. As the cost-effectiveness of ambulatory surgery has been documented, and as studies have found equivalent or lower rates of complications and mortality, and as third-party payers continue pressure to cut costs, more and more surgery is being done on an outpatient basis—more than 60 percent of all surgical procedures are now done on an outpatient basis. The most common outpatient surgeries are cataract surgery, gynecological diagnostic procedures, and minor ear, nose, and throat procedures.

Surgery performed in offices/clinics and freestanding facilities typically is less expensive and more convenient and is done in an atmosphere where a higher priority is assigned to the physician–patient relationship. However, hospital-affiliated services have a more readily available emergency backup system and, if necessary, easier transfer to an inpatient unit.

The cost-efficiency of outpatient surgery is traceable to several factors. First, hospital stays are extremely expensive. Therefore, when recovery can occur at home or in a recovery center with minimal staff, less capital investment, and lower overhead than a hospital, substantial savings result. A surgicenter can also be more cost-effective because it is designed to accommodate only the less complex and low-risk surgical procedures and thus can avoid the purchase of some of the most sophisticated and expensive equipment. Moreover, ASCs operate with fewer legal regulations, thus eliminating associated costs.

Community Health Centers. In the last few decades a variety of neighborhood and community health centers—many focusing on specific population groups—have been created. **Community and migrant health centers (C/MHCs)** are programs funded by the Public Health Service to provide primary care to medically underserved populations. Originally conceived in 1965 as part of the War on Poverty, these centers are located in underserved areas, usually in inner-city neighborhoods and in rural areas, and primarily serve uninsured or publicly insured racial and ethnic minorities. Studies show that a large majority of C/MHC users consider the centers to be their primary source of care.

Free Health Clinics. A **free health clinic** movement emerged in the United States in the late 1960s to establish free health centers for people unable to afford private care and/or for those estranged from the conventional medical system. The early clinics were targeted to people experiencing drug-related illnesses, problem pregnancies, and venereal disease. Free clinics evolved through the 1970s, 1980s, and 1990s as the focus of the clinics shifted more and more to serving either the very poor or the medically indigent (those just above the poverty level who do not qualify for Medicaid).

Although there are many variations in the approximately 600 free clinics in existence in 2004, most (1) offer primary health care services; (2) are staffed largely by volunteer physicians, other health care providers, and laypersons; (3) serve people unable to afford private medical care; and (4) provide an atmosphere that emphasizes treating each patient with dignity and a supportive, nonjudgmental attitude. Financial support for free clinics comes from several sources, including local governments, United Way, church groups, private donations, contributions (often in-kind) from the medical community, and patient donations. The box, "Focus on a Free Health Clinic," describes the evolution of a particular free clinic.

Reasons for the Emergence of New Ambulatory Care Sites. The emergence of

Free clinics emerged in the 1960s but have increased rapidly in the last decade as a community-based means for providing health care for the working poor.

IN THE FIELD

FOCUS ON A FREE HEALTH CLINIC

The Bradley Free Clinic in Roanoke, Virginia, was established in 1974 with $250 in seed money, one volunteer physician, one volunteer nurse, and the free rental of the first floor of an old house (donated by the adjacent church). With the dedication of a small group of concerned citizens and the energy and enthusiasm of a barely paid director, the clinic was able to offer free health services to the local medically indigent two nights per week. The commitment of the director and volunteers was noticed in the medical community, by other lay volunteers, and by local governments—important factors in the clinic's subsequent support.

In 2000, the clinic provided free care for more than 14,000 patient visits; prescribed more than 35,000 medications (almost all of which were given at no charge out of the clinic's own pharmacy—filled mostly with drugs donated by pharmaceutical companies and local physicians); offered extensive dental services (most out of its own fully modern dental operatories—supplied by donations from dental equipment companies and local dentists); provided countless hours of mental health counseling (by local professionals volunteering their time); and performed basic lab tests (in its own small laboratory of mostly donated equipment). The clinic now sits in its own medical building (purchased with funds from a $1 million donation by a local philanthropist). The estimated value of services provided in 2000 was more than $1 million.

Supplementing a small paid staff are a host of volunteers: 80 physicians who volunteer some time at the clinic, plus 40 specialists who accept free referrals of clinic patients; 60 nurses; 30 pharmacists; 12 laboratory technicians; 20 dentists; 15 dental assistants; a dozen mental health counselors; and scores of lay volunteers. Care is provided at no charge in an atmosphere of respect for the dignity of each patient. By 2002 the Bradley Free Clinic had provided care valued at more than $20 million for more than 200,000 patients.

these ambulatory care sites is rooted in several changes within society and within the medical profession. Like so many other changes, these new sites represent efforts to offer health care at a lower cost (walk-in clinics and surgicenters) or to deter the medically indigent from using the very expensive care of the hospital emergency room as a primary care provider (community/migrant health centers and free health clinics). Lowell-Smith (1994:277) ties the development of walk-in clinics and surgicenters to other factors:

> Patient-consumers have become more mobile and thus less likely to establish a long term relationship with a physician. Patient-consumers have also become more knowledgeable in terms of their health needs and thus less likely to rely solely on the advice of a physician. In addition, there is the rise of convenience as a "cultural value." This desire for health care when the patient wants it rather than when the physician is available has aided the growth of walk-in clinics and outpatient surgery centers . . . [Also] improvements in medical technology have made it possible for many tests and procedures to be performed outside the hospital and in ambulatory settings.

The community/migrant health centers and free health clinics are founded primarily on the desire to provide accessible health care (both financially and geographically) for persons not able to afford private medical care. Patients typically opt for these clinics not out of convenience but out of need, and without programs of these types, even more persons would go without needed care.

THE FLOURISHING OF MANAGED CARE ORGANIZATIONS: HMOs AND PPOs

As discussed in the previous chapter, **managed care organizations**—such as health maintenance organizations and preferred provider organizations—have moved to a position of dominance in the American health care system. At their core, these systems are contractual arrangements that offer care at reduced prices to patients who enroll (or are enrolled by their employer) in a system where patient care is managed. Most of these organizations contract with existing health care providers in the community

rather than creating new health care sites. The stated goal of managed care organizations is to limit unnecessary, inappropriate, and expensive services while continuing to provide appropriate care. This part of the chapter describes the basic structure and experiences with these managed care organizations.

Health Maintenance Organizations

Health maintenance organizations are comprehensive, prepaid, managed care networks. HMOs guarantee specified health care services to a defined population who voluntarily enroll in the plan for a fixed monthly fee. The underlying rationale for HMOs is clear. Because patients pay a fixed premium regardless of the amount of health care services used (though patients now typically have a small copayment for services used), the HMO and its physicians have an incentive to keep patients as healthy as possible. This incentive is expressed through encouragement to lead healthy lifestyles, the provision of preventive health care, and regular checkups—all less time consuming and far less expensive than treatment of acute and chronic diseases, especially those that lead to a hospital stay. Furthermore, cost-effectiveness is maintained by having the HMO manage the care for each patient and by making greater use of primary care physicians and less use of more expensive specialists. The attraction for the patient is the security of knowing that the agreed-upon premium will cover all contracted health care services—even a catastrophic health problem.

Participation in HMOs. The first HMOs—Kaiser Permanente in California and the Health Insurance Plan (HIP) in New York—were created more than five decades ago. Development of other HMOs progressed slowly until about 1970 (when about 3.6 million Americans were enrolled in HMOs). Then, enrollment grew tenfold from 1970 to 1990 and continued to grow very rapidly in the 1990s. During this time, HMOs represented the majority of managed care plans. However, due to mergers of some HMOs and failures of others, the number of HMOs has now decreased to 410 (in 2004). These plans cover 69 million persons in the United States—about 39 percent of all persons enrolled in managed care plans. (see Table 14–3 in Chapter 14).

HMO development traditionally has been strongest on the West Coast and in the Northeast, but they now heavily penetrate all parts of the country. States with the largest enrollments are California, New York, and Florida.

Types of HMOs.   There are four main types of HMOs in existence today:

1. *Staff models,* in which the HMO owns all the health care facilities within the HMO system and hires physicians and other providers who are full-time HMO employees. This is the only model in which physicians are required to see only patients of the HMO.
2. *Group models,* in which the HMO contracts with a single physician group practice to provide health care services to the enrolled HMO population.
3. *Network models,* in which the HMO contracts with two or more existing physician group practices to provide health care services to the enrolled HMO population.
4. *Individual practice associations (IPAs),* in which the HMO contracts with individual physicians (solo, partners, or group) to provide health care services to the enrolled HMO population. This is the most common type of HMO because it offers the most options in provider choice and location.

HMO Ownership.   Although ownership of HMOs remains highly diversified, the clear trend is toward HMOs that are run for profit. Growth in ownership has been fastest among commercial health insurance companies like CIGNA, Aetna, and Prudential. More than two-thirds of HMOs are controlled by for-profit companies, and some predict that the figure eventually will be 100 percent.

Do HMOs Save Patients and Employers Money?   Yes. Although variations in coverage by traditional insurance programs and HMOs make it difficult to calculate precise cost comparisons, most studies have determined that HMOs now represent the lowest cost option—with typical savings of 10 to 20 percent over traditional insurance.

Do HMOs Offer High-Quality Care?
The evaluation literature is decidedly mixed on the quality of care in HMOs. Some indicators are positive and some are negative, and there is much variability on each (Mechanic, 2001). Assessing the technical quality of health care provided is difficult. Many of the indicators used—chart reviews and checks for indicated tests and treatments—are helpful, but they are not a totally valid means for measuring delivery of clinically appropriate and skillful care.

Most HMOs market their plans by playing up the quality of the health care providers they use. However, some have contracted with almost any physician interested in signing on, and individual quality control is not possible when the contract is with an existing group. Many HMOs have now begun a system of "credentialing"—examining prospective physicians' qualifications and requiring certain credentials (e.g., board-certification). Clearly, some HMOs are more sensitive to these quality indicators than are others.

Analysis of several studies comparing HMO participation with traditional fee-for-service plans has determined that, in general, HMO enrollees receive more preventive care, have the same or slightly more physician visits, receive fewer expensive tests and procedures, have lower hospital admission rates, have a shorter length of stay when hospitalized, have less use of costly technology, and have mixed but generally better health outcomes (Wholey and Burns, 2000). However, significant variations in the provision of services exist among HMOs.

What are the concerns about quality of care in HMOs? The most heated controversy surrounds the issue of whether HMOs are apt to deny needed services in order to maximize short-term profit. Recall that the traditional fee-for-service system generated funds (and maximized profit) when services were performed, but, in managed care, profit is maximized when services are not performed. Some HMOs have developed explicit incentive systems that could easily discourage physicians from ordering services. Some HMOs have given telephone clerks (people typically with little or no medical training who answer phone calls from patients wanting to make an appointment) cash bonuses for keeping calls short and limiting the number of appointments that they make. Many HMO enrollees have publicized cases in which they were denied care that they considered to be important or necessary.

This concern was exacerbated by a 2004 U.S. Supreme Court decision that forbids patients from suing managed care companies for negligence. Two Texas patients who ended up in an emergency room after the managed care organization denied them services that had been recommended by a physician wished to bring suit against the HMO. Their lawyers argued that because patients can sue physicians and hospitals for not providing needed care, they ought to be able to sue HMOs that refuse to authorize needed care. But, the Supreme Court ruled that federal law prohibits patients from suing HMOs in state courts for malpractice. The judgment was, of course, well-received by managed care organizations but decried by physicians, consumer groups, and patients' rights groups.

A second issue that has received considerable media attention is the "gag rule" that some HMOs have imposed on their member physicians. This rule has taken different forms but has included such requirements as prohibiting physicians from criticizing the HMO to a patient or to a public body or objecting too strenuously to an HMO decision not to cover a particular service for a particular patient.

How do HMO members evaluate the quality of care received? Surveys have found that most patients in some HMOs are satisfied with the care that they receive, but that most patients of other HMOs are dissatisfied. Satisfaction levels reported range from as high as 75 percent to as low as 35 percent. These differences have led some of the best HMOs to conduct marketing plans that attempt to distinguish themselves from more lowly rated plans.

The dissatisfaction with HMO policies has led to various actions being taken by state legislatures. Some states now require HMOs to define ob-gyns as primary care physicians so that women can access them directly and not have to go through a gatekeeper. Some states require HMOs to publicize their restrictions and limitations. Legislation has been passed to prohibit HMOs from exiting new mothers within the first 24 hours after birth. Aspects of the gag rule have been struck down. In 2003 the U.S. Supreme Court ruled that states could require managed care organizations to admit any willing, qualified provider to its network.

Dissatisfaction with HMOs is increasing among physicians. Many physicians claim that the utilization management features of HMOs limit physicians' autonomy and sometimes interfere with providing the highest quality of care to patients. Participation in an HMO requires a significant amount of paperwork in exchange for what some physicians say is inadequate compensation/reimbursement. Organizational changes within the HMO that force physician-employees to become more dependent on the organization can require significant adaptation on the part of the physician and often are resisted (Hoff, 2003). Despite what can be rather intense economic pressures to participate in HMOs, many physicians around the country now refuse to affiliate (Feldman, Novack, and Gracely, 1998).

Preferred Provider Organizations

Preferred provider organizations (PPOs) are networks of physicians and hospitals that agree to give price discounts to groups who enroll in their program, use their services, and agree to follow specified managed care procedures (such as preadmission hospital review). Though patients typically pay for care received on a fee-for-service basis (unlike HMOs) as members of a PPO, they pay lower fees than do other patients. In exchange for discounting fees, PPO providers are likely to see more patients.

Participation in PPOs. PPOs evolved rapidly through the 1980s and early 1990s and are escalating very rapidly in the early 2000s. Enrollment in PPOs grew from 1.3 million in

1984 to 38 million in 1990 to about 113 million in 2003. PPOs are most successful in areas in which there is competition among providers who are therefore willing to discount their services in order to get patients (Kertesz, 1995).

Structure and Ownership of PPOs. PPOs are looser confederations than HMOs. Most physicians are paid on a fee-for-service basis though some are paid by capitation (the number of PPO patients they agree to see rather than the number of services provided), and almost all see patients covered by traditional insurance as well as PPO enrollees. More than 80 percent of PPOs are run on a for-profit basis with commercial insurance companies accounting for most PPO ownership.

Do PPOs Save Patients Money? While less cost analysis has been conducted on PPOs than on HMOs, most research has documented a cost savings in the 5 to 15 percent range. PPOs do not save as much money as HMOs because they offer fewer restrictions on physicians' and patients' behaviors. This feature and the fact that PPOs typically have a larger base of providers from which patients can select make this option very appealing to many employers, individuals, and families (Hurley, Strunk, and White, 2004).

The Point-of-Service Variation

A **point-of-service (POS) plan** is a feature that can be attached to either an HMO or a PPO. It creates the additional option that participants can go outside the system for care (that is, use a provider who is not part of the plan) by paying a higher premium or absorbing a larger share of the cost. Some have described POS as having the benefits of the network discount of PPOs

---

IN COMPARATIVE FOCUS

THE EXPORTATION OF MANAGED CARE TO LATIN AMERICA

The health of people in Latin America has improved substantially in the last 50 years following the establishment of universal public health programs. The disease profile in most countries resembles that in the United States with heart disease, cancer, and stroke being the most common causes of death. Life expectancy has increased, and maternal and infant mortality have decreased. In some countries, childhood immunization rates exceed those of the United States. Most countries have a surplus of medical doctors.

In most countries, pension plans funded by the government and employers provide basic health care coverage for most of the population in a system called *seguro social*. Governments in most countries have accepted responsibility for providing care for those not covered in a pension plan. This arrangement works well in some countries, but is underfunded in others, so that both access and quality of care are uneven.

In recent years, rapidly escalating costs have led many governments to promote the privatization of health care and to look for managed care organizations to play a larger role in the system. Facing mostly saturated markets in the United States, seeing the huge funds available in *seguro social*, and recognizing the relative lack of regulations in the health care market in Latin America, U.S. for-profit managed care organizations have jumped at the opportunity to compete. Some observers, however, are concerned that these companies are demonstrating greater interest in profit-making than in enhancing access to high-quality medical services. In some countries, new co-payments for care have created a barrier to services. New, lengthy means tests have been devised. Primary attention has been given to enrolling the healthiest members of the population. These increased barriers have forced more patients on the already overburdened public hospitals, so that access to care is diminishing (Perez-Stable, 1999; Waitzkin and Iriart, 2000).

and the gatekeeper process of HMOs but with the possibility that the participant can receive partially subsidized care outside the network. Because they add flexibility for participants, POS plans have become quite popular and are expected to become more prevalent.

EMERGENCE OF THE MODERN HOSPITAL

History

Though the first American "hospital" was founded by William Penn in Philadelphia in 1713, it was primarily created to provide shelter for the poor. The first hospital designed primarily to serve the sick was Pennsylvania Hospital, founded in Philadelphia in 1751 by Thomas Bond, a local physician, and Benjamin Franklin. The hospital began in a small, rented house that was capable of housing no more than 20 patients but grew in stages till the early 1800s. The hospital was always crowded as the average length of stay was weeks- or months-long, but its main problem was a large influx of mentally ill persons who occupied most of the beds. These patients were eventually moved to a new facility in 1835.

Most of the general hospitals that were built in the late 1700s and through most of the 1800s provided care primarily for people without family or financial means. Most were financed by charitable contributions, and many physicians volunteered their time. A steward or matron generally controlled the small staff and the patients, and a small number of women, assisted by a few volunteers, performed "nursing" duties. Most of the care focused on making the patients comfortable and preparing them for death.

Gradually, with advances in science and the development of medical technologies, hospitals changed. By 1900, hospitals mostly admitted only curable patients while other resources were sought for the elderly and the homeless. Religious appeals for funding gave way to a more secular rationale, in which communities were convinced that hospitals were necessary to treat illnesses and to protect residents against

epidemics. As a result, cities of all sizes began to build community hospitals.

By 1920, the hospital had become the primary center of acute care treatment. Surgery was the key to both the growth and the increased status of hospitals, along with the development of a skilled nursing force and the introduction of ancillary services such as X-rays and laboratories. As the size of the hospital and the scope of its services increased, administrators were added to coordinate this work and the complex, bureaucratic hospital of today emerged (Rosenberg, 1987). Expansion in the number of community hospitals was spurred by the Hill-Burton Hospital Construction Act of 1946. This massive program committed nearly $4 billion of federal monies and over $9 billion of state and local government monies for the construction of new hospitals and the renovation of existing ones.

During the middle years of the twentieth century, the hospital became the primary acute health care organization and the center for the distribution of modern medical technologies. Advances in life expectancy and shifts in morbidity patterns from acute, infectious diseases to chronic, degenerative diseases resulted in a greater number of older patients who were chronically ill. This led to an enlargement of diagnostic services, an increased number of surgical procedures, and the development of rehabilitation units. In the remaining part of this section of the chapter, we will discuss developments in hospitals in the last few decades and especially in the last few years.

Organizational Structure

Today's hospitals are highly bureaucratic and hierarchical social organizations exemplifying the key characteristics of bureaucracies explicated by Max Weber. They typically contain an authority hierarchy (though not pyramidal in shape), extensive rules and regulations, fixed areas of responsibility based on competence, recruitment based on merit, regular remuneration, promotion based on objective criteria, and separation between the power of a position and of the

The United States has almost 6,000 hospitals employing more than 3 million full-time workers. Physician-owned clinics (like the one pictured on the left) often locate adjacent to hospitals.

incumbent. However, superimposed upon these bureaucratic traits are twin lines of authority that run throughout hospital decision making.

Dual Line of Authority.   These twin lines are referred to as the **dual line of authority**. Figure 15–1 provides one model of hospital organizational structure. Most hospital departments report either to the first line of authority, the hospital administrator (generally a person trained in hospital or health administration and with a strong background in business) or to the second line of authority, the medical director or other person who is medically trained. Both the hospital administrator and the medical director ultimately are responsible to the hospital's governing body—generally a board of trustees.

This dual system of authority frequently results in tension between the business orientation of the administrator and the clinical orientation of the medical director. Although both the administrative and the medical staff share the primary goal of patient care, they do not always agree on related goals and the methods by which

to achieve quality and efficient patient care. Fundamental to this conflict is that the administrator is responsible for the fiscal survival of the institution and that the medical staff is most concerned with clinical efficacy.

Related to this dispute is the struggle between professional autonomy and bureaucratic control. Given their medical expertise, physicians maintain that only they are competent to make decisions regarding patient care and to issue instructions to the medical staff. However, many issues related to patient care also involve administrative decisions and thus physicians may perceive an impingement on their clinical autonomy.

Nurses and other ancillary health care providers can be placed in an awkward situation by this structure. They are expected to carry out physicians' orders at the same time that they are obligated to follow hospital protocol. Being responsible to both can lead to stressful overlapping responsibilities.

Division of Labor.   Hospitals employed 5.3 million employees in 2002, a number that

Figure 15–1 Typical Hospital Structure

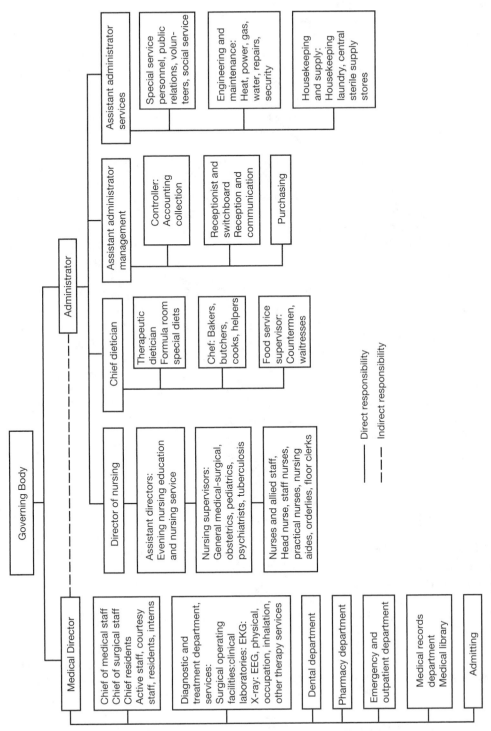

Source: Department of Labor, *Technology and Manpower in the Health Service Industry.* Washington, DC: Government Printing Office, 1967.

has been increasing each year in the early 2000s. As medical science has become more technologically sophisticated, health care practitioners have become increasingly specialized and numerous new allied health occupations have emerged. In the last decade, most hospitals have added new technologies to their roster of services. For example, magnetic resonance imaging did not exist in the early 1980s, but today MRI is found in most hospitals.

The Number of Hospitals and Hospital Beds

The number of hospitals in the United States increased each year from the mid-1940s through 1979 when the number began to decline to a total of 5,810 in 2000 (Table 15–1). Of these, 4,915 are short-term, general hospitals. Since 1980, the number of hospitals has declined by about 15 percent due primarily to the closing of rural and inner-city facilities.

The total number of hospital beds began to decline earlier than the number of hospitals, peaking in the mid-1960s at about 1.7 million and declining to just under one million in 2000. The total number of hospital admissions increased each year until 1985 (when there were 36.3 million admissions) but has decreased since then to 34.8 million in 2000.

Why are the number of hospitals and the number of hospital beds shrinking? The answer is health care reform. Hospital care is the most expensive form of health care. In order to keep their prices as low as possible, private insurance companies and managed care organizations have applied pressure, where feasible, to substitute other forms of care (e.g., outpatient surgery) for hospital care and to keep the number of days of hospitalization as low as possible. In addition, levels of reimbursement for hospitalized care, including from Medicare and Medicaid, are increasingly tightly controlled. These efforts have led to a reduction in hospital admissions and to a declining average length of stay. With demand down, fewer hospitals and fewer hospital beds are needed.

Hospital Ownership

There are three major types of hospital ownership in the United States (Table 15–2).

1. **Voluntary (nonprofit) hospitals** are the most common type of short-term general hospital in the U.S.; in 2000, there were 3,003 nonprofit hospitals in the United States—61 percent of all short-term hospitals. As non-profitmaking facilities, they answer to a board of directors typically comprised of community leaders, and end-of-year financial surpluses are reinvested in the hospital (as opposed to being paid to investors).

2. **Proprietary (for-profit) hospitals** accounted for approximately 15 percent of all short-term hospitals in 2000. These hospitals are created by individual or corporate entrepreneurs; they are sometimes "public" in the sense that shares in the hospital (or controlling agent) are bought and sold on the stock market and are sometimes simply privately owned. These hospitals are expected to have

TABLE 15–1 Trends Among U.S. Hospitals

Year	Hospitals	Beds (millions)	Admissions (millions)
1950	6,788	1.46	18.48
1960	6,876	1.66	25.03
1970	7,123	1.62	31.76
1980	6,965	1.37	38.89
1990	6,649	1.21	33.77
2000	5,810	.98	34.89

Source: American Hospital Association. *Hospital Statistics: Annual Survey of Hospitals* (2003 edition). Chicago: Author, 2003.

TABLE 15–2 Number of Community (Short-Term) Hospitals

Ownership Type	1980	1985	1990	1995	2000
Total	5,830	5,732	5,384	5,184	4,915
Voluntary (nonprofit)	3,322	3,349	3,191	3,052	3,003
Proprietary (for-profit)	730	805	749	752	749
Government	1,778	1,578	1,444	1,380	1,163

Source: National Center for Health Statistics. *Health, United States, 2003*, United States Department of Health and Human Services: Hyattsville, MD, 2003.

greater revenues than expenses each year so that the difference can be returned to investors as profit.

3. **Government (public) hospitals** represent the third type of ownership. They accounted for approximately 24 percent of all short-term hospitals in the United States in 2000. Most federally funded hospitals are for veterans and their families; state-funded hospitals tend to be part of the mental health system; and locally funded hospitals typically are designed to serve the general population but end up being the primary care site for the poor and medically indigent—government hospitals have charity caseloads about four times larger than those of other hospitals. All of these hospitals rely on funding from the sponsoring government.

Until shortly after the start of the twentieth century, the majority of American hospitals were small, proprietary institutions owned primarily by physicians. Gradually these were replaced by larger and more sophisticated community or church-owned nonprofit hospitals. Beginning in the 1970s, considerable (and often heated) debate about the role of profit-making hospitals was inspired by the growth of large conglomerates that purchased and ran multiple for-profit hospitals.

For several years, experts predicted that the proprietary hospitals would again assume control of the market. During the mid-1980s, however, cost-containment efforts reduced the profitability of hospitals and discouraged significant expansion of the profitmaking sector. Since that time, the operating profit margin for

hospitals (based on what is left of operating income after paying expenses) has been unstable. This helps to explain the fact that the percentage of hospitals that are for-profit has remained at about 15 percent.

Multihospital Chains

The year 1968 is often cited as the key point in the development of large **multihospital chains** in the United States. In that year, two men—one a physician and the other an entrepreneur—joined forces to create the Hospital Corporation of America (HCA) to provide funds for capital expansion for the physician's hospital and to acquire additional hospitals. At that time, few of the nation's short-term, general hospitals were part of a chain (Light, 1986). In the intervening years, there has been significant growth of hospital chains—they are now a dominant form of organization.

Megamergers

Perhaps the most significant trend of the 1990s was the hospital **megamerger**—the merger of hospital chains. As an example, in 1993, the second largest chain, Columbia Healthcare (94 hospitals) acquired the largest chain, Hospital Corporation of America (96 hospitals) for $5.7 billion, creating a gigantic Columbia/HCA Healthcare company. Two months later, Healthtrust and Epic Holdings, two other large chains, merged to create a new company with 116 hospitals (a $1 billion deal); it became the second largest chain. Then, in 1995, Columbia/HCA Healthcare acquired Healthtrust for

$5.6 billion—creating a corporation with 320 hospitals (both had continued to grow), more than 60,000 hospital beds in 31 states and two countries, and an estimated value of $15 billion. Each year, there are hundreds of mergers and acquisitions.

Several of these large corporations have been under federal investigation, criminal indictments have been filed, and a mega-corporate shakeup has occurred. For example, in 2002 HCA agreed to pay $631 million to settle allegations of health care fraud (filing false claims for Medicare and Medicaid and paying kickbacks to doctors so that they would refer patients to its hospitals). This settlement brought to more than $1.7 billion that HCA has paid in recent years in civil fines and criminal penalties.

Key Issues in Hospitals in the Early 2000s

The Relative Contributions of Not-For-Profit and For-Profit Hospitals.   Advocates of not-for-profit hospitals typically argue that it is inappropriate to make a profit from patients' ill health. They contend that managers of non-profit hospitals are able to focus on the needs of patients and the resources necessary to meet those needs without having to consider the profitability of choices made. Because they do not need to earn a profit, their fees reflect only the amount needed to cover all expenses plus additional money necessary for capital and service improvements. Nonprofits spend much more money than for-profits to provide services for patients unable to pay—thus making a significant community contribution. The total annual value of uncompensated hospital care is more than $20 billion—holding relatively steady at about 6 percent of expenses.

Proponents of not-for-profit hospitals have charged that the for-profits use a variety of techniques to discourage access by poor patients. Included among these charges are (1) for-profits tend to locate in more affluent suburban areas where many patients have private insurance and that they then target marketing campaigns to these middle- and upper-class persons (a process called **cream skimming**), and (2) for-profits

conduct "wallet biopsies" in order to refuse uninsured patients access to the hospital. If the patient needs to be seen, the for-profit arranges a transfer to a nonprofit or public hospital, assuming it will accept the patient (a process called **patient dumping**), which some analysts believe happens to thousands of persons per year. Prompted by reports that hospitals sometimes turned away even emergency patients because they would be unable to pay for medical care, the federal government passed legislation in 1986 to stop this "patient dumping." The law requires hospitals to medically screen all emergency patients and prohibits them from transferring patients with unstable medical conditions or women in labor to other facilities for economic reasons. The maximum penalty for each violation is $50,000 and the possible loss of Medicare funding. However, patient dumping continues.

On the other hand, advocates of for-profit hospitals contend that the business approach that they bring to health care leads to both the highest quality of care (because they must attract enough patients to earn a profit) and to greater efficiencies (because eliminating waste maximizes profit). For-profit advocates also emphasize that the considerable taxes they pay make an important contribution to their communities, a contribution that is not made by the tax-exempt nonprofit hospitals.

Recently, many local, state, and federal government officials have expressed concern that some local nonprofit hospitals have failed to invest enough of the difference between their income and expenses to provide services for the community's indigent. For some voluntary hospitals in recent years, this margin (even after deductions for depreciation, overhead expenses, and community service projects) has approximated that of for-profit hospitals. Voluntary hospital administrators report that much of this money has been placed in reserve accounts that may be needed should an increasing number of persons lack the ability to pay for care. However, the tax exemption for nonprofit hospitals is in jeopardy in a few states. Both for-profits and not-for-profits are devising more sophisticated means of calculating the value of service rendered to community.

Both for-profit and not-for-profit hospital administrators acknowledge that the large number of uninsured persons unable to pay for hospital care is a significant problem within the health care system. As an example, in the late 1980s a young man in Georgia, without medical insurance, suffered burns over 95 percent of his body and was taken to the closest medical center (which did not have a burn unit). The medical center contacted more than 40 hospitals with burn units—both within the state and in neighboring states—both proprietary and voluntary—asking each to accept the patient. All refused, mainly due to the anticipated high costs associated with treatment and the likelihood of not being paid. Finally, a hospital in Baltimore, Maryland, accepted the patient, and he was flown there.

A case with some similarity occurred in 1998 at a California hospital. A woman who was having painful contractions and breathing problems due to asthma, and was about to give birth, requested an epidural (which allows a woman to remain awake during labor while blocking pain in the lower part of the body). The anesthesiologist demanded $400 in cash on the spot and refused the woman's offer of a credit card, check, or Western Union number for cash confirmation. The epidural was not given.

The Effect of Multihospital Chains on Independent Hospitals.   Hospitals that are members of multihospital chains have several advantages over independent hospitals. Among the most important advantages are: (1) economies of scale in purchasing—the chains buy more of products and get a lower per-unit cost; (2) greater negotiating leverage with managed care networks and health insurance companies, which can offer more favorable rates due to the number of people being covered; (3) greater ability to share the costs of new technologies; and (4) elimination of some duplication of services.

Lacking these benefits, independent hospitals have been put into a squeeze. Especially hard-hit have been black-owned hospitals.

Between 1961 and 1988, 57 of the country's 83 black-owned hospitals closed and an additional 14 others either merged, converted, or consolidated. Today, there are only a few black-owned hospitals in the United States, and some of these are in serious financial difficulty. Traditionally, these hospitals have served the uninsured who could not receive care elsewhere. Their demise has left a significant gap in hospital services for the poor and medically indigent ("Crisis of the Disappearing Black Hospital," 1992).

Recognizing the problem, many of the nation's independent hospitals have responded with a strategy that includes both horizontal and vertical integration of services. To capture some of the same economies of scale and other advantages of the hospital chains, many independent hospitals have themselves consolidated—a process referred to as **horizontal integration**. Theoretically, this creates the same bargaining and powers of leverage that exist in the for-profit chains. Many not-for-profit hospitals have also engaged in **vertical integration** activities. A common procedure is the creation of a corporation (often a holding company) that owns both non-profitmaking (including the hospital), and profitmaking enterprises. Sometimes the profitmaking companies are health related (e.g., hospital supply companies), which gives the conglomerate control over various levels of health care, and sometimes they are unrelated to health care (e.g., real estate companies). These arrangements allow the hospital to retain its nonprofit, tax-exempt status while it secures access to the funds raised by the profitmaking companies (although taxes are paid on these profits).

In the last decade many not-for-profit hospitals have been acquired by for-profit chains and converted to profitmaking status. With many nonprofits struggling financially to compete and with "acquisition fever" running at a high level, several voluntary hospitals have chosen to sell. This has resulted in some very bitter debates between profitmaking companies and community representatives who wish to retain the hospital's not-for-profit basis, and also between the companies and groups of physicians affiliated with the hospital, who do not wish ownership of the hospital to change (Claxton et al., 1997). Physicians in New York City, Los Angeles, and other cities have gone to court in attempts to halt these mergers and acquisitions.

The Survival of Public Hospitals. While many voluntary hospitals have found means to compete with the multihospital chains, public-supported hospitals have fared less well. Public hospitals are confronted with twin problems: (1) The number of patients unable to pay their hospital bills is escalating rapidly (more than one-third being unable to pay their bills) and (2) more competition exists for patients able to pay (and whose payments traditionally have helped subsidize the charity cases). Fewer paying patients and more nonpaying patients have placed many public hospitals—which often provide the only available hospital care for the medically indigent—in a desperate situation.

To help take up the slack, public hospitals have postponed needed capital improvements and service developments, and thus have become a less desirable care option for insured patients. Even at that, many public hospitals lose money year after year. Can this situation continue indefinitely? No—the survival of public hospitals is at stake.

Reconfiguration of Patient Care Services. Today's economic marketplace for hospitals is different from that which existed only a decade ago. The days of rapid expansion of facilities, services, staffing, and prices are rapidly disappearing. In order to compete in the new managed care environment, hospitals realize that they need to become far leaner, more efficient, and more diversified than they have been in the past. In what ways is this happening?

First, most hospitals are attempting to significantly *reduce expenditures*. They are doing this by eliminating inefficiencies (e.g., reusing supplies that once were discarded) and downsizing staffs. Studies show that not only the positions of hourly wage workers have been cut, but that positions of nurses, senior and middle managers, and medical technicians have also been cut back.

This downsizing has been controversial, but hospitals determined that labor costs had to be reduced. In addition, hospitals are beginning fewer construction projects and purchasing less large equipment. At the turn of the twenty-first century, however, much of the downsizing had already occurred, and most hospitals now anticipate steady staffing levels at the new, lower level.

In recent years, a new medical specialist—the hospitalist—has emerged. Hospitalists are physicians who work in and for a hospital and focus just on hospitalized patients. Currently, there are about 8,000 hospitalists in the United States, but that number is expected to increase to as many as 20,000. Hospitals hope that these specialists will help to closely manage the care of each hospitalized patient, improve patient outcomes, and be economically efficient.

Second, many hospitals are *diversifying patient care services*. Prompted by the cost containment environment and the increased willingness of Medicare, Medicaid, and private insurance companies to pay for low-tech, out-of-hospital services, hospitals are offering a wider variety of nonacute care services. The best illustration of this shift is the increasing number of outpatient primary care departments in hospitals and the increasing propensity of hospitals to do outpatient surgery. In 2000, outpatient revenues accounted for about one-third of total hospital revenues—about three times higher than the percentage in 1980—and most analysts expect the percentage to continue to increase.

Hospitals were rather slow in recognizing the desirability of outpatient surgery, and the percentage of all outpatient surgeries done in hospitals declined in the late 1980s and early 1990s. Each year now, however, the percentage of hospital-based surgeries done on an outpatient basis increases (it is now more than 60 percent). Hospitals also are becoming major purchasers of surgicenters. While the reimbursement for outpatient procedures done outside the hospital is less, the costs to the hospital are far less, so that the hospital profit margin is greater.

Part of this diversification has not been of hospitals' choosing. A current and potentially significant trend is the movement of diagnostic treatment technologies to private clinics. Services such as nuclear medicine, once only available within hospitals, are increasingly becoming available in private clinics. In many cases, the movement has been created by the bottom-line mentality in many hospitals, which is not focused on optimum patient care or a professional working environment (Stoeckle, 1995).

More Efficient Use of the Emergency Room. Almost all (95 percent) acute care hospitals in the United States have emergency units open 24 hours a day. Designed to provide care for acutely ill and injured patients, the emergency room has become something of a family physician for many people. In 2001, more than 107 million visits were made to emergency rooms—and in almost half of the cases, urgent care was not needed. Nearly as many patients complained of coughs and sore throats as those who felt chest pain. Nonemergency visits are highest in areas where physicians are least willing to provide primary care to uninsured and Medicaid patients.

Hospital emergency rooms appeal to people for several reasons: Access is relatively easy because it does not depend on affiliation with a physician, an appointment, or time of day; the availability of advanced technology leads to a public perception of high-quality care; and third-party payers have historically covered emergency room visits. But, on average, it costs two to three times more to treat someone in an emergency room as it does in a physician's office. With cost-consciousness now at a high level, services, such as hospital outpatient

---

IN THE FIELD

THE ROLE OF HOSPICE CARE

Hospices provide medical and nursing care, support services, and bereavement counseling for terminally ill patients and their families. The focus of hospices is to provide **palliative care**—that is, care intended to keep patients emotionally and physically comfortable and pain-free while they await death. Many hospices are in independent facilities, whereas others are administered in the patient's home, in hospitals, and in nursing homes. Hospices have a long history in many areas of the world but only began to flourish in the United States in the mid-1970s. Several factors have contributed to the growth of hospices, including the "aging" of American society with more people experiencing and dying from chronic illnesses, the difficulties of patients and families having to contemplate death through a long period of dying, the increasing cultural value of "death with dignity," and popular support for the humaneness of the hospice philosophy.

Only recently have hospitals begun to identify hospice care as being part of the diversity of services that they could offer and have recognized that hospice care meshes with efforts to control medical costs. In 1983, Congress approved Medicare reimbursement for hospice services, which run about 10 percent of average inpatient hospitalization costs. By the late 1990s, there were almost 3,000 hospice programs in the United States; more than 1,100 of these were run by hospitals.

Perhaps the main controversy surrounding hospices today is whether or not their existence eliminates any need for euthanasia. Some supporters contend that the management of pain and emotional support offered in hospices means that no one should have to suffer through the dying process and that euthanasia should never be necessary. Other supporters of hospice care argue that, in some cases, relieving significant pain can be very difficult and can only be accomplished through heavy sedation, and some dying persons also experience other unpleasant emotions such as frustration with confinement and psychic pain accompanying the loss of independence and body control. They contend that some of these patients may still prefer euthanasia (Levy, 1989; Logue, 1994; Burns, 1995).

IN THE FIELD

MEDICAL ERRORS IN HOSPITALS

Without question, errors happen in medicine. But, in the space of just a few months in 1995, an alarming and embarrassing series of serious errors occurred in hospitals around the country. At one hospital in Tampa, Florida, in the space of three weeks, arthroscopic surgery was performed on the wrong knee of a female patient, the wrong leg was amputated on a 51-year old male patient, and a 77-year old man died after a hospital employee mistakenly removed his respirator. Around the same time, the wrong breast was removed from a mastectomy patient in Michigan, the prostate gland was removed from the wrong patient in Maryland, a drug overdose killed an award-winning health columnist in Massachusetts and a male patient in Illinois, and oxygen was accidentally shut off to dozens of patients for up to 15 minutes in a Florida hospital.

The number and severity of these cases raised the issue of the adequacy of precautions and safeguards taken by hospitals to minimize the chance of error. Investigators immediately promised to determine if particular kinds of hospitals or hospitals with particular structures or formal and informal protocols have greater likelihood of being the site of serious error.

But, many analysts contended that the errors were a symptom of a larger systemic problem. This viewpoint was supported in early 1998 when another flurry of reports was published. Over the course of a couple of weeks, the Centers for Disease Control and Prevention reported that 2 million persons each year contract an infection while in the hospital and nearly 90,000 of them die from it. Several studies reported increasing evidence of drug errors in anesthesia and medications administered to patients. And research revealed the continuation of a previously documented problem: that hospital workers are negligent about washing their hands—and that physicians are among the biggest offenders. In the last few years several additional studies have found high rates of medical errors within hospitals with consequent morbidity and mortality.

---

departments, are being developed so that people feel less need to obtain primary care in the hospital emergency room.

HOME HEALTH CARE

Informal Home Health Care

Though often overlooked in scientific research, much health care still takes place in the home—either by self or by family members. Almost all care for minor illnesses is taken care of without formal entry into the health care system. Symptoms are monitored, activity may be restricted, medications are taken, and special attention may be given to eating nutritious foods and taking in fluids. More intensive home care is provided for persons with chronic illnesses, disabilities, and mental retardation, and for persons who are dying (Freund and McGuire, 1991).

Informal home care offers clear benefits: It may be more personal and nurturing, there is continuity of care, and it is usually not as isolating as institutional care (Freund and McGuire, 1991). But, there are disadvantages. Some families are not able to provide the needed nurturance and many family members may be resentful of giving their time, energy, and resources to caring for another. Because this resentment may be difficult or awkward to express, inner tensions may develop that ultimately are vented through verbal or physical abuse.

The obligation to care for ill family members tends to fall disproportionately upon females in the family, especially the wife/mother. Studies confirm that in most families, the adult female assumes the caring/nursing role, and this is true regardless of work and other commitments outside the home. Employed mothers report three times as many hours missed from work due to family illness as are reported by employed fathers (Carpenter, 1980).

Formal Home Health Care. Formal **home health care services** began 100 years ago with the Visiting Nurse Society of New York. Other home care agencies developed over the years, but by the mid-1960s, there were just 1,300 such agencies in all of the United States. The enactment of Medicare in 1965 spurred phenomenal growth in the home care industry—to more than 20,000 agencies today spending almost $40 billion annually on formal home health care. Other factors responsible for the growth of this industry were the increased number of elderly persons with chronic conditions, the increased number of AIDS patients requiring home care, and cost-containment efforts by third-party payers that led to earlier hospital discharges of sicker patients. However, 1997 reductions in Medicare reimbursement for home health care carved into the financial viability of many agencies, and the field has shrunk significantly since then.

Registered nurses provide most of formal home health care, while home-care aides assist many persons with more modest needs. To date, physician involvement in home health care has been minimal. However, physicians are being called upon more frequently to participate in the planning and management of elderly patients at home, and many hospitals have initiated home care departments.

SUMMARY

The sites in which health care services are delivered have changed with the development of modern medical technology and in response to economic conditions. Ambulatory care is still most often delivered through physicians' offices or clinics and increasingly through group practices. However, the number of freestanding ambulatory care facilities has increased dramatically in recent years, providing both walk-in centers and surgicenters, especially appealing to young and middle-aged adults. The number of community health centers and free health clinics, designed to serve the poor and medically indigent, have also increased.

Managed health care systems—such as health maintenance organizations and preferred provider organizations—are now a dominant component of the health care system. They have inspired significant cost-containment efforts throughout the health care industry and provide cost savings to individuals, families, and employers, but they have come under increasing attack for some of their policies.

As cost-containment efforts and managed care have stimulated efforts to deliver care at lower cost, the number of admissions to hospitals and the average length of stay have declined. Many hospitals have closed, and most hospitals have downsized staffs and capital expenditures and diversified patient care services.

Home health care is experiencing a revitalization, as the population continues to age and the demands for lower cost services increase. Home care is much less expensive than alternative hospital and nursing home services.

HEALTH ON THE INTERNET

The American Hospital Association Web site is located at:

http://www.aha.org

What is the American Hospital Association? What is its mission? Click on "Resource Center," and then click on "Patient Care Partnership." What rights are emphasized in the AHA's Patients' Bill of Rights?

KEY CONCEPTS AND TERMS

ambulatory care

ambulatory surgical centers (surgicenters or ASCs)

community and migrant health centers (C/MHCs)

cream skimming

dual line of authority

free health clinics

freestanding ambulatory care centers

government (public) hospitals

group practice

health maintenance organizations (HMOs)

home health care services

horizontal integration

individual practice association (IPA) HMOs

managed care organizations

megamerger

multihospital chains

palliative care

patient dumping

point-of-service plan (POS)

preferred provider organizations (PPOs)

proprietary (for-profit) hospitals

urgent care centers (walk-in centers)

vertical integration

voluntary (nonprofit) hospitals

DISCUSSION CASE

As the chief executive officer of a small-to-medium size company (100 employees), you are concerned about continued substantial increases in the premiums you are paying for health insurance for your employees. In the last few years, you have switched back and forth among commercial companies (depending on who offered the best rates in each year). Service has been good and your employees are satisfied, but you are concerned about escalating costs.

Last week, three representatives of a new, local health care corporation specializing in managed care visited you in your office. They are becoming established in your city, want to create a managed care network (either an HMO or PPO with the possibility of a POS option), and

have asked which type of managed care system is most appealing to you and your company.

You are not sure that you prefer a managed care system, but you realize it is important to consider one. To answer their question, you have decided to list all of the important considerations in choosing a health care plan for your employees. What are these considerations? List the factors that you believe must be taken into account in choosing a plan. Once you have listed these factors, consider each of the alternatives previously listed. All things considered, would you switch coverage to a managed care system? Why or why not? If you would switch, which specific approach would be your preference?

REFERENCES

American Hospital Association. 2003 *Hospital Statistics: Annual Survey of Hospitals.* Chicago: American Hospital Association.

Burns, John. 1995 "Hospices Play Bigger Role in Care Continuum." *Modern Healthcare,* 25:96.

Carpenter, Eugenia S. 1980 "Children's Health Care and the Changing Role of Women." *Medical Care,* 18:1208–1218.

Claxton, Gary, Judith Feder, David Schactman, and Stuart Altman. 1997 "Public Policy Issues in

Nonprofit Conversions: An Overview." *Health Affairs,* 16:9–28.

"Crisis of the Disappearing Black Hospitals." 1992 *Ebony,* March, pp. 23–28.

Department of Labor. 1967 *Technology and Manpower in the Health Service Industry.* Washington, DC: Government Printing Office.

Feldman, Debra S., Dennis H. Novack, and Edward Gracely. 1998 "Effects of Managed Care on Physician-Patient Relationships, Quality of Care, and the Ethical Practice of Medicine." *Archives of Internal Medicine,* 158:1626–1632.

Freund, Peter E. S., and Meredith McGuire. 1991 *Health, Illness and the Social Body: A Critical Sociology.* Upper Saddle River, NJ: Prentice Hall.

Hoff, Timothy J. 2003 "How Physician-Employees Experience Their Work Lives in a Changing HMO." *Journal of Health and Social Behavior,* 44:75–96.

Hurley, Robert E., Bradley C. Strunk, and Justin S. White. 2004 "The Puzzling Popularity of the PPO." *Health Affairs,* 23:56–68.

Kertesz, Louise. 1995 "PPOs Diversify, Accept Some Risk to Ensure Survival." *Modern Healthcare,* 25:41–48.

Levy, Judith A. 1989 "The Hospice in the Context of an Aging Society." *Journal of Aging Studies,* 3:385–389.

Light, Donald W. 1986 "Corporate Medicine for Profit." *Scientific American,* 255:38–45.

Logue, Barbara J. 1994 "When Hospice Fails: The Limits of Palliative Care." *Omega,* 29:291–301.

Lowell-Smith, Elizabeth G. 1994 "Alternative Forms of Ambulatory Care: Implications for Patients and Physicians." *Social Science and Medicine,* 38:275–283.

Mechanic, David. 2001 "The Managed Care Backlash: Perceptions and Rhetoric in Health Care Policy and the Potential for Health Care Reform." *The Milbank Quarterly,* 79:35–54.

National Center for Health Statistics. 2003 *Health, United States, 2003,* United States Department of Health and Human Services, Hyattsville, Maryland.

Perez-Stable, E. 1999 "Managed Care Arrives in Latin America." *New England Journal of Medicine,* 340:1110–1112.

Rosenberg, Charles E. 1987 *The Care of Strangers–The Rise of America's Hospital System.* New York: Basic Books.

Starr, Paul. 1982 *The Social Transformation of American Medicine.* New York: Basic Books.

Stoeckle, John D. 1995 "The Citadel Cannot Hold: Technologies Go Outside the Hospital, Patients and Doctors Too." *The Milbank Quarterly,* 73:3–17.

Waitzkin, Howard, and Celia Iriart. 2000 "How the United States Exports Managed Care to Third-World Countries." *Monthly Review,* 52:21–35.

Wholey, Douglas R., and Lawton R. Burns. 2000 "Tides of Change: The Evolution of Managed Care in the United States," pp. 217–239 in *Handbook of Medical Sociology,* (5th ed.). Chloe E. Bird, Peter Conrad, and Allen M. Fremont (eds.). Upper Saddle River, NJ: Prentice Hall.

16

THE SOCIAL IMPLICATIONS OF ADVANCED HEALTH CARE TECHNOLOGY

The development of **technology**—the practical application of scientific or other forms of knowledge—is a major stimulus of social change in most modern societies. Western cultures subscribe to a belief system that prioritizes "technical rationality"—a mindset that "essentially all problems are seen as manageable with technical solutions, and rationality (reasonableness, plausibility, proof) can be established only through scientific means using scientific criteria" (Barger-Lux and Heaney, 1986:1314). However, social scientists believe that technology not only is influenced by cultural values but in return has a powerful and deterministic effect on culture and social structure—a theory known as **technological determinism**.

HEALTH CARE AND TECHNOLOGICAL INNOVATION

Today's health care system reflects the rapid rate of technological innovation in the last few decades. Hospitals and physicians' offices contain sophisticated pieces of equipment and specially trained personnel to operate them. The benefits of advanced health care technologies are apparent: more accurate and quicker diagnoses, effective treatment modalities, and increased life expectancy. However, there are also negative consequences of technological innovations, including increased costs, inequities of access, technological "advancements" that fail (e.g., the artificial heart and thalidomide), and troubling ethical issues.

Societal Control of Technology

Advocates view technological development as a means for society to fulfill its needs and to create a better life for its citizens. The need for more powerful means of information storage and processing produced the computer revolution. The need for faster food preparation techniques for on-the-go families led to the microwave oven. Automobile air bags are a safety innovation in a society where thousands lose their lives each year in traffic accidents. According to this view (sometimes referred to as *utopian* view), society controls the introduction of new technologies; technological advancements continue because they are beneficial to society.

Others, however, are concerned that technologies also create problems (a *dystopian* view). They critique modern societies (especially the United States) for a failure to systematically assess potential technologies in order to determine whether or not they should be pursued. Instead, American society is said to be controlled by a **technological imperative**—the idea that "if we have the technological capability to do something, then we should do it…. [it] implies that action in the form of the use of an available technology is always preferable to inaction" (Freund and McGuire, 1999:243).

Critics charge that this technological imperative is clearly demonstrated in medicine: in the desire of individual physicians to do the newest and most sophisticated procedures—even if more conservative treatment would be as appropriate; in health insurance companies' greater willingness to pay for high-tech medicine rather than low-tech or non-tech care; in the march of hospitals to create (and thus be forced to use) high-tech wards (such as coronary intensive care units) even when they are shown not to offer any consistent advantage over more conservative, lower-tech, less expensive forms of treatment (Barger-Lux and Heaney, 1986; Freund and McGuire, 1999). Historian David Rothman argues that the insistence of the middle class to unfettered access to medical technologies has been the most important influence on America's health policy for at least the last 60 years (Rothman, 1997).

HEALTH CARE TECHNOLOGY

Advancements in health care technology have occurred throughout this century, but the pace of development in the last few decades has been phenomenal. Bronzino, Smith, and Wade (1990)

identify the following key advancements during these years:

1. *Cardiac technology.* Important innovations include the cardiac pacemaker, which senses the heart's own electrical activity and paces it appropriately; the defibrillator, which maintains the rhythmic contractions of the heart to avoid a "heart attack"; and heart transplants.
2. *Critical care medicine.* Significant advances have been made in handling ICU cardiopulmonary patients (those with insufficient heart and lung capacity). An estimated 20 percent of all hospital patients require some form of respiratory therapy or support, including administration of oxygen to patients who cannot maintain adequate oxygen levels in their blood with their own breathing; performance of physical therapy to break up secretions and mucus in the lungs; and mechanical ventilation for patients unable to breathe on their own.
3. *Medical imaging.* Noninvasive techniques such as nuclear medicine, ultrasound, computer tomography (CT) (also called computerized axial tomography—CAT), and magnetic resonance imaging (MRI) allow pictures to be taken of internal bodily organs.
4. *Health care computers.* These are used throughout the modern health care facility—in the clinical laboratory, in instrumentation, in building patient databases, and in diagnostic support systems. See the box, "Telemedicine."

The Social Implications of Advanced Health Care Technology

Sociologists and other social scientists have identified at least five specific social implications of advanced health care technologies.

First, advanced health care technologies create options for people and for society. These include using today's sophisticated emergency personnel and equipment to sustain a life that once would have expired; cardiac bypass surgery

IN THE FIELD

TELEMEDICINE

The information superhighway has created many new opportunities for sharing, obtaining, and discussing information. Although development and use of this technology in medicine (like in other fields) is still in its infancy, some of the potential is already evident. Research has found that up to one-third of adults in the United States have used the Internet for health-related information retrieval, and the number of people doing so continues to increase (Murray et al., 2003). Following are some ways that the Internet affects health care:

- Some dot.com physicians ("cyberdocs") have established Web sites where patients (sometimes referred to as "guests") can contact and chat one-on-one with available physicians; these sessions are viewed as an alternative to an office visit; many physicians are very skeptical of these sites.
- Home health care nurses can "virtually" visit patients through monitors that enable the two to see each other while talking on the telephone and even allows the nurse to check the patient's heart rate (the patient uses a stethoscope; the nurse uses a headset attached to the computer).
- Anyone with Internet access can retrieve information about any health care condition and treatment from a variety of Web sources. This reduces the traditional dominance of the physician as gatekeeper to

medical knowledge and enables individuals to directly access information. However, because well-educated middle- and upper-income individuals have the most Internet access, they will continue to obtain the most information.
- Electronic files of patient data can be created, stored, and easily communicated to other involved health care professionals.
- Medical journals can place abstracts or full text of articles on the Internet.
- Public health organizations and patient advocacy groups can place patient education materials on the Internet.
- Professional and lay groups can sponsor Internet discussion groups on health-related topics.
- Electronic mail can be used to enhance communication, especially among those located in rural areas without a wide support network.
- Educational courses can be offered on the Internet—as is already occurring in efforts to bring more public health information to health professionals and patients in Third World countries.

As reviews of health-related sites begin to be published, it is clear that there is a wide range in the accuracy and quality of information provided. As with all information on the Web, the consumer must be careful in selecting reputable sites (Goldsmith, 2000).

(where blocked cardiac arteries can be replaced by arteries taken from the leg); and procreation through the use of some form of new reproductive technology.

Second, advanced health care technologies alter human relationships. The existence of technological apparati that are able to sustain life after consciousness has been permanently lost have caused families throughout the country to discuss their personal wishes and have created difficult decisions for family members of

individuals whose wishes are unknown. Physicians and other health care professionals consider the option of "DNR" ("do not resuscitate") or "no code"—and engage family members in discussions about it.

Many people are concerned that the continuing introduction of advanced health care technologies has led to a dehumanization of patient care. Patients complain that physicians concentrate so much on the disease (in anticipation of selecting and using the appropriate technology) that they lose sight of the patient as a person. Feeling that they are being treated more like a thing than a person, patients despair that the warmth and empathy demonstrated by many physicians in the pre-high-tech era are being lost (Barger-Lux and Heaney, 1986). Discussion today of "cyberdocs," "robodocs," and "virtual doctors" indicates the increasing use of modern computer wizardry in medicine but suggests to many an increasingly distant physician–patient relationship.

Renee Anspach's ethnographic work, *Deciding Who Lives: Fateful Choices in the Intensive-Care Nursery* (1993), illustrates this concern. Anspach discovered that the different ways in which physicians and nurses relate to infants in an IC nursery affect their medical interpretations. Physicians, who have more limited contact with the infants and whose interaction is primarily technologically focused, rely on diagnostic technology to develop prognoses. Nurses, whose contact with the infants is more continuous, long term, and emotional, develop prognoses more on the basis of their interaction and observations. Although Anspach does not suggest that either prognostic technique is superior, her analysis demonstrates that one's position in the social structure of the nursery influences perceptions and that, to a certain extent, technology may distance the physician from the patient.

Third, advanced health care technologies affect the entire health care system. For example, technology has been one of the most important stimuli for the rapid increase in health care costs. Up to half of recent health care inflation is attributed to new technologies. Much of the problem relates to increasingly expensive equipment like CT scanners and nuclear medicine cameras, which cost upwards of $500,000. All told, the price tag for medical technologies in the world's developed countries in 2001 was an estimated $675 billion.

The United States is now confronting the realization that it cannot afford every potentially helpful medical procedure for every patient. Increasing the amount of funds spent on health care (already considered by many to be at an unacceptably high level) would mean reducing the amount of money spent on education, the environment, and/or other areas of government funding. When the country (i.e., the government or health insurance companies) chooses to subsidize new technologies, it is explicitly or implicitly choosing not to subsidize other health care programs.

These macroallocation decisions have led to increasingly sophisticated means of technology assessment and cost-benefit analysis. Efforts have been undertaken to quantify the outcomes of implementing specific technologies and to compare these outcomes with those expected from other health care programs. For example, should the government fund 50 organ transplant procedures or offer prenatal care to 5,000 low-income women? The box, "Technology Assessment in Medicine," discusses this process.

These decisions also include value questions related to such issues as the amount of money spent on preventive care versus curative measures, the amount of money spent on people near the end of their lives, the amount of money spent on newborns who will require extensive lifetime care, the amount of money spent on diseases related to "voluntary lifestyles," and mechanisms to provide equal access to available programs.

Fourth, advanced health care technologies stimulate value-clarification thinking. Medicine continues to raise issues that force individuals to confront provocative value questions about life and death.

As discussed in Chapter 4, the United States and other countries have recently mapped and sequenced the human genome (the complete set of human genes). The knowledge gained is dramatically increasing our understanding of human evolution and humans' genetic relatedness with other organisms, the connection between genes and human behavior, and the relationship between specific genes and particular diseases. It is conceivable that this knowledge will enable the elimination or control of all genetic diseases.

However, this process also raises value questions. For example, if all genetic diseases can someday be diagnosed and eliminated during

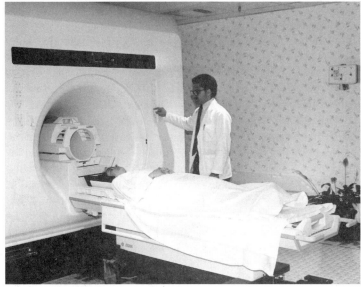

Noninvasive diagnostic imaging techniques, such as magnetic resonance imaging (MRI), represent a key development in health care technology of the last 20 years.

fetal development, will such action be required? Would broad genetic screening programs with mandatory participation for all prospective parents or pregnant women be established? Would it be illegal or immoral to produce a child with an unnecessary genetic disease? Could such a child file a "wrongful life" suit against her or his parents?

Who should (or likely would) have access to genetic information about individuals? Would an employer have a right to a genetics background check of prospective employees? Would health insurance companies be able to require a genetics check-up when deciding whether or not to offer insurance to someone or in calculating the cost of the insurance policy? How would

IN THE FIELD

TECHNOLOGY ASSESSMENT IN MEDICINE
***

What is health technology assessment (HTA)? According to Lehoux and Blume (2000:1063), it is "a field of applied research that seeks to gather and synthesize the *best available evidence* on the costs, efficacy, and safety of health technology." Littenberg (1992:425–427) recommends that any proposed medical technology be assessed on these five levels:

1. *Biologic plausibility* assesses whether "the current understanding of the biology and pathology of the disease in question can support the technology."
2. *Technical feasibility* assesses whether "we can safely and reliably deliver the technology to the target patients."

3. *Intermediate outcomes* assesses the immediate and specific "biological, physiologic, or clinical effects of the technology."
4. *Patient outcomes* assesses "overall and ultimate outcomes for the health of the patient."
5. *Societal outcomes* assesses the external effects of the technology on society including the ethical and fiscal consequences. All technologies include social, ethical, and political dimensions, and the sociopolitical implications for individuals and societies must be examined by social scientists.

discrimination in hiring or insuring be proven and be handled?

In addition to doing prenatal therapy to correct defective genes, will it be permissible to do therapy to provide for genetic enhancements? For example, would it be legal to attempt to "boost" the intelligence gene(s), or would it be ethical to abort any (all?) fetuses with low intellectual potential? Should the government subsidize prospective parents who want therapy to produce a taller offspring or a shorter one? What are the long-term implications for altering the gene pool? These questions exemplify the difficult value questions that are created by this new knowledge.

Finally, advanced health care technologies create social policy questions. Of course, issues that raise difficult value questions for individuals often raise complicated social policy questions for societies. Critics have charged that legislatures and courts have shaped policy regarding ethical issues in medicine prior to adequate public debate. This is beginning to change as these issues are now receiving greater public scrutiny.

An example of an advanced medical technology forcing social policy consideration occurs with **fetal tissue transplants**. The vast majority of abortions are performed in the first trimester

by the suction curettage method in which the fetus is removed by suction through a vacuum cannula. While the fetus is fragmented in this procedure, cells within tissue fragments can be collected. In about 10 percent of abortions using suction curettage (about 90,000 per year), the fragment containing the fetal midbrain can be identified and retrieved.

Research has demonstrated that transplantation of an aborted fetus's midbrain could relieve or even cure certain diseases, including diabetes, Parkinson's disease, and Alzheimer's disease. A high rate of successful transfer is due partially to the fact that this immature tissue is unlikely to be rejected by the recipient. In the early 2000s the issue became focused on the retrieval of stem cells—a universal cell residing in embryos and fetuses where is it called upon to construct hearts, lungs, brains, and other vital organs and tissues. When retrieved, stem cells can be transformed or molded into any type of organ or tissue. The created organ or tissue would then be implanted into a child or adult and would potentially cure a wide range of diseases.

However, fetal tissue and stem-cell transplants are opposed by those who oppose abortion. They believe that use of tissue from an

aborted fetus or embryo (even for such beneficial results) is an act of complicity in the abortion or destruction of a human life. Presidents
Ronald Reagan and George H. W. Bush placed
a moratorium on publicly sponsored research on
fetal tissue transplants. President William
Clinton overturned this ban in his first week in
office in 1992. President George W. Bush enacted a policy that allows research on a relatively small number of stem-cell lines already in
existence but prohibits public support for research
on additional lines, thus restricting and reducing
research in this area.

The relative rights of patients and physicians
vis-a-vis health care technology are examined in
the next section of the chapter by looking at
three questions: Do patients have a legal right to
refuse medical treatment—including artificial
means of nourishment? Can patients demand a
particular medical treatment even if physicians
judge it to be futile? Can physicians participate
in patient suicides?

THE RIGHT TO REFUSE OR DEMAND
ADVANCED HEALTH CARE TECHNOLOGY

Health care technology is at a stage of development in which it often is able to keep people
alive but without being able to cure their disease, relieve their pain, or, at times, even restore
consciousness. As this critical care technology
(especially the artificial ventilator) has been developed and incorporated in hospitals, the customary practice has been to use it whenever
possible.

Gradually, however, patients and their families have begun to challenge the unquestioned
use of technology and have asked (in the words
of the book and film) "Whose life is it, anyway?" Patients and/or their proxies have become more assertive in requesting, and
sometimes demanding, that the technology be
withheld or withdrawn. In some circumstances,
physicians and hospitals have complied, but, in
other circumstances, requests have been refused. These situations have often ended in
court hearings, and it has been the court system

rather than legislators that has primarily dealt
with the rights of patients and families versus
the rights of hospitals and physicians to determine the use of, or refusal to use, advanced
health care technologies.

Do Patients Have a Legal Right to Refuse
Medical Treatment?

Do competent patients, and incompetent
patients through their representatives, have a
right to refuse medical treatment? Or, are physicians and hospitals required (or, at least, law-
fully able) to use all forms of medical treatment,
including high-tech medicine, whenever they
deem that to be appropriate? This is the fundamental "rights" question that was addressed in
the landmark New Jersey Supreme Court decision regarding Karen Ann Quinlan.

Karen Ann Quinlan.   In April 1975, 21-
year-old **Karen Ann Quinlan** was brought to a
hospital emergency room. She had passed out at
a party and temporarily stopped breathing (during which time part of her brain died from lack
of oxygen). Blood and urine tests showed that
she had only a couple of drinks and a small
amount of aspirin and Valium, but that significant brain damage had occurred. Karen was
connected to an artificial ventilator to enable
respiration (see the box, "Defining Death").

After four months, the Quinlans acknowledged that Karen was unlikely ever to regain
consciousness, and that she would be severely
brain damaged if she did. Their priest assured
them that the Catholic church did not require
continuation of extraordinary measures to support a hopeless life. The family asked that the
artificial ventilator be disconnected. The hospital refused, arguing that Karen was alive and
that it was their moral and legal obligation to act
to sustain her life. The Quinlans went to court
asking to be designated as Karen's legal guar-
dians in order to disconnect the ventilator. Part
of the rationale offered by their attorney was
that the Constitution contains an implicit right
to privacy that guarantees that individuals (or
people acting on their behalf) can terminate

IN THE FIELD

DEFINING DEATH

The brain consists of three divisions:

1. The *cerebrum* (with the outer shell called the cortex; also called the "higher brain") is the primary center of consciousness, thought, memory, and feeling; many people believe it is the key to what makes us human—that is, it establishes "personhood."
2. The *brain stem* (also called the "lower brain") is the center of respiration and controls spontaneous, vegetative functions such as swallowing, yawning, and sleep-wake cycles.
3. The *cerebellum* coordinates muscular movement.

Historically, death was defined as the total stoppage of respiration and pulsation. Any destruction of the brain stem would stop respiration, denying needed oxygen to the heart, which would stop pulsation; death would typically occur within 20 minutes.

This definition was rendered inappropriate by the artificial respirator which, in essence, replaces the brain stem. It enables breathing and therefore heartbeat.

In 1968, the brain death definition of death was developed at Harvard Medical School. It defines death as a permanently nonfunctioning whole brain (cerebrum and brain stem) including no reflexes, no spontaneous breathing, no cerebral function, and no awareness of externally applied stimuli. Thus, if breathing persists, but only through means of an artificial respirator, the person is officially dead. Many persons today would prefer a higher-brain oriented definition of death like that suggested by Robert Veatch (1993:23), "an irreversible cessation of the capacity for consciousness." One effect of this definition would be that patients in a persistent (or "permanent") vegetative state would be declared to be dead.

---

extraordinary medical measures even if death results.

The Superior Court ruled against the Quinlan family, but the case was appealed to the New Jersey Supreme Court, which overruled the prior decision and granted guardianship to Mr. Quinlan. The court ruled that patients have a constitutionally derived right to privacy that includes the right to refuse medical treatment, and this right extends to competent and incompetent persons.

Mr. Quinlan again asked the hospital to disconnect. They again refused, though eventually they agreed to wean her from the respirator. When they did, surprisingly, Karen began breathing on her own. After a protracted series of events, Karen was moved to a chronic care institution, where she continued breathing until June ll, 1985.

Nancy Cruzan. Does this right to privacy extend to the refusal to accept artificial means of nourishment? (Artificial nourishment is typically provided through a nasogastric tube that delivers fluids through the nose and esophagus; or a gastrostomy in which fluids are delivered by tube through a surgical incision directly into the stomach; or intravenous feeding and hydration in which fluids are delivered through a needle directly into the bloodstream.) Or, is the provision of nutrition and hydration so basic that it is not considered to be "medical treatment"?

In a poignant and lengthy travail through the court system, the case of **Nancy Cruzan** provided a judicial answer to the question. In January 1983, Nancy was in an automobile accident and suffered irreversible brain damage. She entered a **persistent vegetative state (PVS)**. In PVS, the patient is not conscious, is irretrievably comatose, is nourished artificially, *but* is respirating on his or her own. This happens when the brainstem is functioning, but the cerebrum is not. The eyes are open at times; there are sleep-wake cycles; the pupils respond to light; and gag and cough reflexes are normal. However, the person is completely unconscious and totally unaware of surroundings and will

IN THE FIELD

ADVANCE DIRECTIVES

A **living will** is a document signed by a competent person that provides explicit instructions about desired treatment if the person is unconscious or unable to express his or her wishes. Now legal in all 50 states and the District of Columbia, the living will is commonly used to authorize the withholding or withdrawal of life-sustaining technology and provides immunity to health care professionals who comply with the stated wishes. Approximately 20 percent of adult Americans have completed a living will. Ironically, in most situations, physicians and hospitals ignore the living will if family members request medical treatment.

A *health care power of attorney* can be signed by a competent person to designate someone who will make all health care deci-

sions should the person become legally incompetent. It requires the person to be available in the needed situation but allows the person to consider the particulars of the situation before making a decision. Most experts agree that both types of advance directives have some benefit and encourage people to do both.

The *Patient Self-Determination Act* (sometimes called the "medical Miranda warning") went into effect on December 1, 1991. It requires all health care providers who receive federal funding to inform incoming patients of their rights under state laws to refuse medical treatment and to prepare an advance directive. The law should ensure that more people are aware of their rights vis-à-vis life-sustaining medical technology.

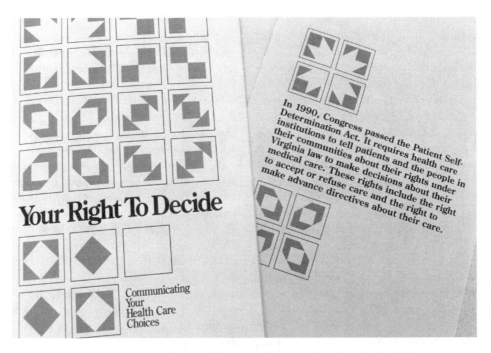

Many hospitals now provide patients with a pamphlet that describes their right to compose a living will and/or to authorize a health care power-of-attorney. The Patient Self-Determination Act requires that hospitals make these options known to patients.

remain in this state till death (which may not occur for many years). At any one time, about 10,000 people in the United States are in persistent vegetative states. It is not the same as **brain death**, in which neither the cerebrum nor the brainstem is functioning.

After four years, Nancy's parents asked the Missouri Rehabilitation Center to withdraw the feeding tube. The center refused; the Cruzans filed suit. They informed the court that Nancy had indicated that she would not want to be kept alive unless she could live "halfway normally." The Circuit Court ruled in favor of the Cruzans, but under appeal, the Missouri Supreme Court overruled, disallowing the feeding tube from being disconnected. The court concluded that there was not "clear and convincing evidence" that Nancy would not have wanted to be maintained as she

was. Missouri law required such evidence for the withdrawing of artificial life-support systems.

The Cruzans appealed to the United States Supreme Court, and, for the first time, the Court agreed to hear a "right to die" case. On June 25, 1990, the Court handed down a 5–4 decision in favor of the state of Missouri. States were given latitude to require "clear and convincing evidence" that the individual would not wish to be sustained in PVS—meaning that families could not use their own judgment to decide to discontinue feeding.

However, the Court did acknowledge a constitutional basis for **advance directives** (see the box, "Advance Directives and Navajo Culture") and the legitimacy of surrogate decision making. Its rationale cited the Fourteenth Amendment's "liberty interest" as enabling individuals to

---

IN THE FIELD

THE CASE OF TERRI SCHIAVO

In 2004 and 2005 the nation's attention was riveted on a Florida case that once again raised issues regarding persistent vegetative states, the role of proxy decision makers, and the power of the media and politicians to dramatize complex medical issues. On February 25, 1990, 26-year-old Terri Schiavo suffered a cardiac arrest that was, at least in part, brought on by an eating disorder. The disruption of oxygen caused permanent brain damage. Like Nancy Cruzan, Terri entered a persistent vegetative state and was kept alive by artificial nutrition and hydration.

For several years her case was similar to that of thousands of other PVS patients as both her husband, Michael, and her birth family did all they could to provide support. In 1994 the relationship between Michael and Terri's parents and siblings broke down over the manner in which a medical malpractice judgment would be spent. Four years later, in 1998, having become resigned to the fact that Terri's brain damage was permanent, Michael asked that the feeding tubes be withdrawn. Like

Nancy Cruzan, Terri did not have any form of advance directive, and Michael was the legal guardian and proxy.

Her family opposed this decision and filed a series of court cases over the next several years to remove Michael as guardian. All judgments found that Michael was acting within his legal rights. In the early 2000s the media picked up on the case, and details of the situation were reported on a routine basis. Florida Governor Jeb Bush, the Florida state legislature, and eventually, President George W. Bush and the Republican leadership in Congress became involved in the case and sought all available means to overturn the several court rulings in the case and to prevent the withdrawal of the feeding tube. Twice, the feeding tube was withdrawn and then reinserted. Congressional Republicans passed a bill that pertained just to Terri, but federal judges immediately found it to be unconstitutional. Ultimately, every court involved in the case ruled in favor of Michael's right to decide. The feeding tube was once again removed, and Terri died.

IN COMPARATIVE FOCUS

ADVANCE DIRECTIVES AND NAVAJO CULTURE

Discussion of ethical issues outside the context of particular cultures means that vital information is not considered. On a broad level in the medical context, it increases the likelihood of social policies that conflict with important values of particular groups. On an individual level, it creates potential for misunderstandings and frustration between health care providers and their patients and may lead to suboptimal care.

This is the case with regard to discussions about advance directives with Navajo patients. An important Navajo cultural norm is avoidance of discussion of negative information. In the Navajo belief system, talking about an event increases the likelihood of the event occurring. This belief obviously comes into conflict with several norms in medical settings: discussing risks as well as benefits of intended procedures, telling patients the truth about a negative diagnosis or prognosis, and preparing an advance directive. Ignoring the cultural val-ues of a Navajo patient almost inevitably means that care and treatment will be interrupted and perhaps discontinued.

On the other hand, acting with cultural sensitivity can enable the values of the patient to be respected while the medical responsibilities are discharged. Health care providers who work with the Navajo have been encouraged to pursue situations of this type in four ways: (1) determining if the patient is or is not willing to discuss negative information; (2) preparing the patient by building rapport and trust, involving the family, giving an advance warning that bad news is coming, and involving traditional Navajo healers in the encounter; (3) communicating in a kind, caring manner that is respectful of traditional beliefs—for example, referring to the patient in third party language rather than directly; and (4) following through in a manner that fosters reasonable hope (Carrese and Rhodes, 2000).

reject unwanted medical treatment. Because the decision did not distinguish between the provision of nutrition and other forms of medical treatment, the feeding tubes could have been removed had the qualifications of the Missouri law been met.

Ultimately, another hearing occurred in the Circuit Court; friends of Nancy came forward to offer additional evidence that Nancy would not have wanted to be maintained in a persistent vegetative state; and the judge again ruled for the Cruzans. No appeal was filed, and the feeding tubes were removed on December 14, 1990. Nancy died 12 days later.

Can Patients Demand a Particular Medical Treatment?

The cases of Karen Ann Quinlan and Nancy Cruzan illustrate circumstances in which a patient or her or his proxy wishes to refuse medical treatment. In 1991, an unusual twist occurred in the Helga Wanglie case: The hospital wished to stop medical treatment and the family demanded that it continue. This created the reverse of the usual question: Does a patient or her or his representatives have the right to demand medical treatment?

Helga Wanglie. In December 1989, **Helga Wanglie**, an active, well-educated 85-year-old woman tripped over a rug and broke her hip. During the next several months, she experienced several cardiopulmonary arrests. In May 1990, she suffered severe anoxia and slipped into a persistent vegetative state. Her breathing was reinforced by a respirator, and she was fed through a feeding tube. By year's end, her medical bills approached $500,000.

In December, the medical staff recommended to Oliver Wanglie, her husband of 53 years, that the ventilator be disconnected. He refused on the grounds that he and his wife believed in the sanctity of life and that, in good conscience, he could never agree to have the ventilator disconnected.

The hospital petitioned the court to have Mr. Wanglie replaced as Helga's legal guardian. The rationale was that Mr. Wanglie had made some statements that indicated that Helga had never voiced an opinion about being sustained in PVS and that he was not legally competent to serve as guardian. The hospital justified its request to disconnect by stating that it did not feel it should be obligated to provide "medically futile" medical treatment.

On July 1, 1991, the judge issued a narrow ruling that the hospital had not demonstrated that Mr. Wanglie was incompetent, and therefore he was the most appropriate legal guardian. Without the tubes being removed, Helga died three days later.

Medical Futility. Although the judge did not address the "medical futility" issue, the concept caught the attention of social scientists, medical ethicists, health care practitioners, and the lay public, and significant attention is now being given to it. It has proven to be an elusive concept to define. Schneiderman, Jecker, and Jonsen (1990) have defined **medical futility** as "an expectation of success that is either predictably or empirically so unlikely that its exact probability is often incalculable" (p. 950). In a quantitative sense, "when physicians conclude... that in the last 100 cases, a medical treatment has been useless, they should regard the treatment as futile" (p. 951). In a qualitative sense, "any treatment that merely preserves permanent unconsciousness or that fails to end total dependence on intensive medical care should be regarded as nonbeneficial and, therefore, futile" (p. 952). If a treatment fails to appreciably improve the person as a whole, they argue, physicians are entitled to withhold the treatment without the consent of family or friends.

While courts have supported patients' "negative rights" to refuse medical treatment, the issue of a "positive right" (the request for a particular intervention) is far different. It raises two questions: (1) a resource-allocation question (the more dollars spent on nonbeneficial treatment, the fewer dollars available to spend on those who would benefit), and (2) the reasonableness of requiring health care practitioners to engage in actions they consider to be unwarranted (and possibly harmful). Some believe that unless some benefit is anticipated, specific measures cannot be demanded.

However, successful intervention may be defined differently by different people. Families may be satisfied as long as everything possible is done—even if the patient dies. Their values may rest more on effort than outcome, and they may never define effort as being futile. Some view the issue as showing respect for the autonomy of patients and their families by honoring these value differences.

Physician-Assisted Suicide

An Anonymous Resident. In the last several years, three very dramatic cases of **physician-assisted suicide** have been brought to public attention. In 1988, an anonymous editorial entitled "It's Over, Debbie" appeared in the *Journal of the American Medical Association*. Written by a medical resident, it describes his administration of a lethal dose of morphine to a 20-year-old woman dying in anguish from ovarian cancer. The action was praised by some, condemned by many.

Dr. Timothy Quill. A few years later, Dr. Timothy Quill, a 41-year-old general internist in Rochester, New York, published an article in the *New England Journal of Medicine* (1991) in which he described how he assisted "Diane," a 45-year-old woman with leukemia, who had been his patient for eight years, to end her life. Diane had rejected the option of chemotherapy and bone marrow transplantation, which had a 1-in-4 chance of success, due to the certain negative side effects. After they had a thorough discussion and he was convinced of her full mental competence, Quill prescribed barbiturates and made sure Diane knew how much to take for sleep and how much to take to end her life. They continued to meet regularly, and she promised to meet with him before taking her life—which she ultimately did. While reaction was mixed, Dr. Quill received

Dr. Jack Kevorkian is pictured here with two women in whose suicides he assisted.

considerable praise for his action with Diane and his courage in describing the events in print.

Dr. Jack Kevorkian.   By far, the most public attention has been drawn to a third case; that of Dr. **Jack Kevorkian,** a retired Michigan pathologist who assisted more than one hundred people in ending their lives by providing a painless means to do so and by being present at the time of death. Each of the persons contacted Kevorkian (none were patients of his) and convinced him that they had made a rational choice to die. The particular means used varied from case to case. Ultimately, Kevorkian was convicted of violating Michigan's ban on physician-assisted suicide, and he is now serving a prison sentence.

Arguments Favoring Physician-Assisted Suicide.   Proponents of the legalization of physician-assisted suicide offer the following rationale:

1. It is perfectly appropriate to have physicians and other health care professionals create a comfortable and peaceful environment in which death occurs.
2. People have a right to self-determination; if one has reflected on life circumstances and made a rational, competent decision to die, the assistance of physicians in the act is appropriate. People should not be required to undergo mental and physical decline, to endure emotional and physical pain, and to incur sizable medical expenses for treatment not desired.
3. In order to prevent abuse, laws could require certain safeguards (e.g., there is intolerable suffering; the patient is mentally competent; a written, witnessed request is provided; the patient consistently and repeatedly over time requests death; and two physicians—one of whom has not participated in the patient's care—agree that death is appropriate).
4. An extremely high rate of suicide already exists. In addition to that which occurs without medical contact, it is clear that many deaths in hospitals occur with some "assistance." An estimated 70 percent of the 1.3 million deaths that occur in American hospitals each year involve some preliminary discussion or consideration and, at the least, an agreement not to take aggressive action to sustain the patient.
5. Public opinion polls show a majority of Americans favor the legalization of physician-assisted suicide and that in certain circumstances as many as half would consider it for themselves. Derek Humphry, president of the

Hemlock Society, a national organization in favor of legalized euthanasia, wrote *Final Exit: The Practicalities of Self-Deliverance and Assisted Suicide for the Dying* in 1991. It is a how-to-commit-suicide guidebook, and it became an overwhelming best-seller.

In recent years, voters in both Washington (1991) and California (1992) defeated referenda that supported laws that would permit active euthanasia and provide legal immunity for physicians participating in a physician-assisted suicide. However, in 1994, voters in Oregon approved (by 51 percent to 49 percent) the Death with Dignity Act that would permit physicians in the state to prescribe, but not administer, lethal doses of medication to terminally ill patients. The law was immediately challenged and ultimately heard by the U.S. Supreme Court.

In 1997, the Court ruled unanimously that terminally ill persons do not have a constitutional right to physician-assisted suicide, but that states could enact legislation consistent with their own constitution that permits it. A second referendum was conducted in Oregon later in 1997 and passed by 60 percent to 40 percent. In June, 1998, Attorney General Janet Reno removed the last legal obstacle to implementation of the Oregon law by indicating that physicians who participate would not be prosecuted. In a series of moves the George W. Bush administration, especially former Attorney General John Ashcroft, has continued to challenge Oregon's law and to threaten physicians who comply with it. Between 1998 and 2003, 171 individuals in Oregon selected physician-assisted suicide.

Arguments Opposing Physician-Assisted Suicide. Opponents of physician-assisted suicide offer the following rationale:

1. Traditionally, we have considered the physician's responsibility to be to sustain life and to relieve suffering. While actions taken by physicians may sometimes have the opposite effects, their intention is to do good. The primary purpose of physician-assisted suicide, however, is to cause death. The American Medical Association, the American Bar Association, and some medical ethicists believe this to be inconsistent with the physician's professional obligations.

2. Patients considering physician-assisted suicide may be sufficiently ill or so worried that they are not capable of genuine contemplative thought or the exercise of a true informed consent. The depression that might lead to consideration of this act might itself be treatable.

3. The legal possibility of physician–assisted suicide may interfere with a good physician–patient relationship. A physician's willingness to participate may be interpreted by the patient that society (and the physician) would prefer that suicide occur. This interpretation may place implicit pressure on the patient to request the act. Elderly and dying patients may be especially vulnerable psychologically. On a broader scale, a climate may be created in the country in which terminally ill people are expected to end their lives.

4. There could be a slippery slope argument—by legalizing physician-assisted suicide for patients with terminal illnesses, we increase the likelihood that suicide will become acceptable for other people—the mentally retarded, those with physical disabilities, and the very old, for example.

Reactions to "Debbie," Quill, and Kevorkian. While Dr. Quill's courage in assisting his patient's suicide and writing openly about it has been praised, the other two physicians have received a very mixed reaction with much condemnation. Arnold Relman, former editor of the *New England Journal of Medicine* called Debbie's case, "a grotesque distortion of the real issue," and "something that few if any doctors in their right mind would do" (Relman, 1991:45). Arthur Caplan, now a University of Pennsylvania medical ethicist, said of Dr. Kevorkian, "What we've got on our hands now is a serial mercy killer. Some people will say [he] is still providing an overdue service and…we should commend him—but I think we should jail him" (Caplan, 1991:2A).

The primary point of distinction in the cases is that Dr. Quill assisted in the suicide of a patient that he had known for many years and with whom he had long and engaging discussions about life and death. In that context, he agreed to participate. On the other hand, the resident who euthanized Debbie did not know her, had not talked with her, and had one, possibly nebulous, statement on which to base his or her decision. Dr. Kevorkian spoke at some length with all of his suicides but did not have long-standing physician–patient interaction with any of them. Many physicians, medical ethicists, and laypersons believe the lack of a personal relationship with the patients is the most troubling aspect of the resident's and Kevorkian's behavior, though many others believe that Kevorkian had adequate assurance of the competent desires of each person.

ORGAN DONATION AND TRANSPLANTATION

The ability to successfully transplant organs from a cadaver or living related donor is a relatively recent health care technology. The first documented successful transplant occurred in Boston in 1954 when a 23-year-old man received a kidney from his genetically identical twin brother. The recipient recovered completely and lived another eight years before dying of an unrelated cause. Bone marrow was first successfully transplanted in 1963 (Paris), the same year as the first liver transplant (Denver); the first pancreas was transplanted in 1966 (Minneapolis), the first heart in 1967 (Capetown, South Africa), and the first heart-lung in 1981 (Palo Alto, California).

Social Policy Issues Related to Organ Transplantation

The success of these sophisticated medical technologies has prolonged the life of many recipients but has created several complex ethical and social policy issues. Nancy Kutner (1987) and Renee Fox and Judith Swazey (1992) have identified the key issues as follows:

1. Do the medical and quality-of-life outcomes for organ recipients (and donors) justify organ transplantation procedures? The question, to be asked before all questions, is whether organ transplants have been shown to have sufficient therapeutic value that they should be continued. If the answer to the first question is affirmative, then the four following additional questions, at least, need to be addressed.

2. Given that the demand for transplant organs exceeds the supply, how should recipients be selected? Should a complex formula be devised to prioritize potential donees, or would a first come–first served (or random) policy be more consistent with democratic principles?

3. How can the supply of organs be increased? Organ donation policy has evolved during the last three decades, but demand continues to exceed supply. What policy might increase motivation to donate while maintaining a noncoercive nature?

4. How much money should be allocated to organ transplant procedures? Given the finite amount of money available to be spent on health care, how much should be directed to these very expensive procedures (most cost between $100,000 and $200,000) that benefit a relatively small number of people versus less dramatic, less costly procedures that might benefit a much larger number?

5. Who should pay for organ transplant procedures? Should (or can) the government be willing to pick up the tab because these procedures are so expensive? Should health insurance companies guarantee coverage? Today, the federal government's Medicare program pays for kidney, heart, and some liver transplants, and some health insurance policies cover transplants—people not covered in these ways are on their own, and those unable to pay are turned away.

This section focuses on the evolution of organ donation policy in the United States, assesses the current and alternative donation policies, and discusses the psychosocial dimension of organ donation.

Organ Donation Policy in the United States

The success of the early transplant efforts in the 1950s and 1960s forced the United States to establish a formal organ donation policy. The initial policy was one of **pure voluntarism**—donation was made legal and it was hoped that volunteers would come forward. Courts ruled that competent adults could voluntarily donate organs to relatives, which at first seemed like the only possibility. Organs could be donated by minors only with parental and judicial consent.

Donations did increase, but as the supply was increasing, so was the demand. The success rate for transplants improved with the development of the artificial respirator and the heart-lung machine and with the discovery of effective immunosuppressive drugs to suppress the body's immune system, thereby making the recipient's body less likely to reject a transplanted organ.

In 1968 the United States adopted "brain death" as the legal standard for death determination; this definition allowed organs to be taken from those who had suffered irreversible loss of brain function (and therefore were legally dead) but were being sustained on artificial respirators. Death could be pronounced, the organs taken, and the respirator disconnected.

These changes forced the United States to develop a more assertive organ donation policy: **encouraged voluntarism**. This occurred in 1968 with the passage of the Uniform Anatomical Gift Act (UAGA), which was adopted in every state and Washington, DC, by 1971. The UAGA permitted adults to donate all or part of their body after death through donor cards and living wills, and gave next-of-kin authority to donate after an individual's death, as long as no contrary instructions had been given. The UAGA was praised for maintaining the country's allegiance to a voluntaristic approach and was successful in increasing the number of donors. However, about 90 percent of the 20,000 to 25,000 people who were potential donors each year in the United States still failed to donate; no centralized system for identifying those needing and those willing to make a donation existed; and hospitals had little involvement in the program.

A dramatic change in organ donation policy occurred in 1987 with the establishment of a **weak required request** policy. To receive essential Medicare and Medicaid reimbursements, each of the nation's more than 6,000 hospitals must make patients and families aware of the organ donation option and must notify a federally certified organ procurement agency (OPA) when there is consent to donation.

Also, a national central registry (now called the *United Network for Organ Sharing—UNOS*) was created in Richmond, Virginia, to maintain a national list of potential donors and donees. To receive Medicare and Medicaid funding, all of the country's more than 260 transplant centers and 60 procurement agencies are required to affiliate with UNOS. When an organ for transplant becomes available, UNOS engages a matching process considering medical need, medical compatibility (size and blood type), and geographic proximity. Much of the physical work is performed by the OPAs: They encourage donation, contact UNOS when an organ becomes available, send teams to collect and process the organ, and deliver it to its designee.

The weak required request policy maintains the voluntaristic and altruistic nature of organ donation but seeks to ensure that potential donors are aware of the donation option. The request is sometimes handled very sensitively and sometimes with little enthusiasm and little tactfulness.

Studies indicate that few physicians and nurses have received any education or training in how to make a request for organ donation, and many feel uncomfortable doing so. Many physicians have been unwilling to be the asker, citing such reasons as uncertainty about their own attitudes regarding organ donation, lack of knowledge about organ donation criteria and processes, reluctance to bother a family during a time of grief, not knowing how to make the request, and lack of time and reimbursement for the donation request (May, Aulisio, and DeVita, 2000).

Yet studies indicate that more than 90 percent of health care professionals approve of organ donation, and many are willing to donate their own organs. A study of more than 700 physicians in a variety of specialties suggested that organ donation information programs for physicians would alleviate some of their concerns and make them more willing to make the request (McGough and Chopek, 1990).

These attitudes are extremely important because the comfort level of the requestor has been shown to have a significant impact on the likelihood of donation. When families are approached with lines such as, "I don't suppose you want to donate, do you?" or "The law says I have to ask if you want to donate," a refusal is very likely.

Has the 1987 legislation succeeded? The level of criticism directed at UNOS has been minimal; it seems to be well run. The number of organ donations did increase after the policy was implemented—but only to a 25 to 30 percent consent level. In 2003, more than 25,000 organ transplants (including the heart, liver, kidney, heart-lung, lung, and pancreas) occurred—the most ever. Moreover, organ transplants are more likely to be successful than ever before, and recipients are living longer. Yet, half of the families that are asked to consider donation after a relative has died do not give their consent.

As of 2004, there were almost 90,000 people on the waiting lists in Richmond who had been medically and financially approved for transplants, and the American Council on Transplantation estimates that more than 100,000 people in the country would benefit from some type of organ transplant (most of those not on the list have been rejected because they do not have the means to pay for a transplant). It is estimated that about one-third of the people on the waiting list will die before receiving a transplant.

Alternative Directions for Organ Donation Policy

There is some support in the United States for adopting a different or enhanced policy regarding organ donation. A recent study of transplant surgeons, coordinators, and nurses found that the current policy of altruistic donation was rated as being the most morally appropriate policy but that several alternative, more aggressive policies were also considered to be morally appropriate (Jasper et al., 2004). If the United States chooses to revise its organ donation policy, five main alternatives exist.

1. **Strong required request:** Every citizen would be asked to indicate her or his willingness to participate in organ donation—either on income tax returns or through a mandatory check-off on the driver's license. This policy retains the voluntaristic/altruistic nature of the system but is more aggressive in forcing people to consider organ donation and to take a formal position.

2. **Weak presumed consent:** Hospitals would be required by law to remove and use all suitable cadaver organs for donation unless the deceased had expressly objected, through a central registry, a nondonor card, or if family members objected. Sometimes called "routine salvaging of organs," this remains a voluntaristic/altruistic system but with a very significant change—the presumption is that donation will occur. In presumed consent, the person must take an action to prevent donation. Several European countries employ this policy.

3. **Strong presumed consent:** Physicians would be given complete authorization to remove usable organs regardless of the wishes of the deceased or family members. Also referred to as "expropriation," it is the only alternative that eliminates the voluntary dimension of organ donation policy, but it is also the policy that retrieves the largest number of transplantable organs. This policy is in effect in several European countries.

4. **Weak market approach:** Individuals or next-of-kin for deceased donors would receive a tax benefit for the donation of organs (perhaps a one-year deduction from federal and state taxes) or a cash payment of sufficient size to offset some funeral expenses. This approach adds financial incentive to a volunteer-based system, thus reducing the role of altruism. Proponents argue that offering financial benefit for the good being extended to others is fair and sensitive, but

opponents prefer altruistic motivation, and they worry that some likely donors would be so offended by the suggestion of payment that they would choose not to donate. Pennsylvania became the first state to incorporate this technique in 2000, when it began offering $300 to help families of organ donors cover their funeral expenses.

5. **Strong market approach:** Individuals or next-of-kin would be able to auction organs to the highest bidder. Like the weak market approach, this system places greater emphasis on increasing the number of organs donated than on retaining altruistic motivation for donation.

Critics of the strong market approach worry that the financial incentive may place undue pressure on low-income persons and people in the Third World to donate. Once organs are on the market, the wealthy clearly would have easier access.

The buying and selling of organs is unlawful in the United States at this time but is an available option in some European countries. A company in Germany routinely sends a form letter to all persons listed in the newspaper as having declared bankruptcy. The individual is offered $45,000 (plus expenses) for a kidney (which is then sold for $85,000). In 1995 India, the country in which the most people have sold organs to strangers, banned the practice and now restricts living donor-related transplants to relatives.

The Psychosocial Dimension of Organ Transplantation and Donation

Some of the most insightful work done in medical sociology has pertained to attitudes, motivations, and consequent feelings related to organ donation. Renee Fox and Judith Swazey (1978, 1992), leaders in this field of study, have written forcefully that the organ donation decision needs to be placed within a social-structural context. Based on years of systematic observation in transplantation settings and countless interviews with physicians, patients, donors, and families, they have raised three important concerns with donation and transplantation:

1. We have often engaged in the practice of organ transplantation while there was still too much "uncertainty" about its therapeutic value. Although there has been significant progress made in the 1980s and 1990s, organ transplantation continues to carry several limitations. For example, there is still a high incidence of long-term (5 or 10 years posttransplant) or chronic rejection of transplanted organs; many organ recipients are prone to redeveloping the same life-threatening medical conditions that led to the transplant; and repeated failures have occurred with certain transplant modalities (e.g., animal to human transplants and the totally implantable artificial heart). Fox and Swazey despair that these types of questions have not been given adequate and genuine reflection.

2. We have been so overwhelmed by cases of technological success in organ transplantation and the optimism and euphoria expressed by the medical and government transplant communities that we have neglected to fully consider the psychosocial dimensions of the organ donation and receipt processes. The focus of attention has become so fixed on the "organ shortage problem" and the "allocation of scarce resources" (as we discussed earlier) that the human dimensions of the process have seemed inconsequential. The very idea of the "gift-exchange" relationship between donor and donee has given way to discussions of "supply and demand" and compensation for donors. Fox and Swazey contend that this way of thinking commodifies body parts and reconceptualizes the "gift of life" idea.

3. The high price of transplant procedures and the fact that more people seek an organ than have been willing to donate one have created real, and not yet fully answered questions, of distributive justice and the public good.

The Donor–Recipient Relationship

Although research has shown that the decision to donate a kidney to a relative is typically made very quickly and with little regret, the decision to donate and the decision to receive an organ is governed by often unspoken but powerful social norms. In their studies, family members expressed an "intense desire" to make a potentially lifesaving gift to someone close, and they sometimes felt that donating was part of a family obligation (even sensing some family pressures). With this "gift of life," an incredible bond was established between the giver and receiver. In addition, some cases of "black sheep donors" surfaced, in which individuals who felt remorse for previous wrongs against the family wished to make amends through donation of an organ (Fox, 1989). For those who donate to strangers, there is often enhancement of self-image—a feeling of having actualized traits of helpfulness and generosity to others, and of having demonstrated their own altruistic nature (Simmons, Schimmel, and Butterworth, 1993).

Just as prevailing norms may motivate organ donation, they also motivate accepting it. Rejection of an offer to donate constitutes a form of rejection of the donor. When the donation and transplant occur, a type of "obligation to repay" is incurred by the recipient. Having received something so profoundly important, the recipient becomes, in a sense, a debtor—owing something back to the donor. Fox and Swazey (1978) referred to this as the **tyranny of the gift**.

Similar considerations occur in family members' decisions to offer cadaveric organs. These decisions are almost always made in traumatic situations, such as automobile accidents, in which the death is sudden and there is no preparation for it. Family members often consent to donation as a way of bringing meaning or some sense of value into a senseless tragedy. The altruistic and humanitarian aspects of organ donation become powerful motivating forces (Simmons, Klein, and Simmons, 1977; Fox and Swazey, 1978).

Fox and Swazey's *Spare Parts: Organ Replacement in American Society* (1992), is a powerful critique of organ donation and organ transplantation in American society. They indict society for the extent to which it has become obsessed with rebuilding people and sustaining life at all costs and for doing so while failing to fully consider quality of life considerations and the psychosocial aspects of donation and transplantation. The final chapter of their book describes their decision to leave this entire field of inquiry.

> By our leave-taking we are intentionally separating ourselves from what we believe has become an overly zealous medical and societal commitment to the endless perpetuation of life and to repairing and rebuilding people through organ replacement—and from the human suffering and the social, cultural, and spiritual harm we believe such unexamined excess can, and already has, brought in its wake. (Fox and Swazey, 1992:210)

NEW REPRODUCTIVE TECHNOLOGIES

Infertility

The reported incidence of **infertility**, defined as the absence of pregnancy after one year of regular sexual intercourse without contraception, is increasing in the United States. An estimated 10 to 15 percent of American couples of childbearing age are defined as being infertile. However, this percentage may give an exaggerated picture; up to half of the couples not pregnant after one year get pregnant on their own in the second year. The increased incidence of infertility is due to several factors: an actual increase in infertility (likely due to increased exposure to radiation and pollution and higher levels of venereal disease); the number of older women now trying to get pregnant (peak fertility occurs between 20 and 29); and more couples seeking assistance with lack of fertility.

The specific reason for a couple's infertility is traceable to the female partner in approximately 40 percent of the cases. The most common specific causes are: inability to produce eggs for fertilization; blocked fallopian tubes (so that the eggs cannot travel to meet the sperm); and a sufficiently high level of acidity in the vagina that kills deposited sperm. In another 40 percent of infertility cases, the specific cause is traceable to the male partner—typically, low sperm count and/or low sperm motility. The specific cause of the remaining 20 percent of infertility cases is either undeterminable or traceable to both partners.

The Development of New Reproductive Technologies

To enable infertile couples to produce children biologically related to at least one of the partners, several new reproductive technologies have been developed. These "assisted procreation" techniques have in common that at least one of the four traditionally essential steps of procreation—sexual intercourse, tubal fertilization, utero implantation, and utero gestation—is eliminated. More than 3 million couples seek medical help for infertility each year, and more than 100,000 attempt a new reproductive technology. This section briefly discusses four techniques—intrauterine insemination, in vitro fertilization, ovum donation (surrogate embryo transfer), and surrogate motherhood. Most of the section focuses on surrogate motherhood—the most controversial of the four new reproductive technologies.

Intrauterine Insemination. Technologically, the least complicated technique is **intrauterine insemination (IUI)**. During the time of the month when the woman is ovulating, she receives three inseminations of sperm through a catheter inserted into the uterus. The sperm may have been provided by her husband or consort, by an anonymous donor, or by a mixture of the two. An overall success rate is reported as 85 percent, though success on the first attempt is rare.

IUI typically is used: (1) when the male cannot produce a sufficient number of healthy sperm to fertilize an egg (it only takes one, but the higher the concentration of sperm, the more likely is fertilization); (2) when the female's vaginal environment is biochemically inhospitable to sperm or the position of the uterus is such or the size of the opening to the uterus is sufficiently small that fertilization is unlikely; (3) if both partners are carriers of a recessive gene for a genetic disorder (e.g., Tay-Sachs) or the male is a carrier of a dominant gene (e.g., Huntington's Chorea); or (4) increasingly, for single women.

More than 70,000 births per year in the United States occur to women who have been inseminated. The cost of an insemination is approximately $200 to $300 per cycle, but up to five cycles may be necessary (about 60 percent of women will become pregnant by the fifth cycle). All states deal with paternity by statute; in most states, insemination by donor sperm for married couples is legal with the husband's consent, and the offspring is considered his legal responsibility.

In Vitro Fertilization (Embryo Transfer). When infertility is due to the female's blocked fallopian tubes or low motility or low count of the male's sperm, **in vitro fertilization (IVF)** may be used. In this process, the woman is given a reproductive hormone to stimulate her ovaries to produce multiple eggs. A few hours before ovulation is expected, a small incision is made in the abdomen. A laparoscope (an instrument with a lens and a light source) is inserted to examine the ovaries. When mature eggs are located, they are removed by a vacuum aspirator and transferred to a petri dish (the so-called test tube) with the male's sperm and a nutrient solution where fertilization occurs about 80 to 90 percent of the time. About two days later, at an appropriate time of cell development, the fertilized egg is introduced through the vagina into the uterus. If the cell continues to divide naturally, it will attach itself to the uterine wall.

For women less than 35, about one attempt in two now results in a pregnancy, but some women try several times before achieving pregnancy. Each attempt may cost from $8,000 to $10,000. To increase the likelihood of a pregnancy, many fertility clinics implant multiple eggs. However, this has led to a sharp increase in multiple births—25 to 30 percent of fertility treatments (including IVF) now result in multiple births. The concern is that multiple births increase the incidence of life-threatening prematurity, low birth weight, and birth defects. From 1981 through 2002, approximately 120,000 IVF babies were born in the United States.

A modification of this technique is **GIFT (gamete intrafallopian transfer)** whereby eggs are retrieved from the woman's ovary and implanted with a sample of the male's sperm in her fallopian tube where fertilization may occur.

This technique has a slightly higher success rate and is no more expensive.

Ovum Donation (Surrogate Embryo Transfer).

Some female infertility is traceable to the absence of ovaries or to nonfunctional ovaries. Since eggs are not produced, there can be no genetic offspring. If the uterus is functional, however, there is no biological obstacle to gestating a fetus and giving birth. If the couple wishes to have the offspring genetically related to the male, **ovum donation** can be used. This procedure can occur in any one of three ways: (1) transfer of a donor egg to the woman's fallopian tube followed by sexual intercourse; (2) in vitro fertilization of a donor's egg with the male's sperm followed by insertion in the woman; and (3) artificial insemination of an egg donor with the male's sperm producing fertilization and then washing the embryo out of the donor and transferring it to the woman's uterus.

Surrogate embryo transfer is the most recently developed technique (early 1980s), the most expensive (approximately $10,000 per attempt), and the least commonly used, but it has a higher rate of success than IVF.

Surrogate Motherhood.

While all of the new reproductive techniques carry some controversy, **surrogate motherhood** has been the most controversial. In this process, a woman who is not capable or not desirous of carrying a pregnancy and her male partner contract with another woman (the surrogate) to carry the pregnancy. The surrogate is artificially inseminated with the male's sperm. If fertilization occurs, the surrogate gestates the fetus, bringing it to term and then gives it to the couple. The woman receiving the baby must adopt it.

The process usually occurs with the assistance of a lawyer/broker who develops an extensive contract. Early in its history, a payment of $10,000 to the surrogate was typical. Many experts distinguish between surrogate motherhood, which is "commercialized" (done for payment), and that which is "altruistic" (most commonly done for a sister). Between 1980 and 1990, about 2,000 births occurred in the United States using the surrogate motherhood process, but legal restraints have sharply reduced the number since then.

Considerable public attention was brought to the surrogate motherhood technique in the mid-to-late 1980s in the *Baby M* case. A New Jersey couple (the Sterns) contracted through a broker with another New Jersey woman (Mary Beth Whitehead) to be a surrogate. Whitehead had registered to be a surrogate with the Infertility Center of New York, saying that she wanted to help another couple. A contract was signed. The Sterns accepted all responsibilities for the baby even if there were birth defects; amniocentesis was required; an abortion was agreed to if problems were detected; $10,000 for Whitehead was put in escrow; and the baby would be given to the Sterns. IUI was performed, and a pregnancy resulted.

After the baby's birth, Whitehead changed her mind about surrendering the baby and refused the payment. When authorities came for the baby, she took her and fled to Florida. This prompted a three-month search by the FBI, police, and private detectives. When they were caught, the baby was returned to the Sterns, and the legal battle began. Ultimately, the New Jersey Supreme Court ruled that surrogate motherhood contracts are illegal; that both the Sterns and Whitehead had claim to the baby but that the baby would be awarded to the Sterns based on the perceived best interests of the child; and that Whitehead would get visitation rights.

Gestational Surrogacy.

A modification of surrogate motherhood occurs when a woman is hired only to gestate an embryo created from the sperm and egg of a contracting couple. In other words, the egg is not contributed by the surrogate, who agrees only to have the embryo implanted, to provide gestation, and to give the resulting baby to the contracting couple.

Analyzing Surrogate Motherhood

The Case for Surrogate Motherhood.

Proponents of surrogate motherhood base their position on two primary points. First, there is a constitutionally protected right to **procreative liberty**. Although some recent Supreme Court decisions have limited full access to abortion services, there is a tradition of judicial and legislative action that suggests a fundamental right not to procreate. The right to procreate has not received the same explicit judicial endorsement because states have not challenged married couples' efforts to give birth. Nevertheless, the Supreme Court, on several occasions, has indicated strong support for procreative liberty, especially for married persons.

Proponents of surrogate motherhood and the other new reproductive technologies contend that this right to procreate extends to noncoital as well as coital reproduction and extends to the use of donors and surrogates. Noncoital assisted procreation would be supported by the same values and interests that have always supported coital reproduction (e.g., a right to privacy and a belief that families provide emotional and physical support). Infertility ought not to be allowed to unnecessarily restrict a couple from procreation.

Second, use of surrogate motherhood is an expression of the involved parties' autonomy and may directly benefit everyone involved. All of the new reproductive technologies assist couples in procreation. Couples unable to procreate without such technology are given the expanded option of producing an offspring genetically related to at least one of the parents. The offspring will be born into a situation where he or she is very much desired, for the parents have gone to considerable lengths to have the child. The surrogate mother has the opportunity to make a contribution to others' happiness and to earn a not insignificant sum of money (though paltry if considered by the hour). All new reproductive technologies are freedom-enhancing procedures (Robertson, 1994).

The Case Against Surrogate Motherhood.
Opponents of surrogate motherhood level three main criticisms. First, surrogate motherhood is not in the best interests of the surrogate mother, the baby, and even the contracting couple. The deliberate separation of genetic, gestational, and social parentage places everyone involved in an awkward and improper position. Reproductive arrangements are negotiated between nonspouses;

the surrogate mother conceives without an intention to raise the baby, who could foreseeably be denied important medical information about lineage and could be psychologically harmed when told about the circumstances surrounding the birth. Both families could experience tension due to the unusual status of the surrogate offspring.

The legal and ethical requirement of an informed consent (see Chapter 12) may inherently be violated in the surrogate motherhood contract. Critics charge that it is impossible for a woman to know at the time a contract is being signed how she will feel about surrendering the offspring once he or she is born. Moreover, the requirement for voluntariness may be violated by the lure of the $10,000 payment. A payment of that size may place considerable pressure on low-income women to enter into surrogacy arrangements. If so, surrogate motherhood creates the possibility of exploitation of poor women.

Second, surrogate motherhood has a negative effect on the status of women within society. Woliver (1989) is critical of the extent to which discussions of new reproductive technologies (NRTs) focus on questions of individual rights and are presented as expanding options for women. She contends that the NRTs may expand options for individual women, but they restrict choices for women as a group.

Women's freedom to make parenting choices must be understood to occur within a culture that remains, in many respects, patriarchal. The zeal with which some women desire children and the vestiges of stigma attached to those who do not are culturally influenced. The growing movement to consider the individual rights of the fetus relative to the mother could restrict women's autonomy over their own bodies. In this environment, technologies have significant potential for abuse and oppression (Rothman, 1989).

Third, surrogate motherhood devalues people and creates a "**commodification of life**—treating people and parts of people as marketable commodities" (Rothman, 1988:95, emphasis added):

> This commodification process is very clearly seen in the notion of "surrogate" motherhood. There

we talk openly about buying services and renting body parts—as if body parts were rented without the people who surround the part, as if you could rent a woman's uterus without renting the woman. We ignore our knowledge that women are pregnant with our whole bodies, from the changes in our hair to our swollen feet, with all of our bodies and perhaps with our souls as well. (pp. 96–97)

According to this line of reasoning, the child—the contracted-for baby—also is commodified in that it is the subject of a contract and, in the end, will be surrendered in exchange for a cash payment. The transaction is tantamount to "baby selling" as the potential baby is "ordered precisely as one orders a car or buys pork futures" (Holder, 1988:55).

Surrogate Motherhood and Public Policy. Laws pertaining to surrogate motherhood are the responsibility of each state. There are three main options: (1) to legalize without restriction; (2) to legalize with restriction; and (3) to prohibit.

Strong proponents of surrogate motherhood believe it is inappropriate to place any greater restriction on it than on coital reproductive methods. If (at the least) married couples have a constitutionally based right to reproduce coitally, and if that right extends to noncoital techniques, then the case is made that these techniques ought to have the same lack of restrictions. However, few states have adopted this approach.

Most advocates of surrogate motherhood acknowledge that one or the other (or both) of two restrictions may be appropriate. The first is that states may restrict the ability of the contracting couple to demand specified behaviors during pregnancy and (more significantly) may insist that the surrogate have the right to change her mind by some specified point in time and retain maternal claim to the baby.

The second is that states may prohibit surrogacy for cash payment. The commercial dimension of the technique is the most objectionable part to many people. Macklin (1988) does not believe that surrogacy violates any fundamental moral principle but believes commercialism in the process does. Rothman (1989) would identify the gestational mother as the mother, who would not be able to sell or trade the offspring though she could give it to a couple in an arrangement that would be tantamount to an adoption. In this case, all parties would be governed by the traditional rights and responsibilities of an adoption proceeding. Many states are following this policy direction, which makes surrogacy legal but only without financial payment. In Great Britain, commercial surrogacy is banned, but the surrogate may receive expenses (usually in the $15,000 to $20,000 range) for time, lost earnings, and costs associated with the pregnancy.

Finally, many states have banned surrogacy altogether and have established a fine or imprisonment for anyone participating in the surrogacy arrangement.

SUMMARY

The myriad of new health care technologies has several social consequences: (1) It creates new options for people, (2) it can alter human relationships, (3) it can affect the entire health care system, (4) it stimulates reflection on important value questions, and (5) it raises social policy questions that must be resolved.

Advances in critical care medicine enable us to keep people alive even though we cannot cure them, relieve all their pain, or sometimes even restore consciousness. The cases of Karen Ann Quinlan and Nancy Cruzan have clarified the judicial right for competent and incompetent persons to refuse medical treatment—even food and hydration. Despite the reluctance of many health care professionals to provide medically futile treatment—even when demanded by patients' families—the courts refused to allow a hospital to stop treatment for Helga Wanglie.

The ability to successfully transplant organs and the demand for transplants have raised several complex questions regarding the nation's organ donation policy and the consequences for individuals who are involved. The United States now has a policy of weak required request—patients or their families must be notified about the option of organ donation. Because many people die before an organ becomes available, there is discussion about going to a more aggressive policy: presuming that people wish to donate or enabling donors to financially benefit.

Many American couples who are infertile seek one of the new reproductive technologies for assistance. The most controversial of the assisted procreation techniques is surrogate motherhood. Proponents argue that there is and should be procreative liberty and that patient autonomy demands that couples have access to this technique. Opponents argue that surrogacy is not in the best interest of the surrogate, the child, and even the contracting couple; that the process demeans women and reduces them to their reproductive capacity; and that it leads to a commodification and cheapening of life. Some states have retained the legality of surrogacy but outlawed payment to the surrogate; other states have banned the practice.

HEALTH ON THE INTERNET

The United Network for Organ Sharing makes available to the public updated information about transplant programs and services. Connect to their Web site at:

http://www.unos.org/

Click on "Data" and then "View summary U.S. transplantation data" and answer the following questions: How many transplants have been done in the last year? How many donors were used? Of the donors, how many were deceased and how many living? How many individuals are currently on the waiting list for a transplant? Go back to "Data" and click on the link to specific organs. Select an organ and determine the kinds of information that are available about the transplantation of this organ.

KEY CONCEPTS AND TERMS

advance directives
brain death
commodification of life
encouraged voluntarism
fetal tissue transplants
GIFT (gamete intrafallopian transfer)
Helga Wanglie
infertility
intrauterine insemination (IUI)
in vitro fertilization (IVF)
Jack Kevorkian
Karen Ann Quinlan
living will
medical futility
Nancy Cruzan
ovum donation

persistent vegetative state (PVS)
physician-assisted suicide
procreative liberty
pure voluntarism
strong market approach
strong presumed consent
strong required request
surrogate motherhood
technological determinism
technological imperative
technology
tyranny of the gift
weak market approach
weak presumed consent
weak required request

DISCUSSION CASE

In 1993 the Dutch Supreme Court officially acted to decriminalize active euthanasia, a practice that had been occurring for more than 25 years. The 1993 ruling protects physicians who engage in physician-assisted suicide or in any form of active euthanasia so long as basic guidelines are followed. The guidelines include:

1. The patient's request is the result of sound, informed consent (the patient is competent, the request is voluntary and made without undue pressure) and is reviewed, discussed, and repeated.
2. The patient's suffering, both physical and mental, is severe and cannot be relieved by any other means.
3. The attending physician must consult with a colleague regarding the patient's condition and the genuineness and appropriateness of the request for euthanasia.

4. Only physicians may engage in euthanasia.

Requests for physician-assisted active euthanasia come mainly from patients with incurable cancer (70 percent), chronic degenerative neurological disorders (10 percent), and chronic obstructive pulmonary disease. Patients seeking euthanasia report both physical and psychological pain. Though Dutch law requires physicians to report the causes of death, some critics charge that euthanasia is underreported. Estimates are that more than 5,000 cases of euthanasia occur each year. Public opinion polls have found that more than 60 percent of Dutch citizens favor physician-assisted euthanasia.

What arguments favor physician-assisted active euthanasia and what arguments oppose the practice? Should the United States adopt the Dutch policy? What would be the social ramifications of adopting this policy?

REFERENCES

Anspach, Renee. 1993 *Deciding Who Lives: Fateful Choices in the Intensive-Care Nursery.* Berkeley: University of California Press.

Barger-Lux, M. Janet, and Robert P. Heaney. 1986 "For Better and Worse: The Technological Imperative in Health Care." *Social Science and Medicine,* 22:1313–1320.

Bronzino, Joseph D., Vincent H. Smith, and Maurice L. Wade. 1990 *Medical Technology and Society: An Interdisciplinary Perspective.* Cambridge, MA: The MIT Press.

Caplan, Arthur. 1991 Quoted in Patricia Edmonds and Carol J. Castaneda, "Debate Over Right-to-Die Rekindled." *USA Today,* October 25, pp. A1–A2.

Carrese, Joseph A., and Lorna A. Rhodes. 2000 "Bridging Cultural Differences in Medical Practice." *Journal of General Internal Medicine,* 15:92–96.

Fox, Renee C. 1989 *The Sociology of Medicine: A Participant Observer's View.* Upper Saddle River, NJ: Prentice Hall.

Fox, Renee C., and Judith P. Swazey. 1978 *The Courage to Fail: A Social View of Organ Transplants and Dialysis,* 2nd ed. Chicago: University of Chicago Press.

———. 1992 *Spare Parts: Organ Replacement in American Society.* New York: Oxford University Press.

Freund, Peter E. S., and Meredith B. McGuire. 1999 *Health, Illness, and the Social Body* (3rd ed.). Upper Saddle River, NJ: Prentice Hall.

Goldsmith, Jeff. 2000 "How Will the Internet Change Our Health System?" *Health Affairs,* 19:148–156.

Holder, Angela R. 1988 "Surrogate Motherhood and the Best Interests of Children." *Law, Medicine, & Health Care,* 16:51–56.

Humphry, Derek. 1991 *Final Exit: The Practicalities of Self-Deliverance and Assisted Suicide for the Dying.* Los Angeles: The Hemlock Society.

Institute of Medicine. 1985 *Assessing Medical Technologies.* Washington, DC: National Academy Press.

"It's Over, Debbie." 1988 *Journal of the American Medical Association,* 259:272.

Jasper, J. D., Carol A. E. Nickerson, Peter A. Ubel, and David A. Asch. 2004 "Altruism, Incentives, and Organ Donation: Attitudes of the Transplant Community." *Medical Care,* 42:378–386.

Kutner, Nancy G. 1987 "Issues in the Application of High Cost Medical Technology: The Case of

Organ Transplantation." *Journal of Health and Social Behavior,* 28:23–36.

Lehoux, Pascale, and Stuart Blume. 2000 "Technology Assessment and the Sociopolitics of Health Technologies." *Journal of Health Politics, Policy, and Law,* 25:1063–1120.

Littenberg, Benjamin. 1992 "Technology Assessment in Medicine." *Academic Medicine,* 67:424–428.

Macklin, Ruth. 1988 "Is There Anything Wrong with Surrogate Motherhood? An Ethical Analysis." *Law, Medicine, & Health Care,* 16:57–64.

May, Thomas, Mark P. Aulisio, and Michael A. DeVita. 2000 "Patients, Families, and Organ Donation: Who Should Decide?" *The Milbank Quarterly,* 78:323–336.

McGough, E. A., and M. W. Chopek. 1990 "The Physician's Role as Asker in Obtaining Organ Donations." *Transplantation Proceedings,* 22:267–272.

Murray, Elizabeth, Bernard Lo, Lance Pollack, Karen Donelan, Joe Catania, Martha White, Kinga Zapert, and Rachel Turner. 2003 "The Impact of Health Information on the Internet on the Physician-Patient Relationship." *Archives of Internal Medicine,* 163:1727–1734.

Quill, Timothy E. 1991 "Death and Dignity: A Case of Individualized Decision Making." *New England Journal of Medicine,* 324:691–694.

Relman, Arnold. 1991 Quoted in "Account of Assisted Suicide in Journal Advances Debate." *Medical Ethics Advisor,* 7:45.

Robertson, John A. 1994 *Children of Choice: Freedom and the New Reproductive Technologies.* Princeton, NJ: Princeton University Press.

Rothman, Barbara K. 1988 "Reproductive Technology and the Commodification of Life." *Women and Health,* 13:95–100.

———. 1989 *Recreating Motherhood: Ideology and Technology in a Patriarchal Society.* New York: W.W. Norton.

Rothman, David J. 1997 *Beginnings Count: The Technological Imperative in American Health Care.* New York: Oxford University Press.

Schneiderman, Lawrence J., Nancy S. Jecker, and Albert R. Jonsen. 1990 "Medical Futility: Its Meaning and Ethical Implications." *Annals of Internal Medicine,* 112:949–954.

Simmons, Roberta G., Mindy Schimmel, and Victoria Butterworth. 1993 "The Self-Image of Unrelated Bone Marrow Donors." *Journal of Health and Social Behavior,* 34:285–301.

Simmons, Roberta G., Susan D. Klein, and Richard L. Simmons. 1977 *Gift of Life: The Social and Psychological Impact of Organ Transplantation.* New York: John Wiley.

Veatch, Robert M. 1993 "The Impending Collapse of the Whole-Brain Definition of Death." *Hastings Center Report,* 23:18–24.

Woliver, Laura R. 1989 "The Deflective Power of Reproductive Technologies: The Impact on Women." *Women & Politics,* 9:17–47.

17

COMPARATIVE HEALTH CARE SYSTEMS

Studying the health care systems of other countries offers three valuable benefits: (1) an understanding of the diversity of approaches that exist to meet health care needs; (2) an understanding of the variety of factors that have shaped the development of these approaches; and (3) an understanding of how the health care system in the United States compares and contrasts with those in other countries. Donald Light, who has written extensively on health care systems around the world, has said that the health care system in the United States "is so unusual that only by comparing it with other systems can those of us who live inside it gain the perspective we need to understand how it works" (Light, 1990:429).

MAJOR INFLUENCES ON HEALTH CARE SYSTEMS

Comparative studies of public policy have taught at least one clear principle: Every public policy in every country is shaped by a unique configuration of forces. Whether the subject is policy as it relates to education, the environ-

ment, or health care and whether the focus is the United States, China, or Canada, a host of factors are important determinants.

> The range and number of factors that influence or determine what governments do or, for that matter, what they choose not to do, are virtually infinite. Public policy may be influenced by prior policy commitments, international tension, a nation's climate, economic wealth, degree of ethnic conflict, historical traditions, the personality of its leadership, the level of literacy of its people, the nature of its party system, and whether it is governed by civilian or military leaders. . . . Virtually anything can influence or determine what governments do. (Leichter, 1979:38)

To clarify this myriad of forces, we have created "A Framework of Major Influences on Health Care Systems" (see the box) that is based on the work of Alford (1969), Leichter (1979), and Lassey, Lassey, and Jinks (1997). The framework includes factors related to:

1. *The physical environment* (e.g., the presence of environmental pollutants and the resources needed to combat them),

IN THE FIELD

A FRAMEWORK OF MAJOR INFLUENCES ON HEALTH CARE SYSTEMS

I. Physical Environmental Factors

A. Availability of natural resources, including land, water, fertile soil, and minerals
B. Exposure of population to harmful pollutants in the air or in the water
C. Control of disease agents such as rodents and noxious substances in the environment

II. Situational-Historical Factors

A. Specific political events and conditions such as achieving independence or a major change in the ruling political regime or political leadership
B. Major economic changes such as depression or rapid inflation
C. Significant technological development

III. Cultural Factors

A. Norms and values concerning the emphasis on individual versus community responsibility
B. Norms and values concerning science and the incorporation of new technologies
C. Norms and values concerning social inequality and the just distribution of social resources

IV. Structural Factors

A. Political factors, including extent of government centralization or decentralization, influence of professional and popular interest groups, nature of the political process
B. Economic factors, including the type of economic system (free market or planned), whether the economic base is more agrarian or industrial, national wealth and distribution of income
C. Demographic factors, including age structure, birthrate, level of education, degree of urbanization
D. Social factors, including conditions of housing and neighborhoods, reliance on family versus formal organizations, nature of incentive and reward system

Source: Framework drawn from the work of Robert Alford, *Bureaucracy and Participation: Political Culture in Four Wisconsin Cities.* Chicago: Rand McNally, 1969; Howard M. Leichter, *A Comparative Approach to Policy Analysis: Health Care Policy in Four Nations.* Cambridge: Cambridge University Press, 1979; and Marie L. Lassey, William R. Lassey, and Martin J. Jinks, *Health Care Systems Around the World.* Upper Saddle River, NJ: Prentice Hall, 1997.

2. *Historical and situational events* that influence health care policy (e.g., America's depression in the 1920s and 1930s),
3. *Cultural norms and values* (e.g., Lynn Payer (1989) relates the propensity of American physicians to order more drugs, do more diagnostic procedures, and do more surgery than their European counterparts to the aggressive "can do" spirit that is part of the cultural makeup of the United States), and
4. *The structure of society,* including political factors (the extent of government centralization), economic factors (the level of national wealth), demographic factors (age structure and degree of urbanization), and social factors (reliance on family versus social organizations).

Even within the same country and at the same time, these factors may differentially affect public policy choices. Often, analysts assign differing weights to them. For example, in the United States, many economists hold to a *popular choice* position—that we have the type of health care system we do because it is the type of system people want. People's preferences are expressed through individual decisions in the marketplace and through voting behavior. Others, including many sociologists and political scientists, favor a *power group* explanation—that health policies have largely been shaped by the power and influence of certain groups (e.g., the AMA, hospitals, and insurance companies). Some analysts emphasize

IN THE FIELD

RATING THE WORLD'S HEALTH CARE SYSTEMS

In recent years, several impressive efforts have been undertaken to evaluate and rate the world's health care systems. In 2000 the World Health Organization evaluated the health care system of 191 nations on health care delivery. The report took into consideration the overall health of each country, health inequities in the population, how nations respond to problems in their health care systems, how well people of varying economic status within a country are served by their system, and how costs are distributed. What country earned the highest score? The top scorer was France, which was followed in the rankings by Italy, San Marino, Andorra, Malta, Singapore, Spain, Oman, Austria, and Japan. Despite spending much more money on health care than any other nation—both in absolute and relative terms—the United States finished 37th.

Another study compared the current performance of the health care systems in 29 modern, industrialized nations relative to studies conducted in 1960 and 1980. Evaluation focused on six categories of performance: (1) preventive health care (e.g., immunization, promotion of healthy lifestyles); (2) health care use and services (e.g., number of physician visits per year); (3) sophisticated technology (e.g., availability of high-technology equipment); (4) mortality; (5) health system responsiveness; and (6) stability of per capita health spending relative to national income. On most indicators, the United States fared poorly. The overall relative performance of the United States and its relative performance on most individual categories declined since 1960, and the United States did not improve its relative ranking in a single category (Anderson and Hussey, 2001).

the influence of economic development and demographic makeup (e.g., the influence of available resources and the percentage of elderly within the society). Marxist analysis focuses on the role of class formation, class interests, and the political behavior of the classes and explains America's lack of universal health care coverage as being due to the weakness of labor unions and the absence of an influential and broadly based socialist party (Navarro, 1989).

HEALTH CARE SERVICES IN DEVELOPING AND INDUSTRIALIZED COUNTRIES

The world's developing countries experience a doubly difficult situation with regard to providing for the public health: more health problems and considerably fewer resources to invest in the health care system (see Table 17–1).

Over the next several decades, developing countries are expected to undergo an epidemiological transition as their disease and illness

TABLE 17–1   Global Distribution of Population, Income, and Per Capita Health Spending, 2001

	Population (%)	Income (%)	Per Capita Health Spending
Distribution by Income Group			
High-income countries	15	80	$2,841
($8,500+ per capita income)			
Low- and middle-income countries	85	20	72

Source: *The World Bank Health, Nutrition, and Population Database,* Washington, DC: World Bank, 2002, with permission.

pattern comes to more closely resemble that of developed countries. Part of this transition will occur should there be reductions in under-age-five mortality, as rates today are about 10 times higher in developing countries. Expected improvements in prevention of communicable (acute infectious) diseases should lead to a decline in mortality from these causes. Due to the high rate of death at relatively early ages from communicable diseases, the overall mortality rate today is twice as high in developing countries as in developed countries. Even among developing countries, wide variations exist; for example, adult mortality in sub-Saharan Africa is more than twice that found in Latin America and the Caribbean. As populations live longer, they will be more likely to experience the same kinds of noncommunicable (chronic, degenerative) diseases, such as heart disease and cancer, that now dominate in developed countries (Schieber and Maeda, 1999).

It will be a major challenge for developing countries to inject sufficient money into the health care system to keep pace with already existing problems and those created by the transition. Today, developing countries spend only about 4 percent of their income on health care—about one-half of what most developed countries spend. This has led to developed countries having about three times more physicians per capita than developing countries and about six times more hospital beds (Schieber and Maeda, 1999). As an example, in 1998, India spent about $17 billion on health care for its population of 1 billion persons—about the same amount as Medicare spent on its 2.7 million recipients in the state of Florida alone.

Health system reform movements in developing countries are already facing some of the same problems as those in developed countries: access to care, quality of care, and system efficiency. More resources need to be invested in the public health infrastructure, especially in rural areas. Given the government's lesser revenue-raising ability, pressures mount to turn more of the system over to the private market. This may work to the benefit of the middle and upper classes, but it forces many in the lower classes out of the health care system (as occurs in the United States). Throughout the world, countries are watching closely the American experience with managed care, and most have already implemented some aspects of it.

TYPES OF HEALTH CARE SYSTEMS

To examine variations in health care systems around the world, Milton Roemer (1991) developed a typology which has been modified by Don Light and is portrayed in Table 17–2. Based on a country's level of affluence (ranging from affluent to poor) and the degree of government

TABLE 17–2   Health Care Systems by Wealth and Control

| Affluence (GNP/capita) | The Degree of Governmental Control | | | |
| | Decentralized | | | Centralized |
	Private insurance, Private, Entrepreneurial Services	National insurance, Private, Regulated Services	National Insurance, Public, Regulated Services	National insurance State-run System
Affluent	United States	Germany Canada	Great Britain Norway	former East Germany former Soviet Union
Wealthy but Developing	—	Libya	Kuwait	—
Modest and Developing	Thailand	Brazil	Israel	Cuba
Poor	Ghana	India	Tanzania	China

Source: Donald W. Light, "Comparative Models of Health Care Systems," pp. 455–470 in *The Sociology of Health and Illness*, 4th ed., Peter Conrad and Rochelle Kern (eds.). New York: St. Martin's Press, 1994. From Milton I. Roemer, *National Health Systems of the World*, Vol. 1, New York: Oxford University Press, 1991, with permission.

TABLE 17–3   Vital Statistics by Level of Development and for Five Countries,
2000–2005 Average (Rounded)

Country	Crude Birth Rate	Crude Death Rate	Life Expectancy	Infant Mortality Rate
World	21	9	66	55
Developing countries	24	9	65	61
China	15	7	71	30
Developed countries	12	10	75	6
Canada	10	8	79	5
Great Britain	11	10	78	5
Russia	9	15	67	18
United States	15	8	77	7

Source: World Resources Institute. 2005 *Earth Trends:* The Environmental Information Portal. Available at http://earthtrends.wri.org. Washington, DC: World Resources Institute

control (ranging from decentralized to centralized), four types of health care systems are identified: (1) private insurance with private, entrepreneurial services, (2) national insurance with private, regulated services, (3) national insurance with public, regulated services, and (4) national insurance state-run system.

Having already examined the United States health care system, the four countries selected for review in this chapter represent a cross-section of the other approaches. Each of the country's health care systems is described by (1) its historical, political, and philosophical foundation, (2) the organization of the health care system, (3) the extent to which health services are accessible to the people, (4) indicators of the performance of the health care system, and (5) recent developments in the system. Table 17–3

TABLE 17–4   Comparative Analysis of the Health Care System in Five Countries

Country	Level of Advancement of Health Care System		
	Technology	Resources	Access
China	Low	Low	Moderate
Russia	Low	Low	Moderate
Canada	High	High	High
Great Britain	High	Moderate	High
United States	High	High	Moderate

Source: Marie L. Lassey, William R. Lassey, and Martin J. Jinks. 1997 *Health Care Systems Around the World.* Upper Saddle River, NJ: Prentice Hall.

compares these four countries with the United States on four important demographic indicators, and Table 17–4 compares the level of advancement in health care of technology, resources, and access.

As you are reading about the individual countries, note how each is affected by the same key forces (e.g., rapidly escalating health care costs), and note the similarities and differences in the types of responses being made. For each country, consider how its health care system has been influenced by environmental, situational-historical, cultural, and structural factors, as described in the box, "A Framework of Major Influences on Health Care Systems."

CHINA

The Historical, Political, and Philosophical Foundation

With a population exceeding 1.3 billion people, China has about one-fifth of all the people in the world and more than any other country. These people live on a land mass that is similar in size to the mainland United States. China is an agricultural country with more than 70 percent of its population living in rural areas. Despite recent modernization efforts, China remains a poor nation.

Relative to health care, three distinct phases are apparent in China's recent history: (1) the focus on improving health care from the time that

Mao Zedong came to power in 1949 until 1965; (2) the radical restructuring of the health care system during the Cultural Revolution from 1965 through 1977; and (3) the initiation of reform efforts and movement toward free market entrepreneuralism from the late 1970s until today.

Mao inherited a China in desperate condition. Plagued by years of both civil war and war with Japan, the economy was in shambles with both agricultural and industrial productivity at low levels. Food shortages were common, as were disease epidemics. About one baby in five died in the first year of life; almost one in three before age five. Hospitals and other health facilities were in desperately short supply in urban areas with even fewer in rural areas. Most physicians practiced only traditional Chinese medicine that had been learned through apprenticeships (Peterson and Peterson, 1990).

At the first National Health Congress, Mao presented four precepts as the ideological basis for health services:

1. Health care must be directed to the working people.
2. Preventive medicine must be given priority over curative medicine. By the mid-1960s, the government had conducted several Patriotic Health Movements in which millions of Chinese worked at getting rid of the "four pests" (flies, mosquitoes, bed bugs, and rats), improving general sanitation, preventing parasitic diseases, and eliminating venereal disease.
3. Modern health care needed to be added to traditional Chinese approaches. The Chinese adage "China walks on two legs: one traditional and one modern" is nowhere more true than in medicine.
4. Health workers must be involved with mass movements. An example is the family planning movement in China with the mandatory "one-child per family" objective.

Considerable efforts were directed to increasing access to medical care for the massive rural population. Rural areas were divided into communes (which averaged between 15,000 and 50,000 people) which were subdivided into *production brigades* (1,000 to 3,000 people), each of which had its own health station. These health stations were staffed by public health workers, midwives, and barefoot doctors. **Barefoot doctors** (later called *countryside doctors*) were peasants who had received a few months of medical training and then returned to their commune to treat minor illnesses (including colds, gastrointestinal ailments, and minor injuries); to provide immunizations and birth control; and to improve sanitation. Their existence compensated for the critical shortage of physicians in rural areas.

Within a decade and a half, substantial progress had been made. However, in 1966, frustrated and angered that his ideas were being incorporated too slowly and mistrustful of various societal institutions, including medicine, Mao launched the Cultural Revolution—a violent campaign of political and social repression. Those who were suspected of having ideological differences with Mao were imprisoned, tortured, and sometimes murdered. Schools and medical colleges were closed; medical research was halted; and health expenditures were reduced. Mao proclaimed that the health care system was not sufficiently directed toward rural areas, that medical education had become too Westernized (meaning theoretical) and not sufficiently practical, and that many physicians were shunning traditional Chinese medicine in favor of Western approaches.

During these years and even for a few years following the death of Mao in 1976, China was committed to a socialist economic system with extensive government control of all areas of the economy. This system was believed to offer the most effective strategy for ensuring that the basic needs of the people were met. Access to health care was deemed a right of all people, and there was a strong moral commitment to providing health care free or at little charge. Emphasis was placed on preventive care, the use of minimally trained health care personnel, and the combining of traditional Chinese and Western-style medicines.

However, Chinese leaders became frustrated at the slow pace of modernization. For the last two decades, leaders have insisted that, while China remain a socialist country politically, efforts to accelerate economic development should occur by shifting from a planned economy with extensive control by the national government to a market-oriented economy. Private ownership of enterprises and private investments in health care, as in all sectors, have been encouraged. This has created a dramatic transformation for the country, rapid industrialization and considerable economic development, but a health care system less accessible to its people.

Organization of the Health Care System

China is comprised of three centrally administered metropolitan areas (Beijing, Shanghai, and Tianjin), five autonomous regions, and 22 provinces. Although the Ministry of Health in Beijing formulates health care policies, establishes prices that physicians can charge, and supervises medical research for the entire country, it is now the health department in each province that oversees health resources within the jurisdiction and local governments that are primarily responsible for the financing and

delivering of health care services (Hsiao, 1995). This system has been described as having "highly decentralized control with increasingly decentralized responsibility" (Lassey, Lassey, and Jinks, 1997).

China has a three-tiered system for delivering health care in both rural and urban areas. In rural areas, the tiers consist of *village health stations* (staffed by physicians with three to six months of medical training after junior high school), *township health centers* (with 10 to 20 beds and staffed by physicians with three years of training after high school), and *county hospitals* (with 250 to 300 beds and staffed by physicians with four to five years of training after high school) (Hsiao and Liu, 1996).

Before the economic reforms, township health centers and county hospitals received most of their funding from the government with only supplemental payments from patients and health insurance. This **cooperative medical care system** ensured that most everyone had access to care. After the reforms, the government share was cut back to just 20 to 25 percent of hospital expenses, so that the remainder had to be collected from patients on a fee-for-service basis and from

China's health care system is currently undergoing a major privatization.

health insurance (which is owned by only a small percentage of the population). Government funds for preventive care and public health also were scaled back (Hsiao and Liu, 1996).

The government does continue to set the prices that providers can charge, and for all services except drugs and high-technology care, these are set at below cost. So, in order to make money, physicians tend to overprescribe drugs and overuse high-tech care—both of which have a steep markup.

In urban areas, the three tiers are *street health stations, community health centers,* and *district hospitals.* About half of China's urban population are covered under one or the other of two different insurance systems, one of which covers all government employees, retirees, disabled veterans, and university teachers and students, and the other of which covers employees (and their dependents and retirees) of state enterprises with more than 100 employees. These are basically health insurance plans that provide comprehensive benefits with minimal cost-sharing (Yip and Hsiao, 1997).

Accessibility of Health Care

The advent of capitalism into health care largely led to the dissolution of the cooperative medical care system. Local governments cut subsidies to rural hospitals and clinics. The decreased funding led to many countryside doctors entering farming and other occupations where they could make more money or entering the private practice of medicine, so that they could charge fees.

Rural peasants, who had been able to receive services for no payment or only a small payment, became subject to a fee-for-service system in which they pay the village doctor out-of-pocket. In this respect, accessibility to care now depends largely on the patient's ability to pay, and many persons are unable to afford the fees. By the year 2000, almost 90 percent of the rural sick had to pay for all of their own medical care.

Performance of the Health Care System

Partly as a result of these changes in health care delivery, disease patterns in China vary considerably between urban and rural areas. In urban China, the major health concerns are the same as in the industrialized world: heart disease and cancer (Hsiao, 1995). Lung cancer has become a particular problem in China. About 300 million Chinese smoke cigarettes (70 percent of adult males but just 7 percent of adult females) and death and illness from smoking-related causes has become a paramount health concern. In addition, the typical diet contains an increasingly high percentage of fat (there are many fast-food restaurants), lifestyles are becoming much more sedentary, once unheard-of obesity is increasing, and excessive alcohol consumption is becoming more of a problem. HIV/AIDS, long ignored by the government, is now acknowledged as a significant problem. The recent SARS epidemic brought worldwide attention to the lack of adequate health preparedness in China.

In rural areas, environmental pollution and the absence of safe drinking water (a major source of stomach, liver, and intestinal cancers) continue to be tremendous problems. Nutrition-related diseases, parasitic diseases, tuberculosis, and hepatitis B are common. After decades of significant health progress, the inattention given to the health care system since economic reform is now showing up in declining health indicators. Although overall mortality rates and infant mortality rates decreased significantly in the 1960s and 1970s, they have been relatively stable since then despite improvements in living standards and in nutrition and sanitation.

China has rapidly increased its number of physicians in recent years, but a serious shortage remains in rural areas. Some progress in assimilating advanced medical technology has been made, but expansion has come slowly, and few high-technology services are offered outside large, urban areas. Overall, China spends only about 5 percent of its gross domestic product on health care—a percentage that is high for developing nations but considerably less than what is spent in industrialized countries.

Recent Developments in Health Care

The commitment to a socialist market economy remains strong in China, but some efforts are being undertaken to redress concerns created by its establishment. In response to the diminished access to health care services in rural areas—the most serious problem—the government has designed a significantly revised cooperative medical care system. The system, which will pay for about half of the medical costs of those in rural areas, will be gradually implemented throughout the country and will be in place by 2010.

RUSSIA

The Historical, Political, and Philosophical Foundation

Russia, with a population of about 145 million people (but decreasing each year), is the largest of the countries that formed the Soviet Union. In many respects, it falls between the level of modernization of the United States and Western Europe, on the one hand, and developing countries like China, on the other. Since the breakup of the Soviet Union in 1991, Russia has struggled to develop a sound economy and a workable health care system.

The socialized health care system of the Soviet Union traced its roots to the 1917 revolution. Overthrowing the tsar, Lenin and the Bolsheviks moved to establish a working-class society based on communist principles. Given both the unstable political situation at home and throughout the world and the economic chaos within the country, the Bolsheviks moved quickly to consolidate their power in a totalitarian government. The power of the Communist party emerged from these events.

The health of the people was a primary concern of Lenin and the new government, and one of their priorities was to establish adequate preventive measures to counter the rampant disease epidemics of the time. In 1913, the mortality rate was 29 per 1,000 people; the infant mortality rate was 269/1,000; and average life expectancy no more than 32 years—all indicators of grave health problems (Leichter, 1979).

Lenin also determined to sharply reduce the power of the medical profession. Under the tsar, physicians had substantial autonomy and had organized themselves into a medical corporation. This body was political as well as medical and often spoke out against the tsar. Following the 1917 revolution, physicians attempted to alter the structure of medicine to make it more amenable to centralized planning (in accord with Lenin's wishes), but they also attempted to retain extensive professional control over clinical practice. This effort was denounced by the Communists who were convinced that physicians would always serve the interests of the ruling class. In an effort to deprofessionalize physicians, the government created a medical union in which physicians had no greater say than other health care workers. By the mid-1920s, the medical profession had been transformed into a group of medical experts employed and largely controlled by the government.

The philosophical foundation for the health care system was developed in the first years after the revolution. The guiding principles were: (1) the state has responsibility for public health and the provision of health care; (2) administration of the health care system is highly centralized and bureaucratized but includes public participation; (3) health care is defined as a right of citizenship, and health care services are provided at no cost; (4) preventive medicine is to be emphasized; and (5) medical research must be oriented toward the solution of practical problems—for example, the reduction of industrial absenteeism (Barr and Field, 1996).

These principles guided the health care system in the succeeding decades. Although the government released little information to the outside world about health indicators, the general perception was that the health care system worked adequately if not better.

However, when President Mikhail Gorbachev began to open Russian society to the outside world in 1985, it became obvious that the health care system was in a badly deteriorated condition due to underfunding. While Soviet leaders had painted a glowing picture of their health care system, in reality they had concentrated their attention on rapid industrialization and militarization and had failed to adequately support health care. Although the Soviet Union claimed (accurately) to have more physicians and more hospital beds per capita than any other country, their quality often was of a very low standard. Unqualified students bribed their way into medical school; severe shortages of pharmaceuticals and other medical supplies existed; and many medical facilities were crumbling (Barr and Field, 1996).

During the summer of 1991, people throughout the Soviet Union demanded an end to centralized government control and insisted on autonomy for the republics. Their focus was largely on political and economic structures, but changes were initiated in every institutional sector. In medicine, an end was signaled to highly centralized decision making, and planning and efforts commenced to establish more free market principles in the system. But, the transition to a workable and efficient health care system has been very difficult.

Organization of the Health Care System

Historically, the chief organizational characteristic of the health care system was its centralized administration. The ultimate authority in the system resided in the national Health Ministry led by a minister of health (typically a physician) and a Council of Health Ministers. This body had responsibility for all planning (which is extensive), coordination, and control of medical care and medical research; for medical education and standards of medical practice; and for formulating the health care budget and allocating funds to republic, regional, district, and local medical resources. The government owned all health care facilities and employed all health care workers.

In urban areas, a network of **polyclinics** (large, multi-service clinics) continues to represent the core of the health care system and serves most of the population. Until recently,

each person was assigned to a particular polyclinic, but this requirement has been eliminated. About 30 percent of the population, including the police, railroad employees, university employees, and high-level government officials have their own clinics and hospitals.

The key ambulatory care providers in rural areas are the midwife and the **feldsher**—a mid-level practitioner approximately equivalent to a physician's assistant (but with even more responsibility) who provides immunizations, primary care, normal childbirth, and minor surgery.

The hospital sector contains both general and specialized hospitals (e.g., maternity or emergency or infectious diseases), most of which are fairly small. Few contain modern medical technology, adequate pharmaceuticals, or high sanitary standards. Periodic reports of shortages of rubber gloves, surgical instruments, sterile needles, and other necessary supplies still occur. The emergency medical system—once the pride of the system—is in total disarray with ambulances sometimes arriving many hours after being called.

Physicians enjoy some prestige in Russia, but they are not among the highest paid professionals. Salaries are approximately the same as those for starting teachers but only 70 percent as much as that of industrial workers. This situation helps to explain the under-the-table payments from patients to physicians that have become common in order to secure more expedient care or additional services or even to have an operation performed or medication prescribed. It should be noted that the government does provide many physicians with certain fringe benefits (e.g., preferred apartments, vacation benefits, access to better schools for their children) not accorded to others (Lassey, Lassey, and Jinks, 1997).

About 70 percent of all physicians in Russia are female, and most of these women work out of the polyclinics. Male physicians are more likely to hold the more prestigious specialist positions in hospitals, academic positions, and most of the positions in the Ministry of Health. These patterns developed during the early 1930s at a time of an overall shortage of workers that was especially acute among physicians. Medicine was determined to be an area where women could adequately replace men. The Soviet government perceived many of these new female physicians (who had been nurses or even hospital orderlies) as being satisfied with a small paycheck and an occupation with little professional status.

Accessibility of Health Care

According to the Russian constitution, free health care is guaranteed to all citizens (at the publicly funded polyclinics and hospitals), but only a small part of services are actually free. Services are provided on a first come–first served basis (often with long queues) and are limited by the chronic shortage of supplies and equipment. The primary problem with the public system is that it continues to be underfunded. Russia continues to spend only about 4 percent of its GDP on health care, and this is not sufficient to elevate standards.

Laws passed in the early 1990s created a two-part government-run health insurance system. Workers were covered under one part (financed by a payroll tax), and nonworkers (e.g., the unemployed, retirees, and children) were covered in the second part, which is financed through the national government's budget. Thus far, however, the program has not worked as anticipated and has not generated the desired amount of funds (Barr and Field, 1996).

In recent years, a private system has begun to emerge beside the public system. Physicians are permitted to treat private as well as public patients, and patients with adequate personal resources may prefer to pay fee-for-service in order to get faster, more personalized, or more thorough care. A few pay-polyclinics have been started, and private health insurance is now available to help subsidize these costs. Many patients avoid both the public and private systems by relying on informal access to physician-friends/relatives. Not surprisingly, this resource is most available to people in upper socioeconomic groups (Brown and Rusinova, 1997).

Performance of the Health Care System

Russia today has substantial problems with its health care system and tremendously worrisome health indicators. Mortality rates are higher than in other industrialized countries and have increased since the early 1960s. Life expectancy is actually decreasing, and infant mortality rates are 2 to 3 times higher than in Western countries. The death rate from heart disease is the highest in the developed world, and AIDS is increasing rapidly (now more than one million cases). Epidemics of diseases once thought to be under control in developed countries, e.g., tuberculosis, hepatitis, typhoid, cholera, and diphtheria, are all on the rise and occasionally are at epidemic levels. Drug-related health problems are up, whereas public sanitation, childhood immunizations, and health education programs are down.

These conditions relate to the deterioration of the health care system but are traceable to a variety of other sources. Mark Field (1995) places the problem within the broad context of the collapse of the Soviet empire and the "systemic" breakdown of Russian society. He casts Russia as a country in a "post-war" mindset having experienced a humiliating national defeat. The deteriorating economic condition with high rates of inflation, political instability, and feelings of social isolation and alienation have contributed to a tearing of the social fabric.

Cockerham (1997) systematically analyzed the possible influence of Soviet health policy, social stress, and health-related lifestyles on the rise of adult mortality. He determined that poor health lifestyles—heavy alcohol consumption, increased consumption of tobacco, lack of exercise, and high-fat diets—are the main culprit in the upturn of deaths. The integration of the Field perspective and the Cockerham research offer an excellent illustration of how macro and micro factors combine to influence social patterns.

Recent Developments in Health Care

The leaders in Russia and in many of the countries that formed the Soviet Union intend to focus heavily on the application of free market principles to the health care system. Many health care providers believe that the main problem with the system in the past—in addition to underfunding—has been its centrally controlled nature and now believe that the highest priority is to complete the transition to a new health care financing system. However, the focus thus far in Russia has been on the economic system, and little attention has been directed to reforming the health care system and acquiring the basic medical supplies and equipment needed for quality clinical services.

CANADA

The Historical, Political, and Philosophical Foundation

The nation of Canada is a federal system—its 32 million people are spread across a loose confederation of 10 provinces, from Newfoundland off the east coast to British Columbia in the west, and two territories, the Yukon and the North West territories. Much of the political structure of Canada was created in the British North America Act (BNA), which was passed by the British Parliament in 1867. It guarantees considerably greater autonomy to the Canadian provinces than that held by individual American states. The BNA allocated to the federal government all matters of national concern plus others thought likely to be most costly; it allocated to the provinces more local and (presumably) less costly activities such as education, roads, and health care.

Throughout the early decades of the twentieth century, limited programs for health insurance were offered by local governments, industries, and voluntary agencies. These programs covered only selected services and left much of the population uninsured. Not until the mid 1940s did Canada begin to earnestly consider universal health insurance. This consideration was stimulated by three factors: the extreme prevalence of indigency brought on by the depression, the inability of local governments to offer substantial help (due to their own state of near-bankruptcy), and the despair of physicians who were frequently not paid. Significant disparities in wealth among the provinces led to additional inequalities in health services.

Though a universal plan was defeated at this time because of fears of federal infringement of provincial authority, the widespread health problems of Canadian people and the inadequacy of available health care facilities and programs were well documented. As a beginning but precedent-setting step, the federal government initiated financial assistance to the provinces for creating additional health care resources.

The transition to a universal health insurance plan occurred gradually. In 1946, the Saskatchewan government enacted legislation for a universal, compulsory hospital care insurance plan for all its citizens. The success of this program led additional provinces to enact similar programs. These were quite successful and well received but expensive—prompting the provinces to encourage the federal government to develop a national plan. However, as the concept was becoming more popular with the general citizenry and with political leaders, increasing reservations were expressed by physicians fearing a loss of professional autonomy and by private insurance companies fearing their own elimination (Graig, 1993).

Finally, in 1968, Canada passed the **Medical Care Act**, which brought all the provinces together in a universal national health insurance program. The federal government agreed to pay for half of the health care costs in each province as long as their health care services complied with four conditions: (1) they provided *comprehensive* services with no benefits limitations, (2) benefits were *universal*—available to all—and provided uniformly, (3) benefits had to be *portable* so that citizens were covered wherever they were in Canada, and (4) the plans had to be *publicly financed and administered by an agency accountable to the provincial government.*

Though the system worked well, the federal government soon realized it not only lacked control over the amount of funds expended by the provinces (and the provinces had little incentive to control costs), but it also received little political credit for its substantial contribution. In 1977, a key compromise, **Bill C-37**, was enacted. This legislation enabled the federal government to reduce its financial contribution to

25 percent, with a corresponding reduction in federal and corporate taxes. The provinces, whose share increased to 75 percent, were able to increase their taxes so as to generate sufficient revenue to fund the program. In addition, the provinces were provided greater latitude in managing the program, with the desired effect that they became more cost conscious.

The law pertaining to health insurance was modified again in 1984 in the Canada Health Act. Concerned that some physicians were "extra-billing" (i.e., directly charging patients fees above the reimbursement amount), this law mandated that physicians accept the reimbursement as their total payment. This legislation was not well received in the medical profession. For example, although only about 10 percent of physicians in Ontario were extra-billing, a series of general strikes occurred to protest the government's increased regulation of physicians (Graig, 1993).

Two key values underlie the Canadian national health insurance system. First, Canada has established a "right" to health care for all of its citizens and eliminated financial barriers to care. In doing so, the Canadian people have made an important statement about the social unity of the country, the high value placed on social equity, and the worth of people independent of their ability to pay for a service. Many would say that these values are more reflective of Canadian than American culture.

At the same time, Canada has maintained the private nature of the medical profession. Canadian physicians are not government employees and have considerably greater autonomy than their counterparts in Russia or even Great Britain. Canada's intention has been to offer publicly funded insurance for health care in a privately controlled system.

Organization of the Health Care System

Within the national government, the ultimate authority on health care is the health minister who directs national health care policy, works with the Parliament on relevant legislation, and serves as an important liaison with the health minister of each of the provinces. Because health is still primarily a provincial responsibility, much of the work related to medical education and medical licensure, hospitals, and public health occurs at the provincial level. While policies, procedures, and standards among provinces tend to be comparable, this is not required and variations do occur.

About 75 to 80 percent of Canadian physicians are in office-based private practice with most of the remainder based in hospitals. As in the United States, however, most office-based physicians (generalists and specialists) have hospital privileges and admit and tend to patients there. Patients have free choice of physicians, and physicians have the option of accepting or rejecting any new patient.

The national health insurance plan is funded from federal and provincial tax revenues and insurance premiums paid by all taxpaying citizens. The government utilizes a variety of "supply-side" cost-containment measures. The most important of these mechanisms is prospective budgeting, whereby hospitals are financed on the basis of annually negotiated prospective budgets within each province. Capital expenditures are handled separately and do not come out of the assigned allocation but do require government approval.

Other key mechanisms used to control costs by controlling the supply of health care services include: (1) determining the level of reimbursement for physicians (currently at 75 percent of established fees); (2) controlling the number of physicians by limiting enrollments in medical schools; and (3) minimizing the presence of private health insurance, which is available only to cover supplemental benefits (e.g., a semiprivate room in a hospital, dental and eye care, and prescription drugs).

A key issue within medicine in Canada is the degree of autonomy held by physicians. Policy discussions regarding national health insurance have typically been sensitive to preserving the "private" nature of the profession and have avoided language that suggests that physicians are government employees.

In reality, however, the line is not so distinct. Physicians are reimbursed directly by the provincial government on a fee-for-service basis, but these fees are established in annual negotiations between the provincial medical association and the provincial government. Through these negotiations, prices are set for each medical service. The negotiated reimbursement schedules are binding, include little variation by medical specialty or complexity of care delivered to individual patients, and prohibit extra-billing. Even physicians who have entirely "opted-out" of national health insurance (an option taken by only a small percentage of Canadian physicians) are prevented from charging patients more than the specified reimbursement level. All of this has led to continuing criticism that the medical professional has in reality been "de-privatized." Provincial governments reimburse physicians for only a percentage of the fee schedules set by the medical associations. This has been acceptable to most physicians, however, because they know that they spend considerably less time on billing and other administrative paperwork and pay significantly less for malpractice insurance than physicians in the United States.

Physicians enjoy high esteem in Canada, which is reflected in salaries in the top 1 percent of all professions. Though some physicians have complained that national health insurance has depressed their incomes, incomes have continued to increase at a reasonable level (Marmor, 1990).

Accessibility of Health Care

All basic hospital and physician services and other services deemed to be necessary are covered for Canadian citizens. The only out-of-pocket health care expenses are for private insurance or direct payment for eye care, dental care, medication purchases for ambulatory patients and, if a person desires, a semiprivate versus ward room in a hospital.

This system has enabled broad access to the health care system. Research has documented a greater use of physician and hospital services by Canadians than Americans—especially among lower income persons. One recent study found that residents of Ontario averaged 19 percent more visits than Americans to physicians and that this difference was even greater among those with low incomes (who averaged 25 to 33 percent more visits) (Katz, Hofer, and Manning, 1996).

Critics of the Canadian system counter that accessibility to care in Canada is limited by reduced availability of physicians, surgical procedures, and high-technology equipment. The relative lack of equipment and resources means that patients are not seen as promptly as they are in the United States, that queues (i.e., waiting lists) exist for many high-tech diagnostic and surgical procedures, and that fewer of these procedures are provided. A recent study of comparable hospitals in the United States and Canada found that U.S. medical patients received 22 percent more diagnostic tests than their Canadian counterparts—with almost all of the difference resulting from greater use of MRI and CT (Katz, McMahon, and Manning, 1996). These delays in service provision lead some Canadians to cross the border to obtain services in the United States, though this practice is much less common than often portrayed (Katz et al., 2002).

Performance of the Health Care System

Standard health indicators for Canada are very favorable. Canada is among the upper echelon of countries in the world with regard to life expectancy (longer than in the United States) and infant mortality (lower than in the United States).

The extent to which Canada has been able to maintain control over costs, while providing high-quality comprehensive services to its people, is an issue that has generated considerable controversy. Many advocates of the Canadian system emphasize that it has been able to guarantee services to all of its people while spending a considerably smaller percentage of its Gross Domestic Product (now less than 10 percent) than does the United States (at about 14 percent). As economist Robert Evans (1986) explains, Canada's willingness to provide universal coverage for health care has given it the bargaining leverage to include mechanisms of cost control. Compared to the United States, Canada invests significantly less money per capita in administrative costs (the uniform billing system alone saves billions of dollars each year), profits,

TABLE 17–5   Public Opinion of One's Own Health Care System in Canada and the United States, 1988 and 1998

View	Canada (%)		United States (%)	
	1988	1998	1988	1998
Only minor changes needed	56	20	10	17
Fundamental changes needed	38	56	60	46
Completely rebuild system	5	23	29	33

Source: Karen Donelan, Robert J. Blendon, Cathy Schoen, Karen Davis, and Katherine Binns, "The Cost of Health System Change: Public Discontent in Five Nations." *Health Affairs*, 18:206–216, 1999.

marketing, legal involvement in medicine, and other "medically irrelevant" areas. As noted in Chapter 14, while as much as 30 percent of the American health care dollar goes for administrative costs, the corresponding figure in Canada is about 16 percent (Woolhandler, Campbell, and Himmelstein, 2004).

Critics of the Canadian system contend that these cost efficiencies come with a price. They argue that even after restricting the availability of services and sacrificing investment in sophisticated high-technology equipment, Canada has not had sufficient money to run this type of health care system. The recent lack of growth in the Canadian economy along with a high rate of inflation and the aging of the Canadian population (producing greater medical needs and less tax revenue to fund the system) led to significant budget slashing in the mid 1990s. Provincial governments and their health authorities closed or merged some hospitals; removed selected, nonessential medical services from the health care plans; made significant reductions in the number of health care jobs; became more assertive in negotiations for physician fee reimbursement (physicians in some provinces received pay cuts); and reduced budgets for outpatient diagnostic services.

Both physicians and patients have lamented these developments. To protest the budget cuts, several groups of physicians have conducted brief strikes and work slowdowns, and migration to the United States has increased. A 1991 survey of physicians who have practiced in both Canada and the United States found that physicians who had ended up in the United States slightly preferred the U.S. system, while physicians who had ended up in Canada rated the Canadian system significantly better (Hayes, Hayes, and Dykstra, 1993).

Canadian citizens have long expressed great pride in their health care system (surveys show that Canadians see it as being superior to that offered in other countries). After a dip in approval in the late 1990s, surveys again report sharply favorable attitudes (Abelson et al., 2004). Table 17–5 compares public opinion of the health care system in Canada and the United States in 1988 and 1998 with the level of satisfaction being higher in Canada.

Recent Developments in Health Care

The Canadian system will need to address two major pressure points in the coming years. First, a decision will have to be made about the level of funding for the system. After several years of budget slashing, cutbacks in available services, and increased dissatisfaction among providers and patients, the government did commit increased funding to health care in the early 2000s—a development that was received favorably.

This issue relates to the other pressure point: the public/private mix in the health care system. Some medical professionals and ideological conservatives have long sought to reprivatize the system by shifting financial responsibility away from the government and back to patients (through private insurance); by establishing less universal and less comprehensive health insurance plans; and by emphasizing market forces in health care by deregulating the field. This position has not been supported either by a majority of the population or the government.

There is currently increased discussion of allowing a private health care system to develop along side the public system. Proponents argue that this direction is already occurring (private health insurance has grown in Canada and now pays for more than one-fourth of all health care), and that by allowing patients who want to pay for care to do so, that some pressure would be relieved from the public system. Opponents argue that this "two-tier" system would eventually lead to the destruction of the public system by eroding broad-based public support and increasing its costs. This issue will test the commitment of the Canadian people to their traditional health care system during the first decades of the new century (DeCoster and Brownell, 1997; Hutchinson, Abelson, and Lavis, 2001).

GREAT BRITAIN

The Historical, Political, and Philosophical Foundation

Great Britain, which consists of England, Scotland, Wales, and Northern Ireland, has a total population of about 60 million persons. The population is overwhelmingly urban as less than 10 percent of the people live in rural areas. Though not extremely wealthy, Great Britain is thoroughly modernized.

Britain's strong commitment to public responsibility for the health and welfare of its citizens dates back to at least the mid-1800s. The foundation for today's National Health Service (NHS) was laid in 1867 when Parliament passed the Metropolitan Poor Act—a bill that obligated local governments to provide free hospital care for the poor. The measure appealed both to people's charitable interests and to a desire to protect the rest of society from contracting diseases from the untreated sick.

By the early 1900s, however, many were dissatisfied with the limited scope of the Poor Act, as Great Britain was confronted with the same pressures that were occurring throughout

Europe to increase social welfare programs. The National Health Insurance Act of 1911 (NHI), one of several social reforms sponsored by the Liberal government, provided medical and disability benefits and income protection during sickness. The program was compulsory for all wage earners between the ages of 16 and 65 earning less than a designated sum per year. However, the plan was less generous than similar programs in Germany and Japan in that it did not cover dependents of wage earners (except for a maternity plan), self-employed persons (including farmers), or the unemployed. Though NHI achieved its objectives as a limited plan, there was continued interest in a more comprehensive program (Graig, 1993).

In the early- and mid-1940s, Great Britain suffered from the devastation of World War II. Major sections of cities were destroyed, the economy was in chaos, a severe housing shortage existed, and the general health of the population was poor. The prevailing system could not adequately handle these problems.

The **Beveridge Report** of 1942 analyzed these social problems and recommended major reform through increased government involvement in the economy, education, and health care. Strong sponsorship by the Labour Party and broad popular support for significant reform in health care existed, though not among physicians, who fiercely resisted change. Eventually, the National Health Service Act of 1946 was passed by a wide margin and the NHS was implemented in 1948. It provided for the entire range of health care services to be available at no charge to the entire population in a system financed by general tax revenues. Despite several major adjustments, the basic health system inaugurated in 1948 continues today.

Britain has a long history of extensive government involvement throughout society's institutions and a commitment to providing for the basic needs of all citizens. Within this "welfare state," the NHS expresses the social value placed on a just distribution of essential resources (like health care). While the current health care system is not without its critics, **the "National"** is a source of great pride in Britain.

Organization of the Health Care System

Great Britain's health care system has largely been government owned and government run. The government sets health care policy, raises funds and budgets for health care, owns health care facilities, employs physicians and other health care professionals, and purchases medical supplies and equipment. Ultimate authority rests with the Department of Health.

The British system underwent several significant changes in the 1990s and early 2000s. In the late 1980s, Prime Minister Margaret Thatcher commissioned a report, *Working for Patients,* which advocated making greater use of private market forces to increase competition and efficiency in the system while maintaining universal and free access to the system.

At the heart of the reform are two basic changes. First, as of 2002, decision-making power is decentralized with localized Primary Care Trusts (PCTs) given the responsibility for running the NHS and improving health in their areas; the PCTs receive 75 percent of the NHS budget. Regional Strategic Health Authorities oversee the PCTs and engage in health planning. Second, increased competition among hospitals and other facilities is created in hopes of reducing costs and increasing quality of services.

Medical settings in Great Britain are like those in the United States: Physicians work out of offices or clinics or in hospitals. As is true in some managed care networks in the United States, Great Britain mandates that an initial contact in the health care system be made with a general practitioner (GP).

The NHS is largely (more than 80 percent) financed by general tax revenues with only about 4 percent of funds coming from out-of-pocket expenses. Patients do pay fees for eyeglasses, dentures, and prescription drugs. Health care from physicians and hospitals is provided to all British citizens at no charge.

Traditionally, there has been a small private health care sector in Great Britain. Recently, however, private health insurance has become more popular; about 12 percent of the population had a private policy in the early 1990s. Physicians are not obligated to register with the NHS (only a handful have not), and registered physicians may accept private patients though rarely do private patients exceed 5 percent of the total patient load. Private insurance companies do exist and sell private health insurance for a premium. Hospitals reserve a small number of beds ("pay beds") for private patients. Why would anyone purchase private insurance? The primary answer can be traced to the long waits ("queues") that typically exist for elective surgery and that sometimes exist for more urgent surgery or even primary care.

Practicing physicians in Great Britain become either general practitioners or consultants. Patients have a free choice of GPs but must get placed on one's roster in order to be seen. Once on a roster, that is the only GP that the patient can use. A patient can switch to another GP by registering with another physician, but this is rare. The GP offers comprehensive primary care and can prescribe medications but must refer patients to a consultant for hospital care.

General practitioners in Great Britain contract with the NHS for reimbursement, which occurs in three ways. Each GP receives a base salary to cover the fixed costs of operating a practice; a certain amount of salary based on the number of patients accepted on the roster (called a **capitation system**); and additional income based on services such as vaccinations for which a fee is charged. The capitation system is the most controversial of the three sources of income. The NHS has established 3,500 patients as the maximum on a roster, though physicians average only about 1,900. Physicians are obligated to provide care for all patients on the roster though neither the number of patients actually seen, nor the duration of the encounter, nor the type of treatment dispensed affects salary. Physicians do get a supplement for having certain kinds of people— for example, the elderly or low-income persons— on their roster (Graig, 1993).

Consultants, all of whom work in a hospital, are physicians trained in a medical or surgical specialty. They are salaried employees of the NHS. Salaries are the same for all specialties in all hospitals and are determined in an annual negotiation with the NHS. Neither the number of patients seen nor the type of treatments rendered affects salary earned.

Physicians in Britain are held in high esteem. Surveys report confidence in physician care; few patients seek a second opinion; and medical malpractice suits are rare. This high prestige is not reflected in salaries to the extent that it is in the United States. Physicians earn considerably above the average income in Britain, but not several times greater as they do in the United States.

Accessibility of Health Care

British citizens can receive comprehensive health care without payment at the point of delivery. In this sense, services are maximally accessible. Moreover, the government offers incentives to physicians who establish practice in medically underserved areas, which has helped to ease the shortage of physicians in rural areas.

However, the British government maintains an important control by determining the amount of money allocated to the health care system. By limiting these funds (Great Britain spends less money per capita on health care than any other country in Europe), the number of health care employees is restrained, and demand for services typically exceeds supply. When patients attempt to make an appointment, often they are forced to wait in a long line. This situation is primarily responsible for the development of the private insurance sector because the privately insured are seen promptly.

> The major advantage to the patient of the private sector in Britain seems to be the opportunity to "jump the queue." In parts of the country where waiting lists for elective surgery may be very long, the private patient can enter the hospital for surgical care at times convenient to the consumer rather than wait upon the convenience of the system. . . . Those who can afford private care can be treated at their convenience and are thus able to sidestep one of the most unpleasant characteristics of the system, waiting time. (Gill, 1994:482)

Performance of the Health Care System

Standard health indicators reflect positively on the general health of the British people. Overall life expectancy is among the highest in the world (higher than in the United States), and infant mortality is very low (less than that in the United States). Though no person is ever turned away due to an inability to pay, the NHS is considerably less expensive than the U.S. health care system. In recent years, Britain spends about 8 percent of its gross domestic product on health care, far below the U.S. level (and a level that has been criticized as being inappropriately low).

Recent Developments in Health Care

It will not be possible to fully analyze the recent reform efforts for many years. Proponents seem generally pleased and believe the decentralization and added competition are creating a more efficient health care system. Critics of the changes express concern that the emphasis on competition and profitmaking will supersede the traditional closeness of the GP-patient relationship. For example, the increased importance of the capitation system gives physicians an incentive to take more patients on to the roster—thereby reducing the time available for each patient. Some suggest that the system may even increase rather than decrease costs if employers are forced to pay higher salaries in order to attract the best people. These are issues that will be followed closely in the twenty-first century.

COMMON CHALLENGES TO HEALTH CARE SYSTEMS AROUND THE WORLD

Despite their profound differences, nations around the world are struggling with some of the same issues and questions with respect to their health care systems. Having briefly examined the health care systems of China, Russia, Canada, and Great Britain, the following emerge as common and important issues that countries are dealing with now and will continue to deal with in the new century.

1. What is the optimal level of involvement of the national government in the health care system and in what ways should the government be involved?

2. Should there be both a public and private health care sector? What is the optimal relationship between the government, employers, insurers, and providers?

3. What is the optimal number of physicians within the system and what should be the distribution between primary care physicians and specialists?

4. Given considerations of cost and equitable distribution, what is the optimal commitment that should be made to the incorporation of health care technologies?

5. How can health care cost increases be most reasonably controlled?

SUMMARY

Studying health care systems around the world offers insights into policy alternatives and an enhanced ability to understand the forces that shape health care. Although every health care system is unique, all are shaped by some configuration of environmental, situational-historical, cultural, and structural factors.

The four systems examined in this chapter represent alternative ways of structuring a health care system. China is an agriculturally based country with a huge rural population. Unable to afford universal access to health care, China is now utilizing a system that relies on a combination of government, cooperative, and private financing. Recently, the government has increased emphasis on private market mechanisms in the health care system.

In past years, Russia has exemplified a state-run, highly centralized, highly bureaucratized health care system. Russians took much pride in the emphasis on preventive care and on the provision of free care for all citizens. However, the transition to a private market economy has been very difficult, the health care system is in desperate condition, and several health indicators remain major concerns.

Canada's health care system has undergone a significant transformation that has shifted more financial and managerial control to the provincial governments while maintaining a commitment to providing universal access to care. Health care personnel in Canada are not government employees, although the federal and provincial governments exercise significant influence on the conditions of medical practice. Health indicators are very positive, but difficult economic times in Canada have led to recent system cutbacks.

Great Britain guarantees universal access to health care through a system that is substantially publicly owned and run. Health indicators for the British people are very favorable, and there is considerable pride in the "National." However, rapidly increasing costs in the 1980s led to significant organizational changes and focused efforts on using competition and private market forces to control cost increases.

HEALTH ON THE INTERNET

To obtain information about a country not covered in this chapter or to learn about the latest trends in world health, check out the World Health Organization's Web site at:

http://who.int

What is the purpose of the World Health Organization? How is it governed? What does WHO have to say about gender and reproductive rights and about child and adolescent rights?

KEY CONCEPTS AND TERMS

barefoot doctor
Beveridge Report
Bill C-37
capitation system
cooperative medical care system
cultural factors
feldsher

Medical Care Act
the "National"
physical environmental factors
polyclinic
situational-historical factors
structural factors

DISCUSSION QUESTIONS

1. Use the "Framework of Major Influences on the Health Care System" to analyze each of the four health care systems presented in this chapter. For each country, which of the factors have been most important in shaping the current system?

2. What are the common denominators in these four health care systems? How is each system unique?

3. Identify two major strengths and two important concerns about each of the four systems. Can you identify at least one feature in the health care system of each country that you would like to see incorporated in the United States and that you believe could be feasibly integrated with our current system (or could feasibly replace the current system)?

REFERENCES

Abelson, Julia, Matthew Mendelson, John N. Lavis, Steven G. Morgan, Pierre Gerlier Forest, and Marilyn Swinton. 2004 "Canadians Confront Health Care Reform." *Health Affairs,* 23:186–192.

Alford, Robert. 1969 *Bureaucracy and Participation: Political Culture in Four Wisconsin Cities.* Chicago: Rand McNally.

Anderson, Gerard, and Peter S. Hussey. 2001 "Comparing Health System Performance in OECD Countries." *Health Affairs,* 20:219–232.

Barr, Donald A., and Mark G. Field. 1996 "The Current State of Health Care in the Former Soviet Union: Implications for Health Care Policy and Reform." *American Journal of Public Health,* 86:307–312.

Brown, Julie V., and Nina L. Rusinova. 1997 "Russian Medical Care in the 1990s: A User's Perspective." *Social Science and Medicine,* 45:1265–1276.

Cockerham, William C. 1997 "The Social Determinants of the Decline of Life Expectancy in Russia and Eastern Europe: A Lifestyle Explanation." *Journal of Health and Social Behavior,* 38:117–130.

DeCoster, Carolyn A., and Marni D. Brownell. 1997 "Private Health Care in Canada: Savior or Siren?" *Public Health Reports,* 112:298–305.

Donelan, Karen, Robert J. Blendon, Cathy Schoen, Karen Davis, and Katherine Binns. 1999 "The Cost of Health System Change: Public Discontent in Five Nations." *Health Affairs,* 18:206–216.

Evans, Robert G. 1986 "Finding the Levers, Finding the Courage: Lessons from Cost Containment in North America." *Journal of Health Politics, Policy and Law,* 11:585–616.

Field, Mark G. 1995 "The Health Care Crisis in the Former Soviet Union: A Report from the 'Post-War' Zone." *Social Science and Medicine,* 41:1469–1478.

Gill, Derek. 1994 "A National Health Service: Principles and Practice," pp. 480–494 in *The Sociology of Health and Illness,* 4th ed., Peter Conrad and Rochelle Kern (eds.). New York: St. Martin's Press.

Graig, Laurene A. 1993 *Health of Nations: An International Perspective on U.S. Health Care Reform.* Washington, DC: Congressional Quarterly, Inc.

Hayes, Gregory L., Steven C. Hayes, and Thane Dykstra. 1993 "Physicians Who Have Practiced in Both the United States and Canada Compare the Systems." *American Journal of Public Health,* 83:1544–1548.

Hsiao, William C. 1995 "The Chinese Health Care System: Lessons for Other Nations." *Social Science and Medicine,* 41:1047–1055.

Hsiao, William C., and Yuanli Liu. 1996 "Economic Reform and Health—Lessons from China." *The New England Journal of Medicine,* 335: 430–431.

Hutchinson, Brian, Julia Abelson, and John Lavis. 2001 "Primary Care in Canada: So Much Innovation, So Little Change." *Health Affairs,* 20:116–131.

Katz, Steven J., Timothy P. Hofer, and Willard G. Manning. 1996 "Physician Use in Ontario and the United States: The Impact of Socioeconomic Status and Health Status." *American Journal of Public Health,* 86:520–524.

Katz, Steven J., Laurence F. McMahon, and Willard G. Manning. 1996 "Comparing the Use of Diagnostic Tests in Canadian and U.S. Hospitals." *Medical Care,* 34:117–125.

Katz, Steven J., Karen Cardiff, Marina Pascali, Morris L. Barer, and Robert G. Evans. 2002 "Phantoms in the Snow: Canadians' Use of Health Care Services in the U.S." *Health Affairs,* 21:19–31.

Lassey, Marie L., William R. Lassey, and Martin J. Jinks. 1997 *Health Care Systems Around the World.* Upper Saddle River, NJ: Prentice Hall.

Leichter, Howard M. 1979 *A Comparative Approach to Policy Analysis: Health Care Policy in Four Nations.* Cambridge, MA: Cambridge University Press.

Light, Donald W. 1990 "Comparing Health Care Systems: Lessons From East and West Germany," pp. 449–463 in *The Sociology of Health and Illness,* 3rd ed., Peter Conrad and Rochelle Kern (eds.). New York: St. Martin's Press.

Light, Donald W. 1994 "Comparative Models of Health Care Systems," pp. 455–470 in *The Sociology of Health and Illness,* 4th ed., Peter Conrad and Rochelle Kern (eds.). New York: St. Martin's Press.

Marmor, Theodore R. 1990 "Canada's Path, America's Choices: Lessons from the Canadian Experience with National Health Insurance," pp. 463–473 in *The Sociology of Health and Illness,* 3rd ed., Peter Conrad and Rochelle Kern (eds.). New York: St. Martin's Press.

Navarro, Vicente. 1989 "Why Some Countries Have National Health Insurance, Others Have National Health Services, and the U.S. Has Neither." *Social Science and Medicine,* 28:887–898.

Payer, Lynn. 1989 *Medicine and Culture.* New York: Holt, Rinehart and Winston.

Peterson, Caryl E., and Ronald G. Peterson. 1990 "Chinese Medicine and Politics: Mao to Tiananmen." *Maryland Medical Journal,* 39:1075–1079.

Roemer, Milton I. 1991 *National Health Systems of the World,* Vol. 1. New York: Oxford University Press.

Schieber, George, and Akiko Maeda. 1999 "Health Care Financing and Delivery in Developing Countries." *Health Affairs,* 18:193–205.

The World Bank. 2002 *Health, Nutrition, and Population Database.* Washington, DC: World Bank.

Woolhandler, Steffie, Terry Campbell, and David U. Himmelstein. 2004 "Health Care Administration in the United States and Canada: Micromanagement, Macro Costs." *International Journal of Health Services,* 34:65–78.

World Resources Institute. 2004 *Earth Trends.* Washington, DC: World Resource Institute (www.wri.org).

Yip, Winnie C., and William C. Hsiao. 1997 "Medical Savings Accounts: Lessons from China." *Health Affairs,* 16:244–251.

PHOTO CREDITS

NAME INDEX

SUBJECT INDEX

Academic health centers, 179,
    182–184
Acquired immune deficiency
    syndrome (AIDS)
    definition, 74
    etiology, 77
    Health Belief Model, 123
    obligation to treat AIDS patients,
        277–282
    prevalence, 74–77
    trends, 77–78
Acupuncture
    current and future status,
        230–231
    history, 229
    and organized medicine, 229–230
    origin, 229
    principles, 229
Advance directives
    among the Navajo, 342
    health care power of
        attorney, 340
    living will, 340
    Patient Self-Determination
        Act, 340
Age
    and Alzheimer's disease, 79
    disability, 54–55
    morbidity, 49–52
    rationing, 301–302
    use of health services, 141
Allied Health Workers, 199–200,
    210–211
Alternative medicine. See
    complimentary and
    alternative medicine
Alzheimer's disease
    definition, 78
    etiology, 79

prevalence, incidence,
    mortality, 79
trends, 79
Ambulatory care
    ambulatory surgical centers
        (surgicenters), 313
    free-standing centers, 312
    group practice, 311–312
    urgent-care centers (walk-in
        centers), 313–313
American Medical Association
    decline, 156–157
    founding, 28–29
    history, 28–29
American Nurses Association,
    200–201, 205–206
Americans with Disabilities
    Act, 150
Anatomical concept of disease,
    20–21
Animals and health, 146
Arabic medicine, 18
Asian and Pacific Islanders
    life expectancy, 43
    morbidity, 53
Attention Deficit/Hyperactivity
    Disorder, 134–135

Baby M case, 352
Binge drinking, 114
Blackwell, Elizabeth, 178
Blue Cross-Blue Shield, 291
Bouvia, Elizabeth, 250

Canada
    accessibility, 371
    Bill C-37, 369–370
    history, political, philosophical
        foundation, 369–370

Medical Care Act, 369
organization, 370–371
recent developments, 372–373
system performance, 371–372
Cancer
    definition, 67
    etiology, 69–72
    incidence and mortality, 67, 69
    trends, 72–74
Capitalism
    medical entrepreneuralism,
        297–299
    medical-industrial complex,
        297–299
Cardiovascular disease. See Heart
    disease
Centers for Disease Control and
    Prevention (CDC), 35–36, 38,
    74–75
Certified Nurse Midwife
    (CNM), 209
Certified Registered Nurse
    Anesthetist (CRNA), 209
China, People's Republic of
    accessibility, 365
    barefoot doctor, 363
    history, political, philosophical
        foundation, 362–363
    organization, 364–365
    recent developments, 366
    system performance, 365
Chiropractic
    current and future status,
        227–228
    history, 226
    and organized medicine,
        226–227
    origin, 223–224
    principles, 224–226